Hospitality and Travel Marketing

www.hospitality-tourism.delmar.com

Hospitality and Travel Marketing

THIRD EDITION

Alastair M. Morrison, Ph.D.

DELMAR

THOMSON LEARNING

Australia Canada Mexico Singapore Spain United Kingdom United States

Hospitality and Travel Marketing, Third Edition
by Alastair M. Morrison, Ph.D.

Business Unit Director:
Susan L. Simpfenderfer

Executive Editor:
Marlene McHugh Pratt

Acquisitions Editor:
Joan M. Gill

Developmental Editor:
Melissa Riveglia

Editorial Assistant:
Lisa Flatley

Executive Production Manager:
Wendy A. Troeger

Production Manager:
Carolyn Miller

Project Editor:
Amy E. Tucker

Production Editor:
Elaine Scull

Production Coordinator:
Matthew Williams

Executive Marketing Manager:
Donna J. Lewis

Channel Manager:
Nigar Hale

Cover Design:
Joseph Villanova

Cover Images:
PhotoDisc, Eyewire Illustration

For permission to use material from this text or product, contact us by
Tel   (800) 730-2214
Fax (800) 730-2215
www.thomsonrights.com

Library of Congress Cataloging-in-Publication Data
Morrison, Alastair M.
    Hospitality and travel marketing / Alastair M. Morrison.— 3rd ed.
        p. cm.
    Includes bibliographical references and index.
    ISBN 0-7668-1605-2
    1. Hospitality industry—Marketing. 2. Tourism—Marketing. I. Title.
    TX911.3.M3 M67 2001
    647.94'068'8—dc21

                                                    2001028449

NOTICE TO THE READER

Contents

Preface

This book began evolving on my very first day as a college teacher at Purdue University in August 1985. Like many of my peers in hospitality and travel education, there was no introductory marketing textbook that quite fit my needs and those of my students. The existing texts in the field were either too narrowly focused, dealing only with restaurants, hotels, or travel agencies, or were written for practitioners rather than college students. They lacked many of the essentials of an effective college text, including learning objectives, assignments, glossaries, instructor's manuals, test banks, and other ancillaries. The content tended to be slanted in one direction, usually the authors' pet areas, resulting in unbalanced treatment of many other important marketing issues.

Hospitality and Travel Marketing, Third Edition, is designed to fill a void in the marketing textbooks for our industry. It is unique because it avoids the compartmentalized thinking characteristic of various segments of our business. In the twenty-first century, the need and value of cooperative marketing efforts among hotels, airlines, restaurants, travel agents, and others will increase. This accelerating push for "partnership" is a major theme of *Hospitality and Travel Marketing, Third Edition.* Our students are tomorrow's managers and need to share with us a broader perspective of our industry than just restaurants, lodging, or the travel agency business. Surely, marketing is one of the areas of study in which students should be encouraged to take a broad, long-term view of their chosen industry and career field.

The target market for this book is the student in two- or four-year college courses in hotel, restaurant, tourism, or travel industry marketing. It was written with the student in mind and was extensively reviewed by college students as well as college marketing teachers. Several special features are included to increase student learning and interest.

SYSTEMATIC SEQUENCE OF BOOK

One of the major strengths of *Hospitality and Travel Marketing, Third Edition,* is its clear structure and organization. Students new to marketing often fail to grasp how each element fits together and get lost in the jargon of our discipline. This book is organized around the **hospitality and travel marketing system** model. The model serves as a road map for students in understanding how the various marketing functions and techniques are related. It reflects a simple, common-sense approach to marketing that students can easily follow and comprehend. The text's five parts and twenty chapters follow the chronological flow of the hospitality and travel marketing system.

Part I (Introduction to Marketing) clearly explains marketing and its evolution in our industry. It highlights the important differences between marketing services and marketing products. This part also introduces the hospitality and travel marketing system. **Part II** (Planning: Research and Analysis) provides a detailed description of the research and analysis techniques that are an essential first step in planning the marketing effort. **Part III** (Planning: Marketing Strategy and Planning) looks at the alternative marketing approaches available to hospitality and travel organizations. Detailed coverage of market segmentation is included, as well as an extensive review of consumer and industry trends. The concept of positioning also receives in-depth treatment. **Part IV** (Implementing the Marketing Plan) discusses how each element of a marketing plan is developed and implemented. Chapters are devoted to product development and partnership, services and service quality, packaging, programming, distribution channels, communications, advertising, sales promotion, personal selling, public relations and publicity, and pricing. **Part V** (Controlling and Evaluating the Plan) discusses the final steps in marketing planning and implementation—marketing management, control, and evaluation.

FEATURES

Learning Objectives and Review Questions

Every chapter opens with a comprehensive set of learning **objectives** addressing the main points covered in the chapter. **Review questions** allow students to review how well they have learned the material related to each objective. The test bank supplied to adopting teachers has been carefully prepared to match the text's learning objectives and review questions.

Key Terms

Marketing is a discipline with a language almost its own. To help students cope with the many new words and ideas, a list of **key terms** is located at the beginning of each chapter. Every listed item is also boldfaced and defined in the chapter when first mentioned. For easy review of all key terms, a glossary is included near the end of the text.

Excellence Cases

All chapters include an **excellence case** describing an organization that has enjoyed great success in applying marketing approaches and techniques related to the chapter's topic area. Each case is carefully linked to chapter materials so that students have real-life examples of how organizations in our industry have made excellent applications of the various elements of marketing. Cases are drawn from a broad range of industry segments, including food service, lodging, destination marketing, car rentals, and tour wholesaling. They cover a wide spectrum of organizations, from industry giants like Disney Enterprises and McDonald's to a small country inn.

A Touch of Technology

This new feature provides a glimpse of the latest technologies in hospitality and tourism marketing as they relate to the topics covered in individual chapters.

Did You Know?

This feature presents interesting facts and figures in an easy-to-follow format that stimulates interest in chapter materials.

On the Web

To illustrate the importance of the Internet in hospitality and travel marketing, many of the figures in the text were downloaded from actual hospitality and travel and tourism websites.

Color Insert

Hospitality and Travel Marketing, Third Edition, includes a color insert showing some of the best examples of advertising and sales promotions in our industry. Not only is this an attractive visual aid for students, but it also highlights why these promotions are so effective.

Chapter Assignments

Hospitality and Travel Marketing, Third Edition, contains 80 **chapter assignments**. These are provided to give students another type of learning experience and the opportunity to apply what they have learned in the chapter. Teachers may also find the chapter assignments useful as individual or group projects. Many of the assignments require students to do a combination of secondary (library) and primary research.

World Wide Web Resources

This new feature acknowledges the important role that technology plays in today's world. Web addresses are provided at the end of each chapter for students who wish to further explore topics presented in the text.

> The authors and Delmar affirm that the Web site URLs referenced herein were accurate at the time of printing. However, due to the fluid nature of the Internet, we cannot guarantee their accuracy for the life of the edition.

SUPPLEMENTS

Instructor's Manual

The Instructor's Manual includes answers to review questions, assignments, suggested resources, transparency masters, and test bank.

Computerized Test Bank

The computerized test bank is comprised of multiple choice and true/false questions, for each chapter.

Instructors can use the computerized test bank software to create sample quizzes for students. Refer to the CTB User's Guide for more information on how to create and post quizzes to your school's Internet or Intranet server. Your students may also access sample quizzes created by Delmar from their Web site for Online Resources™ for Students at http://www.Hospitality-Toursim.delmar.com.

Online Resources

The Online Resources™ to accompany the third edition of *Hospitality and Travel Marketing* is your link to hospitality, travel, and tourism on the Internet. The Online Resources™ contain many features to help focus your understanding of hospitality and travel marketing:

- **Chapter Objectives Review**— provides an overview of the key topics presented in the chapter.
- **Web Activities**—These activities direct you to a Web site(s) and allow you to conduct further research and apply content related to hospitality and travel marketing.
- **Web Links**—For each chapter, a summarized list of Web links is provided for your reference. A listing of travel trade intermediaries and publications is also provided.
- **PowerPoint Presentation**—For each chapter, a detailed PowerPoint slide presentation is provided.

The Online Resources™ icon appears at the end of each chapter to prompt you to go online and take advantage of the many features provided.

You can find the Online Resources™ at http://www.Hospitality-Tourism.delmar.com. The Online Resources™ requires the following username and password to enter the restricted area.

username: httr7258
password: 8527rtth

ACKNOWLEDGEMENTS

A textbook like this one is never a one-person effort but is the result of a variety of creative minds. There are many people who have helped or inspired me in my career as a management consultant and later as a professor. I would like to offer special thanks to the following individuals:

Melissa Riveglia of Delmar Thomson Learning, who expertly guided the book through the development of the third edition.

Rodney Lindsey and **Jim Carpenter,** former students, who were such a great help in acquiring photographs and advertisements and in reviewing manuscript drafts.

Kimberly Risk, former student, for her insightful comments in reviewing manuscript drafts.

Amy So, David Wimbiscus, Troy Bennett, and **Liz Berry,** former students, for their help in acquiring photographs and advertisements. An added thanks is due to Troy for shooting some of the photographs.

Joe Cioch and **Brother Herman Zaccarelli** for coaxing me to come to Purdue
University. A special thanks is due to Brother Herman for his insightful guidance
in choosing the best publishing company.

Patrick Wilson of Hospitality Marketing in Toronto for the initial idea that sparked
all five steps in the hospitality and travel marketing system.

I would also like to thank the following reviewers whose helpful comments and
suggestions helped shape the final product:

Nancy Chappie, CTC
Travel University International
San Diego, California

John W. O'Neill, MAI, CHE, PhD
Johnson and Wales University
Providence, Rhode Island

Leslie Furr, PhD
Georgia Southern University
Statesboro, Georgia

David Schoenberg, PhD
La Guardia Community College
Long Island, New York

Kathryn Hashimoto, PhD
University of New Orleans
New Orleans, Louisiana

Maria A. McConnell, CTC
Lorain County Community
College
Elyria, Ohio

Alastair M. Morrison, Ph.D.
West Lafayette, Indiana

ABOUT THE AUTHOR

Alastair Morrison is a Professor in Purdue University's Department of Hospitality and
Tourism Management. He also serves as the Director of the Purdue Tourism & Hospitality Research Center and is the Director of International Programs for the School of
Consumer & Family Sciences. Dr. Morrison has hospitality and travel industry experience in the United States, Canada, the United Kingdom, and Australia. Most recently he
has conducted training programs and provided tourism marketing and development
advice in Australia, Bahrain, Ghana, Honduras, India, Jamaica, Malaysia, New Zealand,
Poland, Scotland, Singapore, Slovenia, Sri Lanka, Thailand, Trinidad & Tobago, and
Vietnam. He was a Visiting Professor at the Scottish Hotel School, University of Strathclyde in 1999 and during 1992 was the Queensland Tourist & Travel Corporation Visiting Lecturer at James Cook University in Queensland, Australia.

Prior to joining the Purdue University faculty, Dr. Morrison spent 11 years in
Canada as a management consultant specializing in the hospitality and travel industry.
In 1980, along with two partners, he established a private consulting firm called The
Economic Planning Group of Canada, now one of the leading companies in the field.
This book reflects Dr. Morrison's international background and his unique blend of
practical and academic experience. A native of Scotland, he has both lived and worked
in four different countries. His work and educational background have given him the
basic ingredients for an effective marketing textbook—an in-depth knowledge of marketing theory plus a clear understanding of what actually works in practice.

Dr. Morrison has had extensive experience in publishing, including 11 years of
writing hospitality and travel manuscripts on behalf of Tourism Canada and other

government agencies. He is the co-author with Robert Christie Mill of *The Tourism System* and with Philip Pearce and Joy Rutledge of *Tourism: Bridges Across Continents*. He has also written a variety of journal articles related to marketing and market segmentation in the hospitality and travel industry.

Career Summary

1985–2001 Professor, Associate Professor, Assistant Professor, Hospitality and Tourism Management Department, Purdue University, West Lafayette, Indiana

1980–85 President, The Economic Planning Group of Canada, Management Consultants, Ottawa, Ontario

1979–80 Vice-President, Inntrec Group Inc., Management Consultants, Waterloo, Ontario

1974–79 Senior Consultant and Consultant, Pannell Kerr Forster, Toronto, Ontario

PART

I

INTRODUCTION TO MARKETING

WHERE ARE WE NOW?

WHERE WOULD WE LIKE TO BE?

HOW DO WE GET THERE?

HOW DO WE MAKE SURE WE GET THERE?

HOW DO WE KNOW IF WE GOT THERE?

1

Marketing Defined

What Is Marketing?

Objectives

Having read this chapter, you should be able to:

- Define marketing and explain the six marketing fundamentals used in this book.

- Explain "the price of marketing" concept.

- Compare and contrast the roles of marketing during four evolutionary "eras" and describe the digital marketing era.

- Describe the symptoms of a production and sales orientation.

- Explain the marketing myopia concept.

- Describe the characteristics of a marketing (or customer) orientation and its benefits.

- Explain the core principles of marketing.

- Describe the environment for marketing in the hospitality and travel industry.

- Explain the reasons for the increasing importance of marketing in the industry.

Overview

Why is marketing such a hot topic in today's hospitality and travel industry? Why is it expected to be the key management function in this new century? This chapter addresses these questions by explaining the evolution of marketing. It describes the differences between production and marketing orientations, and emphasizes the importance of adopting a mar-keting orientation in today's competitive climate.

The core principles of marketing are identified and described. This chapter also outlines the benefits of marketing and shows that the hospitality and travel industry has been slow to recognize these benefits.

Key Terms

baby boomers
competition
core principles of marketing
customers' needs
customers' wants
database marketing
digital marketing
e-commerce
economic environment
exchange process
external environment
4 Ps
hospitality and travel industry
hospitality and travel marketing
   environment
Internet

legislation and regulation
market segmentation
marketing
marketing-company era
marketing-company orientation
marketing concept
marketing-department era
marketing environment factors
marketing manager
marketing mix
marketing myopia
marketing orientation
marketing-orientation era
marketing strategy factors
organizational objectives and
   resources

product life cycle
production orientation
production-orientation era
relationship marketing
sales orientation
sales-orientation era
service industries
societal and cultural environment
societal-marketing-orientation era
target markets
technology
value
World Wide Web

You are probably new to marketing, wondering how this subject might help further your career objectives. What if you knew that marketing would be the most important management activity in our industry in this new century? What if we told you that every manager will need to be familiar with the basic principles of marketing?

Are you now more interested in marketing? Well, what is so magical and dynamic about this powerful subject? The best place to start seems to be with a definition of the term.

DEFINITION OF MARKETING

How would you define marketing? Write down your ideas on what you think is involved and compare them later with this book's definition. If you are like most people unfamiliar with marketing, you probably listed such things as advertising, selling, and other sales promotions (e.g., coupons, in-store displays). As you will soon realize, these aspects of marketing are only the tip of the iceberg. Even more marketing work goes on behind the scenes. For example, how and why does a company decide to spend millions of dollars on advertising? What are the reasons for promotions? Why does each organization do things just a little differently? These are just a few of the many behind-the-scenes marketing decisions that companies must make.

This book's definition is based on the following six marketing fundamentals.

1. **Satisfaction of Customers' Needs and Wants**—The primary focus of marketing is on satisfying customers' needs (gaps between what customers have and what they would like to have) and customers' wants (needs of which customers are aware).

2. **Continuous Nature of Marketing**—Marketing is a continuous management activity, not a one-time set of decisions.

3. **Sequential Steps in Marketing**—Good marketing is a process of following a number of sequential steps.

4. **Key Role of Marketing Research**—Using marketing research to anticipate and identify customer needs and wants is essential for effective marketing.

5. **Interdependence of Hospitality and Travel Organizations**—There are many opportunities for cooperation in marketing among organizations in our industry.

6. **Organization-Wide and Multidepartment Effort**—Marketing is not the sole responsibility of one department. To work best, it takes the effort of all departments or divisions.

When you combine these six marketing fundamentals the following definition of marketing emerges:

> Marketing is a continuous, sequential process through which management in the **hospitality and travel industry*** plans, researches, implements, controls, and evaluates activities designed to satisfy both customers' needs and wants and their own organization's objectives. To be most effective, marketing requires the efforts of everyone in an organization and can be made more or less effective by the actions of complementary organizations.
>
> *A group of interrelated organizations providing personal services to customers who are away from home.

You may have noticed in this definition that the five tasks of marketing are planning, research, implementation, control, and evaluation. What do you notice about these five words when arranged in this order? Give yourself a pat on the back if you saw that their first letters spell out the word *PRICE*. The *price of marketing* is that all organizations must do planning, research, implementation, control, and evaluation.

THE PRICE OF MARKETING

P	Planning
R	Research
I	Implementation
C	Control
E	Evaluation

EVOLUTIONARY ERAS OF MARKETING

Now that you know what marketing is, you might be interested in some historical background of the subject. There are differences between the way marketing evolved in nonservice industries and the way it developed in **service industries** (organizations primarily involved in the provision of personal services), which includes the hospitality and travel industry.

Marketing in Nonservice Industries

Among manufacturing and packaged-goods companies, marketing has evolved during four distinct *eras:* (1) production, (2) sales, (3) marketing, and (4) societal marketing (Figure 1-1). The changes in management thinking about marketing developed during these

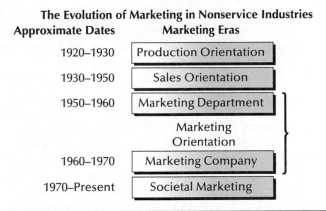

The Evolution of Marketing in Nonservice Industries

◆ FIGURE 1–1   *The evolution of marketing in nonservice industries.* (Adapted from Perreault, William D., and E. Jerome McCarthy, *Essentials of Marketing: A Global Managerial Approach,* 8th ed., 2000. Reproduced with permission of the McGraw-Hill Companies.)

four eras because of technological advances, productivity improvements, intensified competition, expanding market demand, increased management sophistication, changing societal values, and other factors.

1. **Production-Orientation Era.** The production-orientation era was the first evolutionary stage in the development of marketing. It began with the Industrial Revolution and lasted into the 1920s. During this era, the production capacities of factories could not keep pace with demand. Demand exceeded supply. Every item that was manufactured could be sold, and management's emphasis was on producing as many goods as possible. Customers' needs and wants were of secondary importance. Henry Ford summed up production orientation when he said, "They (customers) can have any color they want, as long as it's black." The Ford Motor Company has come a long way since then.

2. **Sales-Orientation Era.** Gradually, technological advances in production and increased competition changed the emphasis of marketing. Beginning in the 1930s, there was enough capacity to meet demand. As competition intensified, the emphasis switched from production to selling. Customers' needs and wants were still of secondary importance. Beating the competition by outselling them was first priority. This was the sales-orientation era, which lasted until the 1950s.

3. **Marketing-Orientation Era.** The marketing-orientation era resulted from even more intense competition and technological advances. Supply now exceeded demand. It was also a result of greater management sophistication and the advancement of marketing as an academic discipline. Organizations began to realize that selling alone did not guarantee satisfied customers and more sales. Customers had more choices than ever before and could select the products and services that best matched their needs. It made good sense to give customers' needs a higher priority than just selling. During this time organizations began adopting the marketing concept (acting on the assumption that satisfying customers' needs and wants is first priority).

   This era had two stages—the marketing-department era and marketing-company era. In the marketing-department era, the need to set up new departments to coordinate marketing activities gained acceptance. Sales departments and divisions were renamed and reorganized, and their responsibilities were expanded to include the related functions of advertising, customer service, and other marketing activities. It was more effective to have all marketing responsibilities in one department, rather than dividing them among several different departments. Marketing was not yet looked at as a long-term activity.

"That's not our problem. It's the marketing department's." This might have been a typical statement of a chef or front-desk supervisor in the marketing-department era. It shows an attitude that satisfying customers' needs is solely a marketing department responsibility and not the concern of other departments.

An organization-wide change of attitude occurred with the onset of the marketing-company era in the 1960s. "It's everyone's problem if our customers are not satisfied" is a statement that typifies this attitude. The marketing department might have had the prime responsibility for marketing-related activities, but all departments played a role in and were affected by customer satisfaction levels. Marketing was seen as a long-term, organizational concern. Survival of the company hinged not only on satisfying customer needs in the short term, but also in the long term. The definition of marketing used in this book is based on a marketing-company orientation.

4. **Societal-Marketing-Orientation Era.** The societal-marketing-orientation era is the final evolutionary era to date. Beginning in the 1970s, organizations started to recognize their social responsibility in addition to their profit and customer-satisfaction objectives. A prime example in the hospitality industry is brewers and distillers that use advertising to fight drunk driving, alcoholism, and under-age drinking (Figure 1–2). Another example is Royal Caribbean International that has created its own environmental management program known as "Save the Waves." The program includes, among other things, the appointment of an Environmental Officer on each of its cruise ships and measures aimed at reducing waste.

Almost all basic marketing textbooks describe these eras by chronicling the histories of a few major manufacturing companies. After reading these books, you are left with the impression that there are no organizations in existence today with production or sales orientations. This is definitely not true. Another misleading impression you might have is that if an organization has a marketing orientation, it automatically follows that managers and staff of the organization have the same orientation. This is not always the case. You might also assume that all organizations must have passed through these evolutionary stages, and at roughly the same time. This confusion is caused by mixing two slightly different concepts—the evolutionary stages in the development of marketing as a management activity (which you have just read about) and the orientations of individual organizations and their employees (which are discussed later).

The Digital Marketing Era?

Some industry observers have suggested that the 1990s witnessed another new era of marketing in which digital technologies were rapidly adopted. No doubt you already know that the Internet revolutionized the way business was done in the 1990s and early 2000s, causing a huge growth in electronic or e-commerce. Hospitality and travel marketers are now making heavy use of the World Wide Web for providing information and accepting reservations. The use of e-mail for communications is a norm in today's marketing environment. Cellular or mobile phones are helping marketing and sales people stay in touch with their clients and home offices. Compact discs (CDs) and digital videodiscs (DVDs) are gaining ground as a digitized alternative to traditional videotapes

◆ **FIGURE 1–2** *Budweiser fights against teenage drinking—an example of societal marketing and social responsibility.* (Courtesy of Anheuser-Busch, Inc.)

EXCELLENCE CASE

Societal-Marketing Orientation:
Ben & Jerry's Homemade, Inc.

Eating ice cream can serve a good cause if your favorite brand is Ben & Jerry's. This Vermont-based company manufactures ice cream, frozen yogurt, sorbet, and other novelty products and has more than 230 franchised and company-owned "scoop shops" in the U.S. It is a great example of a societal-marketing orientation in action in the hospitality and travel industry. Started in 1978 in Burlington, Vermont, with just a $12,000 investment, Ben & Jerry's takes its name from its two founders, Ben Cohen and Jerry Greenfield. The company's societal orientation is embedded in its mission statement:

"Ben & Jerry's is dedicated to the creation and demonstration of a new corporate concept of linked prosperity. Our mission consists of three interrelated parts.

Product

To make, distribute and sell the finest quality all natural ice cream and related products in a wide variety of innovative flavors made from Vermont dairy products.

Economic

To operate the Company on a sound financial basis of profitable growth, increasing value for our shareholders, and creating career opportunities and financial rewards for our employees.

Social

To operate the company in a way that actively recognizes the central role that business plays in the structure of society by initiating innovative ways to improve the quality of life of a broad community—local, national, and international.

Underlying the mission of Ben & Jerry's is the determination to seek new and creative ways of addressing all three parts, while holding a deep respect for individuals inside and outside the company and for the communities of which they are a part."[1]

"Giving away a portion of our profits is nice, but it is a minor thing compared to the positive social impact we can have by making the way we run our business every day a reflection of our conscious caring for the people around us."
Ben Cohen

Ben & Jerry's is one of very few organizations to have a Social Performance Report included as part of its Annual Report. The 1998 report covered eight areas—workplace, manufacturing operations, environment, franchise operations, marketing and sales, international operations, social mission and philanthropy, and finance and shareholders. In 1998, the company allocated $792,595 for giving to nonprofit organizations, or 7.5 percent of its pre-tax profits. Ben & Jerry's has three different ways of giving: through the Ben & Jerry's Foundation, employee community action teams, and corporate grants by the company's Director of Social Mission Development.

This societal orientation, along with great ice cream, has paid off handsomely for Ben & Jerry's. In 1984, the company's sales were just over $4 million. By 1999, they were about $237 million. The company now has scoop shops in

EXCELLENCE CASE *continued*

several other countries, including Canada, France, Israel, the Netherlands, Peru, and the United Kingdom.

A small business that started in 1978 as an ice cream scoop shop in a renovated garage in Burlington, Vermont, has become a multimillion-dollar global ice cream giant. The next time you see Ben & Jerry's distinctive black-and-white Friesian cow logo, you may remember how a good product mixed with a good amount of corporate caring can be a recipe for a great marketing success story.

Discussion Questions

1. How has Ben & Jerry's demonstrated a societal-marketing orientation?
2. What can other hospitality and travel companies learn from the Ben & Jerry's example?
3. Which other hospitality and travel companies have shown they have a societal orientation and how have they demonstrated this orientation?

Web Site

http://www.benjerry.com/

References

1. Ben & Jerry's Web site.

for marketing presentations. Personal digital assistants (PDAs), such as the Palm Pilot, are quickly replacing traditional business calendars and time management systems.

The digital marketing era is fundamentally changing how travelers get information about hospitality and travel services, and how they book them. Airlines like Northwest are providing e-tickets in this new age of *ticketless travel,* and on-line travel agencies and services such as Expedia, Travelocity, and Yahoo Travel are booming.

Computer software programs are changing how marketers look at their customers, and they are leading the transition from mass marketing to database marketing. Database management software allows marketers to gather and use information to form closer relationships with individual customers and to customize appeals to them. In hospitality and travel, frequent-traveler clubs and programs are a key strategy in implementing database-marketing programs.

Is the digital marketing era replacing the societal-marketing-orientation era? The answer is certainly *no* since most organizations continue to realize their social responsibilities while making greater use of digital technologies.

Marketing in the Service Industries

The hospitality and travel industry, along with other service industries, has not followed the same historical evolution in marketing that you have just read about. In fact, the industry is lagging behind manufacturing and packaged-goods firms in its use of marketing by perhaps as much as 10 to 20 years.

Why, you ask, has the hospitality and travel industry let this happen? Many different reasons for this fact are explored in this book, the principal one being that many managers have come up through the ranks. Former chefs and cooks manage restaurants, ex-airline pilots create airline companies, hotel company presidents were front desk clerks, and tour wholesaling company executives used to be tour guides. As these managers advanced, their individual business environments, training, and education stressed the technical details of the business, rather than customers and their needs. Few marketing managers (managers responsible for marketing) with manufacturing and packaged-goods firms have ever worked on the floors of their factories. The statement "In order to market this business, you must know it inside out" reflects a common management attitude in our industry. To modify an old saying, "If you don't know how to cook, you shouldn't be in the marketing department."

A second reason that our industry lags behind is that major technological breakthroughs came later than they did in the manufacturing and packaged-goods industry. The introduction of mass production as a manufacturing concept is normally credited to Henry Ford in the early 1900s. Mass production did not arrive in the hospitality and travel industry until three or four decades later. For example, Pan American offered the first transatlantic passenger flight—in a flying boat—in 1939 (Figure 1–3a). The inaugural flight of British Airways, then BOAC, came even later—in 1946. The year 1952 marked the advent of the Holiday Inn concept (Figure 1–3b) and the now-familiar golden arches of McDonald's first welcomed customers in 1955 (Figure 1–3c). That same year, Walt Disney revolutionized the commercial attraction business by opening North America's first theme park—Disneyland. The first wide-bodied jet took to the air in 1970. Because of this technological time lag, our managers have had 30 years or less to perfect their marketing skills. Others in the manufacturing and packaged-goods industries have had 60 to 70 years. In addition, a large part of these 30 years has been spent perfecting technology and operating systems in the hospitality and travel industry for greater efficiency and profitability.

(a)

(b)

(c)

◆ **FIGURE 1–3** *Technological breakthroughs came later in the hospitality and travel industry. (a) 1939: The first transatlantic passenger flight.* (Courtesy of Pan American) *(b) 1952: The first North American family-oriented motor hotel chain.* (Courtesy of Holiday Inns Inc.) *(c) 1955: The first McDonald's store, Des Plaines, Ill.* (Courtesy of McDonald's Corporation)

DEVELOPING A MARKETING ORIENTATION

You have probably noticed how many times the words *marketing orientation* have already been used. Being the intelligent person that you are, you may have been alerted to the fact that this is a key aspect of this field of marketing. If we tell you it may also be the key to your future career success, you might like to hear more.

Unfortunately, none of us are born with a marketing orientation. It is to be learned and polished through constant practice. Surprisingly, some successful managers have never heard of marketing orientation, but they act as if they had. You might wonder how this can be. The answer is simple. A marketing orientation is such a common-sense approach to business today that some people develop it through their experience, knowledge of what works, and natural intuition, without ever having read a single marketing book or come within 100 miles of a business school. Other people are not as lucky. They may be exposed to the same stimuli, but still emerge with a production orientation or sales orientation.

EXCELLENCE CASE

Marketing Orientation:
The Walt Disney Company

One look at the consolidated income statement for this much-loved company quickly shows the importance of its theme parks and resorts. They accounted for 27 percent of revenues and 59 percent of operating income in 2000.[1] The tremendous success of Disneyland and Walt Disney World, followed by Tokyo Disneyland, The Disney-MGM Studios, Paris Disneyland, Disney's Wild Animal Kingdom, and Disney's California Adventure is one of our industry's premier examples in the application of *marketing orientation.*

Walt Disney himself was the father of the theme park concept, having come up with the idea after a day at an amusement park with his two daughters. He noticed that while his children had a great time on the rides, there was nothing for parents to do but sit and watch. He responded to customers' needs with the Disney-land development—an innovative entertainment concept for the entire family. Since Disneyland's debut in 1955, what has happened at Disney's theme parks and resorts has, to say the least, been *magical.* While the public is just beginning to enjoy a new attraction, resort hotel, or other feature, the company announces plans for others. There is recognition at Disney that entertainment always has to be fresh. It can lose its interest value if it remains unchanged for a long time.

Although the Disney development history is a story in itself, what happens behind the scenes is what fascinates those of us in the industry. As you will see in Chapter 2, one of the greatest difficulties with services like ours is that of *standardizing quality.* As one person said, "You can't paint a smile on a human being." Yet friendly, cheerful employees are so important in ensuring customer satisfaction. Given this human factor, how does an organization such as Disney do such an excellent job with its staff? The answer is a carefully orchestrated orientation and training program.

All new employees are required to attend the Disney Traditions Program, an all-day orienta-tion at Disney University. They are schooled in the company's philosophies and operating procedures, and they learn that Disney is in the entertainment business—the business of making people smile and be happy. Disney has even concocted a new language to make sure its employees remember the basic principles:

- Backstage = Behind-the-scenes areas
- Casting = Personnel services
- Cast Members = Disney employees
- Costumes = Uniforms
- Disney Theme Show = Entire experience at theme park and resorts
- Guests = Customers
- Hosts/Hostesses = Every Disney employee
- Onstage = Customer-contact areas
- Presenting the Show = Serving and enter-taining guests
- Role = Work position

New cast members also learn about the importance of their appearance and the need for them to reflect *The Disney Look.* To help clarify this, a multi-page, four-color booklet provides details on such items as costumes, hair and hair coloring, sideburns, fingernails, jewelry, nametags, and even the use of aftershave and deodorant. From bottom to top, Disney is a first-name organization, and employees must wear a nametag showing their names.

Another indication of Disney's marketing orientation is the constant surveying of guests to determine their satisfaction levels. Hundreds of guests are surveyed each week at theme parks to ensure that the company's high standards are being maintained.

There probably is no better example in the world of a hospitality and travel organization that exudes a marketing orientation than the Walt Disney Company. From their extremely careful research of new marketing opportunities to their elaborate procedures for delivering consistent, friendly service, the company is definitely a model for all facets of modern marketing.

EXCELLENCE CASE *continued*

Discussion Questions

1. Has the Walt Disney Company suffered from the condition known as *marketing myopia (shortsightedness in thinking and planning)*? What evidence is there to support your answer in the Excellence Case or in your own knowledge about this company?
2. Which of the nine characteristics of marketing/ orientation are demonstrated in the Walt Disney Company case?

Web Site

http://disney.go.com/

Reference

1. The Walt Disney Company Annual Report 2000.
   http://disney.go.com/investors/annual99/

Production and Sales Orientation

Many organizations and managers within the hospitality and travel industry have either a **production orientation** or a **sales orientation.** How can you spot them? Production- and sales-oriented organizations have a very strong internal focus. Their entire world revolves only around what goes on within the walls of their business premises. A production-oriented organization puts most of its emphasis on selling services that are the easiest and most efficient to produce. They tend to emphasize sales rather than profits. These companies may provide only the services their executives like best or the ones they think customers like based on their managers' opinions.

There are 13 symptoms that can be used to diagnose production and sales orientations:

1. Planning is short term. Little value is attached to long-term planning.
2. Long-term decisions are made only when serious problems are encountered. When things are going well, no such decisions are made.
3. There is a definite reluctance to change.
4. Business growth is seen as being assured, and current business volumes are viewed as guaranteed.
5. Providing the best or highest quality service is assumed to be an automatic guarantee of success. This is the *better-mousetrap fallacy.*
6. Little is known about the specific characteristics and needs of customers. Research on customers' needs is not given a high priority. Managers assume they know what customers need without any research.
7. Promotions stress service or product features, rather than the customer needs they satisfy.
8. Customers are given only what they ask for and what is normally provided—no more, no less.
9. Decisions are made from a production or sales perspective, not with customers' needs in mind.
10. The organization or department is seen as an *island unto itself.* Cooperation with other departments and complementary organizations (those providing related travel services) is not considered to be very valuable. Only when there is an emergency is the need to cooperate recognized.

11. Departments or divisions have overlapping activities and responsibilities related to marketing. There are open or hidden conflicts between departments concerning these activities and responsibilities.

12. Department or division managers tend to be very defensive and protective of their *domains.*

13. The organization is set up and the services are offered because the owners themselves like them. This is known as the *share-the-wealth syndrome.*

Figure 1–4 shows a set of actual statements from managers in our industry that reflect some of these symptoms. Look at these statements and see if you can spot any of the 13 symptoms of production and sales orientations.

The phrase marketing myopia was coined in 1960 to describe many of these 13 symptoms of production- and sales-oriented orientations.[2] The dictionary meaning of myopia is "shortsightedness or lack of discernment in thinking or planning."[3] Another way of putting this is being unable or unwilling to think, see, and plan beyond the short term. Managers often fail to realize there's no such thing as a perpetual growth industry. Those who act as if growth is inevitable run the risk of failure in the long term, because it is not the ability to produce that guarantees success, but being able to identify and adapt to customer needs and wants.

Lodging Example

"The demand for rooms will always keep growing in this community. In any case, our rooms and restaurants will be the best available."
- Assumes that growth is inevitable (symptom #4).
- Assumes that having the best or highest quality is a guarantee of success (#5).

Food-Service Example

"My sister and I love French food. We are going to open a French restaurant because there are enough people in every town that share our love for the French cuisine."
- Assumes that customers have the same needs, wants, and preferences as the organization (#6, #13).

Travel Agency Example

"I'm sorry, Mrs. Jones, but that was the airline's fault, not ours. You never asked me to recommend any alternative routes or carriers."
- Assumes that customers view the travel industry as a group of independent suppliers and do not blame all for the mistakes of others (#10).
- Assumes that it is only necessary to provide what customers themselves ask for (#8).

Cruise Line Example

"Our ships are the largest and most expensive to build. These are the features we stress most in our advertising, because we think this is important to our cruise patrons."
- Assumes that stressing product features is of greatest importance. This is not usually the case (#7).

Travel Destination Example

"We really can't handle any more visitors in the summer months, so we're switching all our promotional efforts to other periods of the year."
- Assumes that current success is guaranteed for the future (#1, #2, #4).

◆ **FIGURE 1–4** *Typical statements reflecting production and sales orientations.*

Can you think of any examples of marketing myopia in the hospitality and travel industry? There certainly have been some. One occurred in domestic and foreign travel in the 1970s and 1980s. During the 1960s and early 1970s, world tourism was expanding at an annual rate of at least 10 percent. Everyone confidently predicted a continuation of this growth into the 1980s, 1990s, and beyond. Tourism was touted as a growth industry, and no one saw a downturn in this expansion. The United States hotel industry, fueled by favorable tax laws, went through an unprecedented expansion of supply in the early 1980s, and a wide array of new hotel brands were launched. The future seemed to be rosy for our industry.

The so-called energy crisis, widespread economic problems, terrorism, changes in tax laws, and military conflict altered tourism's growth pattern in the mid-1970s to the mid-1990s. Year-to-year increases fell in percentage terms, and in some areas travel volumes actually decreased. United States hotel occupancies plummeted as the industry struggled to absorb the building boom of the 1980s.

The early 1990s brought another period of incredible change worldwide. On August 1, 1990, Iraq and Saddam Hussein invaded Kuwait. This incident far from the shores of North America was to have a major negative impact on the hospitality and travel industry around the world. In August 1991, almost two years after the Berlin Wall fell, the 74 years of Communist Party rule in the USSR was effectively ended. The collapse of communism welcomed a significant new tourism destination—Eastern Europe—to the already competitive world tourism scene. In 2001, foot-and-mouth disease threatened to cause a major decrease in international travel to Europe.

There are also frequent cases of marketing myopia in the restaurant business. New concepts rise and fall in popularity at an alarming rate. Management often becomes preoccupied with expansion and production efficiency when demand for a particular concept is rising, but fails to prepare for an eventual downturn in popularity. New and different ways of satisfying customer needs must be found before the decline occurs.

As these events show, it was a strategic error for management in the hospitality and travel industry to assume that domestic and international travel would always be a growth industry. As Levitt suggested in 1960, without proper planning and an acceptance of change as inevitable, nothing is assured. History has proven the wisdom of his words in our industry. Some of our industry's former *giants,* including Pan American, Eastern Airlines, and Howard Johnson are now its *dinosaurs.*

Production-oriented organizations also define their industries too narrowly and miss lucrative marketing opportunities. For example, if The Walt Disney Company had defined its business as just movies instead of the *entertainment* industry, it would have missed the opportunity to get into the profitable theme park field. Holiday Inns, now part of Bass Hotels & Resorts, could have stuck closely to its original formula of providing affordable family accommodations in roadside locations, missing the lucrative all-suite hotel concept and the Embassy Suites brand (now owned by Hilton).

The dangers of a production orientation are serious, the ultimate being eventual organizational failure. The inability to understand customer needs and changes in these needs is the most serious long-term threat. Loss of market share, falling business volumes, increased customer dissatisfaction, and missed marketing opportunities are some of the results of such an orientation. Management and staff energies tend to be focused inwardly. Profitable opportunities for cooperation between departments and with complementary organizations are neglected.

Experts use the words orientation, attitude, philosophy, and perspective interchangeably to describe an organization's or person's view of marketing. Whichever stance managers or their organizations adopt, this view tends to trickle down to all employees. If an organization is production oriented, then its managers usually follow suit. If managers are production oriented, their staffs mimic them.

Marketing Orientation

Being marketing oriented is essential in today's competitive environment. It will also be a great help to you in your career! So what does it involve? **Marketing orientation** means acceptance and adoption of the marketing concept—customer needs are first priority. Marketing-oriented organizations and managers always have a long-term perspective.

How can you spot an organization with a marketing orientation? Just as there are symptoms of production or sales-orientation, there are nine principal characteristics that can be used to identify marketing-oriented organizations:

1. Customer needs are a first priority and understanding these needs is a constant concern.
2. Marketing research is an ongoing activity assigned a very high priority.
3. Customers' perceptions of the organization are known.
4. Frequent reviews are made of strengths and weaknesses relative to competitors.
5. The value of long-term planning is fully appreciated.
6. The scope of business or activities is broadly set, and change is seen as inevitable.
7. Interdepartmental cooperation is valued and encouraged.
8. Cooperation with complementary organizations is recognized as worthwhile.
9. Measurement and evaluation of marketing activities are done frequently.

1. **Customer needs are a first priority and understanding these needs is a constant concern.** Examples of this are a restaurant chain that places an oversized suggestion box near the door of its stores. Another example is a travel agency that holds periodic focus group meetings with 10 to 15 of its customers. McDonald's and other fast-food companies' introduction of biodegradable packaging reflects customer concerns for our environment. Marriott's concern for the plight of the homeless is another good example of a company exercising its social responsibility. These examples clearly show the organizations' concern for the customer's *two cents*. With such a focus on the customer's needs and their actual experiences with the organization's services, the result is usually more-satisfied customers. Satisfied customers return and tell their friends about their experiences with marketing-oriented hospitality and travel organizations. A second benefit is that this gives all departments, managers, and staff a common goal—the satisfied customer.

2. **Marketing research is an ongoing activity assigned a very high priority.** An example of this is a theme park company that interviews hundreds of park guests each week to see if these customers feel they received value for money. Another example is the computerized guest comment system introduced by Marriott for its Fairfield Inn properties. A third example is the hotel general manager who drives the airport limousine once or twice a week to find out what guests think of the hotel. One benefit of this type of ongoing marketing research is that it provides an *early warning system* for changes in customer needs and expectations. It also gives an accurate indication of how well the organization is satisfying customer needs.

3. **Customers' perceptions of the organization are known.** It is very important in business to find out customers' images of the organization. As companies such as Ramada Inns and Club Med found out through customer surveys, customers' perceptions are not always favorable, nor are they always the same as management's

image of their own companies. If customers' perceptions are identified, facilities, services, and promotions can be designed to match these images.

4. **Frequent reviews are made of strengths and weaknesses relative to competitors.** One of the biggest dangers in business today is complacency. As Holiday Inn found out, yesterday's strengths (standardized properties, highway locations) can become tomorrow's weaknesses (lack of variety, high gasoline prices). Club Med's wide assortment of recreational activities for its guests (a strength) gave some potential customers the perception that they would be forced to participate in them (a weakness). Future marketing success usually comes from accentuating strengths and eliminating weaknesses.

5. **The value of long-term planning is fully appreciated.** Always thinking "long term" is a key ingredient for success in the hospitality and travel industry. Building lasting relationships with individual customers, distribution channels, and other industry partners—called relationship marketing[4]—is much more important than making a one-time sale or deal. The travel agent who finds a customer the lowest-priced airfare, knowing full well that a higher-priced ticket would produce a higher commission, demonstrates an investment in long-term customer satisfaction. As well as building lasting relationships, marketing-oriented organizations are always looking five or more years into the future, deciding how they will adapt to change. In so doing, changes in customer needs are anticipated and acted upon, and marketing opportunities are realized.

6. **The scope of business or activities is broadly set, and change is seen as inevitable.** If the passenger railroad companies throughout the world had defined their business as *transportation* and not *railways,* they would probably be operating some of the largest airline companies today. The railways could have been more successful if they had adopted Disney's lead of a broadly set industry definition. Entertainment became Disney's industry definition, not movies. This gave Disney much greater flexibility to adapt to future trends and opportunities. The marketing-oriented organization does not resist but adapts smoothly to change. It capitalizes on opportunities that serve customers more comprehensively or those that tap into related fields.

7. **Interdepartmental cooperation is valued and encouraged.** For marketing to work at its best, all the departments in an organization must play a role. Jan Carlzon's now famous turnaround of the Scandinavian Airline System (SAS) is an excellent example of *team play* in a marketing organization. By giving all its customer-contact employees, even the baggage handlers, the power to make their own decisions to serve customers better, SAS became a highly profitable airline. Empowering staff to provide quality customer service was Jan Carlzon's key to interdepartmental cooperation.[5]

8. **Cooperation with complementary organizations is recognized as worthwhile.** Hospitality and travel is an industry with great opportunities for marketing partnerships between different companies. It makes sense for companies to cooperate because each of them provides only part of the experience that customers desire. The synergy that comes through cooperation normally benefits the customer. Disney's cosponsorship concept in its theme parks has meant more entertainment for park guests. The thousands of vacation and tour packages now available to travelers provide much greater customer choice. In short, increased cooperation leads to better services and greater customer satisfaction.

9. **Measurement and evaluation of marketing activities are done frequently.** The marketing-oriented organization always prepares a *report card* of the successes and failures in its marketing activities. Effective marketing activities are identified and

- Changes in customer needs and characteristics are known.
- Cooperation among an organization's departments increases.
- Cooperation with complementary organizations increases.
- Customers are more satisfied.
- Departments, managers, and staff share a common goal.
- Effective marketing programs are repeated or enhanced; ineffective ones are dropped.
- Marketing expenditures and human resources are used most effectively.
- More marketing opportunities are realized.
- Services, products, and promotions match the customer's image of the organization.
- Strengths are accentuated and weaknesses addressed.
- Viability of new services and products are identified.

◆ **FIGURE 1–5**   *Benefits of having a marketing orientation.*

then repeated or enhanced. Ineffective activities are reevaluated or dropped. Doing this ensures that marketing dollars and staff are used as effectively as possible. Despite the resounding successes of its marketing programs in the *Crocodile Dundee* era, in 1991, the Australian Tourist Commission conducted one of the most extensive evaluations of marketing by a national tourism organization. The successful marketing organizations do not rest on their laurels!

The benefits of having a marketing orientation are shown in Figure 1–5.

CORE PRINCIPLES OF MARKETING

Now you are ready to hear about the seven core principles of marketing that will be so important to your career. They are as follows:

1. The marketing concept
2. Marketing orientation
3. Satisfying customers' needs and wants
4. Market segmentation
5. Value and the exchange process
6. Product life cycle
7. Marketing mix

1. **The Marketing Concept.** When hospitality and travel managers adopt the *marketing concept*, it means they act on the belief that satisfying customers' needs and wants is first priority. They constantly put themselves in their customers' shoes, and ask, "How would I react if I were one of our customers?" They continually force themselves to put resources and effort toward satisfying customer needs and wants. Walt Disney demonstrated the rich rewards of "wearing his customers' shoes" when he came up with the Disneyland theme park concept. Sitting, rather bored, on a bench in an amusement park watching his two daughters playing on the rides, he realized there was a need for parks with entertainment for the whole family, not just children.

♦ **FIGURE 1–6** *Successful application of the core principles of marketing, the late J. Willard Marriott, Sr. exemplified customer orientation.* (Courtesy of Marriott International.)

2. **Marketing Orientation.** Having a *marketing orientation* implies that the manager or organization has accepted the marketing concept and acts according to it. The late J. Willard Marriott, Sr. exemplified customer orientation by reading daily every single comment card from guests staying at Marriott's many properties, Figure 1–6.

3. **Satisfying Customers' Needs and Wants.** To ensure long-term survival in today's competitive business environment, all hospitality and travel organizations must realize that the key to their existence is the ongoing satisfaction of *customers' needs and wants*. In this marketing-orientation era, they must always be alert for new opportunities to convert customers' needs and wants into sales.

4. **Market Segmentation.** All customers are not alike. Experts have come up with the term **market segmentation** to describe this concept. It is better to pick out specific groups of people—or **target markets**—and market only to them. Some call this the *rifle* approach, as compared with the *shotgun* approach. Assuming you are a good shot, you can aim at a specific target and hit it. If you use a shotgun, you might also hit the target, but a lot of precious buckshot would be wasted. Hospitality and travel marketers can't afford wasted buckshot, because marketing dollars and resources are limited. They must take aim at specific target markets to ensure the highest returns. Contiki, for example, is a tour wholesaler that puts together vacation packages specifically for 18 to 35 year olds who belong to the so-called Generation X.

5. **Value and the Exchange Process.** *Value* and *value for money* are terms often used in today's business and in our daily lives. Although easy to say, these terms are hard to define. Value is the *V* in the four pillars of McDonald's *QSCV,* a concept on which the corporation built an enormously successful business. Quality, service, and cleanliness are the other three. But what specifically does McDonald's mean when it says value? **Value** represents a mental estimate that customers make of a hospitality or travel service's ability to satisfy their needs and wants. Some customers equate value closely with price; others do not. Price is not the only indicator of value.

   Marketing is an **exchange process.** Suppliers of hospitality and travel services trade items of value with their customers. The industry provides services and experiences that customers find valuable when they are away from home. In return,

(a)   (b)

◆ **FIGURE 1–7**   *Atlantic City has had two product life cycles. (a) Atlantic City's new life as a casino gambling destination.* (Courtesy of the Atlantic City Convention & Visitor's Bureau) *(b) Atlantic City in pre-casino era.* (Courtesy of the Atlantic City Free Public Library)

customers make reservations and pay money, which satisfies the industry's financial objectives.

6. **Product Life Cycle.** The product life cycle idea suggests all hospitality and travel services pass through four predictable stages: (1) introduction, (2) growth, (3) maturity, and (4) decline. Marketing approaches need to be modified with each stage. Avoiding a decline is the key to long-term survival. Atlantic City, New Jersey, is a great example of a travel destination that went through one life cycle (from a fashionable to a rather seedy seaside resort) and then got a completely new lease on life as an exciting gambling destination (Figure 1–7).

7. **Marketing Mix.** Every organization has a marketing mix. It includes the marketing strategy factors **(the Ps of marketing)** that are used to satisfy the needs of specific customer groups. Traditionally, four such factors are identified. They are product, place, promotion, and price—the 4 Ps. This book adds another 4 Ps that are especially important in hospitality and travel marketing: people, packaging, programming, and partnership (Figure 1–8).

THE HOSPITALITY AND TRAVEL MARKETING ENVIRONMENT

Marketing success is based both on marketing strategy factors (the marketing mix) and marketing environment factors. These factors make up the hospitality and travel marketing environment (all the factors to be considered when making marketing decisions).

> **Traditional 4 Ps of Marketing**
> Product
> Place
> Promotion
> Price
>
> **Additional 4 Ps of Hospitality and Travel Marketing**
> People
> Packaging
> Programming
> Partnership

◆ **FIGURE 1–8**   *Marketing strategy factors.*

The marketing mix can be changed in many different ways. For instance, an organization can switch from magazine to television advertising, or from radio advertising to coupon promotions. Time, marketing dollars, and customer response are the limiting factors.

Marketing environment factors are events completely beyond the direct control of the marketing manager. Some people call these events the external environment that shapes the way business is done. The six marketing environment factors are as follows:

1. Competition
2. Legislation and regulation
3. Economic environment
4. Technology
5. Societal and cultural environment
6. Organizational objectives and resources [6,7]

1. **Competition.** Marketing managers can influence the actions of competitive organizations, but they cannot control them. The number and size of competing companies are also uncontrollable. Competition has expanded rapidly in our industry. There are more lodging and restaurant chains, airlines, travel agencies, attractions, tour wholesalers, and convention and visitors bureaus than ever before. Destinations are pouring more money into attracting visitors. Hospitality and travel's growth potential has been the main reason for intensifying competition. Competition is also becoming global as more companies expand into foreign countries.

Competition is a dynamic process in the industry. One company will implement a marketing strategy, and then its competitors will react with counter-strategies. One-upmanship seems to be a constant. An airline will introduce a frequent flyer program, and then its competitors will do the same. One hotel company will provide executive floors in its properties, only to be matched a little later by other companies. Salad bars will be added by a fast-food chain, and the same feature will then appear in competitive outlets. "If it works for them, we'll copy it" seems to be the rule.

No one can afford to stand still in our industry. Marketing managers constantly need to keep track of competitors' marketing activities, as well as their own. There has to be enough flexibility to modify an organization's marketing programs to react to competitive moves.

There are three levels of competition in the industry: (1) direct competition, (2) substitute services, and (3) indirect competition. What we have been talking about is the most direct type of competition—organizations with similar services competing to satisfy the needs of the same customer groups. The second level of competition comes from substituting certain services and goods for others. Instead of going on vacation, for example, a family could stay at home, maintain the lawn, swim in the backyard pool, watch movies on cable television, or travel *virtually* on the World Wide Web. A telephone conference call is a substitute for a meeting at a central location. Home-cooked meals compete with trips to fast-food restaurants.

The third level consists of those companies and nonprofit organizations that are competing against our industry for the customer's dollar. Mortgage payments; grocery, medical, and dental bills; insurance costs; and home improvement expenses are just some of these indirect competitors. The fight for the individual consumer's disposable income (what is left after taxes) is fierce. Competition for corporate travel and entertainment dollars is no less intense. Companies can spend money in many different ways, including cutting out some of their travel costs. This cutback can be even more devastating than the effects of direct industry competition. Marketing managers must accept the fact that they face both direct and indirect competition. They have to be on top of what competitors are doing and be flexible enough to react to change when the time comes.

2. **Legislation and Regulation.** Marketing is also affected directly and indirectly by the legislation and regulation of the land. There are specific laws concerning how services and products can be advertised, how contests and sweepstakes must be structured, who can and cannot drink, and much more. Marketing must be performed within the bounds of these laws and regulations, yet these laws are beyond an individual organization's control.

Some pieces of legislation or certain regulations have a greater impact on the industry than others. Deregulation of the United States' airline industry had an enormous impact. Discounted fares and more commercial airlines routes were just some of the outcomes of deregulation. Changes in the tax deductibility of travel and entertainment expenses also have major impacts, as do changes in the minimum-age provisions of drinking laws. As mentioned earlier, the tax laws regarding hotel investments had a major impact on the expansion of the United States hotel industry in the 1980s.

Laws and regulations dictate how business is done. They directly affect the ways that services and products can be marketed, and they are constantly changing. Sometimes a piece of legislation, such as airline deregulation, is passed that completely changes an industry. Organizations and marketing managers need to keep up to date on legislative and regulatory adjustments. Industry and trade association membership helps achieve this goal, but this association membership has to be backed up with internal monitoring of these trends.

3. **Economic Environment.** Inflation, unemployment, and recession are three economic environment factors that plagued the economies of developed countries in the 1970s and 1980s. They also hurt the hospitality and travel industry. Less money was available for business and pleasure travel, and the dining-out dollar was more tightly guarded. In poor economic times, companies and individuals tend to look for substitute services and goods. Conference calls replace meetings, national meetings

become regional, and staying at home is substituted for vacations. A return to these necessionary conditions was predicted for 2001.

There are local, regional, national, and international components of the economic environment. Changes in the local and regional economies can have a very direct impact on hospitality and travel organizations. The opening of new industrial plants can be very positive. Industrial closures may have the opposite impact. In a one-industry community, a plant closure can be fatal for its hospitality and travel businesses. International economic events have an indirect impact on the industry. The OPEC-induced energy crisis in the mid-1970s was a turning point for travel within North America. Shorter vacation trips taken closer to home became the predominant trend. Gone was the two- to three-week family touring trip in the car. The energy crisis changed the pattern of travel and indirectly influenced many people and businesses in our industry.

4. **Technology.** Technology is a constant frontier of change. Hospitality and travel marketers need to watch two aspects of the technological environment. First, using new technology may provide a competitive edge. Bass Hotels & Resorts is a technological leader in the lodging industry, because it has made a major commitment to satellite and videoconferencing systems. This is not surprising since in 1957, the corporation became the first chain to have a black-and-white television in every guest room. Computer technology is advancing rapidly in the industry. As a result, airlines, travel agents, and hotels, to name but a few, provide better customer service and enjoy many other advantages that computers offer.

   A second aspect is the impact of technology on customers (see figure 1-9). People are inundated with technological changes. Sophisticated in-home entertainment systems, including VCRs, rented movies, CDs and DVDs, personal computers, and satellite dishes, have become a viable substitute for out-of-home entertainment and travel. A threat on one side, technology is a friend on the other. Advances in home-maintenance-equipment technology have reduced the time required for household chores, making more time available for out-of-home entertainment and travel.

5. **Societal and Cultural Environment.** There are also two sides to societal and cultural environment. First, an organization must consider how customers will react to marketing activities based on societal and cultural norms. For example, showing X-rated

A Touch of Technology

Hertz NeverLost System

- Consits of an in-car satellite navigation system based on global positioning (GPS) technology.
- Daily fee is charged for rental of the system.
- Shows drivers their exact locations.
- Provides directions and distance between two points.
- Visual and audio prompts are given.
- Audio prompts are in English, Dutch, French, German, Italian, and Spanish.
- More information is available at http://www.hertz.com

Lost? Never!

Only Hertz has NeverLost.®
The revolutionary GPS in-car
satellite navigation system
that tells you the best
way to get there.

When traveling, if you don't know where
you're going, then you're going nowhere,
fast. That's why there's NeverLost from Hertz.
Even when your plans take you from city
to city, you'll always know exactly where
to go. That's because NeverLost is the most
technologically advanced way to find
the smartest distance between two points.
The visual and audio prompts and turn-
by-turn guidance make it simple to know
where you're going. And knowing where to
go means always getting there on time.
NeverLost. Another reason nobody does it
exactly like Hertz.

Find us on the web at **hertz.com** or AOL
Keyword: **hertz.**

Hertz
exactly.®

Hertz rents Fords and other fine cars.
®REG. U.S. PAT. OFF. ©HERTZ SYSTEM INC., 2000/013-00.

For Your Information: Nominal daily fee. Subject to availability.

◆ **FIGURE 1–9** *Rental car navigation made easier with the Hertz NerverLost system.*
(Courtesy of Hertz System, Inc. © 2001 Hertz System, Inc. Hertz is a registered service
mark and trademark of Hertz System, Inc.)

movies might be popular with some as in-flight entertainment, but it is socially unacceptable. Although popular in France, horsemeat still has not found a place at the
North American restaurant table.

Second, customers themselves are affected by changes in society and culture. Economic pressures and social change have combined making it essential and more acceptable for women to work outside the home. The Protestant work ethic is also under siege. Hedonistic (pleasure is good for you) vacations are now popular. Club
Med's ascent to being the second-largest hotel/resort outside the United States attests
to this fact.[8] In addition, more people want to learn useful skills during their vacations and on weekends.

6. **Organizational Objectives and Resources.** Organizational objectives and resources represent the final uncontrollable factor. Marketing is not the only organizational concern, although it is a key to long-term success and survival. Marketing ac-

tivities need to be weighed against competing priorities for resources. A new brochure might have to go head-to-head with a site on the Web, a proposed sales force against more reservationists.

A great marketing idea can run contrary to an organization's objectives or policies. Airlines could capitalize on fatal crashes of competitive jets. Countries promoting tourism could cash in on acts of terrorism and civil disturbances in competing destinations. Restaurants and hotels could criticize specific competitive chains in their media campaigns. These negative approaches are seldom followed because they clash with a company's overall policies and objectives. There is an unwritten code of professional conduct in the industry that discourages these "great" ideas.

INCREASED IMPORTANCE OF MARKETING IN THE INDUSTRY

When you add up what has just been said, it is easy to see that the hospitality and travel industry has undergone rapid change. Continuing change is inevitable. Marketing plays a key role in an organization's ability to cope with change.

Marketing is now more important to our industry than ever before. Greater competition, increased market fragmentation and complexity, and more experienced customers have created a greater emphasis on marketing. Marketing in the industry has become more professional and aggressive.

Let us consider increased competition first. There are now more hotels, restaurants, bars, airlines, theme parks, car rental outlets, and cruise lines than there have ever been. Another supply-side trend heating up competition has been the growth of chain, franchise, and referral/consortium organizations. These groups are present in all parts of the industry. By pooling resources in national programs, they have added to their marketing clout, and have increased competition. Mergers and acquisitions are also a constant, tending to put more marketing power in the hands of fewer organizations.

The market used to be easy to describe. Vacations meant Mom, Dad, the two kids, and the station wagon. The business traveler was a man in his forties who stayed in a Holiday Inn on every trip and ate New York strip steak and french fries. This normal world has turned upside down since then. The advent of the **baby boomers** (those born between 1946 and 1965) changed all the rules. Their reach for *experiences* in travel caused major changes in our industry. The baby boomers also instigated many changes in our society. Women are now the major growth market in business travel. People are eating far less red meat. Family travel groups have lost ground to couples and singles. Overall, the market has become more segmented. The causes are many. The economy; technology; and social, cultural, and lifestyle changes all played a role. The hospitality and travel industry reacted with new services and products, further splintering the market. The end result is that marketers must be more knowledgeable about customer groups and more specific in choosing their targets.

There are more sophisticated travelers and out-of-home eaters in the market today than ever before. They get their sophisticated tastes from traveling and eating out more often than earlier generations did. They have much more experience in sizing up hospitality and travel organizations. These people see slick promotion and advertising campaigns every day at home, at the office, on the Web, and on the road. To get through to these people requires better quality services and products and more sophisticated marketing.

A fourth factor increasing the priority given to marketing is the acquisition of hospitality and travel companies by firms in other industries. For example, several companies, including General Mills, PepsiCo, and Pillsbury, were attracted by the growth record of the restaurant industry. These large parent organizations, long familiar with the benefits of marketing, were quick to pass on their marketing-oriented philosophies and approaches to the newly acquired subsidiaries. For example, what does Burger King have in common with Johnnie Walker scotch whiskey, Tanqueray gin, and Haagen Daz ice cream? They are all owned by Diageo, a large consumer products company.

All of these factors mean that marketing has become increasingly important in the hospitality and travel industry. Success now comes only with the ability to satisfy the needs of particular customer groups, and to do an excellent job of it.

CHAPTER CONCLUSION

Marketing in the hospitality and travel industry is maturing and becoming more sophisticated. There is increasing recognition of the importance of marketing to an organization's ultimate success. Although many years behind manufacturing and packaged goods, our industry has begun to adopt the seven core principles of marketing—the marketing concept, marketing orientation, satisfying customers' needs and wants, market segmentation, value, product life cycle, and marketing mix. This has happened because more people understand the benefits of marketing. An emphasis on marketing is also being forced on our industry because of the intensified competition and the effects of marketing environment factors.

New managers entering our industry must have some knowledge of marketing and what it takes to succeed in today's marketplace. Product-related skills and knowledge, although necessary, are not enough.

REVIEW QUESTIONS

1. How is marketing defined in this book and what are the six fundamentals on which it is based?
2. What is *the price of marketing?*
3. What are the four evolutionary eras of marketing? How has marketing changed in these eras?
4. What is the digital marketing era?
5. Has the hospitality and travel industry passed through these eras at the same pace as other industries? Why or why not?
6. What are the 13 symptoms of production and sales orientation?
7. What is *marketing myopia* and how can it be avoided?
8. What does it mean to have a marketing orientation? Is this the same as a production or sales orientation?
9. What are the characteristics of marketing orientation?
10. What are the benefits of adopting a marketing orientation?
11. What are the seven *core principles of marketing?*
12. There are six marketing environment factors in the hospitality and travel marketing environment. What are they?
13. Why has marketing increased in importance in the hospitality and travel industry?

CHAPTER ASSIGNMENTS

1. Assume you are the manager of a hotel, travel agency, restaurant, auto rental agency, or other customer-contact, travel-related business. Describe the program you would use to make your supervisors and other staff members more marketing oriented. Also show how you could act as a role model in this respect.

2. Pick an organization in the part of the hospitality and travel industry in which you are most interested. Arrange an interview with one or more of its executives to discuss the organization's marketing approaches. Does it seem to have a marketing or a production/sales orientation? What symptoms or characteristics led to your conclusions? Have the seven core principles of marketing been applied? If you were asked to make recommendations to the management team based upon what you have found, what would they be?

3. Select three to five major airlines, hotel or restaurant chains, car rental firms, cruise lines, or other hospitality and travel organizations, and analyze how they have adapted their operations and marketing based on the six marketing environment factors. Which company has done the best job in changing with the hospitality and travel environment?

4. Prepare a standardized list of criteria for evaluating the marketing approaches of hospitality and travel organizations based on the information presented in this chapter.

WORLD WIDE WEB RESOURCES

Atlantic City Convention & Visitors Authority
http://www.atlanticcitynj.com/

Australian Tourist Commission
http://www.atc.net.au/

Bass Hotels & Resorts/Holiday Inns
http://www.basshotels.com/holiday-inn/

Ben & Jerry's
http://www.benjerry.com/

British Airways
http://www.british-airways.com/

Budweiser
http://www.beeresponsible.com/

Club Med
http://www.clubmed.com/

Contiki
http://www.contiki.com/

Diageo PLC
http://www.diageo.com/

Disney
http://www.disney.go.com/

Expedia
http://www.expedia.com/

Hertz
http://www.hertz.com/

Marriott International
http://www.marriott.com/

McDonald's
http://www.mcdonalds.com/

Northwest Airlines
http://www.nwa.com/

Ramada
http://www.ramada.com/

Royal Caribbean International
http://www.rccl.com/

Scandinavian Airlines System(SAS)
http://www.flysas.com/

Travelocity
http://www.travelocity.com/

Yahoo! Travel
http://travel.yahoo.com/

REFERENCES

1. Perreault, William D., Jr., and E. Jerome McCarthy. 2000. *Essentials of Marketing: A Global Managerial Approach.* 8th ed. Boston: Irwin McGraw-Hill.
2. Levitt, Theodore. "Marketing myopia." *Harvard Business Review* 38 (4):45–56 (1960).
3. Morris, William, ed. 1973. *The American Heritage Dictionary of the English Language.* New York: American Heritage Publishing Co., Inc. and Houghton Mifflin Co., 867.
4. McKenna, Regis. 1991. *Relationship Marketing: Successful Strategies for the Age of the Customer.* Reading, Mass.: Addison-Wesley Publishing Co., Inc.

5. Kotler, Philip. 2000. *Marketing Management: Millennium Edition.* 10th ed. Upper Saddle River, N.J.: Prentice-Hall, Inc.

6. Boone, Louis E., and David L. Kurtz. 2001. *Contemporary Marketing.* 10th ed. Fort Worth, Tex.: Harcourt College Publishers.

7. Perreault, William D., Jr., and E. Jerome McCarthy. 2000. *Essentials of Marketing: A Global-Managerial Approach.* 8th ed. Boston: Irwin McGraw-Hill.

8. Kartun, Derek. "Club Mediterranee's growth and policies." *International Journal of Tourism Management* 2 (2):113 (1981).

For additional hospitality and travel marketing resources, visit our Web site at **www.Hospitality-Tourism.delmar.com**

Marketing Hospitality and Travel Services

What Is Marketing?

Objectives

Having read this chapter, you should be able to:

◆ Explain the meaning of services marketing.

◆ Identify four reasons that marketing in the service industries has lagged behind marketing in other industries.

◆ List and describe six generic differences between the marketing of services and the marketing of products.

◆ List and describe six contextual differences between the marketing of services and the marketing of products.

◆ List and explain eight specific differences affecting the marketing of hospitality and travel services.

◆ Explain five unique approaches required in hospitality and travel marketing.

◆ Identify three unique relationships among hospitality and travel organizations.

Overview

This chapter describes the emerging field of services marketing. It emphasizes that, although product and service marketing are similar in many ways, there are important differences between them. These differences are identified and described. For the hospitality and travel industry, generic, contextual, and specific differences are discussed. The unique marketing approaches required in the service industries are also described. One of the distinct features of the hospitality and travel industry is the dependency that exists among companies and organizations. The chapter ends by reviewing these relationships.

Key Terms

carriers	hospitality and travel industry	service industries
contextual differences	inseparable (inseparability)	services marketing
destination marketing	intangible (intangibility)	suppliers
organizations (DMOs)	packaging and programming	travel trade
destination mix	partnership	variability
evidence	perishability	word-of-mouth advertising
generic differences		

Now that you know what marketing is, you are probably anxious to learn the steps involved. So what is the point of having to read another introductory chapter on services marketing? Well, not including this material would be like selling you a car without giving you a maintenance manual. You would probably know how to drive the vehicle, but not much about why it operates the way it does and why things sometimes go wrong.

To be an effective marketing manager, you need to understand the *big picture*. You have to visualize the broad scope of the industry and be aware of the many different organizations within it. Think of our business as a car engine, with many parts working together to ensure high performance. As you know, it takes a problem with only one small auto part to give you that sinking feeling when you turn the ignition key and nothing happens. The same is true in our industry. If one of the providers in the chain provides bad service, all suffer.

Take a trip to your local supermarket and then think about the differences between its merchandise and what we provide. You will realize there is no shelf space in the hospitality and travel industry, nor can you put what we produce in a brown bag. Because of these and other differences, our organizations have to use marketing approaches not required by supermarkets and other product suppliers. You need to understand these differences and unique approaches before moving on.

WHAT IS SERVICES MARKETING?

The United States is recognized as having the world's first service economy. More people are employed in providing services than they are in manufacturing. Almost 60 percent of an average U.S. family's budget is devoted to buying services. In 1998, 71 percent of all Americans, or 99.5 million people, were employed in service-producing occupations.[1] The U.S. Bureau of Labor Statistics estimates that 94 percent of the 24.6 million new jobs created between 1990 and 2005 will be in the service industries. Other countries are moving in the same direction as the United States. Increasing affluence and more leisure time are two of the reasons for the growing economic importance of services.

The **hospitality and travel industry** (a group of interrelated organizations providing personal services to customers who are away from home) is just one part of the **service industries** (organizations primarily involved in the provision of personal services). Other service industries include banking; legal, accounting, and management consulting services; insurance; health care; laundry and dry cleaning; education; and entertainment. National, state, provincial, and local government agencies are also major providers of services. **Services marketing** is a concept based on a recognition of the

A Touch of Technology

The World Factbook, Central Intelligence Agency
http://www.odci.gov/cia/publications/factbook/

◆ This WWW resource provides a treasure trove of information for tourism and hospitality students.

◆ The *World Factbook* includes data on all countries in the world and provides the following statistics on the contribution to Gross Domestic Product (GDP) by the services portion of the economy in ten countries.

◆ Australia: 65% (1997)

◆ Bahamas: 92% (1997)

◆ Canada: 66% (1998)

◆ Denmark: 69% (1998)

◆ Netherlands: 69.3% (1998)

◆ New Zealand: 66% (1997)

◆ South Africa: 56% (1996)

◆ Sweden: 67.3% (1997)

◆ United Kingdom: 67% (1997)

◆ United States: 75% (1998)

uniqueness of all services. It is a branch of marketing that specifically applies to the service industries.

Chapter 1 discussed the evolution of marketing in the manufacturing and packaged-goods industries. Services marketing has not developed at the same pace, but has lagged behind by as much as 20 years. Why did this happen? One reason is that marketing terms and principles were defined with the manufacturing industry in mind. Most marketing textbooks are written for manufacturing and hardly scratch the surface of services marketing. Few marketing textbooks devote special chapters to services.

We cannot blame only authors and marketing managers in manufacturing for the slow evolution of services marketing. A second reason for the delay involves certain characteristics of the industry and management. Parts of the hospitality and travel industry have been highly regulated. United States domestic airlines are a prime example. For one-half century, the Civil Aeronautics Board (CAB) dictated what fares could be charged and what routes flown. This stifled the development of airline marketing. Between 1978 and 1984, the CAB was phased out. The Airline Deregulation Act of 1978 opened the floodgates to marketing creativity in the domestic airline industry, about 30 years after manufacturers first discovered the marketing concept.

A third reason is the composition of the hospitality and travel industry. It is dominated by small businesses. Small family-run restaurants, motels, resorts, campgrounds, travel agencies, attractions, and tour wholesalers significantly outnumber larger chain and franchised businesses. Most small businesses cannot afford full-time marketing managers and have limited marketing budgets. Many of them regard marketing as a luxury that only big business can afford.

There really were no big businesses in our industry in 1950, when large manufacturers began using the marketing concept. McDonald's, Burger King, Wendy's, Holiday

Inns Inc., Marriott, Ramada, Howard Johnson, Travelodge, and Best Western—all household names now—did not get going until after 1950. Most of the major airlines, travel agencies, rental car firms, tour wholesalers, and theme parks have been in operation for less than 40 years. Big-time marketing by government tourism-promotion agencies, convention and visitors bureaus, and other nonprofit groups is in its infancy. For example, the United States did not have a national tourism marketing agency until 1961 when the United States Travel Service (now the Tourism Industries Office of the Department of Commerce) was established. Compared with Pillsbury, Procter & Gamble, General Motors, and the Ford Motor Company, our industry's leaders have had much less time to practice marketing.

As Chapter 1 mentioned, a fourth reason for the lag in services marketing is the historical tendency for technically and operations-oriented people to create and manage hospitality and travel organizations. Few of these people had any formal training in marketing. They learned it on the job. Manufacturers were creating full-blown marketing departments in the 1950s, when our industry was in its infancy.

Why is an understanding of services marketing so important? The answer is simple. Some of the approaches to marketing manufactured goods need to be modified to fit the service industries. For example, packaging in the hospitality and travel industry is quite different from the packaging of cereals and other packaged goods. A package of cereal serves as a container and visual merchandiser of the product, whereas a hospitality and travel package is a combination of our industry's services. The distribution system for hospitality and travel services is also much different from the physical transportation of products from manufactures to retailers and then to customers. A travel agent, for example, does not physically pass a hotel or air trip to the customer. The customer must go to the hotel or airport to use the service.

WHY IS SERVICES MARKETING DIFFERENT?

The marketing of hospitality and travel services has several unique characteristics. Some are shared with all service organizations (generic differences). Others exist because of the ways in which service organizations are managed and regulated (contextual differences). Generic differences affect all organizations in the service industries and will never be eliminated. Contextual differences are also unique to service organizations, but they may eventually disappear through changes in management, legislation, and regulation. Generic differences are common to all service organizations. Contextual differences vary by type of service organization. There are six generic and six contextual differences.[2]

Generic: Unchangeable differences that affect marketing of services:

1. Intangible nature of the services
2. Production methods
3. Perishability
4. Distribution channels
5. Cost determination
6. Relationship of services to providers

Contexual: Correctable differences common among service organizations that affect marketing:

1. Narrow definition of marketing
2. Lack of appreciation for marketing skills
3. Different organizational structures
4. Lack of data on competitive performance
5. Impact of government regulation and deregulation
6. Constraints and opportunities for nonprofit marketers

Generic Differences

Let us take a closer look at the six generic differences that affect the marketing of services.

1. **Intangible Nature of the Services.** Before you buy products, you can evaluate them in various ways. If you go into a grocery store, you can pick up, feel, shake, smell, and sometimes taste many products. The packaging and contents can be examined closely. In a clothing store, for instance, you can try on merchandise for fit and size. Products such as automobiles and personal computers can be tested before you buy them. You can do so much evaluation because products are tangible. On the other hand, services cannot be tested and evaluated in the same way. They are intangible and you have to experience them to know how they work. Since customers cannot physically evaluate or sample most services, they tend to rely on other people's experiences with these services. This is usually referred to as *word-of-mouth* information and is of great importance in the hospitality and travel industry. Customers also place great value on the advice of hospitality and travel experts, such as travel agents, who tend to have more previous experience with travel destinations and companies.

2. **Production Methods.** Products are manufactured, assembled, and physically transported to the point of sale. Most services are produced and consumed in the same location. Passengers have to board airplanes, guests need to stay in hotels, and people must visit restaurants to experience the services they purchase. The fast-food outlet is the closest thing our industry has to a manufactured product, but even then the service is consumed on-site or is picked up by the customer. The fast-food outlet that provides a home-delivery service is one step closer. Most services are not mass-produced.

   The manufacturing process can be precisely and comprehensively controlled. Checkers, inspectors, and even robots ensure that rigid production and quality standards are met. Factory workers have the equipment and training to produce exactly the same quality and quantity of goods each time. No customers are around to worry about. Quality control of services is neither as precise nor as easy to achieve because of the human factors that are involved in supplying them. All staff members cannot consistently provide the same levels of service as their colleagues. Variability of service levels is a fact of life. Although standardized service is an admirable target that all organizations should try to achieve, it is unrealistic. A robot cannot yet provide effective personal service, and the ever-present stare of an inspector would surely take something away from a service experience.

   Customers are more involved in the *production process* of services. Manufacturers keep customers out of their factories for safety and proprietary reasons. Service organizations cannot bar people from their *factories*. If they did, most companies would be bankrupt before long. Hotels, restaurants, airplanes, theme parks, and travel agencies are some of the "factories" in our business. The behavior of one customer can ruin the service experience of others. A boisterous drunk on an airline flight; a noisy, all-night party in an adjoining hotel room; a smoker in a nonsmoking area; or a loud quarrel at the next table in a restaurant can result in dissatisfied customers. In other words, our own customers can stop us from achieving marketing objectives. For example, drunks do enter retail stores, and such stores get their share of quarrels, but shoppers in retail stores do not get as upset by such disruptive behavior as they would if they were celebrating a special occasion in a local restaurant. They can leave their shopping carts, having spent some time but no money in the store. However, customers make a significant emotional, financial, and time investment in most hospitality and travel services. Once a service experience begins, the customer is more committed to completing it. If the experience is spoiled by other customers or service staff, the customer cannot totally recoup the investment, especially its emotional and time components.

Our industry offers various self-service options, including salad bars, cafeterias, airline-ticket-dispensing machines, and so on. How well customers serve themselves can affect how well they are satisfied with the service. Many bars, resorts, restaurants, and amusement and entertainment facilities depend on the behavior of some guests to influence others positively. If guests have a good time, it rubs off on others. People attract people, especially the ones who are visibly enjoying themselves. An empty restaurant parking lot, an empty dance floor, or an attraction ride with no riders is less likely to attract people than ones thronged with customers. Such is human nature.

When customers buy toothpaste in supermarkets, they are almost 100 percent sure that the toothpaste will clean their teeth. When they purchase a service, they have far less assurance. The same standardization cannot be provided. The actions of service staff, other customers, and the customers themselves make the experience more variable.

EXCELLENCE CASE

Standardizing Services:
Red Lobster, Darden Restaurants, Inc.

One of the great differences between manufacturing products and providing services is the control over quality standards. It is much more difficult to standardize services. The seafood dinner chain, Red Lobster, is one of our industry's finest examples of a company that makes an extra effort to give its customers consistency in menu items and personal service.

Red Lobster is a subsidiary of Darden Restaurants, Inc. of Orlando, Florida. Darden also operates the Olive Garden, Bahama Breeze, and Smokey Bones BBQ & Sports Bar restaurants. Bill Darden, a restaurateur, founded Red Lobster in 1968 as a single unit in Lakeland, Florida. Red Lobster was acquired by General Mills in 1970 and was operated by them until 1995. It served its one-billionth guest in 1998 and expected to serve 136 million guests in 2001. Red Lobster has 650 restaurants in the United States and Canada and has more than 60,000 employees.

Part of the secret of Red Lobster's success has been its moderate prices, giving it a strong family appeal. The company has also built a reputation for offering both consistent quality and a wide variety of seafood and fresh fish. The consistent quality is no accident. It comes from a combination of strict quality specifications for purchasing seafood and fish, a test kitchen facility, and a unique way of communicating preparation details to individual restaurants.

Red Lobster is now one of the largest restaurant buyers of seafood in the world, drawing its

continued

EXCELLENCE CASE *continued*

(Photo courtesy of Red Lobster)

supplies from many different countries. Its buying specifications are the strictest of any large buyer in the United States and Red Lobster tries to establish long-term relationships with suppliers. Red Lobster has buyers positioned in Thailand, Singapore, Canada, Brazil, Los Angeles, Indianapolis, Orlando, and Jacksonville. These buyers are not only familiar with the restaurant business, but are required to be knowledgeable about oceanography, marine biology, aquaculture, finance, and food processing. They work with suppliers and processors to ensure that harvesting and processing meet Red Lobster's high quality standards. Every vendor is inspected twice per year by Red Lobster's Field Quality Assurance Managers.

Red Lobster has ensured a high-quality supply, but how is it possible to have 650 seafood restaurants prepare dishes consistently? An important part of the answer is through the operation of a test kitchen. Here, different preparation methods are tried out, and recommended recipes and preparation guidelines are developed, including portioning and the arrangement of items on plates. How does Red Lobster communicate all of these fine details to its far-flung units? One way is through the creation of

detailed training aids filled with visual cues and clear directions on the preparation of proven performing recipes. The Culinary Center, along with Purchasing, Quality Assurance, and Red Lobster Training Department, ensures that crew members and managers at each restaurant have self-directed training aid support that covers raw product specifications, product and storage handling, and detailed procedures for food preparation and cooking. Colored photographs in training aids and charts picture how meals should look in both the raw and cooked state, along with the plate configuration and garnishes. The format of the training package is consistent with previous packages to promote ease of deployment by the management staff.

Red Lobster's worldwide search for quality seafood and fish has also resulted in the discovery of items not offered before in North American restaurants, including popcorn shrimp, snow crab legs, and langostinos. Despite the company's size and sophistication, most of its deals with suppliers are based on a handshake rather than written contracts.

There is little doubt that Red Lobster has been one of North America's most successful chain restaurant concepts. As evidence, its

continued

EXCELLENCE CASE *continued*

weekly customer counts are among the highest in the dinner house category. The company's past and continuing growth has been due in large part to its excellent procedures for ensuring consistent, standardized menu items and service at a reasonable price.

Discussion Questions

1. What has Red Lobster done to standardize its production methods and standards of personal service? How successful has it been with these efforts?
2. Do you know of any other organizations in the hospitality and travel industry that try to introduce greater standardization of their production methods and service

standards? Who are they and what approaches have they used?
3. What are some of the key disadvantages of standardizing hospitality and travel services? For example, do services that are highly standardized lose some of their appeal for the customer? Is service becoming too mechanical? How would you blend the benefits of standardization with the appeal of the unexpected?

Web Site

http://www.redlobster.com/

Reference

Corporate Fact Sheet.
http://www.redlobster.com

3. **Perishability.** Products can be stored for future sale—services cannot. A product such as a VCR can be purchased any day the store is open—now, next week, next month, or even next year. Services are subject to **perishability**. They are "like a running tap in a sink with no plug."[3] An unsold "inventory" of service is just like water down the drain. Time cannot be saved. The sale of an empty hotel room, airline seat, or convention center room is lost forever. Services and, more importantly, the time available to experience them, cannot be stored. There is only one chance to enjoy a summer vacation in any given year. An anniversary or birthday dinner only has value at a specific time. Their shelf lives are only one day or less. There are no warehouses for service experiences.

4. **Distribution Channels.** Trucks, railroad cars, ships, and airplanes physically transport manufactured goods to warehouses and retailers, and directly to customers. Marketing managers in manufacturing have to devise distribution strategies for the most effective movement of products. There is no physical distribution system in our industry. Customers, in fact, have to come to the service *factory* to buy, rather than vice versa. There are a few exceptions to this rule, including home delivery of pizza and other prepared foods.

There are many intermediaries in the hospitality and travel industry. Travel agents, tour wholesalers and operators, corporate travel managers, incentive travel planners, and convention/meeting planners are examples. The items being purchased, however, are not physically shipped from producers through the intermediaries to customers. They cannot be because they are intangible.

The chain of distribution for most products consists of three distinct locations: a factory, a retail store, and a place of consumption (home or business). There is often only one location involved when hospitality and travel services are bought. For example, customers come to a restaurant (the factory) where food and beverages are merchandised (the retail store), and leave after consuming the food and drinks of their choice (the place of consumption).

Most manufacturers do not own the retail outlets that merchandise their products. The opposite is true in our industry. Chains, franchisors, and other similar groups have direct control over the individual outlets that provide the services.

5. **Cost Determination.** Fixed and variable costs can be precisely estimated for most manufactured goods. Such goods are physical, known commodities. Services are both variable and intangible. Some customers may require more attention than others, and the nature of the service needed may not always be known exactly. Factory output can be carefully programmed and predicted. Business volumes in our industry cannot.

6. **Relationship of Services to Providers.** Some services are inseparable from the individuals who provide them, for example, the many restaurants whose chefs or owners have developed unique reputations for their food, personalities, or both, like K-Paul's in New Orleans. Dolly Parton's Dollywood theme park in Tennessee

Did You Know?

About K-Paul's Louisiana Kitchen

✓ Chef Paul Prudhomme started the restaurant in 1979 in New Orleans' French Quarter.

✓ Paul Prudhomme was the youngest of 13 children in his family.

✓ The original restaurant only had 62 seats.

✓ The restaurant did not take reservations when it began operations.

✓ The restaurant now has 200 seats.

✓ Chef Prudhomme now has his own line of herbs and spices—Magic Seasoning Blends.

✓ He has authored several cookbooks and appeared many times on national television.

About Dollywood

✓ The Dollywood theme park is located in Pigeon Forge, Tennessee.

✓ Dollywood was formerly called Silver Dollar City.

✓ Dolly Parton, the singer, songwriter, and actress, became an owner of the park in 1986.

✓ In its first year of operation (1986) as Dollywood, the park had 75 percent more guests than in the previous year (1985) as Silver Dollar City.

✓ Dollywood had more than 2.2 million guests in 1998.

About AJ Hackett

✓ AJ Hackett is considered to be the originator of bungee jumping.

✓ Bungee jumping was based on a manhood ritual in Pentecost Island, Vanuatu, in the Pacific. In the ritual, the bungee cord is made of vine leaves.

✓ He bungee-jumped from the Eiffel Tower in 1987.

✓ AJ opened his first jump site near Queenstown, New Zealand in 1988.

✓ He was the first person to bungee-jump from a helicopter in 1990.

and A J Hackett Bungy in New Zealand are also inseparable. Other examples include tennis camps at resorts hosted by professional stars, shows by famous performers, and tours guided by noted experts in their fields. These individuals are the major attraction. Without them, the services would not have the same appeal.

Contextual Differences

Generic differences between products and services exist because of their inherent natures, production processes, distribution, and consumption. Contextual differences are caused by variations in organizations' management philosophies and practices, and in external environments. Now let us take a closer look at six common contextual differences that affect the marketing of services:

1. Narrow definition of marketing
2. Lack of appreciation for marketing skills
3. Different organizational structures
4. Lack of data on competitive performance
5. Impact of government regulation and deregulation
6. Constraints and opportunities for nonprofit marketers

1. **Narrow Definition of Marketing.** Chapter 1 explained that marketing-organization and societal-marketing orientations are the most sophisticated and advanced. Few hospitality and travel organizations have progressed this far. Many still have to fully adopt a marketing-department orientation. Their so-called marketing departments are really only responsible for promotion (advertising, sales promotion, merchandising, personal selling, and public relations). Pricing, new site selection, development of new service concepts, and research are still done by other departments or by general managers. This is changing, and many marketing specialists are reaching top management positions in our organizations.

   There is less emphasis on marketing research in the hospitality and travel industry than there should be. Its value to marketing decisions is not yet fully appreciated.

2. **Lack of Appreciation for Marketing Skills.** Marketing skills are not yet as highly valued in our industry as they are in manufacturing. Technical skills such as food preparation, innkeeping, destination/supplier knowledge, and ticketing still tend to be held in higher regard. There seems to be a feeling that everybody has the skills to be a marketer, if they really want to be. Marketing skills and talent are not seen as unique, and they are not fully appreciated.

3. **Different Organizational Structures.** Many hospitality and travel organizations are run by persons with the title *general manager.* Most hotels and other lodging properties follow this pattern. Similar management positions exist in travel agencies, airlines, restaurants, tour wholesaler companies, and attractions. When the businesses belong to chains, general managers usually report to the operations division at the head office. These managers are involved in pricing, developing new services, and managing customer-contact personnel. Marketing or sales managers/directors, who handle other marketing management functions, report to them. In the hotel business, there has been a tendency to name the manager in charge of marketing as the Director of Sales rather than Director of Marketing. Many manufacturing companies use a different organizational model, with all marketing activities assigned to one executive and department at both the corporate and field level.

4. **Lack of Data on Competitive Performance.** A large amount of sales data on competitive brands is available for most consumer goods. A packaged-goods manufacturer can access years of sales history on competitive products through various research services. This is not the case in most parts of the hospitality and travel industry. Where data are available, the information tends to be on an aggregated, industry-average basis. Unit sales figures for various companies and their *brands* are nonexistent except for airlines.

5. **Impact of Government Regulation and Deregulation.** Parts of the North American hospitality and travel industry have been highly regulated by government agencies. Tight government control has tended to limit the marketing flexibility of many organizations, including airlines, bus companies, travel agencies, and tour wholesalers. Pricing, distribution channels, routes, and even services provided have required government approval. Most manufacturing businesses have not been as comprehensively controlled. However, a definite move toward the deregulation of parts of the industry in both the United States and Canada occurred in the 1970s, 1980s, and 1990s.

6. **Constraints and Opportunities for Nonprofit Marketers.** Nonprofit organizations, including government tourism promotion bodies, convention and visitors bureaus, regional tourism promotion associations, and various volunteer groups, play a key role in our industry. They normally have a unique set of marketing constraints imposed upon them. Politics, particularly what is politically acceptable, tends to influence the marketing decisions made by nonprofit organizations—decisions that would be unacceptable or unprofitable for profit-making firms. For example, a state or province may have one tourist attraction or region that draws the vast majority of its visitors. It is usually politically unacceptable for a government tourism promotion agency to feature only that attraction or region in its promotional campaigns. Favoritism is not tolerated, and all regions and attractions must be promoted. The opposite is true in profit-making organizations, where the philosophy is push the winners, drop the losers.

WHY ARE HOSPITALITY AND TRAVEL SERVICES MARKETING DIFFERENT?

Hospitality and travel services have specific characteristics that are not found in other services. It is also true that all hospitality and travel services are not the same. They range all the way from companies that offer mass-produced hamburgers to those that prepare individual, foreign tour excursions. There are eight specific differences in hospitality and travel services:

1. Shorter exposure to services
2. More emotional buying appeals
3. Greater importance on managing *evidence*
4. Greater emphasis on stature and imagery
5. More variety and types of distribution channels
6. More dependence on complementary organizations
7. Easier copying of services
8. More emphasis on off-peak promotion

Let us look more closely at each of these differences.

1. **Shorter Exposure to Services.** Customers are exposed to, and can use, most products and many services that they buy for weeks, months, and sometimes years. Consumer durables such as refrigerators, stereos, and automobiles are multiyear investments. So are educational programs, residential mortgages, bank accounts, and personal investment consulting. Most items bought at the supermarket can be deep-frozen for months, or, if it is a nonfood item, it can be used and stored for years. The customer's exposure to most hospitality and travel services is usually shorter. In many cases our services, including trips to fast-food restaurants, short commuter flights, and visits to travel agencies, are consumed within an hour or less. There is less time to make a good or bad impression on customers. Most manufacturers offer warranties and guarantees on their products, sometimes covering several years; however, not many similar assurances of quality are available with hospitality and travel services. Whereas inadequately cooked menu items can be sent back to the restaurant kitchen, many hospitality and travel services that do not *work* cannot be returned and exchanged for similar ones since they are more intangible.

2. **More Emotional Buying Appeals.** You buy products knowing that they will perform a specific function for you, using rational (logical or fact-based) rather than emotional (feeling-based) reasoning. There are a few exceptions where some people form a close emotional bond with specific products and brands. The *Coke-Classic Coke* case is a prime example. This emotional bonding happens more frequently with hospitality and travel services because, above all else, ours is a *people* industry. People provide and receive our services. A person-to-person encounter always takes place. Emotions and personal feelings are generated by these service encounters, and they influence future purchase behavior. In our industry, a single employee may determine if a customer uses our services again.

   People also tend to buy hospitality and travel services that match their self-images. They fly first class and stay at a Four Seasons Hotel because it fits the mental picture of themselves as successful business people. They use a combination of rational (more services and giveaways) and emotional (status or class) reasons when they buy these services.

3. **Greater Importance on Managing *Evidence*.** Whereas a product is basically a tangible object, a service is in essence a performance. Customers cannot see, sample, or self-evaluate services because of their intangibility, but they can see various tangible factors associated with these services.[4] Customers then rely more heavily on these tangible clues or evidence when they are purchasing services.[5] The combined effect of these tangible clues determines their assessment of the service's quality and how well it will meet their needs.

   What tangible clues or evidence do you think are available to hospitality and travel customers when they are deciding what to buy? How do you form an impression of a hotel, restaurant, or airline without having been a customer? You might have guessed that the evidence falls into four categories:

   1. Physical environment
   2. Price
   3. Communications
   4. Customers

   The physical environment can include the types of furniture, carpeting, wall coverings, staff uniforms, and signs that a hotel or restaurant uses. An enormous crystal chandelier hanging over a beautiful Oriental rug on a gleaming hotel-lobby floor is a clue to a top-quality operation. The price of a service also influences customers' perceptions of quality. High prices are often assumed to indicate luxury and high quality, while low prices reflect lesser luxury and quality. Communications about a company's services come from the company itself, through word-of-mouth information, and through expert advisers such as travel agents. Web sites, brochures, and printed advertisements provide customers with tangible evidence, since they *picture* what the customer can expect. The types of customers a service business currently has provides signals to potential new customers. For example, if an 18- to 25-year-old notices that a local restaurant's customers are mostly elderly, she may not see the restaurant as a good place to dine with her friends. Service marketers must *manage* these four types of evidence to ensure that customers make the right decisions. They have to be sure that all the evidence they provide is consistent and that it is matched by the quality of personal service they provide.

4. **Greater Emphasis on Stature and Imagery.** A related concept is the stature and image of hospitality and travel organizations. Because the services provided are mainly intangible and customers frequently have emotional reasons for buying them, organizations put great effort into creating the desired mental associations. In one advertising campaign, Hyatt showed a brightly shining lightbulb among a group of drab green pears. The headline was, "There are hotels, and there is Hyatt." The impression, obviously intended, was that Hyatt hotels are something special and really stand out from other chain properties. Figure 2–1 shows another attempt to establish a distinct image for a hotel chain through advertising. In this case, Starwood Hotels & Resorts Worldwide tries to portray its W Hotels as providing a chic and trendy new type of lodging for business travelers.

5. **More Variety and Types of Distribution Channels.** There is no physical distribution system for hospitality and travel services. Instead of a distribution system, our industry has a unique set of travel intermediaries, including travel agents and companies that put together vacation packages (tour wholesalers). Products also have intermediaries, but these intermediaries seldom influence customers' purchase decisions. Warehousing and trucking companies have no impact on which products customers select in retail stores. In contrast, many travel intermediaries greatly influence what the customer buys. Travel agents and incentive travel and convention planners are looked to for advice on destinations, hotels, attractions, vacation packages, tours, and transportation. Customers see them as experts and take their recommendations seriously.

6. **More Dependence on Complementary Organizations.** A travel service can be extremely complex, beginning when customers notice the advertising for a particular destination. These advertisements may be promotional campaigns funded by government tourism promotion agencies or convention and visitors bureaus. Customers may then visit travel agencies for more detailed information and advice. Travel agents may recommend a destination package consisting of round-trip airfare, ground transportation, hotel accommodations, local sightseeing tours, entertainment and attractions, and meals. While on vacation, the customers may go shopping, try a few restaurants, rent a car, buy gas, and visit the hairdresser. What this adds up to is that many different organizations provide the travel service *experience*. The *experience suppliers* are interdependent and complementary. Travelers evaluate the overall quality of their experiences based on the performance of every organization involved. If one does not perform up to the standards of others, it reflects badly on all.

◆ **FIGURE 2–1**   *Starwood Hotels & Resorts tries to put across a distinctive image for its W Hotels.* (Courtesy of Starwood Hotels & Resorts Worldwide, Inc.)

7. **Easier Copying of Services.** Most hospitality and travel services are easy to copy. On the other hand, products are usually patented or difficult to replicate without detailed knowledge of production processes and materials. Competitors can be kept out of factories to protect industrial secrets. We cannot keep competitors out of our *factories*, since they are free to visit the places where our services are consumed. Most services our industry provides cannot be patented. Services are provided by people and can be imitated by other people. There are only a handful of situations in which trade secrets have been maintained in the hospitality and travel industry. Colonel Sanders' famous recipe for fried chicken is one of these. And if you know much about Cincinnati, Ohio, then you're probably aware of another one—Skyline Chili. The company's founder, Nicholas Lambrinides, brought the secret recipe to the United States from Greece in 1949 (Figure 2–2). The mixture of "secret spices" helped produce the distinctive dish, now known as Cincinnati-style chili. The company has gone to great lengths to guard the secret for more than 50 years. The recipe is locked away in a safe and is known by only a few people. The company also prohibits these people from flying together on the same flights. These extreme measures have paid off. Skyline Chili enjoys a *cult-like* following and can now be bought in grocery stores and online via the Web.

ON THE WEB

It's Skyline Time!

UC XU CROSSTOWN SHOOTOUT 2000 2001

- Order Online
- Talk to us!
- Franchising
- History
- Menu
- Locations
- Grocery
- Fan Page
- Jobs @ Skyline
- Recipes
- Nutritional Info
- Skyline Home
- Links

SKYStuff

Please Tell Us Your Skyline Story.

Since 1949, Skyline Chili has enjoyed what can only be described as a "cult-like" popularity. And for good reason. Skyline Chili is a combination of "personalized" service and a unique taste sensation that's been imitated by countless competitors over the years, but never duplicated. That's because Skyline Chili is made according to a secret family recipe that's been handed down for generations.

Referred to as "Cincinnati-style" chili, Skyline Chili is unlike anything you've ever tasted. Much different than traditional or "Texas-style" chili, our chili's consistency is more like a topping, which makes it ideal for pouring over coney dogs or onto spaghetti, creating our unique signature dish—the 3-Way. Made from 100% top-grade beef and spices from around the world Skyline Chili is a dining experience beyond compare.

Just ask anyone moving away from Cincinnati. They'll undoubtedly report that one of the main things they miss about the Queen City is Skyline Chili. And that's one of the principal reasons we now offer Skyline Chili in frozen and canned varieties. Both are perfect ways for Skyline aficionados to get their "fix" when they're not able to dine in a Skyline restaurant. If you'd like to experience the taste of Cincinnati, or to send Skyline Chili to a friend or loved one, just click on the "Order Online" icon.

ad.MOJO.com

Site design by Mojo @ adMojo.com • Secure hosting by Digital Bang
©Skyline Chili Inc. All rights reserved.

digital BANG LLC

◆ **FIGURE 2–2** *Skyline Chili markets its unique products online.* (Courtesy of Skyline Chili, Inc.)

8. **More Emphasis on Off-Peak Promotion.** Products are promoted most aggressively when there is peak demand. Christmas cards, decorations, and trees in December; garden and pool supplies, suntan oil, and boats in summer; and snowblowers, cold remedies, and warm clothes in winter are all examples. With few exceptions, there is a need for an entirely different schedule of promotions in our industry. Heavy off-peak promotion is the rule, rather than the exception. There are

three reasons for this. First, customers make a large emotional investment in their vacations. These vacations represent precious time away from work and other, everyday responsibilities. Vacations frequently involve major cash outlays. With so much time and money invested, prepurchase planning is a must and is normally enjoyable. The best time to promote a service is when customers are in this planning stage. To start promoting when their vacation dates arrive is too late.

Second, the capacity to *produce* is usually fixed. If resorts, hotels, airplanes, ships, and restaurants are full, their capacities cannot be expanded quickly. Factories can run extra shifts and stockpile inventory to cope with above-peak demand. This is impossible in most parts of our industry.

The third reason is that there is more pressure to use available capacity in off-peak periods. Christmas-decoration manufacturers can spend January to November producing and storing inventory. Hospitality and travel services *inventories* cannot be stored for later sale. They must be consumed when they are available for consumption. There are often wide variations in business volumes during a year, or even a month, week, or day. Since peak capacity is fixed, the emphasis has to shift to promoting the off-peak period. The one notable exception is the fast-food industry, where there is a traditional peak of business from April to September. With such a short time between the decision to buy and to purchase, it makes more sense to promote the hardest when demand is at a peak.

DIFFERENT MARKETING APPROACHES NEEDED FOR HOSPITALITY AND TRAVEL

What is the point of talking about all these differences? Basically, it is because products and services cannot be marketed in exactly the same ways. Many of the contextual differences between products and services should disappear in the future. For example, marketing in our industry is becoming more sophisticated and the industry is steadily becoming less regulated. However, the generic and specific hospitality and travel service differences will remain forever. Time cannot change them. It is because of these ever-present differences that unique marketing approaches are required in our industry. These include the following five unique approaches in hospitality and travel marketing:

1. Use of more than 4 Ps
2. Greater significance of word-of-mouth information
3. More use of emotional appeals in promotions
4. Greater difficulties with new-concept testing
5. Increased importance of relationships with complementary organizations

1. **Use of More Than 4 Ps.** Most books identify the 4 Ps (product, place, promotion, price) as marketing mix elements. One of the assumptions of this book is that there are another 4 Ps in our industry: People, packaging, programming, and partnership.

   a. *People.* Hospitality and travel is a people industry. It is a business of people (staff) providing services to people (customers), who share these services with other people (other customers). Industry marketers have to be very selective both in terms of who they hire—particularly customer-contact staff—and who they target as customers. Some potential employees are just not suitable because their people skills are poor. Some customer groups are not appropriate because their presence conflicts with the enjoyment of others.

Technically, employees are part of the *product* offered by hospitality and travel organizations. However, they are different enough from inanimate products and of such great importance in marketing that they require separate consideration. Staff recruitment, selection, orientation, training, supervision, and motivation all play an exceptionally important role in our industry.

Managing the *customer mix* is also very important to service marketers.[6] One reason is that customers are often part of the experience purchased. Customers share airplanes, restaurants, hotels, attractions, buses, and resorts with other customers. Who they are, how they dress, and how these customers behave are part of the experience. Customers have to follow stricter dress and behavior codes in many hospitality and travel businesses than they do in grocery stores. Marketing managers not only have to think about which target markets will produce the best profits, but also if these customers are compatible.

b. *Packaging and Programming.* These two related techniques—packaging and programming—are significant for two reasons. First, they are very customer-oriented concepts. They satisfy a variety of customer needs, including the desire for convenience found in all-inclusive packages. Second, they help businesses cope with the problems of matching demand with supply or reducing unsold inventory. Unsold rooms and seats and unused staff time are like pouring a rare wine down the sink. They cannot be recaptured for reconsumption. Two ways of dealing with this problem are to alter demand and to control supply.[7] Packaging and programming help alter demand. Weekend packages at downtown hotels, early-bird discounts for seniors in restaurants, computer clinics at resorts, and residents' days at theme parks are all good examples. Marketing creativity is at a premium in our industry because of the perishable nature of the services.

c. *Partnership.* Cooperative marketing efforts among complementary hospitality and travel organizations are referred to as partnerships. It is suggested as the eighth P because of the interdependence of many organizations in satisfying customers' needs and wants. This complementary nature of organizations can be either positive or negative. Customer satisfaction often hinges on the actions of other organizations over which we have no direct control. Relationships with complementary organizations need to be carefully managed and monitored. It is in the best interests of the industry's suppliers (lodging facilities, hotels, restaurants and food service facilities, cruise lines, car rental companies, attractions, and casinos) to maintain good relations with travel intermediaries (travel agents, tour wholesalers and operators, corporate travel managers and agencies, incentive travel planners, and convention/meeting planners) and carriers (airlines, railways, bus, ship, and ferry companies). The opposite is also true. When various parts of the industry cooperate more effectively, the result is predictible—more satisfied customers. When they do not cooperate, the result is equally obvious.

Marketers also need to understand the value of cooperation and interdependency at the travel destination itself. A travel experience is shaped by many organizations as a destination. When these organizations see that they are all in the same boat, the result again is usually more satisfied customers.

2. **Greater Significance of Word-of-Mouth Information.** The opportunities for customers to sample services prior to purchasing them are limited in our industry. People have to rent hotel rooms, buy airplane tickets, and pay meal checks to find out if these services meet their needs. The rule is, "You have to buy to try." This places a premium on word-of-mouth advertising (information about a service experience

passed from past to potential customers). Although the term *advertising* is used along with *word-of-mouth,* technically it is not advertising. Because there are few sampling or testing opportunities in our industry, people have to rely partly on the advice of others, including friends, relatives, and business associates. Positive *word-of-mouth* information is crucial to the success of most hospitality and travel organizations.

Providing a consistent quality of service and associated facilities is a key ingredient in getting *good word-of-mouth.* It is also a basic fundamental of marketing in this industry. The importance of managing evidence (tangible clues) was discussed earlier. Inconsistent evidence detracts from the quality of a customer's experience. A waitperson with a soiled uniform in a top-quality restaurant or a so-called luxury hotel with few in-room guest amenities are two simple examples of inconsistency. Consistency (of evidence) ensures that customers leave with a consistent impresion of an organization's quality standards.

Consistency is also needed in multiunit organizations, because customers tend to make decisions about the entire company based on their experiences in individual units. Most packaged-goods firms have successfully developed separate brand images for their products. If customers have bad experiences with one brand, it does not usually carry over to the company's other brands. The customer does not associate the brand with the parent company or its other brands as closely as they do in our industry. A bad experience at one Westin property, for example, can create a negative predisposition to all its other chain properties. Branding as a concept is only in its infancy in our industry.

3. **More Use of Emotional Appeals in Promotions.** Because of the intangible nature of services, customers tend to make more use of emotional appeals when they buy. This means that it is often more effective to emphasize these appeals in promotional campaigns. In order to make a hotel or restaurant chain, airline, travel agency, destination, vacation package, or attraction appeal to customers, it must be given a distinctive personality. It is not enough to talk about the number of guest rooms, aircraft types, ride configurations, and other rational facts and figures. A dash of color and personality must be added. Thus the name Fun Ships conjures up the phrase Carnival Cruise name, United Airlines becomes the "Friendly Skies," and so on. Companies must be given *personalities* with which customers can associate.

4. **Greater Difficulties with New-Concept Testing.** Services can be copied more easily than products, and this makes it essential for hospitality and travel organizations to be ever-alert for new and innovative customer services. Leading corporations are aware of this and are constantly test marketing new concepts. With the increasing dynamics of North American society, it is unwise to stand still in our business.

5. **Increased Importance of Relationships with Complementary Organizations.** There are three unique relationships among organizations in our industry that have a significant impact on the marketing of hospitality and travel services. These relationships are described in the following paragraphs.
   a. *Suppliers, Carriers, the Travel Trade, and Destination Marketing Organizations. Suppliers* are organizations that operate facilities, attractions and events, ground transportation, and other support services in or between travel destinations. Facilities include the lodging, food and beverage, and support industries (retail shopping, tour guiding, and recreation). Attractions and events are divided into six categories: natural resource, climatic, cultural, historical, ethnic,

and accessible.[8] Ground transportation organizations provide car rental, taxi and limousine, bus, and other related services. *Carriers* are those companies providing transportation to the destination. They include airlines and railway, bus, ship, and ferry companies. The travel trade contains the intermediaries that suppliers and carriers use to get their services to customers, including retail travel agents and tour wholesales. Destination marketing organizations (DMOs) market their cities, areas, regions, counties, states or provinces, and countries to travel trade intermediaries and individual and group travelers. They work on behalf of the suppliers and carriers serving their destinations. Through various types of packages and tours, the services of these four industry groups (suppliers, carriers, travel trade, and DMOs) are combined for greater customer appeal and convenience.

Although some tour or package providers are at greater financial risk than others, all have a stake in the package's success or failure. All are mutually dependent from a marketing standpoint. If the airline or hotel fails to honor reservations, this reflects badly on the travel agent and the tour wholesaler. If the travel agent misrepresents the resort's vacation package, the customer develops a negative impression of the resort. Hospitality and travel marketers in different organizations need to appreciate their mutual dependence and to ensure that their *partners* consistently deliver a level of service that is equal to their own.

b. *The Destination Mix Concept.* The destination mix is another unique, relational concept with five components: attractions and events, facilities, infrastructure, transportation, and hospitality resources.[9] Attractions and events play the pivotal role in travel destinations—they draw visitors. There are both business and pleasure travel attractions. Business travelers are drawn to a destination by the industrial and commercial bases in communities, while pleasure travelers are drawn by the six attraction categories mentioned earlier. Facility and ground transportation organizations such as hotels, restaurants, and car rental firms need to realize that the demand for their service is *derived* from the demand for attractions. Without the commercial/industrial base or pleasure-traveler attractions a large portion of their business would disappear.

c. *Visitors and Residents.* A third unique and important relationship exists between visitors and local residents. Both intermingle and share the same services and facilities. Positive resident attitudes are a major plus for the hospitality and travel industry. When developed, this attitude can enhance the marketing efforts of industry organizations. The opposite is equally true if residents have unfriendly or hostile attitudes toward visitors. Nonprofit organizations, such as government tourism promotion bodies and convention and visitors bureaus, need to be especially aware of this important relationship.

Figure 2–3 shows each of the three relationships just discussed. Managing these three relationships is an added role that hospitality and travel marketers must play. With the first two relationships, the key is to understand that others outside one's own organization have a direct impact on our customers' satisfaction. We not only have to be consistent in providing our own services, but we must also ensure that other partners do likewise. The third relationship, the interaction of visitors with a destination's residents, must also receive careful attention from marketers. Unfriendly or inhospitable local residents can spoil the visitor's experience. As the experience in Miami and Egypt has shown, serious crimes committed by residents and involving visitors can have a very adverse effect on tourism. From the resident perspective, increasing tourism can cause a

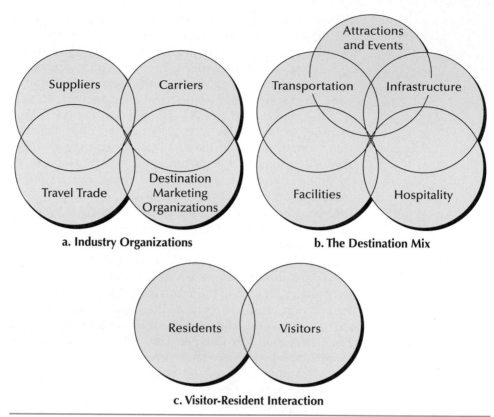

a. Industry Organizations

b. The Destination Mix

c. Visitor-Resident Interaction

◆ FIGURE 2–3　　*Three unique relationships in hospitality and travel.*

feeling of resentment toward visitors because of the overcrowding of popular attractions, traffic congestion, degradation of natural features, increased commercialization and a growth in crime rates.

CHAPTER CONCLUSION

There is a growing recognition that services marketing is a separate and distinct branch of marketing. This is based on the belief that unique marketing approaches are required in the services industry, of which hospitality and travel are just one element. Services share common features that make them quite different from manufactured and packaged goods. Services are intangible, highly perishable, inseparable from providers, and difficult to cost. They have different production processes and distribution channels.

Marketing in the services industry has evolved at a slower pace than it has in the manufacturing and packaged-goods industry, and in several instances has been influenced by government regulation. Service managers and executives have been more reluctant to adopt the core principles of marketing.

The hospitality and travel industry is, above all, a *people industry*. Those organizations that have climbed to the top are known for their high concern for both customer and employee satisfaction.

REVIEW QUESTIONS

1. What does services marketing mean?
2. Should services be marketed exactly the same as manufactured products and packaged goods? Why or why not?
3. What are generic and contextual differences between services and products? Explain the meaning of each concept.
4. What are the six generic and six contextual differences between the marketing of services and products?
5. Are these differences expected to continue in the future? Why or why not?
6. What are the eight specific differences affecting the marketing of hospitality and travel services?
7. This book suggests four additional Ps in marketing hospitality and travel services. What are they?
8. What are the four other unique approaches required in hospitality and travel marketing?
9. What are three key relationships among organizations and individuals in the hospitality and travel industry?

CHAPTER ASSIGNMENTS

1. You have just been hired by an automobile manufacturing company that has recently acquired a chain of resort properties. One of your initial tasks is to meet with the company's corporate marketing executives and to explain the difference between marketing resorts and marketing cars. Highlight the points you will make, including the common approaches both types of marketing share and the unique approaches required to market resorts.

2. Your instructor has asked you to visit the local supermarket and other retail stores and to bring back to class some items that demonstrate the generic differences between services and products. What would you collect, and how would you demonstrate the differences?

3. You have been asked to conduct a workshop in your community to highlight the close relationships between various organizations and individuals involved with hospitality and travel. Who would you invite? What things would you emphasize in the workshop and how would you do this? How would the workshop effectively demonstrate the importance of cooperation and mutual dependency among various organizations and individuals?

4. A major manufacturing company has just acquired a chain of travel agencies. You have been hired as the marketing director of the new travel agency division and have been asked to explain the differences between the distribution systems for products and services. What differences would you emphasize and how would you put your points across effectively?

WORLD WIDE WEB RESOURCES

AJ Hackett
  http://www.ajhackett.com/

American Express
  http://www.americanexpress.com/

Best Western
  http://www.bestwestern.com/

Burger King
  http://www.burgerking.com/

Coca Cola
  http://www.coca-cola.com/

Dollywood
  http://www.dollywood.com/

Four Seasons Hotels and Resorts
  http://www.fourseasons.com/

Greater Miami Convention & Visitors Bureau
  http://www.miamiandbeaches.com/

Howard Johnson
http://www.hojo.com/

Hyatt
http://www.hyatt.com/

KFC
http://www.kfc.com/

K-Paul's Louisiana Kitchen
http://www.kpauls.com/

Red Lobster
http://www.redlobster.com/

Skyline Chili
http://www.skylinechili.com/

Starwood Hotels & Resorts Worldwide
http://www.starwoodhotels.com/

Tourism Industries Office (U.S. Department of Commerce)
http://tinet.ita.doc.gov/

Travelodge
http://www.travelodge.com/

United Airlines
http://www.ual.com/

W Hotels
http://www.whotels.com/

Wendy's
http://www.wendys.com/

Westin
http://www.westin.com/

World Factbook, Central Intelligence Agency
http://www.odci.gov/cia/publications/factbook/

REFERENCES

1. Bureau of Labor Statistics. February 9, 2000. Employment Projections. http://www.bls.gov/news.release/

2. Lovelock, Christopher H. 2000. *Services Marketing: People, Technology, Strategy.* 4th ed. Upper Saddle River, N.J.: Prentice-Hall, Inc.

3. Lovelock, Christopher H. 2000. *Services Marketing: People, Technology, Strategy.* 4th ed. Upper Saddle River, N.J.: Prentice-Hall, Inc.

4. Berry, Leonard L., and A. Parasuraman. 1991. *Marketing Services: Competing Through Quality.* New York: The Free Press, 93–115.

5. Shostack, G. Lynn. "Breaking free from product marketing." *Journal of Marketing* 41(2): 73–80 (1977).

6. Lovelock, Christopher H. 2000. *Services Marketing: People, Technology, Strategy.* 4th ed. Upper Saddle River, N.J.: Prentice-Hall, Inc.

7. Sasser, W. Earl. "Match supply and demand in service industries." *Harvard Business Review* 54 (6):133–140 (1976).

8. Mill, Robert Christie, and Alastair M. Morrison. 1998. *The Tourism System: An Introductory Text.* 3rd ed. Dubuque, Iowa: Kendall/Hunt Publishing Company.

9. Mill, Robert Christie, and Alastair M. Morrison. 1998. *The Tourism System: An Introductory Text.* 3rd ed. Dubuque, Iowa: Kendall/Hunt Publishing Company.

For additional hospitality and travel marketing resources, visit our Web site at **www.Hospitality-Tourism.delmar.com**

3

The Hospitality and Travel Marketing System

What Is Marketing?

Objectives

Having read this chapter, you should be able to:

- Describe what a system is.
- Explain the hospitality and travel marketing system.
- List the four fundamentals of the hospitality and travel marketing system.
- List the benefits of using the hospitality and travel marketing system.

- List and arrange, in order, the five key questions in the hospitality and travel marketing system that must be answered.
- Define long- and short-term marketing planning.
- Distinguish between a strategic market plan and a marketing plan.

Overview

Is there a common way to market all the diverse organizations within the hospitality and travel industry? This chapter starts by exploring this question and suggests that there is a systematic process that everyone can use—the hospitality and travel marketing system. It describes the

general characteristics of all systems and identifies the benefits of using a systematic marketing approach. The need for both long- and short-term planning is emphasized. The chapter ends by describing the five-step hospitality and travel marketing system.

Key Terms

feedback	microsystems	short-term planning
hospitality and travel marketing system	mission	strategic market plan
interdependency (interdependent)	mission statement	strategic marketing planning
long-term planning	open systems	system
macrosystem	planning	tactical planning
marketing plan	plans	vision
	relationship marketing	vision statement

You may have been attracted to the hospitality and travel industry because of its great diversity. For example, lodging businesses range from the smallest mom-and-pop motel to the mega-hotels that contain several thousand rooms. Food service establishments run the gamut from elegant, table-service restaurants to roadside hamburger stands. There are small, local travel agencies with a staff of three or four, as well as major national brands such as American Express and Carlson Wagonlit Travel. Air services range from national airlines such as American, Air Canada, British Airways, and Qantas to one-man bush pilots. Among attractions, there are theme parks such as Walt Disney World and Universal Studios Florida, and small museums with a few hundred attendees a year.

Chapter 1 reviewed core principles of marketing common to all for-profit and non-profit groups. Chapter 2 discussed features shared by all hospitality and travel organizations. Despite this common ground, you are probably still thinking that totally different marketing approaches are needed within our industry. What if we told you that you are both right and wrong? You are right in thinking that businesses as different as hotels and travel agencies need to tailor their services, prices, distribution systems, and promotions to fit their customers. But there is a systematic process to marketing that every hospitality and travel organization can use—the hospitality and travel marketing system. Think about it. You are going to learn this process and will be able to use it in any facet of our industry. Before describing this system, we thought you should be aware of the confusion that exists in our industry about who we are.

MANY DIFFERENT APPROACHES TO DEFINING OUR INDUSTRY

The list of definitions for this industry is enormous. You are left wondering which definition is correct, or if they are all right. Before answering these questions, let us look at some of the definitions.

It Is the Hospitality Industry!

Many educators and writers, particularly in the United States, agree that the correct name is the hospitality industry. Nykiel says that this industry provides products and services to customers who are away from home. According to him, the industry includes travel, lodging, eating, entertainment, recreation, and gaming facilities.[1] Other authors agree with the use of the term hospitality industry, but list additional types of organi-

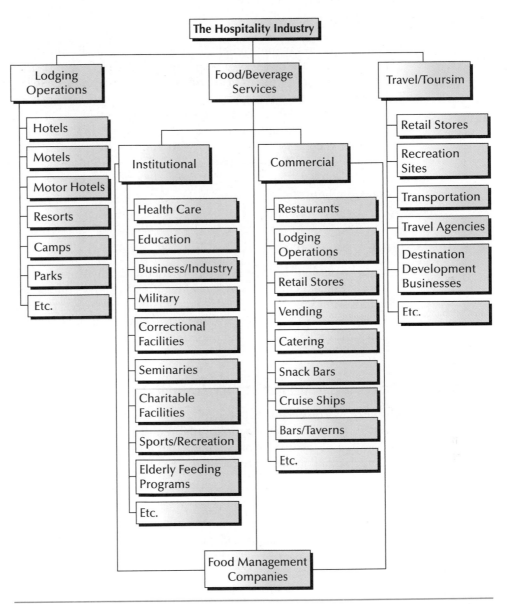

◆ **FIGURE 3–1** *Ninemeier's definition of the hospitality industry.* (From Ninemeier, Jack, *Managing Foodservice Operations,* West Lafayette, Ind., Dietary Managers Association and Restaurant, Hotel and Institutional Management Institute, 1985, p. 2)

zations. For example, Lane and Dupré pinpoint travel distribution channels and transportation.[2] Reid sees the hospitality industry as including restaurants and food service operations, hotels and motels, private clubs, food brokers and distributors, manufacturers, professional associations, and hospitality education.[3] Ninemeier divides the industry into lodging operations and food/beverage services (commercial and institutional), but adds another segment called travel/tourism.[4] Figure 3–1 shows Ninemeier's hospitality industry definition.

It Is the Food Service Industry!

Many companies are not content to be under an umbrella called the hospitality industry. They are in the business of preparing and serving food and, incidentally, beverages as well. They are in the food service industry. The National Restaurant Association (NRA) divides the food service industry into three parts: commercial, institutional, and military feeding. Others see a difference between restaurants and food service and like to use the term restaurant and food service industry. In Canada, NRA's counterpart is known as the Canadian Restaurant and Foodservices Association. The International Foodservice Manufacturers Association defines the food service industry as including all establishments that prepare and generally serve food, meals, snacks, and beverages away from home.[5]

It Is the Lodging Industry!

Not to be outdone by their food service colleagues, there are those who see themselves as part of the lodging industry. Goeldner, Ritchie, and McIntosh believe that the lodging industry is made up of hotels, motels, suites, resorts, bed and breakfasts, and time-sharing units.[6] Others have an even narrower focus, using such terms as the hotel industry, the resort industry, and the campground industry.

It Is the Food Service and Hospitality Industry!

Some draw a distinction between food service and hospitality. They either use the words food service and hospitality, or hospitality and food service industry. The reason for the separation of the two terms is usually that hospitality organizations are profitmaking enterprises and food service facilities are nonprofit.

It Is the Travel and/or Tourism Industry!

Another school of thought is that there is a travel and/or tourism industry. Gee, Makens, and Choy have even written a textbook titled *The Travel Industry.* These authors view the travel industry as including public and private organizations that are involved in the development, production, and marketing of products and services to serve the needs of travelers.[7] *Travel Weekly* bills itself as "the national newspaper of the travel industry."[8] Hodgson has written a book titled *The Travel and Tourism Industry: Strategies for the Future.*[9] Some feel that travel or tourism industry rather than hospitality should be the *umbrella* term. They would take Figure 3–1 and substitute the words "the travel (or tourism) industry" for "the hospitality industry." In their book, Lane and Dupré place five components "under the hospitality umbrella." These five components are lodging, food service, entertainment/attractions/recreation/special events, travel distribution channels, and transportation. Under the heading of travel and tourism, those providing different types of services often see themselves as being distinct industries. For example, the Cruise Lines International Association sees itself as representing the cruise industry, and the National Tour Association represents the group travel industry.

Did You Know?

✓ The Australian Tourist Commission (ATC) is responsible for marketing Australia worldwide as a tourism destination.

✓ ATC calls the industry tourism and says that it benefits more than hotels, airlines, and tourist attractions.

✓ Tourism employs more than one million Australians or 12 percent of the workforce.

✓ Tourism is Australia's largest earner of foreign exchange.

✓ Tourism accounts for 14 percent of Australia's export earnings.

✓ Australia had 4.5 million international visitors in 1999, a new record.

✓ North Americans spend an average of 28 days in Australia on trips; Europeans spend 38 days in the land down under.

✓ Just over 50 percent of international visitors to Australia are on return trips.

✓ In 1999, Australia was the first Western destination where residents of China could take vacations.

It Depends Where You Are!

If you live outside the United States in places such as the United Kingdom, Australia, or New Zealand, you will be exposed to another layer of industry *labels*. In Britain, hospitality and food service becomes the *hotel and catering industry*. In Australia, New Zealand, and Canada, the term *tourism industry* is well accepted as the umbrella term for the entire industry, including hospitality businesses.

It Is Not an Industry at All!

Many economists and statisticians disagree with these authors. They lump commercial restaurants in with department and corner grocery stores under the retail trade heading. Nonprofit food service facilities are scattered among hospitals, colleges/universities, nursing and personal-care facilities, and other institutions. Lodging operations are pigeonholed with other services, including health care, legal services, and insurance services. Airlines, motor coaches, cruise and sightseeing boats, and railways, as well as travel agents and tour operators, find themselves under the transportation and communications heading. This method of categorization, known as Standard Industrial Classification (SIC), is a very convenient way of looking at the industrial structure of a country. However, by neatly fitting every establishment into a box, the strong relationships that exist between hospitality and travel organizations are not reflected. This system also ignores situations in which an organization fits into more than one category. Is a typical city hotel with many restaurants and bars a part of the service industries, or should it be in the retail trade category? Is an airline company that owns hotels in transportation and communications or in the service industries?

A detailed look at the United States Standard Industrial Classification system shows that hospitality and travel organizations are scattered among at least 16 of the two-digit SIC codes known as "major groups" and are in 35 or more of the four-digit SIC codes.[10]

SIC Code	Names of Major Groups
40	Railroad transportation
41	Local and suburban transit and interurban highway passenger transportation
44	Water transportation
45	Transportation by air
47	Transportation services (including travel agents and tour operators)
55	Automotive dealers and service stations
58	Eating and drinking places
59	Miscellaneous retail
60	Depository institutions (including banks and foreign currency exchanges)
70	Hotels, and other lodging places
73	Business services (including convention and visitor bureaus and tourist information bureaus)
75	Automotive repair, services, and parking (including car rental firms)
79	Amusement and recreation services
84	Museums, and botanical and zoological gardens
86	Membership organizations (including Chambers of Commerce)
95	Administration of environmental quality and housing programs

◆ FIGURE 3–2   *Hospitality and travel organizations by SIC codes.* (From Government Sales Specialists, http://www.govtsales.com/sics/sicgroups.htm)

Among the 16 major groups in 1998, the largest number of employees were found in the categories of eating and drinking places (SIC Code 58) and hotels and other lodging places (SIC Code 70), with 7,760,000 and 1,776,000 employees, respectively.[11] Figure 3–2 provides the complete list of the sixteen major groups.

No Universally Accepted Definition

What can you learn from these different definitions? You should see that there is no universally accepted definition of the *industry* that this book covers. The word industry itself is used very loosely. People working *in the industry,* and those who try to educate them, feel a sense of unity and belonging by using a common definition of their fields of endeavor. Influencing legislation and government policy is another practical reason for dividing the industry into groups that share common characteristics. Thus, airlines belong to the Air Transport Association of America, travel agents to the American Society of Travel Agents, lodging facilities to the American Hotel & Lodging Association, restaurants to the National Restaurant Association, theme parks to the International Association of Amusement Parks and Attractions, and so on.

The former United States Travel Data Center, which uses the term travel industry, described it as a collection of diverse products sold by a fragmented industry to segmented markets through a complex distribution chain.[12] This more or less sums up the state of the art in defining the industry. If we have an industry at all, it is one that puts more emphasis on internal differences than on common concerns and opportunities. The economists, by carving hospitality and travel up into many different pieces of an SIC jigsaw puzzle, have not helped us resolve these differences or recognize the relationships that should bind our organizations. In the global marketplace of this new century, it is the cultivation of these relationships with other hospitality and travel organizations as well as with customers that will lead to marketing success.[13]

THE SYSTEMS APPROACH

Definition

The systems approach is an alternative way of looking at industries and organizations. It is the approach recommended in this book. A system is a collection of interrelated parts that work together to achieve common objectives. Our industry consists of a group of interrelated organizations with a common purpose and goals. Likewise, each individual organization is a system—a collection of interrelated departments, divisions, or activities with the same overall purpose and goals. What is it that our industry and its organizations have in common? It is the satisfaction of customer needs while these customers are out of their homes or normal environments (in the case of tourism or travel). Customers may be thousands of miles from home on an overseas vacation, or simply down the road at a local fast-food restaurant. Our industry is set up to meet all types of away-from-home needs.

There is a macrosystem and many microsystems in hospitality and travel. The macrosystem exists at the industry level. As you saw in Chapter 2, there are a number of unique relationships among hospitality and travel organizations. It might be helpful for you to think of the hospitality and travel macrosystem as being like a car. The attractions, for both pleasure and business travelers, are the engine of that car. Without an engine, a car does not run. Without attractions, a hospitality and travel destination is unlikely to draw visitors. However, an engine alone does not constitute a car! A chassis, axles, tires, a body, seats, and many other parts must be added. Likewise, a hospitality and travel destination needs facilities (hotels, restaurants, shopping), transportation and infrastructure, and hospitality resources to run with the maximum effectiveness. Those who operate attractions and events need help from other suppliers of facilities, transportation carriers, and travel trade intermediaries in attracting customers and meeting customer needs.

Microsystems are found at the individual organization level. This book primarily deals with microsystems and discusses how individual hospitality and travel organizations market their services. The term hospitality and travel marketing system is used to describe a microsystem—a process for marketing an organization that involves everyone who works for that organization.

Characteristics of Systems in the Hospitality and Travel Industry

To understand marketing, you must know the characteristics of systems. There are six major characteristics of the systems in our industry:

1. Openness
2. Complexity and variety
3. Responsiveness
4. Competitiveness
5. Interdependency
6. Friction and disharmony

1. **Openness.** The industry and its organizations are open systems. Unlike mechanical and electrical closed systems, they are not rigid, and the system parts are not precisely organized in a definite way. The systems are dynamic, constantly undergoing change. People are always coming up with new and creative ways of marketing hospitality and travel services. Airlines' frequent-flyer and hotels' frequent guest programs are two examples from the 1980s. Global partnerships and strategic alliances among airlines, hotel companies, travel agencies, tour operators, and destination marketing organizations were the hallmark of the 1990s. The Internet and e-commerce started to become a way of life in the late 1990s and early 2000s. The external, strategic environment continually affects our systems, reshaping the way we do business. For example, drive-through restaurants developed because of people's need for greater convenience and less time-consuming service.

   This book recommends a carefully sequenced series of steps in marketing—the hospitality and travel marketing system. But it does not suggest a rigid approach to marketing. The steps can be compared to a human skeleton. They are a basic framework required for effective functioning. A skeleton must have body tissue and a mind before it can be considered to be a human being. Likewise, each organization must have a unique personality and set of marketing activities to survive.

2. **Complexity and Variety.** A great variety of hospitality and travel organizations exist. They range from the smallest mom-and-pop businesses to multinational conglomerates. The interrelationships among the different organizations are complex. One prime example is the diversity of distribution channels that exists. A resort can market directly to customers or it can choose a variety of intermediaries, including traditional or online travel agencies, tour wholesalers, incentive travel planners, and others. There are many different ways to promote, sell, and price hospitality and travel services. No fixed success formula exists.

3. **Responsiveness.** The marketplace is constantly changing. So, too, must our industry and organizations change. We must be responsive to change, or we will not survive. All systems must have feedback mechanisms. Information must be gathered from customers and others to make decisions about changes in both customer needs and competitive activities. Standing still in our industry is fatal. Marketing research provides a nourishing supply of information to help us adapt and survive. Ramada Inn's history provides a good example. Marketing research carried out in the 1970s showed that the chain had a poor image among lodging customers. Facing the prospect of a declining market, company officials decided that a major facelift was required in Ramada properties and that the chain should be divided into three distinct brands. Likewise, Club Med, Inc., a company long associated with swinging singles, made a complete about-face toward families and couples in the 1980s after doing research and studying future population projections.

4. **Competitiveness.** Ours is an industry of intense competition. New organizations throw their hats into the ring almost daily. Competitive power and intensity increase as large corporations acquire related firms. Smaller organizations collaborate to improve their competitive positions. They form consortia, referral groups, and marketing cooperatives and make other joint efforts to gain more clout in the marketplace. Change from within the system is as important as change caused by external factors. The 1980s are remembered for the large number of airline mergers that took place, as well as for the joining of airlines, hotels, car rental firms, and others in offering frequent traveler awards. The 1990s saw the true beginning of global competition in the

hospitality and travel industry. National boundaries lost importance as organizations formed strategic marketing alliances and partnerships with other organizations both within and outside of the hospitality and travel business. The Star Alliance, One World Alliance, Sky Team Alliance, as well as Northwest Airlines and KLM, are good examples of what is ahead in the era of the global marketplace.

5. **Interdependency.** Our industry (the macrosystem) includes a variety of interdependent and interrelated businesses and organizations involved in serving the needs of customers who are away from home. Lodging, restaurant, attraction, transportation, travel agency, tour wholesaling, and retail shopping businesses are part of the industry. Other organizations involved are government tourism promotion agencies, convention and visitors bureaus, chambers of commerce, and other destination marketing groups.

   Many people have a myopic view of the scope of our industry. A broader perspective is required. Many businesses and organizations, even countries, are interdependent. They complement one another, working together to produce results greater than the sum of their individual efforts. A travel agent may never book a meal for a customer at a Burger King restaurant, but may have made the customer's reservation at the nearby hotel. A full understanding of marketing in this industry requires knowledge and acceptance of these interrelationships. Relationship marketing is a term that emphasizes the importance of building long-term relationships with customers and with other organizations in the distribution chain.

   Interdependency also exists at the individual organization level. Marketing is not the only function of hospitality and travel managers. Other areas of responsibility are operations, finance and accounting, human resources management, and maintenance activities. Marketing has to be coordinated with these other areas and is dependent on them for its success.

A Touch of Technology

> ### Online Travel Information and Reservation Services
>
> - The bypassing of traditional travel agencies through online travel services is causing some friction in our industry.
> - The Travel Industry Association of America (TIA) in its report, *Travelers' Use of the Internet,* estimated that 59.4 million online travelers used the Internet in 2000.
> - This was a 1,700 percent increase over 1996.
> - In 2000, 42 percent of online travel planners made online reservations.
> - The most popular sources of online travel information and reservations were Yahoo! Travel, Excite, Lycos, Microsoft Expedia, Travelocity, and Priceline.
> - Travelocity is the third largest e-commerce site in reach and unique visits after Amazon.com and eBay.com.
> - Travelocity completed a merger with Preview Travel in early 2000; the combined online sales of the two services in 1999 were $1.2 billion (http://www.sabre.com).

6. **Friction and Disharmony.**   Within both our industry and individual organizations, there are many points of conflict, stresses, and tensions. We do not have perfect systems. They do not perform exactly as we think they should. In the United States, the topic of airline companies bypassing travel agents and marketing directly to large corporate clients is causing a strain between agents and airlines. The often-tardy submission of agent commissions by hotels and resorts is a source of tension between agents and lodging companies. Lodging companies are often frustrated by tour wholesalers who deliver less than promised. Destinations and businesses that should be cooperating are working against one another.

This imperfect world of hospitality and travel extends to individual organizations. Unhealthy internal competition, personality clashes, and communication problems cause the system to function differently than it should. Marketing can promise the customer something that cannot be delivered due to these types of internal problems. Much of the job of marketing is showing everyone that they are all in the same boat.

THE HOSPITALITY AND TRAVEL MARKETING SYSTEM

Figure 3–3 shows the hospitality and travel system model. This model applies to all organizations, from the largest to the smallest. Whether we are marketing hotels restaurants, travel agencies, or airlines, five key questions require answers. They are:

1. Where are we now?
2. Where would we like to be?
3. How do we get there?
4. How do we make sure we get there?
5. How do we know if we got there?

System Fundamentals

Before discussing each of the questions in the system model, you need to have some idea of the system's fundamentals and benefits. There are four fundamentals of the system:

1. Strategic marketing planning
2. Marketing orientation
3. Differences between product and services marketing
4. Understanding customer behavior

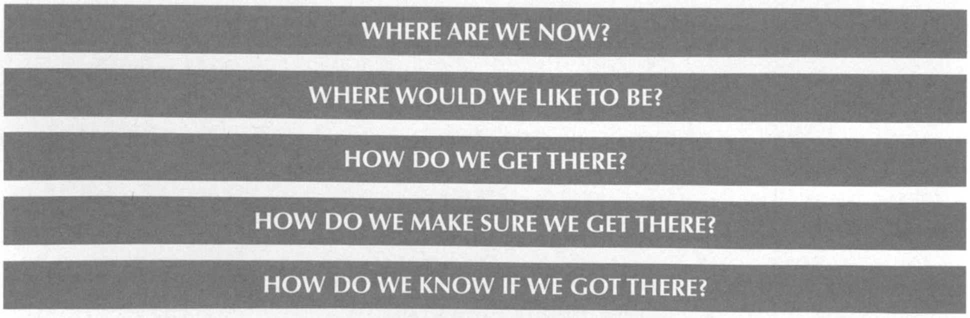

WHERE ARE WE NOW?

WHERE WOULD WE LIKE TO BE?

HOW DO WE GET THERE?

HOW DO WE MAKE SURE WE GET THERE?

HOW DO WE KNOW IF WE GOT THERE?

◆ FIGURE 3–3   *Hospitality and travel marketing system model.*

1. **Strategic Marketing Planning.**   The hospitality and travel business is very dynamic, constantly experiencing change both from within and from outside. Long-term planning is required to guarantee success. "Those who live in the present, will die in the very near future" is a most appropriate statement about our business. Strategic marketing planning is the term used to describe the process of developing long-term (three to five or more years ahead) plans for marketing. It involves selecting a definite course of action for long-term survival and growth. Using strategic marketing planning is the first of the system's fundamentals.

2. **Marketing Orientation.**   Adopting a marketing orientation is the second fundamental. This was discussed in Chapter 1. It means that satisfying customer needs and wants has the top priority in an organization.

3. **Differences Between Product and Services Marketing.**   There are differences between marketing services and marketing products. Ours is a business of marketing and providing services. Using the hospitality and travel marketing system assumes that we are aware of these differences. Chapter 2 reviewed this subject.

4. **Understanding Customer Behavior.**   The fourth fundamental is the need to understand customer behavior. This is the main focus of Chapter 4. The system is most effectively used if we fully appreciate the personal and interpersonal factors that influence customer behavior.

Benefits of Using the System

There are three main benefits for organizations that use the hospitality and travel marketing system:

1. A priority on planning
2. A logical flow of efforts
3. A better balance of marketing activities

1. **A Priority on Planning.** Planning is a must in today's business environment. Organizations that use the hospitality and travel marketing system are forced to plan ahead and to anticipate future events. If we can be sure of just one thing, it is that tomorrow will not be exactly like today. Planning one year ahead is not enough. Multiyear, strategic market plans are required.

   Whether plans are short term (two years or less) or long term (more than two years), they have at least six basic purposes:
   a. Identifying alternative marketing approaches
   b. Maintaining uniqueness
   c. Creating desirable situations
   d. Avoiding undesirable situations
   e. Adapting to the unexpected
   f. Facilitating the measurement, monitoring, and evaluation of results

   The first purpose is to identify all alternative marketing approaches available. There is always more than one way to achieve objectives. It is essential to consider them all and to pinpoint the most effective approach.

   A second purpose is to maintain an organization's uniqueness. Part of the secret of marketing success is having customers perceive that we provide something different. Creating this image means work and maintaining it requires even more effort.

The third purpose is to create several desirable conditions. These include maintaining a high awareness of the service among potential customers, making effective and balanced use of marketing resources and techniques, capitalizing on new market opportunities, adding services that increase market share (proportion of total demand available), and taking full advantage of cooperative marketing ventures.

Avoiding undesirable future conditions is the fourth purpose. Typical situations that most organizations want to avoid include losing market share, continuing to provide services that dilute profitability, and conflicting with interrelated organizations and competitors.

The fifth purpose is to be in a better position to adapt to the unexpected. We said earlier that the hospitality and travel marketing system was an open system. It can be dramatically affected by economic, social, cultural, political/legal, technological, and competitive changes and events. Organizations have to be prepared for the unexpected, and forward planning helps.

A good plan facilitates the measurement, monitoring, and evaluation of results, since it incorporates measurable objectives. Success can be judged by determining how close the organization comes to achieving these objectives.

2. **A Logical Flow of Efforts.** The second system benefit is that it produces a logical flow of effort. Marketing dollars and human resources are more effectively used because the right questions are asked at the right time. Many organizations become lazy and skip over basic marketing questions such as "Where are we now?" and "Where would we like to be?" They jump into implementing a program before they consider the basics. Others fail to coordinate and control marketing efforts. They just let things happen. They ignore the question, "How do we make sure we get there?" Often no feedback mechanism is used. The organization has no idea if their marketing is effective or not. They do not ask the question, "How do we know if we got there?" As you can see, the five key marketing questions in the system logically flow from one to the other.

3. **A Better Balance of Marketing Activities.** A better balance in marketing activities results from using the system. The five questions are given equal priority. All available marketing techniques are carefully considered. There is a constant reevaluation of activities, rather than a continuous repetition of past efforts.

Effective marketing decisions are based on sound research. The hospitality and travel marketing system assumes that organizations recognize the value of marketing research and realize its great benefits. Pinpointing new marketing opportunities is one of these benefits. Research helps us identify new services and customer groups. It lets us know where we stand relative to competitors. Research assists in measuring the results of marketing activities. It shows us what worked and what did not. Research helps us understand what has been most effective, and points out our mistakes. We learn how customers look at us. We find different ways to increase their satisfaction. Research provides a constant source of nourishment for the hospitality and travel system.

The system is used continuously and experience is gained from every use. Something different is learned each time.

Steps in the System

Most traditional textbooks suggest that there is a logical and sequential flow to marketing. However, the authors of these books try to outdo one another in the sophistication of the terminology they use for each step and technique. Students are left confused by the jargon of marketing and wonder which definitions and terms are correct. We will not add to your confusion! The hospitality and travel marketing system uses a more commonsense practical approach that reduces marketing to five basic components expressed as questions that have to be answered.

Let us start looking at the system by comparing it to a commercial airline flight. Try to answer the following questions:

1. Does the flight crew of a commercial aircraft know where they are when their plane lands?
2. Does the flight crew know where they are going as their plane takes off?
3. Does the flight crew have a flight plan for each trip?
4. Do the pilot and copilot monitor their progress and make adjustments to their original flight plan as necessary?
5. Does the pilot evaluate each trip and fill in a flight log?

You should have answered yes to all five questions. If you did not, look them over again. We think you will agree that we are right. Why is a commercial airline flight like the marketing of a hospitality or travel organization? The answer is simple. The key questions that ensure a safe and successful flight are identical to those needed for effective marketing. They are shown in Figure 3–4.

The hospitality and travel marketing system is a systematic process of planning, researching, implementing, controlling, and evaluating an organization's marketing activities. It is systematic because five questions are repeatedly answered in the same order. Figure 3–5 relates the marketing tasks in the system (the PRICE of marketing—planning, research, implementation, control, and evaluation) to the system's steps or questions.

1. **Where Are We Now?** Every airline pilot and flight deck crew knows their current location and the course they have followed. So, too, must an organization assess where it is and where it has just been. If an organization is to succeed in the long run, it must always be assessing its strengths and weaknesses. A great deal must be known about

STEPS	HOSPITALITY AND TRAVEL MARKETING	AIRLINE FLIGHT
1. Where are we now?	• Current situation	• Current airport location
2. Where would we like to be?	• Desired future situation	• Destination airport
3. How do we get there?	• Marketing plan	• Flight plan
4. How do we make sure we get there?	• Monitoring and adjusting marketing plan	• Monitoring and adjusting flight plan
5. How do we know if we got there?	• Evaluating and measuring results of marketing plan	• Evaluating flight plan and filling in pilot's log

◆ FIGURE 3–4   *The hospitality and travel marketing system and airline flight analogy.*

TASKS/FUNCTIONS		STEPS/QUESTIONS
Planning and	**P**	• Where are we now?
Research	**R**	• Where would we like to be?
Implementation	**I**	• How do we get there?
Control	**C**	• How do we make sure we get there?
Evaluation	**E**	• How do we know if we got there?

◆ FIGURE 3–5   *Hospitality and travel marketing system tasks and steps. The PRICE model.*

present and potential customers, and about competitors. It is similar to putting the organization under a microscope. The day-to-day things that get overlooked are magnified and carefully examined. A technique called the situation analysis and various marketing research tools are used. These help answer the question, "Where are we now?" It is not enough to answer this question once, but it must be answered at least once or twice every two years.

2. **Where Would We Like To Be?** Theodore Levitt said that if an organization does not know where it is going, any route will take it there.[14] An organization that does not know what it wants to achieve is like an aircraft taking off without knowing its destination. There are many alternative marketing routes that an organization can follow. The key is to determine which one is most effective. Every organization must try to identify where it wants to be as a result of its marketing activities. Specific techniques are used to achieve this goal, including market segmentation, target marketing, positioning, marketing mixes, and marketing objectives. These techniques help an organization chart the course that it will take to get where it wants to be.

3. **How Do We Get There?** Having decided where it wants to be, the organization must next turn to the question of how it is going to get there. The marketing plan is the key tool here. It acts like a blueprint for action. The marketing plan documents how the organization will use the 4 Ps (product, place, pricing, and promotion) and the other 4 Ps of hospitality and travel marketing (packaging, programming, partnership, and people) to achieve its marketing objectives. An organization without a marketing plan is like an aircraft taking off without a flight plan. It does not know exactly how it will get to where it wants to be.

4. **How Do We Make Sure We Get There?** Having a marketing plan does not automatically guarantee that an organization will be successful. Checks and controls have to be built in to ensure that things go as planned. There is a need for marketing management, budgeting, and controls. Every aircraft that takes off has pre-check and in-flight checking procedures. If an aircraft encounters adverse weather conditions, it may alter its route, speed, or altitude with air traffic control's permission. If an organization finds that parts of its marketing plan are not working, it may have to make changes to get to where it wants to be.

5. **How Do We Know If We Got There?** Many organizations put great effort into developing marketing plans and very little into measuring the results of these plans. This is unfortunate because they can learn from both their mistakes and their successes.

EXCELLENCE CASE

Using the Hospitality and Travel Marketing System and the PRICE Model:
The Calgary Convention & Visitors Bureau

If you wanted to find an example of applying the hospitality and travel marketing system, along with the PRICE model, it would be hard to find a better one than in Alberta, Canada. The Calgary Convention & Visitors Bureau has applied the system in its three-year strategic marketing plan, called the *CCVB 2000–2002 Marketing Plan.* Following is a summary of how CCVB adapted the system and the PRICE model to its situation.

1. **Planning: Follow a System that Works**
   At every step of the strategic plan, there is a reflection of the basic CCVB philosophy, mission statement, and goals as they relate to key industry priorities.

   Destination marketing research shows that marketing strategies work best with extended lifespans, provided there is a clear evaluation of their effectiveness and of the changing opportunities in the marketplace. Choosing a long-term direction and system that works requires a marketing plan that involves the following:

   - **Planning**—Where are we now and where would we like to be? Gathering, analyzing, and translating information into decisions and actions to reach common objectives.
   - **Research**—What are our markets? Matching the right market with travel products and services.
   - **Implementation**—How do we get there? Strategies and marketing tools to employ.
   - **Control**—How are we doing? Monitoring performance daily to stay on track or adjust accordingly.
   - **Evaluation**—How do we know if we got there? Detailed measuring, tracking, analysis, and reporting of marketing performance.

2. **Research: Maintain Traditional Markets, Expand into Growth Markets, Develop New Markets**
   CCVB partners identify leisure and business travel promotion opportunities in three geographic markets that include the following:

   A. **Traditional Markets—Canada and the United States**
   B. **Growth Markets—Europe and Asia-Pacific**
   C. **Emerging Markets—Latin America, South America, and Southeast Asia**

A. **Traditional Markets—Canada and the United States**
   The CCVB partnership dedicates most of its resources to *bread and butter* North American markets, where traditional presence guarantees a steady flow of business. To service an established market this size requires significant resources, which reduces the return on investment.

   - **Leisure Travel—North America:** The North American leisure market is a traditional market that consumes a significant amount of resources. Vacation/pleasure visits represent more than 30 percent of the North American market to Calgary and area. CCVB partners target both group and independent travel markets, and position Calgary and area as a clean, safe, friendly, unique, and unspoiled destination.
   - **Business Travel—Canada and the United States:** Through a new initiative, the CCVB will work with the TELUS Convention Center, the Calgary Stampede, and other partners to target conventions, corporate meetings, and trade shows from the United States and

continued

EXCELLENCE CASE *continued*

Canada. Partners will combine resources to promote new hotel and meeting products in Calgary and area.

B. Growth Markets—Europe and Asia-Pacific
CCVB partners develop high-yield growth markets because offshore visitors stay longer and spend more money. These markets harbor major populations of travel trade buyers and leisure travel consumers such as group, consumer summer touring, or winter skiing.

- **Leisure and Business Travel—Europe:** The European market is a growth market for Calgary with tremendous promise. The CCVB partnership primarily targets the United Kingdom, Germany, and France.
- **Leisure and Business Travel—Asia-Pacific:** The Asia-Pacific region is a vast market that represents the greatest growth opportunity for Calgary and area. Within this region, the CCVB targets the leisure (group and independent travel), student, and incentive travel markets.

C. Emerging Markets—Latin America, South America, and Southeast Asia
High-yield, emerging markets receive the fewest CCVB promotional resources.

Marketing investment is driven primarily by major private sector players. A guide to CCVB involvement in emerging markets is visitor spending potential, market size, opportunity to influence, ability to track and evaluate, and especially partner investment in marketing consortia and travel package development.

- **Leisure and Business Travel—Latin America, South America, and Southeast Asia:** Calgary and area partners will continue to develop opportunities and expand initiatives in the high-spending markets of Mexico, Brazil, and Southeast Asia. Western Canada is becoming more popular for travelers from this market who traditionally search for unique touring vacations with scenery, hospitality, shopping, entertainment, and culture.

3. Implementation: Target Travel Trade Buyers
CCVB marketing staff attend trade events and arrange appointments in cities populated by tour wholesalers, tour operators, meeting planners, and other travel trade influencers.

The CCVB partnership does not have the budget needed to launch an effective consumer advertising campaign. Therefore, the primary marketing strategy of the CCVB is to meet and show travel trade buyers that Calgary and area as a destination will be attractive to their clients and will improve their business margins.

Attendance at consumer shows allows some direct contact with consumers. CCVB partners do double duty in most markets, promoting both leisure travel and business travel opportunities.

CCVB partners also pool dollars into marketing consortia, which maximizes budgets and boosts awareness of the entire destination.

Partners promote the destination through marketing activities that include the following:

- **Personal contact**—CCVB partners attend trade events and call on clients in cities populated by travel trade buyers.
- **Familiarization tours**—These tours introduce tour operators, meeting planners, and media to Calgary.
- **Publications**—CCVB partners produce publications that promote Calgary and area to specific sectors of the visitor market.
- **Media marketing**—The CCVB replaces costly advertising purchases with media marketing. In 1998, media coverage for the destination reached $4 million.
- **Internet marketing**—The destination Web site serves as an inexpensive and effective way to penetrate and service the enormous North American and international consumer market and travel trade buyers, such as meeting planners.
- **Client servicing**—CCVB partners assist visitors and convention delegates year-round with visitor counseling, accom-

continued

EXCELLENCE CASE *continued*

modation services, registration staff, publications, White Hat welcome ceremonies, gift items, and souvenirs.

4. Control and Evaluation: Maintain a Clear Marketing Focus

CCVB partners measure marketing initiatives and are held accountable for results.

The CCVB evaluation program involves detailed measuring, tracking, and analysis of marketing performance and market statistics.

Staff conducts tracking and analysis projects to produce and maintain a clear marketing focus on high-yield opportunities and to enhance market success. Market research on each geographic and economic sector ensures CCVB partners target each market in the most effective manner possible. Market changes mean adaptation and readjustment.

In 1999, CCVB partners began to develop a process to evaluate each marketing activity of the CCVB. The new *score card* will allow CCVB marketing partners to analyze current and new markets, identify and compare marketing activities, and evaluate the effectiveness of activities. The evaluation rating that results will determine whether to repeat activities or reveal more effective ways to market the destination.

CCVB partners receive reports that detail statistics of interest and include the following:

- Leads developed by CCVB partners
- Leads converted into confirmed businesses
- Confirmed business projected spending
- Destination Web site visitors
- Visitors counseled at CCVB Visitor Centers
- Phone line counseling calls

Discussion Questions

1. In your opinion, how well did the CCVB address each of the five questions in the hospitality and travel marketing system?
2. How could CCVB's usage of this system be improved?
3. What could other hospitality and travel marketers learn from this application of the hospitality and travel marketing system?

Web Site

http://www.visitor.calgary.ab.ca/

References

The author acknowledges the assistance of W. A. "Pat" Bell, former Vice President of Strategic Marketing & Planning at CCVB and his staff in preparing this case. Materials from the CCVB plan are reprinted with their permission.

Just as an airline pilot evaluates each trip and fills in a flight log, measuring and evaluating results of a marketing plan produce useful information that is fed back into the next attempt to answer the question, "Where are we now?"

RELATIONSHIP OF THE SYSTEM TO STRATEGIC AND TACTICAL MARKETING PLANNING

Most books use the terms *strategic* and *tactical* to refer to the two branches of planning required for effective marketing. We also use long term and short term in this book. **Long-term planning** is a period of more than two years. **Short-term planning** means two years or less.

To be most effective, marketing has to be viewed as a long-term management activity. It needs to be planned three or more years ahead. Long-term strategic marketing planning is required. Because change is so rapid, short-term, tactical planning is also needed. What is a plan? It is a procedure, worked out in advance, for achieving an objective or objectives. In this book, plans are assumed to be written, but not in stone. There are often good reasons to modify plans. What is planning? It is a management activity of looking into the future and developing procedures in advance to achieve objectives. Marketing planning is an activity of marketing managers who try to anticipate future events and develop procedures for realizing marketing objectives.

The term marketing plan is widely used in industry to mean a short-term plan for two years or less. This book adopts the same definition. A strategic market plan is different. It covers three or more years. A marketing plan is short term and needs to be more detailed. A large part of this book is devoted to developing marketing (short term) plans. This does not mean that marketing plans are more important than long-term (strategic market) plans. It is just the main focus selected for the book.

Before discussing strategic marketing planning, we need to get some basics out of the way. Above all, you need to realize that there is more to the success of an organization than marketing alone. Marketing is just one of several management functions. Every organization has many different objectives and plans, and ways of accomplishing them.

A hierarchy of objectives and plans exists in all organizations (Figure 3–6). At the foundation of the hierarchy is the organization's vision. A vision and vision statement describe where the organization wants to be at some future time. A mission is a broad statement about an organization's business and scope, services or products, markets served, and overall philosophy. It summarizes the organization's role in society. Overall organizational objectives or goals are next in the hierarchy. They support the mission

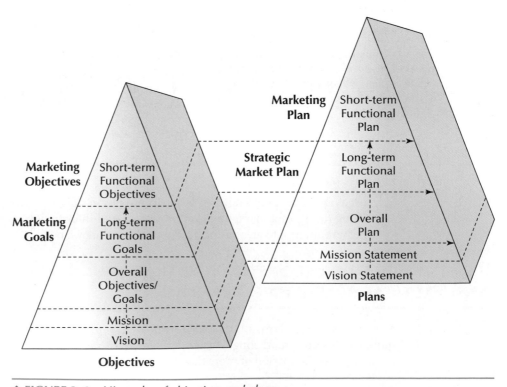

◆ FIGURE 3–6   *Hierarchy of objectives and plans.*

statement. Corporations usually set these as profitability, market share, and sales volume targets. Next come the long-term (strategic) goals for each management function. In our case, these are long-term marketing goals. These must be consistent with the vision, mission, and overall objectives. Last in the hierarchy are the short-term (tactical) goals for each management function. For us, they are short-term marketing objectives.

Planning and plans are needed to achieve objectives. For each level of the objectives hierarchy, there is a corresponding plan. This means that there is a hierarchy of plans as well. Figure 3–6 illustrates this point.

Where does strategic marketing planning fit in? It is the second level from the top in Figure 3–6. Strategic (long-term) marketing planning involves establishing long-term marketing objectives and a (strategic market) plan to achieve them. How does the hospitality and travel marketing system tie in to strategic marketing planning? It does so in two ways. First, strategic marketing planning itself uses the process of the system. It addresses the same five questions, but it does so with a longer-term perspective. Second, a strategic market plan is achieved by repeating the system several times.

Let us clarify one more important point. For planning to be most effective, it must be continuous. Strategic market and marketing plans have to be reassessed and adjusted constantly. We do not start on the first day of Year 1 with a strategic market plan and then not touch the plan again until the first day of Year 4. Likewise, it is wrong to start on January 1 with a marketing plan and assume that it need not be changed. We do not begin with a strategic market plan, follow with two or more marketing plans, and then implement a new strategic plan. Because change can happen almost instantaneously, strategic market and marketing plans are always subject to revision.

ORGANIZATION OF THIS BOOK

This book has been written so that it follows the sequential steps in the hospitality and travel marketing system. The first three chapters start with the fundamentals. Chapters 4, 5, and 6 are devoted to the question, "Where are we now?" Chapters 7, 8, and 9 ask, "Where would we like to be?" These six chapters (4 through 9) discuss the planning and research activities that are required for effective marketing. Chapters 10 through 19 answer the question, "How do we get there?" They provide specifics on how marketing activities are carried out. Chapter 20 addresses the questions, "How do we make sure we get there?" and "How do we know if we got there?" (See Figure 3–7.)

TASKS/FUNCTIONS		STEPS/QUESTIONS	CHAPTERS
Planning and	**P**	• Where are we now?	4–6
Research	**R**	• Where would we like to be	7–9
Implementation	**I**	• How do we get there?	10–19
Control	**C**	• How do we make sure we get there?	20
Evaluation	**E**	• How do we know if we got there?	

◆ FIGURE 3–7   *Organization of this book.*

CHAPTER CONCLUSION

There is a common approach that can be used to market any hospitality and travel organization. It is a five-step process termed the hospitality and travel marketing system. This systematic process involves finding the answers to five questions: "Where are we now?" "Where would we like to be?" "How do we get there?" "How do we make sure we get there?" and "How do we know if we got there?"

Effective marketing requires careful planning, both long term and short term. Planning helps an organization identify alternative marketing approaches, maintain uniqueness, create desirable situations, avoid undesirable situations, adapt to the unexpected, and measure success. If used, the hospitality and travel marketing system ensures that the needed priority is given to planning.

REVIEW QUESTIONS

1. What are the six characteristics of systems?
2. Why are most definitions of our industry inadequate for marketing purposes?
3. What five key questions make up the hospitality and travel marketing system?
4. What are the four fundamentals of the hospitality and travel marketing system?
5. What are the benefits of following the procedure suggested in the hospitality and travel marketing system?
6. In marketing, how would you define short term and long term?
7. Is a strategic market plan the same as a marketing plan? If not, explain the difference.
8. Is there a need for both short-and long-term marketing planning in our industry? Why or why not?

CHAPTER ASSIGNMENTS

1. You have just been hired as the marketing manager of a hospitality or travel organization. You find out quickly that the company has never used a systematic approach to marketing. How would you change the situation, employing the hospitality and travel marketing system? Which departments and individuals would you involve in the process? How would you sell your suggested changes to upper management?

2. Select an existing hospitality or travel organization and examine its marketing procedures and practices. Is the hospitality and travel marketing system being used? If not, what problems exist and what opportunities are being missed? If the system is being used, have

any modifications or additional steps been added? Write a short report summarizing your findings and suggested improvements.

3. This chapter lists the six characteristics of systems in the hospitality and travel industry as openness, complexity and variety, responsiveness, competitiveness, interdependency, and friction and disharmony. Identify three real-life examples or indications of these characteristics in our industry. Use a combination of library research and interviews with hospitality and travel professionals to prepare your paper.

4. "There is a time for competition, but there is also a time for cooperation." Discuss this statement in the context of the hospitality and

travel industry. When does it make sense for organizations to cooperate? Cite at least three actual examples where potentially competitive organizations have joined together in co-

operative marketing in our industry. Why do you think they decided to join forces?

WORLD WIDE WEB RESOURCES

Air Canada
http://www.aircanada.ca/

Air Transport Association
http://www.air-transport.org/

American Airlines
http://www.aa.com/

American Express
http://www.americanexpress.com/

American Hotel & Lodging Association
http://www.ahlaonline.org/

American Society of Travel Agents
http://www.astanet.com/

Bureau of Labor Statistics
http://www.bls.gov/

Calgary Convention & Visitors Bureau
http://www.visitor.calgary.ab.ca/

Canadian Restaurant and Foodservices Association
http://www.crfa.ca/

Carlson Wagonlit Travel
http://www.carlsonwagonlit.com/

Cruise Lines International Association
http://www.cruising.org/

Excite Travel
http://travel.excite.com/

Expedia
http://www.expedia.com/

International Association of Amusement Parks and Attractions
http://www.iaapa.org/

International Foodservice Manufacturers Association
http://www.ifmaworld.com/

KLM Royal Dutch Airlines
http://www.klm.com/

Lycos Travel
http://travel.lycos.com/

National Restaurant Association
http://www.restaurant.org/

One World Alliance
http://www.oneworld.com/

Qantas Airways Limited
http://www.qantas.com/

Sabre, Inc.
http://www.sabre.com/

Sky Team Alliance
http://www.skyteam.com/

Standard Industrial Classifications (U.S.)
http://www.govtsales.com/sics/sicgroups.htm/
http://www.osha.gov/oshstats/sicser.html/

Star Alliance
http://www.star-alliance.com/

Thomas Cook
http://www.thomascook.co.uk/

Travelocity
http://www.travelocity.com/

Travel Weekly
http://www.twcrossroads.com/

Universal Studios Florida
http://www.universalstudios.com/themeparks/

US Airways
http://www.usairways.com/

Yahoo! Travel
http://travel.yahoo.com/

REFERENCES

1. Nykiel, Ronald A. 1997. *Marketing in the Hospitality Industry.* 3rd ed. New York: Educational Institute of the AHMA.

2. Lane, Harold E., and Denise Dupré. 1997. *Hospitality World! An Introduction.* New York: Van Nostrand Reinhold, 32–35.

3. Reid, Robert D., and David Bojanic. 2000. *Hospitality Marketing Management.* 3rd ed. New York: John Wiley & Sons, Inc.

4. Ninemeier, Jack D. 1985. *Managing Foodservice Operations: A Systems Approach for Healthcare and Institutions.* West Lafayette, Ind.: Dietary Managers Association and Restaurant, Hotel, and Institutional Management Institute, 1.

5. International Foodservice Manufacturers Association Market Data Committee. 1985. *Foodservice Industry Segment Categorization and Definitions.* Chicago: International Foodservice Manufacturers Association, 3.

6. Goeldner, Charles R., Brent J. R. Ritchie, and Robert W. McIntosh. 1999. *Tourism: Principles, Practices, Philosophies.* 8th ed. New York: John Wiley & Sons, Inc.

7. Gee, Chuck Y., James C. Makens, and Dexter J. L. Choy. 1997. *The Travel Industry.* 3rd ed. New York: John Wiley & Sons, Inc.

8. *Travel Weekly.* Seacaucus, N.J.: Reed Travel Group.

9. Hodgson, Adele. 1987. *The Travel and Tourism Industry: Strategies for the Future.* Elmsford, N.Y.: Pergamon Press.

10. Office of Management and Budget. 2000. Employment Projections. http://www.govtsales.com/sics/sicgroups.htm

11. Bureau of Labor Statistics. 2000. Employment Projections. Washington, D.C. http://www.bls.gov/

12. United States Travel Data Center. 1985. *The 1984–85 Economic Review of Travel in America.* Washington, D.C.: United States Travel Data Center, 2.

13. Webster, Frederick E., Jr. "The changing role of marketing in the corporation." *Journal of Marketing* 56 (October 1992):1–17.

14. Levitt, Theodore. "Marketing myopia." *Harvard Business Review* 38(4):56 (1960).

For additional hospitality and travel marketing resources, visit our Web site at **www.Hospitality-Tourism.delmar.com**

Planning: Research and Analysis

WHERE ARE WE NOW?

WHERE WOULD WE LIKE TO BE?

HOW DO WE GET THERE?

HOW DO WE MAKE SURE WE GET THERE?

HOW DO WE KNOW IF WE GOT THERE?

Customer Behavior

Where Are We Now?

Objectives

Having read this chapter, you should be able to:

◆ List and describe six personal factors that influence customer behavior.

◆ List and describe four factors that influence customers' perception of hospitality and travel services.

◆ List and explain the role of stimulus factors in perception.

◆ List and describe five interpersonal factors that influence customer behavior.

◆ List and describe the five steps in customer buying processes.

◆ Explain the three categories of decision processes that customers follow.

Overview

Why do customers behave the way they do? This is a question everyone involved in marketing must answer. If we can understand customers' behavior, we are in a much better position to tailor services, prices, promotions, and distribution channels to fit customers' needs.

This chapter explains that people's behavior is influenced both by personal and interpersonal factors. The key factors in each of the two

categories are discussed. The relative importance of information from commercial and personal sources is examined.

All customers go through a series of steps when they decide to buy a hospitality or travel service. This chapter emphasizes that marketers need to understand the decision process that customers are using.

Key Terms

attitudes	lifestyles	product adoption curve
buying process	motivation	psychographics
cognitive dissonance	motives	reference groups
commercial information sources	need	secondary groups
culture	noncommercial sources	self-concept
customer behavior	objective criteria	social class
evoked set	opinion leaders	social information sources
family life-cycle	opinions	subcultures
individual customers	organizational buying behavior	subjective criteria
interests	perception	VALS™ 2
internal sources	personal factors	wants
interpersonal factors	personality	word-of-mouth information
learning	primary groups	

ave you ever thought about the goods or services you buy? What about some of your most prized possessions, such as your computer system, car or bicycle, or stereo? Did you decide to buy these items completely on your own, or did you ask friends for advice? Did you take more time to make these decisions than you do when you choose a fast-food place, for example? Have you ever bought things because you thought your friends would approve of them?

Why are we asking you so many questions? Simple! We want you to realize what a complex decision-making unit you are. Multiply yourself as an individual decision maker by a factor of over 440 million and you will have some idea of the enormous task that marketing decision makers face in North America (United States, Canada, Mexico). This chapter looks at why people do the things they do.

Marketing managers must understand customers' behavior patterns and why they occur. This means not only knowing how customers act when they are consuming services, but also their prepurchase and postpurchase behavior.

BEHAVIOR OF INDIVIDUAL CUSTOMERS

Customer behavior is the way customers select, use and behave after they have purchased hospitality and travel services. Two types of factors influence the behavior of individual customers: personal and interpersonal. Personal factors are the psychological characteristics of the individual. They include the following:

1. Needs, wants, and motivation
2. Perception
3. Learning
4. Personality
5. Lifestyle
6. Self-concept

Personal Factors

1. **Needs, Wants, and Motivation.** Customer needs are the foundation of marketing. Satisfying them is the key to long-term success. But what are needs? Kotler says that a human need is a state of felt deprivation of some basic satisfaction.[1] A need exists when there is a gap between what customers have and what they would like to have. We call these *need deficiencies*. These *gaps* may be in customers' needs for food, clothes, shelter, feeling of safety, or their sense of belonging and esteem. Needs result from customers' physiological and psychological *persons*. Flying first class, staying in the most expensive hotel suite, or ordering the most expensive dish on the menu may be based on a need for esteem (a psychological need), indicating one's importance to others. Hunger or thirst (two physiological needs) may be the reason for a visit to a fast-food restaurant.

   Wants are the customers' desire for specific satisfiers of their needs.[2] For example, a person may need affection but want to visit friends and relatives. Another customer needs esteem from friends and neighbors but wants a transatlantic trip on the Concorde. Whereas people's needs are relatively few in number, they usually have many more wants. For each need, there can be several wants.

   The reasons people give for their travel and dining-out behavior are often insufficient. They do not tell us about the basic needs they are trying to satisfy. Why? Customers may be unaware of the true reasons or do not want to divulge them.[3] It is easier for people to say they are flying first class because of the extra services provided, than to say they are looking for esteem. Surveys of why people select hotels, restaurants, airlines, and other hospitality and travel services can be incomplete and misleading. Customers are more likely to supply rational (price, cleanliness, facilities, and services) than irrational (emotional) reasons. Marketing managers need to understand both types of reasons in developing and promoting their services.

   An understanding of human motivation is essential to knowing how customers become aware of their needs. There are several motivation theories. Before discussing them, we will look at the process of motivation and how the customer and marketer interact.

   Every person has needs, both physiological and psychological. People may or may not be aware of them, however. Marketers have to make customers recognize their need deficiencies and provide the means to eliminate them. This awareness must exist for customers before they can begin the process of satisfying their needs. A need is a conscious or unconscious disparity between a present and desired physiological or psychological state. Marketers are in the business of reminding and making customers aware of their needs.

   Customers have to be motivated to act to satisfy their wants. Marketers have to supply objectives and potential motives for doing so. Objectives are the services that the hospitality and travel industry supplies—hotel accommodations, restaurant meals, cruises, flights, travel counseling, inclusive tours, and entertainment. Motives are customers' personal desires or drives to satisfy their wants. Marketers have to suggest motives to customers involving the use of objectives. McDonald's "Have you had your break today?" commercials are an excellent example of creating need awareness (you deserve to relax), supplying objectives (meals at a McDonald's restaurant), and suggesting motives (eating sandwiches and fries at a restaurant table). Figure 4–1 illustrates the relationship of needs, wants, motiva-

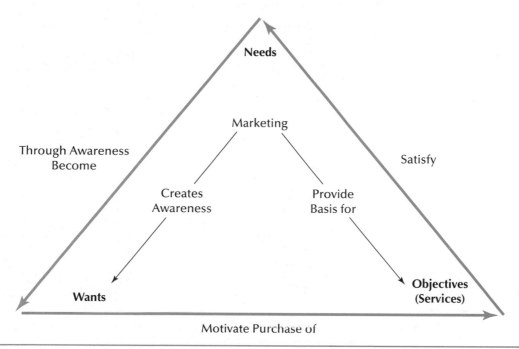

Figure caption:

◆ FIGURE 4–1 *The relationship of needs, wants, motivation, and objectives.* (Adapted from Mill, Robert Christie, and Alastair M. Morrison. 1998. *The Tourism System: An Introductory Text.* 3rd ed. Dubuque, Iowa: Kendall/Hunt Publishing Company. Used with permission.)

tion, and objectives (i.e., needs → through awareness become → wants that → motivate purchase of → objectives (services) → and satisfy → needs).[4]

Two popular motivational theories have been suggested by Maslow and Herzberg. They partly explain how individual customers are motivated to make purchase decisions.

Maslow's "hierarchy of needs" is one of the *cognitive* theories of human motivation. It assumes that customers think before they act, using a rational, decision-making process.[5] Maslow suggests five categories of needs:

a. Physiological
b. Safety
c. Belonging (social)
d. Esteem
e. Self-actualization

Physiological needs are the most basic, including the need for food and liquids, shelter, clothing, relaxation, and physical exercise. They must be satisfied before the individual moves on to thinking about other needs. Most people have a strong desire to feel safe and secure and to be free from the unexpected. These are safety needs. The desire to be accepted by various social groups represents our belonging or social needs. You will hear about these later in the discussion on interpersonal factors. Esteem needs represent the desire to attain status, respect, accomplishment, and achievement in one's own and others' eyes. Realizing our growth potential and discovering our own selves are self-actualization needs.

Maslow's hierarchy concept is usually illustrated in the form of a pyramid, as shown on the left side of Figure 4–2. Customers must satisfy the lower-level needs

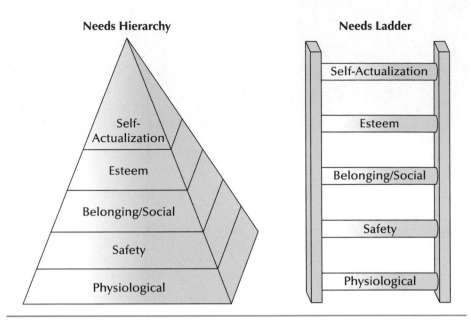

◆ FIGURE 4–2 *Maslow's Hierarchy of Needs and the Needs Ladder.* (Sources: Kotler, Philip. 2000. *Marketing Management: Millennium Edition.* 10th ed. Upper Saddle River, N.J.: Prentice-Hall, Inc.; Boone, Louis E., and David L. Kurtz. 2001. *Contemporary Marketing.* 10th ed. Fort Worth, Tex.: Harcourt College Publishers.)

such as physiological and safety needs before moving on to the higher-level, psychological needs of belonging, esteem, and self-actualization. Another way of looking at Maslow's needs hierarchy is to view it as a needs ladder as shown on the right side of Figure 4–2. A more detailed description of the motives associated with these needs and travel is provided in Figure 4–3. Physiological needs are on the lowest rung; they must be satisfied before others can be dealt with. Once each type of need is satisfied, the person moves on to the next highest need on the ladder. Maslow believes that once a need level has been satisfied, it no longer serves as a motivator. For example, if customers perceive that all hotel chains provide a sufficient guarantee of food, shelter, and security, then physiological and safety needs are no longer significant to them. What this implies is that it would be more effective to appeal to the higher-level needs. It is generally accepted that most of society in the developed world has progressed beyond great concern for physiological and safety needs.

A ladder is for climbing down as well as climbing up. We are constantly driven to ascend the needs ladder, but problems at the lower levels may cause us to descend. One excellent example is the massive wave of cancellations of European travel trips by U.S. residents in 1985. Terrorist attacks on commercial airplanes, airport terminals, and a cruise ship, together with an acceleration in the United States–Libya conflict, severely undermined the perceived safety of Europe and the Middle East as foreign travel destinations. This made many people climb down the needs ladder to its second-lowest rung, the need for safety. Similarly, the Desert Storm conflict in Kuwait and Iraq during 1991 had a very adverse effect on international travel that year. The shelling of Dubrovnik, a popular Adriatic resort, and the civil disturbances in Sri Lanka are other examples in which military conflict

NEED	MOTIVE	TRAVEL LITERATURE REFERENCES
Physiological	Relaxation	Escape
		Relaxation
		Relief of tension
		Sunlust
		Physical
		Mental relaxation of tension
Safety	Security	Health
		Recreation
		Keep oneself active and healthy for the future
Belonging	Love	Family togetherness
		Enhancement of kinship relationships
		Companionship
		Facilitation of social interaction
		Maintenance of personal ties
		Interpersonal relations
		Roots
		Ethnic
		Show one's affection for family members
		Maintain social contacts
Esteem	Achievement	Convince oneself of one's achievements
	Status	Show one's importance to others
		Prestige
		Social recognition
		Ego-enhancement
		Professional/business
		Personal development
		Status and prestige
Self-actualization	Be true to one's own nature	Exploration and evaluation of self
		Self-discovery
		Satisfaction of inner desires

◆ **FIGURE 4–3**   *Maslow's needs and motives listed in hospitality and travel literature.* (Source: Mill, Robert Christie, and Alastair M. Morrison. 1998. *The Tourism System: An Introductory Text.* 3rd ed. Dubuque, Iowa: Kendall/Hunt Publishing Company. Used with permission.)

raised fears among travelers and caused major decreases in tourist arrivals. Outbreaks of diseases can also cause downturns in tourism as did the foot-and-mouth scare in Europe in 2001. These types of events make many people climb down the needs ladder to its second lowest rung, the need for safety. People's lower-level needs may also be aroused by such events as airplane crashes, natural disasters, crimes and fires within hotels, and restaurant food-poisoning incidents. The San Francisco earthquake of 1989, the impact of Hurricane Andrew on the Miami area, and the damage caused by Hurricane Iniki in Kauai, Hawaii, in 1992 are examples of natural disasters that raised travelers' concerns for safety and security in California, Florida, and Hawaii. The advertisement in Figure 4–4 was designed to reassure travel agents that the Fort Myers/Sanibel area of Florida was unaffected by Hurricane Andrew in 1992. The murders of foreign tourists in Miami and New Orleans led to an increasing concern for safety among Europeans contemplating trips to the United States during the 1990s.

◆ **FIGURE 4–4** *The Lee Island Coast assures travel agents that it has not been affected by Hurricane Andrew during 1992.* (Courtesy of the Lee County Visitor & Convention Bureau)

Look through any number of travel magazines or in the travel sections of newspapers and you will find many examples of hospitality and travel advertisers drawing the reader's attention to the needs on Maslow's hierarchy. Following are a few examples for you to consider. Try to determine the advertisers' message by studying Figure 4–5 and then looking at the wording and the graphics in the following advertisements:

Physiological
- North Carolina: "These waters separate our islands from the coast. And you from your cares."
- Four Seasons Hotels/Resorts: "Introducing Four Seasons Resorts. The perfect environment for relaxing everything but your expectations."

Safety
- American Express: "There's one Travelers Cheque for couples who have tied the knot, just not around each other."
- Qantas/Australian Airlines: "Actually, the plane is under his wing."

Belonging
- "Sandals: Where Love Comes to Stay." (Figure 4–5)
- "Princess Cruises: It's more than a cruise, it's the Love Boat."

◆ **FIGURE 4–5** *Sandals kindles thoughts of romantic Caribbean vacations.* (Courtesy of Sandals Resorts)

Esteem	• "The Province of Beverly Hills."
Self-actualization	• Outward Bound: "Our courses are limited to 12 students, but our classrooms are quite large."

Now let us turn to the second theory of motivation. Herzberg's "two-factor" motivation theory states that customers are concerned with satisfiers (things that create satisfaction) and dissatisfiers (things that create dissatisfaction).[6] Herzberg's theory can be explained by the classic hotel swimming pool example. The availability of a swimming pool in a hotel is seldom the primary motivator for its guests' visits, nor is it a satisfier of their needs. But the absence of a pool can be a dissatisfier, causing guests not to select the hotel without a pool. Another simple example is that, although passengers may not select an airline based on the availability of a complimentary beverage service, they may decide against airlines that do not provide it.

The implication of Herzberg's theory is that marketers need to know their primary satisfiers, the services and facilities that meet customers' most important needs. However, that is not enough. They must also identify the common turnoffs or dissatisfiers, the factors that will keep customers away.

2. **Perception.** Customers use their five senses—sight, hearing, taste, touch, and smell—to size up hospitality and travel services and the industry's promotional messages. This sizing-up process is known as **perception**. The phrase "perception counts more than reality" expresses a most important customer behavior concept: decisions are made more on how customers perceive the facts than on the facts

themselves. Customers must not only be motivated to buy, but they must perceive that a service will satisfy their needs and wants.

Perception is "the process by which an individual selects, organizes, and interprets information inputs to create a meaningful picture of the world."[7] It is almost impossible to find two people who share the exact same view of the world. Why? Experts talk about four perceptual processes that make the difference:

    a. Perceptual screens or filters
    b. Perceptual biases
    c. Selective retention
    d. Closure

a. ***Perceptual Screens or Filters.*** People are literally bombarded with stimuli every day, most of them commercially oriented. The morning radio and television are loaded with commercials. The kids show up at the breakfast table wearing T-shirts promoting their favorite brands of soft drinks, clothes, and hosts of other products and services. Even the cereal box tries to grab our attention. The drive-times to and from work are heavily assaulted by advertising. Radio shows; billboards; and even buses, trains, trucks, vans, and buildings are laden with commercial messages. To supplement the daily diet of commercials, the newspapers, magazines, and mail that we read and the evening television that we watch make sure that we get our promotional quotas. The Web is also full of banner advertisements. The average person is exposed to between 1,500 and 2,000 advertisements each day. There is just no way that the human brain can register and remember all of these messages.

Customers screen out the majority of the stimuli or messages to which they are exposed. They notice and retain information from only a small portion of these messages. Some experts call this selective exposure; others choose the words perceptual screens or filters. Marketers must do everything in their power to be sure that their services are among the select few that get noticed.

b. ***Perceptual Biases.*** All customers have perceptual biases; customers twist the information to match their pictures of the world. Even if an advertising message makes it through perceptual screens, people may alter it so much that it bears no resemblance to what was intended. The reshaped information may run contrary to the advertiser's objectives.

c. ***Selective Retention.*** Even if messages make it through the perceptual screens and biases intact, they may not be retained for a long time. Customers practice something called selective retention; they hold on longer to information that supports their predispositions, beliefs, and attitudes.

d. ***Closure.*** Customers tend to see what they want to see. The human brain does not like to deal with incomplete images of objects, people, or organizations. Where information is unavailable to round out an image, the mind adds the missing data, whether the information is right or wrong. A state of psychological tension exists until the missing information is added (closure). Tension forces attention, and the marketer can take advantage of temporarily missing information. A few classic examples are United Airline's "Fly the friendly skies of United," American Express' "Don't leave home without it," and McDonald's "You deserve a break today." Later we will use the title *positioning statements* for these tag lines. Constant repetition of advertisements using these statements, along with the companies' names, have ingrained them in most people's minds. So familiar are these statements that people automatically add the companies' names, whether or not they are specifically mentioned in the messages. People round out their images of the companies created by advertising. Positioning, covered in Chapter 8, is mostly concerned with trying to create desired images in the customer's mind. Effective positioning relies on the closure concept.

Research has demonstrated a degree of predictability about customer perceptions. Some of the key findings show that customers are more likely to do the following:[8]

- Screen out information with which they are already familiar.
- Notice and retain information related to a need of which they are aware (a want) or one that they are actively trying to satisfy.
- Buy services that match their perceived images of themselves (we talk about this later under the self-concept theory).
- Notice and retain things that stand out from the norm (e.g., advertisements that are much larger than average).
- See things that they anticipate seeing (e.g., tour brochures in a travel agency).
- Notice information from hospitality and travel organizations and destinations with which they have had successful previous experiences.
- Attach greater credibility to interpersonal rather than commercially generated information.

On the other hand, customers are less likely to do the following:

- Use perceptual biases to distort information received from interpersonal sources (family, friends, business associates, reference and social groups).
- Absorb information that is too complicated and requires a great deal of effort to fully comprehend.
- Notice and retain information about competitive hospitality and travel service brands if these customers are satisfied with another brand.

Marketing managers can use a variety of tools and techniques to navigate their way around the perception barrier. They need to recognize that two groups of factors influence customer perception—personal and stimulus.[9] Personal factors are the subject of this part of the chapter. They include needs, wants, motives, learning, lifestyle, self-concept, and personality—the customer's individual overall makeup and frame of mind. Stimulus factors are those related to the service itself and the way in which it is promoted.

Stimulus factors are interrelated with the concept of managing the evidence that was discussed in Chapter 2. Customers make deductions using all the *clues* we give them about the quality, price, and uniqueness of our services and facilities. They use the five senses (sight, hearing, taste, touch, and smell) to evaluate the evidence presented. Stimulus factors are a large part of the evidence they review.

Stimulus factors can be expressed through the service itself and through supporting facilities, or in a symbolic way through words and pictures (e.g., advertisements and other promotions).[10] For maximum effect, both approaches should be used, and a consistent impression should be conveyed to customers. As an example of the first group of stimulus factors, a business hotel that provides a business center, swimming pool, tennis courts, health club, and several international-class restaurants supports a perception of a luxury or high-quality property. This also conveys an impression of high room rates.

Size, color, intensity, movement, position, contrast, isolation, texture, shape, and surroundings can be used to support a desired perception. These factors can also be used simply to get through customers' perceptual screens.

a. *Size.* Many customers equate size with quality. The bigger the travel agency, hotel or restaurant chain, airline, attraction, or tour wholesaler, the better their services are perceived to be. Greater size also usually means greater attention in print advertising.

b. *Color.* Color also has perceptual connotations. The use of color in advertisements is far more effective in getting customers' attention than is black and white. Subdued, earth-tone colors carried a perception of quality during the 1990s; pastels carried one of being old-fashioned. Airplanes with colorful paint jobs and identifying logos have been shown to leave the impression that the airline is dynamic and progressive. Rental car companies make extensive use of color to make their services and advertisements stand out (e.g., yellow for Hertz, red for Avis, and green for National).

c. *Intensity.* The intensity of an advertising message can attract above-average attention. Many of the public-service commercials aired on television about drugs, AIDS, drunk driving, using seatbelts, helping the hungry, and crimes against people and animals are very strong in intensity. The use of fear appeals in advertisements fits into this category. American Express' series featuring couples who lost their travelers checks was an excellent use of a fear appeal. Being stranded in a foreign country with no cash is not a thought that many travelers relish.

d. *Movement.* As a stimulus, moving objects are more likely to attract attention than stationary objects. This is one of the reasons that television and the Web have become popular advertising media. They display visual movement; print and radio ads do not. Signs and point-of-sale displays with moving parts also are noticed more frequently than stationary ones.

e. *Position.* The position of advertisements, point-of-sale displays, and signs affects their perception. For example, certain pages and parts of pages in newspapers, magazines, and menus are read more frequently than others.

f. *Contrast.* Contrast can also be used effectively to get customers' attention by making a promotional message or service facility stand out from its competitors. Examples include using an exceptionally large headline in a print advertisement, trick photography (American Hawaii Cruises showed one of its ships parked between skyscraper hotels on Waikiki Beach), or a predominant color that other ads do not feature (e.g., black, silver, or gold).

g. *Isolation.* The use of *white space* to isolate print advertisements from competing messages is an effective perceptual technique. Actually, it can be white, black, red, yellow, or any other color; the effect is the same. The idea is to provide a visual border, and enough separation from other items on a page, to make the ad stand out.

h. *Texture.* Texture is another factor that affects perception. Chair and wall coverings, carpeting, letterhead stationery, brochure and direct mail materials, and menu paper stock are just a few of the items that can create an impression with customers.

i. *Shape.* Designing service facilities or promotional pieces in a distinctive or unusual shape can make them stand out from the competition. For example, many restaurants use odd-shaped menus—on bottles, brown paper bags, and carving boards—to make their operations unique.

j. *Surroundings.* Surroundings as a stimulus factor refers to the physical location of service facilities and promotional materials. For example, locating a restaurant or hotel in an exclusive area, or placing an advertisement in a high-class magazine, connotes quality and high prices.

3. **Learning.** We tend to learn a little from everything we do. We then adjust our behavior patterns after each learning experience. Buying hospitality and travel services is similar to reading and writing; it has to be learned through experience. Learning comes through a combination of factors—needs, motives, objectives, cues, responses, and reinforcement.

Needs, motives, and objectives were discussed earlier in this chapter. A simple example follows to explain the other three factors. Susan Jones is an up-and-coming executive in an electronics company. Long hours and a heavy out-of-town travel schedule have made her very tired. Watching television one night, she notices a Club Med ad that stresses its villages' relaxation qualities. This ad suggests a motive (relaxation) to overcome her need to be less tired (physiological). But she's not ready to call her travel agent just yet. During the next few weeks, she receives some cues that dictate when, where, and how she will respond. At a business meeting she talks to two other young executives, and the subject of vacations comes up. It turns out that both of the other executives have been to Club Med villages, and they loved them. Susan then bumps into an old sorority sister who sports a great tan, along with a Club Med T-shirt. The cues have a cumulative effect, so Susan visits the travel agent and books a one-week trip to a Club Med village in Mexico (her response to the cues).

Susan has a great time on vacation and returns rested and relaxed. After her next bout of executive burnout, she flies to a Club Med village in the Caribbean. Again, she has a wonderful time, and this reinforces her first positive experience at the Mexican resort. The circle of learning is completed once again.

4. **Personality.** A customer's personality is a combination of most of the factors we have already discussed, including motivations, perceptions, learning, and emotions.[11] In essence, it represents all the things that make a person unique, the different ways that every person thinks and acts.

The two common ways of describing personalities is by traits and types. Individual people tend to react in a similar way to things that happen to them and to stimuli. They have traits, or ways of acting and behaving. The types of personality labels we tend to stick on people include outgoing, self-confident, quiet, domineering, sociable, happy-go-lucky, defensive, flexible, and many others.

Although psychologists agree that there is a strong link between personality and buying behavior, research results are inconclusive on the relationship. Using personality traits or types as a predictor of buying behavior is still an inexact science.

5. **Lifestyle.** You will not find the word lifestyle in any dictionary published before 1980. But everybody came to know this word well in the 1980s and 1990s. People began saying such things as, "That doesn't fit in with my lifestyle," "I'd like to have a better lifestyle," "The lifestyle is quite different in. . .," or "I wouldn't like to have their lifestyle." Asked to define this trendy word of the 1980s and 1990s, most people would say, "Well, isn't it just the way we live?"

The answer is yes; lifestyles are the way we live. And the way we live is a function of our attitudes, interests, and opinions. An attitude is a "predisposition to evaluate some symbol, object, or aspect of the world in a favorable or unfavorable manner."[12] Our interests are things that we spend time on and that get our attention. They include our families, homes, jobs, hobbies, recreational pursuits,

A Touch of Technology

The PRIZM Zip Code Look-Up Program

◆ The PRIZM lifestyle cluster system, developed by Claritas, categorizes neighborhoods in the United States into 62 distinct market segments (clusters).

◆ Using Claritas' *PRIZM Zip Code Look-Up Program* on the Web, you can find the top five PRIZM clusters for any zip code. The address for the program is http://yawyl.claritas.com/

◆ Using West Lafayette, Indiana's 47906 zip code, the top five PRIZM lifestyle clusters identified were Second City Elite, Middleburg Managers, Boomtown Singles, Towns & Gowns, and River City, USA.

◆ You can then get a brief profile for each of the five clusters including some demographic characteristics and what they are most likely to own, watch, or read.

◆ The Towns & Gowns group is described as being college town singles, aged 18–34, with annual incomes of $19,700. They are most likely to own a $1,000+ computer and to be a college basketball fan. This fits very well for the Purdue University area!

communities, clothes, food and drink preferences, and other items. Opinions are beliefs that we have, accurate or inaccurate, about a wide variety of subjects, including the political scene, the economy, the educational system, products, future events, sports, countries, and so on. The interaction of attitudes, interests, and opinions—often shortened to the AIOs— determines how we live.

Marketers have come to believe that customers' lifestyles or **psychographics** provide a more complete and more accurate predictor of their purchase behavior than just their geographic locations and demographics (age, income, occupation, etc.).[13] Dividing the market according to lifestyles, or psychographic segmentation, was trendy in the 1960s and 1970s. Eventually, experts agreed that it was better to use psychographic and demographic segmentation together. It was too difficult to pinpoint people based just on lifestyles. An organization that pioneered the joint-factor approach was SRI International. They developed the original VALS (Values and Lifestyles) system based on a large research study conducted in 1978–79. This time the consumer segments were defined using underlying psychological traits correlated with purchase behavior. The revised VALS™ system (VALS™2) has eight segments and uses concepts of resources (for example, age, household income, education, self-confidence, health, energy) and self-orientation (for example, principle-, status-, or action-oriented), Figure 4–6. Self-orientation shows how consumers' inner desires press them toward external gratifications. No single self-orientation prevails across the Actualizer and Struggler segments. Actualizers operate across the self-orientations because of their abundant resources. Strugglers do not express an orientation because their low resources prevent them from being active consumers.

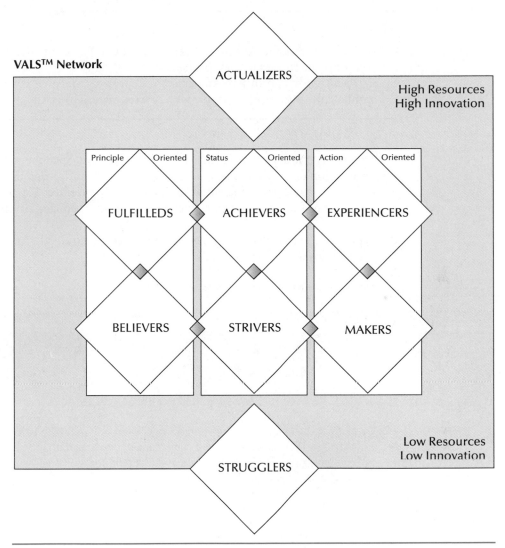

◆ **FIGURE 4–6** *VALS™ Network.* (© 2001 by SRI Consulting Business Intelligence)

VALS™ PSYCHOGRAPHIC CONSUMER SEGMENTS

1. *Actualizers:* Successful, sophisticated, active, take-charge people. Purchases often reflect cultivated tastes for relatively upscale, niche-oriented products.

PRINCIPLE ORIENTED

2. *Fulfilleds:* Mature, satisfied, comfortable, reflective. Favor durability, functionality, and value in products.
3. *Believers:* Conservative, conventional, and traditional. Favor familiar products and established brands.

STATUS ORIENTED

4. *Achievers:* Successful, career- and family-oriented. Favor established products that demonstrate success to their peers.
5. *Strivers:* Trendy, approval seeking, resource constrained. Favor stylish products that emulate the purchases of people with greater material wealth.

ACTION ORIENTED

6. *Experiencers:* Young, vital, enthusiastic, and impulsive. Spend a comparatively high proportion of their income on clothing, fast food, music, movies, and video.
7. *Makers:* Practical self-sufficient, traditional, family-oriented. Favor products with a practical or functional purpose such as tools, utility vehicles, fishing equipment.

8. *Strugglers:* Elderly, passive, risk-averse, resource constrained. Cautious consumers who are loyal to favorite brands.

Courtesy of SRI Consulting Business Intelligence (SRIC-BI)

EXCELLENCE CASE

Understanding Customer Behavior:
Patchwork Quilt Country Inn

In our fast-paced society, many people use their weekends and vacations to escape the stresses and strains of everyday life. They have a need to relax—to have a change of pace in their lifestyles. Bed & breakfast and farm vacation operations have grown in popularity because of this need and behavioral characteristic. Their increased use is also a result of the high value offered for the same amount of money when compared to other lodging alternatives.

The Patchwork Quilt Country Inn, located in Northern Indiana near Middlebury, is an excellent example of a small bed & breakfast operation. It has enjoyed great success by capitalizing on some basic human needs and motivations. It began in 1962 on the Lovejoy Farm when the Lovejoys started taking people in for vacations at their 260-acre dairy farm. Mrs. Lovejoy's recipes and cooking proved so popular that the family decided to open a small restaurant. After the restaurant became successful, a three-room bed & breakfast operation was started in the converted farmhouse. The Inn's facilities now include 15 guest rooms, each with

a private bathroom and a sitting room. The dining areas have a total of 80 seats. Bed & breakfast guests are served a full breakfast. At lunch and dinner, the dining rooms are open to the public. The Inn is renowned for the healthy, fresh ingredients in its menu items, and for the fact that all cooking and baking is done "from scratch" on the premises. Several recipes are unique, including the Buttermilk Pecan Chicken and some pies (Cherry Walnut Torte and Buttermilk Pie). The Inn has a strict no-smoking policy and does not serve or allow any alcoholic beverages.

Why the name Patchwork Quilt Country Inn? First, the operation is located in the heart of "Northern Indiana's Amish Country," a 150 square-mile area around Goshen that's the second largest Amish settlement in the United States. (For more information see the Elkhart County Convention & Visitors Bureau Web site at http://www.amishcountry.org) Quilting, of course, is a craft closely associated with the Amish people of North America. Additionally, the theme is carried through in the Inn's décor

continued

EXCELLENCE CASE *continued*

(Photo courtesy of Patchwork Quilt Country Inn)

and advertising materials. Beds are covered with beautiful patchwork quilts, and quilts also adorn dining room walls and other parts of the Inn. Even the Inn's logo incorporates the patchwork quilt theme. Quilts and other local crafts can be purchased at the Inn.

The main advertising slogan (or *positioning statement*) is "Prepare to be Pampered" and the invitation to "Enjoy a Taste of the Country" is added in the Inn's main brochure. These statements suggest *motives* to potential guests involving a visit to the Inn. Seeing the brochure or other advertising, readers may become aware of their need to "get away from it all;" to relax and escape to a simpler life in the country. This is an excellent example of the process shown in Figure 4–1. The Inn's *objectives* (services) are marketed to potential customers, and these customers' *needs* become *wants* through having been made aware of the services. Several of these potential customers will be so highly *motivated* by the Inn's marketing and services, along with the recognition of their *need deficiencies,* that they will make reservations.

The Patchwork Quilt Country Inn has received national recognition through various

feature articles and listings in popular bed & breakfast/country inn guidebooks such as *Country Inns* and *BackRoads.* While most of the Inn's advertising is targeted in the surrounding Midwest region, especially in Michigan and Indiana, guests come from all over the country. Ads are placed in magazines such as *Great Lakes Travel, Country Homes,* and *Midwest Living,* and in newspapers in Kalamazoo, Grand Rapids, and Fort Wayne, and in local newspapers. The current innkeepers, Ray and Rosetta Miller, are also experimenting with radio advertising. Although the Inn does not use television advertising, it receives many requests from TV stations to do feature stories. Two types of guests tend to predominate: older and retired persons, and younger couples on weekend getaways. A significant amount of business comes through word-of-mouth *(social information sources).*

In the early 1980s, the Inn began to offer Amish Backroad Tours. These are three-hour guided tours in a van or car, involving sightseeing and visits to several Amish homes and businesses. Guests get a first-hand look at Amish craft making and other facets of the Amish way

continued

EXCELLENCE CASE *continued*

(Photo courtesy of Patchwork Quilt Country Inn)

of life. This *programming* feature fits well with the Inn's overall appeal to travelers' *motivations,* allowing them to take a step back to an even simpler lifestyle.

Bed & breakfast is available year round at the Inn. The restaurant is closed in January. Dinner is served on Friday and Saturday evenings in February, March, and April, and Tuesday through Saturday from April to December. Lunch is served from May to December on Tuesday through Saturday. Lunches and dinners are not served on Sundays, Mondays, or public holidays. The 2000 B&B rates were $70–$110 (per day, per room on a double occupancy basis). Sales tax is added, and a 15 percent gratuity is also put on meals.

It is easy to see how the simple, healthy lifestyle offered by the Patchwork Quilt Country Inn and other similar bed and breakfast operations is a perfect antidote for the city dweller whose life moves at a rapid pace. While they must be resigned to spending most of their lives in traffic jams and with hectic work schedules, it is refreshing to return for a day or two to a more relaxed environment. The Patchwork Quilt Country Inn is an excellent example of a business that makes people aware of their needs, and then satisfies those needs with caring, quality service, and beautiful facilities.

Discussion Questions

1. To which of the six personal factors does an operation like the Patchwork Quilt Country Inn appeal? What types of people would be most interested in country inns and bed & breakfast establishments?
2. Do you believe that any of the interpersonal factors influence people to visit these types of establishments? How do they influence their selection?
3. Has the Patchwork Quilt Country Inn been successful in exploiting the relationship of needs, wants, motivation, and objectives? What has the operation done in this respect?

Web Site

http://www.patchworkquiltinn.com/

◆ FIGURE 4–7   *A trip aboard the famed Orient Express. A vacation that will definitely impress your friends.* (Courtesy of Venice Simplon-Orient Express)

6. **Self-concept.** Customers buy things that they perceive as matching their images of themselves. Two psychological processes are at play at the same time—perception and self-concept. A customer's self-concept is a mental picture, consisting of four different elements: the real self, ideal self, reference-group (or looking-glass) self, and self-image. Simply stated, they represent the following:
    a. The way we really are (real self).
    b. The way we would like to be (ideal self).
    c. The way we think other people see us (reference-group self).
    d. The way we see ourselves (self-image).

    Few people know their real selves, and many do not want to. They are even more reluctant to talk about their real selves to others. On the other hand, customers like to think and talk about their ideal selves. The ideal self is a strong motivating influence. We are constantly trying to get closer to this vision of ourselves. How we think others see us is our reference-group self. Reference groups, discussed later in the chapter, are the social groups to which we belong or aspire to belong.

    A person's self-image is the most important element of the self-concept theory for marketing. It is usually a combination of the real, ideal, and reference-group selves. We often buy something to make a positive impression on our reference groups; keeping up with the Joneses is a favorite activity of many. A flight on the Concorde, a stay at Paris' George Cinq, or a trip on the Orient Express might raise our stock with friends and business associates, Figure 4–7. We also make purchases to get closer to our ideal selves, and sometimes we just plain give in to our real selves.

Interpersonal Factors

Interpersonal factors represent the outside influence of other people. Personal and interpersonal influences are at play at the same time. The interpersonal factors include the following:

1. Cultures and subcultures
2. Reference groups
3. Social classes
4. Opinion leaders
5. The family

1. **Cultures and Subcultures.** A culture is a combination of the beliefs, values, attitudes, habits, traditions, customs, and forms of behavior that are shared by a group of people. We are born into a culture, but we are not born with these components of culture. We learn our culture from our parents and others in previous generations. The cultural lessons we absorb affect our decisions about buying hospitality and travel services. They do so by influencing our motivations, perceptions, lifestyles, and personalities, the personal factors we just talked about.

Cultures are the broadest social groups to which customers belong. For example, there are many different social groups in the United States, but just one American culture that everybody shares. A culture affects society in a general way, and it also influences society's social groups and individual customers. It dictates what types of behavior and motives are socially acceptable, which social institutions and conventions we adopt, and how we communicate through language and body movements.[14] Equal opportunity for all and individual initiative are two major social institutions in the United States.

Social conventions are practices that tend to be universally followed by people within a culture; for example, sending birthday cards to family and friends, not eating the flesh of certain animals, and bringing gifts to parties. Hospitality and travel providers must be sensitive to these conventions; for example by not serving pork to people of the Muslim faith.

Each individual customer is affected by the prevailing culture, which determines what is normal and acceptable and what is not. The frenetic pace of life in major cities is quite tolerable and normal but would be unacceptable to people in more rural societies. A culture affects the way we express our feelings. For example, Britons tend to hide their inner feelings with the "stiff upper lip," whereas Americans "let it all hang out" by freely showing their emotions.

Cultures are not static. They constantly have to weather the effects of new generations, as well as economic, technological, environmental, political, and social change. But there are certain threads of a culture that tend to endure, no matter how severe the pressure to adapt. For example, the Puritan or Protestant work ethic is deeply ingrained in U.S. and Canadian society, as is the never-ending quest for material possessions and individual achievement. Although there have been trends that run counter to these, and they are not valued by everyone, these two values still remain almost intact.

Both the United States and Canada have their distinctive cultures, but their citizens do not share exactly the same beliefs, values, attitudes, habits, and behavior patterns. They are both melting-pot societies made up of a collection of unique subcultures (cultures within a culture). The U.S. subcultures include black Americans, Hispanics, various people from Asia, and certain religion-based groups

(Mormons, Jews, Mennonites, and others). Canada has French and English sub-cultures, black Canadians, and various religious groups.

Traditionally, black Americans were the largest racial/ethnic subculture in the United States, followed by Hispanics (persons of any race who either speak Spanish or have Spanish-speaking ancestors).[15] However, according to the 2000 Census, 13 percent of the U.S. population was Latino and 12 percent was African American.[16] It is dangerous and wrong to assume that all persons within a subculture act exactly the same way. A large proportion of the people in a subculture, however, have certain behavior patterns that are different from the norm. For example, studies show that black and Hispanic Americans are more loyal to national brands than are the rest of the U.S. population. Getting these people to buy our brands of hospitality and travel services may be more effective in terms of encouraging repeat purchases.

2. **Reference Groups.** All customers belong to several reference groups with which they identify. There are two broad types of reference groups—primary and secondary. Primary groups include a person's family and friends; secondary groups include those at church and work, and ones to which membership dues are paid (e.g., country clubs, hobby clubs, service clubs, and professional societies). Most of us are also affected by aspirational and disassociative groups. Many people wish they were professional athletes or entertainers and will purchase services and products with which their idols are associated (an example of aspirational groups). Disassociative groups are ones that we want nothing to do with, and we avoid services and products that these groups buy.

These social units are called reference groups because they have certain codes of behavior to which members adhere. In other words, customers use them as a reference point to determine both acceptable and unacceptable purchase behavior. Reference groups vary widely; some exert much more influence than others. The purchase of hospitality and travel services can be affected by these reference groups. People can come back from vacations with suntans, souvenirs, clothing, slides, videos, art, and miscellaneous other items to show off to other group members. They may feel that they win esteem by having others see these items, or by having been to places or having done things that others have not. Travel, although an intangible service, can be made conspicuous to the reference groups with which we closely identify.

3. **Social Classes.** Although people in North America are not quite as class conscious as those on other continents, there is a definite social class system in existence. Researchers believe that the United States class system has six divisions:[17]

    a. Upper-upper
    b. Lower-upper
    c. Upper-middle
    d. Lower-middle
    e. Upper-lower
    f. Lower-lower

Social class is determined by such things as occupation, sources of income and accumulated wealth, highest level of education achieved, place of residence, and family history. The different social classes demonstrate distinct product and brand preferences for clothing, home furnishings, automobiles, and leisure activities.[18] Therefore, these social classes are significant to the hospitality and travel industry because of their relationship to leisure activities. Social classes have different media preferences and habits and ways in which individuals communicate with one another.

4. **Opinion Leaders.** Every social group contains opinion leaders, who act as channels of information for all members. They set the trend by seeking information or

Did You Know?

✓ In Roper Starch's study of *influential Americans,* it was estimated that there were about 20 million opinion leaders or 10 percent of the U.S. adult population.

✓ These people (the *influentials*) are identified based on their social and political activism and not on their demographic or economic characteristics.

✓ In the past year, 82 percent of the *influentials* have recommended a restaurant, and 51 percent a vacation destination.

✓ If the *influentials* like a vacation destination, they recommend it an average of 5.8 times. That is 58 million destination recommendations for the whole group.

✓ They are usually the first to adopt new technologies, and have two or three computers at home.

✓ These facts were from a presentation by Carolyn E. Setlow, group senior vice president of Roper Starch Worldwide, titled "The Future Is Now, and It Looks Good."

purchasing services and products before others do. There are very few general opinion leaders. Instead, there are several opinion leaders in every social group, each with specialized knowledge and information on different types of hospitality and travel services. For example, in a club of fishing enthusiasts, there may be opinion leaders with knowledge on where to fish for trout, bass, walleye, and pike. In a yacht club, these leaders may be divided into power boating, racing sailboat, and cruising sailboat enthusiasts. Opinion leaders tend to seek out and soak up more information on their specialty area. Being recognized as an expert in the group serves as an incentive to become even more knowledgeable. Roper Starch Worldwide of New York has done research on American opinion leaders for approximately 60 years. They estimate that about 10 percent of Americans are role models and opinion leaders. These people have above-average incomes and are more likely to have attended college.[19]

There are two major sources of information on hospitality and travel services— commercial and social. Commercial information sources are the advertising and other promotional materials designed by corporations and other organizations. Social information sources are the interpersonal channels of information, including opinion leaders. Information from commercial sources flows to targeted customers in different ways. Sometimes it goes directly, with no opinion leaders involved. Other information goes to one group of opinion leaders and then is passed on to other customers. This is called a two-step communication flow. Multistep communication occurs when information is passed through two or more groups of opinion leaders.

The product adoption curve is a concept closely associated with the subject of opinion leaders and interpersonal communication flows, Figure 4–8. The idea of this curve is that the population can be divided into innovators (2.5 percent of the population), early adopters (13.5 percent), early majority (34 percent), late majority (34 percent), and laggards (16 percent).[20] Opinion leaders tend to be among the innovators and early adopters, because they are more ready than others to try out new products and services.

Opinion leaders are most important to marketers. Because they influence how others behave, it pays to take time to identify and appeal to them.

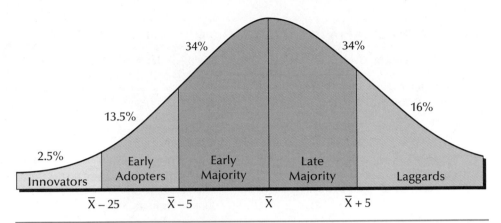

◆ FIGURE 4–8   *The product adoption curve.* (From Rogers, Everett M. 1995. *Diffusion of Innovations.* 4th ed. New York: Free Press.)

5. **The Family.** The family is among the strongest interpersonal influences on customer behavior. The traditional wife-husband-children family unit has been buffeted by many pressures in recent decades. Its proportion of all U.S. households has declined from 38.7 percent in 1970 to 26.7 percent in 1990.[21] Although now second in size after married couples without children, at 28.4 percent of all United States households in 1990, the traditional family unit still represents a significant market.

Traditional families pass through predictable stages over time; experts term this the family life-cycle concept. Purchasing behavior varies with life-cycle stages. Murphy and Staples have identified nine life-cycle stages:[22]
a. Bachelor
b. Newly married
c. Full nest I (youngest child under age 6)
d. Full nest II (youngest age 6 or older)
e. Full nest III (older married couples with dependent children)
f. Empty nest I (household head working)
g. Empty nest II (household head retired)
h. Solitary survivor (working)
i. Solitary survivor (retired)

Free from the responsibilities of child rearing, the bachelor, newly married, and empty nest I groups are less restricted in their vacation choices and spend more time and money on vacations. Other characteristics of the nine groups are summarized in Figure 4–9.

Relative Importance of Social and Commercial Information

You have just read about five interpersonal factors influencing customer behavior: cultures/subcultures, reference groups, social classes, opinion leaders, and the family. These are the social sources of information about services and products, but how important are these social sources of information, compared to the information generated by hospitality and travel organizations?

Interpersonal information is considered to be more objective and accurate than that received from hospitality and travel organizations, because the social source has no

AN OVERVIEW OF THE FAMILY LIFE CYCLE AND BUYING BEHAVIOR

Stage in Family Life Cycle	Buying or Behavioral Pattern
1. Bachelor stage: young, single people not living at home.	Few financial burdens. Fashion opinion leaders. Recreation oriented. Buy: basic kitchen equipment, basic furniture, cars, equipment for the mating game, vacations.
2. Newly married couples: young, no children.	Better off financially than they will be in near future. Highest purchase rate and highest average purchase of durables. Buy: cars, refrigerators, stoves, sensible and durable furniture, vacations.
3. Full nest I: Youngest child under six.	Home purchasing at peak. Liquid assets low. Dissatisfied with financial position and amount of money saved. Interested in new products. Like advertised products. Buy: washers, dryers, TV, baby food, chest rubs and cough medicines, vitamins, dolls, wagons, sleds, skates.
4. Full nest II: Youngest child six or over.	Financial position better. Some wives work. Less influenced by advertising. Buy larger-sized packages, multiple-unit deals. Buy: many foods, cleaning materials, bicycles, music lessons, pianos.
5. Full nest III: Older married couples with dependent children.	Financial position still better. More wives work. Some children get jobs. Hard to influence with advertising. High average purchase of durables. Buy: new, more tasteful furniture, auto travel, unnecessary appliances, boats, dental services, magazines.
6. Empty nest I: Older married couples, no children living with them, household head in labor force.	Home ownership at peak. Most satisfied with financial position and money saved. Interested in travel, recreation, self-education. Make gifts and contributions. Not interested in new products. Buy: vacations, luxuries, home improvements.
7. Empty nest II: Older married couples, no children living at home, household head retired.	Drastic cut in income. Keep home. Buy: medical appliances, medical-care products that aid health, sleep, and digestion.
8. Solitary survivor, in labor force.	Income still good but likely to sell home.
9. Solitary survivor, retired.	Same medical and product needs as other retired group: drastic cut in income. Special need for attention, affection, and security.

◆ FIGURE 4–9 *An overview of the family life cycle and buying behavior.* (From Kotler, Philip. 2000 *Marketing Management: Millennium Edition.* 10th ed. Upper Saddle River, N.J.: Prentice-Hall, Inc. Reprinted by permission of Pearson Education, Inc. Upper Saddle River, N.J. 07458)

vested interest in the information. Socially relayed information is less likely to be distorted by a person's perceptual biases, again because it is more credible. The more important the purchase, the higher the emphasis customers will attach to interpersonal information about that purchase. The same is true when a customer thinks of trying out a service for the first time or is uncertain about the benefits of alternative services.

Chapter 2 showed that it is more difficult to evaluate services than it is to evaluate products before purchasing them. Thus, customers place more weight on social sources of information when they buy services than they do when they buy products. Most research studies confirm this, and they refer to the information as word-of-mouth. In other words, the information on which the purchase is based is passed orally from social contacts to buyers. The hospitality and travel industry is one of the industries that is most dependent on word-of-mouth information.

BUYING PROCESSES OF INDIVIDUAL CUSTOMERS

The customer's buying or decision process describes another important aspect of behavior. This process describes the stages customers go through when making purchases. Understanding the process is most important to marketers, since the effectiveness of different types of advertisements and promotions varies with the buying process stage. Most experts agree that there are five distinct buying process stages:[23, 24]

1. Need awareness
2. Information search
3. Evaluation of alternatives
4. Purchase
5. Postpurchase evaluation

Customers do not always follow each of the five stages, however. Sometimes one or more are skipped.

1. **Need Awareness.** For the process to get going, there must be a stimulus that leads customers to action. A need deficiency must be recognized. Under the topic of motivation, it was shown that organizations can use promotions (information from commercial sources) to make potential customers aware of need deficiencies. On the other hand, the stimulus might come from an interpersonal (social) source, such as an opinion leader, friend, relative, or business associate. A third source of the stimulus is an internal drive, such as hunger or thirst. Most people do not need to be told when they are hungry or thirsty.

   A customer might recognize a need deficiency because of the combined impact of several stimuli. Do you remember Susan Jones, the up-and-coming electronics executive? She saw her need to unwind as a result of several cues: a Club Med advertisement and word-of-mouth recommendations from two business associates and a former sorority sister.

2. **Information Search.** When a customer is made aware of a need, that need becomes a want. If a want exists, the customer normally begins an information search. Four different sources of information may be tapped: commercial, noncommercial, social, or internal. Commercial and social sources were discussed

earlier. Noncommercial sources are independent, objective assessments of hospitality and travel services, such as ratings by the American Automobile Association, Consumer Reports, Mobil, Michelin, and restaurant critics. Internal sources are those stored in the customer's own mind, including past experiences with a service and recollections of related promotions.

The intensity of the customer's search varies, ranging from heightened attention to an active information search.[25] Returning to Susan Jones, she reached a state of heightened awareness when she saw the Club Med ad. She was more attuned and interested in listening to information and conversations about similar resort vacations. But she was not yet ready to visit travel agencies to pick up specific details. What triggered her to begin an active search was the word-of-mouth recommendations from her college friend and business associates.

Customers become aware of alternative services that might satisfy their needs during their information searches. These alternatives might be vacation destinations, hotels, resorts, airlines, attractions, restaurants, rental car firms, or packaged tours. Not all the alternatives available are always considered. Lack of awareness, perception of prohibitive costs, previous bad experiences, and negative word-of-mouth information are the reasons that some alternatives do not make the customer's final short list. This final list is often called the customer's evoked set, the alternatives that are chosen for further consideration.

The advertisement of Residence Inn by Marriott shown in Figure 4–10 provides an excellent example of how advertising can influence the choice of lodging. It clearly and cleverly appeals to a common customer need, what to do with your relatives when they come to visit. Residence Inns obviously wants to become one of the lodging alternatives in the customer's evoked set in these situations. It catches the readers attention by literally *turning the house upside down* and by posing the question, "Does this remind you of your house when relatives come to visit?"

3. **Evaluation of Alternatives.** The next stage involves evaluating the short-listed alternatives using the customer's own criteria. Some people write these factors down on paper; others just consider them in their heads. Criteria can be objective or subjective. Objective criteria include prices, locations, physical characteristics of facilities (e.g., number of rooms, diversity of restaurants, availability of swimming pool), and services offered (e.g., free continental breakfast, complimentary limousine service from the airport). Subjective criteria are intangible factors, such as the image of the service organization.

Customers make judgments using their evaluation criteria. They develop attitudes and preferences for each alternative service. They may even rank the services from their first to their last choice. At the end of this process, one service is favored over the others.

4. **Purchase.** Customers now know which hospitality and travel services best meet their criteria. They develop a definite intention to buy these services, but their decision-making process may not be complete. Whether or not they buy can still be influenced by other factors. Customers may discuss their intentions with family members and other social contacts. There may be some people who disagree with their choices. This may lead to postponing the purchase or completely reevaluating it.

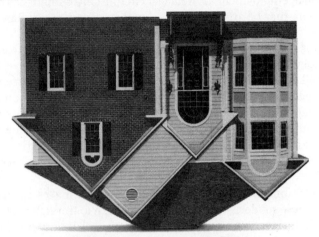

Does this remind you of your house when relatives come to visit?

Make reservations for them at Residence Inn® by Marriott® this holiday season, and keep your sanity. All our rooms are suites: a living area, a kitchen, and in many cases, a fireplace. That's 50% bigger than an ordinary hotel room. Just call your travel agent or 800-331-3131 and ask for the special holiday rate. Or visit us at residenceinn.com.

Marriott. Residence Inn

Room to relax, room to work, room to breathe.

Holiday Special $69 a night.

Earn airline miles* at Residence Inn by Marriott through Marriott Rewards.®

Residence Inn Orlando Airport

7100 Augusta National Drive • (407) 888-2666

Rate available Friday–Sunday from 11/12/99–2/13/00. Rate applies to studio and one-bedroom suites. During holiday weeks, 11/19–11/28 and 12/16/99–1/2/00, rate is available seven days a week except 12/31/99. Rooms are limited and some restrictions apply, including a limited number of blackout dates. Advanced reservations required. *Earn airline miles beginning 10/04/99. © 1999 Residence Inn by Marriott, Inc.

Customers' personal, employment, or financial circumstances might change. A job may be lost, or there may be an illness in the family. Again, the purchase decision may be delayed.

Another factor that often holds up purchases is the concept of perceived risk. All purchases involve risk. The risk can be financial (will my money be well spent?), psychological (will it improve my self-image?), or social (will my friends think more of me?). If the risk is considered too high, customers usually do something to reduce it. They may postpone their purchases, keep searching for more information, or choose a service organization with a national image and reputation. Risk can also be reduced by continually using the same service organizations or destinations. Marketers have to do everything they can promotionally to reduce perceived risk.

Various subdecisions have to be made before a customer makes a purchase. For a family vacation, these subdecisions might include when to travel, how to pay, how and where to make reservations, how long to stay, how much to spend, how to get there, what routes to take, and what to do at the destination. These decisions are not simple, and several different people may be involved in making them (e.g., mother, father, and children).

5. **Postpurchase Evaluation.** Cognitive dissonance is a state of mind that many customers experience after making a purchase. Customers are unsure whether they have made a good or bad decision. The level of dissonance increases with the importance and dollar value of the purchase. A customer is likely to experience less dissonance having chosen Burger King over McDonald's than when selecting an expensive restaurant for a 25th anniversary dinner. Dissonance is also greater when the purchased service lacks some of the appealing features of the rejected alternatives. Let us say that Susan Jones selected Club Med knowing that she would have to pay for all her cocktails, although these were complimentary at some other resorts. It is the marketer's job to reduce dissonance by providing information that confirms the wisdom of the customer's purchase.

When customers have used services, they evaluate them against their expectations. Expectations are based on the information they received from commercial (advertising and promotions) and social (family, friends, associates) sources. If expectations are met, customers are satisfied. If not, customers are usually dissatisfied. The secret for the service organization is never to promise more than can be delivered. It is a much better policy to promise less, knowing that you can probably exceed customer expectations. When customers are satisfied with services, the payoffs are great. Satisfied customers are much more likely to be repeat buyers. They have learned that the services they purchased meet their needs and expectations. By telling friends, relatives, and acquaintances about their positive experiences, satisfied customers influence others to buy because of word-of-mouth recommendations. The reverse is also true. Dissatisfied customers are less likely to be repeat customers. They will tell others of their experiences, discouraging them from buying.

Information from social sources often carries more weight than that from commercial sources. Because we provide intangibles in this industry, marketers have to be especially concerned about dissatisfied customers. Chapter 2 mentioned that quality control is much harder to achieve in the service industry than it is in the manufacturing and packaged-goods industry. Ours is a people-to-people business. People and their behavior cannot easily be standardized. Monitoring customer satisfaction is vital. Chapter 6 discusses how this is done through research.

Classification of Decision Processes

Not all buying decisions are the same. They require different levels of effort from customers. Decisions can be broken down into three categories:

1. Routine decisions
2. Limited decisions
3. Extensive decisions

1. **Routine Decisions.** A routine buying decision is one that customers make frequently and with little effort. Customers buy as the result of habit, almost in a mechanical way. One or more of the buying process stages are skipped. Little perceived risk is involved, and little information is needed. The services are inexpensive. Customers know about all alternative services and have set criteria for evaluating them. Choosing a fast-food outlet for hamburgers is a routine decision for many. Most customers have a clear idea of what they will get when they buy a hamburger at McDonald's, Burger King, or Wendy's. They do not need to ask other people for information. Eating at any of these restaurants is inexpensive, and customers tend to make frequent visits.

2. **Limited Decisions.** Limited decision making takes more time and effort because customers go through all five buying process stages when they make a purchase. Although customers do not buy these services frequently, the services, or similar services, have been tried before. The perceived risk and level of spending are higher than they are for routine purchases. Customers know the evaluation criteria and most alternative services, and may ask other people for information on some alternatives. Eating out at a fine-dining restaurant often involves limited decision making. Customers know what kinds of food, service, and ambience they like. But they know they will spend more than they would at a fast-food outlet. They visit fine-dining restaurants less frequently and have less information about them. Limited decision making will also be used if the customer is thinking about trying one of these services for the first time.

3. **Extensive Decisions.** Extensive decision making takes the most time and effort. Customers get heavily involved in the process. The services are expensive and complex; perceived risk is high. Customers start with little information and previous experience and have not yet developed evaluation criteria. All of the stages in the buying process are followed, and the customers conduct an extensive information search among both commercial and social sources. Customers are more inclined to postpone or reevaluate purchase decisions. First-time cruises, European vacations, honeymoon trips, African safaris, and round-the-world trips are good examples of extensive decisions. Customers will also use the services of experts, including travel agents and government tourism officials, and may search for information on the Web.

BEHAVIOR OF ORGANIZATIONAL CUSTOMERS

Both organizations and individual customers face similar types of decisions about hospitality and travel services. How they make their decisions is different. Organizational buying behavior tends to be more complex because more people are involved in decision making, competitive bids may be required, and objective factors such as costs and service facility amenities may weigh more heavily than emotional ones.

Traditional textbooks classify the market into two groups: individual and organizational. Because of different constraints and influences, these groups do not act in exactly the same way. For example, an individual pleasure traveler can choose any vacation destination. However, an association convention planner faced with a site rotation policy cannot consider certain destinations.

The four components of the organizational market are as follows:[26]

1. The commercial market
2. Trade industries
3. Governments
4. Institutions

The industrial market includes private-sector, profit-making organizations that purchase goods and services to produce other goods and services. Trade industries are wholesalers and retailers that buy goods and services to resell to others. Institutions include hospitals, universities, colleges, schools, associations, and other nonprofit groups.

Suppliers, carriers, and ground transportation companies are our industrial (producer) market. Restaurants buy food and beverages, which they process before selling to customers. Airlines buy planes to produce services (flights) for customers. Hotels buy bricks and mortar, furniture, and equipment to create services. There are many other firms in the industrial (producer) market that are not part of the hospitality and travel industry. Examples include those that are involved in manufacturing, construction, mining, agriculture, finance, insurance, real estate, forestry, and fisheries.

The travel trade represents our trade industry. Retail travel agents and tour wholesalers are the two predominant groups in this industry. Unlike other wholesalers and retailers, these groups do not usually pay for their inventory until after the final purchaser has consumed the services. They buy service inventories from our industrial (producer) market for resale to individual and organizational customers. There are many other retail and wholesale businesses operating outside the hospitality and travel industry.

Governments and institutions are major consumers of hospitality and travel services. Federal, state/provincial, and local agencies generate constant flows of travelers among themselves, their constituents, and their associates. Association conventions are the largest demand component of the institutional market.

CHAPTER CONCLUSION

Understanding how individual and organizational customers behave is a prerequisite for effective marketing. Personal and interpersonal factors influence customers' choices of hospitality and travel services. The personal factors include needs, wants, and motivation; perception; learning; personality; lifestyle; and self-concept. Interpersonal influences come from cultures and subcultures, reference groups, social classes, opinion leaders, and the family. Customers place more weight on the recommendations they receive from their friends and associates than they do on the information supplied by hospitality and travel organizations. Word-of-mouth information is, therefore, a powerful force in our industry.

Customers go through different steps in making purchase decisions. The actual steps followed, and the sequence of these steps, vary according to the amount of the purchase and the perceived degree of difference between alternatives. To be successful, marketers must understand their customers' decision processes.

REVIEW QUESTIONS

1. Why is it important for a hospitality or travel organization to understand the behavior of its customers?
2. What are the personal factors that influence customer behavior?
3. What are the interpersonal factors that affect customer behavior?
4. What are stimulus factors and how do they affect customers' perceptions?
5. What steps do customers usually go through when they make decisions about buying hospitality and travel services?
6. Do customers always go through the same steps when they make decisions? Why or why not?
7. Why is it important for marketers to understand the decision process their customers are following?
8. Why are organizational customers different from individual customers?

CHAPTER ASSIGNMENTS

1. Take a close look at yourself and your family. What interpersonal factors affect the buying decisions made by members of the family? What personal factors tend to influence these choices? How could a hospitality or travel organization effectively appeal to you and other members of your family?

2. Select a hospitality or travel business and try to characterize the behavior patterns of its customers. What decision stages do its customers go through? What are their demographics, lifestyles, cultural backgrounds, social classes, and family life-cycle stages? How can the business best appeal to these groups?

3. Gather a selection of hospitality and travel advertisements. Which of the stimulus fac-

tors have been used in these ads to attract customer attention? How effectively have these factors been used? What could have been done to improve the impact of these ads on customers' perceptions?

4. Think about some major and minor purchases you have made in the past year. Which of the three decision-making processes did you use? How important were social information sources in your decision making? How important were commercial information sources? How can you apply what you have learned from this assignment to the marketing of hospitality and travel services?

WORLD WIDE WEB RESOURCES

American Automobile Association
http://www.aaa.com/

American Hawaii Cruises
http://www.cruisehawaii.com/

Avis
http://www.avis.com/

Claritas
http://www.claritas.com/

Consumer Reports
http://www.consumerreports.org/

Hertz
http://www.hertz.com/

Lee Island Coast Visitor & Convention Bureau
http://www.leeislandcoast.com/

Michelin Travel Guide
http://www.michelin-travel.com/

Mobil Travel Guide
http://www.mobil.com/

National Car Rental
http://www.nationalcar.com/

Outward Bound
http://www.outwardbound.org/

Patchwork Quilt Country Inn
http://patchworkquiltinn.com/

Roper Starch Worldwide
http://www.roper.com/

Sandals
http://www.sandals.com/

SRI Consulting Business Intelligence
http://www.future.sri.com/VALS/VALSindex.shtml

REFERENCES

1. Kotler, Philip. 2000. *Marketing Management: Millennium Edition.* 10th ed. Upper Saddle River, N.J.: Prentice-Hall, Inc.

2. Kotler, Philip. 2000. *Marketing Management: Millennium Edition.* 10th ed. Upper Saddle River, N.J.: Prentice-Hall, Inc.

3. Mill, Robert Christie, and Alastair M. Morrison. 1998. *The Tourism System: An Introductory Text.* 3rd ed. Dubuque, Iowa: Kendall/Hunt Publishing Company.

4. Mill, Robert Christie, and Alastair M. Morrison. 1998. *The Tourism System: An Introductory Text.* 3rd ed. Dubuque, Iowa: Kendall/Hunt Publishing Company.

5. Horton, Raymond L. 1984. *Buyer Behavior: A Decision-Making Approach.* Columbus, Ohio: Charles E. Merrill Publishing Company, 126.

6. Kotler, Philip. 2000. *Marketing Management: Millennium Edition.* 10th ed. Upper Saddle River, N.J.: Prentice-Hall, Inc.

7. Berelson, Bernard, and Gary A. Steiner. 1964. *Human Behavior: An Inventory of Scientific Findings.* New York: Harcourt Brace Jovanovich, 88.

8. Mill, Robert Christie, and Alastair M. Morrison. 1998. *The Tourism System: An Introductory Text.* 3rd ed. Dubuque, Iowa: Kendall/Hunt Publishing Company.

9. Mayo, Edward J., and Lance P. Jarvis. 1981. *The Psychology of Leisure Travel: Effective Marketing and Selling of Services.* Boston: CBI Publishing Company, 24.

10. Mill, Robert Christie, and Alastair M. Morrison. 1998. *The Tourism System: An Introductory Text.* 3rd ed. Dubuque, Iowa: Kendall/Hunt Publishing Company.

11. Mayo, Edward J., and Lance P. Jarvis. 1981. *The Psychology of Leisure Travel: Effective Marketing and Selling of Services.* Boston: CBI Publishing Company, 108–109.

12. Mayo, Edward J., and Lance P. Jarvis. 1981. *The Psychology of Leisure Travel: Effective Marketing and Selling of Services.* Boston: CBI Publishing Company, 179.

13. Michman, R. D. 1991. *Lifestyle Market Segmentation.* New York: Praeger, 20.

14. Mill, Robert Christie, and Alastair M. Morrison. 1998. *The Tourism System: An Introductory Text.* 3rd ed. Dubuque, Iowa: Kendall/Hunt Publishing Company.

15. Braus, Patricia. "What Does 'Hispanic' Mean?" *American Demographics* 15(6):46–58 (1993).

16. Riche, Martha F. "We're All Minorities Now." *American Demographics* 13(10):26–34 (1991).

17. Boone, Louis E., and David L. Kurtz. 2001. *Contemporary Marketing.* 10th ed. Fort Worth, Tex.: Harcourt College Publishers.

18. Kotler, Philip. 2000. *Marketing Management: Millennium Edition.* 10th ed. Upper Saddle River, N.J.: Prentice-Hall, Inc.

19. Piirto, Rebecca. "The Influentials." *American Demographics* 14(10):30–38 (1992).

20. Rogers, Everett M. 1995. *Diffusion of Innovations.* 4th ed. New York: Free Press.

21. American Demographics. "The Changing American Household." *American Demographics Desk Reference* 14 (July 1992):2–3.

22. Murphy, Patrick E., and William A. Staples. "A Modernized Family Life Cycle." *Journal of Consumer Research* 6(1):12–22 (1979).

23. Kotler, Philip. 2000. *Marketing Management: Millennium Edition.* 10th ed. Upper Saddle River, N.J.: Prentice-Hall, Inc.

24. Boone, Louis E., and David L. Kurtz. 2001. *Contemporary Marketing.* 10th ed. Fort Worth, Tex.: Harcourt College Publishers.

25. Kotler, Philip. 2000. *Marketing Management: Millennium Edition.* 10th ed. Upper Saddle River, N.J.: Prentice-Hall, Inc.

26. Boone, Louis E., and David L. Kurtz. 2001. *Contemporary Marketing.* 10th ed. Fort Worth, Tex.: Harcourt College Publishers.

For additional hospitality and travel marketing resources, visit our Web site at **www.Hospitality-Tourism.delmar.com**

Analyzing Marketing Opportunities

Where Are We Now?

Objectives

Having read this chapter, you should be able to:

◆ Define the terms situation analysis, market analysis, and feasibility analysis.

◆ Explain the relationship and differences between situation, market, and feasibility analyses.

◆ Explain the five benefits of doing a situation analysis.

◆ List in order and describe the steps in a situation analysis.

◆ List in order and describe the six major steps in a market analysis.

◆ List and describe the four additional steps in a feasibility analysis.

Overview

This chapter begins by stressing the importance of research and analysis as the foundation of sound marketing decisions. It looks at three analysis techniques—situation, market, and feasibility analysis. A situation analysis is a very important element of the first of the five systematic steps in the hospitality and travel marketing system.

The benefits and products of preparing a situation analysis are identified. The fact that situation analysis results are the foundation for long- and short-term marketing planning is emphasized. Sample worksheets for a situation analysis are provided.

Situation analyses are used for existing operations. Market and feasibility analyses are used for proposed new businesses. The relationship among the three analysis techniques is emphasized.

Key Terms

capital budget	marketing position and plan	secondary research
economic feasibility	analysis	services analysis
feasibility analysis	market potential analysis	situation analysis
location and community analysis	positioning	SWOT analysis
management contract	primary competitors	trade-area analysis
market analysis	primary (original) research	zip-code demographics analysis
marketing environment analysis	*pro forma* (projected) income	
	statement	

ANALYSIS FOR SUCCESS

We begin this chapter with a catchy heading to get your attention quickly. Analysis for success—what does it mean? The analysis of marketing opportunities and problems is the foundation for starting and keeping a successful business. No new venture should be launched without a thorough market or feasibility analysis. Likewise, no organization should be without at least an annual situation analysis.

What is a market or feasibility analysis, and why are they different from a situation analysis? A situation analysis is similar to a market analysis, but is done for an existing business. It is a study of the marketing strengths, weaknesses, opportunities, and threats of a business or other type of organization. A market analysis is a study of the potential demand for a new hospitality or travel business. It determines whether market demand is large enough. A feasibility analysis is a study of the potential demand for *and* economic feasibility of a business or other type of organization, and it includes a market analysis plus a few additional steps. It looks at the total investment required to start a business, and the expected financial returns. Market and feasibility analyses are done for new businesses that people are considering starting.

Most writers talk about either the situation analysis or the feasibility and market analysis. Nobody ever links all three techniques. Why then put them together in one chapter? The answer is simple; they are related. The first situation analysis should be built upon a market or feasibility analysis. The second situation analysis is founded on the first, and so on (Figure 5–1). If the initial market or feasibility analysis is placed on a shelf and ignored, the business loses an opportunity to use valuable research information and analysis. If each situation analysis does not build on prior ones, effort is wasted. Using these analysis tools has to be a continuous process. Just like marketing itself, performing these analyses has to be accepted as a long-term activity. Chapter 3 pointed out that long-term marketing planning is a fundamental of the hospitality and travel marketing system. There is a strong link between planning and these analysis techniques. A market analysis should be the basis for a strategic (long-term) market plan. The situation analysis updates the initial market analysis. The new information is then used to prepare the marketing (short-term) plan and to update the strategic market plan. The situation analysis does this by answering the question, "Where are we now?" Because the situation analysis is included in the first step in the hospitality and travel system described in Chapter 3, we will start with it.

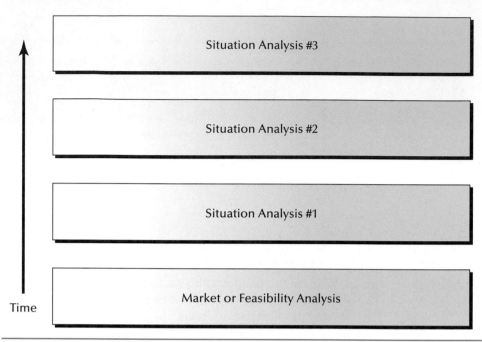

Time

♦ **FIGURE 5–1**   *Relationship of situation, market, and feasibility analyses.*

THE SITUATION ANALYSIS

We have already defined this term as a study of an organization's marketing strengths, weaknesses, opportunities, and threats. It is included in the first step in the hospitality and travel marketing system for an existing organization. It answers the question "Where are we now?" Sometimes the terms *marketing* or *market audit* and *SWOT analysis* are used instead of situation analysis. Before telling you what a situation analysis includes, let us look at five of its advantages:

1. Focuses attention on strengths and weaknesses
2. Assists with long-term planning
3. Helps in the development of marketing plans
4. Puts a priority on marketing research
5. Has spin-off benefits

1. **Focuses Attention on Strengths and Weaknesses.** The greatest benefit from doing a situation analysis every year is that it continually focuses attention on an organization's strengths and weaknesses. In busy organizations it is easy to lose track of the big picture and get caught up in day-to-day operations. It is convenient to accept the status quo and to believe that things will not change. Doing a situation analysis is similar to going to the dentist for a checkup or to the doctor for a physical. Both professionals examine you thoroughly and may tell you to change habits. Although you may not like the advice they give you, you know it will do you good. Giving an organization a routine *checkup* is just as beneficial and important to the continued health of an organization.

2. **Assists with Long-Term Planning.** The second benefit is that the completed situation analysis contributes to strategic marketing planning. The situation analysis makes sure that the long-term planning process remains current. It does so by reviewing recent trends in the marketing environment.

3. **Helps in the Development of Marketing Plans.** The situation analysis plays an important role in structuring marketing plans. The results of the situation analysis are the base upon which plans are built. Preparing a plan without first doing a situation analysis is similar to trying to put a roof on a building with no walls. It is bound to fall flat. Marketing plans must reflect an organization's strengths and opportunities, and the situation analysis identifies them.

4. **Puts a Priority on Marketing Research.** Situation analyses rely heavily on research and place a premium on marketing research results. Research is needed to investigate new marketing opportunities, track customer satisfaction levels, evaluate competitors' strengths and weaknesses, and measure the effectiveness of past marketing plans. The human body continues to function as intended with continual nourishment from food and liquids. Marketing research plays the same role for an organization. The situation analysis focuses attention on the value of research and requires an ongoing research effort.

5. **Has Spin-off Benefits.** The fifth benefit is the *by-products* of the situation analysis. It provides an inventory, a status report on conditions, and a list of improvements needed in an organization's facilities and services. The inventory is useful for preparing press kits and information packages, such as convention brochures for hotels. The more obvious products of the situation analysis are as follows:
   a. An identification of strengths, weaknesses, opportunities, and threats
   b. An identification of primary competitors' strengths and weaknesses
   c. A community profile, including an indication of the opportunities and problems presented
   d. An assessment of the impact of marketing environment factors
   e. An historical record of marketing activities, successes, and failures

Like the marketing plan, the situation analysis should be a written document. It needs to be updated each time a new marketing plan is required.

Steps in a Situation Analysis

A situation analysis should include six steps. The procedure used is much like taking a photograph of someone. It starts by viewing *the big picture* (marketing environment analysis), focuses on the next level (location and community analysis), and then eventually *zooms in* more tightly on the organization's marketing position and plan. The situation analysis often goes by the name SWOT analysis, meaning an analysis of strengths, weaknesses, opportunities, and threats. The sequence in which the situation analysis steps are completed is slightly different than that followed in a market analysis, as can be seen in Figure 5–2.

As you can see, the order of the location and community analysis and the market potential analysis is reversed in these two types of analysis. The reordering of the steps is possible because in a situation analysis the business location is set and information is

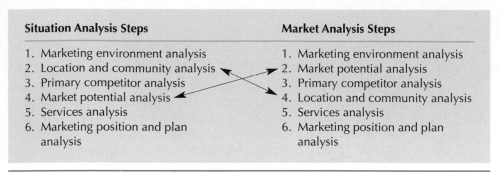

Situation Analysis Steps	Market Analysis Steps
1. Marketing environment analysis	1. Marketing environment analysis
2. Location and community analysis	2. Market potential analysis
3. Primary competitor analysis	3. Primary competitor analysis
4. Market potential analysis	4. Location and community analysis
5. Services analysis	5. Services analysis
6. Marketing position and plan analysis	6. Marketing position and plan analysis

◆ FIGURE 5–2   *Situation and market analyses steps.*

available on past customers. Since a market analysis is done for a proposed new business, the exact characteristics of customers are not known, and the location may not be established.

Now let us take a step-by-step look at how the situation analysis is done. Before doing this, you should know that because hospitality and travel organizations are very diverse, their situation analyses can be very different. For example, a hotel may have hundreds of rooms and other physical facilities to evaluate in its services analysis, but a travel agency may only have one small office. A cruise line company may have several ships with thousands of berths among them, whereas a convention and visitors bureau has no physical facilities directly serving the public except for its office space and perhaps a visitor information center. Despite these differences, the same six steps should be followed by all hospitality and travel organizations.

1. **Marketing Environment Analysis.** Marketing is a long-term activity that requires constant planning and updating. Chapter 1 highlighted the need for marketers to carefully consider the marketing environment. No organization totally controls its future direction. Marketing environment factors often dictate the path to follow. A marketing environment analysis looks at these factors and their impacts. Chapter 1 identifies six marketing environment factors: competition, economics, politics, and legislation (government), society and culture, technology, and organizational objectives and resources. Analyzing these factors helps highlight long-term marketing opportunities and threats. It can be fatal for an organization to lose sight of the marketing environment that shapes the way future business is done. Checking and rechecking each marketing environment factor during the situation analysis is an effective way to anticipate important future events.

Let us go back to the basics. What factors, other than an organization's internal operations, affect its marketing success and future direction? We can divide them into controllable and marketing environment factors. Controllables are factors over which complete control is possible. Marketing environment factors are beyond the total control of an individual organization. The economy, society, culture, government, technology, and population (demographic) trends certainly cannot be controlled. Competitors' and customers' behavior patterns can be influenced but cannot be completely controlled. The same is true of the hospitality and travel industry, suppliers, creditors, distribution channels, and other publics. The marketing mix and the other elements of the hospitality and travel system are the only items that can be totally controlled.

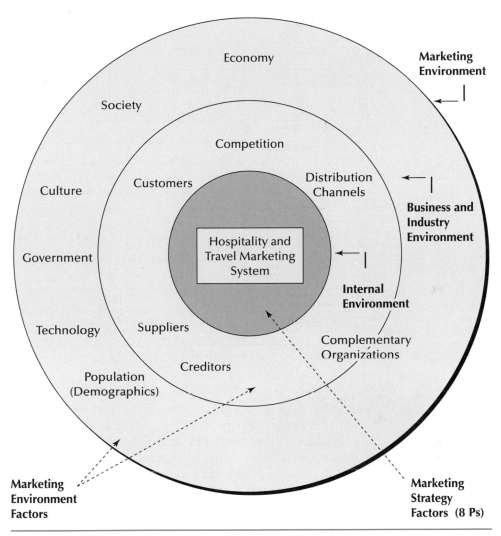

◆ FIGURE 5–3   *The hospitality and travel marketing environment.*

What this discussion shows is that the marketing environment has three levels (Figure 5–3). The first is the internal environment (the hospitality and travel marketing system), which can be controlled. The second, called the business and industry environment, can be influenced but is uncontrollable. The marketing environment is the third level. It cannot be influenced and is also uncontrollable.

Preparing a situation analysis for an existing organization takes a combination of research, forecasting, and judgment. Updating a situation analysis is easier if preprinted worksheets are used. This means anticipating the questions that require answers.

Figure 5–4 is an example of a marketing environment analysis worksheet, which can be modified to suit the needs of individual organizations. The five marketing environment factors, excluding organizational objectives and resources, are listed in the left column. Two or three questions are then supplied to focus attention on the major trends for each factor. The people doing the situation analysis

UNCONTROLLABLE FACTORS	QUESTIONS	ANSWERS	IMPACT ASSESSMENT How will this affect our organization?	+	−	Rating (+10 to −10)
1. COMPETITIVE AND INDUSTRY TRENDS	What has been the pattern of growth in the industry?					
	Which parts of the industry have enjoyed the greatest success recently?					
	Are there any new viable substitutes for our types of services?					
2. ECONOMIC TRENDS	What are the economic forecasts for the country?					
	What are the economic prospects for this region?					
3. POLITICAL AND LEGISLATIVE TRENDS	Are there any regulatory or legislative proposals that will directly affect us?					
4. SOCIETAL AND CULTURAL TRENDS	What lifestyles are gaining in popularity?					
	What sections of the population and subcultures are growing fastest?					
	What trends are happening in our target markets?					
5. TECHNOLOGICAL TRENDS	What has been the major technological advances in the country as a whole?					
	What have been the major technological advances in our industry?					
	What new technologies are in their developmental stage?					

◆ FIGURE 5–4   *Marketing environment analysis worksheet.*

respond to these questions by writing in the "Answers" and "Impact Assessment" columns. They must have an ongoing tracking and research program to supply the answers. Most information for the analysis comes from secondary (previously published) research. There are specialized research organizations, such as the Travel Industry Association of America, that track major trends in the hospitality and travel industry. Buying their periodic reports is an alternative to in-house research.

Will these trends have a negative or a positive effect on the organization? This is the next item to be noted on the worksheet in Figure 5–4. The people doing the situation analysis have to use their judgment in deciding whether there will be any impact at all and whether the effects will be positive or negative. Is the result of the trend viewed as an opportunity or as a threat? If the effect is seen as being positive (an opportunity), the "+" column is checked. The "−" column is checked if the effect is viewed as negative (a threat). Next, each opportunity or threat is assigned a score from −10 to +10 in the "rating" column to reflect the expected magnitude of the effect of the trend. The bigger the opportunity or threat, the higher the assigned score.

2. **Location and Community Analysis.** The scope of the situation analysis then narrows to the local community and site location. Although a site location analysis is an accepted part of a market or feasibility analysis, it is seldom mentioned as an element of the situation analysis. However, assuming that a site location's advantages will last forever is dangerous. Changes in highway design, new building construction, new primary competitors, and other factors can all make a site less attractive. Remember that a site can make or break a hospitality and travel business. A site's market-related features must constantly be reevaluated. Of particular importance are proximity, accessibility, and visibility for potential customers.

LOCATION AND COMMUNITY PROFILE		TRENDS	IMPACT
INDUSTRIAL AND OTHER EMPLOYMENT BASE	Major Employers: Employees (#): 1. _____ _____ 2. _____ _____ 3. _____ _____ 4. _____ _____ 5. _____ _____		
POPULATION CHARACTERISTICS (DEMOGRAPHICS)	Population Size: _____ Age Distribution: _____ Income Distribution: _____ Ethnic Distribution: _____ Sex Distribution: _____ Occupational Distribution: _____ Households: _____ Household Size Distribution: _____		
RESIDENTIAL NEIGHBORHOODS	Single Family: _____ Multi–Unit: _____		
TRANSPORTATION SYSTEM AND FACILITIES	Airport: _____ Expressways: _____ Bus Terminal: _____ Other: _____		
VISITOR ATTRACTIONS AND RECREATIONAL FACILITIES	1. _____ 2. _____ 3. _____ 4. _____ 5. _____		
EVENTS	1. _____ 2. _____ 3. _____ 4. _____ 5. _____		
HEALTH FACILITIES	Hospitals: _____ Medical / Dental Centers: _____ Nursing Homes: _____		
EDUCATIONAL FACILITIES	College / Universities: _____ High Schools: _____ Elementary Schools: _____ Trade Schools: _____		
LOCAL MEDIA AND NEWSMAKERS	Newspapers: _____ Radio: _____ T.V.: _____ Newsmakers: _____		

◆ **FIGURE 5–5**   *Location and community analysis worksheet.*

The location and community analysis is a two-part process. Part one is the profile, which inventories community resources. Part two is an assessment of community trends and their impact. Figure 5–5 shows a sample location and community analysis worksheet. This form is most suitable for hospitality and travel organizations that derive significant business either directly or indirectly from their local communities. These businesses include hotels, restaurants, attractions and theme parks, travel agencies, car rental agencies, and shopping facilities. The factors analyzed in Figure 5–5 are the community's industrial and other employment base, population characteristics, residential neighborhoods, transportation system and facilities, visitor attractions and recreational facilities, events, health facilities, educational facilities, and local media and newsmakers.

The people conducting the situation analysis first complete the community profile by writing answers in the "Location and Community Profile" section of Figure 5–5. Much of this information can usually be obtained from local economic development agencies, chambers of commerce, or convention and visitor bureaus. Next, they record in the "Trends" column any changes that have occurred in the nine location and community factors since the last situation analysis was completed. For example, this might include the opening of a new industrial plant or the expansion of an existing visitor attraction. Finally, the "Impact" column is filled out by indicating how each trend is expected to affect the business. Layoffs at local factories might be seen as having a potential negative effect, whereas the construction of a new residential subdivision might have a positive impact.

3. **Primary Competitor Analysis.** Competition as a whole is considered in the marketing environment analysis. It is also important to take a detailed look at

NAME:
ADDRESS:
PHONE NUMBER:
OWNER:
MANAGER:

SITE LOCATION		PROXIMITY ACCESS VISIBILITY	STRENGTHS:
Located close to (check):	Travel Time (min)	+ − + − + −	
Downtown			
Major Employers			
Expressway			WEAKNESSES:
Airport			
Suburbs			
Shopping Centers			
Other Shopping Districts			
Restaurant District			COMPARISON:
Attraction #1:			
Attraction #2:			
Attraction #3:			
University / College			
Hospital / Medical			
Other #1:			
Other #2:			
Other #3:			

| TARGET MARKETS AND MARKETING ACTIVITIES: | | | COMMENTS: | STRENGTHS: |

1. TARGET MARKETS SERVED:

	Guest Rooms	(Percentages) F&B	Convention/Meeting	
Target Market #1	[ ]	[ ]	[ ]	WEAKNESSES:
Target Market #2				
Target Market #3				
Target Market #4				
Target Market #5				COMPARISON:
Target Market #6				
Target Market #7				
Target Market #8				
Target Market #9				
Target Market #10	[ ]	[ ]	[ ]	

| 2. MARKETING ACTIVITIES: | COMMENTS: | STRENGTHS: |

Major activities:

Advertising _____
Sales Promotion _____
Personal Selling _____   WEAKNESSES:
Public Relations _____
Merchandising _____   COMPARISON:
Travel Trade _____

◆ **FIGURE 5–6**   *Primary competitor analysis worksheet.*

primary competitors. These are usually businesses in the local community with a large share of the target markets identified in the market potential analysis. We say usually because there are some hospitality and travel organizations who compete on a broader geographic basis. Included are resorts, theme parks, airlines, tour wholesalers, incentive travel planners, and destinations. Their primary competitors are more dispersed and may be located in several different foreign countries.

Primary competitors are put under the microscope to discover their major strengths and weaknesses. Different sources of information should be used to make this assessment. The first is obvious! Studying competitors' advertising, Web sites, and other promotional materials is the best place to start. What services and advantages do they promote the hardest? If their marketing is effective, these are their major strengths. Physical inspection, observation, and sampling should come next. Most hotel and restaurant consultants use a standardized checklist to physically inspect competitive operations. Physically observing business patterns and customers is another technique. What is wrong with counting the cars passing through a competitive restaurant's drive-through? How about adding up the people inside a competitor's restaurant? These are just two useful tricks among many. Sampling the competitor's services is another good way of evaluating them.

An example of a primary competitor analysis worksheet is provided in Figure 5–6. This particular form has been designed for a lodging facility. By modifying the form in the "Target Markets and Marketing Activities" section, it can be adapted for use by restaurants, attractions, travel agencies, rental car agencies, and shopping facilities.

FACILITIES AND SERVICES INVENTORY

COMMENTS:

STRENGTHS:

1. GUEST ROOMS (#):

[ ] Singles   [ ] Suites with Parlors
[ ] Twin (Singles)   [ ] Convertible Parlors
[ ] Twin (Double)   [ ] Studios
[ ] Single and Double   [ ] Connecting
[ ] Queens   [ ] Other: _____
[ ] Kings   [ ] Other: _____

WEAKNESSES:

OPPORTUNITIES/
IMPROVEMENTS:

2. FOOD AND BEVERAGE FACILITIES (#): (# seats)

COMMENTS:

STRENGTHS:

	1	2	3	4
Restaurant	[ ]	[ ]	[ ]	[ ]
Coffee Shop	[ ]	[ ]	[ ]	[ ]
Snack Bar	[ ]	[ ]	[ ]	[ ]
Lounge Bar	[ ]	[ ]	[ ]	[ ]
Pub	[ ]	[ ]	[ ]	[ ]
Cabaret	[ ]	[ ]	[ ]	[ ]
Licensed Patio	[ ]	[ ]	[ ]	[ ]
Other	[ ]	[ ]	[ ]	[ ]

WEAKNESSES:

OPPORTUNITIES/
IMPROVEMENTS:

3. CONVENTION, MEETING, AND BANQUET FACILITIES (#):

COMMENTS:

STRENGTHS:

(# seats)

	Banquet	Theatre	Other
Room_____	[ ]	[ ]	[ ]
Room_____	[ ]	[ ]	[ ]
Room_____	[ ]	[ ]	[ ]
Room_____	[ ]	[ ]	[ ]
Room_____	[ ]	[ ]	[ ]
Room_____	[ ]	[ ]	[ ]
Room_____	[ ]	[ ]	[ ]
Room_____	[ ]	[ ]	[ ]
Room_____	[ ]	[ ]	[ ]
Room_____	[ ]	[ ]	[ ]

WEAKNESSES:

OPPORTUNITIES/
IMPROVEMENTS:

4. RECREATIONAL FACILITIES (Provided on–site):

COMMENTS:

STRENGTHS:

INDOOR

[ ] Pool
[ ] Whirlpool / Hot Tub
[ ] Sauna / Steam Room
[ ] Tennis Courts
[ ] Exercise Room
[ ] Games Room
[ ] Squash Courts
[ ] Racquetball / Handball Courts
[ ] Dance Floor
[ ] Jogging Track
[ ] Other _____
[ ] Other _____

OUTDOOR

[ ] Pool
[ ] Whirlpool / Hot Tub
[ ] Golf Course
[ ] Tennis Courts
[ ] Beach
[ ] Boat Rentals
[ ] Boat Docks
[ ] Marina
[ ] Alpine Skiing
[ ] Cross–country skiing
[ ] Other _____
[ ] Other _____

WEAKNESSES:

OPPORTUNITIES/
IMPROVEMENTS:

5. GUEST SERVICES:

COMMENTS:

STRENGTHS:

[ ] Airport Limo
[ ] Complimentary Coffee
[ ] Babysitting
[ ] Bilingual Staff
[ ] Room Service
[ ] Doormen
[ ] Bell Staff
[ ] Beauty / Barber Shop
[ ] Shoe-Cleaning
[ ] Office Center
[ ] Other _____

[ ] Free Parking
[ ] Valet Parking
[ ] Executive Floor (s)
[ ] Executive Lounge
[ ] Wake–up calls
[ ] Massage
[ ] Dry Cleaning
[ ] Turndown Service
[ ] Free Paper
[ ] Other _____
[ ] Other _____

WEAKNESSES:

OPPORTUNITIES/
IMPROVEMENTS:

◆ FIGURE 5–7   *Services analysis worksheet.*

A separate primary competitor analysis worksheet should be completed for each primary competitor. The people doing the situation analysis should first provide the information on the site location, target markets, and marketing activities of the primary competitor. Completing this form should not be looked at as just a fact-finding exercise. While the facts are important, it is their interpretation that is of even greater importance. This interpretation is accomplished by filling out the right column in Figure 5–6. What are competitors' major strengths that they use effectively in marketing? What are their weaknesses, and how do we compare these factors? These are three key questions that the primary competitor analysis worksheet should specify for each primary competitor.

To complete the primary competitor analysis, a form such as that shown in Figure 5–7 (services analysis worksheet) should be completed for each primary competitor. Again, this form was designed for a lodging facility, but it can be adapted to suit other hospitality and travel businesses. It provides for an inventory of each competitor's facilities and services (left side) and an analysis of competitive strengths and weaknesses.

4. **Market Potential Analysis.** A market potential analysis for an existing hospitality and travel organization considers both the organization's past and potential customers. It is a research study of the market potential, or target markets, upon which the business is built.

   Chapter 6 discusses marketing research techniques in detail. In this chapter, these tools are mentioned where they apply. Some important research terminology should be discussed before we go further. A market potential analysis uses a combination of secondary and primary research. Secondary research is already published information available from other sources, either internally (e.g., a hotel's guest registration data) or externally. Primary or original research is data collected for the first time, by a method other than secondary research, to answer specific questions.

   The people doing the situation analysis should use a systematic, six-step process in preparing the market potential analysis. This process is also used where research is required in other parts of the situation analysis. The seven steps involved are as follows:

   a. Decide on research questions.
   b. Collect and analyze secondary information.
   c. Design primary research, data collection method, and forms.
   d. Design sample and collect primary information.
   e. Analyze and interpret primary information.
   f. Draw conclusions and make recommendations.
   g. Present results.

   Figure 5–8 provides ideas on how this process is applied in a market potential analysis. Listing the key questions for which answers are needed is the logical starting point for the research process. The following is a list of the seven key research questions about past and potential customers that the situation analysis must address.

   a. **WHO?** Who are the customers?
   b. **WHAT?** What needs are they trying to satisfy?
   c. **WHERE?** Where do the customers live and work? Where do they buy?
   d. **WHEN?** When do they buy?
   e. **HOW?** How do they buy?
   f. **HOW MANY?** How many customers are there?
   g. **HOW DO?** How do they feel about our organization and about primary competitors?

   We now know the types of information we need. Next, we have to make a choice. Should we use secondary research, primary research, or a combination of both? The best answer is always a combination of both. Secondary information is less expensive and is available more quickly. Primary research is more difficult to do, is more expensive, and takes longer to gather, but it provides more specific and reliable information.

   The best place to start the market potential analysis is by collecting secondary research information. It does not make any sense to reinvent the wheel! If someone has already gathered the data and it is readily available, primary research is not required. Secondary information also helps us plan primary research. It pinpoints

---

STEP 1   Decide on research questions.

[   ]   **WHO?** Who are the customers?
[   ]   **WHAT?** What needs are they trying to satisfy?
[   ]   **WHERE?** Where do the customers live and work? Where do they buy?
[   ]   **WHEN?** When do they buy?
[   ]   **HOW?** How do they buy?
[   ]   **HOW MANY?** How many customers are there?
[   ]   **HOW DO?** How do they feel about our organization and about primary competitors?

STEP 2   Collect and analyze secondary information.

[   ]   What information do we have on customers in our own organization's records?
[   ]   What information have other organizations gathered on these customers?
[   ]   Do we need to do any further or new (primary) research?

STEP 3   Design primary research data collection method and forms.

[   ]   Which research method should be used to collect data (experimental, observational, survey, or focus groups)?
[   ]   Which specific research techniques should be used (e.g., mail, telephone, personal interview, online, or in-house, self-administered surveys)?
[   ]   What questions and other materials should be included on data collection forms?
[   ]   How should data collection forms be administered and analyzed?

STEP 4   Design sample and collect primary information.

[   ]   Who are the research subjects (e.g., in-house customers, corporate travel managers, travel agents, or householders)?
[   ]   How many research subjects are there?
[   ]   What sample selection method and sample size should be used?

STEP 5   Analyze and interpret primary information.

[   ]   What procedures should be used for coding, editing, and entering or tabulating the data?
[   ]   Which statistical analysis techniques and programs should be used to analyze the data?
[   ]   What are the results and how should we interpret these results?

STEP 6   Draw conclusions and make recommendations.

[   ]   What types of conclusions can we draw from the results?
[   ]   What types of recommendations can we make?
[   ]   What form of report or reports are required?

◆ FIGURE 5–8   *Steps in the research process of a market potential analysis of past and potential customers.*

information gaps, ways of segmenting the market, and profiles of average customers. It helps in structuring primary research questions. *Get smart quick* is the key principle in making effective use of secondary information. Chapter 6 looks at major information sources and quick ways of using them.

Now let us take a more detailed look at what is involved in both the past customer analysis and the potential customer analysis.

a. ***Past Customer Analysis.*** Every hospitality and travel organization should have an ongoing program to track customer volumes and characteristics. This is essential for measuring success and for planning future marketing activities. Past customers are usually an excellent source of new business. Many become repeat users and influence others to become customers. Knowing as much as possible about past customers is one of the best investments of an organization's time and money. With so much emphasis now being placed on *relationship marketing* and *database marketing,* it has become extremely important for organizations to develop an in-depth understanding of their past customers.

Figure 5–9 provides an example of a market potential analysis worksheet for past customers. The people completing the situation analysis provide answers in the lined section on the right of the worksheet and check off each topic after it has been covered.

b. ***Potential Customer Analysis.*** Organizations constantly have to be alert for new sources of customers. A situation analysis helps achieve this in several different ways. The location and community analysis can point out new market opportunities arising from the site location (proximity) and from cooperation with complementary businesses. The primary competitor analysis pinpoints competitors' target markets and successful marketing activities. Businesses can certainly duplicate successful techniques. There is no law against imitation! The services analysis highlights strengths and opportunities, some of which may not have been fully capitalized upon. The past customer analysis may produce methods of increasing repeat use and customer spending. Finally, the marketing environment analysis may indicate new potential markets.

Once identified, potential markets must be researched. This may take place during the situation analysis or at some other time. Researching new markets is a constant activity of a marketing-oriented organization. The situation analysis is one of the best sources of ideas for research programs.

- ***Who are the potential customers?*** How do we select the potential customers to research? Usually this is done by specifying a market segment or segments in which the organization sees some business potential. Market segmentation is a subject that Chapter 7 reviews in detail. In general, there are many ways to segment a market. Some methods are *traditional,* having become the norm in the industry for years. Dividing lodging customers by purpose of trip is an example. Purpose-of-trip segmentation is also popular with airlines, travel agencies, restaurants, and others. Purpose-of-trip segmentation first divides customers into business and pleasure travelers and then subdivides these two segments further using factors such as price and group size. *Nontraditional,* or newer, methods include lifestyle and benefit segmentation. They are more sophisticated and are slowly gaining popularity.

- ***What needs are potential customers trying to satisfy?*** This is a much more difficult question to answer! It often gets skipped over because it is hard to answer. Remember our definition of marketing as satisfying customer needs and wants? How can an organization satisfy potential customers' needs if it does not know what these needs are? It is easy to fall into the trap of assuming that all hospitality and travel businesses of a given type (hotels, restaurants, travel agencies, theme parks, etc.) are alike and, therefore, all their customers must also be alike. Secondary research information

WHO?   1. Who are our past customers?

[   ]   Target markets   ———————————————
[   ]   Demographic profile   ———————————————
[   ]   Purposes of trips   ———————————————
[   ]   Lifestyle/psychographic profile   ———————————————
[   ]   Party or group sizes   ———————————————
[   ]   Number of previous visits or uses
        of our business   ———————————————

WHAT?   2. What needs have past customers tried to satisfy?

[   ]   Needs   ———————————————
[   ]   Benefits sought   ———————————————
[   ]   Services purchased   ———————————————
[   ]   Dollar volumes purchased   ———————————————

WHERE?   3. Where do past customers live and work?

[   ]   Place of residence   ———————————————
[   ]   Place of work   ———————————————
[   ]   Location before use   ———————————————
[   ]   Location after use   ———————————————

WHEN?   4. When have past customers bought?

[   ]   Day part, daily, weekly, monthly   ———————————————
[   ]   Weekday versus weekend   ———————————————
[   ]   Lengths of stay or visit   ———————————————

HOW?   5. How have past customers bought?

[   ]   Travel agents, tour operators, and
        other intermediaries used   ———————————————
[   ]   Sources of information   ———————————————
[   ]   Internet Use   ———————————————
[   ]   Decision-makers and influencers   ———————————————
[   ]   Reservations methods used   ———————————————
[   ]   Routes/transportation used   ———————————————

HOW MANY?   6. How many past customers do we have?

[   ]   Total number of customers
[   ]   Number of customers by market   ———————————————
        segment   ———————————————
[   ]   Number of repeat customers
[   ]   Customer counts by day part,   ———————————————
        day, week, month, and year   *continued*

◆ FIGURE 5–9   *Market potential analysis worksheet: past customers.*

HOW DO?   7. How do past customers feel about our organization and about primary competitors?

[   ]   How well are we meeting their needs?   ———————————

[   ]   How can we improve to better serve
         their needs?   ———————————

[   ]   Will they recommend us to others?   ———————————

[   ]   What is different about the way we do
         business that customers like?   ———————————

[   ]   What image do they have of us?   ———————————

[   ]   How well are competitors meeting
         their needs?   ———————————

[   ]   What problems have they had with
         competitors?   ———————————

[   ]   Would they recommend competitors
         to others?   ———————————

[   ]   What is different about the way
         competitors do business that customers
         like?   ———————————

[   ]   How are competitors different from us? ———————————

◆ FIGURE 5–9   *continued*

points the way. But there is only one surefire way of getting good information on potential customers' needs—go right to the source! Using the primary research method, ask potential customers about their needs and the
benefits they want.

• ***Where do potential customers live and work?*** Secondary information
comes first in determining where potential customers live and work. A few
examples help explain the process. The Lodging Market Analysis (LMA) is
a secondary research source for hotel market analysis.[1] Trade-area and
zip-code demographics analysis are two secondary sources for restaurant, travel agency, and retail shopping market analysis. These three tools
provide data on where potential customers live and work.

American Express provides the LMA service to hotels accepting their credit
card. This source does not answer all the questions in a potential customer
analysis, but it does help plan primary research. Reports from the LMA provide
information on customers' origin markets (where they live or work) as well as
on the hotel bills they pay by American Express. Data, as well as combined figures for all participating hotels in the surrounding area, are provided for each
individual hotel. Reports from the LMA suggest which geographic markets
generate the highest percentages of hotel business volumes in the area. Primary
research should be conducted in these major business-generating areas.

Trade-area and zip-code demographics analysis are two related secondary research tools. They both consider customer demographics, are based on
census data, and can be used individually or together. These tools are most
useful to businesses with a strong local market, including restaurants, travel
agencies, shopping facilities, and many attractions. One leading restaurant
expert believes that 75 to 80 percent of most restaurant customers come from

A Touch of Technology

SiteReports.com

◆ The World Wide Web is making it easy to do trade area analyses through services like Claritas' SiteReports.com.

◆ Reports and maps can be ordered on-line using either a one-, three-, or five-mile radius from the site or a standard geographic unit like a zip-code area.

◆ The following reports are available for on-line delivery (pop-facts demographic snapshot, pop-facts full demographic data report, pop-facts summary demographic data, demographic trend, age by income, daytime employment, retail trade potential, shopping center list, Micro Vision area segment profile, Micro Vision area group profile, restaurant top chain, daytime occupation).

◆ These maps can be prepared and delivered on-line (current-year population, current-year household, median household income, population growth 1990 to current year, daytime population).

within a three- to five-mile radius (about 10 minutes away).[2] A restaurant does not usually have to look far for its potential customers; they are in its *backyard*. A trade area is geographic and is often specified as a radius around a business location from which the business draws the majority of its customers. A zip-code analysis provides demographic statistics for specific zip codes in the United States. Trade areas can be identified as one or several zip codes. Several research firms provide customized trade area analysis.

• ***Where, when, and how do they buy?*** To answer these questions, we again get some clues from secondary research, but the most precise answers come from primary research. Primary research is harder to collect and is more expensive and time-consuming: it must be carefully planned. Many primary research tools are available. Choosing the right ones for the job is the key planning task. Chapter 6 discusses the alternatives. It divides these tools into four groups: survey, observational, experimental, and simulation research. The survey method is by far the most frequently used in the analysis of potential customers. Personal, telephone, and mail surveys are the most used survey techniques.

   Let us carry through with our lodging and restaurant examples to show how a primary research plan is put together. We will assume that the people doing the analysis of potential customers have analyzed LMA reports and picked out the biggest business-generating markets (areas). The next step is to conduct interviews with corporate travel and meeting planners, travel agents specializing in corporate accounts, association convention planners, tour wholesalers, and incentive travel executives.[3] An interview is another name for a survey carried out in person or on the phone. The author's own experience in doing potential customer analyses for lodging facilities indicates that personal interviews (surveys) are more effective than telephone interviews.

Some of the key questions that need to be answered in these interviews are the following:

i. WHERE DO THEY BUY?
- To which destinations are trips made?
- What types of lodging formats are preferred (e.g., luxury, first-class, moderate-price, all-suite, budget)?
- Which types of location are preferred (e.g., downtown, airport, resort)?
- Which specific lodging properties are used frequently?
- What do travelers like most about these specific properties?
- What major problems or weaknesses have they experienced at these specific properties?

ii. WHEN DO THEY BUY?
- When are trips made?

iii. HOW DO THEY BUY?
- Who makes the decision on choices of destinations and specific lodging choices?
- Who else has a say in the decision-making process?
- Are frequent-guest or frequent-flyer programs important?
- Are travel agents used?
- Are other travel intermediaries used?

Figure 5–10 provides an example of a market potential analysis worksheet for potential customers.

As the follow-up to a trade-area or zip-code demographics analysis, interviewers may survey people in specific parts of the area. These people may live in a single zip-code area or in a certain *band* around the business. They may also be selected because of demographic characteristics such as age, household income, household composition, or occupation. With some wording changes, the same types of where, when, and how questions should be asked. For example, the second question becomes "What restaurant formats are preferred?"

- ***How many potential customers can we attract?*** With all the secondary and primary research completed, it is time to draw conclusions and make recommendations. About what? Remember the who, what, where, when, how, how many, and how do questions? These are the key questions that the accumulated research must answer. Answering the "how many" question is particularly important since the answer determines if the potential market is big enough for the organization to pursue. Whatever the answer, it is only an estimate. The best estimates require a combination of research results, experience with the types of business under consideration, and excellent judgment.

5. **Service Analysis.** What are the organization's strengths and weaknesses? What opportunities and problems do they present? These are the two most important questions the services analysis addresses. This self-analysis is more realistic and beneficial if it comes after the analysis of primary competitors and market potential. It is a two-part process involving an inventory of facilities and services and a physical inspection of their condition.

6. **Marketing Position and Plan Analysis.** The last situation analysis step draws from all previous ones. It is the culmination of the information-gathering and analysis process. Two key questions are considered: "What position do we occupy in the minds of past and potential customers?" and "How effective is our marketing?"

Did You Know?

✓ Arthur Andersen's Hospitality Consulting Services group conducted a large study on the use of technology by hotels, the *Hospitality 2000—The Technology* study.

✓ The hotel organization respondents indicated the percentage of their guest rooms that contained the following technologies:

✓ Voicemail (84%)

✓ On-demand movies and dual phone lines (67%)

✓ In-room Internet access (57%)

✓ Fax/copier/printers (38%)

✓ Interactive television (26%)

✓ Cordless phones (17%)

✓ E-mail (16%).

WHO?   1. Who are the potential customers?

[ ]	Market segments	_____
[ ]	Demographic profile	_____
[ ]	Lifestyle/psychographic profile	_____
[ ]	Party or group sizes	_____
[ ]	Frequency of visits/uses of business like ours	_____

WHAT?   2. What needs are potential customers trying to satisfy?

[ ]	Needs	_____
[ ]	Benefits sought	_____
[ ]	Services sought	_____
[ ]	Expenditures/spending	_____

WHERE?   3. Where do potential customers live and work?

[ ]	Place of residence	_____
[ ]	Place of work	_____
[ ]	Location before use	_____
[ ]	Location after use	_____

WHEN?   4. When do potential customers buy?

[ ]	Day part, daily, weekly, monthly	_____
[ ]	Weekday versus weekend	_____
[ ]	Lengths of stay or visit	_____

continued

◆ FIGURE 5–10   *Market potential analysis worksheet: potential customers.*

HOW?   5. How do potential customers buy?

[   ]   Use of travel agents, tour operators,
         and other intermediaries   _____
[   ]   Sources of information   _____
[   ]   Use of Internet   _____
[   ]   Decision-makers and influencers   _____
[   ]   Reservations methods   _____
[   ]   Routes/transportation   _____

HOW MANY?   6. How many potential customers are there?

[   ]   Total number of potential customers   _____
[   ]   Number of potential customers by
         market segment   _____

**HOW DO?   7. How do potential customers feel about our organization and about primary
                competitors?**

[   ]   How well can we meet potential
         customers' needs?   _____
[   ]   What is different about the way we do
         business that potential customers
         may like?   _____
[   ]   What image do potential customers
         have of us?   _____
[   ]   How well are competitors meeting
         potential customers' needs?   _____
[   ]   What problems have potential
         customers had with competitors?   _____
[   ]   Would potential customers recommend
         competitors to others?   _____
[   ]   What is different about the way
         competitors do business that potential
         customers like?   _____
[   ]   How are competitors different from us?   _____

◆ FIGURE 5–10   *continued*

These two topics are discussed in detail in later chapters. For now it is sufficient to look at the information requirements and results.

Figure 5–11 shows a sample market position and plan analysis worksheet for a lodging facility. It provides a history of past marketing activities and their effectiveness.

In the first part of the worksheet, strengths, unique features, and customers benefits are noted. In the second section, marketing expenditures are entered and comments are made on their effectiveness.

1. MARKET POSITION ANALYSIS

Strengths, Unique Features, and Benefits:

All Target Markets

Target Market #1
Target Market #2
Target Market #3
Target Market #4
Target Market #5
Target Market #6

Positioning Statement: _____

2. PLAN ANALYSIS AND HISTORY

MARKETING MIX ELEMENTS

	ACTUAL EXPENSES					TARGET MARKETS						EVALUATION OF EFFECTIVENESS & OTHER COMMENTS
	19__	19__	19__	19__	19__	1	2	3	4	5	6	

1. ADVERTISING
a. Newspapers
b. Magazines
c. Travel Guides
d. Trade Publications
e. Yellow Pages
f. Billboards
g. Transit Ads
h. Radio
i. Television
j. Barter Ads
k. Cooperative Ads
l.
m.
n.
   Subtotal

2. SALES PROMOTION
a. Direct Mail
b. Brochures
c. Post Cards
d. Newsletters
e. Trade / Travel Shows
f.
g.
h.
   Subtotal

3. PERSONAL SELLING
a. Sales Calls
b.
c.
d.
e.
   Subtotal

4. PUBLIC RELATIONS AND PUBLICITY
a.
b.
c.
d.
e.
   Subtotal

5. MERCHANDISE / IN–HOUSE PROMOTIONS
a.
b.
c.
d.
e.
   Subtotal

6. TRAVEL TRADE MARKETING
a.
b.
c.
d.
e.
   Subtotal

7. OTHER MARKETING PROGRAMS
a.
b.
c.
   Subtotal
   TOTAL

◆ FIGURE 5–11   *Marketing position and plan analysis.*

CASE: A situation analysis for New York City

In October 1990, the New York Convention & Visitors Bureau started a process to prepare a strategic (market) plan for tourism in the city. The consulting firm of Hunt & Hunt was employed to oversee the development of the plan. The plan received extensive input from the hospitality and travel industry in New York and elsewhere and was published in 1992 under the name "New York Tourism 2000: A Strategic Plan to Prepare New York City for the Next Generation of Visitors."

A situation analysis was included in New York's strategic plan and selected sections have been reprinted. While the format does not exactly follow that suggested in this

EXCELLENCE CASE

Tourism's Impact on New York City

New York City has always been a major visitor destination. Early visitors coming for trade and business helped make the city a great port and financial center. As time went on, more and more visitors came to New York City to experience the pulse and excitement of one of the most vibrant cities in the world. As a result, the tourism industry has become an important part of the city's economic and cultural picture.

New York City is the favored destination for millions of visitors each year, due to a broad base of visitor segments and trip purpose categories that generate visitation. A prioritized list of the city's strengths was compiled by participants in the New York Tourism 2000 workshops. They are:

—Product diversity. The city offers numerous visitor appeals which motivate high volumes of pleasure traffic, including museums, theater, music, visual arts, ethnic neighborhoods, architecture and historic sites.

—A wide range of world-class shopping and dining options.

—Superior accessibility. New York City is the world's leading land, sea, rail and air transportation center, as well as a major gateway for international arrivals to the United States. The city also boasts an outstanding internal public transportation system.

—An internationally regarded infrastructure of hotels, major meeting facilities and services. New York City currently has nearly 70,000 hotel rooms, from budget to super-luxury, and hosts more conventions than any other United States city.

The above factors contribute to New York City's exceptional inherent value as a visitor destination.

Currently a $13 billion industry, tourism impacts every facet of city life. In 1990, over 25 million visitors, including daytrippers, came to the city. Their impact was significant: according to the United States Travel Data Center, total overnight visitors to New York City numbered 15.9 million and spent $9.6 billion in 1990—up 4.9% over 1989. The secondary impact or "multiplier effect" of this visitor spending generated an additional $3.0 billion during the year.

Total taxes generated by visitor spending stood at $1.8 billion in 1990, an increase of 6.0%. New York City realized $515.7 million of these visitor-generated revenues—funds necessary to support services for city residents. On average, each visitor dollar produces five cents in city tax revenues. More than $433 million in state tax revenues and $835 million in federal tax revenues were also generated by visitor spending in New York.

An estimated 124,100 jobs in all five boroughs are supported by visitor spending, approximately 3.5% of the city's total employment picture. Without these visitor-supported jobs, New York City's 1990 unemployment rate of 6.8% would have stood at approximately 10.1%.

International Visitors to New York City

New York City is the number one international gateway and the number one international visitor destination in the United States. Attracting more than 5.6 million international visitors in 1990, including four million overseas visitors, the city captured 14.4% of all international visitors to the nation.

Although the international visitor market segment has seen record increases in the past few years, New York City's position as the number one port-of-entry to overseas arrivals has weakened. In 1990, growth in arrivals to New York City did not match that of the United States—+3.7% compared to +7.5%. As a result, the city's share of overseas arrivals to the United States slipped from 24.0% in 1988 to 23.2% in 1990.

continued

EXCELLENCE CASE *continued*

**Where the New York City
Visitor Dollar Goes**
(1990)

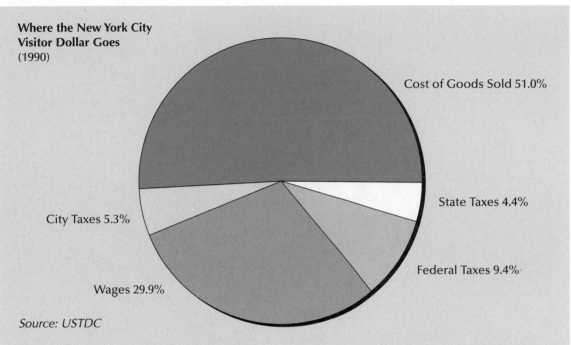

Cost of Goods Sold 51.0%

State Taxes 4.4%

Federal Taxes 9.4%

Wages 29.9%

City Taxes 5.3%

Source: USTDC

The growth in tourism projected through the decade from Eastern Bloc countries will first be felt in Western Europe, primarily through the friends and relatives market. Tourism from Eastern Europe should begin impacting the United States by the end of the century, with New York City as the principal recipient.

Domestic Visitors to New York City

Total visitor spending by United States residents exceeded $6.0 billion, approximately 1/3 of all domestic visitor expenditures in New York State and more than the domestic visitor spending in 36 other states and the District of Columbia. Although domestic spending slowed in 1990, with only a 2.7% rise over 1989, this segment still commands a 63% share of all New York City visitor spending.

Meetings & Conventions

The convention and meetings market is an important component of New York City's tourism industry. More meetings and conventions are held in New York than any other United States city.

In 1990, meetings and conventions booked or confirmed by the New York Convention &

Visitors Bureau numbered 761, a drop of 11.2% from 1989. Convention delegate attendance rose 13% to 3.3 million delegates. Out-of-town delegate attendance fell 14.5% to 1.3 million. Although delegate spending decreased 4.5% during the year, it still topped the $1 billion mark for the third straight year. These declines can be attributed, in part, to economic downturns in the nation. Long term concerns, such as pricing and date availability, threaten a strong recovery in this segment unless addressed.

An emerging world economy will stimulate more international congress meetings and trade shows in the United States, and through aggressive marketing New York City can become a prime recipient.

Future of New York City Tourism

Despite the economic uncertainties of the early 1990s, the future for New York City's tourism industry seems bright.
- Visitor spending in the year 2000 is expected to reach $16.5 billion, a 70.8% increase from 1990.
- City tax revenues are estimated to rise to $825.3 million, up 59.9%.

continued

EXCELLENCE CASE *continued*

Top New York City International Markets
(1990)

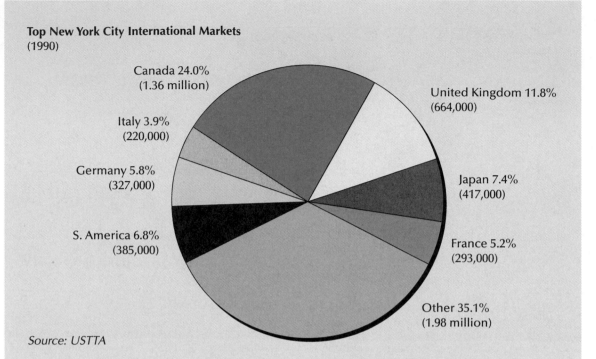

Canada 24.0%
(1.36 million)

Italy 3.9%
(220,000)

Germany 5.8%
(327,000)

S. America 6.8%
(385,000)

United Kingdom 11.8%
(664,000)

Japan 7.4%
(417,000)

France 5.2%
(293,000)

Other 35.1%
(1.98 million)

Source: USTTA

- State tax revenues are expected to rise 56.1% to $660.0 million.
- Visitor-generated payroll is expected to grow to $4.9 billion, a 70.6% increase.*

The Competition

Potential visitors are targets for the increasingly competitive global marketing efforts of numerous destinations. Currently, there are 38 countries that outspend the United States in their efforts to attract the international tourist. Competition closer to home includes those states and cities with marketing budgets larger than New York City and New York State.

Of particular concern is the severely declining budget of the New York State Division of Tourism. In 1989, New York State stood at the top of the 50 states and the District of Columbia with a budget of $21.0 million for advertising, marketing and matching funds programs. Since then the budget has been repeatedly slashed, dropping a total of 73.6% to $5.3 million in 1992. New York State currently ranks 28th in state tourism budgets and is losing much of the equity and competi-

tive advantage gained by the highly successful "I love NY" campaign.

Since New York City benefits greatly from the state's promotion and advertising program, it too is feeling the impact of these drastic budget reductions. Research on state tourism office spending suggests that aggressive budget growth is more important than budget size for capturing market share from other states. New York's budget reductions make the state and the city extremely vulnerable to loss of market share to other destinations.

Until recently, New York's tourism development budget placed the city at a decided disadvantage among its competitors. In fiscal year 1990, New York City ranked last among major United States cities in tourism funding with a budget of $3.5 million. The New York Convention & Visitors Bureau's (NYCVB) budget has increased dramatically in 1991 with a dedicated 7/8 of a 1/4 portion of the 1% city hotel occupancy tax enacted in September 1990. However, the NYCVB must now play catch-up to build the equity long enjoyed by its competitors.

continued

EXCELLENCE CASE *continued*

This will be a difficult task. Even with a near doubling of its tourism development budget, which currently stands at $7.1 million, New York City remains behind major competitors like Miami ($12.7 million), San Francisco ($11 million), Atlanta ($10 million) and Los Angeles ($9.9 million).

An aggressive response to the competition is necessary if New York City is to maintain a growing tourism industry. In addition to the intensification of competition, there are other major trends which must be addressed.

Future Travel Patterns

The United States Travel Data Center's landmark report, *Discover America 2000,* recognizes significant implications to the United States tourism industry in America's changing demographics and attitudes. Organized around seven generational groups in America, it forecasts travel behavior to the year 2000.

- **Depression Babies** and **World War I Babies** will reach 66+ years of age by the year 2000 and comprise about 16% of the population.

Although these groups have a low propensity toward travel, they will be good candidates for "Grand Travel"—traveling with grandchildren.

- **World War II Babies** will reach the ages of 55–65 by the year 2000 and comprise 11% of the population. Active travelers, this group will be a good market for group travel, cruises and travel clubs.
- **Early Baby Boomers** will reach the ages of 46–54 by 2000, and make up 18% of the United States population. Currently among the most prolific travelers, this group will be the premier travel market by the year 2000.
- **Late Baby Boomers** will reach the ages of 36–45 by the year 2000, comprise 21% of the population and exhibit an interest in specialty travel, travel without children and resort destinations.
- **Baby Busters** will comprise 17% of the population by the year 2000, when they reach the ages of 24–35. This group will exhibit a strong desire to travel but will be constrained by a lack of discretionary income, limited time and the responsibilities of family life.

New York City Visitor Spending

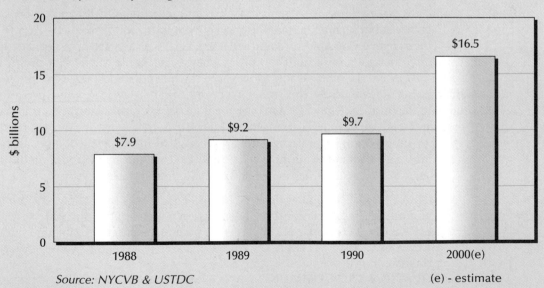

Source: NYCVB & USTDC   (e) - estimate

*These figures are based on an anticipated average annual spending increase of 5.5% for the 1990s. This average increase is based on the past performance of New York City's tourism industry, and overall economic projections for the region and the nation.

continued

EXCELLENCE CASE *continued*

- **Baby Boomlets** will be 12–23 years of age in the year 2000 and will comprise 17% of the population. Their limited resources will render them a relatively small travel market until beyond the first decade of the new century.

Discussion Questions

1. What are some of the problems that may be encountered in doing a situation analysis for a city as large as New York?

2. Which of the six steps in a situation analysis were covered in the New York City example?
3. Which steps did not seem to be covered and how could these steps have been carried out?
4. What other suggestions do you have about how this situation analysis could have been improved?

chapter, the material provides a good case study for you to consider. Once you have read the sections of New York's plan, there are a few discussion questions to answer.

THE MARKET ANALYSIS

Let us face the hard facts right away. Not every organization has a market or feasibility analysis. Some owners and executives do not see the value of these analyses. Others perform these analyses, but not for marketing purposes. Often, they are completed only to satisfy a lender's requirements. Still another group does them for marketing reasons and for lenders, but puts the analyses on the shelf on the day their business opens. Why do people not make greater use of this vital source of marketing information? There is no logical answer, but such people are wasting a good opportunity.

There are many reasons for doing a market analysis. When a new business is being considered, several groups need to see this analysis, including the developers and investors. They are the ones putting money into the business, and they want to be sure their money is spent wisely. Sometimes in our industry the developers and investors do not run the business. They hire a management group to do this. Many new hotels operate in this way under a legal arrangement known as a management contract. Lenders asked to supply loans or mortgages are also interested in seeing the market analysis. They must be sure that the business will be able to repay the loan amount on the date it is due. A market analysis has the same six steps as a situation analysis:

1. **MARKETING ENVIRONMENT ANALYSIS:** How will marketing environment and controllable factors affect the organization's direction and success?
2. **MARKET POTENTIAL ANALYSIS:** Is the potential market big enough?
3. **PRIMARY COMPETITOR ANALYSIS:** What are the strengths and weaknesses of primary competitors?
4. **LOCATION AND COMMUNITY ANALYSIS:** How will the site and community contribute to success?
5. **SERVICES ANALYSIS:** What services can be provided to match the needs of potential customers?
6. **MARKETING POSITION AND PLAN ANALYSIS:** How can the new business carve a niche for itself in the potential market?

Outside experts are usually hired to prepare market and feasibility analyses. Because they have no financial interest in the new business, their opinions and recommendations are objective. They are also very experienced in doing these studies. They have access to information on industry performance and the competition that other interested groups do not. External consultants and researchers have standardized approaches for completing market and feasibility analyses and only do what is asked of them. The marketing managers of the new business often have to do additional analysis. We include this fact so that you will not automatically assume that the outside expert's analysis is the only element of the first strategic market plan.

Completing the six steps in a market analysis is very similar to the process described earlier for the situation analysis. However, there are some differences in the two analysis techniques. Whereas the steps in the marketing environment and primary competitor analyses are almost identical to those used in the situation analysis, the other four analyses are not exactly the same.

1. ***Market Potential Analysis.*** When conducting a **market potential analysis,** a forecast of primary competitors' capacities and total market demand must be made. For a new hotel this refers to how many rooms both existing and new competitors will have in the future. Other organizations may be concerned about restaurant seats, retail stores, airplanes, buses, convention space, or other facilities. Growth rates for each market segment will also have to be projected. Comparing future supply and demand shows whether there is a gap that can be filled by the new business under consideration.

    Approaches for determining the size of the potential market for a new business are many and varied. One is to use the *pro rata* or *fair-share* method. The total market available to all primary competitors is calculated and then projected 5 to 10 years into the future. The new business is then assigned a share of total market equal to its share of total capacity (e.g., available room nights, restaurant seats, aircraft seats, travel agent personnel, etc.). For example, a new hotel with 20 percent of the available room nights in the community is allocated 20 percent of the projected occupied room nights. This method is easy to apply and is often used in this or a slightly modified way. However, it is imprecise and should only be used along with more detailed and sophisticated calculations. One involves estimating the demand from each individual market segment and forecasting the new business share of each one. The market shares projected are based on the results of the primary research into each market segment. Each interviewee or respondent must be asked to estimate his or her likelihood of using the new business.

2. ***Location and Community Analysis.*** The right **location** is a key determinant of the success of a new hospitality and travel business with fixed real-estate sites. The surrounding **community** is usually a major source of business, and its future prospects influence success. A market analyses must consider these two factors in great detail.

    Location and site analysis are extremely important in market analyses for lodging facilities, restaurants, travel agencies, attractions, shopping facilities, and other types of hospitality and travel businesses. For many years it has been accepted that, no matter how good an organization's marketing is, a poor site can lead to failure. The criteria for evaluating and selecting a site vary with the type of business. Urban hotels need to be close to offices and industrial areas. Motor hotels must have easy access and be close to highways. Restaurants usually need a combination of the two, plus a proximity to residential neighborhoods. Resorts must be near major recreational resources or attractions. Whatever the business, the criteria for selecting a site are divided into three groups: market-related, site-related, and other. Market-related factors are those that affect the customers' convenience in using the business. Site-related criteria deal with the physical characteristics of the site. Other criteria include legal considerations and land costs.

Market-related criteria are of primary importance to marketing. Success for many hospitality and travel businesses means being as close as possible to their customers. As we said earlier, one expert believes that 75 to 80 percent of a restaurant's business comes from no more than a 10-minute drive away. New lodging facilities often take market share away from existing properties by locating closer to customers. Without a doubt, the more convenient a location is for customers, the greater its success potential.

Site accessibility and visibility are two other factors related to proximity. How easy is it to get to the site? Is the site clearly visible? The best site location for most hospitality and travel businesses is not only one closest to customers but also one easily accessible and highly visible. Many fast-food restaurants, for example, are highly dependent on their stores' (or their signs') visibility and convenient access.

3. *Services Analysis.* What services can the new business provide to meet the needs of potential customers? This means combining all previous information and judging which services will best satisfy customer needs. Some authors talk about this as a product analysis or the product-service mix. The term *services analysis* better matches the nature of our industry. Combining research findings and a knowledge of what actually works in the business accomplishes this most effectively.

The first step is deciding on the format and quality of the service. Does the market indicate the need for a cafeteria or a table-service restaurant? Will a motor hotel or an all-suite property better satisfy customer needs? Does the community need a full-service travel agency or one specializing in corporate travel? Within each format, different quality levels are possible. Primary research results should be the deciding factor.

Determining the size of the facilities is step two. How big should they be, based on the size of the potential market? For hotels, this means the number of guest rooms, restaurant and bar seats, and convention and meeting rooms. Other interior spaces, such as the lobby and reception area, kitchens, and recreational facilities, are sized and designed next.

4. *Marketing Position and Plan Analysis.* What is the market niche or marketing position that the new business will occupy, and how will it earn this position? These are the last two questions in the market analysis. Again, this step is based on research findings and the judgment of the people completing the market analysis. The answers to these two questions define a number of unique features of the new business that can be used in positioning it. The concept of positioning (developing a service and marketing mix to occupy a specific place in the minds of customers within target markets) is discussed in Chapter 8.

THE FEASIBILITY ANALYSIS OR STUDY

Four more steps are added when completing a feasibility analysis or study: (1) pricing analysis, (2) income and expense analysis, (3) development cost analysis, and (4) analysis of return on investment and economic feasibility. Figure 5–12 shows the

```
┌─────────────────────────────────────────────────┐
│ FEASIBILITY ANALYSIS                              │
│                                                   │
│ ┌───────────────────────────────────────────┐    │
│ │ MARKET ANALYSIS                            │    │
│ │   1.    Environmental Analysis             │    │
│ │   2.    Market Potential Analysis          │    │
│ │   3.    Primary Competitor Analysis        │    │
│ │   4.    Location and Community Analysis     │    │
│ │   5.    Services Analysis                   │    │
│ │   6.    Marketing Position and Plan Analysis│    │
│ └───────────────────────────────────────────┘    │
│                                                   │
│   7.    Pricing Analysis              FOUR ADDITIONAL │
│   8.    Income and Expense Analysis   STEPS ARE   │
│   9.    Development Cost Analysis     INVOLVED IN A│
│  10.    Analysis of Return on Investment and  FEASIBILITY │
│         Economic Feasibility          ANALYSIS    │
└─────────────────────────────────────────────────┘
```

◆ FIGURE 5–12   *Relationship of market and feasibility analyses.*

relationship of the feasibility analysis to a marketing analysis. It indicates that part of the feasibility analysis is, in fact, a market analysis.

1. **Pricing Analysis.** What prices or rates can the new business hope to command? This question is answered by carefully considering the prices of primary competitors, together with the responses of potential customers to price-related questions in the market potential analysis. Again, this usually requires separate analyses for each distinct target market. Hotels, for example, often have special rates for corporate travelers, convention/meeting attendees, people on group tours, and government personnel. In addition, prices normally vary according to a specific time period—by time of day for restaurants, day of the week (or weekend) for city hotels, and season for resorts.

   This type of pricing exercise takes considerable experience and judgment, as well as in-depth knowledge of the pricing system used in the relevant part of the hospitality and travel industry. This is also a facet of analysis with which independent consultants tend to be very effective because of their knowledge and experience with similar situations.

2. **Income and Expense Analysis.** The next step is to estimate the revenues, operating expenses, and profits for the new business. A *pro forma* **(projected) income statement** is prepared that generally covers 5 to 20 years. The demand expected from each target market is multiplied by the applicable rate or price to arrive at a sales forecast for each target market. These figures are then totaled to give an aggregate income estimate. Operating expenses are costs incurred directly in running the business, such as labor, food and other materials, energy, administration, marketing, and maintenance.

   Secondary information can be useful in preparing estimates of prices, sales volumes, and operating costs. Several organizations publish hospitality and travel industry average operating statistics. Arthur Andersen, Ernst & Young, PKF Consulting, D. K. Shifflet & Associates, and Smith Travel Research are five firms that produce periodic reports and statistical data on the United States lodging industry. Smith Travel Research's "Lodging Outlook" provides data on room occupancy percentages, average room rates, room sales, room supply, and room demand for the United States as a whole, by census region, by type and location of hotel, and for selected U.S. cities.[4] D. K. Shifflet & Associates' "DIRECTIONS Travel Intelligence System" provides in-depth information about business and pleasure travelers, including demographics, trip purposes, transportation modes, lodging choices, spending levels, and satisfaction with lodging facilities used.[5] Travel Weekly provides the Louis Harris and Associates "United States Travel Agency Survey" that includes information on U.S. travel agency revenues, revenue sources, and costs.[6]

3. **Development Cost Analysis.** How much will it cost to develop the new business? This forecast is often called a **capital budget** (a projection of the capital investment expected in a new hospitality or travel business). In our industry, development costs normally include building construction, equipment, furniture and fixtures, professional fees (e.g., for architects and designers), infrastructure (e.g., roads, electrical and sewerage service), and contingencies. The most accurate capital budgets result when a multidisciplinary team of consultants, architects, engineers, interior designers, and landscape architects is used.

   Next, capital-related expenses, including long-term financing, property taxes, depreciation, and insurance charges for fixed assets (e.g., buildings and equipment), are estimated. The capital-related expenses are then deducted from operating profits to arrive at net income and cash-flow figures.

4. **Analysis of Return on Investment and Economic Feasibility.** The final feasibility analysis step involves the calculation of the return on investment and, based on this, the **economic feasibility** of the new business. The net income, cash flow figures, and capital budget forecast are then compared. A time-value, financial analysis technique such as the net-present-value or internal-rate-of-return method is best for this type of analysis. These techniques indicate the rate of return the new business will produce. If the return is high enough, the business is considered to be economically feasible.

CHAPTER CONCLUSION

Good marketing decisions usually result from research and careful analysis of research findings. A situation analysis is done for an existing business and represents the first step in the hospitality and travel marketing system.

The situation analysis focuses an organization's attention on its strengths and weaknesses, assists with long-term planning, helps in developing marketing plans, and puts a priority on marketing research. The six steps involved in such an analysis are environmental, location and community, primary competitor, market potential, services, and market position and plan.

Market and feasibility analyses are the techniques available for determining the optimum approaches for proposed new business.

REVIEW QUESTIONS

1. What are the differences between market, feasibility, and situation analyses?
2. Are these three analysis techniques related and, if so, how?
3. How often should each of these analyses be conducted?
4. What is the relationship between these three techniques and marketing research?
5. How does a situation analysis fit into the hospitality and travel marketing system?
6. What are the benefits of completing a situation analysis?
7. What are the steps involved in preparing a situation analysis?
8. What are the six components of a market analysis?

CHAPTER ASSIGNMENTS

1. Pick a hospitality and travel organization and decide how you would prepare a situation analysis for it. Where would you gather the necessary research information? Who would you involve in its preparation? If time permits, try to prepare the situation analysis and assess the organization's major strengths, weaknesses, and opportunities.

2. You have been asked to prepare a market analysis for a proposed new hotel, restaurant, attraction, or travel agency in your home town. Prepare a proposal outlining the steps you would follow in doing the analysis. What sources of information would you use? How long would it take to complete? What recommendations will it produce?

3. There are many similarities between market, feasibility, and situation analyses, but there are also important differences. Write a paper comparing these similarities and differences for an organization in a specific part of the hospitality and travel industry. Be sure to explain how each level of analysis builds upon previous ones.

4. A developer has asked you to prepare a feasibility study for a new restaurant, hotel, travel agency, or other hospitality and travel business. The developer asks you to write a detailed proposal describing the steps to be followed in the study. Prepare this proposal, trying to be as specific as possible about the approaches you would use in each feasibility study step.

WORLD WIDE WEB RESOURCES

Amtrak
http://www.amtrak.com/

Arthur Andersen
http://www.arthurandersen.com/
http://www.hotelbenchmark.com

D.K. Shifflet & Associates
http://www.dksa.com/

Ernst & Young
http://www.ey.com/

New York Convention & Visitors Bureau
http://www.nycvisit.com/

PKF Consulting (Pannell Kerr Forster)
http://www.pkfonline.com/

Site Reports
http://www.sitereports.com/

Smith Travel Research
http://www.str-online.com/

Travel Industry Association of America (TIA)
http://www.tia.org/travel/default.asp

U.S. Travel Agency Survey
http://www.twcrossroads.com/

REFERENCES

1. Suhr, G. Henrik. "The lodging market analysis." *Cornell Hotel & Restaurant Administration Quarterly* 22 (1):81–84, (1981).

2. Feltenstein, Tom. 1983. *Restaurant Profits through Advertising and Promotion: The Indispensable Plan.* New York: CBI Publishing Co., 2.

3. Troy, David A., and Paul Beals. "Hotel feasibility analysis, part II." *Cornell Hotel & Restaurant Administration Quarterly* 23 (3):61, (1982).

4. Smith Travel Research. *Lodging Outlook.* Gallatin, Tenn.: Smith Travel Research (published monthly).

5. American Demographics. "The best 100 sources for marketing information." *1993 Directory of Marketing Information,* 10.

6. Travel Weekly. Travel Weekly's U.S. Travel Agency Market Survey 2000. http://www.twcrossroads.com/

For additional hospitality and travel marketing resources, visit our Web site at **www.Hospitality-Tourism.delmar.com**

Marketing Research

Where Are We Now?

Objectives

Having read this chapter, you should be able to

- Define marketing research.

- Describe the reasons for doing marketing research (the five Cs) and explain why marketing research is sometimes not done.

- Explain how research is used in each step of the hospitality and travel marketing system.

- List and describe the five key requirements for good research information.

- List in order and explain the six steps in the marketing research process.

- Describe the internal and external sources of secondary research data.

- Explain the differences between primary and secondary research and list their respective advantages and disadvantages.

- List and describe the primary research methods and differentiate between quantitative and qualitative research.

- Explain the advantages and disadvantages of personal interviews, mail, telephone, in-house, self-administered, and on-line surveys.

- Explain the focus group approach and how it can be used in making effective marketing decisions.

Overview

*This chapter begins with a discussion of the importance of using research results to make marketing decisions. The reasons for doing and not doing marketing research are covered. The chapter then explains the role of research in each step of the hospitality and travel market-*ing system, and it presents a systematic, six-step procedure for doing marketing research.*

The distinction between primary and secondary research information is described. Various marketing research methods are identified and discussed.

Key Terms

accountability research	exploratory research	on-line surveys
case studies	external secondary research data	primary research
change	Five Cs	probability sampling
comment cards	focus groups	qualitative data
competitors	frequently asked questions (FAQs)	quantitative data
conclusive research	individual depth interviews	questionnaires
confidence	internal secondary research data	response rate
credibility	marketing research	secondary research
customers	marketing research program	simulation
databases	marketing research project	survey research
direct-response advertising	nonprobability sampling	test marketing
evaluation research	observational research	
experimental research	on-line research	

RESEARCH: NOURISHMENT FOR MARKETING

You are probably wondering what is so nourishing about marketing research. How can a subject so statistical and technique-laden be the lifeblood of the hospitality and travel marketing system? Aren't the creative sides of marketing, such as advertising and sales promotion, more important? The answer is an emphatic no. Good marketing decisions are usually based on marketing research.

The following quotes will give you a flavor of the importance of research and how it is used in the hospitality and travel industry:

Amtrak—"An extensive market-based research analysis is now underway to define consumer demand, identify opportunities for growth of rail service, and increase Amtrak's market share of America's travel business."[1]

Australian Tourist Commission—"In the first four months of 1999, use of the ATC Web site is up 167 percent from last year. From January to April, more than 4.3 million pages of www.australia.com were accessed, compared to 1.6 million over the same period last year."[2]

Cruise Lines International Association—"Nearly 1.2 million cruise vacationers are expected to choose Europe and Mediterranean itineraries this year, double the number a mere five years ago, according to Cruise Lines International Association. The European cruise market is flourishing, with a new ship making its debut and several vessels making maiden calls at new ports in 2000."[3]

Las Vegas Convention and Visitor Authority—"Las Vegas drew a record-breaking 33.8 million visitors in 1999, according to the Las Vegas Convention and Visitors Authority. The 10.5 percent increase over 1998's 30.6 million visitors is the highest spike in visitor volume recorded for the destination since 1994."[4]

Marriott International—"We continually solicit guest feedback and perform regular physical inspections to ensure that every property in the Marriott system is upholding the company's high standards."[5]

Pizza Hut—"A national survey commissioned by Pizza Hut revealed that 18–29 year-old males preferred pizza to ice cream, cookies, and candy when indulging their palates."[6]

ON THE WEB

◆ FIGURE 6–1   *The Las Vegas Convention and Visitors Authority uses its research to answer FAQs.* (Courtesy of the Las Vegas Convention and Visitors Authority)

Figure 6–1 shows a great application of the importance of market research information and how it can be distributed globally with the help of the Internet. Through its Web site, the Las Vegas Convention and Visitors Authority (LCVA) answers many **frequently asked questions (FAQs)** about the hospitality and travel industry. Without a good marketing research program, the LCVA would not be able to distribute this information.

DEFINITION OF MARKETING RESEARCH

According to the American Marketing Association (AMA), **marketing research** is "the function which links the consumer, customer, and public to the marketer through information." This information is used to do the following:

1. Identify and define marketing opportunities and problems.
2. Generate, refine, and evaluate marketing actions.

3. Monitor marketing performance.
4. Improve understanding of marketing as a process.

The AMA definition also states that "marketing research specifies the information required to address issues; designs the method for collecting information; manages and implements the data collection process; analyzes the results; and communicates the findings and their implications."[7]

REASONS FOR DOING MARKETING RESEARCH: THE FIVE Cs

Marketing research helps an organization make more effective marketing decisions. This is its primary objective. Good marketing decisions come from being better informed, and research supplies the information. There are five major reasons for doing marketing research and you will notice that these all start with the letter "C"—**the five Cs**:

1. Customers
2. Competitors
3. Confidence
4. Credibility
5. Change

The most important reason for doing marketing research is that it helps an organization develop a detailed knowledge of its **customers**, both past and potential. It gives the organization information on how well it is meeting customers' needs and on the organization's position in the market. New target markets are investigated through research. New services and facilities are assessed and tested through market and feasibility analyses, test marketing, and other product testing.

Competitive research is also a must in today's intensely competitive hospitality and travel industry. Research identifies primary **competitors** and pinpoints their strengths and weaknesses.

Well-designed research increases the **confidence** of an organization as well as its marketing partners when making marketing decisions. The perceived risk is reduced if the organization has developed an in-depth understanding of customer needs and characteristics as well as competitive strengths and weaknesses.

Research results can be used to add **credibility** to an organization's advertising campaigns. For example, research done by the organization itself or by others can be used effectively to back up advertising claims. Figures 6–2 and 6–3 show two examples of this use of research.

Domestic and international travel markets are in a constant state of **change**, as is the global hospitality and travel industry. Travelers' needs and expectations are also changing rapidly. Organizations must constantly keep up-to-date with these changes, and research is the primary tool for doing so.

REASONS FOR NOT DOING MARKETING RESEARCH

Having read this chapter so far, you are probably wondering how an organization survives without marketing research. We want to be totally realistic—many effective marketing decisions have been based on no research at all. The intuition and judgment of

You can expect many happy returns when you recommend Club Med.

Because if your clients are like most of our members, they'll be back an average of 4 times. What's more, they recommend Club Med's unique spirit of conviviality and philosophy of pure enjoyment to all their friends. For more information,

Call 1-800-CLUB MED

◆ FIGURE 6–2   *Club Med uses its research statistics to make a point with travel agents.* (Courtesy of Club Med)

On Maui, rocks talk, hands sing and angels swim.

Hālau Hula O Ka Makani Wili Mākaha O Kaua-ula. Kumu Hula: Keali'i Reichel.

Experience the magic that inspired the readers of Conde Nast Traveler to vote Maui the world's "Best Island" for the past six years. Wonder at petroglyphs carved eons ago into cliff walls and lava boulders. Journey back in time with Maui's traditional *kahiko* hula dancers. Discover an underwater heaven blessed with angelfish and their tropical brethren.

From the bustling whaling town of Lahaina – a National Historic Landmark – to 42 miles of pristine beaches, from the 10,000 ft. summit of Haleakala to soaring rain forest waterfalls, from Molokai's sea cliffs to Lanai's timeless Garden of the Gods, the tri-isles of Maui will surprise you and touch you with their heart of "aloha." Come to a place where the people are warmer than the sun. Maui, Molokai and Lanai – the Magic Isles.

MAUI *the Magic Isles*™
MAUI • MOLOKAI • LANAI

For a free, full-color Maui brochure, call the Maui Visitors Bureau at 1-800-525-MAUI. For an award-winning "Maui, the Magic Isle" video, call us at 1-800-892-MAUI ($5.95 including shipping and handling; please have your Visa or Mastercard ready). For more information on Molokai, call 1-800-800-6367. For more information on Lanai, call 1-800-947-4774. Or visit Maui on the web at: **www.visitmaui.com.**

◆ FIGURE 6–3   *Backing up advertising with others' research. The Maui Visitors Bureau uses the results of Condé Naste Traveler reader surveys to prove its point.* (Courtesy of Maui Visitors Bureau)

the decision-makers have turned out to be extremely accurate in some cases. Does this mean that marketing research is unnecessary? Is management intuition and judgment an acceptable substitute? The answer is no on both counts. Intuition is not a good substitute for research. On the other hand, research cannot take the place of intuition and judgment. The best marketing decisions come from a blend of research, intuition, and judgment. Effective marketing managers know the advantages of marketing research and how to use it. They are also aware of the limitations and the need to inject their own intuition and judgment.

Following are reasons for not doing marketing research.

1. Timing
2. Cost
3. Reliability
4. Competitive intelligence
5. Management decision

A research project such as a survey can take several months to complete. The decision for which the research information is needed may have to be made in just a few weeks. Research can be very expensive, and its costs may outweigh its value. There may also be no reliable method available to answer a specific research question. When conclusions such as these are reached rationally and with full information, research may have to be replaced completely by intuition and judgment.

There is another reason why research is not done. A company considering a new service or product may be concerned that doing a research study in full public view might provide valuable information to its closest competitors. These competitors may try to imitate the new service or product offerings.

There are many managers who do not care for research or understand its value. They are content to fly solo and by the seat of their pants, using intuition and judgment to make a decision. A crash landing is usually not too far ahead. Intuition and judgment tend to be based on past experience. The future often is nothing like the past. These managers seldom see all sides of a problem or opportunity. They frequently fail to identify all alternative approaches. As a result, their marketing decisions may not be as effective as they could have been with some research.

USING RESEARCH IN THE HOSPITALITY AND TRAVEL MARKETING SYSTEM STEPS

Figure 6–4 indicates that research must be done during all five steps in the hospitality and travel marketing system (Chapter 3). It shows the relationship of marketing research to the five marketing tasks (PRICE—planning, research, implementation, control, and evaluation) and to the five steps in the hospitality and travel marketing system.

Now let's take a quick look at how research is used in each step of the hospitality and travel marketing system.

1. Where Are We Now? (Research for Planning and Analysis)

The first step in the hospitality and travel marketing system requires researching and analyzing the marketing environment, location and community, primary competitors,

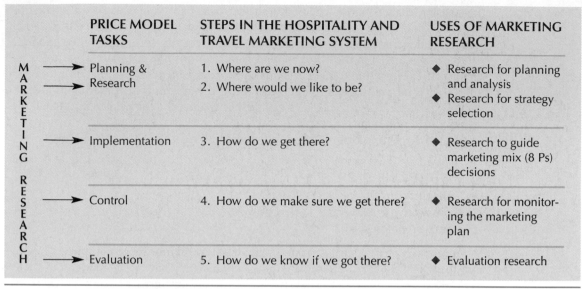

	PRICE MODEL TASKS	STEPS IN THE HOSPITALITY AND TRAVEL MARKETING SYSTEM	USES OF MARKETING RESEARCH
M A R K E T I N G R E S E A R C H	Planning & Research	1. Where are we now? 2. Where would we like to be?	◆ Research for planning and analysis ◆ Research for strategy selection
	Implementation	3. How do we get there?	◆ Research to guide marketing mix (8 Ps) decisions
	Control	4. How do we make sure we get there?	◆ Research for monitoring the marketing plan
	Evaluation	5. How do we know if we got there?	◆ Evaluation research

◆ **FIGURE 6–4** *Relationship of marketing research to hospitality and travel marketing system.*

past and potential customers, services, market position, and past marketing plans—the research for a situation analysis. Figure 6–4 shows the research needs and questions for all five steps in the system.

2. Where Would We Like to Be? (Research for Strategy Selection)

Marketing research helps an organization select target markets, marketing mixes, and positioning approaches. It assists with the development of a marketing strategy. Here research looks at the advantages and disadvantages of alternative courses of action, another element of planning. Organizations use this type of research when considering possible new marketing strategies—new target markets and ways of attracting customers in these markets. A restaurant chain may be considering adding a delivery service, whereas a hotel chain may investigate the addition of a new brand of property. Many "What if we did this?" questions can be tackled in this way, using marketing research.

3. How Do We Get There? (Research to Guide Marketing Mix Decisions)

Marketing research assists an organization in the development of the marketing plan by assessing the potential effectiveness of specific promotional campaigns and other specific marketing mix activities. This research helps with decisions on how to use the 8Ps (product, price, place, promotion, packaging, programming, partnership, and people) in the upcoming marketing plan by investigating and testing out alternative approaches.

4. How Do We Make Sure We Get There? (Research for Monitoring the Marketing Plan)

You should realize that once the marketing plan is implemented, marketing research does not stop. It takes great effort to research, analyze, and develop a marketing plan.

This effort does not stop on day one of the marketing plan. In fact, a plan must be constantly monitored to see whether its marketing objectives are being achieved and to determine if adjustments are needed. Research is used to check progress at specific times during the implementation of the marketing plan.

5. How Do We Know If We Got There? (Research for Evaluation)

Although often overlooked, this is a crucial application of marketing research. A marketing plan is effective only if it achieves stated objectives. Research assists in measuring the results of the plan. This is often referred to as evaluation research or accountability research.

When the marketing plan comes to an end, one major question must be answered. Did we reach our objectives? Research helps measure and evaluate the results. The plan's objectives may have been expressed in numbers of customers by target market, in dollar sales volumes, or in a variety of other ways. Measuring the results of a marketing plan is rather like tallying the votes in a political election. But it is not just a simple yes-no process. The results also have to be evaluated. What do the results mean for future marketing plans? How should marketing activities be adjusted for greater effectiveness? What worked? What did not work?

Figure 6–5 shows the specific research needs and questions for each of the five steps.

---

1. WHERE ARE WE NOW? RESEARCH FOR PLANNING AND ANALYSIS

Needs	Research Questions
1. Trends in the marketing environment	• How will marketing environment factors affect the organization's direction and future success?
2. Trends affecting location and community	• How will the location and community contribute to the organization's future success?
3. Strengths and weaknesses of primary competitors	• What are the strengths and weaknesses of the organization's primary competitors?
4. Current target market characteristics and penetration	• Who are the organization's customers and what are they like?
5. Characteristics and size of potential target markets	• Should the organization pursue specific new target markets?
6. Current market position	• What images do the organization's customers have of the organization?
7. Evaluation of past marketing plans	• How effective have the organization's past marketing programs been?

2. WHERE WOULD WE LIKE TO BE? RESEARCH FOR STRATEGY SELECTION

Needs	Research Questions
1. Needs and characteristics of overall market	• How should the market be segmented?
2. Market trends by segment	• What recent trends have occurred in each market segment?

continued

◆ FIGURE 6–5   *Research needs and questions for steps in the hospitality and travel marketing system.*

3. Benefits and services that match needs of segments' customers

4. Likelihood and amount of use by customers in a given target market

5. Potential effectiveness of alternative approaches to positioning

6. Potential effectiveness of alternative marketing mix approaches for each target market

- Which market segments are available to the organization?

- Which market segments should the organization target?

- How effective are different positioning approaches for the organization likely to be?

- How effective are different marketing mix approaches for each target market likely to be?

3. HOW DO WE GET THERE? RESEARCH TO GUIDE MARKETING MIX DECISIONS

Needs	Research Questions
1. Potential effectiveness of specific promotional activities or campaigns	• Which promotional activities or campaigns should the organization use?
2. Potential effectiveness of specific distribution mix approaches	• Which distribution channels should the organization use?
3. Potential effectiveness of specific pricing approaches	• Which pricing approaches should the organization use?
4. Potential effectiveness of specific packaging and programming approaches	• Which packaging and programming approaches should the organization use?
5. Potential effectiveness of specific partnership arrangements	• Should the organization cooperate with other organizations in certain marketing programs?
6. Potential effectiveness of specific service quality training programs	• What service quality training approaches and programs should the organization use?

4. HOW DO WE MAKE SURE WE GET THERE? RESEARCH FOR MONITORING THE MARKETING PLAN

Needs	Research Questions
1. Progress in achieving marketing objectives	• Does it look as if the organization will achieve each of the marketing plan's objectives?
2. Progress in using positioning approaches	• Are the selected positioning approaches working as planned?
3. Progress in using specific promotional campaigns and other specific marketing mix activities	• Are the promotional campaigns and other selected marketing mix activities working as planned?
4. Changes in customer satisfaction levels	• How have customer satisfaction levels changed since the service quality training programs were implemented?

continued

◆ FIGURE 6–5   *continued.*

5. HOW DO WE KNOW IF WE GOT THERE? RESEARCH FOR EVALUATION

Needs	Research Questions
1. Level of success in achieving marketing objectives for each target market	• To what extent did the organization achieve the objectives for each target market?
2. Success of specific marketing mix approaches, campaigns, and other activities	• To what extent were promotional campaigns and other specific marketing mix activities effective in achieving their objectives?
3. Changes in customer satisfaction levels	• How did customer satisfaction levels change since the implementation of the marketing plan?

◆ FIGURE 6–5   *continued.*

KEY REQUIREMENTS FOR GOOD RESEARCH INFORMATION

Before discussing specific techniques, it is important to establish what we mean by good research. The key requirements are as follows:

1. Utility
2. Timeliness
3. Cost-Effectiveness
4. Accuracy
5. Reliability

1. **Utility.** Marketing research can be expensive and time consuming. Money and staff time can be saved by gathering only information that can be used. There is a tendency in many research activities to collect *nice-to-know* as well as *must-know* data. The *nice-to-know* information often has limited value. Having clear research objectives is the key here. These objectives are translated into a number of questions to be answered. Only the information that specifically addresses these questions should be collected.

2. **Timeliness.** Timeliness of the research results is also important. Again, it requires some preplanning to determine when the results are needed for decision making. A decision may be needed by the end of the month, but a survey would take three months to complete. In this case, the decision makers may have to rely on secondary research, because it is available almost immediately.

3. **Cost-Effectiveness.** Some nationwide research projects cost hundreds of thousands of dollars. The expense can be justified because the decisions they affect are worth millions or even billions. However, it does not make any sense to conduct a $100,000 research project on a problem or opportunity worth only $10,000. The research expenditure must be directly related to the expected value of investigating the opportunity or solving the problem.

4/5. **Accuracy and Reliability.** Two related requirements are that research information must be accurate and reliable. Accuracy in both primary and secondary research is essential. The decision maker has to be sure that the methods and calculations used to arrive at the data are technically correct. As we see later, this is easier to do with primary research. Reliability means that if the same or similar research was done, the result should be approximately the same. If research information is unreliable, it is not a good predictor of what will actually happen when an organization tackles a problem or opportunity.

THE MARKETING RESEARCH PROCESS

Before discussing the research process, it is important to realize that each project should be part of a marketing research program. A **marketing research program** is a plan developed by an organization to investigate several opportunities or problems. **Marketing research projects** are different. Programs outline what is to be researched. Projects deal with how the opportunities and problems in the program are to be researched. Programs usually have routine and one-time research components. For example, Walt Disney World decided that its program should collect demographic information on guests and their satisfaction with the park's services. The next decision was that information should be collected routinely because there was a continual need for it. Therefore, their guest survey is repeated several times a year. Walt Disney World's program could also include one or more one-time research studies. Let us assume that a special, one-time season's entrance pass was made available to Orlando residents. The season-ticket purchasers could be surveyed to determine what they liked and disliked about the offer.

Marketing research projects are most effective if they follow the six sequential steps shown in Figure 6–6.[8]

1. **Problem Formulation.** Step 1 in the marketing research process is to define the problem or opportunity to be studied. We just said that the marketing research program outlines what is to be researched. For example, Taco Bell decided that it needed to track customer awareness of its advertising and in-store sales promotions (merchandising). Its research problem is promotional awareness. This is a broad problem statement. More detail is required before a decision can be made on how to research it. This comes from drawing one or more research objectives from the problem statement. By deciding on research objectives, an organization is in a better position to decide what research method to use and what questions to ask. Figure 6–6 actually shows two component tasks for step 1—defining the research problem and deciding on research objectives.

2. **Research Design and Data Collection Method.** Having pinpointed research objectives and related questions, the organization's next steps are to choose a research design and a method for collecting the information. The first question to be asked is whether we should use *primary* or *secondary research*, or both. **Primary research** is data collected for the first time, by a method other than secondary research, to answer specific questions. It is sometimes also referred to as original research. **Secondary research** is previously gathered information available from internal or external sources. Later in this chapter, you will learn about the respective advantages of primary and secondary research and how to use both of them.

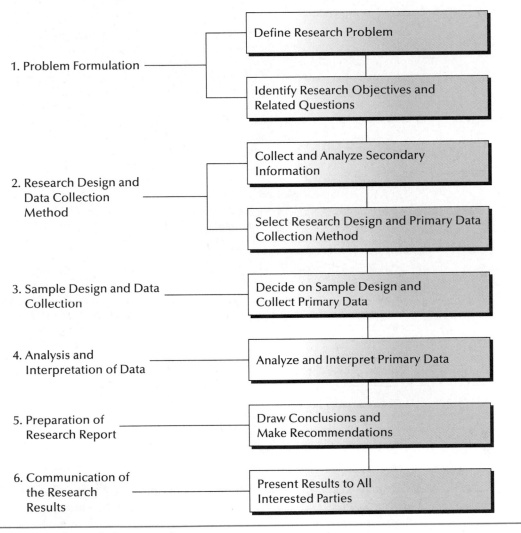

◆ FIGURE 6–6   *The marketing research process.*

3. **Sample Design and Data Collection.** The third step is setting up the sample design and collecting the information. A sample design consists of three elements:

   a. Sample frame
   b. Sample selection process
   c. Sample size

   a. *Sample Frame.* The sample frame determines which groups are to be covered by the research. Walt Disney World uses the sample frame of its in-park visitors. Many hotels and restaurants also do in-house and in-store customer research.
   b. *Sample Selection Process.* Nonprobability and probability sample selection can be used. Nonprobability samples are drawn on the basis of convenience or judgment. They are less accurate than probability samples. **Nonprobability sampling** is a subjective sample-selection approach where every person in the group does *not* have a known probability of being in the sample. Probability samples

1. **SIMPLE RANDOM:** All respondents have an equal chance of being selected. This can be done simply by putting all names into a bowl, mixing them, and then picking out the desired number of names for the sample. Another technique is to use random number tables (a table of numbers randomly generated by computer that correspond to every potential respondent in the sample frame).

2. **SYSTEMATIC:** A system is developed to pick and spread the sample randomly throughout the list of potential respondents. This is common in telephone surveys. A number is selected randomly, let us say seven. The seventh name from the top of each phone book page would be selected for the sample.

3. **STRATIFIED RANDOM:** Here it is recognized that there are distinct subgroupings of respondents (e.g., business versus vacation travelers). The list of respondents is subdivided ("stratified") into these groups and then samples are randomly selected from within each subgroup.

4. **CLUSTER SAMPLING:** Those to be researched are divided into subgroups, and a number of these subgroups (clusters) are randomly selected. *All members* of each cluster are surveyed. For example, a hotel might randomly select days of the year to survey its overnight guests and then survey all the guests on these randomly selected days.

5. **AREA SAMPLING:** This is a type of cluster sampling used when lists of all potential respondents are not available. Areas (e.g., blocks within a city) are randomly selected and all persons or households in the areas are surveyed.[9]

◆ **FIGURE 6–7**   *Probability sampling techniques.*

are arrived at using a more scientific and objective approach. **Probability sampling** (where every person in the group to be researched has a known, nonzero probability of being in the sample) techniques are shown in Figure 6–7.

   c. *Sample Size.* Choosing the sample size depends on how precise the information needs to be. The most precise data come from using an established mathematical formula. Describing these formulae is beyond the scope of this book, but you can find a detailed description in most marketing research texts. So we will move right on to the analysis and interpretation of data.

4. **Analysis and Interpretation of Data.** The *raw* data is of limited value. It has to be analyzed and interpreted carefully to be of any use. Four separate tasks are involved:

   a. **Editing.** Checking the data for errors, omissions, and ambiguities.

   b. **Coding.** Specifying how responses are to be entered into a computer, e.g., for a yes-no question, a yes could be entered as a 1 and a no as a 0.

   c. **Tabulating.** Calculating and arranging the answers to questions in tabular form—often done by a computerized statistical analysis program, but also manually.

   d. **Applying statistical tests and procedures.** Carrying out various types of statistical procedures and tests, such as chi-square statistics, correlation, regression, and factor-cluster analysis.

5. **Preparation of Research Report.** What does the research mean? This step involves drawing conclusions and recommendations for management and presenting them in a report format.

6. **Communication of the Research Results.** The marketing research process is only successful if the research results are effectively communicated to key decision makers and other parties. Having a research report is only part of the answer. The researchers must clearly highlight the key research results and communicate them in a way that the audience fully comprehends.

Secondary Research

Chapter 5 warned against reinventing the wheel in research. Answers may already be available through *secondary research* (previously gathered information available from internal or external sources). Figure 6–8 shows the types of secondary research data that are available to hospitality and travel organizations. The two broad categories are internal secondary research data (information contained within the organization's own records) and external secondary research data (information previously published by an outside organization).

Internal Data

Examples of internal secondary data include registration and reservation records, sales-mix and customer-mix information, databases, inquiry records, and turnaway statistics. Most hospitality and travel organizations, including hotels, airlines, car rental firms, restaurants, tour operators and wholesalers, and cruise lines, take reservations. Of course, travel agencies also make reservations for their customers. Some hospitality and travel organizations, such as hotels, are required by law to *register* guests. This registration information can be an important source of secondary research information. Have you been asked for your zip or postal code lately? Many theme parks and other attractions gather zip/postal code information at their entrances. This not only lets these attractions know where their guests live but, when used along with zip/postal code databases from outside companies, provides demographic and lifestyle information on the attractions' customers.

Sales- and customer-mix records are another important internal secondary research data source, since they are an indicator of business trends and marketing success. As marketing objectives are often expressed in sales or customer volume targets, sales- and customer-mix records are an important tool in marketing control and evaluation. Sales-mix figures provide information on sales volume by profit center (e.g., rooms, food and beverage, telephone, minor operated, and rentals and other income in a hotel). Some measures of supply capacity usage and customer volumes, such as hotel occupancy percentages and occupied room nights, restaurant covers, passenger volumes, and attraction attendance volumes, should be available. Customer-mix figures should include sales revenues and customer counts by target market.

Some hospitality and travel organizations, including casinos, hotels, and airlines, go further than this and maintain large internal databases on individual customers. In creating frequent traveler and other club programs, these organizations have developed powerful databases of information on individual customer sales, demographics, and preferences.

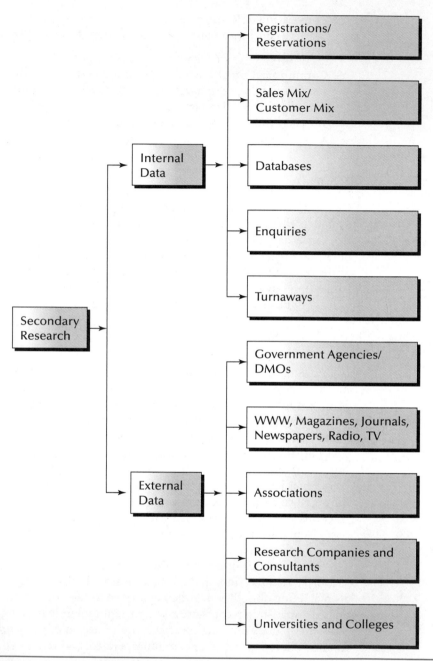

◆ **FIGURE 6–8** *Sources of secondary research data.*

Many hospitality and travel organizations receive enquiries directly from customers or from travel trade intermediaries. These enquiries can be by telephone, mail, fax, e-mail, or in person. Since enquiries are another indicator of marketing success, it is important for an organization to maintain records of them. Much of today's hospitality and travel advertising is **direct-response advertising**, in which the potential customer must call a given telephone number, write to a given address, send back a completed coupon, or complete and submit a Web-based form (Figure 6–12). A good example of measuring the results of direct-response advertising is its use by state and provincial government travel offices. The task of handling these inquiries is often called *fulfillment* and provides the agencies with an important database of potential visitors.

Turnaway statistics represent *frustrated demand* or reservations that cannot be accepted or honored because the organization is already at full capacity. It is important that the organization record turnaways (some of whom are *walks* or *bumps* resulting from the industry's practice of overbooking), since these customers represent another measure of marketing success. The statistics are also useful if the organization is considering an expansion of its capacity.

External Data

Figure 6–8 shows that external secondary research data can be obtained from government agencies and other destination marketing organizations, the World Wide Web, magazines, journals and newspapers, radio and television stations, trade and travel associations, research companies and other private consulting organizations, and universities. Government agencies and other destination marketing organizations, including convention and visitor bureaus, are major providers of hospitality and travel industry research. These include the Bureau of Tourism Research (BTR) in Australia, the British Tourist Authority, The Canadian Tourism Commission, and the U.S. Tourism Industries Office, as well as the many state, provincial, and territorial tourism offices in these countries.

Magazines, journals, newspapers, radio, and television provide marketers with information on their subscribers, readers, listeners, or viewing audiences. In addition, these organizations may conduct specific surveys or other research studies on customer characteristics and preferences as well as *state-of-the-industry* studies. Some of the more prominent state-of-the-industry studies conducted periodically by hospitality and travel industry magazines and newspapers are shown in Figure 6–9. Media research information is also available through certain private research firms including A.C. Nielsen Co., Arbitron, Mediamark Research, Simmons Market Research Bureau, and Roper Starch.

Trade and travel associations sponsor and publish considerable research on the hospitality and travel industry. Some of these research studies are done periodically (Figure 6–9), whereas others are completed on special topics or issues on a one-time basis. The Cruise Lines International Association (CLIA) conducts a periodic study of cruise ship capacity, passenger volumes, and customer satisfaction levels. The National Restaurant Association prepares an annual report of the average operating performance levels of restaurants in the United States.

Research companies and other private consultants are a major provider of hospitality and travel industry research. These companies either sell their research reports or restrict their distribution to a specific group of research sponsors who each pay part of the cost of the research. Some companies specialize in specific parts of the hospitality and travel industry, whereas others provide broader statistics on travel volumes and patterns (Figure 6–9).

Universities and colleges conduct a large volume of research on the hospitality and travel industry. Much of this is published in major academic journals, such as *The Cornell Hotel and Restaurant Administration Quarterly, Journal of Travel Research, Tourism Management,* and *Annals of Tourism Research,* or is presented at major research and educators' conferences.

External Data Sources	**Magazines, Journals, and Newspapers**
Auto Rental News Fact Book	• Auto Rental News
Hotels' 325	• Hotels
Meetings Market Report	• Meetings & Conventions
The NRN Top 100	• Nation's Restaurant News
The State of the Industry Report	• Successful Meetings
Top U.S. Hotel Chain Survey	• Business Travel News
U.S. Consumer Survey	• Travel Weekly
U.S. Travel Agency Survey (Louis Harris)	• Travel Weekly

	Trade and Travel Associations
Amusement Facility Operations Survey	• International Association of Amusement Parks and Attractions (IAAPA)
Annual Report of the U.S. Scheduled Airline Industry	• Air Transport Association
Convention Income Survey Report	• International Association of Convention & Visitor Bureaus (IACVB)
Corporate Travel Survey	• International Air Transport Association (IATA)
Economic Impact Report on the Travel & Tourism Industry	• American Hotel & Motel Association
Incentive Federation Survey	• Incentive Federation
Incentive Travel Factbook	• Society of Incentive & Travel Executives (SITE)
National Travel Survey	• Travel Industry Association of America (TIA)
Restaurant Industry Operations Report	• National Restaurant Association (NRA)
Technology and Travel Report	• TIA
The Cruise Industry: An Overview	• Cruise Lines International Association
The Economic Impact of Conventions, Expositions, Meetings & Incentive Travel	• Convention Industry Council (formerly Convention Liaison Council)
Tour Traveler Index	• National Tour Foundation
U.S. Amusement Industry Consumer Survey	• IAAPA

	Research Companies and Consultants
American Traveler Survey	• Plog Research
DKS&A DIRECTIONS	• D.K. Shifflet & Associates
HOST (Hotel Operating Statistic) Study	• Smith Travel Research
Interactive Traveler Survey	• Plog Research
J.D. Power and Associates Domestic Airline Frequent Flyer Customer Satisfaction Study	• J.D. Power and Associates
Trends in the Hotel Industry	• PKF Consulting
Leisure TRAK	• Leisure Trends Group
Survey of International Air Travelers	• CIC Research/Tourism Industries Office

◆ FIGURE 6–9   *External sources of secondary research data in the hospitality and travel industry.*

	SECONDARY RESEARCH	PRIMARY RESEARCH
ADVANTAGES	1. Inexpensive 2. Easily accessible 3. Immediately available	1. Applicable and usable 2. Accurate and reliable 3. Up-to-date
DISADVANTAGES	1. May not be applicable 2. Potentially unreliable 3. Frequently outdated	1. Expensive 2. Not as readily accessible 3. Not available immediately

◆ FIGURE 6–10   *Advantages and Disadvantages of Primary and Secondary Research.*

As you can see, there is a great amount of secondary research information available in the hospitality and travel industry. It is always a good practice to begin a research project by collecting and analyzing secondary data. This may answer some of the research questions or none at all. However, collecting these data means that the organization knows that research dollars are being used in the most effective way. Having done a thorough search, the organization may find that the information needed is not available through internal and external secondary data. When an organization reaches this conclusion, it must conduct primary research if the funds are available to do so. Before looking at primary research, you would probably like to know about the pros and cons of secondary research, which are shown in Figure 6–10.

Did You Know?

The Gallup Organization/CNN/USA Today did a poll during 1999 on vacations. The following responses were received to the question, "If you were trying to design a perfect vacation on a trip away from home, would each of the following be something you would try to do, or not?"

✓ Seek out good food and restaurants (92% said yes)
✓ See a museum, play, or other cultural activity (82%)
✓ Spend time with friends or family you normally don't see (80%)
✓ Try to meet new people (73%)
✓ Shop (72%)
✓ Participate in a sport or hobby you regularly engage in (63%)
✓ Participate in a sport or activity you don't normally have a chance to do (59%)
✓ Read a book (58%)
✓ Get a suntan (43%)
✓ Engage in vigorous exercise (39%)

Source: *The Gallup Organization, Princeton, NJ.* http://www.gallup.com/

Primary Research

Primary (or original) research is data collected for the first time, by a method other than secondary research, to answer specific questions. When it is done, this normally happens after some secondary research information has been collected and analyzed. The advantages and disadvantages of primary research are shown in Figure 6–10.

So you now want the answer to the question posed earlier: Should we use primary or secondary research, or both? We hope you have already guessed the answer. It is usually *both*. Although there are some occasions when an organization cannot afford the time and expense required for primary research, secondary research is usually insufficient for making major marketing decisions. It can help shape primary research information collection but cannot take its place.

Choosing the primary research method is the next hurdle to be surmounted. Two broad categories of research design exist: exploratory and conclusive. Secondary research falls into the exploratory category, along with several primary research methods (e.g., focus groups). Exploratory research sheds more light on the problem or opportunity. Conclusive research helps solve the problem or assess the opportunity.

Dividing primary research methods by the type of data they provide is another common approach. Figure 6–11 shows that the two major divisions of data are *quantitative* (numerical) and *qualitative* (nonnumerical). Generally, the conclusive research methods produce quantitative data, whereas the exploratory primary research methods provide qualitative information.

Selecting the most appropriate design and method depends on several factors. The selection is based mainly on the research problem and objectives, how much is already known about them, and how the results are to be used. Figure 6–11 displays the alternative primary research methods. Four of these methods—(1) experiments, (2) mechanical observation, (3) surveys, and (4) simulation—can be used to produce quantitative data. The four other methods—(5) focus groups, (6) individual depth interviews, (7) human observation, and (8) case studies—normally provide researchers with qualitative data.

Quantitative Primary Research Methods

1. **Experiments.** You probably associate the word experiment with the science classes you had in school. Scientists, in fact, carry out many experiments to test their beliefs. Experimental research in our industry usually involves tests of various kinds to determine the likely reactions of customers to new services or products. It is extremely expensive for an organization to introduce a new item and have it fail. By using the experimental method, there is less risk of failure. The experiment can be as simple as a concept test, or as complex and expensive as full-blown test marketing (see the Marriott International Excellence Case).

2. **Mechanical Observation.** Human and mechanical observation are the two main forms of observational research. People are used to make the first type of observation, whereas mechanical and electronic devices produce the second type.

   Mechanical observation is used in certain parts of the hospitality and travel industry, usually to provide customer counts or sales information. The turnstiles at the entrance to theme parks and other gated attractions are a good example. Cash registers, especially electronic ones backed up by computer systems, are powerful observers of customers' purchasing behaviors. Bar code technology and related scanning devices are widely used in retail shopping situations. Hand counters are

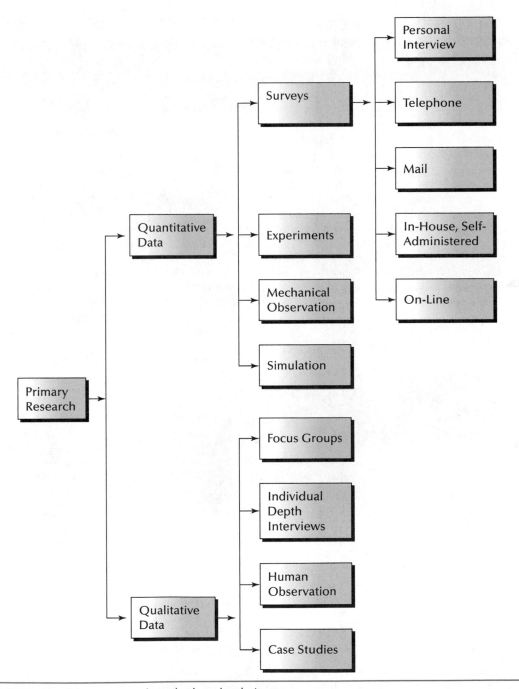

◆ FIGURE 6–11 *Primary research methods and techniques.*

used by ships and some attractions, whereas vehicle counts are taken using a counting device stretched across the surface of roads.

Mechanical observation devices are also used in tracking television viewing and in testing advertisements and other promotions. A variety of devices, including eye-tracking monitors, pupilometers, psychogalvanometers, and voice pitch analysis,

EXCELLENCE CASE

Marketing Research:
Marriott International

In our industry, Marriott represents one of the best examples of a company that places a high priority on marketing research. It has continued the legacy of its late founder, J. Willard Marriott, Sr., of understanding the importance of listening to customers. He epitomized marketing orientation by personally reading every guest comment card from his rapidly expanding lodging chain. The way the company developed the Courtyard by Marriott concept is an excellent example of how research can be used to pinpoint new marketing opportunities.

Announced in 1980, the first Courtyard by Marriott was opened in 1983 in Atlanta. Prior to 1980, hundreds of thousands were spent on *surveys and focus groups* to determine what gaps existed in lodging offerings. Before beginning construction on the Atlanta Courtyard, Marriott built a prototype guest room with movable walls, showed different configurations to selected travelers, and then surveyed them for their opinions on the different room setups. The research process continued with the first Atlanta opening, as it was used to *test market* the Courtyard concept.

Marriott used both *secondary* (mainly competitor analysis) and *primary research* in coming up with Courtyard. Additionally, it employed all four of the primary information collection methods: *experiments* (by test marketing in Atlanta), *observation* (watching the reactions of customers to mock-up rooms), *survey* (including a major segmentation study and a product-attribute preference survey using cluster analysis), and *simulation* (mock-up rooms).

After years of research and analysis by the development team, the main conclusion was that there was a niche for a new type of lodging property. Frequent travelers were willing to trade some of the extras at the typical hotel, such as large lobbies and extensive food and beverage areas, for a better guest room, a more residential feel, and lower rates.

The Courtyards are relatively small (about 150 rooms) and generally have one 90-seat restaurant and lounge. They look more like a low-rise apartment or condominium complex than the typical hotel. Not unlike residential developments, guest rooms surround a centrally located pool circled by a courtyard (hence the name Courtyard). Guest rooms are laid out with

continued

EXCELLENCE CASE *continued*

the traveling businessperson in mind. Marriott's research showed that guests disliked working on their beds and having no comfortable seating areas to talk to business associates. Each Courtyard room, therefore, includes a work desk and a separate seating arrangement conducive to sit-down conversations.

Marriott has continued its research-test-and-introduce approach to development with other lodging concepts, including its Marriott Suites, compact hotel, and Fairfield Inns economy-oriented concepts. The first Marriott Suites opened, after considerable consumer research, in Atlanta in March 1987.

Marriott also increased its emphasis on promoting weekend packages based on the results of a nationwide survey done on its behalf. The survey showed that about 73 percent of all pleasure travel trips in the United States were of three days or less, and approximately 60 percent of these mini trips occurred on weekends. Based on these and other findings, the company first introduced its *Two For Breakfast* packages in the winter of 1986–1987 and has repeated the program every year since then. The packages include a room for two people for two nights and full breakfasts for two persons on two consecutive weekend mornings (Thursday night through Sunday morning). Marriott's research confirmed that American lifestyles were changing away from the traditional two- or three-week vacation toward shorter, more frequent trips. With these packages, they were in fact practicing a form of lifestyle segmentation discussed in the next chapter.

(Photos courtesy of Marriott International, Inc.)

Discussion Questions

1. Which categories of research methods did Marriott use? Which specific marketing research techniques were employed? How were the findings of these research techniques applied?
2. Does Marriott International's use of marketing research represent a good model for other hospitality and travel organizations? Why or why not?
3. What are the strengths of Marriott's approach to conducting and applying research?
4. How could Marriott's research approaches be applied in other parts of the hospitality and travel industry?

Web Site

http://www.marriott.com/

---

are used to evaluate consumers' physical and psychological reactions to advertisements and other promotional materials.[10]

While all these devices are capable of producing very accurate, quantitative data, they do not provide the in-depth, qualitative information that human observation gives. They describe rather than explain customer behavior and give little indication of people's motivations, attitudes, opinions, and perceptions.

3. **Survey.** Most of you are already familiar with surveys. Perhaps you have been stopped in the local shopping mall and asked about your favorite brand of shampoo. Or maybe you received a form in the mail from your high school asking for your opinions on various programs offered there. How about that phone call from the life insurance company asking you all kinds of personal questions about your future plans? What about the comment cards you have seen on many restaurant tables or the questionnaire on the Web site you visited? You have just identified the five principal ways of completing surveys.
   a. Personal interviews
   b. Mail
   c. Telephone

    d. In-house, self-administered

    e. On-line

      Survey research is the most popular research method in our industry because it is flexible and easy to use. Despite their great popularity, though, many poor and ineffective surveys are completed every day. Knowing how to *field* a good survey is definitely a science, but also a bit of an art.

    a. ***Personal Interviews.*** A questionnaire received in the mail can simply be tossed in the garbage. It is also easy to hang up the phone on a researcher. Human nature, however, makes it much more difficult to refuse to give answers in a one-on-one interviewing situation. One of the advantages of personal interviewing, therefore, is the relatively high **response rate**—the percentage of all people surveyed who supply answers to the researcher's questions.

        Another advantage is its high degree of flexibility. Once committed to paper, the questions in mail and in-house, self-administered surveys cannot be modified. Although telephone researchers can reword questions, they cannot get visual clues from the respondent's behavior and body language. The personal interviewer can show or demonstrate more things. Let us assume we are a hotel company considering a new video-based checkout system. We might write up a description of the system (remember concept testing?) and get past guest opinions on it via a mail or telephone survey. Much more effective, however, would be a personal interview. We could show the description to some of our current guests and ask them for their reactions.

        Interviewers can provide fuller explanations of the meaning of certain questions. They can also gather more complete answers by rephrasing questions and probing further.

        Personal interviews can provide very timely data, as can telephone surveys. However, there is always a lag time in mail surveys between the mailing date and receipt of completed questionnaires. Thus, if information is required quickly, in-person or telephone surveys are preferable.

        Following are some of the disadvantages of personally-administered surveys.

- They are relatively expensive.
- There can be interviewer bias in questioning.
- Respondents may be reluctant to answer personal questions.
- Respondents may not answer in a relaxed way.
- The time of the interview may inconvenience the respondent.

    b. ***Mail Surveys.*** Surveys done by mail lack the personal touch of one-on-one, personal interviews. Despite this, they offer several distinct advantages.

- They are relatively inexpensive if the response rate is high.
- There is no interviewer bias.
- There is a consistency in the questions and responses.
- They can survey a large number of respondents.
- They can reach every respondent by mail.
- Respondents can remain anonymous.
- Respondents can choose the most convenient time to answer questions.

        One of the major drawbacks of mail surveys, apart from their impersonal nature, is the relatively low response rate. Although personal interviewing and telephone surveys usually generate answers from 50 percent or more of the respondents, a response rate of 30 percent to 40 percent is quite good for a mail survey. Response rates below this range are also quite common. In many ways, this survey technique suffers from most of the same disadvantages as direct-mail advertising, particularly the *junk mail syndrome* (a commonly held perception that much of one's daily mail is purely commercial solicitation). Like direct mail, however, there are procedures that help improve the response to mail surveys. These include the following:[11]

- Using highly personalized approaches and avoiding the mass-mailing look (e.g., individually typed addresses on envelopes, personalized salutations on cover letters, respondents' names in the body of the cover letter, postage stamps rather than metered mail)
- Following up several times after the initial request to remind respondents about completing the questionnaire
- Promising respondents something for completing the questionnaire (e.g., a copy of research findings or a monetary or nonmonetary incentive)
- Using accurate and up-to-date mailing lists
- Avoiding lengthy questionnaires
- Including a postage-paid, preaddressed envelope for returning the questionnaire

By following these guidelines carefully, a hospitality and travel organization can increase the response rate so that it approaches that of personal and telephone surveys.

c. **Telephone Surveys.** Telephone surveys share many of the advantages of personal interviews. They are more flexible than mail surveys, since the researcher can reword questions for greater clarification and skip questions that are not applicable. Information can be gathered quickly and inexpensively if only local dialing is required. High response rates can be achieved with good contact lists and trained telephone interviewers.

On the other hand, like personal interviews, telephone surveys are more obtrusive than mail. Many people regard telephone solicitations and surveys as an invasion of their privacy and quickly hang up the phone. It is more difficult to build a good rapport with the respondent on the telephone than it is in personal interviews. Telephone surveys also become expensive when long-distance calls have to be made. In this case, the number of questions asked usually has to be kept to a minimum.

As with mail surveys, there are specific telephone survey procedures that help improve response rates and data quality. These procedures are borrowed mainly from the field of telephone selling or telemarketing, which Chapter 17 discusses.

d. **In-house, Self-administered.** These are surveys that are provided for customers to complete while they are within the premises of hospitality and travel organizations. They include the comment cards often found on restaurant tables as well as the survey forms left in hotel guest rooms and cruise ship staterooms. These surveys can be extremely helpful in determining guest satisfaction with service quality, facilities, and equipment.

In-house, self-administered surveys have many of the same disadvantages as mail surveys, the primary one being that they usually generate a low response rate. One study on the use of comment cards in hotels found that many hotels had response rates of less than 1 percent.[12] How many comment cards have you filled out in restaurants in the past few months? Your answer is probably "none" or "very few." Unfortunately, many customers feel that nobody is interested in their two cents, and, in most cases, there is really no other incentive for taking the time to express their opinions.

In the era of relationship marketing in which current and past customers are seen as the key resource for future marketing, this situation is unacceptable. The organization must do all it can to motivate customers to fill out in-house questionnaires. One novel solution used at Marriott's Fairfield Inn is to have guests, at the time of checking out, type in their answers to a computer-based survey at the front desk. Other astute marketers offer incentives for completion such as free desserts or other small rewards.

e. **On-line.** The Internet has introduced some exciting new ways of conducting surveys. The two main alternatives are using either e-mail or the World Wide Web to deliver and receive questionnaires. For example, many hospitality and travel organizations have placed HTML (hypertext markup language) questionnaires on their Web sites to collect information from people visiting their sites. Figure 6–12 shows an example of a Web form used by the Australian Tourist Commission.

Researchers are still experimenting with on-line surveys, and there are as yet no conclusive guidelines on the strengths and weaknesses of on-line research. However, the relative speed and flexibility of on-line surveys are seen to be two major advantages. Additionally, there is the potential of reaching a large and growing audience of people on-line. The limitations of on-line research are the technical skills and time required to develop questionnaires for Web-based administration.

ON THE WEB

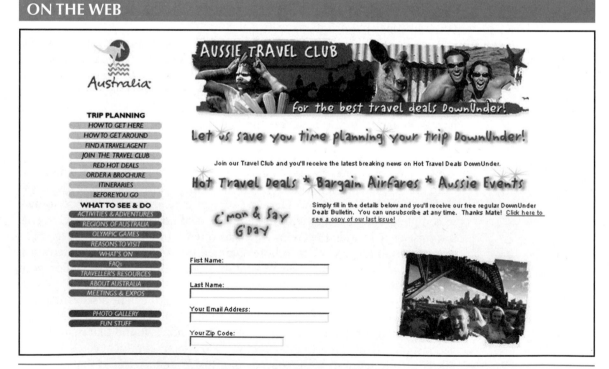

◆ **FIGURE 6–12**　*The ATC uses this HTML questionnaire on its Web site to collect information on potential visitors.* (Courtesy of the Australian Tourist Commission)

A Touch of Technology

Frequently Asked Questions about Conducting On-line Research from CASRO

- The Internet, particularly the World Wide Web and e-mail, is a relatively new way of collecting survey data.
- CASRO, the Council of American Research Organizations, has developed a set of FAQs on conducting on-line research through surveys.
- The three types of on-line surveys are completed through, (1) e-mail surveys, (2) HTML form surveys, and (3) downloadable surveys.
- CASRO believes that on-line research can be completed quite quickly compared with other types of surveys, especially mailed questionnaires.
- CASRO estimates the following times to complete on-line research from final questionnaire until the production of *topline* data; e-mail surveys from 1 to 10 days; HTML form surveys, 3 to 15 days; downloadable interactive surveys, 7 to 20 days.
- CASRO recommends that an on-line survey should not take more than 20 minutes to complete.

Questionnaire Design.

All four survey techniques—personal interviews, mail, telephone, and in-house, self-administered surveys—normally require a printed form that lists the questions and provides space for answers. These come in all shapes and sizes and are referred to as **questionnaires**. A good questionnaire is one of the keys to getting quality research information. It is surprising then that many poorly-designed questionnaires are used in our industry. Figure 6–13 lists common faults found in questionnaires and Figure 6–14 presents guidelines for designing effective questionnaires.

- Questions that use jargon or technical terms (e.g., check average, occupied room nights, AP/MAP/EP, covers)
- Too many questions
- Questions that are long and wordy
- Questions that are really two questions in one
- Questions that are vague and general
- Failure to tell the respondent how to fill in each question (e.g., how many items to check, how to rank alternatives)
- Questions that are personal and embarrassing
- Questions that do not cover the full range of possible responses (e.g., no "don't know" or "no opinion" responses)
- Questions that give management answers that are too general (e.g., rating broad areas of service as excellent to poor)

◆ FIGURE 6–13   *Common faults in questionnaire design.*

The following guidelines are suggested for designing effective questionnaires:

LENGTH

1. Keep it as short as possible.
2. Be sure individual questions are short and to the point.

ORGANIZATION

3. Include a date.
4. Place personal questions (e.g., income level, age) at the end.
5. Provide instructions on how the interviewer or respondent should answer each question.
6. If appropriate, always supply "don't know" or "no opinion" options.

WORDING OF QUESTIONS

7. Ask only one question in each question.
8. Be as specific as possible.
9. Avoid technical terms.
10. Use words whose meanings are clear.
11. Make sure there are no overlaps in possible responses (e.g., use $1–$1.99 and $2–$2.99, rather than $1–$2 and $2–$3).

◆ **FIGURE 6–14**   *Guidelines for effective questionnaire design.*

4. **Simulation.** The fourth research method involves using computers to simulate marketing situations. A mathematical model is developed that is a simulation of the real-life situation. The model can be used to predict sales volumes, customer counts, or other variables important to management.

Qualitative Primary Research Methods

1. **Focus Groups.** A focus group is a method in which the researcher directs questions to a small group of people, usually between eight and twelve. The word *focus* means that the researcher draws the group's attention to a specific subject or set of questions and invites a discussion about them. From then on the researcher listens, watches people's behavior, refocuses the discussion if necessary, and tries to summarize the group's opinions, comments, and suggestions.

   The real strength of focus groups is that they can provide an in-depth understanding of customers' opinions, attitudes, perceptions, and behavior. Researchers can probe even further than they can in one-on-one, personal interviews.

   In an article about using focus groups for restaurant research, Joe L. Welch came up with an impressive list of uses for this versatile research method.[13] With some slight modifications and additions, they can be used to help make effective marketing decisions in the following ways:

   a. Generating ideas for new services or products
   b. Evaluating an organization's ideas for new service or product concepts

c. Determining customer attitudes toward the organization and its services and products

d. Coming up with questions to be used later in surveys

e. Testing proposed advertisements or sales promotions

f. Examining, in greater depth, customer responses to previous surveys

g. Identifying the criteria that customers use in selecting a specific type of hospitality or travel business

h. Determining customer attitudes toward competitive organizations

i. Testing new or modified products or services

j. Identifying the decision process that customers use in making buying decisions

The focus group method is widely used in the hospitality and travel industry, especially to explore people's images of specific companies and travel destination areas. Despite their versatility, focus groups produce only *qualitative* information. The information collected from a focus group session cannot be called *representative*. It may not accurately represent the opinions, attitudes, perceptions, or behavior of all customers. If an organization needs to have numerical data that represent the collective opinions of all its past or potential customers, then the survey method is preferable.

2. **Individual Depth Interviews.** The individual depth interview (IDI) has objectives and procedures similar to the focus group, but involves only one interviewee (subject) and one interviewer. These one-on-one sessions usually last between 45 minutes and one hour.[14] During the interview, the researcher asks many questions and probes for additional elaboration after the subject answers.[15] Individual depth interviews may be favored over focus groups when the topic being discussed is confidential or sensitive, or when logistical problems make focus groups impractical.[16]

3. **Human Observation.** Using human observation in research means watching and noting how customers behave. It is a great technique for evaluating competitors. The following are just a few other creative ideas for using human observational research.

   - Count how many times people refill their plates from buffet or salad bars.
   - Tally the number of cars and the license-plate origins in a competitor's parking lot.
   - Watch how many people take brochures from a rack.
   - Add up the number of people using a pool during different times of the day.
   - Calculate the average amount of time customers spend eating meals in a restaurant.

   Try to come up with a few more ideas yourself. Is this not a really useful technique? It is surprising then that it often gets overlooked as a source of research information. Whether we watch our own or competitors' customers, the observational method provides a relatively inexpensive and rich supply of data for decision making.

4. **Case Studies.** The purpose of the case study method is to get information from one or more situations that are similar to the organization's problem situation.[17] The word *situations* often means other organizations that are similar to the organization doing the case study and that have had experience in dealing with the same or

a similar research problem. Case studies are usually done in the hospitality and travel industry when an organization is investigating the addition of new services or facilities and when potential new target markets and marketing mix approaches are being evaluated. Effective case studies are dependent on obtaining the cooperation of the organizations to be studied and can provide rich and in-depth information on their experiences.

CHAPTER CONCLUSION

Properly conducted marketing research helps hospitality and travel organizations make effective decisions. It does not replace the need for managerial experience and judgment, but lessens the risk of poor decisions being made without adequate prior research. Marketing research must be done in every step of the hospitality and travel marketing system.

The two major divisions of research information are primary and secondary. There are many research and statistical techniques available. Selecting from among them should be done using a systematic marketing research process. The steps in this process are problem formulation, selection of research design and data collection method, sample design and data collection, analysis and interpretation of data, preparation of research report, and communication of the research results.

REVIEW QUESTIONS

1. How is marketing research defined in this book?
2. What are the reasons for doing marketing research?
3. Sometimes managers do not do marketing research when it seems they should. What are the reasons for not doing marketing research? Are these justifiable?
4. How is research used in each of the steps of the hospitality and travel marketing system?
5. What are the five key requirements for good research information?
6. What are the six steps in the marketing research process?
7. What are the sources of secondary research data?
8. What are the broad categories of primary research methods?
9. What are the advantages and disadvantages of personal interviews, mail, telephone, in-house, self-administered, and on-line surveys?
10. What are focus groups and how can they be used to assist with marketing decisions?
11. What steps can be taken to develop the most effective questionnaires?

CHAPTER ASSIGNMENTS

1. Interview the owner or manager of a local, independent restaurant. What types of ongoing market research does the business carry out? Does it make use of primary or secondary research? What suggestions do you have for improving or expanding the restaurant's market research program?

2. Gather a selection of comment cards and guest surveys from airlines, hotels, restaurants, and other travel businesses. What common questions or other features do you notice? Can you see any similar faults or weaknesses? Which is the strongest and why? What recommendations would you make to improve these types of in-house, self-administered surveys?

3. You have been approached by a hospitality and travel business to do some research for them. They have been experiencing a growing number of complaints about their service, but cannot pinpoint the specific reasons. Which research method would you use and why? How would you design your research procedures? Draft a questionnaire or questionnaires you would use. How would you suggest that management use your research information?

4. You have just started work in the marketing department of a hospitality and travel organization. To your surprise, you learn that no marketing research has been done because your boss—the director of marketing—thinks research is a waste of time and money. How would you justify a marketing research program to your boss, and what research projects would you include? Can you prove that your research program and projects may save money and lead to increased sales? If so, how?

WORLD WIDE WEB RESOURCES

A. C. Nielsen
http://www.acnielsen.com/

American Marketing Association
http://www.ama.org/

Amtrak
http://www.amtrak.com/

Annals of Tourism Research
http://www.elsevier.nl/inca/publications/store/6/8/9/

Arbitron
http://www.arbitron.com/

Australian Tourist Commission
http://www.australia.com/

Bureau of Tourism Research
http://www.btr.gov.au/

Business Travel News
http://btnonline.com/

CIC Research
http://www.cicresearch.com/

Club Med
http://www.clubmed.com/

Council of American Survey Research Organizations
http://www.casro.org/

Cornell Hotel and Restaurant Administration Quarterly
http://www.elsevier.nl/inca/publications/store/5/2/3/0/4/0/

Cruise Lines International Association
http://www.cruising.org/

D. K. Shifflet & Associates
http://www.dksa.com/

Gallup Organization
http://www.gallup.com/

J. D. Power and Associates
http://www.jdpower.com/

Journal of Travel Research
http://www.sagepub.com/

Las Vegas Convention and Visitor Authority
http://www.vegasfreedom.com/

Leisure Trends Group
http://www.leisuretrends.com/

Marriott International
http://www.marriott.com/

Maui Visitors Bureau
http://www.visitmaui.com/

Mediamark Research Inc.
http://www.mediamark.com/

Meetings & Conventions
http://www.meetings-conventions.com/

National Tour Foundation
http://www.ntaonline.com/

NPD Group
http://www.npd.com/

PKF Consulting
http://www.pkfonline.com/

Pizza Hut
http://www.pizzahut.com/

Plog Research
http://www.nfow.com/

St. Petersburg/Clearwater Area Convention and Visitors Bureau
http://www.stpete-clearwater.com/

Simmons Market Research Bureau
http://www.smrb.com/

Smith Travel Research
http://www.str-online.com/

Successful Meetings
http://www.successmtgs.com/

Tourism Management
http://www.elsevier.nl/inca/publications/store/3/0/4/7/2/

REFERENCES

1. http://www.amtrak.com/
2. Siskin, Jonathon. "Net is the key to Aussie marketing." *Travel Weekly* 58(51):18 (1999).
3. Orban, Diana. 2000. "Cruise industry adds more destinations." http://www.cruising.org/
4. http://www.lasvegas24hours.com/
5. http://www.marriott.com/
6. http://www.pizzahut.com/
7. Bennett, Peter D. 1988. *Dictionary of Marketing Terms.* Chicago: American Marketing Association.
8. Churchill, Gilbert A. 2000. *Marketing Research: Methodological Foundations.* 7th ed. Orlando, Fla.: Holt Rinehart Winston.
9. Churchill, Gilbert A. 2000. *Marketing Research: Methodological Foundations.* 7th ed. Orlando, Fla.: Holt Rinehart Winston.
10. Zikmund, William G. 2000. *Exploring Marketing Research.* 7th ed. Fort Worth, Tex.: Harcourt College Publishers.
11. Dillman, Don. 1978. *Mail and Telephone Surveys: The Total Design Method.* New York: John Wiley & Sons.
12. Lewis, Robert C., and Abraham Pizam. "Guest surveys: A missed opportunity." *Cornell Hotel and Restaurant Administration Quarterly* 22 (3):37–44 (1981).
13. Welch, Joe L. "Focus groups for restaurant research." *Cornell Hotel and Restaurant Administration Quarterly* 26 (2):81 (1985).
14. Goldman, Alfred E., and Susan S. McDonald. 1987. *The Group Depth Interview: Principles and Practice.* Englewood Cliffs, N.J.: Prentice-Hall, Inc., 7–8.
15. Zikmund, William G. 2000. *Exploring Marketing Research.* 7th ed. Fort Worth, Tex.: Harcourt College Publishers.
16. Goldman, Alfred E., and Susan S. McDonald. 1987. *The Group Depth Interview: Principles and Practice.* Englewood Cliffs, N.J.: Prentice-Hall, Inc., 7–8.
17. Zikmund, William G. 2000. *Exploring Marketing Research.* 7th ed. Fort Worth, Tex.: Harcourt College Publishers.

For additional hospitality and travel marketing resources, visit our Web site at **www.Hospitality-Tourism.delmar.com**

PART III

PLANNING: MARKETING STRATEGY AND PLANNING

WHERE ARE WE NOW?

WHERE WOULD WE LIKE TO BE?

HOW DO WE GET THERE?

HOW DO WE MAKE SURE WE GET THERE?

HOW DO WE KNOW IF WE GOT THERE?

7

Marketing Strategy: Market Segmentation and Trends

Where Would We Like to Be?

Objectives

Having read this chapter, you should be able to:

◆ Define market segmentation.

◆ Explain the importance of segmentation to effective marketing.

◆ Explain the benefits and limitations of market segmentation.

◆ List the eight criteria used to determine the viability of market segments.

◆ List the bases for segmenting hospitality and travel markets.

◆ Describe the major demand and supply trends influencing today's hospitality and travel industry.

◆ Describe the recent trends in the segmentation practices of the hospitality and travel industry.

Overview

A wise person once said that you can please some people all of the time and all people some of the time, but you cannot please all people all of the time. This is the basis for one of marketing's core principles—market segmentation.

This chapter explains the role and benefits of market segmentation. It also looks at the various ways that hospitality and travel markets

can be segmented. Also reviewed are trends that have shaped today's hospitality and travel markets and placed greater emphasis on market segmentation. It explains the traditional methods used to categorize different customer groups and describes the segmentation practices that have recently gained in popularity.

Key Terms

baby boomers	geodemographic segmentation	product-related segmentation
behavioral segmentation	geographic segmentation	psychographics
benefit segmentation	heavy-half segmentation	psychographic segmentation
brand loyalty	lifestyle	purpose-of-trip segmentation
brand segmentation	lifestyle segmentation	segmentation bases
business travel market	market segment	segmentation criteria
channel-of-distribution	market segmentation analysis	segmented marketing strategy
segmentation	multistage segmentation	single-stage segmentation
customer mix	occasion-based segmentation	target market
database marketing	pleasure and personal travel	trading area
demand-led trends	market	two-stage segmentation
demographic segmentation	positioning	undifferentiated marketing
frequent travelers	primary segmentation base	use-frequency segmentation

ave you ever considered to how many groups you and other members of your family belong? A good place to start is to list those elements that you and other people have in common. What about your home? Perhaps you share a street address and zip code with several others. You will agree that thousands of people also share your home town, city, county, state, or province. What about your age? You know that many others are the same age as you are, and they may even have the exact same birthdate. How about other things such as your income, educational background, family composition, and religion? Although you like to think of yourself as a one-of-a-kind person, you must admit that other people also have similar characteristics.

Your list of groups is already long! But we are not finished yet. You might not know it, but you have the same culture, subculture, psychographic and lifestyle characteristics, product and service usage rates and patterns, and favorite activities as many other people. You and other people also look for similar benefits from certain products and services.

Your list is probably on a second page by now, and you are wondering about the point of the exercise. It is simple. Although every human being, even an identical twin, is unique, each person can be grouped with others on the basis of shared characteristics. Effective marketing involves identifying those groups to which our services have the greatest appeal, as well as ruling out others that are unlikely to purchase our services.

MARKET SEGMENTATION

Analyzing market segments is the first step in developing a marketing strategy. This chapter looks at the concept of market segmentation. Chapter 8 discusses the second step in the strategy-setting process: Selecting marketing strategies, positioning approaches, and marketing objectives.

Market Segmentation Analysis

Market segmentation is the division of the overall market for a service into groups of people with common characteristics. These are usually called market segments or target markets. A **market segment** (e.g., business travelers who live in Seattle) is an identifiable component group of an overall market whose members have something in common, and to which a specific service appeals. When the term target market is used, it means a market segment selected by a hospitality and travel organization for marketing attention.

As you can see, there are two distinct and sequential steps in market segmentation:

1. Dividing the whole market into groups (market segments) with common characteristics (using specific segmentation bases).
2. Selecting those market segments (target markets) that the organization is best able to serve (using a set of segmentation criteria).

This process, known as market segmentation analysis (segmenting the market and selecting target markets), requires the types of good research data and analysis that were discussed in Chapters 5 and 6. Before discussing how market segmentation analysis is done, it is important to review the reasons for the increasing importance of market segmentation, as well as segmentation's benefits and limitations.

Reasons for Market Segmentation

Chapter 1 identified market segmentation as one of the core principles of marketing. It contrasted the *rifle* (targeted) and *shotgun* (untargeted) approaches to marketing and strongly recommended the first of the two. Why? The basic reason for market segmentation is that trying to appeal to all potential customers—the untargeted approach—is wasteful. There are groups of customers who are just not interested in buying our services.

The essence of good marketing is to pick out the segments that are most interested in specific services and to aim marketing programs at them. In this way, marketing is similar to shuffling and dealing a pack of cards. Many different hands are dealt and played, but only one is a winner. Cards, like customers, can be grouped in several different ways: similar suits, similar values, similar faces, or royals. Depending on the game, players reorganize their hands in ways that are most likely to win. They know that selecting and grouping their cards is necessary to succeed. Effective marketers recognize the same type of rule. There is, sadly, an end to this analogy. Playing and winning at cards is a gamble. Marketing should not be.

The principal reason for segmentation, therefore, is to focus effort and marketing dollars in the most effective way. There are several choices to be made, and it is helpful to think of the answers to the *who, what, how, where,* and *when* questions:

1. **WHO**? Which market segments should we pursue?
2. **WHAT**? What are they looking for in our types of services?
3. **HOW**? How do we develop our marketing programs to best fit their needs and wants?
4. **WHERE**? Where do we promote our services?
5. **WHEN**? When do we promote them?

Once target markets have been selected, other decisions and alternatives come into better focus. Through research, we can then identify the needs and wants of these groups. What follows is similar to operating a camera. Once the operator selects the subject, he or she adjusts the environment (lighting, speed, arrangement, and position) and focuses. Clear, sharp photographs require good subjects, proper equipment and accessories, the right environment, careful preplanning, and precise timing. Effective market segmentation is much like photography. The marketer must know how, where, and when to appeal to selected target markets. When the camera operator uses the wrong equipment or environment, or hurriedly snaps a picture, the result is predictable—a blurry photograph. Likewise, the marketer who fails to take adequate time to plan how, where, and when to best appeal to target markets will have an out-of-focus marketing program and will waste precious dollars.

The need for segmentation has never been greater than it is today. The market trends discussed later in this chapter have caused great fragmentation in hospitality and travel markets.

Benefits of Market Segmentation

The benefits of using market segmentation are as follows:

1. More effective use of marketing dollars
2. Clearer understanding of the needs and wants of selected customer groups
3. More effective **positioning** (developing a service and marketing mix to occupy a specific place in the minds of potential customers within target markets)
4. Greater precision in selecting promotional vehicles and techniques (e.g., advertising media, sales promotion methods, geographic placement)

The budget hotel concept provides a good example of these benefits. Its developers realized that there are groups of travelers that are not interested in the full range of services provided by the typical, roadside Holiday Inn, for example. These potential customers wanted inexpensive, clean, and comfortable lodging in limited-service and conveniently located properties. These developers responded by positioning a standardized (same across the nation) service, with few of the frills of a typical motor hotel, at a significantly reduced price. The result is history. A completely new sector of the lodging industry was created. Companies such as Days Inns, Super 8, and Motel 6 are now household names. By selecting economy-minded travelers, these companies concentrated on these customers' needs, chose the best ways to appeal to them, and promoted in the right places at the right times. The *no-frills* concept has also been used successfully by other hospitality and travel organizations. Examples include Rent-A-Wreck car rentals, last-minute travel clubs, Southwest Airlines, Easy Jet (U.K.), and WestJet (Western Canada). Even fast-food chain outlets can be considered a variation on the same theme.

Limitations of Market Segmentation

You may now feel that every hospitality and travel organization should use market segmentation. In more than 90 percent of the cases, you are absolutely correct. Most organizations find that a **segmented marketing strategy** (selecting specific target markets, and marketing mixes for each of them) is the most effective. Almost all full-service hotels, table-service restaurants, airlines, and travel agencies recognize that they have customer groups with different needs and wants to whom specific promotional approaches apply. Convention/meeting planners want the right types of meeting rooms with appropriate audiovisual equipment. Pleasure travelers are not at all interested in this service. Pleasure travelers are more likely to be subscribers to *Travel & Leisure*. On the other hand, convention planners have a greater preference for *Meetings & Conventions* magazine. A segmented marketing strategy makes great sense.

Now turn your attention to fast-food operators. The picture is not as clear, is it? McDonald's claims that almost everyone has eaten at least one meal at one of their outlets. When a service's appeal is so broad. does it make any sense to use different approaches for various customer groups, or should the same methods be used for all? We will leave this question for later.

Market segmentation has the following limitations and problems:

1. More expensive than using a nonsegmented approach
2. Difficult to select the best base or bases for segmenting a market
3. Difficult to know how finely or broadly to segment
4. Tendency to appeal to segments that are not viable

1. **More Expensive.** The most obvious limitation of market segmentation is the added expense. Each target market receives individual attention. This means a wider range of services and price structures must be provided. Advertisements and promotions have to be tailored to the habits and preferences of each segment. More than one distribution channel may have to be used. Because each additional target market brings an extra cost, each must be examined individually to determine whether pursuing it is worthwhile.

2. **Difficult to Select the Best Segmentation Base.** You will remember that we began this chapter by asking you to list the different groups to which you belong. The problem facing any marketer comes from the size of the list you probably compiled. Many *segmentation bases* (characteristics used to divide a market into segments) can be used. Geographic location, purpose of trip, demographics, lifestyles, benefits sought, and rate of usage are just a few of the alternative bases. The marketer's dilemma is to decide which base or combination of bases will produce the best return on the marketing dollar. There is no single answer to this question. Each situation requires careful research and planning.

3. **Difficult to Know How Finely or Broadly to Segment.** Market segmentation can be carried too far. It can be as wasteful to have too many as it can be to have too few target markets. Some find that the amount spent to generate business from certain target markets is more than the additional profits generated. On the other hand, if a market is divided too broadly, certain segments are not reached effectively. Here, marketing can be compared to panning for gold. If a sieve with a very fine mesh is used, for example, only the very finest sand will pass through. If the perforations are larger, only larger particles are trapped. Marketing to only a few target markets is similar to mining with the large-mesh sieve—some potential customers pass through the marketer's hands. Selecting a large number of target markets can be compared to using the fine-mesh mining implement. In this case, almost all potential customers are netted, but it is difficult to distinguish the value of individual target markets. Just as the miner may not find that much more gold by using this tool, the marketer may find segmentation of limited value if it is carried too far.

4. **Tendency to Appeal to Nonviable Segments.** There are market segments that are not viable. For example, there may be no specific promotional or advertising vehicle to reach them. Some groups may be too small to justify the investment required. Some segments may not be permanent. They may be fad-oriented. Other segments may be so dominated by one or more large companies that a newcomer that chooses to pursue these segments will find it both expensive and unrewarding.

Criteria for Effective Segmentation

You now know that there are pitfalls to market segmentation. But how can they be avoided? The answer lies in carefully screening potential target markets to make sure they meet the following eight criteria:

1. Measurable
2. Substantial
3. Accessible
4. Defensible
5. Durable
6. Competitive
7. Homogeneous
8. Compatible

1. **Measurable.** It is inadvisable to pick target markets that cannot be measured without a reasonable degree of accuracy. This book stresses the need to set marketing objectives in numerical terms and to measure the results of marketing plans. If the marketer can only guess the size of a target market, then there is no way of knowing what level of investment is justified, or even if *any* investment is worthwhile. Similarly, there is an insufficient basis for measuring success.

2. **Substantial.** A target market must be big enough to warrant a separate investment. How big is big? The answer is that it must produce more in added profits than the amount required to pursue it.

3. **Accessible.** The essence of market segmentation is being able to select and reach specific customer groups. However, there are target markets that cannot be reached with the degree of precision the marketer desires. In this case, noninterested parties also receive communications, resulting in wasted effort and money.

4. **Defensible.** There are situations in which a similar approach can be used with two or more individual target markets. The marketer must be sure that each group requires individual attention. The marketer must also feel confident that the organization's share of each target market can be defended from competitors.

5. **Durable.** Some market segments are short term or medium term, meaning that they exist for less than five years. Some are fads that enjoy brief popularity. Others result from nonrecurrent events. Hula hoops, pet rocks, Michael Jackson mania, discotheques, and roller rinks are examples of fads. Although some ventures are so profitable that they quickly produce a sufficient return on investment, most are not. The prudent marketer should be convinced that each target market has long-term potential.

6. **Competitive.** The sixth criterion is the competitiveness of our service relative to the market segment. Marketers need to take a long, hard look at whether what they offer provides something distinct or unique for these customers. The more precisely the service fits the needs of a particular segment, the more likely it is to succeed. On the other hand, if a service does not match the needs well, there is little point in pursuing the segment.

7. **Homogeneous.** In dividing the whole market into its component market segments, the organization should make sure that the segments are as different from each

other, or as heterogeneous, as possible. At the same time, the people within each segment should be as similar, or as homogeneous, as possible.

8. **Compatible.** When an organization selects a target market it must be sure that this market does not conflict in any way with the markets it already serves. Marketers would say that this means ensuring that a new target market is compatible with the existing **customer mix** (the combination of target markets that an organization serves).

The Role of Segmentation in Marketing Strategies

You will remember our earlier discussion of a segmented marketing strategy, and you may also recall the concept of strategic marketing planning from Chapter 3. The terms *strategy* and *strategic* involve long-term planning, or making choices between alternative courses of action for a period of at least three future years. Although Chapter 8 takes a more detailed look at marketing strategy and positioning, you should know about the function of market segmentation in the strategy-selection process.

Market segmentation plays a key role in selecting and detailing a marketing strategy. In fact, deciding on a strategy usually involves choosing a single target market or some combination of target markets, or, alternatively, consciously deciding to ignore segment differences (**undifferentiated marketing**). Selecting target markets for attention is usually a multiyear decision that is subject to annual reviews using the situation analysis and marketing research.

EXCELLENCE CASE

Market Segmentation:
Contiki Holidays

Contiki Holidays, a tour operator, provides a great example of market segmentation and positioning by user category. Contiki's tours are designed exclusively for 18 to 35 year olds—a form of segmentation using demographics as a base. Launched originally in Europe in 1961, the company has grown to more than 80,000 tour patrons a year on more than 2,000 tour departures. Its 100-plus tours have historically been concentrated on Europe, Australia, and New Zealand. Other destinations now include the United States, Canada, and the Middle East. The company added tours to Africa for the first time in 1995. Tour groups usually consist of 20 to 50 young people from a variety of countries including Australia, Canada, Germany, New

Zealand, South Africa, the United States, the United Kingdom, and other European and Asian nations. Contiki markets its tours in 30 different countries.

On Contiki's tours, everyone is between 18 and 35, even the tour guides. The average age is about 24, and approximately one-third of the participants are from the United States.[1] Once in the country, Contiki uses motorcoaches for transportation. Company officials find that they have to counter the misconceptions that motorcoaches are uncomfortable and that motorcoach tours are only for older people. Contiki's modern fleet of coaches are equipped with aircraft-style reclining seats, panoramic windows, VCRs and TV screens, mega stereo systems, and bathrooms.

continued

EXCELLENCE CASE *continued*

(Photo courtesy of Contiki Holidays)

Many activities are programmed on- and off-coach, including more nightlife entertainment than most tours. While there are many sightseeing and other activities built into Contiki's tours, tour patrons are also able to choose from a list of optional activities and excursions.

Three types of tours are offered. "Superior" tours use superior-quality accommodation, while "budget" tours use shared accommodation in more budget-quality lodging. The pricing of Contiki's tours is certainly reasonable, usually in the range of US $58 to $100 per day (excluding air fare). The daily rate includes lodging, as well as almost complete Modified American Plan (all breakfasts and about half of the dinners), motor coach transport, and sightseeing tours and activities.

The United States office of Contiki concentrates its efforts on trade promotion through travel agents and focuses its consumer marketing on college students, young professionals, and the parents of college students. All of Contiki's business is booked through retail travel agents, and it organizes many agent-training seminars each year to explain its tour programs. The commissions paid to agents are in the range of 10 to 16 percent, based on the number of tour patrons booked by the agency.

Contiki wants to make its name synonymous with youth travel in the country markets it serves. The company feels that its major competition is the type of backpacking that young people have traditionally selected to do when visiting Europe, Australia, and New Zealand. With concerns growing for safety, Contiki believes its standing as a major tour operator with 40-plus years of experience and its highly organized itineraries provide greater assurance for young people and their parents. Contiki is a member of the United States Tour Operator Association and participates in its $1 Million Consumer Protection program. While there are approximately 12 tour operators in the world catering to the 18 to 35 market, only Contiki markets its tours throughout the world. The resulting mix of nationalities on every tour departure is definitely one of Contiki's perceived competitive strengths. On any given trip, there may be as many as 15 different nationalities represented in the tour group.

In an effort to further establish its name as the premier tour operator for youth travel, Contiki is switching its emphasis from trade to consumer and Internet advertising, while maintaining its focus on personal selling and sales promotions to travel agents. This move includes placing ads in consumer magazines such as *Cosmopolitan, Jane, Maxim,* and *Men's Journal,* radio commercials on youth-oriented music stations, and a university newspaper advertising campaign.[2]

Contiki's Web site — http://www.contiki.com — is proving to be very popular with the 18- to 35-year-old niche market. According to Contiki's marketing coordinator, the message board feature on the site "is especially successful as it allows both past, present and future travelers to connect with each other over the Internet."[3] The site also includes brochure information, video clips,

continued

EXCELLENCE CASE *continued*

(Photo courtesy of Contiki Holidays)

virtual postcards, and frequently asked questions (FAQs) for people to learn more about Contiki.

In today's marketing terminology, a large part of Contiki's market would be called Generation X — those young people born between 1965 and 1980, and now mostly in the 20- to 35-year-old age group. According to one source, this is a substantial market with growing spending power. The number of specific media that are targeting this lucrative market is expanding quite rapidly. A substantial proportion of X-ers are either enrolled in college or are

young professionals, which provides companies such as Contiki with a great opportunity to target a substantial portion of the market.

Contiki Holidays is an excellent example of a long-standing commitment to serve a specific target market. With a repeat-business rate of around 30 percent and a steadily growing number of tours and tour patrons, the company clearly demonstrates the success that can result from niche marketing in the highly competitive tour operating business.

Discussion Questions

1. How should a company like Contiki use the World Wide Web and e-mail to appeal to people in the 18 to 35-year-old age group?
2. What new segments of the 18 to 35 market could Contiki explore?
3. What can Contiki do to offset this age group's apparent dislike of traveling by motor coach?

Web Site

http://www.contiki.com/

References

1. Launder, Richard. (1995) Conversation with author.
2. Thompson, Stacy. (1995) Letter to author.
3. Zable, Stacey. 1993. "Getting the word out." *The Travel Agent,* 18 January, 30–31.

SEGMENTATION BASES

What characteristics or bases should be used to divide a market into segments? This is one of the most difficult questions facing all hospitality and travel organizations, yet it is very important in marketing effectiveness. The alternatives are numerous, including the following seven broad categories:

1. Geography
2. Demographics
3. Purpose of trip
4. Psychographics
5. Behavior

6. Product-related
7. Channels of distribution

Each of these seven categories includes several alternative characteristics for carving the market into segments. For example, a restaurant that uses a geographic segmentation base might separate potential customers by their zip code, the first three digits of their phone number, their residential neighborhood, or their street address. Because different combinations of the seven broad categories can be used—for example, geography, purpose of trip, and demographics—the alternatives available increase to well over 100. Choosing from among these extensive possibilities is a major problem in market segmentation, as you have already seen.

Segmentation Approaches

Before describing each segmentation base, you should recognize the three different approaches to segmentation described in the following paragraphs.

1. **Single-Stage Segmentation.** Only one of the seven categories of segmentation bases is chosen in single-stage segmentation. For example, a travel agency might divide groups of potential customers into pleasure and corporate accounts (a purpose-of-trip base).

2. **Two-Stage Segmentation.** After a primary segmentation base (the characteristic most important in determining the customer's choice of a service) is chosen, the market is further subdivided using a second segmentation base. Traditionally, lodging properties use two-stage segmentation when they divide their market by purpose of trip and then use geography to pinpoint target markets more finely.

3. **Multistage Segmentation.** A primary segmentation base is once again chosen, but then two or more other bases are used in multistage segmentation. For example, a hotel divides its market by purpose of trip. One of the segments it identifies is the convention-meeting market. Because of the limited capacity of its meeting rooms, the hotel narrows its focus further by considering only associations and companies that hold meetings of fewer than a certain number of people (a product-related base). Finally, it uses geography to pinpoint where these organizations are located.

   Which is the best of these three approaches? There is no single, correct answer. Generally, it is more effective to use the two-stage or multistage methods. Experts also agree that choosing the first or primary segmentation base is critical to success. This should be the characteristic with the greatest influence on the customer's buying behavior.

Individual Segmentation Bases

1. **Geographic Segmentation.** This is the most widely used segmentation base in the hospitality and travel industry. Geographic segmentation means dividing the market into groups of customers who share the same geographic location. Areas can be very large (e.g., several countries or continents) or very small (e.g., residential neighborhoods). Some travel marketing organizations, including the

Australian Tourist Commission and the British Tourist Authority, use country of origin as a primary segmentation base. On the other hand, restaurants need a much finer and more localized approach, such as the zip codes within their city or town.

Why is geographic segmentation so popular? First, it is easy to use. There are universally accepted definitions of geographic areas. This is not the case, as we shall see, with psychographic and benefit segments. Geographic markets can be easily measured, and usually there are numerous demographic, travel, and other statistics available for these markets. Another reason that this type of segmentation is so popular is that most media vehicles (television and radio stations, newspapers, billboards, Yellow Pages, and some magazines) serve specific geographic areas. Aiming promotional messages at target customers inevitably involves the use of geographic segmentation. Organizations with markets in one or more countries feel that behavior patterns vary with the country or region of residence. Within the United States. some have found differences in the preferences and consumption patterns of residents in the nine census regions.

Figure 7–1 lists the different geographic characteristics used for segmentation. The actual choice of the geographic factor is influenced by trading area (the geographic area from which an organization and/or similar organizations tend to attract the majority of its customers). Many hotels, resorts, attractions, airlines, countries, and destination areas have an international trading area covering several foreign countries. Others, such as fast-food and lodging chains, have a predominantly national or domestic market. More locally oriented businesses, such as independent restaurants and travel agencies, have much narrower trading areas, sometimes consisting of only a few blocks.

2. **Demographic Segmentation.** Demographic segmentation means dividing markets based on population statistics. These statistics—primarily generated from census information—include age, sex, household and per capita income, family size and composition, occupation, educational level, religion, race/ethnic origin, housing type, and other factors. The Contiki Excellence Case in this chapter shows an outstanding application of demographic segmentation at an international level. Other variables, such as family life cycle, effective buying incomes, and buying power indices, are based on a combination of demographic statistics.

1. Community Level
   - Neighborhoods
   - Zip/Postal Codes
   - Metropolitan Statistical Areas (MSAs)
   - Designated Market Areas (DMAs)
   - Local Access and Transport Areas (LATAs)
   - Trading Areas
   - Cities/Towns
   - Population Densities

2. State/Provincial/County Level
   - County
   - State/Province

3. National and International Level
   - Regions
   - Countries
   - Continents

◆ FIGURE 7–1   *Factors used in geographic segmentation.*

Demographic and geographic segmentation are popular for the same reasons. The statistics are readily available, uniformly defined and accepted, and easy to use. It is common for demographic to be used along with geographic segmentation, giving rise to a technique known as geodemographic segmentation (a two-stage segmentation approach using geographic and demographic characteristics).

A Touch of Technology

CACI Demographic Data Comparisons

http://www.demographics.caci.com/free_samples/zip_code_searches.htm

- Marketers often want to compare the demographics of one geographic area with national averages.
- CACI provides comparisons on its Web site for zip codes within the United States.
- When a specific zip code is entered, CACI compares the zip code to the national average for population by race, population by gender, median household income, and median home values and rent.
- The dominant ACORN market segment in the zip code is identified and described.
- Figure 7–2 shows the ZIP code data entry form.

3. **Purpose-of-Trip Segmentation.** Chapter 5 introduced the concept of purpose-of-trip segmentation (dividing hospitality and travel markets according to the primary purpose of the customer's trip). Use of this segmentation base is widespread. Lodging, restaurant, travel agency, cruise line, airline, and destination marketing organizations traditionally apply it as at least part of their segmentation approach.

   The most important consideration in selecting a primary segmentation base should be that it represents the factor with the greatest influence on the customer's behavior. Splitting the hospitality and travel market into two main groups—the business travel market and the pleasure and personal travel market—is a widely accepted practice. It is generally agreed that the needs and wants of business and pleasure/personal travelers are quite different. For example, businesspersons prefer locations close to their place of business. While on vacation, these same people look for lodging near attractions. Pleasure travelers spending their own money are more price-sensitive than businesspersons on expense accounts. Segmentation in the hospitality and travel industry, therefore, often involves two-stage or multistage approaches with purpose of trip as the primary segmentation base.

4. **Psychographic Segmentation.** Psychographic segmentation has recently gained popularity. Psychographics is the development of psychological profiles of customers and psychologically based measures of distinctive modes of living or lifestyles.[1] A lifestyle is a way of living characterized by the manner in which people spend their time (*activities*), what things they consider important (*interests*), and how they feel about themselves and the world around them (*opinions*)—their AIOs.[2] These are all factors used in lifestyle segmentation.

ON THE WEB

Demographic Solutions by CACI

home ▪ about us ▪ products ▪ services ▪ solutions ▪ partnerships ▪ news ▪ order online ▪ mapdata

free samples

contact us ▪ sitemap ▪ free samples

CACI
eBusiness
Solutions

ACORN® cd

download demos

electronic
newsletter

ZIP lookup

mapdata samples

zip lookup

Includes 2000 data and national averages!

Using our search tool to find **demographic data** for a ZIP code, enter the code and click on the "Find my ZIP!" button. This data also contains **national averages** for the same statistics and the dominant ACORN® cluster data for the region. Enjoy!

Please Enter ZIP Code	
Find My ZIP!	

Courtesy of the U.S. Postal Service, you can also search for ZIP Codes by city name.

14151 Park Meadow Drive, Chantilly, Virginia 20151
Phone: 800-292-2224/East or 800-394-3690/West

◆ **FIGURE 7–2**   *A great way to compare demographic data by ZIP codes.* (Courtesy of CACI Marketing Systems)

People's activities, interests, and opinions are diverse. Just think about yourself for a minute. What you do at college is quite different from what you do at home, on vacation, or during a night out on the town. You probably have many interests. Some revolve around your school life and some are favorite hobbies, sports, or other leisure-time interests. You also hold a variety of beliefs about yourself, the educational system, politics and political events, specific products and services, social issues, and other things in the external environment. The following is a list of activities, interests, and opinions shared by most people.[3]

A. Activities	**B. Interests**	**C. Opinions**
• Work	• Family	• Themselves
• Hobbies	• Home	• Social issues
• Social events	• Job	• Politics
• Vacation	• Community	• Business
• Entertainment	• Recreation	• Economics
• Club membership	• Fashion	• Education
• Community	• Food	• Products
• Shopping	• Media	• Future
• Sports	• Achievements	• Culture

When we looked at demographic and geographic segmentation, one of the obvious advantages was that everyone uses the same definitions and rules. In the hospitality and travel industry, most people also have a similar understanding of purpose-of-trip segments. This is not the case with psychographic segmentation. There are many alternative ways of defining and describing psychographic or lifestyle segments.

Chapter 4 identified lifestyle as a personal factor that influences customer behavior. It also describes the VALS™ (Values and Lifestyles) and PRIZM programs developed by professional research firms as psychographic segmentation techniques that many marketers favor.

Instead of using a technique such as VALS™ or PRIZM, an organization can develop its own psychographic segmentation scheme based on marketing research. A battery of questions can be developed that relate to customers' activities, interests, and opinions. Most researchers then use techniques such as factor or cluster analysis to identify specific segments based on the similarity of respondents' answers to certain questions. An example of this in the travel field is a joint study of potential travelers by the U.S. Tourism Industries Office (TI) and Canadian Tourism Commission (CTC). Part of this work involved segmenting travelers in France, Japan, the United Kingdom, Germany, and other countries into *travel arrangement/philosophy* groups. Respondents in these countries were asked to answer questions on their feelings about travel in general, and how they prefer to travel. Using cluster analysis on the results, seven segments were identified (guarded independents, guarded, reluctant, affirmed package, enthusiastic independent, guarded package, and reluctant).[4]

Although psychographic segmentation is a more sophisticated method than geographic, demographic, and purpose of trip and is thought to be a good predictor of customer behavior, one of its major drawbacks is its lack of a uniform approach toward segmentation. Another caution is that it cannot be used on its own. It must be part of a two-stage or multistage segmentation approach. Although psychographics can be the primary segmentation base, other factors such as geography and demographics must be used to pinpoint target markets.

5. **Behavioral Segmentation.** Behavioral segmentation divides customers by their use occasions, benefits, user status, usage rate, loyalty status, buyer-readiness stage, and attitudes toward the product of service.[5] In other words, it uses some dimension of a customer's past, current, or potential behavior toward a specific product or service category (e.g., restaurants, hotels, airlines, travel agencies) or specific brands (e.g., Carnival, Disney, Princess, or Royal Caribbean).

   a. *Use Frequency.* Use-frequency segmentation means dividing the overall market based on the number of times a service is purchased or on each segment's share of the total demand. Some experts use the terms *volume* or heavy-half segmentation instead of use frequency. Like psychographic segmentation, this concept has gained popularity in the hospitality and travel industry. It is based on a very simple concept—there are segments of the population that tend to purchase specific services or products more frequently than others. Because these segments usually account for the lion's share of an organization's business, it makes sense to devote a large proportion of marketing resources to them.

   The classic example used to illustrate this technique is beer consumption. A research study conducted in 1962 suggested that 88 percent of the beer sold in the United States was consumed by only 16 percent of the population.[6] This segment was defined as the *heavy half* (no pun intended), or the 50 percent of users who buy the majority of a product or service. The study also identified the *light half* and *nonuser* segments. In the beer example, nonusers were 68 percent of the population, whereas the light half represented 16 percent of the population consuming 12 percent of the beer.

Until the mid-1970s, the hospitality and travel industry made little use of this type of segmentation. However, intensified competition caused by airline deregulation, overcapacity lodging situations, increasing popularity of database marketing, and other factors changed this. Organizations started to look more closely at sources of past customers and volumes of repeat business. Research studies showed that there were customers who traveled much more often than average. These people have become widely known as the frequent travelers. Almost all major airlines and hotel companies now have special reward programs for frequent users of their services. Holiday Inn's Priority Club, launched in 1983, was the first of its kind among U.S. lodging companies. American Airlines usually receives the credit for originating the concept among the airlines. Car rental companies introduced similar programs, and other suppliers followed suit. The objectives of these programs are simple: To encourage repeat use by frequent travelers and to build brand loyalty for the airline or hotel chain (Figure 7–3).

Not surprisingly, the main focus of frequent-traveler programs is on the business traveler. The 1994 Lodging Guest Survey conducted on behalf of the American Hotel & Motel Association highlights the importance of frequent travelers (defined as people who took five or more trips in the past 12 months) to hotels. Thirty-two percent of these frequent travelers took more than 10 trips in 1994. Some 35 percent of them spent 31 nights or more a year in lodging properties.[7] A survey conducted in 1992 by the Air Transport Association found that 8 percent of the passengers on United States domestic flights had flown at least 10 times during 1992. Although representing a small proportion of all passengers, these frequent flyers accounted for a high 46 percent of the total air trips.[8]

The attractiveness of use-frequency segmentation is clear—a dollar spent on marketing to frequent users should produce a better return on investment than if it is spent on other target markets. Although this seems the best logic in the world, a word of caution is necessary. It is not yet known whether frequent travelers have characteristics—apart from their more regular trips—that make them different from other travelers. Additionally, it is clear that not all frequent travelers are alike and that further segmentation is required for maximum effectiveness. Thus, as with psychographic segmentation, use frequency should be chosen as part of a two-stage or multistage approach. For example, a combination of use frequency, purpose-of-trip, and geographic segmentation might prove effective for many hospitality and travel organizations. Increasing use of computerized databases (database marketing) in our industry is helping marketers pinpoint these lucrative customers.

Another potential drawback is the intense competition for the frequent traveler's business. This approach tends to focus most of the attention on heavy users of services and products and away from medium, light, and nonusers. However, some organizations may find great success in targeting one or more of these other segments.

With over **2,000** hotels now in the Hilton HHonors® family, you'll discover both Points & Miles at more places than ever before.

Only Hilton HHonors makes your travel more rewarding.

The Hilton HHonors family just got bigger. Much, much bigger. Now, in addition to Hilton, Hilton Garden Inn and Conrad International hotels, you'll earn both Points & Miles at Doubletree, Embassy Suites, Hampton Inn, Hampton Inn & Suites and Homewood Suites by Hilton. So, stay with the new Hilton HHonors family of hotels, and discover how "&" can be more rewarding. To enroll in Hilton HHonors or to make reservations, call your professional travel agent or **1-800-HHONORS**. Or, receive a 1,000 point bonus by enrolling online at www.hiltonhhonors.com.

Hilton HHonors
Points & Miles™

◆ **FIGURE 7–3**   *The Hilton HHonors program offers frequent travelers points and miles.* (Courtesy of Hilton HHonors Worldwide)

b. ***Usage Status and Potential.*** Customers can be grouped according to their usage status. Examples of this approach include splitting the market into nonusers and former, regular, and potential users. Another application is to divide customers by the number of times they have purchased an organization's

Did You Know?

Database Marketing by the Aruba Tourism Authority

✓ The Aruba Tourism Authority (ATA) traditionally converted 12 percent of those who asked for information through its 800 number into actual visitors to the island.

✓ In the mid-1990s, ATA introduced the *Hug-and-Hold Inquirer Conversion and Repeat System* to attract prospective and repeat visitors at a lower cost per visitor.

✓ The system scans the zip codes of people who enquire from the United States and compares these codes to a database of household incomes by zip code.

✓ If a person's zip code has an average income equal to or above the U.S. average, they receive three staged mailings of the magazine, *Aruba Holiday Traveler* (the initial mailing and two others after four and twelve months).

✓ ATA checks the names of these people against the island's customs database from the international airport.

✓ The conversion rates from doing this check of names more than doubled, from 12 to 26 percent.

Source: *Direct Marketing*[9]

---

services (e.g., first-time customers, two-time customers, and so on). Different marketing programs are often justified for each of these approaches.

Much attention in travel research and marketing is given to potential travelers and customers, especially to their travel destination areas, which rely on a high percentage of first-time visitors. Some experts even refer to this as *usage potential segmentation*. Usually, research is done on persons who have not visited or used the service before. Based on these people's responses, they are divided into high-, medium-, and low-potential users. Obviously, the high-potential-user segment warrants the greatest attention.

Again, when this approach is used in the hospitality and travel industry, it tends to be part of a two-stage or multistage segmentation approach (e.g., a combination of geographic, purpose of trip, and usage status or potential).

c. ***Brand Loyalty.*** Brand loyalty is a concept just beginning to catch on in the hospitality and travel industry, although it has been around for decades in consumer-goods industries. Customers are divided according to their loyalty to a specific brand and their use of competitive brands. There are four brand-loyalty segments: hard-core loyals, split loyals, shifting loyals, and switchers.[10] Using lodging as an example, a hard-core loyal is someone who always stays at a Holiday Inn when he or she is out of town. A split loyal is someone who consistently uses two or three lodging brands, for example, Holiday Inn Express, Hampton Inn, and Fairfield Inn. This person's loyalties are divided among these three chains. A shifting loyal is someone who shifts loyalties periodically from one brand to another. For example, this customer may stay at a Hyatt on three consecutive occasions, stay at a Marriott the next three, return to the Hyatt, and so on. A switcher has no loyalty to any particular brand. These people are either consummate bargain hunters or simply enjoy a high level of variety. Any effort to attract them usually produces only short-term benefits.

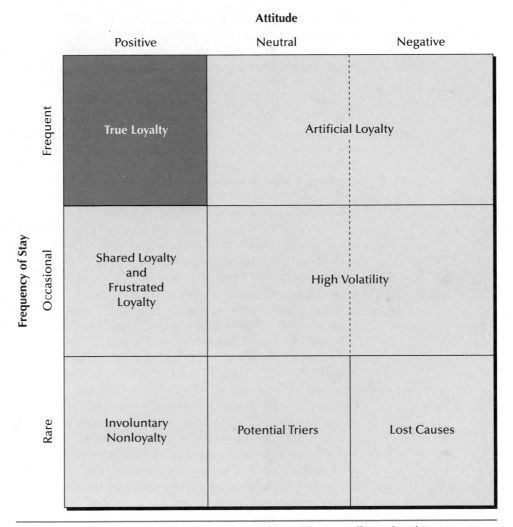

♦ FIGURE 7–4   *Chain-loyalty matrix.* (Reprinted from *The Cornell Hotel and Restaurant Quarterly.* Jarvis, Lance P., and Edward J. Mayo, "Winning at the market-share game," 75, (1986), with permission from Elsevier Science.)

Another approach to brand-loyalty segmentation is illustrated in Figure 7–4. The originators of this matrix feel that even though a guest frequently stays with a particular hotel chain, she may not be loyal to that chain.[11] She may, in fact, have a neutral or even negative attitude toward the chain. *True loyalty,* by their definition, involves frequent stays at chain properties, plus a positive attitude toward the corporation. Figure 7–4 shows nine loyalty segments derived by constructing a three-by-three matrix and using frequency of stay and attitude as the two axes. The main conclusion here is that all nine segments require different marketing approaches, the ultimate goal being to eventually attract a high percentage of *truly loyal* customers.

The concept of brand segmentation has become a hot topic in the hospitality and travel industry, especially among hotel chains, restaurant companies, airlines, and cruise lines. Although the use of brand-loyalty segmentation has been limited, it will become more popular in the future.

d. ***Use Occasions.*** Occasion-based segmentation categorizes customers according to when they buy and the purpose of their purchases. Purpose-of-trip segmentation, discussed earlier in this chapter, is a variant of use-occasion segmentation. Here, the main travel occasions are business, vacation, and other family or personal reasons. One excellent example of a use-occasion segment is the honeymooner market (Figure 7–5). Couples take these trips when they get married to fulfill an age-old tradition. Special banquets to mark anniversaries, birthdays, retirements, holidays, and awards are another form of use-occasion segmentation in restaurants and hotels. Another example is splitting the convention-meeting market (a purpose-of-trip segment) into annual conventions, chapter meetings, board meetings, educational seminars, sales meetings, and so on.

The history of Enterprise Rent-A-Car is perhaps the most outstanding example of a company using occasion-based segmentation to fill a neglected niche in the market. Enterprise supplies vehicles to people who need cars because of accidents, mechanical repairs to their own vehicles, or thefts (the occasions). In the car rental business, this is known as the *replacement* market segment. The company has grown from 17 vehicles in 1963 and an office in St. Louis, Missouri, to a fleet of about 500,000 vehicles and 4,000 locations in the United States, Canada, U.K., and Germany. Using the distinctive slogan, "Pick Enterprise. We'll pick you up," the company offers the unique benefit of taking the car to the customer.

e. ***Benefits.*** Many marketing experts consider benefit segmentation to be the best segmentation base. It groups customers according to similarities in the benefits that they look for in specific products or services. Why is this form of segmentation thought to be so powerful? The answer is that people do not just buy services, they buy a *package* of benefits they will get when they buy the service. You will remember also that the essence of a marketing orientation is to provide customers with what they need and want.

One of the originators of the benefit-segmentation idea said that benefits motivate purchases, and that other segmentation bases are only descriptive.[12] In other words, benefits should always be the primary segmentation base, with other criteria such as purpose of trip, geographic location, and demographics being used to focus more precisely on the best targets (a two-stage or multistage segmentation approach).

Although there have been many studies in the hospitality and travel industry to determine the benefits, attributes, or features that customers look for in certain services, use of benefit segmentation has been limited to date. For example, several studies of lodging customers have pinpointed location, cleanliness, and price as three of the top reasons for selecting accommodations. Convention/meeting planners consistently have been shown to rate the quality of food and foodservice as one of the most important benefits sought. Convenient schedules, lower fares, and on-time departures are very important to business airline travelers. The problem is that, although this type of information exists, few marketers have taken the next step of identifying and pursuing specific benefit segments. It may seem that many are using this approach, but in fact they are simply promoting features corresponding to the benefits that customers typically seek. As with psychographic, a major drawback of this type of segmentation is the lack of uniform definitions of hospitality and travel benefit segments. Although the toothpaste market has almost universally accepted benefit segments, our industry has not.

Hawai'i Honeymoons...

as unique as the two of you

The incredible variety of resorts and activities in Hawai'i allows you to create a honeymoon that's entirely unique and perfectly suited...to you. Choose relaxing or exciting, the beach or the mountains, horseback riding or windsurfing, golf or tennis, economy or deluxe...or maybe a little of everything. It's easy to do here in the Islands of Aloha.

And Aloha means "with love." The Spirit of Aloha, of love, is everywhere in Hawai'i. Aloha will send you home refreshed and renewed, ready to start your new life together. Aloha is the final ingredient for a honeymoon as perfect and as unique as the two of you.

For the *free*
Wedding & Honeymoon Guide
or Official Travel Planner,
call 1-800-GO-HAWAII
www.gohawaii.com

HAWAI'I
The Islands of Aloha

◆ FIGURE 7–5 *Appealing to honeymooners is an example of use occasion segmentation.* (Courtesy of Hawaii Visitors & Convention Bureau)

6. **Product-Related Segmentation.** Product-related segmentation uses some aspect of the service to classify customers. It is a popular approach in the hospitality and travel industry. Stop and think about some of the terms that have become commonplace in our business. What about fast-food customers, the incentive travel market, the cruise market, the ski market, the budget hotel market, the all-suite hotel market, the inclusive tour market, the luxury travel market, the motorcoach market, the casino gambling market, and many others? Common to all of these is the classification of customers according to the degree that specific types of services appeal to them.

Costa Rica and Trinidad & Tobago provide two great examples of destination marketing organizations using product-related segmentation. Costa Rica has very effectively marketed its natural resources to become one of the leading ecotourism destinations in the Americas. A spectacular brain coral is the centerpiece of an advertisement aimed at attracting scuba divers to plumb the depths of Trinidad & Tobago.

Product-related and brand segmentation have become more popular in the industry. This was particularly evident among North American lodging chains in the 1980s and 1990s. Major lodging chains such as Cendant Corp., Bass Hotels & Resorts, Marriott International, Choice Hotels International, Starwood Hotels & Resorts, Hilton, Carlson Hospitality, and Accor opened different types of properties under one corporate umbrella. As you will see in Chapter 10, mergers and acquisitions by the majors also allowed them to add to their brand portfolios. In 1999, Hilton swooped in and acquired Promus, giving it the Hilton, Homewood Suites, Doubletree, Hampton, Conrad International, and Embassy Suites brands.

You might be thinking that this segmentation base smacks of the very production orientation that was criticized earlier. Should not the customer's needs, wants, and benefits sought be more important than the service itself? Pat yourself on the back—you are right. Using product-related segmentation on its own is not recommended. In essence, it is a way of describing customer groups with needs and wants that correspond to certain types of hospitality and travel services. For example, the all-suite hotel concept was created to serve the needs of longer-stay guests, particularly relocated managers and executives. The fast-food restaurant concept emerged to meet the need for inexpensive, quality, standardized, and quick meals.

Product-related segmentation should be used as part of a two-stage or multi-stage approach. It is also useful only when the service's typical users have different characteristics from those of nonusers or can be reached directly with some form of promotion.

7. **Channel-of-Distribution Segmentation.** *Channel-of-distribution segmentation* is different from the six previous segmentation bases since it is a way to divide up travel trade intermediaries rather than customers. Chapter 2 identified distribution channels as a key difference between services and products. Chapter 13 looks at the hospitality and travel industry's distribution channels in detail. The basic concept that both chapters emphasize is that hospitality and travel organizations have the option of (1) marketing directly to customers, (2) marketing through intermediary organizations (e.g., travel agents), or (3) a combination of (1) and (2). Different marketing approaches are required for customers and intermediary organizations.

Channel-of-distribution segmentation means dividing travel intermediaries or the travel trade by function and by common characteristics shared by functional groups. As is true with customers in general, all intermediaries or travel trade companies are not alike. There are groups that perform specific functions, such as retailing hospitality and travel services (travel agents), assembling custom-prepared incentive trips (incentive travel planners), and developing and coordinating tours and vacation packages (tour wholesalers and operators). Within each group, there are major differences in organization sizes, geographic areas served, degrees of specialization, policies in dealing with suppliers, and other factors. Other hospitality and travel organizations using their services must decide which of the many available channel segments match the profile of their target markets. In other words, segmenting customers comes first and is followed by segmenting distribution channels.

An example might further clarify this concept. Suppose that a theme park traditionally has marketed directly to customers, but is exploring the use of travel trade channels to promote new package deals for off-peak periods. By surveying its visitors, the park's management could determine which cities or city districts (geographical segmentation) provide the majority of its business. Management would then identify travel agencies in these cities that either specialize in the theme park's destination area, have high vacation-travel versus corporate-travel volumes, have sufficient total volume, or have some combination of the three. The park's managers would then approach these agencies about marketing a special commissionable (pays commissions to travel agents) program of the park's new packages.

Although there are some organizations that deal exclusively with travel intermediaries (e.g., tour wholesalers), most need to market both to customers and intermediaries. Channel-of-distribution segmentation is a useful method for matching target markets to the most appropriate channel groups. By its very nature, it is always used as part of a two-stage or multistage segmentation approach.

MARKET TRENDS AND SEGMENTATION

Many would-be humorists characterize the post-World War II years from 1946 to the early 1960s as the era of mom, pop, the two kids, the station wagon, a dog, and one very large mortgage. The so-called family market was a well-defined target for most marketers. During this time, many household-name chains, including Holiday Inn, Disneyland, and McDonald's, got their start. You already know that things have changed drastically since then. What has happened in the 1960s, 1970s, 1980s, and 1990s has meant that the hospitality and travel market is much more fragmented or segmented than ever before. Although the family market remains strong, there are many other viable target markets that can be pursued. Thus, the correct use of segmentation techniques is becoming increasingly important in marketing.

Demand- and Supply-Side Changes

In the 1950s, our industry emphasized standardization, or a *sameness* across the country. Today the emphasis is the opposite. There is a focus on diversity. Changes in customers' behavior dictated this move, and our industry is reacting to fill newly emerging needs. Therefore, trends have occurred both on the demand and the supply side. Let us take a brief look at each of the two sides.

Demand-Led Trends

Six demand-led trends are particularly important to the hospitality and travel industry:

1. Changing age structure
2. Changing household structures
3. Changing household roles and responsibilities
4. Increasing importance of minorities
5. Changing social/cultural patterns and lifestyles
6. Increased demand for specific travel alternatives

1. **Changing Age Structure.** The population in the developed world is aging (Figure 7–6). This generally is felt to be a positive trend for our industry, since there will be more customers with the independence and financial means to travel and dine out.

   Two demographic segments that are attracting particular attention because of above-average growth are the baby boomers and those over age 55. A baby boomer is anyone born in the period between 1946 and 1964, that is, following the end of World War II. At the turn of the millennium these people were all between 36 and 54 years of age. The Baby Boomers attract so much marketing attention because of the size of this age cohort. For example, the AARP estimated that there were 76 million Americans in this age group in 1999.[13] Baby boomers are known to be more frequent travelers than their parents and regard travel as a necessity rather than a luxury.

   In the period from 1999 to 2050, the highest population growth rate will be in the traditional retirement age group—those 65 and over. The U.S. Census Bureau

Country	Population in millions (1999)	Age 0–14 (%)	Age 15–64 (%)	Age 65 and over (%)
Developed nations				
USA	272.6	22%	66%	12%
Canada	31.0	20%	68%	12%
UK	59.1	19%	65%	16%
Australia	18.8	21%	66%	13%
France	59.0	19%	65%	16%
Germany	82.1	15%	69%	16%
Developing nations				
China	1,246.9	26%	68%	6%
India	1,000.8	34%	61%	5%
Indonesia	216.1	30%	65%	5%

◆ FIGURE 7–6   *The aging of the population in the developed world. The over 65 group is much more important in developed nations than in developing nations.* (Source: The CIA World Factbook, 2000)

It's roomier. It's comfier. It's a double upgrade.

AARP members can take advantage of a double upgrade with Hertz.

Treat yourself to a first-class ride with a free double upgrade from Hertz. Reserve a midsize through sporty 2-door car, call your travel agent or Hertz at **1·800·654·2210** in advance and mention **CDP# 50075** and the appropriate PC# from the coupon below. If a car from the next two higher classes is available, you'll get it at the discounted, lower car class rate. Even if you rent one-way. You can also visit **hertz.com** or AOL Keyword: **hertz**. Big car luxury at a small car price. Another reason nobody does it exactly like Hertz. **The world's #1 in car rental.**

Two Car Class Upgrade	CDP# 50075

Mention this offer and your Hertz **CDP# 50075** when you reserve a midsize or sporty 2-door car (Class C or D) at Hertz Standard or Leisure Round Trip and One Way Daily, Weekly or Weekend Rates. At the time of rental, surrender this coupon and present your AARP Membership Card, Hertz Member Discount Card or Traveler's Select℠ card for identification. If a car from the next two higher classes is available (Class F or G), you'll be driving it at the discounted lower car class rate. **For reservations, call your travel agent, call Hertz at 1·800·654·2210 or visit hertz.com.** Advance reservations are required as blackouts may apply in some cities at some times, especially during periods of peak demand. If a blackout occurs, you're still entitled to your member discount and can save this offer for another trip as it's good through 6/30/01. This offer is redeemable at participating Hertz locations in the Continental U.S. and is subject to vehicle availability. Highest obtainable upgrade is to a Premium (Class G) car. This coupon has no cash value and may not be used with any other CDP#, coupon, discount, rate or promotion. Hertz standard driver and credit qualifications for the renting location apply and the car must be returned to that location. Minimum rental age is 25 with this offer. Call Hertz for details.
Coupon expires 6/30/01
Round Trip PC# 158620
One Way PC# 158616

AARP APPROVED

Hertz
exactly.

Hertz rents Fords and other fine cars. ® REG. U.S. PAT. OFF. © HERTZ SYSTEM INC., 2001/020-01

◆ **FIGURE 7–7**   *Hertz offers upgrades to AARP members.* (Courtesy of Hertz System, Inc.)

forecasts a 137 percent increase, as this group grows from 34.6 million in 1999 to 82 million in 2050.[14] Together with those aged between 50 and 64, these people represent a sizable and increasingly attractive target for the hospitality and travel industry. They have more money, higher education levels, a greater desire to travel, and better health than did their predecessors.

Many hospitality and travel organizations have developed and are promoting special programs for older customers. For example, Northwest Airlines offers the *NorthBest Senior Travel Coupon Program* for passengers aged 62 years or more. Gray Line Worldwide offers a 10 percent discount to AARP members on its tours. Several cruise lines, hotel chains, and car rental companies (Figure 7–7) offer discounts to AARP members, as does Virgin Atlantic Airways. Many restaurants have also gotten into the act by providing discounted meal or beverage prices and early-bird specials for older persons.

Some companies have gone even further and serve the older traveler exclusively. ElderTreks, a Toronto-based tour operator, serves travelers aged 50 and over "who love adventure" and who do not want "to see a country through the windows of a tour bus." The company's trips are of the "soft adventure" variety and include visits to destinations such as Belize, Borneo, Costa Rica, Ecuador, Nepal, and Vietnam.

2. **Changing Household Structures.** The predictable family structure of the 1950s gave way to greater diversity in household composition at the start of the new millennium. Between 1990 and 2000, non-family and single-parent households increased at a faster rate than married-couple households (see Did You Know?).

The *singles* market has certainly taken much of the limelight off the family market. Later marriages, higher divorce rates, and more older people living alone and longer are factors sparking the significant increases in the number of single adults.

Did You Know?

U.S. Household and Family Characteristics, 1998

The following statistics from the U.S. Census Bureau give a clear idea of the diversity of households that now exist:

✓ 70.9 million family and 31.6 million non-family households total 102.5 million households.

✓ 35 million family households with own children under 18 living at home.

✓ 10 million family households with own children over 18 living at home.

✓ 9.6 million single-parent households with own children under 18 living at home.

✓ 2.1 father-child and 9.8 million mother-child family groups.

✓ 26 million people in non-family households living alone.

Source: *U.S. Census Bureau, Household and Family Characteristics, March 1998.*[15]

Again, many hospitality and travel marketers have honed in on the singles market as a prime target. Club Med pioneered this move among resorts, followed by several others with variations on the same theme. For another demonstration of this point, check the shelves of your local grocery store. You will find that many special packages are available *for singles only.*

3. **Changing Household Roles and Responsibilities.** A revolution has taken place in the role of women in North American society. The major impact of this change has been the substantially larger number of women in the work force. For example, only 19.2 percent of U.S. married-couple families in 1999 were households in which only the husband worked. Some 71.8 percent of mothers with children under 18 were in the labor force.[16] The hospitality and travel industry has felt the full force of this trend. Travel surveys taken about 1970 showed that female travelers made up fewer than 5 percent of all business travelers. By 1993 this figure had catapulted to nearly 40 percent.[17] Some experts believe that in this first decade of the 2000s, females will represent between 45 and 50 percent of all business travelers. Most agree that women business travelers are the fastest-growing segment of the business travel market. To respond to this trend, many hospitality and travel companies have modified their facilities and services to accommodate the special needs of businesswomen more effectively. These changes include extra skirt hangers, more toiletries, hair dryers, full-length mirrors in rooms, and 24-hour room service.

Some organizations have worked especially hard at meeting the needs of the woman business traveler. For example, Delta Airlines and American Express have established the Executive Woman's Travel Network (EWTN). Among other benefits, EWTN provides a Travel Resource Center on the Web with important information for female business travelers. Signature Inns, also through its Website, provides excerpts from Laurie Borman's book, *The Smart Woman's Guide to Business Travel.*

A byproduct of the increasing number of working women has been the growth of two-income families. This has had a profound impact on family eating habits and vacation patterns. Family time is being severely pressured by work schedules and responsibilities, and this has increased the demand for convenience in travel and dining out. Well into the 2000s, some historians may refer to the 1990s as the *drive-through decade,* when more and more North Americans received their nutrition through small

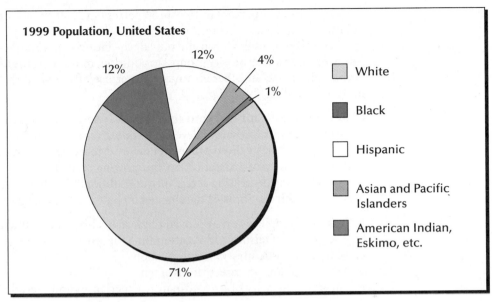

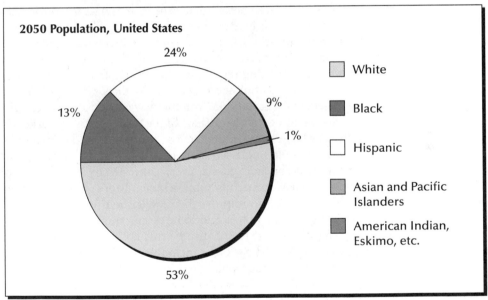

◆ FIGURE 7–8   *Expected shift in ethnic makeup of U.S. population, 1999–2050.* (Source: U.S. Census Bureau, January 2000)

holes in restaurant walls. It may also be remembered as the time when the word *microwaveable* was added to the English language. At the start of the new millennium, many restaurants offered the convenience of ordering food for home delivery or take-out via their Web sites. Recent years have seen an upsurge in the popularity of week-end "getaways" and other minivacations, as busy couples juggle their work schedules.

4. **Increasing Importance of Minorities.** In many developed countries, racial and ethnic minorities are growing at above-average rates and are attracting greater attention from marketers. Figure 7–8 presents an example of this demographic trend for the United States. This shows the traditional majority (white) population

decreasing from 71 percent in 1999 to 53 percent in 2050, with a significant increase in Hispanic and Asian groups.[18]

Several companies within and outside the industry have enjoyed success by targeting one or more minority groups. In addition, more advertisements now feature visible minorities, and there is much greater use of the Spanish language in promotions and directional signs.

5. **Changing Social/Cultural Patterns and Lifestyles.** Sweeping changes have taken place in the cultural mosaic of developed countries, and the population is now more socially and culturally diverse than ever before. Most experts attribute these changes to increased affluence and education, the growing desire to escape the complexity of everyday life, and decreasing acceptance of traditional Puritan/Protestant ethics, beliefs, and principles. Some of the changes include the following:

   a. Increased emphasis on improved physical health, fitness, and appearance
   b. Greater use of leisure and vacation time for self-improvement
   c. More hedonistic lifestyles and vacations
   d. More emphasis on careers for women
   e. Greater popularity of back-to-nature experiences and lifestyles

   You might get a better picture of these trends by considering a few examples. The *fitness craze* is evident throughout the world. People now exercise more, are more nutrition-conscious, and shun health-damaging items such as cigarettes and hard liquor. Non-smoking sections in restaurants, non-smoking hotel rooms, non-smoking rental cars, and smoke-free cruises are now quite common. Sales of lower-alcohol beverages such as wines, wine coolers, and light beers have increased, while hard liquor volumes have dropped. Low-calorie and caffeine-free soft drinks now own a large share of the total soft drink market. Salad bars and low-calorie or low-carbohydrate menus are now featured in many restaurants. In addition, more hotels and motor hotels now offer exercise equipment or full-scale health clubs for their guests. Every town or city has one or more health/fitness clubs, as well as numerous tanning salons. More people each year take vacations at health-spa resorts to improve their looks, their fitness levels, or their diets.

   Many resorts, hotels, and some restaurants have spotted the increased interest in using leisure time to enhance specific skills or to broaden one's education. Many resorts offer special packages, including tennis or golf instruction or classes aimed at improving photographic or gourmet cooking skills. Adults are now more interested in furthering their education. The Mohonk Mountain House in New York satisfies this increasing need by offering seminar packages in cooking, personal health management, foreign languages, and art.[19]

6. **Increased Demand for Specific Travel Alternatives.** Some parts of the hospitality and travel industry have enjoyed growth rates well above average. In part, this has been caused by increased customer demand, coupled with a greater supply. These include cruises, conventions and meetings, incentive travel, motorcoach tours, casino gambling trips, and the already mentioned minivacations and educational/skill-improvement vacations. The number of cruise passengers in 1998, about 5.4 million, was approximately ten times greater than in 1970.[20] For 1999, the meetings industry was estimated to have generated $40.2 billion.[21] Spending on incentive travel has also increased rapidly to the point where the Incentive Federation estimates that it was a $9.8 billion business in 1999.[22] Motorcoach tours are enjoying much greater popularity, particularly because more senior citizens are

choosing this vacation alternative. Travel to participate in casino gambling has grown with the further development of casinos in southern Nevada and Atlantic City, New Jersey, and with the addition of riverboat gambling in the Midwest.

Supply-Side Trends

The public's shifting wants, needs, and preferences during the past 20 to 30 years have opened up a vast store of new marketing opportunities. The hospitality and travel industry has responded with an exciting array of services tailor-made for specific target markets—the industry has learned to practice market segmentation. Ten specific supply-side trends include the following:

1. Increased emphasis on frequent travelers
2. Greater attention to nutritional and fitness needs
3. More marketing to executive and luxury travelers
4. Greater emphasis on weekend packages and other minivacations
5. More attention to women business travelers
6. Greater emphasis on longer-stay travelers
7. More pricing and rate alternatives
8. Greater convenience in services provided
9. Greater variety of ethnic food offerings
10. Increased supply of specific travel offerings

1. **Increased Emphasis on Frequent Travelers.** One supply-side trend already mentioned is the increasing focus on the frequent business traveler by airlines, hotels, car rental firms, and even some credit card companies. Almost every airline and major hotel chain now has an awards program for frequent users of their services. Reciprocal award programs between domestic and international airlines began to be introduced in the late 1980s. Since then, a complicated network of interrelated awards programs has developed (Figure 7–3).

2. **Greater Attention to Nutritional and Fitness Needs.** The industry has really caught on to today's increasingly health-conscious travelers. Even fast-food companies, often criticized for the low nutritional value of their menu items, responded by modifying their offerings or publicizing the contents of their food.

   The strong antismoking movement and governments' growing acceptance of the health dangers of smoking caused major changes in the hospitality and travel industry in the 1980s and 1990s. Smoking is now banned on many countries' domestic flights and is being increasingly restricted on international flights. There is growing public pressure to ban smoking in all public places including restaurants and hotel lobbies. As mentioned earlier, many hotels and resorts began making fitness facilities available to guests.

3. **More Marketing to Executive and Luxury Travelers.** There was a time when most hospitality and travel companies treated all business travelers the same. This practice came to an abrupt end in the late 1970s and early 1980s. Hotel companies, airlines, and some credit card companies started to recognize the lucrative potential of executive-level business and luxury-oriented pleasure travelers. While some airlines upgraded their first-class services, many introduced a new *executive-class* section. Some hotel chains and independents introduced executive or *concierge* floors, where special services such as private lounges, free morning newspapers, complimentary continental breakfasts, upgraded room amenities, and the personal attention of a concierge were provided to guests.

Many special packages have been developed for the pleasure traveler willing to pay for luxury. Companies such as Abercombie & Kent and others specialize in assembling tours to exotic or inaccessible places, or highly pampered trips to other far-off destinations.

4. **Greater Emphasis on Weekend Packages and Other Minivacations.** With more two-income families in the market, the hospitality and travel industry has responded with an increased range of short-duration vacation packages. Among hotel chains, Hyatt, Marriott, and Holiday Inns are especially active in national advertising campaigns to back up these packages.

5. **More Attention to Women Business Travelers.** As already mentioned, airlines, hotels, and restaurants are now devoting more attention to the special needs of female business travelers. Special advertising campaigns now target this group.

6. **Greater Emphasis on Longer-stay Travelers.** One of the major lodging industry innovations of the 1980s was the emergence of the all-suite concept. Although all-suite hotels subsequently broadened their marketing focus, it was their original intent to provide more acceptable accommodations for relocated executives and other extended-duration guests.

7. **More Pricing and Rate Alternatives.** The hospitality and travel industry has bedazzled the traveling public with an ever-increasing range of prices and rates. After deregulation, the only foolproof way to keep track of the huge number of constantly changing air fares was to use computers. Not to be outdone by the airlines, hotels began to offer more special rates based on customer types and time of stay.

8. **Greater Convenience in Services Provided.** Many of us take for granted the extra conveniences and time-saving services provided by the industry. The drive-through window became a permanent fixture at almost all fast-food chain stores. Double drive-throughs (hamburger restaurants with two drive-through lanes that have no sit-down areas inside) or *burger babies* took this idea one step further. Delivery and takeout food services also expanded rapidly, and convenience stores entered the fast-food business. Express check-in and check-out became commonplace at many hotels, and many travel agencies offered extra convenience by delivering tickets.

9. **Greater Variety of Ethnic Food Offerings.** The National Restaurant Association has found that Italian, Chinese, and Mexican are the most popular ethnic foods in the United States, while some less well-known cuisines, such as Japanese sushi, Thai, Caribbean, and Middle Eastern, are reaching a broader audience. In other countries such as the U.K. and Australia, the cuisines of India and other Asian countries have grown rapidly in popularity.

10. **Increased Supply of Specific Travel Offerings.** Among the demand-led trends discussed earlier, we mentioned the greater popularity of certain specific travel alternatives. These included cruises, conventions and meetings, incentive travel, motorcoach tours, casino gambling, and educational/skill enhancement packages. We have also talked about the increased supply of weekend and minivacation packages. The hospitality and travel industry has reacted to customers, changing needs and travel preferences by supplying a much greater inventory of facilities, packages, and services. For example, the number of companies specializing in incentive travel arrangements has grown from a handful to several hundred. Conference centers—specialized resorts catering exclusively to smaller meetings—have sprung up to fill a void in the market. Almost every city now has a convention and visitors bureau

to attract travelers. The so-called move toward *brand segmentation* in the lodging industry is another indication of a response to changing customer needs.

You can see that there has been a push and pull situation between changes in the market and changes in the services provided by the industry. One fact should be clear above all—the need and opportunities for market segmentation have greatly increased in the past 20 years.

CHANGING SEGMENTATION PRACTICES

The hospitality and travel industry has become more sophisticated in its use of market segmentation. Although there is still great room for improvement, the industry is now much more aware of the benefits of effective segmentation and the variety of segmentation bases available.

Traditionally, hospitality and travel marketers have leaned most heavily on demographic, geographic, and purpose-of-trip segmentation, but they are now beginning to add other segmentation bases. With increased use of computers for reservations and customer databases, companies are now in a better position to identify and track their customers' characteristics. This new technology is particularly helpful in pinpointing frequent customers and, therefore, in designing and promoting frequent-traveler award programs.

The industry is also increasing its use of marketing research, including those techniques that pave the way for psychographic/lifestyle, benefit, and brand-loyalty segmentation. Although it is still very much in the experimental stage, the use of these segmentation bases may provide the competitive edge that companies will need in the future.

CHAPTER CONCLUSION

The hospitality and travel industry is maturing in its use of market segmentation. There is growing recognition of the need to select specific target markets and to aim marketing programs at them. At the same time, the market is becoming increasingly diverse, offering more and more possible niches for hospitality and travel marketers. As the industry moves into the twenty-first century, the big winners are most likely to be those organizations that hone in most precisely on their target markets.

Improved marketing research and greater use of computer technology hold great promise for more effective segmentation in the industry. More applications of multi-segmentation also hold good potential for more effective marketing.

REVIEW QUESTIONS

1. How is market segmentation defined in this book?
2. Why is market segmentation so important to effective marketing?
3. What are the benefits of using market segmentation?
4. Does market segmentation have any limitations and, if so, what are they?
5. What are the eight criteria used to determine the viability of market segments?
6. What are the differences between the single-stage, two-stage, and multistage segmentation approaches?

7. What are the seven bases that can be used to segment hospitality and travel markets?
8. Which of the seven segmentation bases have traditionally been used by the industry?
9. Is the hospitality and travel industry becoming more or less segmented? Explain your answer by citing some recent demand and supply trends.
10. Is the industry becoming more or less sophisticated in its use of market segmentation? Justify your answer with a few examples.

CHAPTER ASSIGNMENTS

1. Select an existing hospitality and travel organization and analyze its use of market segmentation. What are the organization's target markets? What segmentation bases are being used? Is the organization employing single-stage, two-stage, or multistage segmentation? Have new services, facilities, packages, or promotional efforts been introduced to more finely key in on target markets? How could the organization improve its market segmentation practices?

2. You have just been hired as the marketing director of an airline, hotel or restaurant chain, travel agency, convention/visitors bureau, or other hospitality/travel organization. As your first assignment, the chief executive has asked you to report on the major demand and supply trends in your field. You have also been asked to outline how the organization can capitalize on these changes. What specific trends would you mention in your report, and how would you try to benefit from them?

3. Select a part of the hospitality and travel industry (e.g., hotels, airlines, car rental agencies, or restaurants) and examine what companies in this industry are doing to attract the frequent traveler or diner. Are the numbers of programs increasing or decreasing? Do companies follow fairly standardized approaches, or is there a great deal of variation? How are programs promoted, and what incentives are offered? Have the programs been effective in increasing brand loyalty?

4. Select a part of the industry and interview several marketing or general managers about their approaches to market segmentation. What segmentation bases are being used? Do the organizations tend to use the same approaches toward segmentation bases? Is it common to find single-stage, two-stage, or multistage segmentation, and why is this? Have approaches to segmentation changed in recent years? Are organizations experimenting with less frequently used segmentation bases (i.e., psychographic, benefit, and behavioral)?

WORLD WIDE WEB RESOURCES

AAdvantage
http://www.aadvantage.com/

Air Transport Association
http://www.air-transport.org/

AARP
http://www.aarp.org/

Abercrombie & Kent
http://www.abercrombiekent.com/

Accor
http://www.accor.com/

American Hotel & Lodging Association (AH&LA)
http://www.ahlaonline.org/

Aruba Tourism Authority
http://www.aruba.com/

CACI Marketing Systems
http://demographics.caci.com/

Canadian Tourism Commission
http://www.canadatourism.com/

Carlson Hospitality Worldwide
http:/www.carlson.com/

Cendant Corp (Hospitality Franchise Systems)
http://www.cendant.com/ctg/

Choice Hotels International
http://www.choicehotels.com/

Contiki
http://www.contiki.com/

Costa Rica
http://www.tourism-costarica.com/

Days Inn
http://www.daysinn.com/

Delta Airlines
http://www.delta.com/

Disney Cruise Line
http://disney.go.com/disneycruise/

EasyJet
http://www.easyjet.com/

ElderTreks
http://www.eldertreks.com/

Enterprise Rent-A-Car
http://www.enterprise.com/

Fairfield Inn
http://www.marriott.com/

Gray Line Worldwide
http://www.grayline.com/

Hampton Inn
http://www.hampton-inn.com/

Hawaii Visitors & Convention Bureau
http://www.gohawaii.com/

Hertz System Inc.
http://www.hertz.com/

Hilton
http://www.hilton.com/

Mohonk Mountain House
http://www.mohonk.com/

Motel 6
http://www.motel6.com/

Northwest Airlines
http://www.nwa.com/

Princess Cruises
http://www.princesscruises.com/

Priority Club
http://www.basshotels.com/priorityclub/

Rent-A-Wreck
http://www.rent-a-wreck.com/

Royal Caribbean
http://www.rccl.com/

Signature Inns
http://www.signature-inns.com/

Southwest Airlines
http://www.southwest.com/

Super 8 Motels
http://www.super8.com/

Tourism Industries Office
http://www.ita.doc.gov/

Travel & Leisure Magazine
http://www.travelandleisure.com/

Trinidad & Tobago
http://www.visittnt.com/

U.S. Census Bureau
http://www.census.gov/

WestJet Airlines Ltd.
http://www.westjet.com/

REFERENCES

1. Mill, Robert Christie, and Alastair M. Morrison. 1998. *The Tourism System: An Introductory Text.* 3rd ed. Dubuque, Iowa: Kendall/Hunt Publishing Company.
2. Assael, Henry. 1995. *Consumer Behavior and Marketing Action.* 5th ed. Cincinnati, Ohio: South-Western Publishing.
3. Plummer, Joseph T. "The concept and application of life style segmentation." *Journal of Marketing* 38 (1):33–37 (1974).
4. Market Facts of Canada Limited. *Pleasure Travel Markets to North America: United Kingdom.* Ottawa: Tourism Canada, May, 50–55 (1987).
5. Kotler, Philip. 2000. *Marketing Management: The Millennium Edition.* 10th ed. Upper Saddle River, N.J.: Prentice-Hall, Inc.
6. Twedt, Dik Warren. "How important to marketing strategy is the 'heavy user'?" *Journal of Marketing* 28 (1):71–72 (1974).

7. "Trends & forecasts." *Business Travel News* 305 (Dec 5):18 (1994).

8. "Business travelers drop to 37% of air passengers." *Travel Weekly* 52 (69):4 (1993).

9. Bono, Jennifer D. "Marketing database heats up tourism for sunny Aruba." *Direct Marketing* 58 (6):18 (1995).

10. Kotler, Philip. 2000. *Marketing Management: The Millennium Edition.* 10th ed. Upper Saddle River, N.J.: Prentice-Hall, Inc.

11. Jarvis, Lance P., and Edward J. Mayo. "Winning the market-share game." *The Cornell Hotel and Restaurant Administration Quarterly* 27 (3):73–79 (1986).

12. Haley, Russell J. "Benefit segmentation: A decision oriented tool." *Journal of Marketing* 32 (3):30–35 (1963).

13. American Association of Retired Persons. 2000. *Baby Boomers Envision Their Retirement: An AARP Segmentation Analysis: Executive Summary Part 1.* http://research.aarp.org/ boomer_seg_1.html.

14. U.S. Census Bureau. 2000. *Census Bureau Projects Doubling of Nation's Population by 2100.* http://www.census.gov/Press-Release/www/2000/

15. Casper, Lynne M., and Ken Bryson. 1998. *Household and Family Characteristics: March 1998.* Washington, D.C.: U.S. Census Bureau.

16. Bureau of Labor Statistics. 1999. *Employment Characteristics of Families Summary.* http://stats.bls.gov/newsrels.htm

17. Gates, Anita. "The best hotels for women." *Working Woman* April, 77–81.

18. U.S. Census Bureau. 2000. *Census Bureau Projects Doubling of Nation's Population by 2100.* http://www.census.gov/Press-Release/www/2000/

19. http://www.mohonk.com/

20. "The cruise industry: An overview: Marketing edition." Cruise Lines International Association August, 2 (1999).

21. "M&C's Meetings Market Report." *Meetings & Conventions.* http://www.meetings-conventions.com/

22. "A study of the Incentive Merchandise and Travel Marketplace, 2000." Incentive Federation. http://www.incentivecentral.org/

For additional hospitality and travel marketing resources, visit our Web site at **www.Hospitality-Tourism.delmar.com**

8

Marketing Strategy: Strategies, Positioning, and Marketing Objectives

Where Would We Like to Be?

Objectives

Having read this chapter, you should be able to:

◆ Identify the six components in developing a marketing strategy and plan.

◆ Define the terms marketing strategy, positioning, and marketing objective.

◆ Explain the concept of segmented marketing strategies and describe the alternative strategies by market focus.

◆ Describe the alternative strategies by product life cycle (PLC) stage.

◆ Describe the alternative strategies by industry position.

◆ Explain the concepts of relationship marketing and strategic alliances.

◆ Identify the reasons that have made positioning essential in today's business climate.

◆ List and describe the steps required for effective positioning (the five Ds).

◆ List and describe the six different approaches to positioning.

◆ Explain the benefits of having marketing objectives and list the four requirements for good marketing objectives.

Overview

What do you do when the market has been segmented and potential target markets are known? The next steps are rather like planning a journey to some exotic or inaccessible place. Any explorers worth their salt recognize the need for a map, a chosen route, the proper types and amount of supplies, a means of access or transportation to their destination, some human (and perhaps an- *imal) help to get there, and day-to-day progress objectives. This chapter begins by describing marketing strategies as the routes to success.*

It looks at the alternative strategies that hospitality and travel organizations can use. The chapter also shows that different strategies work best during the various product life-cycle stages. It describes the strategies that are most effective both for industry leaders and for those trying to catch them.

The chapter examines the technique of positioning and shows how it can be used to obtain

the greatest benefit. It ends by looking at marketing objectives and their importance to successful marketing strategies.

Key Terms

brand segmentation	marketing strategy	segmented marketing strategies
combiners	maturity stage	segmenters
concentrated marketing strategy	nichers	seven core principles
decline stage	niching	single-target-market strategy
differentiated marketing strategies	penetration strategies	skimming strategies
five Ds of positioning	positioning	specific positioning approach
full-coverage marketing strategy	positioning statement	strategic alliances
general positioning approach	preferred suppliers or vendors	undifferentiated marketing
growth stage	product life cycle (PLC)	strategy
introduction stage	relationship marketing	
marketing objective	reposition	

I magine yourself as one of the great explorers of all time—Columbus, Magellan, Raleigh, Scott, Hillary, Marco Polo, Leif Ericson, Livingstone, Baffin, Rasmussen, or even Indiana Jones! All these great men set out to go somewhere and do something that no person had accomplished before. They succeeded. Their great feats took months, sometimes years, of careful planning. In most cases, they had to beg, borrow, and steal to get enough money for their trips. There were many alternate routes to their destinations, but they chose those that involved the least effort and wasted resources. Those who returned alive carefully documented their journeys so that others could retrace their footsteps or find a better route.

Now, you are probably wondering what explorations have to do with marketing. The answer is, as usual, plenty! First, every explorer needs a precise idea of the final destination. For Edmund Hillary, it was the summit of Mount Everest. For Robert Scott, it was the South Pole. All marketers must also know where they want to take their organizations—remember the "Where would we like to be?" question. Both groups need to identify alternate routes and then pick the best ones. Each must also budget for resources needed along the way and choose those that will be most beneficial to reaching the ultimate goal. Explorers and marketers both place a premium on getting the most out of their resources and on having points at which they can check their progress.

THE PROCESS OF DEVELOPING A MARKETING STRATEGY AND PLAN

When marketers are planning how they will get where they want to be, they look at alternative marketing strategies and pick the ones best suited to their organizations and resources. They put their budgets and human resources into activities (marketing mixes) with the greatest expected payoffs. Intermediate progress steps (objectives) are set. If everything works as planned, like explorers who succeed and return alive, marketers will have the privilege of succeeding again.

Before moving ahead, we thought that you would like to know where we are headed. Figure 8–1 is your map, showing how Chapters 7, 8, and 9 link together. Chapter 7 covered market segmentation and the selection of target markets. Chapter 8 describes how a complete marketing strategy is developed and discusses the three concepts of marketing strategy, positioning, and objectives. Chapter 9 talks about the marketing mix (8 Ps) and the marketing plan.

The left colum of Figure 8–1 shows the marketing strategy components and where they are discussed in this book. The steps that marketers must complete are listed in the middle column. The right column shows the outcomes or choices that result from the completion of the steps.

Following are definitions of the three concepts covered in this chapter.

Marketing Strategy

In this book, as in general practice, marketing strategy has a distinct meaning. It is the selection of a course of action from among several alternatives that involves specific customer groups, communication methods, distribution channels, and pricing structures. As most experts would say, it is a combination of target markets and marketing mixes.

Positioning

Often called *product positioning*, positioning is the development of a service and marketing mix to occupy a specific place in the minds of customers within target markets. Usually this means having distinctive service features (e.g., Club Med's ultra, all-inclusive vacations) and/or communicating the position in a distinctive way (e.g., Avis is only No. 2 in rent-a-cars, so why go with us? We try harder.).

Marketing Objective

A marketing objective is a measurable goal that a hospitality or travel organization attempts to achieve for a target market within a specific time period, typically one or two years.

Now let us begin discussing the second component in Figure 8–1—marketing strategy formulation.

MARKETING STRATEGY FORMULATION

Marketing strategy formulation begins by choosing from among alternative strategy options. Three groups of alternatives are discussed in this chapter:

1. Alternative strategies by market focus
2. Alternative strategies for product life-cycle stages
3. Alternative strategies by industry position

Every organization is unique and must select the alternatives that best suit its situation.

MARKETING STRATEGY COMPONENTS	STEPS	OUTCOMES AND CHOICES
1. **Market Segmentation Analysis** (Chapter 7, pages 170–202)	• Divide the market into segments • Select target markets for the organization	♦ Target market or markets
2. **Marketing Strategy Formulation** (Chapter 8, pages 205–221)	• Choose a market focus • Determine industry position • Identify the product life-cycle stage (introduction, growth, maturity, decline)	♦ Single target market, concentrated, full-coverage, or undifferentiated? ♦ Leader, challenger, or follower? ♦ Introduction, growth, maturity, or decline?
3. **Positioning Approach** (Chapter 8, pages 221–228)	• Select a positioning approach (overall and by target market)	♦ Specific product features, benefits/problem, solution/needs, specific usage occasions, user category, against another product, or product class dissociation?
4. **Marketing Objectives** (Chapter 8, pages 228–229)	• Write marketing objectives for each selected target market	♦ Marketing objectives that are target-market specific, results-oriented, quantitative, and time-specific
5. **Marketing Mix (The 8 Ps)** (Chapter 9, pages 249–251)	• Decide on how the 8 Ps are to be used to achieve the marketing objectives for each selected target market	♦ Use of product, partnership, people, packaging, programming, place, promotion, and pricing
6. **Marketing Plan** (Chapter 9, pages 233–252)	• Write up a plan including a marketing plan rationale, implementation plan, and executive summary	♦ Written marketing plan

♦ **FIGURE 8–1**   *The process of developing a marketing strategy and plan.*

1. **Alternative Strategies by Market Focus.** There are four market focus strategies available to hospitality and travel organizations:
   a. Select only one target market from several market segments and market exclusively to it (**single-target-market strategy**).
   b. Select a few target markets from several market segments and concentrate on these (**concentrated marketing strategy**).
   c. Appeal to all market segments in the total market with a tailor-made approach for each of them (**full-coverage marketing strategy**).

d. Recognize that there are different market segments, but ignore these differences when marketing (**undifferentiated marketing strategy**).

Certain names have been coined for organizations that follow these strategies. Groups adopting the single-target-market approach have become known as **nichers**. Organizations using concentrated and full-coverage strategies are often called *segmenters*. The name typically associated with users of the fourth strategy is **combiners**.

a. **Single-Target-Market Strategy.** As we shall see later, this strategy, known as **niching**, is popular with smaller and low-market-share organizations (those with a minor percentage of total demand for the service).[1] A good example in the hospitality and travel industry is *conference-center* resorts, Figure 8–2. The developers of these properties spotted the need for specialized resorts exclusively serving smaller corporate and association meetings and conferences. The real strength of their approach is *specialization* and close attention to the needs of a specific target market. Most other hotels and resorts accommodate convention/meeting groups of all sizes, in addition to other business and pleasure travelers. They rely on demand from several target markets. Unlike most major hotel chains and convention/visitors bureaus, however, conference resorts do not pursue the major association conventions. Instead, they rely on sophisticated audiovisual equipment, purpose-built meeting facilities, and a high level of personal service in arranging and coordinating their customers' meetings. They provide the added touches and services that many larger hotels and resorts overlook or cannot justify.

◆ FIGURE 8–2 *The conference center resort: an application of single-target-market strategy.* (Courtesy of Scottsdale Conference Resort)

There are many other examples of market specialization in the industry. For example, Abercombie & Kent concentrates on offering exclusive, luxury tour packages, often to unusual places. Small, regional air carriers serve specific geographic areas with routes and schedules that major airlines find uneconomical. Cinnabon provides an alternative to fast food with a very narrow line of products (a cinnamon roll plus a few beverages). Most small, independent restaurants specialize by only serving a well-defined local market. A growing number of travel agencies concentrate exclusively on corporate accounts or on cruise vacations.

The essence of the single-target-market approach is to avoid head-to-head competition with industry leaders. The organization selecting this approach chooses one market segment, with the goal of serving its needs more comprehensively than competitive organizations do. In the long term, it is hoped that a strong association with the target market, as well as a reputation for excellent service to that market, will be developed.

b. **Concentrated Marketing Strategy.** This strategy is similar to the single-target-market one, except that a few additional market segments are pursued. Most independent hotels and resorts use this approach. Faced with direct competition from national chains, they provide uniquely designed properties, added services, or personal touches to attract business and pleasure travelers. They offer a single product that serves the needs of several lodging market segments. In contrast, many leading hotel chains have several different brands of properties that they hope will appeal to most, if not all, market segments.

c. **Full-Coverage Marketing Strategy.** The most expensive of the four strategies usually is applied by industry leaders, those nationally based chains with many branch locations. They provide services for every target market and use a unique marketing mix to promote to each one separately.

The concept of brand segmentation in the lodging industry is an application of full-coverage strategy. Marriott International is a prime example. This industry leader stole a page from Procter & Gamble's playbook by offering travelers a complete range of lodging services, from its luxury-oriented J. W. Marriott and Ritz Carlton Hotels to the budget-conscious Fairfield Inns. Recognizing that it is impossible to provide something for everyone under the same roof, Marriott, like Choice Hotels International, Accor, and several others, decided to build properties that appealed strongly to specific market segments.

Other examples in the industry include major North American airlines that gobbled up smaller national and regional/commuter carriers in the 1980s and 1990s. Their objective was to serve all geographic regions with an increased inventory of equipment, personnel, routes, and schedules. In Canada, Pacific Western Airlines created Canadian Airlines by joining with Canadian Pacific Air Lines, Eastern Provincial, and Nordair. Later, Canadian Airlines International was merged with Air Canada. In the United States, US Airways absorbed Allegheny and Piedmont, while Northwest took over Republic. In Australia Qantas added a domestic route system by merging with Australian Airlines.

d. **Undifferentiated Marketing Strategy.** All three previous approaches are examples of segmented marketing or differentiated marketing strategies —

MARKET FOCUS STRATEGIES	ALSO KNOWN AS	MAIN CHARACTERISTICS	EXAMPLES
Single-target market	*Nichers*	• Smaller organizations • Specialized expertise or services for one market segment • Avoid head-to-head competition with industry leaders	• Conference center resorts • Contiki • Couples Resorts • Spa resorts
Concentrated	*Segmenters*	• Organizations serving a local market	• Local hotels and restaurants • Four Seasons Hotels & Resorts
Full-coverage	*Segmenters*	• Industry leaders and challengers	• Accor • Choice Hotels International • Marriott International
Undifferentiated	*Combiners*	• Have products with a very general appeal	• Major quick-service/fast-food chains

◆ FIGURE 8–3   *Summary of the characteristics of the four market-focus strategies.*

methods that recognize differences between target markets by using individualized marketing mixes (Figure 8–3). An *undifferentiated marketing strategy* is one that overlooks segment differences and uses the same marketing mix for all target markets. You might be thinking that organizations using undifferentiated marketing must have a production orientation because they do not recognize the market segmentation concept. You are both right and wrong. Some start out trying to be all things to all people and end up meaning nothing to anyone. On the other hand, some industry leaders use undifferentiated marketing very effectively.

These combiners focus on similarities among customers and try to add product options and promotional appeals with one marketing mix.[2] Combiners are aware of differences in the needs of various target markets, but concentrate on the common needs they share. These target markets are then combined into one *super target market,* and a marketing mix is designed for it.

What are the benefits of the undifferentiated strategy? As mentioned in Chapter 7, market segmentation has drawbacks (added cost, difficulties in choosing the best segmentation base, knowing how finely or broadly to segment, and appealing to nonviable segments). These problems are lessened by combiners, because they aim at several target markets with only one marketing mix.

Are there any combiners in the hospitality and travel industry? If your answer was yes, please accept a little applause. You might remember that we purposely did not answer one question about fast-food operators in Chapter 7. The question was, "When a service's appeal is so broad, does it make any sense to use different approaches for various customer groups, or should the same methods be used for all?" We mentioned McDonald's claim that almost every U.S., Canadian, U.K., and Australian resident has eaten at least once at one of their restaurants. McDonald's and other leading fast-food chains use partially undifferentiated marketing strategies. Their national advertising and promotions are designed to appeal to several target markets. Highly standardized, limited-choice menus are provided to meet common away-from-home eating needs. They use heavy television advertising featuring typical customers from all walks of life. We said partially undifferentiated because McDonald's and some of its competitors allow their franchisees to develop local marketing programs. These local advertising, public relations, and sales promotion efforts have a definite geographic target market. McDonald's also has customized advertising programs for certain minority markets, including black and Hispanic Americans.

Can you imagine the horrendous marketing budgets that KFC, Burger King, and McDonald's would need to advertise in all newspapers and magazines, and on all radio and television stations to reach each and every market segment? It is much more economical for them to use broad-scale promotions. To keep people coming back, these combiners frequently add new menu items, modified items, or packages of items.

2. **Alternative Strategies for Product Life-Cycle Stages.** Chapter 1 identified the product life cycle (PLC) as one of marketing's seven core principles. The basic idea of the PLC is that all products and services pass through the same stages during their histories. They are rather like people—they are born; go through infancy, childhood, and adolescence; reach maturity; and finally attain old age. Services and products also go through four stages. The effectiveness of different marketing approaches varies with product life-cycle stage. Marketing strategies need to be adapted to meet the new challenges of each stage (Figure 8–4).

   a. Introduction
   b. Growth
   c. Maturity
   d. Decline

   a. **Introduction Stage.** The introduction stage begins when a new service is first offered to the public. Traditionally, this has been considered a period of low profits because of the high promotion and other costs required to establish a firm foothold in the market. Often the service or product is priced high and appeals to more adventurous, higher-income customers and other *innovators*.

   Can you think of any new and revolutionary services recently introduced in the hospitality and travel industry? What about all-suite hotels, timesharing condominiums, and frequent-stay programs? In the airline business, there are frequent-flyer programs, and Concorde has initiated supersonic air travel. Others include McDonald's prepackaged salads, video check-out in hotels

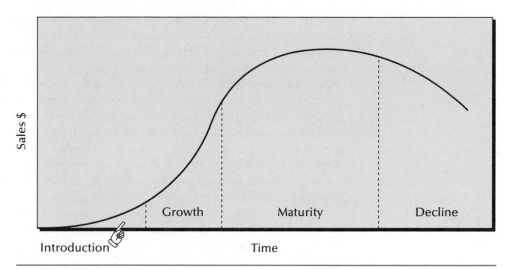

◆ FIGURE 8–4   *The product life cycle.*

(checking out of rooms using in-room television), electronic airline tickets, double drive-through restaurants, theme parks, salad-only restaurants, discotheques, and resort conference centers. One thing you will notice about all of these (except Concorde) is that competitors were very quick to copy the originators' services. Remember from Chapter 2 that services can be copied more easily than products. The introduction stage for any new service tends to be quite short.

    There are four strategies that companies can use in the introduction stage (Figure 8–5).[3] They are based on two different pricing approaches—skimming strategies (using high prices) and penetration strategies (using low prices):

- *Rapid-Skimming Strategy* (high price/high promotion). Skimmed milk is milk from which all the fat has been removed. Market skimming works on

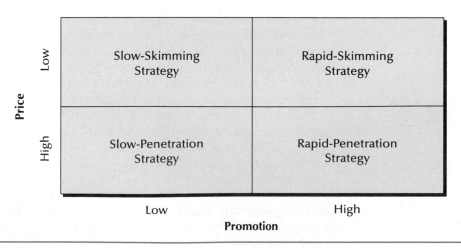

◆ FIGURE 8–5   *Strategies for the introduction stage of the product life cycle.*

exactly the same principle. A high price is charged and the "fat" of the buyers purchase the new service or product. The objective is to earn the highest possible gross profit. A rapid-skimming strategy means the new service is highly promoted when it is first introduced.

- *Slow-Skimming Strategy* (high price/low promotion). The difference between slow and rapid skimming is in the amount spent on promotion. A low promotion budget is used in slow skimming. There are a small number of potential customers, but most are aware of the new service. Competitive services are not expected to be introduced for a considerable time.
- *Rapid-Penetration Strategy* (low price/high promotion). The price level is the key difference between penetration and skimming strategies. With a penetration strategy, prices are initially set low to capture as much of the market as possible. The market for the new service is large, but most buyers are price sensitive (they like lower rather than higher prices). Rapid penetration means teaming low introduction prices with a high level of promotion. Most of the potential purchasers are unaware of the new service. There is a strong threat that competitors will quickly copy it.
- *Slow-Penetration Strategy* (low price/low promotion). Here the new service is introduced at a low price with a low level of promotion. Again, the potential market is large and price sensitive. Unlike with rapid penetration, these customers are highly aware of the new service. There are some potential competitors, but the competitive threat is not as great.

b.   **Growth Stage.** In the growth stage, sales climb rapidly, profit levels improve, and more competitors enter the fray. For the organization pioneering the new service, the following strategies can be used:[4]

- Improving service quality and adding new service features and service elements
- Pursuing new target markets
- Using new channels of distribution
- Lowering prices to attract more price-sensitive customers
- Shifting some advertising emphasis from building awareness to creating desire and action (purchase)

An excellent example of this is the approach taken by Club Med in North America in the 1980s and 1990s. In the late 1970s and 1980s, Club Med enjoyed year-to-year sales increases of 15 percent to 25 percent. To sustain this growth, the company used several of the above-listed strategies. New resorts were opened to ensure sufficient capacity to permit growth. New target markets were pursued, including corporate groups, families with children, honeymooners, sports enthusiasts such as scuba divers and tennis players, and theme weeks. Advertising strategies were shifted from *the one world, one club* theme to pinpoint specific target markets and what each could do at the Club Meds of their choice. Approaches in a price-sensitive environment were made to various market segments including seniors, reunion groups, singles, couples, and families. Club Med also began offering weekend packages in the North American market. Additional features were added at existing and new resorts, including special facilities for young children and babies, personal computer instruction, and boardsailing. The traditional direct-to-customer sales approach was expanded to place much greater emphasis on travel agents.

c. **Maturity Stage.** Many parts of the hospitality and travel industry are now in the **maturity stage** of development. Hotels, fast-food restaurants, car rental companies, and airlines are four examples. This stage is characterized by a slowdown in the rate of sales growth. There are overcapacity situations; too much supply is chasing too little demand. An organization can use three strategies if it wants to maintain its sales growth during this stage:[5]

- *Market-Modification Strategy.* The organization goes after its competitors' customers, adds new target markets, or tries to convert nonusers into users. Other actions that can be taken include encouraging more frequent use or greater use per purchase, or creating new and more varied uses. The frequent-traveler programs of airlines and hotels are a prime example of this, as are the somewhat scathing, comparative advertising attacks by Burger King, Wendy's, Hardee's, and the VISA card.

- *Product-Modification Strategy.* The essence of this approach is rejuvenating the organization's services or products to make them seem new. Have you ever watched what airlines do to their equipment? A new paint job now and then, flashy logos one after the other, constant uniform changes for flight attendants, and games of musical chairs with seating layouts are all examples. Hotels also actively try to keep their customers from becoming jaded. Concierge service, executive floors and lounges, express checkout, and business centers are a few added hotel features.

   Some companies find it necessary to shake off a rather tired image. Ramada, Best Western, and Holiday Inn are good examples.

- *Marketing-Mix-Modification Strategy.* Sales can be stimulated by changing the marketing mix. For example, hotels faced with mature markets can place more emphasis on finding new distribution channels such as travel agents, tour wholesalers, incentive travel planners, or on-line. Restaurants can use coupons and other sales promotions to increase their volumes. Travel agencies may employ commissioned or outside sales agents to bring in more business.

d. **Decline Stage.** What do you do when the sales of your service begin to fall in the **decline stage**? There are alternatives to going out of business completely. Most marketing experts recommend reducing costs and *milking* the company, product, or service as sales decline further. Selling out to someone else is another alternative.

Limitations of the Product Life-Cycle Concept

One of the major criticisms of this concept is its assumption that all sales of all products and services eventually decline to zero or to a very low level. Experience has shown that this is not necessarily true. Many old hotel and resort properties have been restored and rejuvenated to recapture former glories. Consider the *Queen Mary,* which has been transformed from a fabulous ocean liner to a convention and trade show facility in Long Beach, California. Think about the restaurant concepts and menu items that have come and gone, only to be replaced by others. The best answer to the decline-stage dilemma is to rejuvenate the service by finding new uses and customers, picking new channels of distribution, or repositioning (changing perceptions).

Did You Know?

The Story of the *Queen Mary*

✓ The *Queen Mary* was built in Clydebank, Scotland, by Cunard and launched in 1934. She was 67 years old on September 26, 2001.

✓ Her maiden voyage was in 1936.

✓ The *Queen Mary* was longer and heavier than *Titanic* (and made many more successful journeys!). *Titanic,* unfortunately carried more passengers.

✓ The *Queen Mary* made 1,001 transatlantic crossings and on each trip carried up to 1,957 passengers and 1,200 crew.

✓ She was put into war service from 1940 until 1946 and carried more than 765,000 military personnel. The *Queen Mary* was painted all in grey and was known as "The Grey Ghost."

✓ The *Queen Mary* was removed from regular passenger service in 1967 and was purchased by the City of Long Beach, California.

✓ The City of Long Beach had to construct a special landfill, 900-foot pier, parking lot, boarding ramps, and shore protection to accommodate The *Queen Mary.*

✓ She was renovated into a hotel and tourist attraction and opened in 1971. The *Queen Mary* is close to the Long Beach Convention Center.

✓ The *Queen Mary* has 365 staterooms, three restaurants and cafes, 85,000 square feet of meeting space in 14 Art Deco salons (including a 50,000 square foot Exhibit Hall), an art gallery, and shops.

✓ The *Queen Mary Seaport* also functions as a tourist attraction with a separate admission fee.

✓ More information is available at http://www.queenmary.com/

3. **Alternative Strategies by Industry Position.** If you take a look at the hospitality and travel industry, you will find that certain organizations dominate all others. Examples include McDonald's in fast food; The Walt Disney Company in theme parks; Carnival in cruise lines; Florida, California, and Hawaii in travel destinations; Hertz in rental cars; and so on. You will also recognize that other groups—we will call them *challengers and followers*–are not as big or successful, but still have a large slice of the business. In this category are organizations such as Burger King, Wendy's, Hardee's, Avis, Budget, National, and Six Flags. There are still others—let us use the term *nichers* for them—that are even smaller and target a small number or only one specific target market. To recap, there are four industry role or position categories:

   a. Leaders
   b. Challengers
   c. Followers
   d. Nichers[6]

   a. **Market Leaders.** Winning is habit-forming. Once an organization becomes the leader in its field, it rarely decides to give up the number one position. Many of its competitors, however, would also like to be number one or to grab market share away from the leader. Staying on top is perhaps one of marketing's biggest challenges, but some organizations excel at it.

There are three different strategies for market leaders:

- Expanding the size of the total market (or increasing "*primary demand*")
- Protecting market share
- Expanding market share

- ***Expanding the Size of the Total Market.*** The total or primary market can be increased in three ways:

  i. Find new target markets.
  ii. Develop new uses for the services or facilities.
  iii. Convince customers to use the services or facilities more frequently.

The market leader has the most to gain if the total demand for its services grows. It can identify target markets that are not using these services as frequently as they could be, or are not using them at all. Marriott International, in a bid to increase its share of frequent travelers, launched the "Marriott Miles" program in early 1993. Members of the program received 500 frequent-flier miles with the airline of their choice each time they stayed at a Marriott.[7] This program is now even more extensive and is called "Marriott Rewards." Club Med, the originator of the all-inclusive concept added a cruise ship and introduced its *Rent-a-Village* concept in the mid-1980s. In this program, corporations such as IBM and Sony take over entire Club Med villages for incentive travel trips or meetings.[8] Theme weekends promoted new markets in the shoulder season (the time period on both sides of the peak season) at resorts that needed a boost. The company found new users for its resorts.

Another way to build up the primary market is to find and promote new uses for a service. There are several examples of this in the hospitality and travel industry. Many of the leading cruise lines have been successful in promoting the use of their ships for corporate meetings and conventions. Traditional summer-only and ski resorts have taken the same tack by marketing to meeting planners for fall and spring events.

Convincing customers to use your service more frequently is the third option. An excellent example of this approach is McDonald's Happy Meal concept, which was introduced in 1979. Children, with their parents in tow, are lured back time and time again to the *Golden Arches* for the toys and other items in these meals. The frequent-traveler programs discussed in various parts of this book are another example, as are the *bounce-back* coupons mentioned in Chapter 16.

- ***Protecting Market Share.*** Protecting market share is the second main approach available to the market leader. How do leaders hold on to customers when every competitor is eyeing their business? By far the best way is to continue to be innovative, constantly adding new or improved services. Again, McDonald's and Holiday Inn (now Bass Hotels & Resorts) are two of the industry's brightest stars in this respect. McDonald's introduced the concept of chicken nuggets and was one of the innovators of the drive-through window. Holiday Inn pioneered the frequent-guest award idea and is the leader in using hotel telecommunications systems. Another highly recommended step for the leader is to continually look

◆ **FIGURE 8–6** *Four Seasons Hotels and Resorts acquired the Regent Hotel group and strengthened its position as a luxury hotel chain.* (Courtesy of Four Seasons Hotels and Resorts)

for diversification opportunities. Keeping eggs in only one basket is a dangerous business strategy. Marriott and Holiday Inn are fine examples of lodging companies that diversified to maintain their market shares. Both introduced several new brands of properties in the 1980s and 1990s.

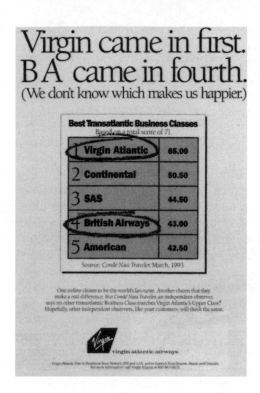

◆ FIGURE 8–7   *Virgin Atlantic claims it has the favorite transatlantic business class.* (Courtesy of Virgin Atlantic Airways)

- **Expanding Market Share.** Leaders can also try to expand their market shares by adding new services, improving service quality, increasing spending on marketing, or acquiring competitive organizations. Four Seasons Hotels and Resorts strengthened its position as a leading international chain of luxury hotels with the purchase of Regent International (Figure 8–6).

b. **Market Challengers.** Market challengers are organizations that decide to take on the leaders in a bid for market share. In the battle of the burgers, Burger King, Wendy's, and Hardee's all have gone after McDonald's commanding market share. Avis and other car rental companies have challenged Hertz. When challengers *attack* the leader, they usually do it through comparative advertising campaigns. Burger King has compared its menu items several times to McDonald's, including the famous broiled versus fried advertising campaign. Wendy's cleverly put down both McDonald's and Burger King in its celebrated "Where's the Beef?" commercials. Not to be outdone by its big brothers, Hardee's had a campaign that spoofed the battle of the burgers.

Avis' run at Hertz is well documented and is often used as one of the best examples of successful positioning. Avis sold the traveling public on the idea that because it was the number two firm, it had to try harder to satisfy its rental customers. Virgin Atlantic used the results of a survey from a consumer travel magazine to show travel agents that it was favored over British Airways, Figure 8–7.

A challenger can mount five different types of attacks on the leader: frontal, flank, encirclement, bypass, and guerilla.[9] Burger King used the frontal or head-on approach when it questioned McDonald's hamburger cooking methods in broiled versus fried. Attacking the leader's flank means hitting them where they are weak. The challenger can concentrate on geographic areas or market segments that the leader has neglected or sees as a low priority. Encirclement means mounting an attack on all fronts, whereas a bypass attack involves avoiding direct confrontation with the market leader. In the guerilla attack, the challenger makes small, periodic raids on the market leader.

c. **Market Followers.** Unlike market challengers, follower organizations shy away from any direct or indirect attacks on market leaders. To date, the lodging industry has behaved in this fashion. For example, there has been very little comparative advertising among hotel companies. Organizations that take this stance try to copy all or some of what the leader does. They go after the same target markets, choose the same advertising media, or add similar services.

This me-too approach is very evident among hotel chains, fast-food restaurants, airlines, and car rental companies. When the leader pioneers a new concept successfully, most of its competitors are quick to follow suit. American Airlines was first to introduce a frequent-flyer program. Now every major airline has one. The same fate befell Holiday Inn's frequent-stay program. Holiday Inn was one of the first of the major organizations to enter the all-suite hotel business. Marriott, Hilton, Sheraton, Radisson, and Choice Hotels International followed. McDonald's Chicken McNuggets have been emulated by Burger King, KFC, and others.

d. **Market Nichers.** A market nicher is a smaller organization that also avoids direct confrontation with the major companies but does not necessarily follow them closely. It finds a niche in which it specializes. Regional and commuter airlines service the routes that major companies find unprofitable. They have geographic niches. Doughnut shops specialize in baking doughnuts and refuse to broaden their lines to include more fast-food items.

RELATIONSHIP MARKETING AND STRATEGIC ALLIANCES

Many experts believe we have entered an era of relationship marketing in the hospitality and travel industry. They suggest that, in developing marketing strategies, all organizations must place an emphasis on building, maintaining, and enhancing long-term relationships with customers, suppliers, travel trade intermediaries, and perhaps even competitors.[10] There are many examples, including airline frequent-flyer and hotel-frequent guest programs, that try to build loyalty among the companies' present customers. The concept of preferred suppliers or vendors is another example. Here, airlines, hotel companies, rental car firms, and cruise lines try to increase their shares of selected travel agencies' business by offering extra commission percentage points (*overrides*). They hope that, by motivating agents through above-the-industry-average rates of commission, they will become their *preferred suppliers*.

Whereas there are many short-term *partnerships* in the hospitality and travel industry—one-time cooperative advertising campaigns or promotions involving two or more organizations—relationship marketing is concerned with building long-term loyalty among customers, distribution channels, and complementary organizations. These long-term relationships include those between Walt Disney World and National Car Rental, and between Walt Disney World and Delta. Several other hospitality companies have also tried to build long-term relationships with specific types of customers. Some companies have tried to build up loyalty among children, including Hyatt Hotels with its "Camp Hyatt" concept and Burger King, which has five million members in the Burger King Kids Club.

Water covers two-thirds of the earth's surface. We cover six-sevenths.

With our global travel partners, we serve over 500 cities in nearly 100 countries on 6 continents. So our new alliance with Continental Airlines has your travel needs covered. With over 3,400 worldwide departures every day, we've got flight selection and flexibility covered, too. Add the ability to earn and redeem WorldPerks® free travel miles on both airlines, shared airport-club privileges and one-stop check-in, and travel has never been easier or more rewarding. All you need now is a ticket. To enroll in the WorldPerks program or to book and buy your tickets, visit www.nwa.com, call your travel agent or call Northwest Airlines at 1-800-225-2525. Go ahead. Because now, the whole world is yours.

Introducing the worldwide Northwest Airlines and Continental Airlines alliance.

1-800-225-2525 / www.nwa.com

◆ FIGURE 8–8 *The Northwest-KLM-Continental strategic alliance.* (Courtesy of *Northwest Airlines*)

Strategic alliances are special long-term relationships formed between two or more hospitality and travel organizations, or between a hospitality and travel organization and one or more other types of organizations. A good example of these special relationships is the partnering of international air carriers, including Northwest Airlines, KLM Royal Dutch Airlines, and Continental (Figure 8–8). One of the main features of a strategic alliance is that the partners wish to achieve a specific, long-term goal.[11] In the case of Northwest, KLM, and Continental this goal appears to be the development of a world-wide global airline system.

Partnerships and strategic alliances will be discussed further in Chapter 10, and both Chapters 10 and 11 talk more about the relationship marketing concept.

A Touch of Technology

Global Strategic Alliances among Airlines

Several strategic alliances have developed among the world's airlines that are described on specific sites on the World Wide Web. They include the following:

◆ **http://www.oneworldalliance.com/**

The participating airlines include Aer Lingus, American Airlines, British Airways, Cathay Pacific, Finnair, Iberia, LanChile, and Qantas. Canadian Airlines left the alliance in early 2000.

Customer benefits include transferability of frequent flyer miles among the individual airline's programs, smoother airport transfers, better value fares, and access to more airport lounges.

◆ **http://www.star-alliance.com/**

Airlines in the Star Alliance are Air Canada, Air New Zealand, All Nippon Airways, Ansett Australia, Austrian Airlines, Lauda Air, Lufthansa, SAS, Thai, Tyrolean Airways, United, and Varig. Singapore Airlines joined during 2000.

Benefits are transferability of frequent flyer miles, priority status, and lounge access for Star Gold members.

◆ **http://www.nwa.com/ and http://www.klm.nl/ and http://www.continental.com/**

Northwest and KLM formed an alliance several years ago and were joined by Continental Airlines in 1999.

As well as the code sharing on flights and exchange of frequent flyer miles, Northwest and Continental began sharing self-service kiosks for customer check-in during 2000 and were planning an Interline E-Ticket program.

◆ **http://www.skyteam.com/**

The participating airlines include Delta, AeroMexico, Air France, Korean Air, and Czech Airlines.

Launched in 2000 by AeroMexico, Air France, Delta Air Lines, and Korean Air.

Benefits include transferability of member airlines' frequent flyer program miles, access to more airport lounges, and guaranteed reservations as part of Sky Team Elite Plus member program.

POSITIONING APPROACH

The technique of positioning is relatively recent and is generally attributed to two advertising executives—Al Ries and Jack Trout. After a series of articles in 1972, they wrote a book titled *Positioning: The Battle for Your Mind,* in which they said that "positioning is what you do to the mind of the prospect."[12] Since then, other marketing experts have endorsed their idea and have expanded on the original concept.

As defined earlier, positioning is the development of a service and marketing mix to occupy a specific place in the minds of customers within target markets. In other words, the marketer sets out to create a definite image by offering an appropriate service and communicating to potential customers in a way that is consistent with this image. To make this technique crystal clear, you just need to think about the Holland America Line in the cruise business. For years it used the tag line, "A Tradition of Excellence," to position itself as an upscale cruising alternative. To this, it has been adding the word "premium" so that potential guests get the intended image that Holland America's ships are in the luxury cruise category.

Reasons for Positioning

There are three main reasons for positioning: human perceptual processes, intensified competition, and the sheer volume of advertising to which most people are exposed every day.

1. **Perceptual Processes.** Chapter 4 described perception as a method used by the human brain to sort out people's images of the world around them and dump unnecessary information. The marketer whose advertising messages communicate an unclear or confusing image to customers will find these messages ending up as a pile of mental garbage, screened out by highly sophisticated consumers. Research has shown again and again that people forget a very high percentage of the commercial messages to which they are exposed. Clear, concise, and simple messages are the key to slipping past perceptual defenses. This, together with well-positioned service offerings, is the essence of positioning.

2. **Intensified Competition.** This book often refers to the growing competitiveness of the hospitality and travel industry. Positioning is a technique used to give a service an image that is unique and different from that of competitors. One of the classic cases cited by Ries and Trout is Avis Rent-a-Car. The company, recognizing that Hertz was the established leader in car rentals, successfully positioned itself as the industry's number two company, and it firmly implanted the idea that it had to try harder to satisfy its customers. Burger King gained on McDonald's with its "Have it Your Way" campaign, as did Wendy's with its humorous "Where's the Beef?" commercials.

3. **Volume of Commercial Messages.** People are exposed to hundreds of commercial messages each day, some from hospitality and travel organizations, but most from other advertisers. The sheer volume of messages makes it impossible for anyone to absorb all they see, hear, and read. To get a person's attention among what many call the *advertising clutter* requires effective positioning. Advertisements must stand

out from the crowd by being distinctive, while also communicating clear, unconfusing ideas.

Essentials for Effective Positioning

Positioning a service comes after market segments have been identified and target markets chosen. The following information is, therefore, essential for effective positioning:

1. Information on the needs of customers in target markets and the benefits they look for.
2. A knowledge of the organization's competitive strengths and weaknesses.
3. A familiarity with competitors' strengths and weaknesses.
4. Information on how customers perceive the organization relative to competitors.

As you will probably realize, marketing research must be done to get this vital information. Some of this comes from the situation analysis and the rest from special research studies. The results of a study by Pizza Hut helped management **reposition** (change the image in customers' minds) the chain. Pizza Hut found people to be very emotional about their pizza and skeptical that a national pizza chain could produce good pizza like local mom-and-pop outlets do. As a result of the findings of a major customer survey in 1987, Club Med significantly altered its marketing strategy. The survey found that customers' perceptions of Club Med were that it was only for singles and young adults, that participation in activities was forced upon you, and that Club Med villages were confining and that guests were not able to explore the host country on their own.[13]

In these two cases, management decided through careful research and analysis that their firms had weaknesses that competitors could exploit. These companies had images in customers' minds that were either confused or not conducive to long-term growth. The answer was to change their images by adding new or modified services, introducing new and consistent promotional campaigns, and concentrating more on the benefits that customers were seeking. These firms are now more effectively positioned.

The Five Ds of Positioning

There are three elements in true positioning:

1. Creating an image
2. Communicating customer benefits
3. Differentiating the brand from competitive services[14]

Another important point is that a position must be chosen on which the organization can, in fact, deliver. For example, a company portraying a top-quality image will not succeed if its employees provide poor-quality service. An airline boasting the best-available record for on-time arrivals had better make sure that its planes arrive on time. Positioning can backfire if what is promised is not what is delivered.

Another aspect of positioning that Ries and Trout considered to be important was deciding which competitors you want to appear different from. Avis' "We Try Harder" pinpointed Hertz, Burger King's "Have it Your Way" singled out McDonald's, and

EXCELLENCE CASE

Repositioning To Change With The Times:
Club Med

Club Méditerranée, or Club Med for short, which was 50 years old in 2000, is one of the world's leading resort chains. Its spectacular success story can primarily be attributed to the company's innovative all-inclusive vacation packages. As with other industry giants, it has shown remarkable skill in anticipating societal and travel trends and responding with the right *products* at the most opportune times and before competitors.

In the late 1980s, Club Med began a major effort to *reposition* the chain and to appeal to a broader range of individual target markets—in other words, to change with the times. Consumer research showed that while people generally had a positive image of Club Med, there were also some negative images, such as that Club Med vacations were too restrictive and confining and that guests were forced to participate in the villages' activities. Club Med was also perceived as being somewhat expensive and more oriented toward youthful and single travelers. While the swinging singles image of the 1960s had served the company well, the baby boom generation was now aging and taking on more domestic responsibilities.

The Club Med packaging formula is to include almost every possible vacation cost in the one price, including air fare, ground transportation to and from Club Med villages, accommodations, meals, entertainment, numerous recreational activities and instruction, and free wine and beer at lunch and dinner. The only extras are for optional side trips, scuba diving, golf greens fees, bar drinks, and clothing and souvenirs bought at villages or elsewhere. Since Club Med innovated these all-inclusive resort packages, many other resorts, especially in the Caribbean, have imitated the idea.

Another unique feature of most Club Med villages is the policy of not having many modern-day *distractions.* Tipping is also not allowed. Guests, referred to as GMs (gentils membres or nice members in English) in Club

Med Parlance, are allowed to concentrate all their energies on enjoying their vacations. The caliber of the instructional and recreational *programming* is excellent. Club Med employees, known as GOs (gentils organisateurs or congenial hosts in English), coordinate these activities. In addition to daytime duties as sports instructors, chefs, and so on, all GOs perform in the nightly cabaret with surprising professionalism. There are more than 10,000 GOs representing more than 80 different nationalities working at Club Med villages.

Who Goes To Club Med?

- Median age: 41.8
- 45% are male and 55% are female
- Median household income is $71,500
- 91% are college graduates
- 28% have post-graduate degrees
- 68% hold professional, executive, or managerial positions
- 63% are married
- 34% are single, divorced, or widowed
- 44% are families
- 51% have children
- 15% are children

If no money changes hands at Club Med villages, how do GMs pay for bar drinks? The answer, in the typically creative Club Med fashion, is through the plastic, pop-it beads, drink tickets, or smart cards.

The term *chain* does not seem to fit well with Club Med. Although the basic *packaging* and *programming* concepts are roughly the same at all villages, each has a unique layout, architecture, and assortment of recreational activities. Like the packages themselves, Club Med villages typically are completely self-contained and include every conceivable facility needed for a one- or two-week resort vacation. Guest accommodations vary by location, always taking on an architectural look reflective of the host country or region. More

continued

EXCELLENCE CASE *continued*

recently, Club Med has introduced a *Trident* ranking system for its villages dividing them into four groups (4 Trident villages, 3 Trident villages, 2 Trident villages, and straw hut villages). Rather than the typical multistory building containing relatively standardized guest rooms, Club Med villages usually feature bungalow-style units in small clusters. Most villages include tennis courts, outdoor pool, dining area, central bar with open-air dance area, a boutique, sailing, boardsailing, scuba diving, snorkeling, picnics, and boat rides.

Like many other of the *greats* in the industry, Club Med has shown an uncanny ability to predict change and to alter its services and facilities accordingly. Prior to the 1980s, Club Med changed many of its villages, as well as its advertising approaches, to give them a broader, whole-family appeal. In other words, it *repositioned* itself. Children and families are now prominently featured in advertising and brochures. Some villages offer separate Mini Clubs for 4 to 12 year olds. Others also offer *Petit* Clubs for children 2 to 4 years old, or Baby Clubs for infants from 4 months to 2 years. During school break periods, Mini Club villages offer Junior Clubs for teenagers. Again, Club Med's creativity in *programming* and *packaging* turned the changing baby boomer challenge into a marketing opportunity. The Mini Club Med concept is a brilliant example of *programming* especially for children. Staffed with dedicated GOs and their own facilities, they usually include a theater, playroom, arts and crafts center, and separate times for water-skiing, sailing, and picnics. Some 23 villages provide Circus Schools, which provide workshops on unicycling, juggling, clowning, walking the tightrope, and flying the trapeze for Mini Club Med members. Some Mini Club villages offer lessons in mountain biking, in-line skating, horseback riding, and soccer.

Club Med was also quick to spot the growing interest of corporations in using resorts for meetings and incentive travel trips. Under the banner of *Rent-A-Village,* Club Med rents entire villages (or its cruise ship, *Club Med 2*) to corporations and often does extensive theming for such events. A special *Club Med Group & Incentive* guide is published and the company has a team of training specialists in its Club Med Business division to handle group needs. Thirty-nine of its villages provide conference rooms.

Noticing the trend toward weekend and mini-vacations, Club Med offers vacationers the opportunity to create their own packages with Club Med providing the land transportation portion and travelers providing their own air fare. Club Med also noted the spectacular growth in cruising and decided to go into the business itself. Its ship, *Club Med 2,* spends the winter in the Caribbean and summers in the Mediterranean and Norway. Introduced in 1992, *Club Med 2* is a five-masted, computer-controlled sail ship with 394-passenger capacity and with a crew of about 200.

As it entered the new millennium, Club Med was playing host to approximately 1.57 million GMs per year at more than 110 villages. The company had annual sales of about $1.5 billion with operations in 40 different countries.

Discussion Questions

1. What factors caused Club Med to change its marketing strategy?
2. How has Club Med's approach to market segmentation been altered?
3. In what ways has Club Med tried to change its image in the minds of potential travelers?
4. What can other hospitality and travel organizations learn from Club Med and its new marketing strategy?

Web Site

http://www.clubmed.com/

Wendy's "Where's the Beef?" picked on both McDonald's and Burger King. Other **positioning statements** (phrases reflecting the image the organization wants to create) try to separate organizations from all competitors. For example, Renaissance Cruises, which operates a group of smaller cruise ships, pointed out its difference by saying,

"There's a Renaissance in cruising. And it's us." They also make it clear whom their market is by stating, "We don't cater to children." Carnival, the industry market share leader, takes the opposite approach by positioning itself as "The Most Popular Cruise Line In The World."

An easy way to remember the steps required for effective positioning is to think of them as the **five Ds of positioning:**

1. **DOCUMENTING:** Identifying the benefits that are most important to the customers who buy your type of service.
2. **DECIDING:** Deciding on the image that you want customers to have within your chosen target markets.
3. **DIFFERENTIATING:** Pinpointing the competitors you want to appear different from and the things that make you different.
4. **DESIGNING:** Providing product or service differences and communicating these in positioning statements and other aspects of the marketing mix.
5. **DELIVERING:** Making good on your promises!

Positioning Approaches

There are several different ways to create unique images in customers' minds, including *specific* and *general* positioning and positioning by information versus imagery.[15] A **specific positioning approach** is where only one customer benefit is selected and concentrated on. The Belize Tourist Board provides a good example of the specific positioning approach when it puts across the image of the country as "Mother Nature's best kept secret." The island of Dominica uses a similar theme by calling itself "The Nature Island of the Caribbean." These destination examples specifically position the countries for people interested in nature-based travel. In the lodging business, Courtyard by Marriott specifically appeals to the corporate market by its statement, "The hotel designed by business travelers." The Hilton Garden Inn communicates quality and value with "four-star lodging at a three-star price." The **general positioning approach** promises more than one benefit that is not as directly obvious. The customer almost has to read into advertising and service offerings to discover the benefits that are available (Figure 8–9).

A position can be created by stating clear, factual information. Positioning can also be done by using images, moods, and symbols. A factual ad from the airline industry was Qantas' "How often do you get the chance to fly Qantas?" Another example of this approach is the one used by Universal Studios Hollywood, who state that they are the "World's Largest Movie Studio and Theme Park." The Sandals Royal Bahamian Resort & Spa says it is "The Only AAA Four Diamond Resort in the Bahamas." In the casino resort hotel business is the MGM Grand's "World's Largest Hotel, Casino & Theme Park." Getting a place in the customer's mind through imagery is shown in the strategies of Hyatt Hotels and Four Seasons Hotels and Resorts. Both hotel companies aim for a top-quality, rather luxurious and prestigious image. For Hyatt, this has been done through its *Hyatt Touch* program, while Four Seasons Hotels and Resorts emphasizes the quality of the service in its Four Seasons and Regent brands.

There are six possible positioning approaches:[16]

1. Positioning on specific product features
2. Positioning on benefits, problem solution, or needs
3. Positioning for specific usage occasions
4. Positioning for user category

Today, some airlines seem more interested in filling planes than cleaning them. In an effort to cut costs, some carriers have cut way back on services.

American doesn't want you to think that all airlines ignore the demands of their customers.

That's why we'd like to address just one of the many steps we take to help assure passenger comfort.

We work hard to keep our fleet clean.

Every year, we spend over $30 million cleaning our planes.

Our 72-point cleaning checklist helps us deliver the quality you've come to expect from American.

Every day we pick up, wash, wipe, scrub, scour, dust, polish, sanitize, refresh, replenish, replace, disinfect, arrange and rearrange our 389 American airplanes.

And that commitment to cleanliness doesn't stop with our interiors.

Next time you see one of our aircraft, take a look at our silver exteriors. That shine on our face is not achieved with a once-over-lightly washing.

We do it all by hand. Even the polishing. Hand-held buffers go over every square inch of our planes. Imagine waxing over 100 cars and you have some idea of the magnitude of polishing just one of our planes.

American is committed to doing the job right. Not just sometimes. But all the time.

That's not to say that on occasion, when we turn a plane fast to make an on-time departure, we won't miss a spot or fail to clean an ashtray or overlook a scrap of paper in the seat pocket. But rest assured, these oversights will be

corrected before the day is out.

Dedicated to superior service.

Cost cutting will never come before cleanliness at American Airlines. Keeping our planes clean is a reflection of an attitude that runs through our entire organization. We are dedicated to giving you superior service on every flight because we know it's something our passengers expect from us.

To be successful, we must continue to deliver a better way to fly. That's the American Way.

Number two is a series about an airline's flying public.

American Airlines
Something special in the air.

If The Plane Is A Mess, What Does That Tell You About The Airline?

◆ FIGURE 8–9   *American Airlines tries to stand out among all major domestic airlines.* (Courtesy of American Airlines)

5. Positioning against another product
6. Positioning by product class dissociation

1. **Positioning on Specific Product Features.** This is exactly the same as the concept of specific positioning discussed earlier. A direct link is usually made between some aspect of the service and a customer benefit. It is, of course, possible to position more than one feature. One very good example of this positioning approach is that used by the increasingly popular resort spas. For example, the Golden Door Fitness Resort in California offers its guests "a week of our renowned mind/body fitness program—the perfect blending of physical and mental challenges with restorative and healing therapies."

2. **Positioning on Benefits, Problem Solution, or Needs.** The travel literature is loaded with examples of this approach. Emirates suggests, "Be good to yourself. Fly Emirates." Enterprise Rent-A-Car clearly states its customer benefit as, "We'll pick you up." As you can see, most positioning statements reflecting this approach include the pronoun *you* for close association with the customer's needs or problems.

3. **Positioning for Specific Usage Occasions.** Here the positioning is based on a specific occasion when the customer may find a use for the service.

4. **Positioning for User Category.** The approach here is to identify and associate with a specific group of customers. Couples, a Caribbean resort, advertises itself "For Couples Only." Northwest Airlines appeals to the gay and lesbian market by stating in its advertising that they were "the first major U.S. airline to join the International Gay and Lesbian Travel Association and we've been a proud member ever since."

5. **Positioning Against Another Product.** As we will see later, another name for this approach is comparative or competitive advertising. We have already talked about the classic examples of Burger King versus McDonald's, and Avis versus Hertz. In its 1995 advertising campaign, "Get your burger's worth," Burger King directly compared the size of its hamburgers and their beef content with those of McDonald's. At the start of the new millennium. Burger King changed to the "It just tastes better" theme. Another more recent media battle between two industry leaders has been that of the Visa and American Express cards. Visa launched television commercials showing events and attractions at which the American Express card was not accepted. For example, Visa was a major sponsor of the Sydney 2000 Olympic Games and the exclusive payment card for that event. Visa frequently used the statement, "We're everywhere you want to be."

6. **Positioning by Product Class Dissociation.** What an organization tries to do here is make its services appear different from all competitors. We have already talked about a few examples, including Renaissance Cruises and Carnival Cruise Lines. Another prime example is World Explorer Cruises' advertising campaign that tries to set it apart from the contemporary cruise ships. Take a look at the ad shown in Figure 8–10. You will notice the quote, "Our sense of adventure runs a little deeper than a cruise ship discotheque." Another ad in the same campaign stated, "I'd rather take my chances kayaking a river than feeding a slot machine." What are they trying to say? They are positioning World Explorer's cruises as being different from the experiences on modern cruise ships with their discos, casinos, and other entertainment.

MARKETING OBJECTIVES

The next step before developing the marketing mix is to establish marketing objectives for each target market. Earlier these were defined as the measurable goals that a hospitality and travel organization attempts to achieve within a specific time period for a specific target market.

Benefits of Marketing Objectives

An organization without marketing objectives can be compared to a plane flying without its black box and pilot's flight log. Remember that two of the five key questions in the hospitality and travel marketing system are, "How do we make sure we get there?" and "How do we know if we got there?" With no marketing objectives, you cannot even begin to answer these fundamental questions. The benefits of marketing objectives are as follows:

1. Giving marketing managers a way to measure progress toward their goals and make timely adjustments to their programs

◆ **FIGURE 8–10**   *World Explorer Cruises stands out from the pack by using effective product class dissociation.* (Courtesy of World Explorer Cruises)

2. Providing a yardstick for management to measure the success of marketing programs
3. Representing a benchmark for judging the potential return on alternative marketing-mix activities
4. Providing a frame of reference for all those involved directly in marketing
5. Giving broad directions for the scope and types of marketing activities required in a specific period

Requirements of Marketing Objectives

There are two main dangers to avoid when setting marketing objectives. The first is not to mechanically set them based totally on previous-period results. If there is one thing that can be predicted with 100 percent confidence in this industry, it is that tomorrow will never be exactly the same as today. Second, objectives must not be built on guesses, wishful thinking, or natural intuition. They must always come from thorough research and analysis, such as that described in Chapters 5 and 6. Additionally, objectives must be consistent with the selected marketing strategy.

All marketing objectives should be:

1. **TARGET-MARKET SPECIFIC:** Objectives should be set for each target market selected for marketing attention. This is a crucial step to ensure that the investment in individual target markets is justified. When an objective is further detailed into tasks, the costs of pursuing a given target market can be determined. This can then be compared to the revenues and profits generated, giving an indication of each target market's worth.

2. **RESULTS ORIENTED:** Objectives must be expressed in terms of desired results. In marketing, an objective usually means an improvement over a current situation (e.g., an increase in volume, revenues, or market share). Results should be written using one of these yardsticks. They provide an essential tool for marketing managers as they control, measure, and evaluate the success of marketing plans.

3. **QUANTITATIVE:** Objectives should be expressed numerically so that progress and results can be measured. When they are set in qualitative or nonnumerical terms, they are almost impossible to measure and subjective judgments enter the picture. By attaching numbers to each objective, the marketing manager is able to set progress points or *milestones* when actual performance can be checked against desired performance. Corrective measures can be taken quickly if required. At the end of a marketing planning period, the manager has a way to gauge success and the amount of variation from desired performance.

4. **TIME SPECIFIC:** Objectives have to be set for specific time periods. They usually span one or two years or the duration of the marketing plan, but they can also be set for a season, weekends or weekdays, a part of the day, or some combination of weeks or months.

A few examples of time-specific marketing objectives will probably help you grasp these criteria for effective marketing objectives:

1. **RESTAURANT**—To increase the average check (*result*) from business lunches (*target market*) by 50 cents (*quantified*) between January 1 and May 31 (*time specific*).
2. **MOTOR INN**—To increase occupied room nights (*result*) by 5,000 (*quantified*) from the corporate meetings market (*target market*) in 2002 (*time specific*).
3. **THEME PARK**—To increase senior citizen (*target market*) ticket sales (*result*) by 1,000 (*quantified*) in fall 2003 (*time specific*).

Setting marketing objectives is the last step in answering the question, "Where would we like to be?" Now that the organization knows precisely what it wants to achieve in the upcoming period, it is time to draw up a specific plan for meeting its objectives.

CHAPTER CONCLUSION

Every organization must decide where it wants to be in the future. Following marketing segmentation analysis, choices have to be made between alternative marketing strategies, positioning approaches, and objectives. Making these decisions is part of planning. The service's product life-cycle stage and the organization's competitive position influence the selection from among alternative approaches. Marketing research information provides the basis for these decisions.

Having a marketing strategy is similar to having a map to help you get where you want to be. Even with a good map, some people get lost. More careful and detailed planning is necessary to get to the final destination.

REVIEW QUESTIONS

1. How are the terms marketing strategy, positioning, and marketing objective defined in this book?
2. What is a segmented marketing strategy?
3. What are the four alternative marketing strategies by market focus and how do they differ?
4. Should marketing strategies be changed in the four stages of the product life cycle? If so, which strategies work best during each stage?
5. Should smaller or lower-share organizations use the same marketing strategies as industry leaders? If not, how should their approaches differ?

6. Why has positioning become so important in today's business climate?
7. What information and steps are required for effective positioning?
8. What are the six positioning approaches?
9. Why are marketing objectives so important in effective marketing?
10. Which four requirements must marketing objectives satisfy?

CHAPTER ASSIGNMENTS

1. Review the recent marketing strategies of three leading hotel chains, restaurant chains, airlines, cruise companies, travel destinations, travel agency chains, or other hospitality/travel organizations. Which types of marketing strategies are they using? What are their target markets? What image have they tried to create and which positioning approach is used? How have their strategies and positioning changed in the past five years? Use illustrations of advertising or other promotions to back up your points.
2. The product life cycle is a good general guide, but it does not always reflect reality. Discuss this statement by describing companies, destinations, services, or facilities that have extended their life cycles or otherwise not followed the PLC exactly.

3. This chapter says that each industry tends to include market leaders, challengers, followers, and nichers. Select one part of our industry and identify the organizations that play these individual roles. What strategies and approaches does each organization use to improve or maintain its competitive position? You can either do this on a national basis, or use your local community as the base. How successful has each selected organization been with its choice of strategy and related approaches?
4. The owner of a small hospitality and travel business has asked you for some help in developing marketing objectives. What general guidelines would you suggest for objective setting? Detail how you would help the owner develop these objectives. Develop a set of hypothetical (or real) objectives for the business.

WORLD WIDE WEB RESOURCES

Abercrombie & Kent
http://www.abercrombiekent.com/

Accor
http://www.accor.com/

Air Canada
http://www.aircanada.ca/

Belize Tourist Board
http://www.travelbelize.org/

Best Western International Inc.
http://www.bestwestern.com/

Burger King
http://www.burgerking.com/

California Division of Tourism
http://www.gocalif.ca.gov/

Carnival Corporation
http://www.carnivalcorp.com/

Choice Hotels International
http://www.choicehotels.com/

Cinnabon
http://www.cinnabon.com/

Club Med
http://www.clubmed.com/

Couples
http://www.couples.com/

Emirates Airlines
http://www.emirates.com/

Dominica
http://www.caribtourism.com/

Four Seasons Hotels and Resorts
http://www.fourseasons.com/

Golden Door Fitness Resort
http://www.goldendoor.com/

Hardee's
http://www.hardees.com/main.html

Hawaii Visitors & Convention Bureau
http://www.gohawaii.com/

Hilton Garden Inn
http://www.hilton.com/hiltongardeninn/
index.html/

Holland America Line
http://www.hollandamerica.com/

Hyatt Hotels and Resorts
http://www.hyatt.com/

International Gay and Lesbian Travel Association
http://www.iglta.org/

Long Beach Convention Center
http://www.golongbeach.org/

McDonald's
http://www.mcdonalds.com/

MGM Grand
http://www.mgmgrand.com/

Marriott Rewards
http://www.marriottrewards.com/

Oneworld Alliance
http://www.oneworldalliance.com/

Renaissance Cruise
http://www.renaissancecruises.com/

Sandals
http://www.sandals.com/

Six Flags
http://www.sixflags.com/

Scottsdale Conference Resort
http://www.scottsconf.com/

SkyTeam Alliance
http://www.skyteam.com/

Star Alliance
http://www.star-alliance.com/

The Queen Mary
http://www.queenmary.com/

Universal Studios Hollywood
http://www.universalstudios.com/unicity2/

US Airways
http://www.usairways.com/

Virgin Atlantic Airlines
http://www.virgin-atlantic.com/

Visa
http://www.visa.com/

Visit Florida
http://www.flausa.com/

World Explorer Cruises
http://www.wecruise.com/

REFERENCES

1. Kotler, Philip. 2000. *Marketing Management: The Millennium Edition.*10th ed. Upper Saddle River, N.J.: Prentice-Hall, Inc.

2. Perreault, William D., and E. Jerome McCarthy. 2000. *Essentials of Marketing: A Global-Managerial Approach.* 8th ed. Boston: Irwin McGraw-Hill.

3. Kotler, Philip. 2000. *Marketing Management: The Millennium Edition.* 10th ed. Upper Saddle River, N.J.: Prentice-Hall, Inc.

4. Kotler, Philip. 2000. *Marketing Management: The Millennium Edition.* 10th ed. Upper Saddle River, N.J.: Prentice-Hall, Inc.

5. Kotler, Philip. 2000. *Marketing Management: The Millennium Edition.* 10th ed. Upper Saddle River, N.J.: Prentice-Hall, Inc.

6. Kotler, Philip. 2000. *Marketing Management: The Millennium Edition.* 10th ed. Upper Saddle River, N.J.: Prentice-Hall, Inc.

7. Golden, Fran. "Marriott's new guest bonus plan comes under fire from Hilton." *Travel Weekly* 52 (30):71 (1993).

8. Reitman, Judith. "Club Med's new 'antidote' mixes fun, families, and business." *Marketing & Media Decisions* Spring 1985 Special Issue, 51–56.

9. Kotler, Philip. 2000. *Marketing Management: The Millennium Edition.* 10th ed. Upper Saddle River, N.J.: Prentice-Hall, Inc.

10. McKenna, Regis. 1991. *Relationship Marketing.* Reading, Mass.: Addison-Wesley Publishing Co., Inc., 85–116.

11. Webster, Frederick E., Jr. "The changing role of marketing in the corporation." *Journal of Marketing* 56 (10):1–17 (1992).

12. Ries, Al, and Jack Trout. 2001. *Positioning: The Battle for Your Mind.* 2nd ed. Boston: McGraw-Hill.

13. ABC News/Prentice Hall Video Library, 1991. *Club Med: Changing with the Times.* Englewood Cliffs, N.J.: Prentice-Hall, Inc.

14. Lewis, Robert C. "The positioning statement for hotels." *The Cornell Hotel and Restaurant Administration Quarterly* 22 (1):51–61.

15. Assael, Henry. 1995. *Consumer Behavior and Marketing Action.* 5th ed. Cincinnati, Ohio: South-Western Publishing.

16. Kotler, Philip. 2000. *Marketing Management: Millennium Edition.* 10th ed. Upper Saddle River, N.J.: Prentice-Hall, Inc.

For additional hospitality and travel marketing resources, visit out Web site at **www.Hospitality-Tourism.delmar.com**

9

The Marketing Plan and the 8 Ps

Where Would We Like To Be?

Objectives

Having read this chapter, you should be able to:

◆ Define the term marketing plan.

◆ Explain the difference between tactical and strategic marketing planning.

◆ List eight requirements for an effective marketing plan.

◆ Explain the benefits of having a marketing plan.

◆ Describe the contents of a marketing plan.

◆ List four approaches to developing marketing budgets and recommend one of these approaches.

◆ Describe the three major steps involved in preparing a marketing plan.

◆ List the 8 Ps of hospitality and travel marketing.

Overview

Where would we like to be? The answer to this question is spelled out in a marketing plan. In Chapter 3, this document was compared to a plane's flight plan that guides its users safely to their final destination. This chapter begins by defining the marketing plan and explaining its role in tactical planning. It lists the contents of a plan and describes the benefits of having one.

The chapter then provides the step-by-step procedure for preparing a plan. It ties in concepts discussed earlier, including market segmentation, marketing strategy, positioning, marketing objectives, and marketing mix. The scene is set for the next ten chapters, as each of the 8 Ps of hospitality and travel marketing are discussed.

Key Terms

competitive budgeting	marketing management	pricing
contingency planning	marketing mix	product
8 Ps of hospitality and travel	marketing plan	product/service mix
marketing	milestones	programming
executive summary	objective-and-task budgeting	promotion
historical budgeting	packaging	promotional mix
hospitality and travel marketing	partnership	rationale
system	people	rule-of-thumb budgeting
implementation plan	place	zero-based budgeting

Would you climb aboard an airliner if you knew that its pilots had no flight plan? Unless you have a great love for danger, you probably answered no. An organization without a marketing plan is like a plane with no flight plan. Both may know where they are and where they want to be, but everything in between is unknown. A plane can stray off course and end up not reaching its final destination because it burns too much fuel. Similarly, a planless organization can find itself going down a series of blind alleys and using up its marketing budget before it achieves its objectives. As the old saying goes, "Failing to plan is planning to fail."

MARKETING PLAN DEFINITION

In this book, a **marketing plan** is defined as a written plan that is used to guide an organization's marketing activities for a period of two years or less. It is quite detailed and specific, and it helps an organization coordinate the many steps and people that play a role in marketing.

DIFFERENCES BETWEEN TACTICAL AND STRATEGIC PLANNING

Marketing plans are what most experts call *tactical* or short term. It is not enough just to have marketing plans, however. Long-term or *strategic* plans are needed. These three year or more plans are more general and less detailed than tactical plans. They ensure that long-term marketing objectives are attained. There must be a close fit between the strategies and objectives in each marketing plan and those in the strategic market plan.

Marketing plans take an in-depth look at the organization's marketing mix and contain detailed budgets and timetables. Strategic market plans are more concerned with the external marketing environment and the opportunities and challenges in the medium and long term.

REQUIREMENTS FOR AN EFFECTIVE MARKETING PLAN

Just as every building needs a solid foundation, a marketing plan must be rooted in careful research and analysis. Earlier chapters discussed the situation analysis, marketing research, market segmentation, marketing strategy selection, positioning, and marketing objectives. The marketing plan builds on all of these, giving management a *blueprint* for action.

There are a few universal truths about all blueprints, whether they are architectural or the ones we are looking at right now. Every architect and construction manager knows that original blueprints must be modified for unexpected occurrences. They realize that many people are needed to turn an on-paper plan into reality. It is accepted that things must be carefully staged and timed. Walls come before roofs and rough carpentry before fine, for example. Building professionals also recognize the value of careful construction budgeting, contingency planning, and objective setting. They are aware that a preselected mixture of materials and human skills is essential to meet specifications.

The requirements of a marketing plan are very similar to those of a construction blueprint. A marketing plan must meet the following criteria:

1. **Fact-Based.** A marketing plan must build on previous research and analysis. A plan established on managerial hunches is like a house of cards—if one key assumption is proven wrong, the whole plan falls apart.
2. **Organized and Coordinated.** A marketing plan must be as specific and detailed as possible. It needs to clearly identify the departments and people responsible for specific tasks; it must also describe the promotional and other materials that are required. The required level of *workmanship* should be clarified, including the quality and level of effort and service from all involved.
3. **Programmed.** A marketing plan must be orchestrated so that activities are carefully sequenced. Timing is vitally important in marketing. Thus, a marketing plan must have a detailed, staged timetable.
4. **Budgeted.** Every marketing plan must be budgeted carefully. In fact, several tentative budgets should be prepared before the organization decides on a final figure.
5. **Flexible.** Unforeseen events will happen. Therefore, no plan should be cast in stone. The marketing plan should be adjusted if it appears that objectives will definitely not be achieved, or if there are unexpected competitive moves. Contingency planning must be built in. This means allowing some room in the plan and marketing budget to take care of unexpected events.
6. **Controllable.** Making a plan work as it was originally designed is perhaps even more difficult than developing it in the first place. Every plan must contain measurable objectives and ways to determine, during the planning period, if adequate progress is being made toward satisfying the objectives. The plan must also define who is responsible for measuring progress.
7. **Internally Consistent and Interrelated.** Most parts of a marketing plan are interrelated and, therefore, need to be consistent. For example, advertising campaigns and sales promotion methods should be tied together for greatest impact.
8. **Clear and Simple.** Detailed does not mean difficult. It is not enough that the plan's *architect* is the only one who understands it. The efforts of many go into creating a successful marketing plan. Objectives and tasks must be clearly communicated. Possible areas of overlap, confusion, or misunderstanding need to be eliminated.

BENEFITS OF HAVING A MARKETING PLAN

A marketing plan is without doubt one of the most useful tools for any organization. Having a written marketing plan as described in this book has the following five key benefits:

1. Activities matched with target markets
2. Consistency of objectives and target-market priorities
3. Common terms of reference
4. Assistance in measuring marketing success
5. Continuity in long-term planning

1. **Activities Matched with Target Markets.** Assuming that a segmented marketing strategy is being used, a plan ensures that activities are focused only on chosen target markets. One of the steps involved in writing the plan is detailing the marketing mix on a market-by-market basis. Budget waste from appealing to unattractive target markets is avoided.

2. **Consistency of Objectives and Target-Market Priorities.** How far should the plan go to meet objectives? Should each target market get equal attention? These are two questions that are resolved by a good marketing plan, which ensures that the level of effort is consistent with the marketing objectives for each target market and the relative size of each market. Generally, the higher the objective, the greater the required effort. Usually it does not make sense for an organization to spend 80 percent of its marketing budget on a target market or markets that contribute only 20 percent to its sales or profits, yet this happens frequently. Although an exact, one-to-one ratio is not absolutely essential, share of budget and a target market's percentage contribution to sales or profits should be quite similar.

3. **Common Terms of Reference.** A marketing plan details activities for many people both within and outside an organization. A good plan provides a common point of reference for all. It carefully coordinates their efforts. It improves communication among those responsible for marketing and is a great help in orienting outside advisors such as advertising agency personnel.

4. **Assistance in Measuring Marketing Success.** A marketing plan is a tool of marketing management, because it provides the basis for controlling marketing activities. It also helps marketing managers evaluate marketing success. In other words, a marketing plan plays a vital role in answering two key questions: How do we make sure we get there? (control) and How do we know if we got there? (evaluation).

5. **Continuity in Long-Term Planning.** Marketing plans complement strategic market plans and provide a link between short- and long-term planning. They ensure that an organization's long-term objectives are always kept in focus. Because they are carefully rationalized and detailed, marketing plans remain useful even if their originators leave the organization.

CONTENTS OF A MARKETING PLAN

There are three parts to a marketing plan, which we can call the executive summary, the rationale, and the implementation plan. The executive summary is a brief summary of the major highlights of the marketing plan. The rationale explains the facts, analyses, and assumptions upon which the marketing plan is based. It describes the marketing strategies, target markets, positioning approaches, and marketing objectives selected for the period. The implementation plan details the marketing budget, staff responsibilities, activities, timetable, and methods of controlling, measuring, and evaluating activities. Figure 9–1 provides a table of contents for the written plan. You will see that a thorough marketing plan addresses all five key questions in the hospitality and travel marketing system.

A. Executive Summary

B. Marketing Plan Rationale

   1. Situation Analysis Highlights (Where are we now?)
      a. Environmental Analysis
      b. Location and Community Analysis
      c. Primary Competitor Analysis
      d. Market Potential Analysis
      e. Services Analysis
      f. Marketing Position and Plan Analysis
      g. Major Strengths, Weaknesses, Opportunities, and Constraints

   2. Selected Marketing Strategy (Where would we like to be?)
      a. Market Segmentation and Target Markets
      b. Marketing Strategy
      c. Marketing Mixes
      d. Positioning Approaches
      e. Marketing Objectives

C. Implementation Plan

   1. Activities Plan (How do we get there?)
      a. Activities by Target Market for Each Mix Element
      b. Responsibilities for Activities
      c. Timetable and Activity Schedule

   2. Marketing Budget (How do we get there?)
      a. Budget by Target Market
      b. Budget by Marketing-Mix Element
      c. Contingency Funds

   3. Control Procedures (How do we make sure we get there?)
      a. Results Expected from Each Activity
      b. Progress Reporting and Measures

   4. Evaluation Procedures (How do we know if we got there?)
      a. Measurements
      b. Performance Standards
      c. Evaluation Timetable

◆ FIGURE 9–1 *Marketing plan table of contents.*

Executive Summary

The executive summary should be no more than a few pages long and should be easy to read. A good approach is to sum up each of the sections and present them in the order in which they appear in the plan.

Marketing Plan Rationale

Although most people remember what is to be done, it is easy to forget why it is being done. The marketing plan rationale draws together on paper all the research and analysis discussed in Chapters 5 and 6. It provides a historic record for those putting together future marketing plans and strategic market plans. The rationale is also very helpful to outside advisors, such as advertising agencies, who are asked to handle only one specific task.

1. **Situation Analysis Highlights (Where are we now?).** The situation analysis is a study of an organization's strengths, weaknesses, and opportunities. Chapter 5 pointed out that the situation analysis plays an important role in structuring marketing plans. Why? Because these plans must reflect the organization's marketing strengths and capitalize on identified opportunities.

   Some groups combine the situation analysis and the marketing plan into one project that is printed in a single document. This book recommends that they be two separate, but closely related entities. Only the situation analysis highlights should be written up, and there is little need to include the detailed worksheets.

   a. *Environmental Analysis.* There are various trends in the external environment that can have a positive or negative effect on hospitality and travel organizations. These trends include competitive and industry-wide, economic, political and legislative, societal and cultural, and technological. The marketing plan should list and briefly discuss the major opportunities and threats presented. It should explain what impact is expected during the planning period.

   b. *Location and Community Analysis.* What are the key events predicted for the local community and immediate surrounding area during the planning period? New plant openings, business closures or workforce reductions, residential development, industrial expansion, and new highway construction or redesign are just a few things that can have a very positive or negative effect on a business in a short time span. These events should be identified and summarized in the plan, and their impacts should be reviewed.

   c. *Primary Competitor Analysis.* What new approaches are expected from our most direct competitors during the next 24 months? Will these organizations add to or improve their services? Are new promotional thrusts expected? These are the main questions that the marketing plan should address. It should also highlight competitive strengths and weaknesses.

   d. *Market Potential Analysis.* What are the major conclusions that have been drawn about past and potential customers? Are new marketing activities required to hold on to our past clientele? Are there ways to encourage greater use of our services from past or existing clients, or to tap into additional target markets? Answers to these questions, including the highlights of special marketing research studies, should be included.

   e. *Services Analysis.* What will be done during the next two years to improve or augment our organization's services? What research findings or subsequent analysis motivate these changes? The marketing plan should discuss such development projects and how they will be integrated with other marketing-mix activities.

   f. *Marketing Position and Plan Analysis.* Have you ever driven in a strange city and gotten lost? What's the best way to reorient yourself and get back on track? Yes, you can ask a friendly policeman or gas station attendant. But another method that many of us use is to retrace the route that we took to get lost in the first place. The marketing plan and position analysis does just that; it goes over what has been done before so important lessons can be learned for future planning. A synopsis of the organization's current positioning in its target markets and the effectiveness of activities in previous marketing plans should also be presented.

    g. *Major Strengths, Weaknesses, Opportunities, and Constraints.* This part of the plan is similar to a summary. It forces marketers to consolidate all key situation analysis findings. It should involve attaching priorities to identified strengths, weaknesses, opportunities, and constraints.

2. **Selected Marketing Strategy (Where would we like to be?).** The second part of the marketing plan rationale details the strategy that the organization will follow in the next period. It explains the facts, assumptions, and decisions influencing strategy choices that were discussed in Chapters 7 and 8.

    a. *Market Segmentation and Target Markets.* The plan should briefly review the segmentation approach (single stage, two stage, or multistage) and bases (geography, demographics, purpose of trip, psychographics, behavior, product-related, or channels of distribution) used to divide the market. Some statistics should be presented on the size of the market segments and the organization's penetration or share of each. The selected target markets should be discussed, along with the reasons for choosing them. It is also useful to briefly review why other market segments are being overlooked.

    b. *Marketing Strategy.* Will a single-target-market, concentrated, full-coverage, or undifferentiated strategy be used? How has the strategy's choice been influenced by product life-cycle stage and the organization's position in the industry? The plan should explain the analysis and assumptions that led to these choices.

    c. *Marketing Mixes.* Which of the 8 Ps (product, people, packaging, programming, pricing, place, promotion, and partnership) will be used, and why? The marketing plan should review these individually for each target market. A more detailed list of activities comes later in the second part of the plan.

    d. *Positioning Approaches.* Will the organization try to solidify its image in each target market, or will repositioning be attempted? Which of the six positioning approaches (specific product features, benefits/problem solution/needs, specific usage occasions, user category, against another product, or product class dissociation) will be used, and why? The marketing plan should address these questions and explain how the positioning approaches will be reflected in each marketing-mix element.

    e. *Marketing Objectives.* The objectives for each target market should be spelled out. They have to be results-oriented, stated in numerical terms, and time specific. A good idea suggested by some experts is to break up each objective into milestones.[1] This means dividing each objective into subobjectives with specific time deadlines (e.g., a 6.5-percent increase for a year may be divided into a 2-percent gain in the first quarter, a 10-percent gain in the next two quarters, and a 4-percent gain in the final quarter).

Implementation Plan

There are many detailed arrangements to be made and steps that are involved in creating a successful marketing plan. The function of the implementation plan is to specify all the required activities, responsibilities, costs, time schedules, and control and evaluation procedures. Many marketing plans fail because they are not detailed enough. Too much interpretation of the plan has to be done by those responsible for activities, often resulting in missed deadlines, unproductive spending, and general confusion. It is a far greater mistake to have too much detail rather than too little in the implementation plan.

A good way to remember the contents of the implementation plan is to think of them as answers to *what, where, when, who,* and *how* questions.

1. **WHAT** activities or tasks will be carried out and what will be spent on them? (activities plan and budget)
2. **WHERE** will the activities be carried out? (activities plan)
3. **WHEN** are activities to commence and be completed? (activities plan)
4. **WHO** is responsible for each activity? (activities plan)
5. **HOW** will the plan be controlled and evaluated? (control and evaluation procedures)

1. **Activities Plan (How do we get there?).** The activities plan builds on the marketing mix or mixes selected. It provides the specifics on all the tasks required for each mix element of each target market.
   a. *Activities by Target Market for Each Mix Element.* All of the activities anticipated for each target market should be listed. It is best to do this separately for each marketing-mix element (the eight Ps), and to arrange tasks chronologically based on when they will be initiated.
   b. *Responsibilities for Activities.* In most cases, several departments or divisions, many organization employees, and some outside firms will play a role in implementing the plan. They all must know what is expected of them. A good way to do this is to write a description of major responsibilities into the plan and to identify each responsible party in the timetable and activity schedule.
   c. *Timetable and Activity Schedule.* This a key part of the plan that is frequently referred to. It should show each activity's starting and completion dates, where the activity is to be carried out (e.g., in-house or outside the firm), and the persons responsible for it. Figure 9–2 is a sample of the type of form that can be used for this schedule.

2. **Marketing Budget (How do we get there?).** Every marketing plan should include a detailed budget that outlines how much will be spent on each marketing-mix element. Knowing how much money to allocate to marketing is one of the most difficult decisions facing an organization. A good marketing budget should meet the following four criteria:
   a. **COMPREHENSIVE**—All marketing activities are accounted for and costed out.
   b. **COORDINATED**—Budgeting for all items is carefully coordinated to avoid unnecessary duplication of effort and to maximize the synergy between budget items.
   c. **PRACTICAL**—The budget specifies where the money and human resources for marketing will come from.
   d. **REALISTIC**—Marketing budgets cannot be set in isolation from other activities. They have to be related to the organization's resources and position in the industry.

   There are at least four ways to establish marketing budgets. The most effective is known as the objective-and-task or empirical method. This process follows the

TIMETABLE AND ACTIVITY SCHEDULE: <u>Sales Promotion and Merchandising</u>
Year: 2003
Page: 1

ACTIVITY	ASSIGNED TO	JAN	FEB	MAR	APR	MAY	JUNE	JULY	AUG	SEP	OCT	NOV	DEC

◆ **FIGURE 9–2**   *Example of a timetable and activity schedule.*

zero-based budgeting idea, which means that every budget starts at zero each year and then builds up activity by activity. A multistage budgeting process is used. The advantages and disadvantages of the four budgeting approaches are discussed in the following paragraphs.

a. ***Historical or Arbitrary Budgeting.*** This is a very simple and mechanical approach. A certain dollar amount or percentage is added to the last marketing budget. The budget increase is often set close to the economy's rate of inflation. This is not a zero-based approach, because the last budget is considered a given.

Historical budgeting is a popular practice in the hospitality and travel industry because it is easy and requires little time and effort. However, you probably see its dangers. This book emphasizes the need to control and evaluate the results of marketing plans. Such a systematic process always suggests ways to modify and improve marketing activities. It pinpoints the organization's successes and failures. Those who use the historical approach, however, tend to perpetuate ineffective marketing activities and fail to act on their real winners.

The hospitality and travel industry is very dynamic. It is changing quickly and constantly. Every organization should remain as flexible and amenable to change as possible. Although it is useful to keep a historic record of marketing spending, past budgets should not provide the primary basis for setting future ones.

b. ***Rule-of-Thumb Budgeting.*** This approach is also known as the percentage-of-sales method. In rule-of-thumb budgeting, the marketing budget is calculated using an established industry average, and is usually a percentage of total revenues. For example, it is common for hotels and motels to budget 3.5 to 5 percent of their total expected sales in the next year for marketing. Why? This is the typical range found in published reports by such firms as PKF Consulting and Smith Travel Research. Again, this is not a zero-based approach, because it assumes that the organization will spend some amount close to industry norms.

Like the historical method, this approach is popular because it does not take very much work and can be done quickly. But it also runs contrary to the principles of the hospitality and travel marketing system. No two organizations and their operating performances are exactly alike. No two organizations have exactly the same target markets and marketing mixes. Additionally, industry averages can be very misleading. They are the combination of a wide range of results. New businesses trying to build market share normally have to budget above-average amounts. Established firms with a large core of loyal and repeat customers may get by with much less. The level of competition in different businesses and geographic areas varies widely. Each requires budgets tailor-made for the situation. For example, the fast-food trade is intensely competitive and requires huge marketing budgets for national television campaigns. McDonald's spent an estimated $1.13 billion on its advertising in the United States in 1999, making it the thirteenth largest advertiser among all United States organizations.[2] On the other hand, dinner-house chains do not engage in the same level of competition.

The rule-of-thumb approach is dangerous and should be avoided. It is a rather sloppy practice handed down by past generations of hospitality and travel marketers. Again, although it is interesting to know what the industry is spending on average, this should not be the primary basis for setting an organization's budget.

c. ***Competitive Budgeting.*** We looked at the strategies for *market followers* in Chapter 8. One way that a lower-share firm can mimic the industry leader is to try to match its spending levels and marketing activities. Some call this the competitive parity approach.[3] Like the previous two methods, this one is easy to use. All that is needed is information on what competitors are budgeting for marketing, which can be found by reading published materials on these organizations or by studying their annual reports. Because this method begins by assuming that some amount will be spent in relation to some competitor(s), it is not a zero-based approach.

Again, the major weakness of competitive budgeting is that it overlooks the unique sets of target markets, marketing mixes, objectives, resources, and market positions of individual organizations. Although keeping a close track of competitors' marketing programs is essential, it is inadvisable to use only the competitive budgeting approach.

d. ***Objective-and-Task Budgeting.*** This works exactly the way it sounds—marketing objectives are set first and then the steps (or tasks) to achieve them are detailed. The budget starts at nothing, which implies that it is a zero-based approach. Some call it the *buildup* method, because an organization establishes the budget from the bottom up, rather than starting with a total dollar amount and then deciding how to spend it.

Using the *objective-and-task* method takes much more time and effort than the historical, rule-of-thumb, and competitive approaches. All the activities in the previous marketing plan are carefully evaluated beforehand. But the primary basis for arriving at the budget are the activities necessary to reach the marketing objectives for each target market.

Although many marketing budgets are less detailed, the ideal method is to show the amount to be spent for each marketing-mix element and for each target market.

a. *Budget by Target Market.* How much of the marketing budget will be devoted to each target market? This is a question that is often skipped over in marketing plans. Nevertheless, it is of great importance. This book suggests that budgets should be apportioned roughly according to each target market's current or expected share of total revenues or profits. Many organizations make the mistake of grossly overspending on small-share target markets at the expense of larger-share customer groups.

b. *Budget by Marketing-Mix Element.* Marketing managers also need to know how much is being spent on each of the 8 Ps. Otherwise, they are unable to measure the effectiveness of each marketing-mix element and to make informed future decisions about how the budget should be allocated.

c. *Contingency Funds.* Always expect the unexpected. The vast majority of budgets end up being exceeded. This is not to say that it is fine to go over budget. It is not! It is essential to make a reserve fund available from the beginning to provide for unexpected competitive moves, media production cost overruns, and other unanticipated increases in marketing expenses. Typically, 10 to 15 percent of the total cost of budgeted activities should be set aside as a contingency fund.

3. **Control Procedures (How do we make sure we get there?).** Controlling the plan is a *marketing management* function. To control effectively, the manager must know what is expected (desired results), when it is expected (progress points or *milestones*), who it is expected of (responsible parties), and how expectations are to be measured (measures). Financial control of the marketing plan is achieved through budgeting and periodic reports that compare budgeted with actual expenditures. Monitoring progress towards objectives is done by measuring sales volumes (e.g., restaurant covers, occupied room nights, clients served, airline seats sold), revenues, and profits. Sometimes special marketing research studies have to be done. For example, these may be needed if the objective is to increase awareness or improve attitudes toward an organization's services.

a. *Results Expected from Each Activity.* How is each marketing activity expected to contribute to its related marketing objective? For example, will the new ad in *Meetings & Conventions* magazine produce 25 percent of the projected 10-percent increase in corporate meeting-room nights? The plan should look at these types of questions on an activity-by-activity basis.

b. *Progress Reporting and Measures. Milestones* have already been mentioned. Real milestones show how far travelers are from their destinations. The *milestones* we are interested in are the interim results or subobjectives that lead toward achieving a marketing objective. A decision should be made on how these will be measured, when they will be checked, and how they will be reported.

4. **Evaluation Procedures (How do we know if we got there?).** The ultimate test of a marketing plan's success is the extent to which its marketing objectives are achieved. Figure 5–11 (marketing position and plan analysis worksheet) shows how the effectiveness of each marketing-mix element can be evaluated. In addition to this type of analysis, results must be reviewed carefully on an objective-by-objective basis. Effective evaluation requires expected results and measurement techniques, performance standards, and a timetable for evaluation.

   a. *Measurements.* How will success be measured? Will it be measured in dollars, customers, number of inquiries, or awareness percentage? Obviously, it is best to tie these directly to marketing objectives.

   b. *Performance Standards.* This is another item that is overlooked in many marketing plans. What deviations from an objective are acceptable and unacceptable? Performance standards should be specified in the marketing plan so that the organization can make an overall judgment on the acceptability of actual results.

   c. *Evaluation Timetable.* Some prior thought should go into the timing of the marketing plan evaluation. To be most useful, evaluation must begin before the planning period ends so it can provide input into the next situation analysis and marketing plan.

STEPS INVOLVED IN PREPARING A MARKETING PLAN

You now know what should be included in a marketing plan. What you have read has shown you that a good marketing plan deals with all five key questions in the **hospitality and travel marketing system** (Chapter 3). You have also noticed that the written plan follows the exact same systematic process. In summary, the steps involved in preparing a marketing plan are as follows:

1. **PREPARE THE MARKETING PLAN RATIONALE**—Review and summarize
   - Situation analysis
   - Marketing research studies
   - Market segmentation
   - Segmentation approach and bases
   - Target-market selection
   - Marketing strategy
   - Positioning approaches
   - Marketing mixes
   - Marketing objectives

2. **DEVELOP A DETAILED IMPLEMENTATION PLAN**—Design and specify
   - Activities by marketing-mix element for target markets
   - Responsibilities (internal and external)
   - Timetable and activity schedule
   - Budget and contingency fund

EXCELLENCE CASE

Marketing Plan:
Tourism Vancouver

Tourism Vancouver is the destination marketing organization responsible for the marketing of the Greater Vancouver area in British Columbia, Canada. Its mission statement is "to lead the cooperative effort of positioning Greater Vancouver as a preferred travel destination in all targeted markets worldwide, thereby creating opportunities for member and community sharing of the resulting economic, environmental, social and cultural benefits." Tourism Vancouver's *"Business and Market Development Plan"* for 1995–1997 represents an excellent application of the steps recommended in this chapter for preparing a marketing plan.

Covering a three-year period, Tourism Vancouver's Plan is a combination of a strategic market plan and a marketing plan. Many of the elements recommended for a marketing plan are included and the three-year strategic market plan is updated annually. The plan, with the title *"Making a Difference,"* was released in December 1994. The plan opens with an **executive summary** which describes its principal highlights. This summary is followed by four sections (called chapters in the plan) that together form the **marketing plan rationale.** The first three of these sections are an introduction, a review of the performance of tourism in Vancouver in 1994, and an analysis of Tourism Vancouver's marketing environment **(situation analysis highlights and environmental analysis).** The fourth section of the plan identifies the "strategic priorities and rationale." The following seven strategic priorities, which we can also call **marketing goals,** are specified:

1. Increase investment in convention marketing to attract city-wide business and to take advantage of future product developments in Vancouver.
2. Focus tour and travel trade marketing through joint ventures with tour operators

in key markets and continue to build Vancouver-Alaska pre- and post-cruise passenger business.

3. Continue to support incentive marketing activities of the membership.

continued

EXCELLENCE CASE *continued*

4. Increase investment leverage in consumer marketing campaigns to offset reduced core funding.
5. Continue to actively pursue joint ventures that extend the product appeal of Vancouver.
6. Develop incremental business with a return on investment by delivering marketing initiatives responsive to growth and emerging markets.
7. Enhance business vehicles and communication programs for membership.

The plan identifies the four target markets (part of the **selected marketing strategies**) of association/corporate meeting planners, travel trade, incentive buyers, and independent travelers. The **positioning approaches** for each of the four target markets are described through a series of "key messages." In the case of the association/corporate meeting planner market the five key messages are an appealing destination for attendance building, pre- and post-meeting activities, quality facilities, scenic and safe, and good value.

Tourism Vancouver's **marketing mixes** and **marketing objectives** are based on a set of twenty-eight specific initiatives for the 1995–1997 period, the majority of which relate to these individual target markets. Tourism Vancouver's "initiatives-based marketing" approach was adopted in 1994 and is described in the plan's sixth section under "review of 1995–1997 initiatives." These initiatives define the broad programs that Tourism Vancouver will undertake. For example, the association (convention) and corporate meeting planner target market has nine initiatives:

- Sport tourism event/meeting marketing
- Canadian association/corporate meeting sales and market development
- Northeastern United States association/corporate meeting sales and market development
- Washington D.C./Atlanta association/corporate meeting sales and market development
- West, Midwest, and Southern United States association/corporate meeting sales and market development
- European congress sales and market development
- BC convention destination cooperative ("Team BC")
- Convention bridge financing support
- Convention services and attendance building program

Matched with these initiatives, Tourism Vancouver's plan specifies the **marketing mixes** to be used for each target market. For example, the Northeastern United States association/corporation meeting component of the association (convention) and corporate meeting planner market is to be targeted through advertising (direct mail), personal selling (sales calls), and sales promotion (trade shows). Three **marketing objectives** are specified for Northeastern United States association/corporate meeting planners:

1. Identify and develop qualified leads from Northeastern United States association and corporate meeting planners.
2. Strengthen Vancouver's image as a convention destination for United States business.
3. Assist members in developing and closing new business in the marketplace.

These objectives are results-oriented, quantitative, and time specific, since Tourism Vancouver identifies "key measures" of marketing success for this target market for 1995 (twenty-four qualified leads), 1996 (twenty-six qualified leads), and 1997 (twenty-eight qualified leads). Tourism Vancouver's **partners** are also specified for the Northeastern United States association/corporate meeting market. These include the Vancouver Trade & Convention Centre, member hotels, destination management companies, and airlines.

Tourism Vancouver's **implementation plan** includes a set of activities, a marketing budget, control and evaluation procedures, and an evaluation timetable. The **activities plan,** which Tourism Vancouver's plan refers to as a "schedule of activities," provides a month-by-month listing of its planned activities by target market and marketing mix element. These are shown in the seventh section of the plan. For example, in April 1995 Tourism Vancouver planned two activities for the Northeastern

continued

EXCELLENCE CASE *continued*

SCHEDULE OF ACTIVITIES

The following schedule lists the 1995 activities for each sector. Although Tourism Vancouver endeavors to complete each activity, changes in dates, postponements and cancellations will occur throughout the year.

CONVENTIONS/CORPORATE MEETINGS AND INCENTIVE		INITIATIVE	ADVERTISING/COMMUNICATIONS	DIRECT SALES/MEETINGS	TRADE SHOWS	SALES MATERIALS	PROMOTIONAL EVENTS	FAMS/SITES	RESEARCH/MONITORING	TRAVEL MEDIA
JANUARY 1	Directories: • CSAE (Canada)	CV2	■							
	• CSAE (USA)	CV5	■							
	• GWSAE	CV4	■							
	• ASAE	CV5	■							
1	Forum Magazine	CV5	■							
1	Association Management Magazine	CV5	■							
5-8	ACOM Educational Conference, Orlando	CV9			■					
7-10	PCMA Atlanta▲*	CV5			■					
7-10	USAE Newspaper (3x)	CV4	■							
15	Convention Schedule	CV9				■				
22-23	CSAE Winter Conference, Toronto▲*	CV2			■					
24-27	Promotion: Toronto, Ottawa, Montreal▲	CV2					■			
	Sites/Hosting (ongoing throughout year, Convention and Incentive)▲	CI#						■		
	Direct Mail (ongoing throughout year)	CV#	■							
	Promotional Items (ongoing throughout year)	CI#				■				
FEBRUARY 9	IACVB Destination Showcase, Washington, D.C.	CV4			■					
13	Kit Folders	CV#				■				
15	CSAE Trade Show, Ottawa▲*	CV2			■					
27	New Lure Brochures	CV#				■				
MARCH 1	PCMA Directory	CV5	■							
1	Forum Magazine	CV5	■							
1	Canadian Consulate "Showcase Canada", Seattle▲*	CV5			■					
2	Canada Meeting Place, London	CV6			■					
7	Canadian Consulate "Showcase Canada", San Francisco▲*	CV5			■					
9	Canadian Consulate "Showcase Canada", Los Angeles▲*	CV5			■					
19-21	USAE Newspaper (4x)	CV4	■							
19-22	ASAE Forum, Opryland, Nashville	CV5			■					
21	Greeting Cards and Postcards	CV#					■			
tba	Sales Calls, Europe	CV6		■						
tba	Team BC Event, Chicago▲	CV7						■		
APRIL 1	Association Magazine	CV2	■							
4	Canadian Consulate "Showcase Canada", Atlanta▲*	CV4			■					
5	Canadian Consulate "Showcase Canada", Houston▲*	CV5			■					
6	Canadian Consulate "Showcase Canada", Dallas▲*	CV5			■					
13	Association for Computing Machinery (attendance building), Denver	CV9			■					
25	Canadian Consulate "Showcase Canada", Minneapolis▲*	CV5			■					
26	Canadian Consulate "Showcase Canada", Pittsburgh	CV3			■					
tba	Japanese Cooperative End User Fam (Incentive)	IN3							■	
tba	Sales Calls, Pittsburgh, Philadelphia	CV3		■						
MAY 1	Corporate Meetings & Incentives Magazine	CV3	■							
1	Insurance Conference Planner Magazine	CV3	■							
1	Convene Magazine	CV5	■							
1	Forum Magazine	CV5	■							
1	Tagungs-Wirtschaft Magazine	CV6	■							
8	Canadian Consulate, Los Angeles "Swing Through Canada" Event, Newport Beach▲*	CV5			■					
15	Blank Tour Shells	CV#				■	■			
16-18	EIBTM, Geneva, Switzerland (Incentive)▲	IN1			■		■			
23	USAE Newspaper	CV4	■							
29	Black and White Downtown Map	CV#				■	■			
31-Jun 3	Five Star Edge Promotion, Montreal (Incentive)	IN2			■			■		
31	PCMA Foundation Dinner	CV5		■						
tba	MPI - Geneva	CV6		■						

▲ Direct membership participation opportunity   * Must register directly with organizer
CV# All conventions/corporate meetings initiatives   IN# All incentive initiatives   CI# All conventions and incentive initiatives

continued

EXCELLENCE CASE *continued*

United States association/corporate meeting planner market (CV3)—participation in the Canadian Consulate's "Showcase Canada" in Pittsburgh (a trade show) and sales calls on meeting planners in Pittsburgh (direct sales/meetings).

The plan includes a **marketing budget** of C$ 2,510,155 separated by target market for "market development" which mainly covers promotional activities. Tourism Vancouver's total budget for 1995 is expected to be approximately C$ 6.5 million. The marketing budget is included in the plan's fifth section titled as "financial investment." The allocations for 1995 for each of the target markets are association meeting planners ($884,440 or 35 percent), corporate meeting planners ($151,254; 6 percent), travel trade ($662,043; 27 percent), incentive buyers ($186,106; 7 percent), and independent travelers ($626,312; 25 percent). The budget is also broken out by origin (Canada, United States, Europe, and Asia Pacific), seasonality (high, shoulder, and low seasons), and life cycle (maintenance, growth, and emerging).

The **control** and **evaluation procedures** for Tourism Vancouver's plan are included in a subsection called "evaluation of plan." The 1995–1997 plan was developed after a thorough evaluation of the previous plan for 1994–1996. This evaluation resulted in a reduction from thirty-six to twenty-eight initiatives and several other plan modifications. Each of the twenty-eight initiatives in the 1995–1997 plan is assigned to a specialist in Tourism Vancouver who is supported by a cross-functional staff team (**responsibilities for activi-**

ties). The two specific control procedures are "monthly initiative review meetings" and "business and market development reports." According to the plan, the monthly initiative review meetings include the review by management of performance in reaching intended targets, budget considerations, and arising opportunities. The business and market development reports summarize monthly and year-to-date performance and are prepared bimonthly and issued to Tourism Vancouver's Board of Directors. The plan evaluation is accomplished at an "annual planning session" and this review of activities forms the basis for the next plan.

Tourism Vancouver's marketing planning approach sets a fine example for other hospitality and travel organizations. The careful thought and execution of this plan may one day lead to the realization of its **vision statement** of being "recognized as the best convention and visitors bureau in North America."

Discussion Questions

1. In what ways has Tourism Vancouver followed the approaches recommended in this chapter for preparing a marketing plan?
2. How does Tourism Vancouver's plan differ from the procedures described in this chapter? Could Tourism Vancouver's plan be improved?
3. What could other hospitality and travel organizations learn from the marketing planning approach used by Tourism Vancouver?

- Expected results
- Measurements
- Progress reporting procedures
- Performance standards
- Evaluation timetable

3. **WRITE THE EXECUTIVE SUMMARY**—Figure 9–3 shows, in flow-chart format, the steps involved in developing the marketing plan.

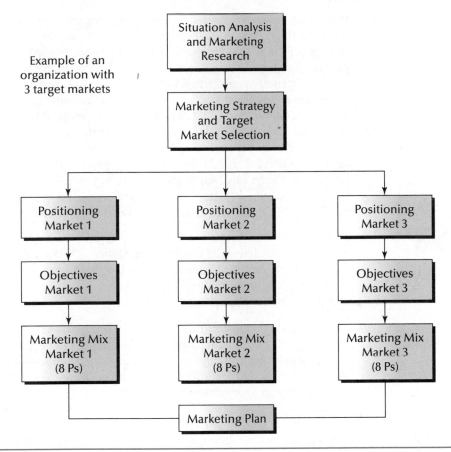

◆ **FIGURE 9–3** *Steps in developing a marketing plan.*

THE 8 PS OF HOSPITALITY AND TRAVEL MARKETING

A large part of a marketing plan concerns how the organization intends to use the 8 Ps of hospitality and travel marketing (marketing mix). Chapters 10 through 19 review each of the marketing-mix elements, or Ps. Before we get into the details of each element, let us take a brief look at how each is integrated into the marketing plan. The 8 Ps include the following:

1. Product
2. Partnership
3. People
4. Packaging
5. Programming
6. Place
7. Promotion
8. Pricing

1. **Product.** Chapter 10 discusses product development in the hospitality and travel industry. It introduces the term product/service mix to describe the range of facilities or products that an individual organization provides to customers. One important point made earlier in this book is that hospitality and travel marketing is a separate branch of marketing, with its own unique requirements. Most traditional marketers lump people, packaging, and programming in with product. Although they are definitely part of the mix of things that hospitality and travel organizations offer, these three factors deserve separate attention.

   How do we define a hospitality and travel organization's product? This is a tough question because, unlike most other products, it is not an inanimate object. People are always involved in the *production* process. It is doubly difficult to pinpoint because many customers buy more on the basis of their emotions than on hard facts. What they buy is not always what we think we are selling!

2. **People.** The ways that people—employees and managers—are involved in the marketing plan have already been discussed. Let us emphasize, however, that a marketing plan must include programs that have been developed to make use of these vital human resources. Chapter 11 discusses the *people* aspect of hospitality and travel marketing.

3/4. **Packaging and Programming.** Chapter 12 reviews the related concepts of packaging and programming. In many ways, packaging epitomizes a marketing orientation. It results from finding out what people need and want and then assembling various services and facilities to match these needs. The related concept of programming is also very customer-oriented.

   The marketing plan should detail the continuing and new packages and programs for the upcoming twenty-four months or less. A financial justification for each package and program should be included, as well as an explanation about how these offerings will be tied in with promotional activities and pricing/revenue objectives.

5. **Place.** How does the organization plan to place the product or to work with other complementary groups in the distribution channel? For suppliers and carriers, this means how they will use travel trade intermediaries (travel agents, tour wholesalers, incentive travel planners, etc.) to achieve marketing objectives. For the intermediaries, it means the relationships they have with other intermediaries, suppliers, and carriers. Chapter 13 introduces the distribution mix concept and describes the travel trade intermediaries.

6. **Promotion.** The marketing plan specifies how each technique in the promotional mix (advertising, personal selling, sales promotion, merchandising, and public relations and publicity) will be used. These techniques are interrelated, and the plan must make sure that each one complements, rather than contradicts, the others. Promotion usually represents the largest percentage of the marketing budget, and it involves the greatest use of outside advisors and professionals. As such, it must be planned in considerable detail, with great emphasis on costs, responsibilities, and timing. Chapters 14 through 18 provide a detailed discussion of all the promotional mix elements.

7. **Partnership.** Technically, it would be correct to include partnership as part of each of the other 7 Ps. However, to give added emphasis to the value of cooperative ad-

vertising and other marketing programs, this book considers it separately in Chapter 10. The marketing plan should spend some time discussing cooperative efforts, their costs, and their financial paybacks.

8. **Pricing.** Pricing often gets inadequate consideration in marketing plans. It deserves a much higher priority because it is both a marketing technique and a major profit determinant. What is recommended is a comprehensive pricing plan that takes into account all special rates, prices, and discounts projected for the upcoming period. Chapter 19 discusses pricing and price planning in the hospitality and travel industry.

CHAPTER CONCLUSION

The marketing plan is a blueprint for action. It shows how the organization will try to reach its marketing objectives. The plan details all the marketing activities to be carried out in the next year or two. It is really a series of plans, one for each of the eight marketing-mix elements, carefully coordinated within one overall plan.

A plan should be written in ink, but not in stone. An organization must monitor implementation of the plan and make adjustments when necessary. Like any airline flight, no organization is guaranteed perfect flying weather. Plans take weeks and sometimes months to draft, but it may take even more time and effort to make them work as effectively as possible.

REVIEW QUESTIONS

1. Is a marketing plan tactical or strategic? What is the difference between the two types of plans?
2. How is the term marketing plan defined in this book?
3. What are the eight requirements for an effective marketing plan?
4. What are the benefits of having a marketing plan?
5. What are the three parts of the marketing plan?
6. Should a marketing plan always be written down? Why?
7. Does the marketing plan address all five questions in the hospitality and travel marketing system? If so, how is this done?
8. What are the 8 Ps of hospitality and travel marketing? Are they the same as the marketing mix?
9. What are the four approaches to preparing marketing budgets? Which is the best and why is it superior to the other three?

CHAPTER ASSIGNMENTS

1. You have just joined a nonprofit organization that has never had a marketing plan. The board of directors is very skeptical of the time and money required to complete a plan. How would you sell your idea to prepare the organization's first marketing plan? How would you justify the time and expense needed to prepare the plan? What would you include in the plan?
2. You have just taken over as the new director of marketing. Using the objective-and-task budgeting approach, you have just calculated the upcoming year's marketing budget to be 30 percent higher than the previous year's. Your company has always used the historic approach in the past, adding 5 to 10 percent each year to the previous year's spending.

How would you justify your position? What drawbacks would you highlight in the historic approach?

3. The owner of a small hospitality and travel business in your community has just asked you to help her prepare a marketing plan. What would you include in the plan? Who would you consult in preparing the plan, and what sources of information would you use? Using Figure 9–1 as a guide, develop a more detailed table of contents for the plan. How long would your plan be? To whom would you give copies?

4. Choose a hospitality and travel organization. How has it made use of the 8 Ps of hospitality and travel marketing? Are all the Ps given equal emphasis, or are some emphasized more than others? Have any of the Ps been overlooked? What recommendation would you make to the organization about improving its use of these eight marketing-mix elements? Use examples from other organizations to back up your recommendations.

WORLD WIDE WEB RESOURCES

PKF Consulting
  http://www.pkfonline.com/

Smith Travel Research
  http://www.str-online.com/

Tourism Vancouver
  http://www.tourism-vancouver.org/

REFERENCES

1. Lovelock, Christopher H. 2000. *Services Marketing: People, Technology, Strategy.* 4th ed. Upper Saddle River, N.J.: Prentice-Hall, Inc.

2. "100 leading national advertisers." *Advertising Age,* http://www.dataplace/index.html

3. Ray, Michael L. 1982. *Advertising & Communication Management.* Englewood Cliffs, N.J.: Prentice-Hall. Inc., 149.

For additional hospitality and travel marketing resources, visit our Web site at **www.Hospitality-Tourism.delmar.com**

PART IV

IMPLEMENTING THE MARKETING PLAN

WHERE ARE WE NOW?

WHERE WOULD WE LIKE TO BE?

HOW DO WE GET THERE?

HOW DO WE MAKE SURE WE GET THERE?

HOW DO WE KNOW IF WE GOT THERE?

10

Product Development and Partnership

How Do We Get There?

Objectives

Having read this chapter, you should be able to

◆ Identify the four major groups of organizations in the hospitality and travel industry.

◆ Describe the roles played by each of these four groups of hospitality and travel organizations.

◆ Identify the trends among each of the four groups of organizations.

◆ Identify five overall trends and industry realities.

◆ Define the product/service mix.

◆ Identify and describe the six components of an organization's product/service mix.

◆ Explain the types of product development decisions that an organization must make.

◆ Define the term partnership and list the potential benefits of marketing partnerships to hospitality and travel organizations.

◆ Identify the types of partners available to hospitality and travel organizations.

Overview

What are the products that the hospitality and travel industry markets to customers? To start with, you already know that we should replace the word products *with* services. *The services provided by the industry are many and varied, ranging from 1,000-plus-room hotels to two- or three-person travel agencies. Understanding the structure of the industry is fundamental for marketing managers. This chapter begins by*

describing the organizations and resources in the hospitality and travel industry. Recent supply trends are then reviewed.

The term product/service mix is introduced and explained, and each of its components is described. The chapter shows how decisions are made to modify an organization's product/service mix.

Key Terms

branding	destination marketing	product/service-mix length
cannibalize	organizations (DMOs)	product/service-mix width
carriers	horizontal integration	relationship marketing
co-branding	macrosystem	strategic alliances
convention and visitors bureaus	megacarriers	suppliers
(CVBs)	microsystem	travel trade intermediaries
database marketing	partnership	vertical integration
	product/service mix	

Have you ever tried to put your finger on a blob of mercury? What happens is quite predictable, right? Whenever you think you have got the mercury pinned down, it squeezes away from you. Describing the hospitality and travel industry is very similar. It is a fast-changing business. If you take a snapshot of it today, the picture is sure to become outdated in a few months. When putting this book together, we gathered the latest statistics, but there probably will be many changes after the book is published.

Some of you are probably most interested in hotel and restaurant careers—others in the airlines and the travel trade. Some may be pursuing other fields such as cruise-line operations, theme parks and attractions, convention and meeting planning, country club management, government or association travel promotion, or ski area management. Whatever your favorite area, you will find this chapter both interesting and informative. You may even see new career opportunities opening up.

Before discussing product development decisions, we will take a look at the overall industry structure. Taking this broader perspective first will help you better understand the role played by various types of organizations.

TYPES AND ROLES OF HOSPITALITY AND TRAVEL INDUSTRY ORGANIZATIONS

There are four major groups of organizations in the hospitality and travel industry:

1. Suppliers
2. Carriers
3. Travel trade intermediaries
4. Destination marketing organizations

This book looks at four groups of organizations in the industry based on the functions they perform. Suppliers—including cruise lines; car rental firms; and lodging, restaurant, casino, and attraction facilities—provide the services that travel trade intermediaries wholesale (or package) and retail, and that customers also buy directly. Carriers, including airlines and train, bus, and ferry companies, provide transportation from the customers' origins to their destinations. Travel trade intermediaries package and retail supplier and carrier services to travelers. Destination marketing organizations (DMOs) promote their cities, counties, regions, states, and countries to travel trade intermediaries and individual travelers. One of the major messages in this book is that all these businesses and organizations are interrelated. Remember from Chapter 3 that we called the industry the macrosystem and said that individual organizations were microsystems. Using these expressions was one way of showing that many hospitality and travel organizations are interdependent.

Trends among Suppliers

Supplier organizations in the hospitality and travel industry can be grouped into the following six categories:

1. Lodging
2. Restaurant and foodservice
3. Cruise lines
4. Car rental
5. Attractions and events
6. Casinos

1. **Lodging.** This huge sector of the industry contains a diverse variety of property types. One leading hotel expert divides lodging facilities into transient hotels, resort hotels, convention hotels, conference centers, motels and motor hotels, and inns.[1] Another more comprehensive classification scheme uses five *development criteria* (price, amenities, location, specific markets served, and distinctiveness of style or offerings) to segment facilities.

   a. *Chain Domination.* Although a large proportion of lodging establishments have fewer than 50 rooms, larger chain-owned properties predominate from a marketing standpoint. In 1999, *Hotels* magazine in its *Hotels' 325* found the top ten lodging chains in the world, in terms of total available rooms, to be Cendant, Bass, Marriott, Choice, Best Western, Accor, Starwood, Promus, Carlson, and Wyndham.[2] Each of these chains had more than 100,000 rooms in 1998. Appendices 1-1a and 1-1b provide more detailed information on the leading lodging chains.

   b. *Increasing Brand Segmentation.* This type of lodging segmentation has greatly expanded the range of property types available. Figure 10–1 shows several of the main lodging companies along with their brands of properties.

       Not all the leading chains have decided to add new brands to further penetrate the lodging market's various segments. Upscale Four Seasons and Ritz-Carlton have chosen to concentrate on the higher-priced and luxury end of the lodging market. As discussed in Chapter 8, you can see that the chains have picked different segmentation and positioning approaches within their marketing strategies.

   c. *Mergers and Joint-Marketing Programs.* Throughout this chapter, you will see mentions of mergers and new cooperative partnerships in different parts of the industry. Companies grouping together for greater marketing *clout* was a pervasive industry trend in the 1970s, 1980s, and 1990s. Some larger lodging chains swallowed smaller ones, while others were acquired by companies new to the industry. During the 1990s, Marriott International and Hilton were especially active in acquisitions, as were the real estate investment trusts (REITs) including Starwood. Bass, the British beer company, took over the Holiday Inn chain and portfolio. In 1999, Hilton acquired Promus and with this added the DoubleTree, Embassy Suites, Hampton, and Homewood Suites brands.

Cendant Corp.	Bass Hotels & Resorts	Marriott International	Choice Hotels International	Starwood Hotels & Resorts Worldwide	Hilton
• Days Inn • Howard Johnson • Knights Inn • Ramada • Super 8 • Travelodge • Villager Lodge • Wingate Inn	• Crowne Plaza Hotels & Resorts • Holiday Inn • Holiday Inn Express • Holiday Inn Family Suites Resorts • Holiday Inn Garden Court • Holiday Inn Select • Holiday Inn SunSpree Resorts • Inter-Continental Hotels and Resorts • Staybridge Suites by Holiday Inn	• Courtyard by Marriott • ExecuStay by Marriott • Fairfield Inn by Marriott • Marriott Conference Centers • Marriott Executive Apartments • Marriott Hotels, Resorts, and Suites • Marriott Vacation Club International • New World • Ramada International • Renaissance Hotels and Resorts • Residence Inn by Marriott • Ritz-Carlton • SpringHill Suites • TownePlace Suites	• Clarion • Comfort • Econo Lodge • MainStay Suites • Quality • Rodeway • Sleep	• Four Points • Luxury Collection • St. Regis • Sheraton • W • Westin	• Conrad International • DoubleTree Hotels, Suites, Resorts, and Clubs • Embassy Suites • Hampton Inns & Suites • Homewood Suites

◆ **FIGURE 10–1**   *Brand segmentation among leading lodging brands.*

In addition to being acquired by other organizations, most major lodging companies are now part of one or more joint-marketing ventures, carrier-supplier reservations networks, or frequent-travel award programs.

d. ***All-Suite Hotels.*** Among the major lodging trends in the early 1980s was the emergence of the all-suite hotel concept, Figure 10–2. This is a property type with a distinctive style and offerings—all rooms are designed as suites. As Figure 10–1 shows, most of the major lodging chains have one or more all-suite (or extended stay) brands.

ON THE WEB

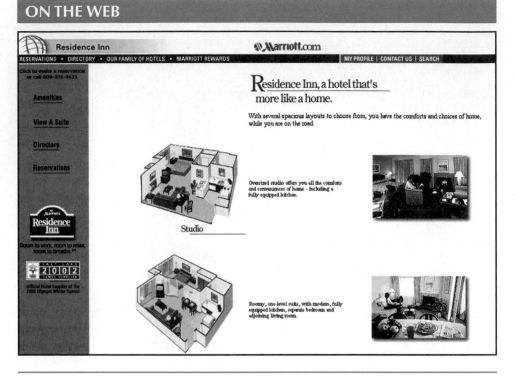

◆ FIGURE 10–2   *Residence Inn's Web site clearly illustrates the benefits of suites.* (Courtesy of Marriott International, Inc.)

   e. ***Frequent-Guest Programs.*** Another significant 1980s and 1990s lodging trend was the increasing number and importance of frequent-guest programs (Figure 10–3). There are several reasons for these programs:
   - To identify frequent guests
   - To allocate marketing dollars to them
   - To reward and provide special services to them
   - To build awareness of the chain

   In the early 1990s, several hotel chains enhanced their frequent-guest programs by offering frequent-flyer mileage points for club members who stayed at their properties.

   f. ***Special Services and Amenities.*** The last 20 years of the twentieth century may be remembered as the era in which lodging companies pampered their guests. Apart from generous reward programs, they provided many new services and amenities.
   - Cable television/free movies
   - Complimentary breakfasts and cocktails
   - Computerized reservation systems
   - Concierge service
   - Data ports for computer modems
   - Executive floors and lounges
   - Express check-out and check-in
   - Free newspapers

ON THE WEB

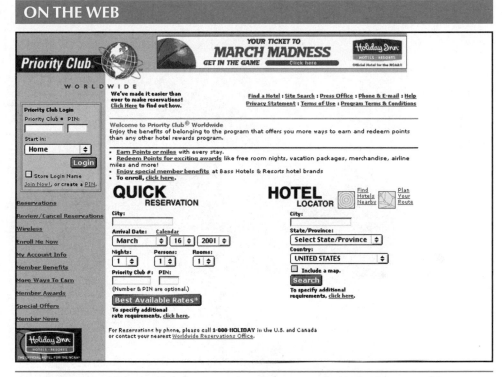

◆ **FIGURE 10–3**   *Priority Club frequent-guest program on the Web.* (Courtesy of Bass Hotels & Resorts, Inc.)

- Health clubs or exercise facilities
- Health-conscious menus
- In-room fax services
- Jogging trail maps
- Nonsmoking rooms and sections
- Office or business centers
- Specially designed facilities for women
- Teleconferencing
- Video check-out
- Video magazines

Figure 10–4 provides a good example of the extras that hotel chains are offering. In this 1999 ad, Westin tried to attract guests with "The Heavenly Bed."

2. **Restaurant and Foodservice.** The restaurant and foodservice sector, like the lodging sector, is dominated by the large chains. Appendix 1–2a shows the top foodservice chains in the United States by total systemwide sales. According to *Nation's Restaurant News,* the top 100 chains had combined sales of $130.55 billion in 1999-2000.[3] Six of the top ten foodservice chains were sandwich restaurants (McDonald's, Burger King, Taco Bell, Wendy's, Subway, and Hardee's). Together the 18-chain sandwich segment accounted for 41.5 percent of the total sales of the top 100 chains.

Figure 10–5 shows a classification of foodservice facilities as suggested by *Nation's Restaurant News.*

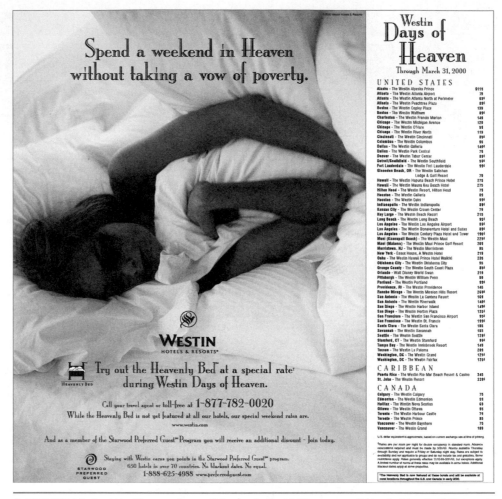

◆ **FIGURE 10–4**   *Westin promises a "Heavenly Bed."* (Courtesy of Westin Hotels & Resorts)

a. ***Major Restaurant-Industry Trends.*** Chapter 7 identified some of the major trends in the restaurant industry. A more complete set of trends includes the following:

- Increased emphasis on home delivery
- More single and double drive-throughs
- Greater emphasis by restaurant operators on the nutritional qualities of menu items
- More restaurants specializing in ethnic or national foods, particularly Mexican
- Entry of convenience stores, such as 7-Eleven, into the fast-food business
- Increased popularity of certain food items (e.g., fresh baked goods, pasta, salads, fish and seafood, poultry and other lean meats)
- Increased popularity of lower-alcohol-content beverages (e.g., wines, coolers, light beers)
- Increased popularity of special-theme restaurants (e.g., fifties-style nostalgia)

Foodservice Segments	Examples
Bagel	• Einstein Bros. Bagels
Buffet	• Old Country Buffet, HomeTown Buffet
Cafeteria	• Luby's Cafeteria, Piccadilly Cafeteria
Chicken	• KFC, Popeye's
Coffee	• Starbuck's
Contract	• Aramark Global Food/Leisure Services, LSG Lufthansa Service/Sky Chef
Convenience store	• 7-Eleven
Dinner house	• Red Lobster, Outback Steakhouse
Family	• Denny's, Shoney's, Cracker Barrel Old Country Store
Fish QSR	• Long John Silver's, Captain D's Seafood
Grill-buffet	• Golden Corral, Ponderosa Steakhouse
Hotel	• Marriott Hotels, Resorts, and Suites
In-store	• Wal-Mart
Italian QSR	• Fazoli's
Pizza	• Pizza Hut, Domino's Pizza
Sandwich	• McDonald's, Burger King, Taco Bell
Snack	• Dunkin' Donuts, Baskin-Robbins
Theme park	• Disney theme parks

◆ FIGURE 10–5 *Restaurant classification by* Nation's Restaurant News. (Courtesy of Lebhar-Friedman, Inc.)

b. ***Restaurant Franchising.*** The restaurant business is one of the fastest growing retail segments in the economy. Much of this growth has been sustained by extensive use of franchising, especially in the fast-food sector. About 75 percent of all fast-food restaurants are franchised. They are owned and run by independent operators under an agreement with the parent firm. This arrangement usually results in two-tiered or other multitiered marketing programs, where the parent mounts a national advertising campaign that is supplemented by regional and local activities.

c. ***Co-branding.*** Another strong trend during the 1990s was the movement toward co-branding or putting two branded services together in one business location. One good example is the KFC, Pizza Hut, and Taco Bell brands, which are all owned by Tricon Global Restaurants. The company had approximately 370 units at the end of 1999 that were *2n1s* or combinations of the KFC-Taco Bell or KFC-Pizza Hut menus.[4]

d. ***New Foodservice Locations.*** This has been a trend allied with co-branding, as the leading chains tried to sustain their growth by finding new locations for their outlets. McDonald's, for example, through its *oil alliances* began combining restaurants with gas station companies. Tricon put express units and kiosks in airports, gas and convenience stores, stadiums, amusement parks, universities, and colleges.

e. ***Increasing Brand Segmentation.*** Foodservice companies followed a trend similar to lodging in adding new brands as a growth strategy. For example, Darden Restaurants introduced the Bahama Breeze concept, and McDonald's has added several new brands.

f. ***Changing Ownership of Major Chains.*** During the 1990s, there were two major divestments of restaurant chains by large companies. Darden Restaurants took over Red Lobster and The Olive Garden from General Mills. Pepsico spun off KFC, Pizza Hut, and Taco Bell to Tricon. This left Burger King as the only leading chain owned by a nonrestaurant company, the multiconsumer brand firm, Diageo PLC.

3. **Cruise Lines.** Although cruise liners are a mode of transportation, cruise line companies are suppliers rather than carriers. The only real difference between cruises and resorts today is that the cruise *resort hotel* moves. Appendix 1–3 lists, in alphabetical order, the major cruise lines that cater to North American customers.

a. ***Rapid Growth in Cruising and Cruise Ship Capacity.*** Cruising has been one of the fastest growing segments of the hospitality and travel industry during the past 30 years. An estimated 6.9 million passengers took cruises in 2000, about fourteen times as many as in 1970.[5] In the late 1950s, scheduled transatlantic ocean liners carried more than 1 million persons between Europe and North America. Today scheduled liner services are almost nonexistent, and ships are being used exclusively for cruises.

Unlike most parts of the North American hospitality and travel industry, cruising is controlled by foreign companies. The Scandinavians have an especially large share of the North American cruise business.

Along with the rapid growth in demand for cruises, there has been a major increase in cruise ship capacity. The International Council of Cruise Lines (ICCL) indicated that the worldwide cruise fleet consisted of 223 ships carrying an estimated 9.5 million passengers in 1998.[6] In 2001, the Cruise Lines International Association estimated that 148 cruise ships with a combined capacity of 155,649 lower berths were serving the North American market (see Appendix 1–3).[7] CLIA estimated that 50 new ships would be added by 2005 to the fleet positioned to serve North Americans.

b. ***Creativity and Expansion of Target Markets.*** The key to the success of cruising has been its repositioning as a viable alternative to traditional resort vacations. Cruise ships are now perceived as *floating resorts* with a full range of accommodations and dining, recreation, and entertainment services. Cruise line companies have been among the most creative in the industry in developing a broad spectrum of cruise packages and programs. In addition to traditional packages, a variety of specialized shipboard packages, ranging from fitness to financial management seminars, are now available.

Cruise line companies have also been quick to spot new target markets and emerging trends. Most now have a significant volume of group business, both in shipboard conventions and meetings, and in incentive trips. Innovative companies have introduced fly-cruise and cruise-land packages. Minicruises, often for weekends, have also become more popular.

c. ***Dependence on Travel Agents.*** One of the best examples of industry interdependency is the cruise line-travel agent relationship. More than 95 percent of North Americans who reserve cruises do so through retail travel agents. Individual cruise lines are, therefore, highly dependent on the positive recommendations of agents.

d. ***Changing Cruiser Demographics.*** For some time, cruises had a reputation of only being for wealthy, elderly people. Recent research has shown that both the average ages and incomes of North American cruise passengers have decreased dramatically since the early 1970s.

e. ***Entry of Hotel/Resort Companies into the Cruise Business.*** If you can manage a shoreside resort hotel successfully, then why not a floating resort hotel? Radisson is one lodging chain that decided to test the waters with its own cruise ships. The Walt Disney Company also operates two cruise ships to serve the Caribbean cruising area. By 2010, it is highly probable that other giants of the hospitality and travel industry will be lured into the cruise business by its great growth potential.

f. ***Consolidation.*** The cruise line business has witnessed many changes in ownership during the 1990s. Carnival Corporation (see "Did You Know?") was especially aggressive in acquiring other cruise lines.

g. ***Internet Service.*** As use of the Internet boomed during the late 1990s, both the cruise lines and lodging firms struggled to keep up with the trend. Several of the leading companies in both supplier groups began providing e-mail and Web services, either in guest rooms or in special Internet Café style facilities.

Did You Know?

The hospitality and travel industry has two emerging industry giants in Carnival Corporation and Virgin.

Carnival Corporation

✓ During the 1990s, Carnival Corporation rapidly became the giant of the cruise line industry.

✓ Carnival bought 100 percent ownership or partial ownership of the following six lines:

✓ Costa

✓ Cunard

✓ Holland America

✓ Seabourn

✓ Sun Cruises

✓ Windstar

✓ These cruise lines, together with the Carnival Cruise Line, had a combined fleet of 45 ships at the beginning of 2000.

Virgin

✓ Virgin started operations as a record label under the direction of Richard Branson.

✓ The company is now a carrier with an airline, Virgin Atlantic, and a passenger train service, Virgin Trains.

✓ Virgin is also a tour operator.

✓ The company operates a number of Megastores selling music, videos, and more.

✓ Virgin even has its own brand of cola and clothing.

◆ **FIGURE 10–6**   *Car rental companies go global. Hertz's signature yellow covers most of the world.* (©1994 Hertz System Inc. Hertz is a registered service mark and trademark of Hertz System Inc.)

4. **Car Rental.** The car rental industry has enjoyed tremendous growth. Today it is a highly competitive, multibillion-dollar business. In the period from 1990 to 1999, the combined revenues of U.S. car rental companies doubled.[8] According to *Auto Rental News,* the total revenues of the auto rental market in the United States in 1999 was just under $18.3 billion, and there were more than 1.73 million cars in the fleet in 1997.[9] The six largest companies (Enterprise, Hertz, Avis, Alamo, Budget, and National) each had 140,000 or more cars. As Figure 10–6 reflects, the major car rental companies are attempting to spread worldwide and to become truly global brand names in this business. Appendix 1–4 lists the major car rental firms in the United States.

   a. *Sales Concentrated among Business Leaders.* Although there are thousands of car rental firms, the majority are small mom-and-pop businesses. The bulk of the sales are made by a small number of leading firms. According to one source, the top six rental car companies had approximately 81 percent of the total 1999 car rental revenues in the United States.

   b. *Dependence on Airlines and Travel Agents.* Car rental companies present another excellent example of a supplier that is highly dependent on other hospitality and travel businesses. A high proportion of rentals are made from airports, making these companies dependent on airline routes and schedules. Travel agents book a large share of domestic airline reservations and usually are asked to reserve the traveler's rental car as well. Therefore, rental car firms are one of the major advertisers in specialized magazines read by travel agents, such as *Travel Weekly, Travel Agent,* and *Travel Trade.* Leading companies also promote heavily to corporate travel managers, who negotiate special rental agreements for their organizations.

   c. ***Participation in Frequent-Traveler Programs.*** All major car rental companies have networked with airlines and hotel chains to provide awards to frequent travelers. Most also have their own *frequent-renter* programs. National, for example, has a program it calls The Emerald Club, and Avis has Club Red.

   d. ***New Services.*** During the 1990s, the car rental companies began introducing a variety of new services. These included the use of global positioning systems in vehicles, and express check-in and drop-off services.

5. **Attractions and Events.** For pleasure travelers, attractions and events usually play the key role in bringing people to destinations. Some attractions are both physical and fixed, such as Paramount Canada's Wonderland north of Toronto, the Grand Canyon, the Rockies, and Niagara Falls. Others are event-oriented, are less permanent, and have locations that, in some cases, can be changed (e.g., the Olympic Games, the Pan American Games, and soccer's World Cup). A wide variety of private-sector, government, and nonprofit organizations operate attractions. They range in size from corporations as big as The Walt Disney Company to small, local museum boards.

   a. ***Theme Park Business Growth.*** Disneyland, opened in 1955, was North America's first theme park. Since Disney pioneered the concept, many other theme parks have been developed, making theme parks one of the fastest growing segments of the hospitality and travel industry. The combined attendance at the top ten theme parks in the United States in 1999 was 81.6 million.[10] Approximately 69 percent of the people visited Disney's five parks in Florida and California (see Appendix 1–6 for more details).

     Although many major theme parks are concentrated in areas where the favorable climate permits year-round operations (e.g., Florida and California in the United States, the Gold Coast of Australia), many smaller and more regionally-oriented parks have been opened. The Northern European location of Disneyland Paris also represented an ambitious venture to serve a multinational market. In addition to the full-scale theme parks, there are a large number of waterplay parks, family recreation centers, and amusement/*hardride* parks.

6. **Casinos.** The increasing popularity of casino gambling has been a major trend in U.S. and international tourism. Although many casino operations are attached to hotel/resort properties and cruise ships, there are a growing number of free-standing casinos internationally and on riverboats and American Indian lands in the United States.

   a. ***Growth in Number of Casino Operations.*** In a few decades in the United States, the number of casino gambling locations has gone from just one state (Nevada) to two states (Nevada and Atlantic City, New Jersey), and now to almost all states. Two factors that seem to have contributed to this growth are a general softening of public attitudes toward gaming and the growing recognition of the profitability of casino operations and their appeal to tourists. Casino development is also being used as an economic development strategy in poorer areas of the United States.[11] In addition, the passage of the Indian Gaming Regulatory Act in the late 1980s opened the doors for casino gambling operations on Indian lands, and many have now developed there (Figure 10–7). Outside of the United

◆ **FIGURE 10–7**   *Foxwoods Resort Casino: A mega resort on native American land.* (Courtesy of Mashantucket Pequot Tribal Nation)

States, most major cities and resort areas in Europe, the Caribbean, Asia, and Australia now have casino operations as part of their mix of tourist facilities.

b. ***Casinos Take to the Water.*** Almost all major modern cruise ships include substantial casino operations as part of their mix of entertainment facilities. Gambling on water is also becoming popular on major inland river systems in the United States and other countries. The growth in riverboat gambling operations on the Mississippi and Ohio Rivers has been especially noticeable in recent years in the United States.

c. ***Casino Resort Diversification.*** The end of the twentieth century saw a trend toward the repositioning of casino gambling destinations and individual casino resort operations to appeal to a broader range of market segments, including families with children. This trend has been particularly evident in Las Vegas, Nevada, where existing and new resorts now offer facilities that are truly combinations of destination resorts, casinos, and theme parks. At the end of 2000, Las Vegas had a total of 124,270 rooms. During 2001–03, it was expected that another 7,500 rooms would be added bringing the total number of guest rooms in Las Vegas to around 135,000.[12]

Trends among Carriers

Airline carriers are a powerful force in the hospitality and travel industry, and their operations significantly influence both travel trade intermediaries and suppliers.

1. **Airlines.** Airline companies play a key role in the hospitality and travel industry. Although this book classifies these companies as carriers, many have diversified into other parts of the industry, have put together their own tours, and offer services similar to those of travel intermediaries.

   a. ***Mergers and Industry Concentration.*** In the topsy-turvy world of hospitality and travel, the airline business is perhaps the most volatile sector. According to the Air Transport Association, there were 12 major U.S. airlines in 1984 with annual revenues of more than $1 billion (American, Braniff, Continental, Delta, Eastern, Northwest, Pan American, Republic, TWA, United, USAir, and Western).[13] The period from 1985 to 1987 was characterized by what several airline experts call *merger fever.* The highly successful and budget-conscious People Express bought Frontier and Britt. It was then, along with New York Air, swallowed up by Continental (Texas Air Corp.). Texas Air made an even bolder step later when it took over Eastern. Other major mergers involved Northwest and Republic, Delta and Western, American and AirCal, USAir and Piedmont, TWA and Ozark, Southwest and Transtar, and Alaska and JetAmerica. United also bought out Pan American's Pacific routes. Since then, two of the airline leaders, Eastern and Pan Am, have gone out of business and Texas Air Corp. is no more.

   The results of the failures of major airlines, along with the acquisitions and mergers of the 1980s, was a major reshuffling of the United States' principal air carriers (Appendix 1–6). The United States now has seven airline megacarriers—Delta, United, American, US Airways, Southwest, Northwest, and Continental. According to the Air Transport Association, each of these airlines carried more than 43 million passengers in 1999.[14] Delta was the industry leader with just over 105 million passengers. Despite the fact that smaller airlines, like America West and American Trans Air have enjoyed good recent success, the powerful and larger airlines have increased their potential to influence the marketing and business fortunes of related industry segments, particularly travel agencies. The top carriers in 1999 in terms of passengers carried internationally were British Airways, Lufthansa, Air France, American Airlines, and KLM.[15]

   b. ***More Regional and Commuter Airlines.*** The Airline Deregulation Act of 1978 changed the whole complexion of the U.S. airline industry. It opened the floodgates for a variety of new carriers to enter the market. Industry competition became fierce. Fare options increased geometrically and many types of fare discounts became available. With greater freedom to select their routes and schedules, most major airlines adopted *hub-and-spoke* systems for greater efficiency. That is, rather than the old point-to-point routes, flights from smaller cities were channelled into a larger, centrally located *hub* airport. This proved to be a boon to the growing number of regional and commuter airlines, especially those that signed cooperative agreements with the major companies. These smaller airlines began servicing the smaller feeder cities in the hub-and-spoke patterns, and bringing in more passengers to the hub from airports not serviced by the major airlines.

c. **Frequent-Flyer Programs.** The airlines ignited our industry's seeming mania for frequent-traveler awards programs. First introduced in the early 1980s, these programs now have millions of members, some of whom belong to more than one airline's program. In a 1993 survey of business travelers, approximately 78 percent of the respondents rated frequent-flier programs as either very important or somewhat important when making travel arrangements.[16] Business travelers have used these programs so frequently that abuse is now a major problem facing many corporate travel managers. The airlines have networked with many suppliers to provide an endless array of rewards for the most frequent travelers. The programs usually team a major domestic carrier with one or more national domestic, foreign, and regional airlines; a hotel chain; and a car rental company. Some airlines have gone one step further by trying credit-card companies, long-distance telephone firms, cruise lines, and hotel/resort chains such as Holiday Inn, Marriott, and Sheraton to their programs. This is an excellent example of the marketing partnership concept (one of the 8 Ps of hospitality and travel marketing).

d. **Strategic Alliances.** The 1990s were the era of airline marketing partnerships, some of which had spanned the entire globe. Commonly referred to as strategic alliances, these are special long-term marketing relationships usually formed between two or more airlines. Some of these alliances have involved investments in one carrier by the other airline (e.g., KLM in Northwest), while others are simply code-sharing agreements for certain city pairs. As was mentioned in Chapter 8, three major global airline alliances were formed in the late 1990s and early 2000s, the Star Alliance (Figure 10–8), the Oneworld alliance, and the Shyteam alliance.

e. **Ticketless Travel and E-ticketing.** During the 1990s, airlines took advantage of technological advances and began the *ticketless* travel era. Airlines and travel agents started to issue electronic tickets (or e-tickets) to passengers. With further advances in cellular phone and personal digital assistant technologies, airline travelers began to use these wireless tools to check flight availability and to book flights.

f. **Changes in Travel Agency Commission Policies.** This trend was initiated in the United States as Delta introduced the concept of *commission caps.* Now almost all U.S. domestic airlines and several international airlines have effectively reduced the rate of commission paid to travel agents for ticket sales. This policy, together with more direct distribution to travelers through the Internet, has allowed the airlines to achieve significant distribution cost efficiencies.

2. **Ferry Services.** Ferries are an especially important carrier for sea passage between countries and among islands and mainland areas. In most cases, they carry local

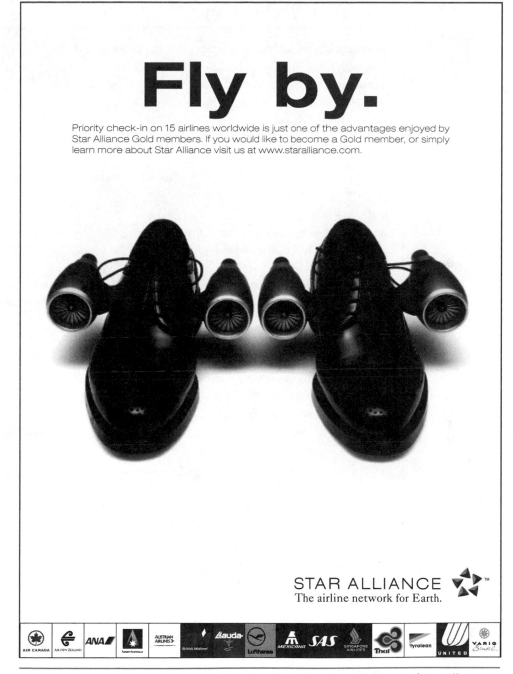

◆ **FIGURE 10–8** *The Star Alliance: A global airline partnership.* (Courtesy of Star Alliance)

passengers as well as visitors. In Western Europe, ferry services are particularly important for crossing the Irish Sea, English Channel, North Sea, and Baltic Sea. Some of the major operators are P&O Ferries and Irish Ferries. There are also major ferry services in Australia, Canada, and the United States. For example, The

A Touch of Technology

Keeping Up with Developments among Airlines and Travel Agencies

The Web is becoming a great source of information for staying on top of what is happening in the airline and travel agency businesses. Here are four Web sites that are particularly useful:

http://www.air-transport.org/

- This is the Web site of the Air Transport Association, the major grouping of U.S. airlines.
- The ATA site provides good information on passenger traffic, airline employment, airfare trends, and airline costs.

http://www.iata.org/

- The International Air Transport Association (IATA) has its headquarters in Montreal and its members include most of the major air carriers worldwide.
- This is the international equivalent of the ATA site. It provides an excellent Frequently Asked Questions (FAQ) section about the operating statistics for international airlines.

http://www.arccorp.com/

- The Airlines Reporting Corporation or ARC is located in Arlington, Virginia.
- The ARC site is the best source available on trends in the U.S. travel agency business in both numbers of agencies and airline commission statistics.

http://www.twcrossroads.com/

- This is the Web site of *Travel Weekly* magazine, a major journal for retail travel agents.
- The site provides comprehensive statistics on the structure and trends of the U.S. travel agency business and details on agency customers.

British Columbia Ferry Corporation carried 21.4 million passengers and 7.9 million vehicles in 1999-2000.[17] The major trends in the ferry business include the introduction of larger, more modern ferries, and the greater involvement of ferry companies in cruise excursions.

3. **Railways.** In many parts of the world, railways are a major carrier linking key centers of population and countries. This is especially true in Europe, where a highly advanced passenger railway system has been developed. This rail system is much more important in the European hospitality and travel industry than railways are in North America.

Two major trends that are evident among passenger railways include the introduction of high-speed trains and the privatization of railway systems. High-speed trains are capable of exceeding 125 miles per hour.[18] These include the Eurostar that links Paris and London, the TGV in France, and ICE in Germany (Figure 10–9). The privatization of railways has resulted in several new railway companies, especially in the United Kingdom.

THE MARKETING MIX

The marketing mix is the heart of the marketing plan. This book characterizes the marketing mix as consisting of the 8 Ps:

1. Product

2. Partnership

3. People

4. Packaging

5. Programming

6. Place

7. Promotion

8. Price

The following color section is designed to give you applications of each of the 8 Ps by hospitality and travel organizations. These examples are presented in the order that the 8 Ps are covered in this book.

Product

What is the product of a theme park like Six Flags Great America in Gurnee, Illinois? The answer includes different types of rides and shows and other forms of entertainment, foodservice, and retail shopping facilities. All theme parks realize that their core service is entertainment, and they must keep adding to and improving their rides and other entertainment programs to keep guests coming back. If they fail to do this, they will quickly lose their appeal as did many of North America's traditional amusement parks.

(Courtesy of Six Flags Great America)

Partnership

This advertisement is an excellent example of the power of partnering among international airlines. At the time this edition was published, 15 different airline companies had joined the Star Alliance, and were cooperatively marketing the concept of global air coverage. The combination of the brand logos at the bottom of this advertisement, clearly illustrates the impact that joining forces can have in the marketplace.

(Courtesy of Star Alliance)

People

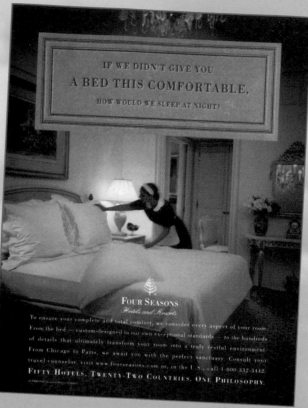

Four Seasons Hotels and Resorts have long been associated with luxury and high levels of personal service. This is expertly emphasized in the advertisement with the heading, "If we didn't give you a bed this comfortable, how would we sleep at night?" The "people" aspect of a Four Seasons' property is demonstrated through the photography and text, which together promise the guest a warm initial welcome, and close attention to individual needs throughout their stay.

(Courtesy of Four Seasons Hotels and Resorts)

Packaging

Contiki clearly depicts its target market of 18–35-year-olds in its European tour brochure for 2000–2001. This cover shot also portrays some of the key features and benefits of a Contiki tour package including sightseeing, the camaraderie of traveling with people of a similar age, and the prospect of participating in unique activities (parasailing). The old phrase "Sell the sizzle, not the steak" is well demonstrated in this brochure. Rather than picturing scenes aboard a motor coach, Contiki "sells" the destinations on its brochure cover (Venice and the Coliseum in Rome).

(Courtesy of Contiki Holidays)

Programming

As these photographs show, programming can be a very valuable asset in effectively marketing a resort property. "Le Club" has been famous since the 1950s for the wide variety of sports and entertainment activities offered at its resorts. Its staff members are known as "gentils organisateurs" in French, or "nice organizers" in English. This means that one of their key roles is to arrange and coordinate the sports and entertainment activities for the guests.

(Courtesy of Club Med)

Place

This advertisement from Galileo headed "Create your Future" demonstrates the market power and flexibility of today's global distribution systems (GDS). With 40,000 subscribers around the world, Galileo promises the travel agent that it is a highly popular GDS. In addition, this advertisement identifies six important agent issues (such as finding more customers and increasing profitability) that Galileo can help agents address with customized solutions.

(Courtesy of Galileo International, Inc.)

Promotion

(Courtesy of Chick-fil-A)

It is a well-accepted axiom in the advertising business that humor gets people's attention and helps the company doing the promotion to break through the increasing level of advertising "clutter." Chick-fil-A's "Eat Mor Chikin" promotions are a great example. Friesian cows are depicted as leading a campaign to convince those eating beef to add more chicken to their diets.

Price

Rail Europe uses a price-off promotional strategy to convince travel agents to recommend the Eurostar Channel Tunnel train. As this is a relatively new rail service, the "introductory" price—with a 33 to 37 percent discount on first and standard classes—may be just what is needed to lure agents to book their customers on the train between England and mainland Europe. Notice how prominently the "Save up to 37%" is displayed in the top right hand corner of the advertisement.

(Courtesy of Rail Europe)

◆ **FIGURE 10–9**   *High-speed trains are whisking travelers across Europe.* (Courtesy of Rail Europe)

Trends among Travel Trade Intermediaries

So important are the industry's distribution channels that Chapter 13 is devoted entirely to them. In this chapter, however, we take only a brief look at the major intermediaries and the role they play within the industry's structure.

1. **Retail Travel Agents.** The growth rate in the number of travel agencies in the United States between 1970 and 1996 was very rapid. At the end of 1996, there were 33,715 full-service travel agencies, almost five times as many as in 1970. However, during 1997 travel agencies began to close. There were 30,026 agencies at the end of 2000.[19] This trend reversal is largely attributed to the reduced commission rates from airlines.

   Traditionally, travel agents were dependent on carriers, suppliers, and other intermediaries for their income (commissions). At the same time, many of these organizations depend heavily on the travel agent's positive recommendations. This two-way relationship and interdependence is one of the most distinct features of hospitality and travel marketing, and provides another example of the partnership concept. Agents can be considered a key target market for most suppliers and carriers, who spend a huge amount of money each year promoting to them. Most carriers and many suppliers have set up preferred supplier or vendor relationships with individual travel agencies in order to secure a larger share of the agencies' bookings. Usually these relationships offer agencies higher commission rates on the preferred supplier's/vendor's services.

2. **Tour Wholesalers and Operators.** Chapter 12 takes an in-depth look at the seemingly endless selection of packages and programs developed by the industry. Many are put together and operated by this second group of intermediaries. Wholesalers and operators negotiate and block space and prices with suppliers and carriers and then add a markup to all the elements to determine an all-inclusive price. They prepare brochures about their tours or packages, which they distribute mainly through travel agencies and on the Web.

    There are thousands of companies that assemble tours, but business is concentrated among a very few. Most of these larger firms belong to the U. S. Tour Operators Association. The Bus Regulatory Reform Act of 1982, which deregulated the bus industry, brought a spate of new tour packages from bus companies that tend to belong to the American Bus Association, National Tour Association, or United Motorcoach Association. Most suppliers and carriers assemble their own tours and packages and, at the same time, participate in those of tour operators and wholesalers.

3. **Corporate Travel Departments.** Corporations and other organizations have become increasingly sensitive to the escalating costs of travel. The traditional approach allowed individual departments, divisions, or even managers to book their own flights, rooms, and rental cars. However, an increasing number of organizations now recognize the inefficiencies of this approach and the financial benefits of negotiating rates and prices based on the combined purchasing power of an entire group.

    Corporate travel department staff have become a key target for many suppliers and carriers, including hotels, airlines, rental car firms, and convention/meeting destinations and facilities. Advertising in specialized journals such as *Business Travel News* has become popular. Many corporate travel managers also belong to the National Business Travel Association or the Association of Corporate Travel Executives.

4. **Incentive Travel Planners.** Although what usually happens on incentive travel trips is definitely pleasurable, the buyers of these specialized vacation-like packages are businesses. More corporations are realizing the increasing value of using travel to reward employees, dealers, and others for outstanding performance. Consequently, the incentive travel business has grown from a very insignificant part of the industry to a multibillion-dollar trade. Many hotel chains, airlines, resorts, government agencies, cruise lines, and others have noticed the trend, and have added in-house incentive specialists or complete incentive departments.

    In addition to the in-house specialists, there are now several hundred incentive travel-planning firms. Of these, there are a handful of major full-service, incentive marketing companies that handle a broad range of incentives, including Carlson and Maritz. Most of these firms belong to the Society of Incentive and Travel Executives (SITE), which defines incentive travel as follows:

a modern management tool used to achieve extraordinary goals by awarding participants a travel prize upon attainment of their share of the uncommon goals[20]

Incentive travel planners are really specialized tour wholesalers who provide services directly to sponsoring organizations. They are compensated by a markup on the various elements of the incentive package.

5. **Convention/Meeting Planners.** The fifth main travel trade group is made up of convention/meeting planners. Some are employed by major national associations, large nonprofit groups, government agencies, educational institutions, and large corporations. Others work for specialized convention management consulting firms. Many of these professionals belong to meeting planning associations, including Meeting Professionals International, the American Society of Association Executives, and the Professional Convention Management Association.

The convention/meeting business is a multibillion-dollar market that has shown continually high growth rates. As a result, it has attracted greater attention from various suppliers (hotels, resorts, cruise lines, car rental firms, and conference and convention centers), carriers (airlines), other intermediaries (travel agents), and destination marketing organizations (state tourism offices and convention and visitors bureaus). Journals such as *Meetings & Conventions, Successful Meetings,* and *Meeting News* are full of advertisements aimed at these planners.

Convention/meeting planners organize events ranging from international conventions with hundreds of thousands of attendees to small board meetings with ten or fewer persons. They select meeting destinations, lodging and convention/meeting facilities, delegate/spouse tours and programs, and official airline carriers. A significant proportion of these planners are also responsible for arranging incentive travel trips.

Trends among Destination Marketing Organizations

Hospitality and travel industry growth has lured many government agencies and other groups into marketing their destinations to pleasure and business travelers. Every state, province, and territory now has a separate body responsible for this task. Nationally, organizations such as the Australian Tourist Commission, British Tourist Authority, and Canadian Tourism Commission are investing millions of dollars in tourism marketing and development. More and more cities, regions, and areas are creating convention and visitors bureaus to handle this type of marketing.

1. **Federal and State Tourism Marketing Agencies.** In the United States, state spending on tourism marketing has grown phenomenally. In1999-2000, the 50 states, the District of Columbia, and Puerto Rico, together spent $644 million.[21] A large portion of these funds goes into advertising aimed at individual and group travelers in other states.

Most of these agencies are government departments, except in Hawaii where the Hawaii Visitors & Convention Bureau is privately run. Their marketing programs target both individual travelers and travel trade intermediaries. Often they enter into cooperative marketing with suppliers, carriers, intermediaries, and other destination marketing organizations. Many also provide *seed money* to other destination organizations for their individual marketing programs.

2. **Convention and Visitors Bureaus.** Almost every community with a resident population of more than 50,000 now has a convention and visitors bureau (CVB). Approximately 400 of the larger bureaus belong to the International Association of Convention & Visitor Bureaus (IACVB). According to the IACVB survey, 274 of their members had combined total budgets of $585 million in 1993, or an average budget

of approximately \$2.2 million per bureau.[22] These bureaus try to bring more conventions, meetings, and pleasure travelers to their communities. They represent a broad group of suppliers in their destination areas and are often funded through local lodging and restaurant taxes. Like government agencies, these bureaus divide their attention between the travel trade—particularly convention/meeting planners and tour operators/wholesalers—and individual travelers (Figure 10–10).

Think little.

Now our little city isn't so much of an unknown.

Hardly anyone has to ask where it is anymore.

More and more people visit here and really enjoy themselves.

In fact, people who convention in Little Rock don't even realize they're "thinking little."

What with 6,500 hotel rooms.

About 100,000 square feet of exhibit and meeting space.

And truly personalized service. (Nothing little about that.)

That's because here you get used to the fact that little doesn't mean less.

In truth, being little has real value.

Like little expense. Short drives to great attractions. And, "big-fish-in-little-pond" advantages.

Little did you know.

Think about it.

Little Rock
full of surprises

Convention & Visitors Bureau • P.O. Box 3232 • Little Rock, Arkansas 72203 • 1-800-844-4781 • (501) 376-4781

◆ FIGURE 10–10   *The Little Rock Convention & Visitors Bureau reprises an old Volkswagen ad in appealing to the meetings and convention market.* (Courtesy of the Little Rock Convention & Visitors Bureau)

Overall Trends and Industry Realities

You have now had a detailed look at the hospitality and travel industry and the diversity of roles played by its key types of organizations. You should have noticed five main points in reviewing this material. Marketing managers must make their product development mix decisions within the context of these five overall trends and industry realities.

1. There has been a trend toward organizations increasing the scope of their operations within their specific field (e.g., lodging brand segmentation, and airline acquisitions and mergers). The technical term for these moves is **horizontal integration**, developing or acquiring similar businesses.

2. More organizations have been diversifying into the hospitality and travel industry (e.g., food companies, soft drink companies, other conglomerates). Organizations already in the industry have also begun to expand up and down the distribution channel (e.g., airline/hotel mergers, tour operator/travel agency mergers). The name for these combinations is **vertical integration**. Carlson Companies, Inc. is one of the best examples in North America. Its companies include Carlson Hospitality, Carlson Wagonlit Travel, Radisson Seven Seas Cruises, T.G.I. Friday's, and Carlson Marketing Group.

3. The hospitality and travel industry has steadily introduced a wide variety of new services, facilities, and travel alternatives.

4. Although demand growth is tapering off in some parts of the industry, there are still great opportunities for new services, facilities, and travel services.

5. The industry is becoming increasingly competitive, forcing all participants to constantly improve, or at least maintain, service levels.

EXCELLENCE CASE

Vertical Integration:
Carlson Companies, Inc.

Founded in 1938 by Curtis L. Carlson, Carlson Companies became one of North America's largest and perhaps the most vertically integrated hospitality and travel organizations by the end of the millennium. In 2000, the company's subsidiaries, all of which are in the service industries, included hotels (Radisson Hotels & Resorts, Regent International Hotels, and Country Inns & Suites By Carlson); several restaurant brands (T.G.I. Friday's, Italianni's, Front Row Sports Grill, Friday's American Bar, Timpano Italian Chophouse, Samba Room, Taqueria Cañtonita, Star Canyon, and AquaKnox); a cruise line (Radisson Seven Seas Cruises); a full-service relationship marketing organization (Carlson Marketing Group); travel agencies (Carlson Wagonlit Travel, Neiman Marcus Travel Services, and Thomas Cook); vacation ownership (Carlson Vacation Ownership); and lifestyle communities (Carlson Lifestyle Living). The company is, therefore, both on the supplier (hotels, restaurants, cruises, vacation ownership) and travel trade intermediary (travel agencies, incentive travel, tour wholesaling and operations) side of our industry.

continued

EXCELLENCE CASE *continued*

Carlson Companies' global brands employ 188,000 people in more than 140 countries and generate more than $30 billion in gross, systemwide sales. It is one of the largest privately held corporations in the United States. The three main parts of the company are Carlson Marketing Group, Carlson Hospitality Worldwide (including the hotels, restaurants, and cruises), and Carlson Wagonlit Travel.

The company's long-term objective for each group is to be the market leader. It bills itself as a group of "companies that are customer and market driven, and dedicated to excellence in carrying out its business mission." Certainly its Carlson Hospitality Worldwide group with its rapid international growth has become one of the industry leaders in the lodging industry.

Begun in Minneapolis in 1962, Carlson Hospitality Worldwide had more than 600 hotels in 53 countries in the year 2000. It has continued to climb the ranks of North America's largest lodging chains and is one of the leaders in brand segmentation with the following types of properties:

- Radisson Hotels
- Radisson Plaza Hotels
- Radisson Suites
- Radisson Resorts
- Country Inns & Suites By Carlson
- Regent International Hotels

Carlson Hospitality Worldwide is a firm believer in the value of marketing research as a tool for marketing decisions, and in the importance of friendly service. Radisson's primary research of frequent business travelers showed that they disliked the typical reactions of hotel employees when asked by a guest for an out-of-the ordinary service. Backed by media advertising, the "Yes I Can"

employee-training program was introduced. The program is one of the most extensive in the industry and features training sessions, skill-building sessions, and monthly team meetings. Radisson clearly recognizes the importance of quality service—the people side of its product.

An aggressive franchising program has fueled expansion in North America. International expansion is also taking place around the world.

With so many facets of the hospitality and travel industry under the same corporate umbrella, Carlson Companies, Inc. has the potential for becoming one of the most powerful forces in our business. It is ideally positioned for further growth and an expanding market share.

Discussion Questions

1. How has Carlson Companies, Inc. used the vertical integration concept to stimulate its growth in the hospitality and travel industry?
2. What can other major hospitality and travel organizations learn from the approaches that Carlson Companies, Inc. employed to increase its power and influence in the industry? Which specific companies might be able to follow these same approaches?
3. How should Carlson Companies, Inc. use its various subsidiaries to increase its market share in each of the parts of the hospitality and travel industry in which they operate (i.e., lodging, restaurant/food-service, vacation ownership, travel agencies, incentive travel, and cruising)?

Web Site

http://www.carlson.com/

THE PRODUCT/SERVICE MIX

The *products* of the hospitality and travel industry are many and varied. Each organization within the industry has its own product/service mix, the assortment of services and products that are provided to customers. This mix consists of every visible element in the organization, including the following:

1. Staff behavior, appearance, and uniforms
2. Building exteriors
3. Equipment
4. Furniture and fixtures
5. Signage
6. Communications with customers and other publics

The many behind-the-scenes facilities, equipment, and personnel cannot be forgotten. Although not outwardly visible, they contribute directly to customer satisfaction and are part of the product/service mix. Technically, the mix includes all services, facilities, and packages and programs provided by the organization. This book separates the last two items (packaging and programming) from the first two because of their unique role in the industry.

1. **Staff Behavior, Appearance, and Uniforms.** Chapter 11 is devoted to the people part of the marketing mix. Here, it is sufficient to mention that the physical aspects of staff appearance must be carefully considered in the marketing plan.

2. **Building Exteriors.** Many hospitality and travel organizations serve their guests in one or more buildings. The overall physical condition and cleanliness of these structures greatly influence the customer's image of the organization and their own satisfaction. A run-down building does not fit well with a luxury positioning. The marketing plan should mention any steps that organizations envisage for the period that will enhance the exterior appearance of their buildings.

3. **Equipment.** Customers evaluate several types of hospitality and travel businesses partly on the upkeep and cleanliness of their equipment. Airline, cruise line, car rental, bus, train, limousine/taxi, and attraction companies are a few examples of the relevancy of this element. Many hotels and some restaurants also use shuttle transportation equipment and should be concerned about maintaining it and keeping it clean. A marketing plan should address scheduled improvements and other changes in such equipment.

4. **Furniture and Fixtures.** Many customers are sensitive to the quality of the furniture and fixtures within buildings and transportation equipment. Many hospitality and travel companies back up their high-quality images with high-quality furniture and fixtures. A section of the marketing plan should be devoted to improvements and changes in furniture and fixtures.

5. **Signage.** This is another part of the product/service mix that is often forgotten. Most organizations have a variety of signs, including billboards, directional signs, and exterior building signs. Customers often equate a broken or poorly maintained sign with low quality and a lax management attitude. The marketing plan should

♦ FIGURE 10–11   *Best Western's new signage program heralds a major change in standards at its properties.* (Courtesy of Best Western International)

address not only advertising-oriented outdoor signs, but all signs used by customers. New signs can also be used to reflect a new positioning approach by an organization or to signal that a company has remodeled or modernized its facilities and equipment, Figure 10–11.

6. **Communications with Customers and Other Publics.** Advertising, personal selling, sales promotion, merchandising, and public relations and publicity activities are often considered only as ways to influence customers to buy. They do, however, play a more subtle role in influencing customers' images of organizations. Negative publicity can detract from an organization's image. Positive publicity can enhance that image. The quality and size of an advertisement, as well as its media placement choice, give customers mental clues to the organization's stature. Promotional giveaways and premiums must be consistent with the organization's image of quality. The organization's Web site is another important element of these communications.

   If there is one single requirement for every hospitality and travel organization's product/service mix, it is that it must be consistent. Customers notice inconsistencies. By considering all aspects, the marketing plan ensures continuity among the various components.

PRODUCT DEVELOPMENT DECISIONS

Most organizations must make product development decisions at two different levels: (1) organization-wide and (2) for individual facilities or services.

1. **Organization-Wide Decisions.**
    a. ***Width and Length of Product/Service Mix.*** When Disney established the Disney Cruise Line, it expanded its product/service-mix width (the number of different services provided by an organization) (Figure 10–12). In marketing jargon, it added a *product line*. In developing the Wild Animal Kingdom, it increased its product/service-mix length (the number of similar services provided by an organization). Figure 10–12 shows other examples of these types of decisions. For example, when Richard Branson's company, Virgin, got into the passenger rail business in the United Kingdom it was diversifying and adding to its product/service-mix width. When Air Canada acquired another airline, Canadian, it increased the length of its product/service mix, as did Marriott when it acquired a part ownership of Ritz-Carlton Hotels.
    b. ***Improving or Modernizing the Product/Service Mix.*** Sometimes a company determines, usually through a situation analysis or marketing research, that the time has come to upgrade all or part of its product/service mix. Airlines do this frequently, often repainting their entire fleets or changing their interior finishes, seating layouts, and cabin crew uniforms. Theme parks are constantly updating and adding to their entertainment mix. They do this to encourage repeat visitation. Cruise lines temporarily remove ships from service in order to undertake necessary maintenance and onboard improvements.
    c. ***Branding.*** There was a time when branding was relatively unimportant in the hospitality and travel industry; the company's name was all that was attached to

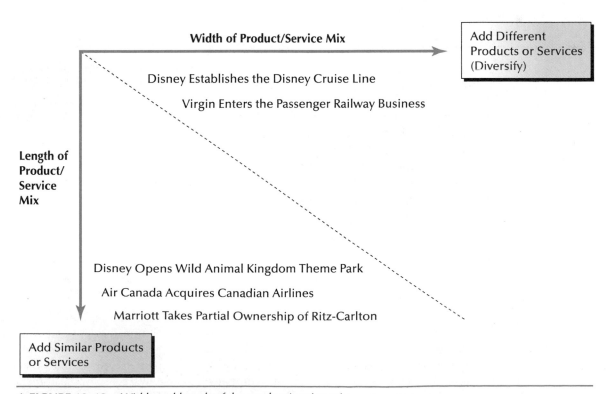

◆ FIGURE 10–12 *Width and length of the product/service mix.*

the service. Branding is becoming more important as many companies expand the width and length of their product service mixes. The advantages of branding include the following:

- Helps the company segment markets
- Gives the company the potential to attract loyal and profitable customers
- Improves the company's image if their brands are successful
- Helps track reservations, sales, problems, and complaints

Increasing brand segmentation in the hospitality and travel industry has already been highlighted in this chapter. It has been occurring in several parts of the industry including lodging, restaurant and foodservices, and cruise lines. This approach offers companies the chance to attract larger shares of specific target markets by giving customers facilities and services that better match their needs. In essence, it broadens the customer base from which each *branding* company draws.

Most of the major lodging chains now use a multibrand approach. Although the advantages are obvious, there are also potential drawbacks. One brand may cannibalize another—take customers away from the other company brand.

2. **Individual Facility/Service Decisions.** Product/service-mix decisions also have to be made by the individual hotel, restaurant, agency, or other hospitality/travel outlet. These decisions concern the quality, range, and design of the facilities and services provided. Again, the situation analysis and other marketing research studies should provide the impetus for changing these elements.

PARTNERSHIP

Marketing partnerships of many varieties have become more popular in recent years in the hospitality and travel industry as more companies realize the advantages of relationship marketing (building, maintaining, and enhancing long-term relationships with customers, suppliers, and travel trade intermediaries). *Partnerships* are cooperative promotions and other cooperative marketing efforts by hospitality and travel organizations. They range from "one-shot" (short-term) cooperative promotions to strategic (long-term) joint marketing agreements that may involve some combination of the products or services of two or more organizations. Chapters 15 to 18 discuss the different types of cooperative promotions that occur in the industry. In this chapter, you will hear about the longer-term marketing partnerships.

Types of Partners

With such a wide variety of organizations involved in our industry, there are almost limitless opportunities for partnerships.

1. **Customers.** Frequent traveler programs are a good example of a partnership program with customers. These were introduced to build customer loyalty to the companies, but now some go much further than this. Some hospitality and travel companies form advisory groups from among their frequent travelers, and others employ them as *advocates* of the company to help attract new customers.

An interesting variation on this theme is the Valued Visitor program developed by the Brown County Convention & Visitors Bureau in southern Indiana. For a small sign-up fee, people join the program and receive a Valued Visitor card and an attractive tote bag with the Valued Visitor logo printed on it. Meanwhile, local shops, restaurants, and lodging places were also recruited to join the program. These businesspeople agreed to post the Valued Visitor decal on their premises and to provide either a gift or a discount to anyone presenting a Valued Visitor card. The bureau mails a Valued Visitor newsletter to members to keep in touch and to promote what is going on in Brown County. The program has been highly successful.

2. **Organizations in the Same Business.** You have already heard about the concept of *strategic alliances* in the airline business. Another good example is the BestCities.net alliance created by the convention and visitors bureaus in Boston, Copenhagen, Edinburgh, Melbourne, and Vancouver. This alliance was formed expressly to better meet the needs of international meeting clients. The alliance's programs included the development of a Web site and a set of best practices in service standards.

   As you will see later, some countries' national tourism organizations have joined forces either for promotions or to share facilities. With the help of American Express, several countries in East and Southeast Asia have joined together in the *Jewels of the Mekong* marketing cooperative. Countries along the famous *Silk Road* in Asia have also banded together for marketing purposes.

   Another concept that was discussed earlier is that of *co-branding*. In this situation, two brands of a similar type of operation (e.g., a Taco Bell and a KFC) are located together.

3. **Organizations in Related Businesses.** Frequent-traveler programs are a good example here as they bring together airlines, lodging chains, car rental firms, and others in the hospitality and travel industry. Industry organizations are also working with credit card companies including MasterCard and Visa, both in joint promotions and in the issuance of specially designed credit cards bearing the hospitality and travel organizations' names.

   Dual branding is another good example. This occurs when a well-known restaurant brand agrees to operate one of its units within a branded hotel property of a lodging chain. An example of this is the strategic alliance formed by Ramada Franchise Systems and Bennigan's Irish American Grill & Tavern in late 1999. Bennigan's, a part of the Metromedia Restaurant Group, became the preferred foodservice provider to Ramada. The arrangement allows Ramada to concentrate on the lodging side of the operation, while Bennigan's gains new restaurant locations.

   Other examples are the alliances between restaurant companies and retailers, in which the companies place outlets within stores, and the oil alliances between McDonald's and gas station companies. Finally, there are several restaurant brands now located in airports, colleges and universities, and sports venues.

4. **Organizations in Non-Related Businesses.** It is also possible for hospitality and travel organizations to work with businesses outside of the industry. An excellent example of this is the relationship between Park West Gallery, a fine art dealer, and several cruise lines. Park West Gallery stages art auctions during the cruises, which provides another form of activity and entertainment for the guests. It is truly a *win-win* proposition for both sides. Park West gets increased sales of its artwork, while the cruise lines are able to offer more to their guests.

5. **Digital Alliances.** The introduction of Internet technology brought with it new forms of potential partnerships among organizations. In hospitality and travel, the main avenue for digital alliances is through reciprocal linking (hyperlinking) of Web sites.

Benefits of Partnership

Partnerships such as these offer many possible benefits to the organizations involved:

1. **Access to New Markets.** A strategic partnership may provide new geographic markets or other new target markets for the organizations involved. For example, the strategic alliance between Northwest, KLM, and Continental has provided each airline with access to geographic markets throughout the world.

2. **Expansion of Product/Service Mixes.** By teaming up with another organization, a company may be able to expand its product/service mix at little or lesser cost. For example, the Carlson Companies entered the lucrative cruise market using its Radisson Hotel brand name by signing an agreement to operate the SSC Diamond on behalf of the ship's owners.[23]

3. **Increased Ability to Serve Customer Needs.** When hospitality and travel organizations or destination areas *pool* their facilities and services, they may be in a better position to serve customer needs. For example, the *code-sharing* agreements between partnered airlines is helping to make international air travel simpler and more convenient for travelers.

4. **Increased Marketing Budgets.** When hospitality and travel organizations agree to cooperate, they increase the total budget amount available for marketing for each individual partner. The countries of Central America and a number of Mexican states have joined forces in promoting the "El Mundo Maya" (the Mayan world) region to the travel trade and consumers. By joining forces in this cooperative venture, the six countries have created a much greater collective marketing budget to promote the historical regions of the former Mayan Indian civilizations. Similarly, four countries (Austria, Germany, Italy, and Switzerland) have combined to promote the Alps, which they all share.

5. **Sharing of Facilities and Facility Costs.** Teaming up with other organizations may help each partner to provide and afford certain physical facilities. For example, in the British Travel Centre in London, the costs of renting office space are shared by several partners, including the British Tourism Authority, Wales Tourism Board, British Rail, and others. A similar arrangement is used by the Scandinavian countries in co-funding the Scandinavian Tourist Boards' office in New York.

6. **Enhanced Image or Positioning.** Associating with other hospitality and travel organizations may improve the image or enhance an organization's positioning. The appointment of Delta as the official airline of Walt Disney World under a joint marketing agreement between the two companies gives the airline an advantageous competitive position for Florida-bound travelers.

7. **Access to Partners' Customer Databases.** You have already heard about the increasing importance of database marketing. The sharing of the partners' proprietary customer databases can be a powerful advantage of cooperation. For example, the tie-ins between airlines, credit card firms, long-distance telephone companies, and hotel chains in frequent traveler programs give each partner the potential to access databases with records on millions of individual customers.

8. **Access to Partners' Expertise.** A partnership may be formed because each of the partners has experience or expertise that the other partners want. This experience or expertise may be well-recognized by customers.

CHAPTER CONCLUSION

The hospitality and travel industry is a complex mixture of interrelated companies, government agencies, and nonprofit organizations. The four main component groups are suppliers, carriers, travel trade intermediaries, and destination marketing organizations. Each industry organization has a unique product/service mix that periodically must be upgraded, augmented, and pruned. Product/service-mix decisions have to be made at two levels: (1) organization-wide and (2) for individual facilities or services.

REVIEW QUESTIONS

1. What are the four major groups of organizations within the hospitality and travel industry?
2. What are the major roles that each of these groups play within the hospitality and travel industry?
3. What are some of the major recent trends in these four groups of hospitality and travel organizations?
4. How is the term product/service mix defined in this book?
5. What are the six components of the product/service mix and what does each component include?
6. What are the steps involved in product development?
7. What is the meaning of the term partnership?
8. What are the potential benefits of marketing partnerships for hospitality and travel organizations?
9. What are the types of partnerships available to hospitality and travel organizations?

CHAPTER ASSIGNMENTS

1. You have been hired by a hotel, airline, attraction, cruise line, or travel trade organization that is interested in expanding both its domestic and international operations. You have been given a project to analyze the benefits and possible disadvantages of marketing partnerships in achieving these growth objectives. What advantages and disadvantages of potential partnerships would you present to the organization's senior executives? Draw upon actual cases of successful and unsuccessful marketing partnerships in our industry to justify your conclusions.

2. Choose a specific part of the hospitality and travel industry. How has the structure of this industry group changed over the past 10 years? Which organizations have made the greatest changes or improvements to their product/service mixes? Who are the leaders in terms of quality of service provided? What

techniques have they followed to earn this reputation?

3. This chapter identifies four distinct parts of the hospitality and travel industry (suppliers, carriers, travel trade intermediaries, and destination marketing organizations). Write a paper describing how each part is related to the others. How important is it for someone involved in hospitality and travel marketing to keep up to date on developments in each of these industry parts?

4. The owners of a small hospitality and travel business have asked you to help them review their facilities and services. They are interested in exploring ways to improve and perhaps also add to their existing facilities and services. Prepare a proposal outlining the steps you would take to review this organization's product/service mix. Be specific about the possible techniques you would use to evaluate facilities and levels of service.

WORLD WIDE WEB RESOURCES

Airlines Reporting Corporation (ARC)
http://www.arccorp.com/

Air Transport Association
http://www.air-transport.org/

Alps
http://www.alpseurope.org/

American Bus Association (ABA)
http://www.buses.org/

American Society of Association Executives (ASAE)
http://www.asaenet.org/

Association of Corporate Travel Executives (ACTE)
http://www.acte.org

Atlantic City Convention & Visitors Authority
http://www.atlanticcitynj.com/

BC Ferries
http://www.bcferries.com/

Bennigan's
http://www.bennigans.com/

British Travel Centre
http://www.visitbritain.com/

Brown County Convention & Visitors Bureau
http://www.browncounty.com/

Business Travel News
http://btnonline.com/

Carlson Companies
http://www.carlson.com/

Cruise Lines International Association (CLIA)
http://www.cruising.org/

Darden Restaurants
http://www.darden.com/

Diageo PLC
http://www.diageo.com/

Foxwoods Resort Casino
http://www.foxwoods.com/

Gold Coast
http://www.goldcoasttourism.com.au/

International Air Transport Association (IATA)
http://www.iata.org/

International Council of Cruise Lines
http://www.iccl.org/

Irish Ferries
http://www.irishferries.ie/

Little Rock Convention & Visitors Bureau
http://www.littlerock.com/

Maritz
http://www.maritz.com/

Meeting Professionals International (MPI)
http://www.mpiweb.org/

Metromedia Restaurant Group
http://www.metromediarestaurants.com/

Nation's Restaurant News
http://www.nrn.com/

National Car Rental
http://www.nationalcar.com/

National Business Travel Association (NBTA)
http://www.nbta.org/

National Tour Association (NTA)
http://www.ntaonline.com/

Norwegian Cruise Line
http://www.ncl.com/

P&O Ferries
http://www.poferries.com/

Park West at Sea
http://parkwestgallery.acmeinfo.com/

Princess Cruises
http://www.princess.com/

Priority Club
http://www.basshotels.com/priorityclub/

Professional Convention Management Association (PCMA)
http://www.pcma.org/

Rail Europe
http://www.raileurope.com/

Residence Inn by Marriott
http://www.residenceinn.com/

Scandinavian Tourist Board
http://www.goscandinavia.com/

Society of Incentive & Travel Executives (SITE)
http://www.site-intl.org/

Travel Weekly
http://www.twcrossroads.com/

Tricon Global Restaurants
http://www.triconglobal.com/

United Motorcoach Association
http://www.uma.org/

Wyndham International
http://www.wyndhamintl.com/

Virgin Rail
http://www.virgin.com/

Westin
http://www.westin.com/

REFERENCES

1. Gomes, Albert J. 1985. *Hospitality in Transition.* New York: American Hotel & Motel Association 29–31.

2. "Hotels' 325." *Hotels.* http://www.hotelsmag.com/hogiants.html

3. Top 100 Chains Ranked by U.S. Systemwide Foodservice Sales. *Nation's Restaurant News.* http://www.nrn.com/resources/

4. Tricon on Global Restaurants. http://www.triconglobal.com/

5. *The Cruise Industry: An Overview: Marketing Edition.* 2001. New York: Cruise Lines International Association. http://www.cruising.org/

6. International Council of Cruise Lines. http://www.iccl.org/

7. *The Cruise Industry: An Overview: Marketing Edition.* 2001. New York: Cruise Lines International Association. http://www.cruising.org/

8. Mill, Robert Christie, and Alastair M. Morrison. 1998. *The Tourism System: An Introductory Text.* 3rd ed. Dubuque, Iowa: Kendall/Hunt Publishing Company.

9. U.S. Car Rental Market: 1999. *Auto Rental News.* http://www.FleetCentral.com/ARN/

10. Top 50 North American Amusement/Theme Parks. *Amusement Business*, December 25, 2000, 84–85.

11. Waters, Somerset R. 1993. *Travel Industry World Yearbook: The Big Picture—1993–94.* Rye, N.Y.: Child & Waters, 16.

12. Las Vegas Convention & Visitor Authority. http://www.vegasfreedom.com/

13. Goeldner, Charles R., Brent J. R. Ritchie, and Robert W. McIntosh. 1999. *Tourism: Principles, Practices, Philosophies.* 8th ed. New York: John Wiley & Sons, Inc.

14. 2000 Annual Report. Air Transport Association. http://www.airtransport.org/

15. World Air Transport Statistics. International Air Transport Association. http://www.iata.org/

16. Lassiter, Eric. "Travelers rank suppliers, importance of frequent flier plans." *Travel Weekly* (May 10, 1993) 58.

17. British Columbia Ferry Corporation Annual Report, 1999-2000. BC Ferries. http://www.bcferries.com/

18. Spritzer, Dinah A. "The read on speed: Just how fast are they?" *Travel Weekly* (February 24, 2000) E4.

19. Fine, Phyllis. "As cap anniversary nears, agents look back—and ahead." *Travel Weekly* (February 7, 2000) 1–2.

20. Society of Incentive & Travel Executives. http://www.site-intl.org/

21. Travel Industry Association of America. *Survey of State Travel Offices: 1999-2000.* http://www.tia.org/

22. *IACVB 1993 Bureau Funding & Expenditure Survey.* 1993. Champaign, Ill.: International Association of Convention & Visitor Bureaus.

23. Blum, Ernest. "Radisson plans to grow diamond cruise brand." *Travel Weekly* 53 (51):6 (1994).

For additional hospitality and travel marketing resources, visit our Web site at **www.Hospitality-Tourism.delmar.com**

People: Services and Service Quality

How Do We Get There?

Objectives

Having read this chapter, you should be able to:

- Identify the two main groups of people involved in hospitality and travel marketing and explain how they interact.

- Explain the key role played by people in the marketing mix.

- Describe the total quality management (TQM) concept, including its key principles.

- Identify the benefits of customer codes and guarantees.

- Explain the importance of employee selection, orientation, training, and motivation programs in delivering service quality.

- Describe the concept of empowering employees and how important this is to customer satisfaction.

- Explain the five dimensions of the SERVQUAL model and how this technique is used to measure service quality.

- Explain why the relationship marketing concept is so important in the hospitality and travel industry and how it is done successfully.

- Describe the customer mix and explain why organizations must manage it.

Overview

People represent one of the 8 Ps of hospitality and travel marketing, and this chapter emphasizes the key role played by people in producing satisfied customers. Guest-host relationships are discussed within the context of the total quality management (TQM) concept. Methods *for improving service quality levels as well as employees' customer-orientation and guest-relations skills are presented. Techniques for measuring service quality are also reviewed. This chapter describes the relationship marketing concept—how organizations can build and maintain long-term relationships with individual customers. It ends with an examination of the customer mix and how this mix affects an organization's image and the quality of the customer's service quality experience.*

Key Terms

customer mix	internal customers	service encounter
empowerment	internal marketing	SERVQUAL
external customers	lifetime value (LTV)	total quality management (TQM)
guests	people	word-of-mouth advertising
hosts	relationship marketing	

THE TWO MAIN GROUPS OF PEOPLE: GUESTS AND HOSTS

What do you like about the hospitality and travel industry? What attracted you to this field rather than to another? Some might say "the opportunity to travel" or "to work in nice places," but is it because you like to work with other people? Many of us are attracted to this industry because of the desire to meet and to serve a wide variety of people, sometimes from an array of different cultures and countries.

There are two groups of people in hospitality and travel marketing—the **guests** (customers) and the **hosts** (those who work within hospitality and travel organizations). Managing this guest-host relationship is one of the key functions in our business; in fact, some say it is the most important. In this chapter the focus is mainly on the hosts and the quality of service they provide. However, you will also read about managing long-term relationships with individual guests (relationship marketing) and about the importance of considering how guests interact with each other in a hospitality and travel business (customer mix).

KEY ROLE OF PEOPLE IN THE MARKETING MIX

In Chapter 2 you learned about the generic and contextual differences between the marketing of services and products. That chapter highlighted the greater difficulties with standardizing services, as well as the relationship of the quality of services to those providing the services. It is much more difficult with services to give the customer a *defect-free* experience because of the human factor involved in service transactions. Services are not mass-produced on a factory line but should be delivered one customer at a time. Services involve person-to-person interactions, both employees with customers and customers with other customers.

To say that people make the main difference in services marketing is perhaps both obvious and an understatement of the real truth. Services marketing is all about people! To borrow a quote from a famous U.S. stock brokerage firm, success in services marketing needs to be measured "one customer at a time." While you will read much about communications and promotion in the rest of this book, the real foundations of a hospitality and travel organization's success and survival are the people it employs and the people it serves. How the organization selects and treats both of these two groups of people has perhaps the greatest impact on its ultimate marketing effectiveness.

The front-line people who provide the services of our industry play a key role. They alone can make or break a guest's experience. An otherwise ordinary occasion can be made extra special by above-average courtesy and attention. On the other hand, a superior environment and facilities can be marred by indifferent, curt, or unfriendly service. People, the service providers, play the pivotal role in hospitality and travel marketing. No amount of slick advertising and catchy promotions can compensate for below-average service. Hospitality and travel organizations must do two things well to satisfy customers: (1) provide a good product (the meal, room, airline seat, vacation package, rental car, etc.) and (2) provide good service.[1] The human dimension of hospitality and travel *products,* although harder to control and standardize, deserves at least equal attention. Most marketing textbooks ignore this human element in marketing, but not this one.

Although much of what the hospitality and travel industry provides involves physical facilities and equipment, most experts believe that it is the level of service provided that separates the successful from the unsuccessful. That is the people element of the marketing mix. Traditional thinking separates marketing and human resources management into two distinct management functions. However, the two are very closely linked in the service industries. Organizations with superior human resources, policies, and practices are usually the most successful marketers. Organizations such as Disney, McDonald's, Singapore Airlines, The Ritz-Carlton Hotel Company, Emirates, and Four Seasons Hotels & Resorts (Figure 11–1) know the rich payoffs that come from positive employee-customer service encounters. They learned years ago that only satisfied customers come back and that positive word-of-mouth advertising is the most powerful force in attracting new customers.

If there is one universal truth about the industry, it is that nothing can make up for poor service. Excellent food, exquisitely decorated guest rooms, or on-time arrival cannot swing the pendulum far enough to make up for unfriendly or inadequate employee service. According to Horst Schulze, president and chief executive of The Ritz-Carlton Hotel Company, "Service can only be accomplished by people. The hotel can be breathtakingly beautiful and the food memorable, but a poor employee can quickly sour the experience."[2] Many in the industry do not fully understand the bond between the quality of the physical product (hotel, restaurant, plane, ship, motor coach, menu items, etc.) and the quality of the service. Customers form their overall evaluations based on a combined assessment of these two factors.

Books such as *Service America! Doing Business in the New Economy* suggest that there is a crisis in the service industries.[3] Poor or indifferent service is the rule, rather than the exception. In this era of mediocre service, those who devote above-average attention to hiring, orienting, training, empowering, and keeping service-oriented employees will have a distinct marketing advantage.

According to Berry and Parasuraman, the essence of services marketing is service, and service quality is the foundation of services marketing.[4] Therefore, hospitality and travel marketers must be concerned with service quality and must be sure that their organizations have a process in place for managing the quality of service provided to customers.

FOUR SEASONS HOTELS AND RESORTS

Our Goals, Our Beliefs, Our Principles

Who we are

We have chosen to specialize within the hospitality industry, by offering only experiences of exceptional quality. Our objective is to be recognized as the company that manages the finest hotels, resorts and resort clubs wherever we locate.

We create properties of enduring value using superior design and finishes, and support them with a deeply instilled ethic of personal service. Doing so allows Four Seasons to satisfy the needs and tastes of our discriminating customers, and to maintain our position as the world's premier luxury hospitality company.

What we believe

Our greatest asset, and the key to our success, is our people.

We believe that each of us needs a sense of dignity, pride and satisfaction in what we do. Because satisfying our guests depends on the united efforts of many, we are most effective when we work together cooperatively, respecting each other's contribution and importance.

How we behave

We demonstrate our beliefs most meaningfully in the way we treat each other and by the example we set for one another. In all our interactions with our guests, customers, business associates and colleagues, we seek to deal with others as we would have them deal with us.

How we succeed

We succeed when every decision is based on a clear understanding of and belief in what we do and when we couple this conviction with sound financial planning. We expect to achieve a fair and reasonable profit to ensure the prosperity of the company, and to offer long-term benefits to our hotel owners, our shareholders, our customers and our employees.

◆ FIGURE 11–1 *Four Seasons Hotels and Resorts' goals, beliefs, and principles emphasize people.* (Courtesy of Four Seasons Hotels and Resorts) (NOTE: Italics added by author to highlight importance of host-guest relationships in this statement.)

THE TOTAL QUALITY MANAGEMENT (TQM) CONCEPT

Total quality management, or TQM as it is sometimes called, is a quality management concept that gained widespread recognition in the 1980s. The impetus for the TQM concept is largely attributed to Japanese manufacturing companies and to quality experts including W. Edward Deming, Joseph M. Juran, and Philip Crosby. A TQM program is designed to cut down on an organization's *defects*, to determine its customers' requirements, and to satisfy these requirements.

A Touch of Technology

Emirates uses technology to please passengers.

- ◆ Emirates is an airline with headquarters in Dubai that is considered by many experienced international travelers to be one of the best in the world. Since it began in 1985, the airline has won more than 190 awards for excellence.

- ◆ The readers of the Official Airline Guide (OAG) voted it Airline of the Year 2000. This was the third time in a row that these frequent travelers placed Emirates as Airline of the Year.

- ◆ Following are examples of how Emirates has used technology to help please its passengers:

- ◆ Emirates provides all passengers on its Boeing 777s with a full range of audio and visual entertainment (18 audio-video and 22 audio channels distributed by a GEC Marconi system).

- ◆ All 777s have a central fax machine and telephones at each seat.

- ◆ First and Business Class passengers are picked up at their home or hotel by chauffeur-driven cars and driven to the airport. Cars are also available at their destination (Figure 11–2).

- ◆ Passengers traveling to the U.K. may request a mobile phone to use while in the U.K. for up to 28 days.

- ◆ Children traveling on Emirate flights receive complimentary Polaroid photos of themselves as a memento of their trips.

Five of the key principles of TQM are:[5]

1. **Commitment to Quality:** Any organization that institutes a TQM program must make a commitment to have quality as a top priority. The senior executives of the organization must actively endorse and direct the TQM process.

2. **Focus on Customer Satisfaction:** TQM organizations recognize that customers care about quality, and they make specific efforts to find out what levels of service quality their customers want. When they determine customers' expected service quality standards, the organizations make every effort to meet or exceed those standards.

3. **Assessment of Organizational Culture:** An organization must examine how consistent its existing organizational *culture* is with the principles of TQM. This is usually done by selecting a team of top executives and employees to conduct this assessment over a period of several months.

4. **Empowerment of Employees and Teams:** Although directed by an organization's top executives, the true success of a TQM program comes through *empowering* employees to satisfy each individual customer.

5. **Measurement of Quality Efforts:** A TQM organization must be able to measure the results of its quality improvement efforts. This means measuring customer sat-

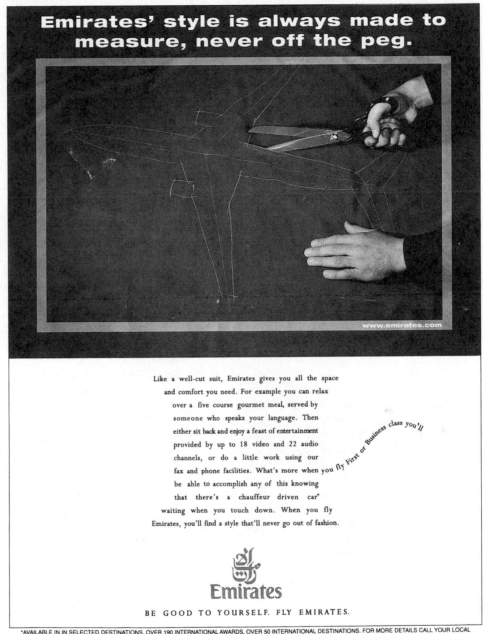

◆ **FIGURE 11–2**   *Emirates stresses service and uses technology to please travelers.* (Courtesy of Emirates)

isfaction levels, employee performance, and the responsiveness of the organization's suppliers, as well as other indicators of service quality.

Later, you will read about The Ritz-Carlton Hotel Company and how it adapted the TQM concept to hotel operations. This example shows how the five key principles of TQM can be used to fit a hospitality and travel organization.

EXCELLENCE CASE

Enhancing Service Quality:
The Ritz-Carlton Hotel Company, L.L.C.

In 1992, The Ritz-Carlton Hotel Company, L.L.C. did something that no U.S. hotel chain had done before—it won the highly coveted Malcolm Baldrige National Quality Award. Named after the late Secretary of Commerce, Malcolm Baldrige, the award was created in 1987 by the U.S. Congress to recognize companies that achieve excellence in their products or services through the use of quality improvement programs. The Atlanta-headquartered Ritz-Carlton achieved this enviable position after only 10 years of operation. In 1999, Ritz-Carlton went one step further by winning the Malcolm Baldrige National Quality Award for the second time. This was an unprecedented event, since no service company has ever earned the award more than once.

W. B. Johnson Properties founded the company when it bought the U.S. rights to the Ritz-Carlton name.[1] W. B. Johnson acquired the rights to the famous hotel name when it bought the Boston Ritz-Carlton. By 2001, the chain had 38 properties in Canada, China, Egypt, Germany, Indonesia, Jamaica, Japan, Korea, Malaysia, Mexico, Puerto Rico, Singapore, Spain, U.S. Virgin Islands, UAE, and the United States.[2]

Ritz-Carlton has adopted many of the principles of *total quality management (TQM)*. It began its efforts toward winning the Baldrige award in 1989. However, Ritz-Carlton's great concern for service quality began when it started operations in 1983 with its self-expressed *born at birth* insistence on high-quality service. The company began operating with two basic quality strategies: (1) the "seven-day countdown" for each new Ritz-Carlton Hotel and (2) the "Gold Standards."

The pre-opening "seven-day countdown" includes seven days of intensive orientation and training by the company's most senior executives, including the president, for the staff of each new hotel.[3] The second central strategy in Ritz-Carlton's quality training and assurance program is the company's *Gold Standards*. The four elements are: (1) The Credo, (2) The Three Steps of Service, (3) The Ritz-Carlton Basics, and (4) The Motto of *Ladies and Gentlemen Serving Ladies and Gentlemen.*

The Credo: The Ritz-Carlton Hotel is a place where the genuine care and comfort of our guests is our highest mission. We pledge to provide the finest personal service and facilities for our guests who will always enjoy a warm, relaxed, yet refined ambience. The Ritz-Carlton experience enlivens the senses, instills well-being, and fulfills even the unexpressed wishes and needs of our guests.

The Three Steps of Service: 1. A warm and sincere greeting. Use the guest name, if and when possible. 2. Anticipation and compliance with guest needs. 3. Fond farewell. Give them a warm good-bye and use their name if and when possible.

The Ritz-Carlton Basics (or 20 Basics):

1. The Credo is the principal belief of our Company. It must be known, owned and energized by all.
2. Our Motto is "We are Ladies and Gentlemen serving Ladies and Gentlemen." As service professionals, we treat our guests and each other with respect and dignity.
3. The Three Steps of Service are the foundation of Ritz-Carlton hospitality. These steps must be used in every interaction to ensure satisfaction, retention and loyalty.
4. The Employee Promise is the basis for our Ritz-Carlton work environment. It will be honored by all employees.
5. All employees will successfully complete annual Training Certification for their position.
6. Company objectives are communicated to all employees. It is everyone's responsibility to support them.

continued

EXCELLENCE CASE *continued*

7. To create pride and joy in the workplace, all employees have the right to be involved in the planning of the work that affects them.

8. Each employee will continuously identify defects (MR BIV) throughout the Hotel.

9. It is the responsibility of each employee to create a work environment of teamwork and lateral service so that the needs of our guests and each other are met.

10. Each employee is empowered. For example, when a guest has a problem or needs something special you should break away from your regular duties, address and resolve the issue.

11. Uncompromising levels of cleanliness are the responsibility of every employee.

12. To provide the finest personal service for our guests, each employee is responsible for identifying and recording individual guest preferences.

13. Never lose a guest. Instant guest pacification is the responsibility of each employee. Whoever receives a complaint will own it, resolve it to the guest's satisfaction and record it.

© 1992 The Ritz-Carlton Hotel Company. All rights reserved. Reprinted with permission of The Ritz-Carlton Hotel Company, L.L.C. The Ritz-Carlton® is a federally registered trademark of The Ritz-Carlton Hotel Company, L.L.C.

continued

EXCELLENCE CASE *continued*

14. "Smile—we are on stage." Always maintain positive eye contact. Use the proper vocabulary with our guests and each other. (Use words like—"Good Morning," "Certainly," "I'll be happy to," and "My pleasure.")

15. Be an ambassador of your Hotel in and outside of the workplace. Always speak positively. Communicate any concerns to the appropriate person.

16. Escort guests rather than pointing out directions to another area of the Hotel.

17. Use Ritz-Carlton telephone etiquette. Answer within three rings and with a "smile." Use the guest's name when possible. When necessary, ask the caller "May I place you on hold?" Do not screen calls. Eliminate call transfers whenever possible. Adhere to voice mail standards.

18. Take pride in and care of your personal appearance. Everyone is responsible to convey a professional image by adhering to Ritz-Carlton clothing and grooming standards.

19. Think safety first. Each employee is responsible for creating a safe, secure and accident free environment for all guests and each other. Be aware of all fire and safety emergency procedures and report any security risks immediately.

20. Protecting the assets of a Ritz-Carlton Hotel is the responsibility of every employee. Conserve energy, properly maintain our hotels and protect the environment.

A few explanations of some of the words and phrases used in the Ritz-Carlton basics help to highlight the company's extraordinary concern for quality service. "MR BIV" is an acronym for Mistakes, Rework, Breakdowns, Inefficiencies, and Variations, which the company has made into an animated, mischievous looking character. The company's employees are reminded to continuously note and report any defects in these areas. The "lateral service" concept means that employees are encouraged to help fellow employees, even if they work in different departments of the hotel, if it means that a higher quality customer service is delivered.

Other key words and phrases in the Ritz-Carlton vocabulary are "doing it right the first time" and "instant pacification" of guests.[4] These two related ideas involve employees in identifying defects in a hotel's operation and doing everything in their power to satisfy guests who have problems or complaints. Ritz-Carlton has identified 720 work areas in a hotel for which daily quality production reports are prepared. Employees complete these reports, noting defects or problems that may adversely affect service quality and guest satisfaction.[5] Employees are required to respond to a guest complaint within 10 minutes of receiving the complaint and to follow up within 20 minutes.[6] Each employee is allowed—or *empowered*—to spend up to $2,000 to make a dissatisfied guest happy.[7]

However you measure it, Ritz-Carlton is a success story in service quality because of its unique approaches. Since winning the Malcolm Baldrige Awards in 1992 and 1999, it has been flooded with requests to share its secrets of success with others. This, like serving its own guests, it has done gladly and with excellence.

Discussion Questions

1. How has The Ritz-Carlton Hotel Company adapted the five key principles of total quality management in its operations?

2. What can other hospitality and travel organizations learn from what Ritz-Carlton has done?

3. How important has employee empowerment been in producing quality service at The Ritz-Carlton Hotel Company?

References

1. 1992 Award winner. The Ritz-Carlton Hotel Company.

2. Application Summary. Malcolm Baldrige National Quality Award. 1993. The Ritz-Carlton Hotel Company.

3. Henderson, Cheri. "Putting on the Ritz." *The TQM Magazine* (November/December 1992): 292–296.

continued

EXCELLENCE CASE *continued*

4. Partlow, Charles G. "How Ritz-Carlton applies TQM." *Cornell Hotel and Restaurant Administration Quarterly* 34 (4):16–24 (1993).
5. The Ritz-Carlton Hotel Company Web site: http://www.ritzcarlton.com/html_corp/about-us/factsheet.asp
6. United Airlines. 1994. "Cultivating quality: the Ritz Carlton." *Hemispheres* (January 1994).

7. Watkins, Edward. "How Ritz-Carlton won the Baldrige Award." *Lodging Hospitality* 48 (11):22–24 (1992).

Web Site

http://www.ritzcarlton.com

CUSTOMER CODES AND GUARANTEES

You now have seen how a few companies have strived for service excellence and succeeded. But how can other organizations emulate what a company like Ritz-Carlton has done in managing its host-guest relationships? One clear lesson that you have no doubt learned from the Ritz-Carlton Excellence Case is that it is important for an organization to articulate its service standards *in writing*. Some hospitality and travel organizations have done this through customer codes or customer guarantees. A few good examples of these will help you get the picture and understand their value:

◆ **Delta Hotels,** Canada. Delta Hotels has a *Great Meetings Guaranteed* program. Figure 11–3 provides the details of this guarantee, which covers response times to telephone inquiries, meeting room set-up and audio-visual equipment, refreshment breaks, and meeting room supplies.

◆ **Hampton Inn,** USA. Hampton's *100% Satisfaction Guarantee* dates back to 1989, and states that "if you're not completely satisfied, we'll give you your night's stay for free."

◆ **ScotRail Railways Limited,** Scotland. ScotRail publishes a booklet titled *Passenger Charter: Scotrail's promise to customers*. The booklet shows ScotRail's Performance Standards and goals (percent of trains arriving within 5 or 10 minutes of scheduled arrival time), its Customer Care guidelines, and what ScotRail will do for customers "When Things Go Wrong."

◆ **Southwest Airlines,** USA. Southwest has developed the *Southwest Airlines Customer Service Commitment*, which can now be accessed online. Figure 11–4 shows Southwest's mission statement and indicates the importance of customer satisfaction to the airline.

Customer codes and guarantees benefit both the organization and its customers. Putting the organization's service commitments in writing is important in communicating to guests what to expect in the service delivery. Additionally, it gives the organization's employees a clear idea of what is expected of them in serving guests. In a way, this becomes a *service contract* between the host and guest.

Now you may be a bit skeptical about these codes and guarantees. Why? No guarantee is foolproof, you might be thinking. We tend to agree with you, because it takes

ON THE WEB

GROUP PLANNER

Great Meetings Guaranteed

Complete our convenient online Meeting Space Inquiry Form.

EVERYTHING YOU NEED TO PULL OFF A GREAT MEETING

High standards, network wide consistency and an ever expanding list of great locations ensure your meeting can't miss. From beginning to end, a Delta meeting planner will work closely with you to ensure everything goes off without a hitch. But that's only half of it.

Delta meeting planners also provide a wealth of experience, and creative solutions that can upgrade your meeting from good to great. They will work with you to customize the event to suit your group's needs. They can also provide advice on how to structure the meeting itself, and how to keep it fresh. But a savvy business person like you probably wants that in writing. OK.

We guarantee: You'll receive a response to your telephone inquiry within one hour.** You'll receive a written response to your inquiry within one business day. Your function room will be set up as agreed. Your audio visual equipment will be delivered on time and in working order. Your refreshment breaks will be ready on time. Your supplies will be in your meeting room.

**between 8:30am - 6:00pm

Here's how to book:
Call our toll free number at
1-800-387-1265
OR
Call one of our national sales offices:
Ottawa (613) 598-0364
Montréal (514) 879-4703
Toronto (416) 874-2171
Vancouver (604) 276-1104
OR
Contact any one of our hotels directly.

◆ FIGURE 11–3   *Delta Hotels' Great Meetings Guaranteed Program improves the service quality for meeting planners.* (Courtesy of Delta Hotels & Resorts)

people to deliver on all of these promises, and people's behaviors tend to be variable. An organization must select, orient, train, motivate, retain, and empower the best customer-oriented people. Those are our next topics.

EMPLOYEES: MANAGING INTERNAL CUSTOMERS FOR SERVICE QUALITY

The main focus of any hospitality and travel organization wishing to improve its service quality must be its employees (called **internal marketing**). It must develop a human resources management program that selects, orients, trains, motivates, rewards, retains, and empowers the best people for the organization's unique culture, positioning, and style of operations. An organization must also consistently require all employees to adhere to policies regarding behavior and personal grooming.

CUSTOMER SERVICE COMMITMENT

Our Mission Statement

The mission of Southwest Airlines is dedication to the highest quality of Customer Service delivered with a sense of warmth, friendliness, individual pride, and Company Spirit.

SOUTHWEST AIRLINES
A SYMBOL OF FREEDOM

Revised March 13, 2000

◆ FIGURE 11–4 *Southwest Airlines' mission statement demonstrates the importance of customer satisfaction to the company.* (Courtesy of Southwest Airlines) *continued*

Table of Contents

◆ FIGURE 11–4　*continued*

Staff Selection, Orientation, and Training

All of a hospitality and travel organization's employees contribute to the quality of its service. Therefore, if an organization wants to maintain or improve its service quality, the place to start is when hiring new employees. Successful service organizations recognize the need to employ people with the following characteristics:[6]

1. Strong interpersonal skills
2. Behavioral flexibility
3. Empathy

Another industry source says that top-notch service employees have superior guest-contact skills, which are a blend of courtesy, communication, response to guest needs, good judgment, and teamwork.[7] Although new employees can be asked to fill out personality inventory forms, there are newer techniques that offer even greater promise. With video-assisted selection, applicants are asked to look at problem-laden service situations and indicate how they would respond.

Whatever route they choose, the successful service companies really *sweat the details* in recruiting the best people. For example, it took The Ritz-Carlton Hotel Company four years to develop its *Targeted Selection Process* for hiring new employees. This involved developing personality profiles for every position within the company, based partly on the traits demonstrated by the best of Ritz-Carlton's existing employees in each position. Generally, these traits included politeness, a friendly personality and positive attitude, and a feeling of belonging to the job and the work environment.[8] The development process produced many written interview guides used in selection interviews. Each person is interviewed by three different levels of management. At each new hotel property, less than one in ten of the people interviewed are selected.[9]

Service-oriented behavior is innate in some people but must be sharpened through good orientation and training programs. Disney has one of the most highly regarded orientation and training programs for new employees. All are required to attend a one-day *Traditions* session at Disney University. This program conveys Disney's operating and guest-service philosophies. New hires at Ritz-Carlton Hotels have a two-day orientation on the company's philosophies and quality standards. So important is this orientation process that at each new hotel opening the president and chief operating officer conduct these two-day sessions. Orientation programs for newly hired employees are a key step in an organization communicating its service quality culture.

Training is the third cornerstone, after selection and orientation, for preparing service-oriented employees. Most experts agree that several days or weeks of supervised, on-the-job training is best. However, this does not mean sink-or-swim training where new employees are thrown in at the deep end and learn the job by themselves. At Ritz-Carlton Hotels, each employee receives at least 120 hours of training on the company's quality standards.[10]

Motivating and Retaining Staff

Keeping highly motivated, service-oriented employees is the next major challenge. Many techniques seem to work for several companies.

1. **Maintaining regular communications with employees.** For example, most major firms have an internal newsletter.
2. **Complimenting or rewarding employees frequently.** Employees should be made to feel important. Many companies have employee-of-the-month awards.

3. **Setting clear objectives and performance standards for employees.**
4. **Making sure that there are advancement opportunities.** Many successful companies have strong promotion-from-within policies and clear, mapped-out career paths.
5. **Using management and supervisory staff who are honest, open, and willing to listen to employees.**
6. **Giving service employees an accurate description of what the typical customer expects from the services that the organization provides.**

Many experts believe that organizations need to treat their employees as internal customers with guests being the external customers.

Empowering Staff to Deliver Guest Satisfaction

How much is a dissatisfied guest worth to a hospitality and travel organization? Too much is probably the best answer to this difficult question. Dissatisfied customers are customers who usually do not return and who share their negative experiences, through word of mouth, with acquaintances. Therefore, coverting potentially dissatisfied guests into satisfied guests is a major challenge for hospitality and travel organizations. Empowering employees to go the extra mile to satisfy guests is recognized as one of the most powerful tools available to a service organization. Empowerment means giving employees the authority to identify and solve guest problems or complaints *on the spot*, and to make improvements in work processes when necessary.[11] How many times have you heard the words "I'm sorry, that's not my job," "I'm sorry, it's company policy," or "I'm sorry, that's the way we always do it" from employees of service organizations? You will not hear these excuses in a service business that effectively empowers its employees.

Empowering employees means decentralizing decision-making and *flattening* organization charts by giving more power to the front-line employees who directly serve guests.[12] Empowerment means that managers must have greater levels of trust in their subordinates and must respect their judgment.[13] In the Excellence Case for this chapter, you read that Ritz-Carlton authorizes its employees to spend up to $2,000 to please a dissatisfied guest. Since employees are given more power to satisfy customers, they should be asked to take *ownership* of guest problems or complaints. This means that if a guest tells an employee about a problem that he or she has experienced, then that employee *owns* the problem and must take action to correct it to the customer's satisfaction, even if the problem occurred in another department or division within the employee's organization.

Staff Behavior, Appearance, and Uniforms

Can you think of one feature that stands out about the employees of our industry's leaders, such as Disney and McDonald's? You are correct if you mentioned employees, attitudes, behavior, appearance, or uniforms. These and other corporations stay on top of the group because of the time and effort they invest in their people. Disney even has a concept known as *the Disney look*, which is written up in a special brochure for all new employees to study. The following quote from the brochure highlights the importance of Disney's people to its theme parks.[14]

> "The Disney look is a tremendously important part of the overall show at Disneyland Park and the Walt Disney World Resort. The combination of our Cast Members' themed costumes and appearance has brought compliments and recognition from people the world over."

The following are two other quotes from the late founders of these two industry giants. Each sums up their philosophies on the importance of people.

"My way of fighting the competition is the positive approach. Stress your strengths, emphasize quality, service, cleanliness and value (Q, S, C, and V), and the competition will wear itself out trying to keep up with you."[15] (the late Ray Kroc of McDonald's)

"You can dream, create, design and build the most wonderful place in the world . . . but it takes people to make the dream a reality."[16] (the late Walt Disney)

There is no place in such companies for soiled uniforms, outlandish hairstyles, or *ad lib* dressing. There are dress codes, rules of conduct, and sometimes even a unique language that everyone knows and uses. Such companies recognize that their people can greatly enhance the customer's image of the company.

What about managers and people who work behind the scenes? Are dishwashers, cooks, mechanics, cleaners, accountants, and other *back-of-the-house* personnel not part of the product because they are not visible to customers? The answer is that managers and non-front-line staff are definitely part of the service-quality team. Front-line, customer-contact staff rely heavily on these people. Effective managers do not spend the majority of their time sequestered in their offices. They recognize the need to be part of the service-quality team—meeting, greeting, and making sure that customers get what they expect and want.

Many marketing plans make no reference to staff and management programs but concentrate entirely on promotional, pricing, and distribution activities. A *take-it-for-granted* attitude seems to prevail about how employees will perform. This is a serious mistake because it ignores the powerful positive (or negative) impacts that people have on an organization's sales and profits. At a minimum, the marketing plan should specify the following:

1. Staff uniform improvements and changes
2. Employee and management recognition and award programs
3. Employee and management incentive and reward programs
4. Sales and guest relations training programs
5. Orientation program on marketing plan objectives and activities
6. Communication mechanisms on marketing progress and results

All hospitality and travel organizations have to be concerned about the quality of their people. This is a particularly difficult challenge because destination marketing organizations (DMOs) employ only limited numbers of people themselves but rely on quality service from the employees of many other organizations in their destinations (e.g., hotels and resorts, restaurants, attractions, etc.). Several DMOs have developed hospitality and service training programs for their members and other local organizations. Others, such as the San Francisco Convention & Visitors Bureau, believe that it is necessary to recognize the many employees who make tourism work for visitors to their communities, Figure 11–5.

MEASURING SERVICE QUALITY

The importance of quality service to positive guest experiences has long been recognized, and many techniques for improving service quality have been developed. However, not as much effort has been put into techniques for measuring service quality.[17] In the mid-1980s, based upon research conducted by Parasuraman, Zeithaml, and Berry, a technique known as SERVQUAL was developed. These three authors defined service quality as the customer's perception of a specific firm's service quality based on

Presenting 600 of the most memorable sights in the world's top travel destination

There's a lot to see in San Francisco. But that's not the only reason we were just named "Best City" in the world by *Condé Nast Traveler* magazine.

Just as important are the thousands of men and women who make our visitors feel so welcome. From the cable-car bell ringer, to the hotel concierge, to the maitre d', to the taxi

driver—the list goes on and on. As does their dedication to hospitality.

So we'd like to say thanks to each and every one of them. They've made San Francisco more than a great place to see.

They've made it a great place to visit.

San Francisco

CONVENTION & VISITORS BUREAU
©1991 SFCVB. Photo: Dan Escobar

◆ **FIGURE 11–5**   *San Francisco Convention & Visitors Bureau applauds the efforts of all the city's tourism employees.* (Courtesy of San Francisco Convention & Visitors Bureau)

a comparison of the performance of that specific firm in providing the service with the customer's general expectations of all firms in the same industry who provide that service.[18]

The SERVQUAL technique uses the following five individual *dimensions* to measure customers' expectations and perceptions:

1. **TANGIBLES:** The hospitality and travel organization's physical facilities, equipment, and appearance of staff.
2. **RELIABILITY:** The hospitality and travel organization's ability to perform the service dependably and accurately.
3. **RESPONSIVENESS:** The willingness of staff to help customers and provide prompt service.
4. **ASSURANCE:** The knowledge and courtesy of staff and their ability to convey trust and confidence.
5. **EMPATHY:** The degree of caring, individualized attention that the hospitality and travel organization's staff provides to its customers.

Did You Know?

✓ The National Institute of Standards and Technology (NIST), an agency of the U.S. Department of Commerce, is responsible for the Malcolm Baldrige National Quality Award.

✓ The American Society for Quality (ASQ) helps NIST with the administration of the program.

✓ In 2000, there were seven criteria for Performance Excellence in the Baldrige awards:

- Leadership
- Strategic planning
- Customer and market focus
- Information and analysis
- Human resource focus
- Process management
- Business results

✓ A detailed description of these criteria can be found at NIST's Web site: http://www.quality.nist.gov/

In their original SERVQUAL model, the authors had seven other factors (competence, access, courtesy, communication, credibility, security, and understanding/knowing). These seven factors were included under *assurance* and *empathy* in the new model. Two different research studies have shown that the relative ranking of quality of service expectations by customers places *reliability* as the most important item, followed in order by *assurance, tangibles, responsiveness,* and *empathy.*[19]

Service quality is measured by SERVQUAL through the use of a special questionnaire, which is usually filled out by the customers themselves (self-administered). The questionnaire contains 22 statements, reflecting the five service dimensions. Customers rate both their expectations and perceptions for each of these 22 statements using a seven-point scale, with one being labeled *strongly disagree.* For example, in the *tangibles* dimension, one of the expectation statements is "their employees should be well dressed and neat" and the parallel perception statement is "ABC organization's employees are well dressed and appear neat." The scores for all of the statements under each of the five service dimensions are averaged and then a *perceived quality score* is calculated by subtracting the expectation average scores from the perceived average scores. More simply stated, this means that perceived service quality is the difference between the quality of service provided by a specific hospitality and travel organization and the quality of service customers expect to receive from similar hospitality and travel organizations (PERCEPTIONS – EXPECTATIONS = QUALITY).

Another method of investigating service quality is that of identifying favorable and unfavorable incidents in service encounters between a customer and service provider. A **service encounter** is a period of time when a customer directly interacts with a service.[20] Bitner, Booms, and Tetreault used the critical incident method with customers of airlines, hotels, and restaurants to identify 12 types of favorable and unfavorable service-encounter incidents.[21] These incidents are categorized into three groups—employee response to service delivery failures (how employees respond to complaints or disappointments), employee response to customer needs and requests, and unprompted and unsolicited employee actions. The first group includes responses to unavailable services, unreasonably slow services, and other core service failures. Customer needs and requests are further divided into *special needs* customers (e.g., guests with language difficulties), customer preferences, admitted customer error, and potentially disruptive others. The third group includes the attention paid to the customer, truly out-of-the ordinary employee behavior, employee behavior in the context of cultural norms, Gestalt evaluation, and performance under adverse circumstances. Figure 11–6 provides examples of these types of satisfactory and unsatisfactory incidents.

Hospitality and travel organizations should conduct periodic checks of overall service quality. A third technique, the *Customer-Service Assessment Scale,* can be used to determine the level of service provided.[22] This scale can be applied in three different ways:

1. **Self-Assessment:** Employees and supervisors assess themselves on the scale.
2. **Managers' Assessment:** The manager completes an assessment for each employee and supervisor.
3. **Group Analysis:** Groups of managers, supervisors, or employees jointly complete the assessments.

The typical guest comment cards found in most hotels and restaurants have been widely criticized as being inadequate indicators of guest satisfaction with service quality, and several companies now supplement this through large-scale surveys of past guests. Marriott randomly picks groups of past hotel guests and mails questionnaires to their homes. Ritz-Carlton does likewise, surveying a significant 25,000 per year.[23]

RELATIONSHIP MARKETING: TREATING GUESTS AS PEOPLE

In the past, there has been a definite tendency for hospitality and travel marketers to place their greatest emphasis on attracting new customers. More recently, the idea of nurturing the individual relationships with present and past customers has received greater attention. Most marketers now accept that it is less expensive to attract repeat customers than to *create* new customers. This is the basic concept behind **relationship marketing**, or building, maintaining, and enhancing long-term relationships with individual customers.[24] You might look at it as treating the individual guest as a person, rather than as a statistic. It means having a long-term interest in an individual customer, which some refer to as customer **lifetime value (LTV)** or treating the individual as an asset rather than as a commodity.[25]

The ultimate goal of relationship marketing is to make the individual guest loyal to the organization. This is particularly important in our business where there are many frequent travelers and where word-of-mouth recommendations have such a great influence. Retaining loyal, repeat customers is also crucial because it is easy for people to switch between carriers, suppliers, and travel trade intermediaries. The key outcome of all relationship marketing efforts is to make individual customers feel special and to make them believe that the organization has singled them out for extraordinary attention.

GROUP 1   SAMPLE INCIDENTS: EMPLOYEE RESPONSE TO SERVICE DELIVERY FAILURES

Incident	
Satisfactory	**Unsatisfactory**

A. Response to Unavailable Service

They lost my room reservation but the manager gave me the V.P. suite for the same price.	We had made advance reservations at the hotel. When we arrived we found we had no room—no explanation, no apologies, and no assistance in finding another hotel.

B. Response to Unreasonably Slow Service

Even though I didn't make any complaint about the hour-and-a-half wait, the waitress kept apologizing and said that the bill was on the house.	The airline employees continually gave us erroneous information. A one-hour delay turned into a six-hour wait.

C. Response to Other Core Service Failures

My shrimp cocktail was half frozen. The waitress apologized, and didn't charge me for any of my dinner.	One of my suitcases was all dented and looked as though it had been dropped from 30,000 feet. When I tried to make a claim for my damaged luggage, the employee insinuated that I was lying and trying to rip them off.

GROUP 2   SAMPLE INCIDENTS: EMPLOYEE RESPONSE TO CUSTOMER NEEDS AND REQUESTS

Incident	
Satisfactory	**Unsatisfactory**

A. Response to Special Needs Customers

The flight attendant helped me calm and care for my airsick child.	My young son, flying alone, was to be assisted by the stewardess from start to finish. At the Albany airport she left him alone in the airport with no one to escort him to his connecting flight.

B. Response to Customer Preferences

The front desk clerk called around and found me tickets to the Mariners' opening game.	The waitress refused to move me from a window table on a hot day, because there was nothing left in *her* section.
It was snowing outside—car broke down. I checked 10 hotels and there were no rooms. Finally, one understood my situation and offered to rent me a bed and set it up in one of their small banquet rooms.	The airline wouldn't let me bring my scuba gear on board coming back from Hawaii even though I brought it over as carry-on luggage.

◆ **FIGURE 11–6**   *Satisfactory and unsatisfactory service incidents.* (Courtesy of Journal Of Marketing)
continued

GROUP 2　SAMPLE INCIDENTS: EMPLOYEE RESPONSE TO CUSTOMER NEEDS AND REQUESTS

Incident	
Satisfactory	**Unsatisfactory**

C. Response to Admitted Customer Error

I lost my glasses on the plane. The stewardess found them and they were delivered to my hotel free of charge.	We missed our flight because of car trouble. The service clerk wouldn't help us find a flight on an alternative airline.

D. Response to Potentially Disruptive Others

The manager kept his eye on an obnoxious guy at the bar, to make sure that he didn't bother us.	The hotel staff wouldn't deal with the noisy people partying in the hall at 3 A.M.

GROUP 3　SAMPLE INCIDENTS: UNPROMPTED AND UNSOLICITED EMPLOYEE ACTIONS

Incident	
Satisfactory	**Unsatisfactory**

A. Attention Paid to Customer

The waiter treated me like royalty. He really showed he cared about me.	The lady at the front desk acted as if we were bothering her. She was watching TV and paying more attention to the TV than the hotel guests.

B. Truly Out-of-the-Ordinary Employee Behavior

We always travel with our teddy bears. When we got back to our room at the hotel we saw that the maid had arranged our bears very comfortably in a chair. The bears were holding hands.	I needed a few more minutes to decide on a dinner. The waitress said, "If you would read the menu and not the road map, you would know what you want to order."

C. Employee Behaviors in the Context of Cultural Norms

The busboy ran after us to return a $50 bill my boyfriend had dropped under the table.	The waiter at this expensive restaurant treated us like dirt because we were only high school kids on a prom date.

D. Gestalt Evaluation

The whole experience was so pleasant . . . everything went smoothly and perfectly.	The flight was a nightmare. A one-hour layover went to 3½ hours. The air conditioning didn't work. The pilots and stewardesses were fighting because of an impending flight attendant strike. The landing was extremely rough. To top it all off, when the plane stopped, the pilots and stewardesses were the first ones off.

E. Performance Under Adverse Circumstances

The counter agent was obviously under stress, but kept his cool and acted very professionally.	

◆ FIGURE 11–6　*continued.*

This individualization or customization can be achieved through the following procedures:

1. **Managing service encounters:** Training hospitality and travel organization staff members to treat customers as individuals, e.g., by using their names, knowing their preferences and interests, etc.
2. **Providing customer incentives:** Giving customers incentives or inducements to make repeat uses of the business, e.g., frequent-flyer and frequent-guest programs, preferred supplier arrangements, etc.
3. **Providing special service options:** Giving special *extras* to repeat or *club* customers, including, for example, upgrades to executive or concierge floors in hotels, airline club lounge memberships, and personalized baggage tags.
4. **Developing pricing strategies to encourage long-term use:** Offering repeat customers special prices or rates, e.g., annual memberships to theme parks, museums, zoos, and other gated attractions.
5. **Maintaining a customer database:** Keeping an up-to-date database on individual customers, including purchase history, preferences, likes and dislikes, demographics, etc.
6. **Communicating with customers through direct or specialized media:** Using non-mass media approaches to communicate directly with individual customers, e.g., direct mail, club newsletters, etc.

Returning to the Ritz-Carlton Hotels example, you can see some concrete applications of these procedures. The chain maintains a computerized guest history profile of thousands of individual repeat guests. This database notes, among other things, each guest's preferences and likes and dislikes. Ritz-Carlton employees are trained to keep track of this information for each hotel guest so that it can be recorded and used to provide more personalized service. Each hotel has at least one *guest-recognition coordinator* whose job is to identify repeat guests and to record new information on each guest within 24 hours of his or her departure. Once entered, this information is distributed system-wide to all other Ritz-Carlton Hotels. When guests visit another Ritz-Carlton, members of the staff already know about their likes and dislikes.[26] Casinos also maintain sophisticated databases of guest preferences, as well as their wagering habits.

THE CUSTOMER MIX

Another important people-related decision for a hospitality and travel organization is its customer mix. The **customer mix** is the combination of customers that use or are attracted to a specific hospitality and travel organization. The term *mix* is most appropriate for our business, since our guests do mix and often interact with one another. Of course, this concept is closely related to market segmentation, which was discussed in Chapter 7, but the customer mix requires the careful management of the interactions between customers, mostly when they are in the process of using hospitality and travel organizations' services. The types of customers who use a hospitality and travel organization definitely influence its image among other present and potential customers. In some cases, certain types of customers attract other similar customers, and the reverse may be true as well. Customers also directly influence other customers' quality of service experiences. The actions and behavior of

africa
asia
australia
canada
uk/europe
latin america
new zealand
united states
other

◆ FIGURE 11–7   *Contiki's customer mix is 18- to 35-year-olds.* (Courtesy of Contiki Holidays)

individual customers (e.g., guests who are loud or rude, who smoke, or who are intoxicated) may also be annoying or offensive to other customers and lead to lowered customer satisfaction levels. Conversely, very considerate or friendly customers may enhance other customers' service experiences.

Some hospitality and travel organizations in their positioning make it quite clear which groups of customers they wish to attract and serve. For example, Contiki explicitly indicates in all of its advertising and other promotions that it is a tour company for persons aged 18 to 35 years (Figure 11–7). Their communications carry photographs of men and women in this age group to emphasize the appropriate youthful image of Contiki. Club Med used a similar strategy in the 1960s and 1970s, featuring many photographs of young adults, which gave the resort company an image of being a place for only youthful singles and couples. Contiki also assures potential tour patrons that all tour staff (tour managers, drivers, and Contiki resort staff) are in the 18 to 35 age group. As the ad shown in Figure 11–8 shows, the new millennium version of Club Med is that of trying to shake off the *young swinger* image it earned in earlier years.

Some exclusive and expensive resorts have *no children* policies or do not allow children under a certain age to stay with them. The reason is that they believe that their typical guests do not like to be bothered by children, who can be noisy and boisterous if not properly supervised by adults. Other resorts advertised as being *for couples only,* have chosen to target only adult guests as part of their marketing strategies. In contrast, a growing number of hospitality and travel organizations, such as Westin and their *Westin Kids Club,* are actively trying to recruit children into their customer mixes. Other examples include the Hyatt Corporation with its *Camp Hyatt* program, Carnival's *Camp Carnival,* and Super Clubs.

For guests who like to vacation in places without all or most of their clothes, some companies offer special tours, resorts, or beach areas. These include a very appropriately named tour company whose site on the Web is bare-necessities.com. Another example of a specific customer mix is the growing number of hospitality and travel organizations that are targeting the gay and lesbian market. Lufthansa, in early 2000 offered 10 percent off the lowest published airfare from its U.S. gateways to the Gay & Lesbian Capitals of Europe, including Amsterdam, Berlin, Cologne, and Hamburg.

◆ FIGURE 11–8 *Club Med shows that families are part of its customer mix.* (Courtesy of Club Med)

CHAPTER CONCLUSION

The interaction of customers (guests) and employees (hosts) has a great influence on marketing success. In particular, the quality of service provided plays the pivotal role in the success of a hospitality and travel organization. Organizations that devote above-average attention to their employees usually prosper the most. Successful organizations train their employees to do things right the first time and empower employees to resolve customer problems and complaints. Service quality must constantly be measured by a hospitality and travel organization, and a variety of techniques can be used to accomplish this.

All hospitality and travel organizations should apply the relationship marketing concept. This means building long-term customer loyalty among individual customers through customized programs that make guests feel extra-special.

An organization's customer mix may affect both its image and the service quality that individual customers experience. Efforts are needed to manage the customer mix, not only for profitability reasons, but also to maximize guest satisfaction.

REVIEW QUESTIONS

1. Who are the two major groups of people involved in hospitality and travel marketing, and what are the most important interactions between these two groups?
2. How important are a hospitality and travel organization's staff members to its marketing success and effectiveness?
3. What is the total quality management (TQM) concept and what are its key principles?
4. Which techniques can be used to make employees provide more consistent and higher quality service to customers?
5. What is empowerment and how does it contribute to increasing service quality?
6. What is SERVQUAL and how is it used in evaluating service quality?
7. What other techniques can be used to measure service quality?
8. What is relationship marketing and what steps should a hospitality and travel organization take to build long-term relationships with individual customers?
9. How does the customer mix affect an organization's image and the quality of its customers' service experiences?

CHAPTER ASSIGNMENTS

1. You have been hired by a hotel, restaurant, travel agency, airline, or other hospitality and travel organization with a reputation for below-average service. Your task is to significantly upgrade the service orientation and service quality of supervisors and other staff members. What steps would you follow in satisfying this objective? Draw on examples of successful companies in the industry. Try to come up with two or more creative ideas of your own.

2. You have been asked by your boss to develop a program for measuring service quality in your organization. What technique or techniques would you recommend be used for this measurement? Write a report to your boss explaining your plan and how it should be implemented.

3. Choose a specific hospitality and travel organization and describe how you would develop a relationship marketing program for it. How would you attract and recognize repeat

customers? What special options or services would you offer repeat customers? What type of database would be developed and how would it be maintained? How would you communicate with past guests?

4. Describe the importance of the customer mix concept to a particular hospitality and travel organization. Explain how the types of customers it attracts affects its image, and how customers' service experiences are either enhanced or made less satisfactory. Make constructive suggestions to the organization's management on how they could manage their customer mix more effectively.

WORLD WIDE WEB RESOURCES

American Society for Quality (ASQ)
http://www.asq.org/

Bare Necessities
http://www.bare-necessities.com/

Delta Hotels
http://www.deltahotels.com/

Disney
http://www.disney.go.com/

Emirates
http://www.emirates.com/

Four Seasons Hotels and Resorts
http://www.fourseasons.com/

Hampton Inn
http://www.hamptoninn.com/

Lufthansa
http://www.lufthansa-usa.com/

National Institute for Quality Standards
http://www.quality.nist.gov/

The Ritz-Carlton Hotel Company
http://www.ritzcarlton.com/

San Francisco Convention and Visitors Bureau
http://www.sfvisitor.org/

ScotRail Railways Limited
http://www.scotrail.co.uk/

Singapore Airlines
http://www.singaporeair.com/

Southwest Airlines
http://www.southwest.com/

REFERENCES

1. Mill, Robert C. "Managing the service encounter." *Cornell Hotel and Restaurant Administration Quarterly* 26 (4):39–46 (1986).

2. Henderson, Cheri. "Putting on the Ritz." *The TQM Magazine* (November/December, 1992): 292–296.

3. Albrecht, Karl, and Ron Zemke. 1985. *Service America! Doing Business in the New Economy.* Homewood, Ill.: Dow Jones-Irwin.

4. Berry, Leonard L., and A. Parasuraman. 1991. *Marketing Services: Competing Through Quality.* New York: The Free Press, 4.

5. Partlow, Charles G. "How Ritz-Carlton applies TQM." *Cornell Hotel and Restaurant Administration Quarterly* 34 (4):16–24 (1993).

6. Mill, Robert C. "Managing the service encounter." *Cornell Hotel and Restaurant Administration Quarterly* 26 (4):39–46 (1986).

7. Jones, Casey, and Thomas A. DeCotiis. "Video-assisted selection of hospitality employees." *Cornell Hotel and Restaurant Administration Quarterly* 27 (2):68–73 (1986).

8. Avery, Lincoln. "Ritz-Carlton: elegance with feeling." *Hotel & Resort Industry* 12 (8):18–21 (1989).

9. Wagner, Grace. "Strategies/employee selection makes Ritz Tradition." *Lodging Hospitality* 47 (7):30 (1991).

10. Watkins, Edward. "How Ritz-Carlton won the Baldrige Award." *Lodging Hospitality* 48 (11):22–24 (1992).

11. Partlow, Charles G. "How Ritz-Carlton applies TQM." *Cornell Hotel and Restaurant Administration Quarterly* 34 (4):23 (1993).

12. Brymer, Robert A. "Employee empowerment: a guest-driven leadership strategy." *Cornell*

Hotel and Restaurant Administration Quarterly 32 (2):58–68.

13. Sternberg, Lawrence E. "Empowerment: trust vs. control." *Cornell Hotel and Restaurant Administration Quarterly* 33 (1):69–72.

14. The Walt Disney Company. 1992. *The Disney Look: Guidelines for Cast Members at the Walt Disney World Resort.*

15. Kroc, Ray. 1990. *Grinding It Out: The Making of McDonald's.* New York: Berkley Publishing Company.

16. The Walt Disney Company. 1992. *The Disney Look: Guidelines for Cast Members at the Walt Disney World Resort.*

17. Fick, Gavin R., and J. R. Brent Ritchie. "Measuring service quality in the travel and tourism industry." *Journal of Travel Research* 30:2–9 (1991).

18. Parasuraman, A., V. A. Zeithaml, and Leonard L. Berry. "A conceptual model of service quality and its implications for future research." *Journal of Marketing* 49:41–50 (1985).

19. Parasuraman, A., V. A. Zeithaml, and Leonard L. Berry. "SERVQUAL: A multiple-item scale for measuring consumer perceptions of service quality." Report No. 86–108. Cambridge, Mass.: Marketing Science Institute; Fick and Ritchie, 1991.

20. Shostack, G. Lynn. "Planning the service encounter." In John A. Czepiel, Michael R. Solomon, and Carol F. Surprenant, Eds., *The Service Encounter.* Lexington, Mass.: Lexington Books, 243–254.

21. Bitner, Mary J., Bernard H. Booms, and Mary S. Tetreault. "The service encounter: Diagnosing favorable and unfavorable incidents." *Journal of Marketing* 54:71–84 (1990).

22. Martin, William B. "Measuring and improving your service quality." *Cornell Hotel and Restaurant Administration Quarterly* 27 (1):80–87 (1986).

23. Watkins, Edward. "How Ritz-Carlton won the Baldrige Award." *Lodging Hospitality* 48 (11):23 (1992).

24. McKenna, Regis. 1991. *Relationship Marketing Successful Strategies for the Age of the Customer.* Reading, Mass.: Addison-Wesley Publishing Co., Inc.

25. Shani, David, and Sujana Chalasani. "Exploiting niches using relationship marketing." *The Journal of Services Marketing* No. 4 (Fall 1992): 43–51.

26. Bergsman, Steve. "Ritz-Carlton aims to know its guests." *Hotel & Motel Management* (May 27, 1991): 24, 75.

For additional hospitality and travel marketing resources, visit our Web site at **www.Hospitality-Tourism.delmar.com**

Packaging and Programming
How Do We Get There?

Objectives

Having read this chapter, you should be able to:

◆ Define the terms packaging and programming.

◆ Explain the relationship between packaging and programming.

◆ List the reasons for the increased popularity of packages and programs in the hospitality and travel industry.

◆ Explain the five key roles of packaging and programming in marketing hospitality and travel services.

◆ Explain the difference between packages developed by intermediaries and packages developed by others.

◆ List and explain four ways of classifying packages.

◆ Describe the steps that should be followed in developing effective packages.

◆ Describe the procedures used to price packages.

Overview

Hospitality and travel services are perishable. A sale not made today is lost forever. Packaging, and the related technique of programming, play a key role in selling services when demand for them is lowest. Packages are popular with customers because they make travel easier and more convenient. In addition, they usually offer a price break on regular rates and

fares. Packages and programs are the epitome of the marketing concept. They are tailor-made offerings to meet specific customer needs and wants.

The packaging of hospitality and travel services is unique. It is very different from the packaging of consumer products found in grocery stores. Our industry's packages usually involve some combination of services from suppliers, carriers, and travel trade intermediaries. They are an excellent example of partner- *ship, because they require the cooperative efforts of several industry groups.*

Key Terms

affinity group packages	destination package	incentive packages
all-inclusive package	double-occupancy basis	Modified American Plan (MAP)
American Plan (AP)	escorted tours	packaging
Bed and Breakfast (B&B)	European Plan (EP)	partnership
blocking space	event packages	programming
break-even analysis	family vacation packages	rail-drive packages
charter tour	fixed costs	shared-room basis
commissionable (packages)	fly-cruise packages	single supplement
continental plan (CP)	fly-drive packages	special-interest packages
convention/meeting packages	fly-rail packages	synergism
destination management	foreign independent tour (FIT)	travel demand generators
companies (DMCs)	group inclusive tour (GIT)	variable or direct costs

When you walk into the local grocery store, you are confronted by thousands of products in a myriad of packages. If you select a box of cereal, you know that it is packaged exactly the same as the other boxes of the same brand on the shelf. Unless the product is visibly damaged, you will not spend even an instant thinking about which box or package of your selected brand to choose. Consumer-goods manufacturers, however, spend millions of dollars designing packages to catch your eye. The hospitality and travel industry's version of packaging is very different, however. Packaging is not physical, but involves blending several services into appealing, convenient customer offerings.

Programming is a related concept that is vitally important to the industry. These are special events and activities with *drawing power* that give a service an added dimension and appeal. Programming is very helpful in creating interest in off-peak times and in maintaining customer interest in the service.

DEFINITION OF PACKAGING AND PROGRAMMING

You have heard the expression *package deal,* which means that the seller throws in a variety of products at a total price that is usually less than the sum of all individual items. Most packages offered by the hospitality and travel industry are of the *package-deal* type. In our industry, packaging is the combination of related and complementary services into a single-price offering.

Programming is a technique closely related to packaging. It involves developing special activities, events, or programs to increase customer spending, or to give added appeal to a package or other hospitality/travel service.

Packaging and programming are related concepts, since a large number of packages include some programming. For example, many golf and tennis packages include some instruction. The instruction portions of these packages are a special activity (program) arranged by the host resort. Computer *camps* at resorts and on cruise ships are another example, in which expert advice on personal computer use (the program) is given to attendees. Of course, not all programming occurs within packages. Parades and holiday celebrations at theme parks and cartoon-character appearances at fast-food outlets are just a few examples.

RELATIONSHIP OF PACKAGING AND PROGRAMMING

As you saw earlier, packaging and programming are related concepts. Many packages include some programming, and often the program is the package's principal travel demand generator. It is also possible to have packages with no programming and to program without packaging. Figure 12–1 shows this relationship.

Packages do not have to incorporate programming. For example, they can simply be accommodation and meal packages, as shown on the left of Figure 12–1. Marriott's weekend package is the example that will be used throughout this chapter to demonstrate this concept. The package rate includes two nights accommodation and American-style breakfasts for two on two sequential weekend mornings. What is the core appeal and travel demand generator? It is simply a price reduction with no added frills. Sometimes a reduced price is enough to sell the package, and no programming is needed.

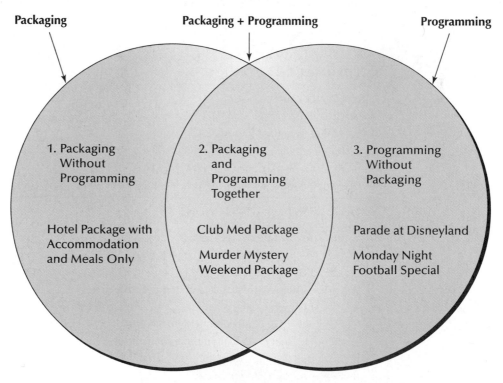

Packaging   **Packaging + Programming**   **Programming**

1. Packaging
   Without
   Programming

   Hotel Package with
   Accommodation
   and Meals Only

2. Packaging
   and
   Programming
   Together

   Club Med Package

   Murder Mystery
   Weekend Package

3. Programming
   Without
   Packaging

   Parade at Disneyland

   Monday Night
   Football Special

Packaging and programming are related techniques.
They can be done together or separately

◆ FIGURE 12–1   *Relationship of packaging and programming.*

But programming can be a powerful ally of packaging, especially when a lower price alone cannot generate enough customer interest. Programming can be the travel demand generator, as in a murder-mystery weekend, or it can be an integral part of the package. As Figure 12–1 shows, the murder-mystery weekend and program-based vacations such as Club Med's are examples of situations where programming and packaging *overlap*.

Programming can also be done on its own, and not in conjunction with packaging. The two examples of this in Figure 12–1 are a parade at Disneyland and Monday-night football nights at U.S. bars and lounges.

REASONS FOR THE POPULARITY OF PACKAGES AND PROGRAMMING

The travel package probably ranks among the concepts that have had the greatest influence on the industry in the past 50 or 60 years. The range of packages available today seems limitless. Why has there been such growth in their popularity? The reasons can be divided into two categories: customer-related and participant-related. (Figure 12–2).

1. **Customer-Related Reasons.** Packages and programs are very user-friendly concepts. They respond to various customer needs, including more convenient vaca-

---

1. CUSTOMER-RELATED REASONS

a. Greater convenience
b. Greater economy
c. Ability to budget for trips
d. Implicit assurance of consistent quality
e. Satisfaction of special interests
f. Added dimension to traveling and dining out

2. PARTICIPANT-RELATED REASONS

a. Increased business in off-peak periods
b. Enhanced appeal to specific target markets
c. Attraction of new target markets
d. Easier business forecasting and improved efficiency
e. Use of complementary facilities, attractions, and events
f. Flexibility to capitalize on new market trends
g. Stimulation of repeat and more frequent usage
h. Increased per capita spending and lengths of stay
i. Public relations and publicity value of unique packages
j. Increased customer satisfaction

◆ FIGURE 12–2　*Reasons for increased popularity of packages and programs.*

tion planning, more economic travel, and a greater desire for specialized experiences. The main customer benefits of travel packages are as follows:

a. ***Greater Convenience.*** Although some people experience great joy from assembling the different pieces of their vacations, meetings, or incentive trips, most prefer the convenience of buying packages. Why? The travel package requires less planning time and effort. For an increasing number of people, time is becoming an even more precious resource than money. This trend toward greater demand for time-saving convenience was highlighted in Chapter 7. The popularity of packages should continue to increase with the growth of two-income families.

b. ***Greater Economy.*** Packages not only make travel and travel planning easier and less time consuming, but also more affordable. For many packages involving air travel, the total package price might be less than the regular, return-trip airfare. You might wonder how this can be. Do the carriers and suppliers involved not lose money? Sometimes they do, but usually they do not. As you will see later, packages are also financially attractive for the industry.

Packages are economical for three reasons. First, if travel intermediaries put them together, they buy in bulk and receive discounts from suppliers and carriers. They pass on part of these discounts to customers. Second, many packages are offered by suppliers and carriers at off-peak periods. The weekend package at a city hotel is a prime example. Most urban hotels that are busy serving business travelers on weekday nights have a sharp drop in occupancies on Friday and Saturday nights. Specially priced weekend packages help fill the void. The third reason is that the industry realizes that customers buy packages partly because of their desire for greater economy.

c. ***Ability to Budget for Trips.*** Most packages are *all inclusive,* meaning that customers know how much they will have to spend weeks or months in advance. This is part of the reason why cruises and resort concepts such as Club Med and Sandals (Figure 12-3) have become so popular. Club Med offers, for one price, everything from return-trip airfare to unlimited free wine at mealtime. Participation and instruction in a wide variety of sports is also included. The only elements not covered are beer and liquor purchased at the bar, optional side trips, and souvenirs purchased in the resorts' gift shops. The tremendous growth in the popularity of cruises is another great example of all-inclusive vacations. Typically, the cruise package includes airfare, accommodations, transfers, meals, on-board entertainment, and a full complement of shipboard activities and amenities.[1] As with Club Med, on most ships drinks and optional, land-based tours are extra. The inclusive nature of packages removes much customer anxiety about how much they will have to spend, and what they will get for their money.

d. ***Implicit Assurance of Consistent Quality.*** Consider the alternative to purchasing a package: customers have to put all the pieces together themselves. Often, they have to buy hospitality and travel services sight unseen. The results can be disastrous if expectations of quality and service are not met.

The travel intermediaries, suppliers, and carriers that assemble packages have more experience and a wider knowledge base. They are professionals in this line of work. Customers can usually rely on this professionalism, in-depth knowledge and experience, and the participants' stake in delivering what is expected. Most organizations recognize the vast power of word-of-mouth

ON THE WEB

◆ **FIGURE 12–3**   *Sandals Resorts offer guests a highly convienent range of Caribbean packages with the "Ultra All-Inclusive" concept.* (Courtesy of Sandals Resorts)

recommendations (positive and negative) and the importance of repeat customers. It is in their best long-term interests to provide consistent quality in all package elements. Customers notice inconsistencies and are apt to judge their entire experiences on the weakest elements. Packages, therefore, offer greater assurance of consistent quality among hospitality and travel elements.

e. ***Satisfaction of Special Interests.*** Along with the numerous, more general packages, there is an ever-expanding menu of special-interest offerings, ranging from weekends for *chocoholics* to guided tour packages featuring the art of China and Tibet. The Specialty Travel Index On-line (http://www.spectrav.com), provides an excellent on-line guide to packages covering about 350 special-interest activities ranging alphabetically from astronomy to zoology.[2] Chapter 7 mentioned the trend toward using vacation time to brush up on or otherwise pursue special interests.

Most of these special-interest packages require considerable prior research, careful programming, and expert instructors or guides. Normally, customers have neither the experience, the time, nor the resources to put these elements together. The packages offer a tailor-made alternative to satisfying their needs.

f. ***Added Dimension to Traveling and Dining Out.*** Programming adds an extra dimension, and sometimes a fresh appeal, to hospitality and travel services. Theme parks are masters of the art of programming. Many of them are highly dependent on repeat use from local residents. How can you get customers to come back if what you have to sell remains essentially the same? The answer lies in programming—constantly offering new entertainment, special events, and activities that renew and heighten customer interest. Parks such as Walt Disney World and Disneyland hold special parades, and birthday and other celebrations, to bring back past guests who otherwise would not return. Many restaurants also use programming successfully to induce customers to return more frequently (the dinner theatre is one good example, as are restaurants offering special-theme meals). Medieval Times is a chain of restaurants in the United States and Canada in which customers are treated to an exciting program of jousting, sword fights, and horseriding among knights while they eat dinner. This is an excellent example of turning a meal into a memorable experience through programming.

Crystal Cruises adds an extra dimension to traveling by cruise ship in its two theme cruises, *Computer University@Sea* and the *Crystal Wine & Food Festival*. In the *Computer University@Sea* cruise, computer industry experts provide lectures and participants are given hands-on instruction on major software programs. At the *Wine & Food Festival*, celebrated chefs provide cooking demonstrations, and wine experts give presentations and hold wine tasting sessions.

Programming adds excitement to the customer's experience and planning. It gives an added dimension to services that they find very appealing. A good example are the themed dinners or parties staged at conventions and other meetings. A specialized group of organizations in the hospitality and travel industry called **destination management companies (DMCs)** arrange these themed dinners or parties. The Association of Destination Management Executives (ADME) defines a DMC as "a professional services company possessing extensive local knowledge, expertise and resources, specializing in the design and implementation of events, activities, tours, transportation and program logistics."[3]

2. **Participant-Related Reasons.** The real beauty of packaging and programming is that they benefit both the customer and the package/program participants. These participants can include travel trade intermediaries (tour operators, travel agents, incentive travel planners), suppliers (lodging, restaurant, car rental, cruise line, and attraction organizations), and carriers (airlines, bus, train, and ferry companies). Whatever the mixture of participants, well-conceived and marketed packages and programs help build customer volumes and improve profitability.

a. ***Increased Business in Off-Peak Periods.*** One of the major reasons for organizing or participating in packages or programs is their ability to create demand at off-peak times. For many restaurants and bars, Mondays and Tuesdays are the

A Touch of Technology

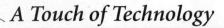

Specialty Travel Index http://www.spectrav.com

◆ The Specialty Travel Index claims to be the #1 source for adventure and special interest travel. It has been published continuously since 1980.

◆ The on-line version allows Web users to search its database either by activity, destination, or tour operator.

◆ This source contains information on more than 600 tour operators.

◆ Approximately 350 different activities and interests are included in the site.

◆ Some of the most obscure and less well-known activities include lloma packing, iceberg viewing, and spelunking.

◆ Other better-publicized activities are birdwatching, cooking schools, dude ranches and farm stays, ecotourism, gambling, and history tours.

◆ Some other interesting activities are brewery and whisky tours, cattle breeding, cigar tours, DHOW sailing, and perfumery tours.

lowest-volume days. Most city lodging properties have their poorest occupancies on weekends. Marriott and Renaissance's "Breakfast and Break-Free Weekend Rates" package is an excellent example of a customer inducement, based on a price reduction of 30 to 45 percent, to boost business at off-peak times (weekends).[4] Airlines experience their lowest load factors on weekends and outside the early-morning and late-afternoon rush times. Most resorts have great swings in business volumes by season. Good packages and programs help even out otherwise cyclical business patterns by creating new reasons for customers to use services.

b. ***Enhanced Appeal to Specific Target Markets.*** Packages and programs help participants hone in on selected target markets. Most of these packages and programs are tailor-made to fit the needs and desires of specific customer groups. There are numerous examples in the resort business, such as skiing packages for alpine and cross-country enthusiasts; golf and tennis packages; offerings for scuba divers, sailors, the health- and fitness-conscious; and many others. Many resorts also put together special package deals for organizations with conventions/meetings and incentive trips.

Two specific examples should help clarify this benefit. The Scottsdale Conference Resort developed a Media Center with $2 million of audio-visual and business office equipment. The appeal of this facility and the high-tech equipment is further enhanced by the availability of in-house skilled technicians and support personnel to help meeting planners stage even the most sophisticated productions.

The second example is Sandals *Wedding Planner* software program and the arrangements resorts make for either weddings or honeymoons at their facilities. The *Wedding Planner* assists in wedding planning and can be downloaded free of charge from Sandals' Web site. By providing this free service, plus all of the onsite arrangements at the resorts, Sandals has increased its appeal to this special-occasion market (see Figure 12–3).

c. ***Attraction of New Target Markets.*** As well as solidifying its appeal to existing target markets, a hospitality and travel business can use packages and programs to go after new target markets. A good example of this is in the cruise line business. Long the exclusive domain of vacationers, cruises are now being used by an increasing number of organizations for shipboard meetings, conventions, and incentive trips. Cruise line companies have developed a new target market by preparing and promoting packages to these groups.

d. ***Easier Business Forecasting and Improved Efficiency.*** Many packages are booked and paid for well in advance of the customer's visit. Because of this fact, the hospitality and travel business is in a better position to predict customer volumes and to schedule staff, supplies, and other resources with greater efficiency. However, there is also a related danger if a large number of cancellations are received close to arrival dates. In recent years, the hospitality and travel industry has done much to encourage *advance bookings* by their customers. This has been especially true among the airlines but has also been used with packaging. For example, First European Cruises offers $100 per person off the brochure fare if bookings and deposits are made 90 days in advance of the sailing date.

e. ***Use of Complementary Facilities, Attractions, and Events.*** This book makes frequent mention of the partnership concept (cooperative marketing of related hospitality and travel services). Many packages and programs provide excellent examples of this approach, as various groups meld their services into more marketable customer offerings.

  Packaging and programming offer a great opportunity to use travel demand generators (primary reasons for travel) creatively. For example, many hotels and restaurants combine their services with visits to key local attractions, events, and other activities. Many hotels in National Football League cities offer packages that include game tickets. Some Napa Valley lodging properties incorporate wine tours into their packages, whereas New York hotels add Broadway shows. Many restaurants offer dining-entertainment packages featuring the performing arts.

  Carriers and travel trade intermediaries also benefit from these arrangements, as do other categories of suppliers and destination marketing organizations. Many airlines, passenger rail, and bus companies themselves offer packages built around special events or attractions in the cities they serve. For example, ScotRail markets a package that includes rail and bus travel, and admission to New Lanark World Heritage Village in Scotland (Figure 12–4). The Greater Pittsburgh Convention & Visitors Bureau developed packages combining lodging with tickets to Pittsburgh Pirates baseball games.

f. ***Flexibility to Capitalize on New Market Trends.*** The physical facilities and equipment of many hospitality and travel organizations are fixed and cannot be altered significantly in the short term. Packaging and programming give these organizations the flexibility to capitalize on new market trends, often without having to make expensive physical changes. The adult-education packages offered by the Mohonk Mountain House in New Paltz, New York, provide an excellent example. The resort hotel, built in 1869, has focused on the trend toward people using vacation time to learn or otherwise enhance their education. It offers several such opportunities, including packages featuring personal health management, language-immersion programs, gardening, and birding.

◆ FIGURE 12–4
Using complementary attractions: Scrathclyde Passenger Transport and New Lanark World Heritage Village. (Courtesy of Strathclyde Passenger Transport)

g. ***Stimulation of Repeat and More Frequent Usage.*** This is the flip side of the previously mentioned customer benefit. New packaging and programming can rekindle and increase customers' interest in the service. Theme parks have already been mentioned as strong believers in keeping their entertainment offerings fresh by holding numerous special events. Several restaurants offer themed meals, gourmet dining and wine-tasting nights, and other events partly to bring customers back more regularly. Red Lobster, for example, features Lobster and Shrimp Festivals each year. The added dimension given to the service through programming and packaging benefits both the customer and the organization.

h. ***Increased Per Capita Spending and Lengths of Stay.*** Used correctly, packages and programs help hospitality and travel organizations increase both the average amount spent by customers and their lengths of stay. Again, many theme parks have perfected this technique. By adding live shows, holiday celebrations, or parades, they encourage guests to remain longer, and the customer who stays longer spends more. Pre- and post-convention tours at hotels and resorts are another excellent example. By offering side trips to local attractions or events, these packages extend convention/meeting guests' lengths of stay.

i. ***Public Relations and Publicity Value of Unique Packages.*** Chapter 18 takes a detailed look at public relations and publicity and their great long-term value to hospitality and travel organizations. Often businesses find that they have a limited variety of newsworthy items for the media to cover. Unique and creative packages grab the attention of newspapers, magazines, television, and radio stations. Packages that latch on to popular issues and trends (e.g., health/fitness packages, using personal computers, lifestyle and stress management, and personal financial management) frequently attract widespread media attention. Others, such as Star Trek Weekends, are so different that they appeal to the public's curiosity. Used correctly, packages can be very effective in generating greater publicity.

j. ***Increased Customer Satisfaction.*** The bottom line on packaging and programming is their contribution to greater customer satisfaction. Both concepts are true reflections of the marketing concept. They are tailor-made to fit specific customer needs and provide many useful benefits to travelers.

ROLE OF PACKAGING AND PROGRAMMING IN MARKETING

What roles do packaging and programming play in the marketing of hospitality and travel services? You already know from previous chapters that they can be part of an organization's marketing mix and, therefore, should figure in its marketing plan (remember the "How do we get there?" question). You may also have a good idea about their roles from the previous discussion on reasons for their popularity. Packages and programs perform the following five key roles in hospitality and travel marketing:

1. Smoothing patterns of business
2. Improving profitability
3. Assisting in use of segmented marketing strategies
4. Complementing other product/service-mix elements
5. Bringing together related hospitality and travel organizations

1. **Smoothing Patterns of Business.** Chapter 2 compared unsold inventories of services to water running down a drain. In fact, the pipe for unused services is eternal. The sale of such services is lost forever. One of the principal roles of packages and programs is to plug the drain and to even out the peaks and valleys in this often-cyclical business.

2. **Improving Profitability.** By smoothing out the kinks in business, packages and programs improve profitability. They also add to profits by doing the following:
   a. Increasing per capita spending
   b. Extending lengths of stay
   c. Generating new business
   d. Encouraging more frequent use and repeat use
   e. Improving efficiency through more accurate sales forecasting

3. **Assisting in Use of Segmented Marketing Strategies.** Chapter 8 highlighted the various marketing strategies, including the segmented approach. Packages and programs are a useful tool for segmenters who are trying to match their offerings to the needs of specific customer groups.

4. **Complementing Other Product/Service-Mix Elements.** Packages and programs are part of an organization's product/service mix. They are an important complement to the other elements, including facilities, equipment, and other services. In a way, they are much like product and gift packages—they make hospitality and travel services more attractive to customers. They *wrap up* the other product/mix elements into more appealing and marketable offerings.

5. **Bringing Together Related Hospitality and Travel Organizations.** When you think about the overall impact of packages and programs, you might come up with the word synergy. Synergism is the combined action of two or more factors, or in our case organizations, that produces a result that individually would not have been possible. A well-conceived, professionally promoted, and well-executed package does this for all its participants. It produces results that they could not match on their own. Packages bring together travel trade intermediaries, carriers, suppliers, and destination marketing groups. They are an excellent example of cooperative marketing (or *partnership*) in the industry.

PACKAGING CONCEPTS OFFERED BY INDUSTRY

Two major categories of packages are available from the hospitality and travel industry.

◆ **Packages Developed by Intermediaries**—Many travel trade intermediaries, including tour wholesalers and operators, incentive travel planners, some travel agents, and convention/meeting planners, put together packages.

◆ **Packages Developed by Others**—Other packages have been developed by suppliers, carriers, destination marketing organizations, various clubs, and special-interest groups. These packages can usually be purchased directly from the source (e.g., a hotel weekend package) and may or may not also be booked through a travel agent. In some instances, like many cruise packages, booking can only be done through travel agencies.

EXCELLENCE CASE

Programming:
Mohonk Mountain House

How can a resort opened in 1870 be a model of current thinking on trends, lifestyles, travel, and leisure activities? The answer, in the form of the Mohonk Mountain House located near New Paltz, New York, is through an innovative assortment of more than 30 vacation packages and programs, mostly featuring skilled instructors.

Some of Mohonk's most interesting *programs* and *packages* are its Tower of Babble, Self in Balance, and the Art of Chocolate. The Tower of Babble is a language immersion program taught by State University of New York professors. The languages offered range from French to Chinese.

Mohonk Mountain House also offers packages and programs found at many other resorts, including tennis camps, a summer tennis program, and a complete children's program. The resort was one of the originators of the *murder mystery* weekend, having begun these in 1977. Approximately 300 guests participate in these plots, whose hosts and speakers have included Stephen King, Martin Cruz Smith, and Donald E. Westlake.

What sets Mohonk Mountain House apart from other resorts is the great variety and topical themes of many of its programs. Mohonk has several packages for people interested in using vacation and leisure time to improve their educations or certain skills. *Programming* gives this property an added dimension by creating activities and events that satisfy the special interests of certain people.

The following theme Programs were scheduled for the Mohonk Mountain House in 2001:

Midweek Rejuvenation Special	Midweek January February, March, April
Argentine Tango and the Dances of Latin America (New)	March 23–25
A Taste of Italy with Kevin Zraly (New)	March 30–April 1
Tower of Babble	March 30–April 1
Cousin Brucie Rocks Around the Clock '50s and '60s Nostalgia Weekend	April 6–8
Children's Easter Special . . . Midweek (Children Stay Free)	April 8–12, 15–19, 2001
Family Festival	April 13–15, 2001
Springtime Awakening: Couples Romantic Getaway	April 20–22, 2001
Birding and Spring Nature	May 11–13, 2001
Hiker's Holiday	May 13–18, 2001
Mohonk Adult Tennis Camps	June, July, August
Senior Tennis Program	June and September
Walker's and Runner's Rally	June 8–10, 2001
Summer Nature Week	June 18–22, 2001
Birding and Spring Nature	May 11–13, 2001
Hiker's Holiday	May 13–18, 2001
Mohonk Adult Tennis Camps	June, July, August
Senior Tennis Program	June and September
Walker's and Runners' Rally	June 8–10, 2001
Summer Nature Week	June 18–22, 2001
Garden Holiday	August 26–31, 2001
Artist's Inspiration	September 7–9, 2001
Hudson Valley Harvest: A Culinary Tribute	September 14–16, 2001
Halloween Haunts and Happenings	October 26–28, 2001
The Wonderful World of Words	November 2–4, 2001
A Celebration of Readers and Their Favorite Books	November 9–11, 2001

continued

EXCELLENCE CASE *continued*

(Photo by and courtesy of Ruth Smiley)

Tower of Babble	November 16–18, 2001
Couples' Romantic Getaway	November 16–18, 2001
Ballroom Dancing	November 30– December 2, 2001
Holistic Way	December 7–9, 2001
Christmas Gala	December 14–16, 2001
Children's Holiday Special (Children Stay Free)	December 20–22, 2001

Notice that these packages and programs generally occur at traditionally off-peak times for most resorts. They fill in the valleys in business for this 12-month operation, and account for about 20 percent of its annual volume. Mohonk Mountain House is truly an artistic case study in blending travel and leisure trends with solid business economics.

Discussion Questions

1. What are the benefits of the programs offered at Mohonk Mountain House to its occupancy rates and profitability?
2. What creative ideas has Mohonk Mountain House used in designing its programs?
3. What could other lodging and travel organizations learn from the packaging and programming done by Mohonk Mountain House?

Web Site

http://www.mohonk.com/

Packages can also be classified in four different ways:

1. By package elements
2. By target market
3. By package duration or timing
4. By travel arrangements or destination

1. **Classification by Package Elements.**
    a. *All-Inclusive Packages.* The all-inclusive package is a generic term for packages that include all or nearly all the elements that travelers require for their trips, including airfare, lodging, ground transportation, meals, recreation and entertainment, taxes, and gratuities. The packages offered by the cruise lines and Club Med are of this type, as are those provided by many other offshore resorts and destinations.
    b. *Escorted Tours.* The key word here is tour. Escorted tours follows a predetermined itinerary, and tour escorts or guides accompany travelers. These packages are usually all inclusive, but may have some optional (e.g., special side trips) or *on-your-own* (e.g., arrange your own meals or activities) elements. Most motor-coach packages fit into this category and include motor-coach transportation, lodging, meals, and admissions to various attractions and entertainment facilities. Even prestigious organizations such as the Smithsonian, American Museum of Natural History, and National Geographic Society are in the escorted tour business. The American Museum of Natural History's Discovery Tours and National Geographic Expeditions provide professional escorts, accommodations, meals, excursions, and expert lectures.
    c. *Fly-Drive Packages.* Fly-drive packages are single-price packages that include return-trip airfare and a rental car at destinations. For example, the Lufthansa/Avis *flyDRIVE Classics* provides air travel from the United States to Germany or Austria, plus a rental car for five or more days. These packages appeal to travelers who like to put together their own travel plans within a destination area.
    d. *Fly-Cruise Packages.* Fly-cruise packages include return airfare to a port of departure, plus a cruise. Many cruise lines advertise *free* or *low-cost* airfares from gateway airports to departure ports. Free air travel is seldom a reality, however. Although it is discounted, the airfare is usually buried in the total package price.
    e. *Fly-Rail Packages.* Fly-rail packages are a combination of air and railway travel. An example in the United States is Amtrak's Air-Rail Travel Plan, in which passengers travel by train on one leg of their trip and by air on the other leg with United Airlines, at one all-inclusive price. Introduced in 1991, this quickly became one of Amtrak's top-selling packages.[5]
    f. *Rail-Drive Packages.* Rail-drive packages involve transportation by train combined with a rental car at the destination.
    g. *Accommodation and Meal Packages.* Most resorts and certain other lodging properties promote packages that incorporate one or more nights of accommodation, plus a specified number of meals. For example, American Plan (AP) rates include three meals each day—typically breakfast, lunch, and dinner. Modified American Plan (MAP) packages provide two meals daily, normally allowing guests to arrange their own lunches (Figure 12–5).
       Bed and Breakfast (B&B) rates combine a night's accommodation with breakfast the following day. A variant of B&B packages is the continental plan (CP), which includes a continental (cold) breakfast. Finally, the term European Plan (EP) rate implies that no meals are provided with the accommodations.
    h. *Event Packages.* Every year, special one-time events, festivals, entertainment and cultural performances, or other occurrences take place in North America

Package Type	Abbreviation	Number of Meals Included	Meal Type
American Plan	AP	3	B, L, D
Modified American Plan	MAP	2	B, D
Bed and Breakfast	B&B	1	B (cooked)
Continental Plan	CP	1	B (cold)
European Plan	EP	0	—

◆ **FIGURE 12–5**　*Summary profile of accommodation and meal packages.*

and throughout the world. They present the industry with a considerable store of packaging and programming opportunities. These include major sports championships such as the Olympic, Pan American, and Commonwealth games, the Americas, World, and Grey cups; the Super Bowl; the World Series; and various NCAA college football bowl games. There are also numerous large festivals and celebrations such as Oberammagau, New Orleans' Mardi Gras, the Rio Carnival, and the Edinburgh Festival. Once-in-a-lifetime occurrences, such as viewing Halley's Comet, also have great packaging potential. Event packages may be simple transportation-plus-admission offerings, but may also provide on-site lodging and meals.

i. *Packages With Programming for Special Interests.* The primary attraction of these packages are the special activities, programs, and events arranged by one or more of the participants. This can be sports and sports instruction (tennis, golf, sailing, boardsailing, scuba diving, mountaineering, etc.), hobbies or other pastimes (gourmet cooking, wine appreciation, photography, fine arts, crafts, etc.), and continuing and self-education topics (e.g., computers, money management, coping with stress, literature, foreign languages, cultural history, medicine, etc.). Just as in the popular movie "City Slickers," you can participate in a cattle drive in the Western United States courtesy of a number of ranch operations who provide this service. Avid fans of baseball can achieve their dreams in the field by attending *fantasy baseball camps,* where they may play against former or current baseball stars.[6] Special-interest packages are normally offered by lodging properties as an extension of basic accommodation and meals packages.

j. *Local Attraction or Entertainment Packages.* These typically do not include a lodging component and are aimed at local area customers. Examples are restaurant/theatre, theme park/meal, and tour/meal packages.

2. **Classification by Target Market.** These are packages specifically developed to meet the needs of certain target markets. They include the following:

a. *Incentive Packages or Tours.* Chapter 7 pinpointed incentive travel as a major growth market. Incentive packages are assembled by a variety of groups and individuals, including travel trade intermediaries (full-service incentive companies, specialized incentive travel-planning firms, travel agents, corporate travel managers, convention/meeting planners), suppliers (lodging chains, cruise lines, and some theme parks), airlines, and destination marketing organizations (some government tourism agencies and convention and visitors bureaus). The packages are all inclusive, and all expenses are paid for the groups or individuals who travel. Companies, associations, and other groups buy the packages, usually as a reward for outstanding sales achievements, new product introductions, or fund raising.

b. *Convention/Meeting Packages.* Almost all resorts, hotels, and conference centers provide packages to attract conventions and other meetings. Normally, convention/meeting packages include accommodations and meals, but they may also include some local tours or attraction admissions, or special events or programs. Programming is often a key feature of meetings and conventions. Earlier, you heard about the special theme parties staged at events. The programs are often recreational—the resort or hotel arranges golf or tennis tournaments for the group.

c. *Affinity Group Packages or Tours.* Affinity group packages are arranged for groups that share some form of *affinity,* usually a close social, religious, or ethnic bond. Examples include packages developed for university alumni associations, church groups, the handicapped, racial and ethnic minorities, service clubs, and other social and recreation clubs or associations.

d. *Family Vacation Packages.* Family vacation packages provide something for everyone in parent-child households. Frequently, they incorporate special programming for the children. For example, several cruise lines including Disney and Carnival have developed specially supervised programs within packages for children. Similarly, Hyatt Hotels' *Camp Hyatt* concept offers special activities and amenities for children.

e. *Packages for Special-Interest Groups.* These were discussed earlier under the first classification scheme. Refer to that section for more information on these types of packages.

3. **Classification by Package Duration or Timing.** A third way to categorize packages is by their length or timing. Some examples follow:
   a. Weekend and minivacation packages (packages for weekends, or for a period of less than six nights)
   b. Holiday packages (packages at public and other holidays. e.g., Christmas, New Year's, Memorial Day, Labor Day)
   c. Seasonal packages (winter, spring, summer, and fall packages)
   d. Pre- and post-convention packages and tours (packages tagged on, before or at the end of conventions or meetings)
   e. Other specific-length packages or tours (e.g., a one- or two-week package)
   f. Off-peak specials (packages advertised as travel bargains because they occur in off-peak periods)

4. **Classification by Travel Arrangements or Destination.** Packages can also be classified by the manner in which they are arranged. Examples include:
   a. Foreign Independent Tour (FIT)—A special package arranged by travel agents or other foreign independent travel specialists that fits individual clients' needs while they are traveling in foreign countries.

Did You Know?

Package Power from USTOA

✓ Early in 2000, the United States Tour Operators Association (USTOA) introduced an Internet-based, e-commerce program called *USTOA Package Power.*

✓ This program is for retail travel agencies, not consumers.

✓ It provides agents with Electronic Brochures on USTOA's members giving each operator's profile and tour itineraries.

✓ *Package Power* allows travel agencies to make online bookings with some USTOA members.

✓ http://www.ustoapackagepower.com/

   b. Group Inclusive Tour (GIT)—An all-inclusive package with a specified minimum size involving one or more groups traveling on scheduled or chartered air service.

   c. Charter Tour—A trip or package where the aircraft or other equipment is chartered by a tour wholesaler, tour operator, other individual, or group.

   d. Destination Package—A package can be categorized by the destination areas it features. Magazines for travel agents often have special inserts on packages to Hawaii, Florida, California, the Caribbean, Bermuda, Europe, South America, the Orient, and other destinations.

STEPS IN DEVELOPING EFFECTIVE PACKAGES

You now have a good idea of why packages are so popular, the roles they play, and the types of packages available. The next item on our agenda is to look at the mechanics of developing packages. What makes a package successful? The simple answer, just as for any good recipe, is the right ingredients, combined and prepared in the best way possible and served in an attractive, appealing manner. Before we look at this step by step, we should address some preliminary questions and concerns.

Potential Packaging Problems and Concerns

Some packages prove to be unprofitable or below customer expectations. Two major concerns are financial viability (will the package produce a profit?) and the loss of total control over the customer's experience (will the other participants deliver a level of service consistent with ours?). Because most packages involve price discounts, suppliers and carriers must also worry about displacing those customers who pay regular rates or fares in favor of lower-paying customers.

There is the risk of blocking space (groups of rooms or seats) and then having cancellations or below-expected package sales. This often happens and there is insufficient time to resell the space set aside.

Another worry is that the package customers will be incompatible with our other target markets. Mixing a planeload of delegates to a Christian conference in with customers on a Las Vegas gambling spree or en route to the Super Bowl may not be the best idea. Simultaneously housing a hunting convention and a Greenpeace conference also seems to be a combination laden with problems.

Will the packaging support or detract from our chosen positioning approach? This is a very real problem for companies that choose to provide luxury hospitality and travel services. Will they turn off their regular customers who pay high prices by offering cutrate packages? On the other hand, can a budget-oriented company modify its image sufficiently to market higher-priced packages successfully?

Although we will leave you to ponder these tricky questions, they do bring us to the main point of this discussion. Packaging and programming must be consistent with and support the chosen marketing strategy, target markets, positioning approach(es), and marketing objectives. Of course, they must also meet the basic goal of marketing—to satisfy customers' needs and wants at a profit.

Ingredients of Successful Packages

A package is a mixture of hospitality and travel elements, often provided by more than one participant organization. Putting together a successful package is similar to cooking, in that a lower-quality ingredient often spoils the flavor and taste of the overall experience. These ingredients are the hallmarks of successful packages, and they must do the following:

1. **Include Attractions or Demand-Generators.** Every package needs one or more core attractions or other demand-generators, whether it is tickets to a New York Giants game or a visit to Lourdes. The simplest core appeal is reduced prices, an approach used in many hotel weekend packages. Some packages, such as escorted tours, include several attractions or destinations.

2. **Provide Value to the Customer.** Customers buy packages because they perceive that they will receive greater value for the travel dollars they spend. For many, value translates into a total package that costs less than the sum of the regular prices of its individual elements. Others measure value by the calibre and variety of the package elements. For example, wine lovers put a high value on hearing lectures from recognized wine experts and having complimentary wine tasting built into the package price. Murder-mystery fanatics attach added value to the presence of a famous author, whereas chocoholics swoon on the quantities of their favorite substance made available.

   Almost all of us can be hooked by the words *free* or *complimentary*. We are intrigued by the prospect of getting something for nothing. Packages with *free* or *complimentary* elements have added value and appeal.

3. **Offer Consistent Quality and Compatibility Among Elements.** Successful packages provide consistent quality and compatibility in their elements. Earlier, we pointed out that customers buy packages partly because they expect this consistency. If inconsistencies are found in the levels of service or in the quality of facilities, customers are very likely to notice them. They are apt to judge the entire *package*

experience on the quality of an inconsistent element or service. Here is an example to prove the point. A young couple bought a one-week package in the Caribbean from a company that offered a high-quality experience on a small sailing ship. They had a fabulous time on the ship. However, service on the airline that carried them to the departure port was below par. Flights were delayed en route, and no one on the airline's staff made a special effort to compensate them for their long waiting time in the airport. Their entire vacation experience was spoiled because the airline's service did not match the personal attention and quality service that they received from the sailing-boat operator.

4. **Be Well Planned and Coordinated.** An excellent package is carefully planned and coordinated to fit the customer's needs as closely as possible. The Club Med concept again provides a great example. Their underlying concept, and packages, are planned to allow vacationers to relax completely and to escape from their humdrum or high-stress everyday lives. Newspapers, televisions, radios, and telephones are banished from all Club Med villages. Sports activities, instruction, and entertainment are very well planned and coordinated. These items are, in fact, programmed for the maximum enjoyment of GMs (Gentils Membres—the Club's name for its guests). From the opening welcome ceremony staged by the GOs (Gentils Organisateurs—the Club's employees) to the seating arrangements that ensure that GMs get to know each other, the Club Med vacation package is planned and coordinated to provide the most enjoyable experience possible.

5. **Provide a Distinctive Customer Benefit.** The best packages give customers something they would not get if they purchased the hospitality and travel elements separately. Often this distinctive benefit is the offer of value for money as shown earlier in the *Two for Breakfast Weekend* offered by Marriott. A lower-than-normal price is not always the benefit that appeals to customers the most. It can be a ticket to see a famous entertainer or a major sports event, a lecture by a famous author or historian, or a gift certificate to a plush department store. The key appeal here is that these features or programs are not readily available to individual customers. The package provides a unique and convenient way for customers to gain access to these programs or services.

6. **Cover All the Details.** In many cases, it is simple to throw together a package, but it is the attention to minute and sometimes seemingly trivial details that make excellent packages stand out. What happens if customers have to cancel because of unexpected circumstances? What if there is no snow when you arrive for your ski vacation? What if you or your companion do not want to visit one of the attractions on the itinerary? What if it rains every day during your tropical vacation? These are just a few of the problems that can happen and that must be anticipated by the package planner.

   Making sure that all the details are covered is almost like assuming that Murphy's Law ("if anything can go wrong, it will") will prevail, a too-gloomy perspective for many people. However, it is the attention to these details that often produces the most satisfied customers and positive word-of-mouth advertising. Another example proves this point. An elderly couple booked an escorted package tour offered by a leading tour operator to the Galapagos Islands and Peru. While on the trip, the woman was advised by a doctor that the side trip to Machu Picchu in the Peruvian Andes might adversely affect her health. The tour wholesaler had anticipated this possibility, and refunded the cost of the Machu Picchu trip. The couple were greatly impressed by the wholesaler's forethought and fairness, and have told many acquaintances about the company's professionalism and high regard for its individual customers. What this illustrates is that it is often the little things that a business does for customers that matter the most.

There are several key factors to be considered in covering all the details:

a. Having a clear policy on deposits, cancellations, and refunds

b. Offering customers the maximum amount of flexibility in booking dates and optional activities

c. Providing complete information on all package elements included in the price, items not included, clothing or equipment needed, substitutions allowed and options available, reservation procedures, minimum group sizes (if applicable), single room supplements (additional charges for a single room), policy and charges regarding children accompanying adults, contingency arrangements in case of weather or other problems, and other specific data

7. **Generate a Profit.** Although packages are a marvelous way to satisfy a customer's needs and wants, they must also generate a profit. Many packages offered by the industry have turned into financial disasters. In most cases, packages really represent a type of price discounting and must follow the same rules. A more detailed look at pricing comes later, but for now it is enough to say that services generally should not be included in packages if they are priced below their variable (direct) costs. The ideal times to offer packages are when other demand sources are at their minimum or are nonexistent, and when they do not displace higher-revenue-generating customers

Pricing Packages

How do you give the customer the right amount of value, yet still make an acceptable profit? The answer lies in a careful, step-by-step approach to package pricing employing the break-even analysis technique (making pricing decisions based upon the consideration of fixed and variable costs, customer volumes, and profit margins):

1. Identify and quantify fixed costs
2. Identify and quantify variable costs
3. Calculate total package costs per person
4. Add a mark-up for profit
5. Calculate the single supplement

1. **Identify and Quantify Fixed Costs.** Fixed costs will be the same no matter how many customers buy the package. They include the costs of developing and mailing special brochures, media advertisements, and certain package elements (e.g., tour escort salary and travel expenses, chartered transportation equipment, speakers' fees, and so on). If the package is unescorted and includes no transportation to the destination (e.g., the typical hotel weekend package), the fixed costs are usually only those for producing and mailing brochures, advertising, and fixed-payment or *lump-sum* elements such as entertainers and blocks of tickets. The real beauty of weekend packages for hotels is that, except for these items, packages add only a very minimal amount to other fixed costs. The hotel only needs to worry about covering

variable costs once the upfront expenses are matched. The hotel may want to add a small amount of overhead expenses to the other fixed costs to cover such items as administrative and maintenance costs.

2. **Identify and Quantify Variable Costs.** Variable or direct costs vary directly with the number of customers who buy the package. For the hotel weekend package, these costs are primarily for the housekeeping of rooms, meals included, *giveaways* (e.g., bottles of wine or champagne, gift certificates, fruit baskets, tote bags), and other items that will be expensed per person or per room. Some hotel weekend packages are commissionable (pay commissions to travel agents who reserve them for their clients) and commission expenses vary directly with the number of travel agent bookings.

   The range of variable costs is more extensive for wholesalers, travel agents, and others who assemble packages and tours. Typically, these costs include the following:[7]
   a. Hotel room rates
   b. Airfares
   c. Meals
   d. Tips, gratuities, or service charges
   e. Entrance or admission fees
   f. Sightseeing tours
   g. Taxes

3. **Calculate Total Package Costs Per Person.** You now have two cost estimates: (1) the total fixed costs that will have to be paid no matter how many packages are sold and (2) the total variable costs per person, which change directly with the number of guests. Because your goal is to come up with a package price per person, you must express the fixed costs on this basis as well. Doing this means estimating the number of customers who are expected to buy the package. But how do you do this? Should you use the maximum, the minimum, or a middle-range figure? The least risky and recommended route is to use the minimum expected or, alternatively, to make your best projection and then cut this by approximately 25 to 30 percent.[8,9] Once you have calculated the expected number of buyers, divide the total fixed costs (plus any allocation of overhead) by that number.

4. **Add a Markup for Profit.** Many different types of organizations in the hospitality and travel industry put together packages. They do so with one common thought in mind—to make a profit. How this profit is made varies by type of organization:
   a. **Packages Developed by Intermediaries**
      - If the package planner is a tour wholesaler or incentive travel company, then none of the package elements has provided a profit thus far. A "markup" must be added, either as a percentage or a fixed amount. Normally, the markup is made on the "land portion" only, meaning that airfares are not marked up.
      - Travel agents who assemble packages are compensated through the commissions earned on various package elements.
   b. **Packages Developed by Others**
      - Suppliers and carriers that develop packages make their money from the elements they supply (e.g., rooms, meals, airfare, car rental, cruise). Their profit is built into the costs they have calculated for these package elements.

   In tour wholesaler and incentive travel-company packages, the markup is usually from 10 percent to 30 percent. The company, therefore, adds an amount equal to this percentage of the variable and fixed costs per person (excluding, if appropriate, the airfare) to arrive at the final per-person package price.

5. **Calculate the Single Supplement.** Most packages and tours are sold on a shared-room or double-occupancy basis, and prices are quoted this way. To give customers maximum flexibility, packages can normally be booked, with an added charge, on a single-occupancy basis. In the travel trade, this additional amount is known as the single supplement. It is equal to the difference between the single- and double-room rate on a per-person basis times the number of nights, plus taxes, service charges/gratuities, and markup (if appropriate).

6. **Calculate the Break-Even Point.** The last step in pricing a package is to calculate the break-even point. This is the point at which the total revenues earned from the package exactly equal the sum of the total costs (fixed and variable) and the desired profits. In the hospitality and travel industry, it is traditional to express the break-even point in terms of a number of guests or tour patrons.[10] The exact formula for calculation is discussed in Chapter 19.

CHAPTER CONCLUSION

The hospitality and travel industry's version of packaging is unique, and the increased popularity of packaging has been one of the major industry trends over the past few decades. Part of the reason is that packages provide benefits to both customers and participating organizations. They make for a better fit between customers' needs and available services. At the same time, packages help the industry deal with the problem of perishability by creating business at otherwise low-volume periods.

Programming is related to packaging, and it also adds to the appeal of hospitality and travel services. Programming often occurs within packages, but it can also be done on its own.

REVIEW QUESTIONS

1. What do the terms packaging and programming mean? Are they related and, if so, how?
2. Why have packages and programs increased in popularity in the past 30 years?
3. What five key roles do packaging and programming play in marketing hospitality and travel services?
4. What are the two main categories of packages found in the industry?
5. Which three additional factors can be used to classify packages? What types of packages are included in these three groups?
6. What are the seven steps to be followed in developing effective packages?
7. What procedures must be followed to establish the price of a package?
8. Does programming always occur within packages and, if not, what are some examples of stand-alone programs?

CHAPTER ASSIGNMENTS

1. You are the marketing director of a small resort. The resort does very well in the summer and winter, but business drops off significantly in the spring and fall. Develop five or six creative packages that you would introduce to boost fall and spring business. What

elements would you include in these packages? What prices would you charge, and how would you market the packages? What would be the target markets? How would you measure the success of each package?

2. Visit a travel agency and collect the brochures for five or six competitive packages (e.g., cruise vacations, resort packages, hotel weekend packages). Compare the elements in each package. Are they exactly the same or, if not, how do they differ? How do the prices compare? Do any of the packages include programming? Which package do you think is the best? Why? How could you improve these packages?

3. The owner of a restaurant or attraction in your community has asked you to suggest some potential programs to increase sales. What steps would you follow in developing these programming ideas? Suggest five or six programs that could be used. Try to prove that the added costs of the programs will be justified by increased profits. How would the restaurant or attraction benefit from offering the programs?

4. This chapter explains that packages can be categorized by package elements, target market, duration or timing, or travel arrangements or destination. Do some research and find at least three examples of each of the four categories of packages (other than those mentioned in the chapter). You may select examples from your local region, or you may want to pick a specific part of our industry (e.g., resorts or airlines). Provide a description of each of the packages you find.

WORLD WIDE WEB RESOURCES

American Museum of Natural History
http://www.amnh.org/

Association of Destination Management Executives (ADME)
http://www.adme.org/

Crystal Cruises
http://www.crystalcruises.com/

First European Cruises
http://www.first-european.com/

Medieval Times
http://www.medievaltimes.com/

Mohonk Mountain House
http://www.mohonk.com/

National Geographic Society
http://www.nationalgeographic.com/

New Lanark Village
http://www.newlanark.org/

Scottsdale Conference Resort
http://www.scottsconf.com/scottsdale/

Smithsonian
http://www.si.edu/

Specialty Travel Index
http://www.spectrav.com/

Strathclyde Passenger Transport
http://www.spt.co.uk/

United States Tour Operators Association (USTOA)
http://www.ustoapackagepower.com/

Via Rail
http://www.viarail.ca/en.index.html

REFERENCES

1. Potter, Everett. "The price is right." *Cruise Vacation Planner,* Volume 2 (1999):62.
2. http://www.spectrav.com/
3. http://www.adme.org/
4. "Hotel executives reveal their winning marketing strategies." *Travel Weekly.* (November 9, 1992):52.
5. "Amtrak: air-rail plan struck chord with agents, consumers." *Travel Weekly* 51(91): 33–34 (1992).
6. Rosen, Fred. "Field of dreams." *Meetings & Conventions* 27(2): 102–106 (1992).
7. Sarbey de Souto, Martha. 1993. *Group Travel.* 2nd ed. Albany, N.Y.: Delmar, 142–145.

8. Sarbey de Souto, Martha. 1993. *Group Travel,* 2nd ed. Albany, N.Y.: Delmar, 140–141.

9. Tourism Canada. 1986. *Tourism is your business: Marketing management.* Ottawa, Ontario: Tourism Canada, 125.

10. Poynter, James M. 1993. *Tour Design, Marketing, & Management.* Englewood Cliffs, N.J.: Regents/Prentice Hall, 34.

For additional hospitality and travel marketing resources, visit our Web site at **www.Hospitality-Tourism.delmar.com**

13

The Distribution Mix and the Travel Trade

How Do We Get There?

Objectives

Having read this chapter, you should be able to:

◆ Define the terms distribution mix and travel trade.

◆ Explain why the distribution mixes in the hospitality and travel industry are different from those in other industries.

◆ List the major travel trade intermediaries.

◆ Explain the roles played by each of the major travel trade intermediaries.

◆ Identify the major on–line travel services and the customer benefits in using them.

◆ List the steps involved in marketing to the travel trade.

Overview

What is the best way to deliver hospitality and travel services to customers? As you already know, except for home delivery of certain foods, there is no physical distribution system in this industry. Services are intangible. They cannot be shipped from point A to point B. Companies and other organizations either provide their services directly to customers or indirectly through one or more travel trade intermediaries.

The industry's distribution system is both complex and unique. It is unique because of the influence that travel intermediaries have on customers' choices. It is complex because of the diversity of organizations involved and their relationships with each other. This chapter takes an in-depth look at the industry's distribution channels and the roles played by the key organizations involved. The new distribution tools via the Internet are discussed. They are quickly changing how distribution is accomplished in the hospitality and travel industry.

Key Terms

appointed	disintermediation	on-line travel services
channel of distribution	distribution channel	preferred suppliers or vendors
commission caps	distribution mix	retail travel agents
convention/meeting planners	e-commerce	tour operator
corporate travel agency	incentive travel	tour wholesaler
corporate travel managers	incentive travel planners	trade advertising
cruise-only agents	indirect distribution	travel trade
direct distribution	inplant	travel trade intermediaries

Drive along any major highway and you will see many trucks delivering products to retail stores, to wholesale warehouses, or to other locations for further processing and manufacturing. Check any good-sized airport and you will notice that several cargo planes are taking off and landing. If a railway passes through your town, you might be acutely aware of the seemingly endless freight trains lumbering by. What you are witnessing is the physical distribution of products from many large companies. The hospitality and travel industry's distribution system is not as visible, however, because our *products* are intangible. The only outward sign of a distribution system may be one or more travel agencies in your area.

Although our industry's distribution system is largely invisible, it is every bit as important as the one for the manufacturing and packaged-goods industry. The travel trade intermediaries in the distribution system provide many benefits, both for customers and the other industry groups. Their knowledge and expertise make the customer's travel experience more satisfying and enjoyable. Their services, retail outlets, and promotions greatly increase sales and awareness for carriers, suppliers, and destinations.

THE DISTRIBUTION MIX AND THE TRAVEL TRADE

This book has already talked about the marketing mix, the promotional mix, and the product/service mix. The **distribution mix** is similar to these concepts. It is the combination of the direct and indirect distribution channels that a hospitality and travel organization uses to make customers aware of its services and to reserve and deliver them. **Direct distribution** occurs when the organization assumes total responsibility for promoting, reserving, and providing services to customers. Generally, this applies to suppliers and carriers when they do not work with any **travel trade intermediaries** collectively known as the **travel trade**. For example, some hotel weekend packages can only be booked directly through the hotel itself. **Indirect distribution** occurs when part of the responsibility for promoting, reserving, and providing services is given to one or more other hospitality and travel organizations. Usually these other groups are travel trade intermediaries. A **channel of distribution** is a particular direct or indirect distribution arrangement used by a supplier, carrier, or destination marketing organization.

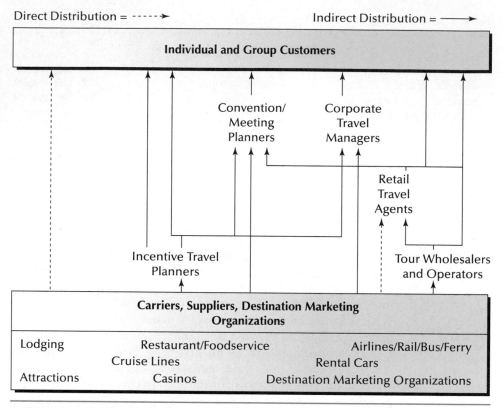

Direct Distribution = - - - - →   Indirect Distribution = ⟶

Individual and Group Customers

Convention/Meeting Planners   Corporate Travel Managers

Retail Travel Agents

Incentive Travel Planners

Tour Wholesalers and Operators

Carriers, Suppliers, Destination Marketing Organizations

Lodging	Restaurant/Foodservice	Airlines/Rail/Bus/Ferry
	Cruise Lines	Rental Cars
Attractions	Casinos	Destination Marketing Organizations

◆ **FIGURE 13–1**   *The hospitality and travel distribution system. NOTE: Direct distribution includes on-line bookings made through the Web sites of suppliers and carriers, as well as those of on-line travel services.*

Figure 13–1 visually displays the concepts of direct and indirect distribution. It also highlights the following five major travel trade intermediaries:

1. Retail travel agents
2. Tour wholesalers and operators
3. Corporate travel managers and agencies
4. Incentive travel planners
5. Convention/meeting planners

Let us take a more detailed look at these intermediaries to clarify the distribution-mix concept further. As Figure 13–1 illustrates, carriers and suppliers are the foundation of the hospitality and travel distribution system, because they provide the transportation and destination services that customers require. Individual carriers and suppliers normally use more than one channel of distribution in their distribution mixes, and they use both direct and indirect distribution. For example, most major airlines promote directly to individual pleasure and business travelers, as well as to corporate and other group customers. They take reservations and issue tickets directly to customers, if customers so desire.

Travelers can also choose to make reservations through retail travel agents and to have their airline tickets delivered by the agencies (an indirect distribution channel for airlines). As you will see later, this constitutes a major portion of most agencies' business volumes. Airlines also frequently work through the other four intermediaries, promoting directly in their specialized trade journals and participating in packages created by tour wholesalers/operators, incentive travel planners, corporate travel managers/agencies, and convention/meeting planners. Again, these are indirect distribution channels for airlines.

Lodging chains can also be used to illustrate this concept. If you choose, you can make a hotel reservation directly with your destination hotel or you can use the chain's Website or central reservation system. You can also book indirectly through a travel agency or airline. Finally, you may get a reservation indirectly through the efforts of a tour wholesaler/operator, incentive travel planner, corporate travel planner, or convention/ meeting planner. Why is it that suppliers and carriers do not use direct distribution all the time? The simple answer is that using several distribution channels and intermediaries generally broadens the impact and effectiveness of in-house marketing plans. Intermediaries function almost like an external reservations and sales staff. Their specific roles and benefits include the following:

1. **Retailing the services of suppliers, carriers, and other intermediaries at locations convenient for travelers.** No supplier, carrier, or other intermediary could afford to have tens of thousands of retail sales outlets such as there are in many developed countries. Independent and chain travel agencies perform this important function, and thus provide a major benefit to other industry groups.

2. **Expanding the distribution network for suppliers, carriers, and other intermediaries.** The net effect of the activities of all intermediaries is to provide more channels for distributing the services of carriers, suppliers, and, in some cases, other intermediaries. This creates greater awareness of their services, while it expands their internal reservations/booking capacity.

3. **Providing specialized, knowledgeable advice to travelers on destinations, prices, facilities, schedules, and services.** Travel trade intermediaries are specialists and experts at their work. Customers view them as being one step removed from carriers, suppliers, and other intermediaries. Travel agents especially are perceived as having large quantities of information and knowledge on hospitality and travel services. Their professional advice and recommendations influence customer choices of suppliers, carriers, and other intermediaries. Positive relationships with agencies often have rich paybacks for other industry groups.

4. **Coordinating corporate travel arrangements to maximize the efficiency of corporations' travel expenditures.** Corporate travel departments and travel agents who coordinate corporate clients' accounts produce rich benefits for the organizations they serve. They are *in-house* advisors to business travelers and perform a function similar to the one that retail travel agents perform for pleasure travelers.

5. **Assembling vacation packages by bringing together an array of destinations and the services of suppliers and carriers at all-inclusive prices.** Chapter 12 highlighted the benefits of packaging for customers and various groups within the hospitality and travel industry. Some travel intermediaries, especially tour wholesalers and operators, are experts at doing this type of thing. They make supplier and carrier services more attractive to customers by tailor-making vacations to fit these customers' needs. Travel agents often assist individual and group travelers by putting together foreign independent tours and packages (e.g., FITs) for them.

6. **Tailor-making incentive travel trips for corporations and others.** Incentive travel planners are professionals at developing these special trips. They fill a need for corporations and other groups by *manufacturing* experiences that are lucrative to potential travel recipients. Again, the suppliers and carriers that participate in incentive packages find that, by using the expertise of this intermediary, their services are better molded to fit client needs.

7. **Organizing and coordinating conventions, conferences, and meetings for associations, corporations, and other organizations.** Corporate, association, government, and other convention/meeting planners package supplier and carrier services for their organizations. Like other professionals who assemble vacation and incentive packages, these experts provide for a better fit between their organizations' needs and the available hospitality and travel services.

8. **Operating and guiding group tours.** Certain travel intermediaries offer guide and escort services. In doing so, they enrich and enhance travelers' experiences.

Although one of the five types of travel trade intermediaries takes the lead in performing each one of these eight roles, many organizations take on more than one role. For example, whereas tour wholesalers play the lead role in assembling vacation packages, many travel agents also perform the tour wholesaling function. Another example of multiple role-playing is the corporate travel manager who also acts as the firm's meeting planner. You might now be getting the idea that the hospitality and travel distribution system is very complex. This complexity is quite evident from the structure of some of the industry's *giants*. Companies such as American Express, Carlson Wagonlit Travel, and Maritz Travel each have several divisions that perform different travel trade intermediary roles, including travel agencies, incentive travel planning, and tour wholesaling.

INDIVIDUAL TRAVEL INTERMEDIARIES

As the new millennium dawned, the distribution of hospitality and travel services was vastly different than it had been just years earlier. The Internet emerged as a viable distribution channel during the 1990s and, along with sophisticated on-line database programs, caused a trend that some call disintermediation (the decreasing importance of traditional travel trade intermediaries, especially travel agents). Now in the early years of the new century, electronic commerce or e-commerce (buying and selling of goods and services on the Internet) is booming, and travel is one of the most popular items to buy on-line. As you read through the following descriptions of individual travel intermediaries, be aware that the Internet and related technologies are affecting the whole distribution apparatus in hospitality and travel.

Retail Travel Agents

Chapter 10 highlighted the spectacular growth in the North American travel agency business up until the mid-1990s, which was followed by a slowdown caused mainly by airline commission *caps*. The late 1990s was a difficult period for travel agencies as they dealt both with the declining airline commissions and the new competition from the on-line travel services. These Web-based information and reservation services were

A Touch of Technology

The Hot New Trend of Buying Travel On-line

- ◆ Travel e-commerce, or buying travel on-line, is one of the hottest trends in business today.

- ◆ PhocusWright, Inc., an independent strategy and research company, estimates that on-line travel sales in the United States will reach $20.2 billion in 2001, up from $2.5 billion in 1998. This is more than 700 percent growth.

- ◆ The distribution of on-line travel sales according to PhocusWright is on-line travel services (52%), airlines (33%), hotels (9%), car rentals (5%), and tours/packages/cruises (1%).

- ◆ The report, *Travelers' Use of the Internet,* by the Travel Industry Association of America (TIA), estimated that 24.7 million Americans booked travel on-line in 2000, a 64 percent increase over 1999.

- ◆ Frequent travelers (people making five or more trips per year) are especially likely to book on-line. The TIA study found that 8.2 million frequent travelers made on-line travel bookings in 1999.

- ◆ Media Metrix produced a ranking of the *Top 10 Travel Sites* for February 2000 based on the number of unique visitors to each Web site. The top-ranked sites were as follows:

  - AOL Travel Channel (6.4 million visitors)
  - Expedia.com (5.3 million)
  - Travelocity.com (5 million)
  - Mapquest.com (4.4 million)
  - Preview Travel (3 million)
  - Southwest.com (2 million)
  - AA.com (2 million)
  - Delta-Air.com (1.6 million)
  - ITN.net (1.6 million)
  - LowestFare.com (1.5 million)

profiled in Chapter 3. Despite the adversity, the *1998 U.S. Travel Agency Survey* found that total travel agency bookings in 1997 were $126 billion, up by 25 percent over 1995.[1] When combined with the increasing hospitality and travel sales on-line, these figures show that our industry represents a strong and growing retail market.

Travel agencies are putting the latest technologies to work for themselves. Some traditional agencies have set up shop on the Internet and are selling their services both in the local market and far beyond their local areas. Of course, there are also many on-line travel services, including new on-line travel agencies that deal with clients exclusively through the Internet.

Computer reservation systems (CRSs), also known as global distribution systems (GDSs), have had a huge impact on travel agency businesses, so much so that agencies cannot function effectively without links to them. The *1998 U.S. Travel Agency*

Survey estimated that 96 percent of agencies were linked to these systems.[2] The major systems are Sabre, Galileo Apollo, Worldspan, and Amadeus (Figure 13–2). Traditionally, travel agencies had exclusive access to the systems, but this is changing. Most of the systems now allow access by individual business travelers or their corporate travel departments.

In recent years, the growing importance of travel agencies to suppliers and destinations has resulted in the establishment of preferred supplier or vendor relationships as well as other programs that promise a special status for individual travel agencies. Preferred supplier or vendor relationships are special arrangements established by suppliers (hotels, rental car firms, cruise lines) in which above-average commission rates (overrides) are paid to particular agencies, usually in recognition of booking certain volumes of business. Other programs include those used by several destinations,

◆ FIGURE 13–2   *Galileo is one of the major global distribution systems.* (Courtesy of Galileo International, Inc.)

including Jamaica, New Zealand, and the Scandinavian countries, that offer a *specialist* or *preferred* status to individual travel agencies who meet certain criteria.

Retail travel agents receive their income directly from suppliers, carriers, and other travel trade intermediaries in the form of commissions (typically 10 percent for car rental and lodging reservations). Normally, customers are not charged for the agent's services. However, since the introduction of commission *caps* on domestic airline tickets, there is a trend toward agencies levying fees for their services. In February 1995, the major domestic U.S. airlines introduced commission caps on their payments to retail travel agencies for domestic tickets. Rather than paying a flat 10 percent on the cost of the ticket, these *caps* placed a maximum amount in dollar terms on the amount of commission paid by the airlines. Delta was the airline that triggered this new airline commission policy by putting a *cap* of a $50 commission payment on a round-trip air ticket of more than $500. The immediate impact on retail travel agencies was that dollar amounts earned and the average rate of commission on domestic air tickets fell. According to the Airlines Reporting Corporation (ARC), the average rate of commission on domestic tickets dropped from 10.05% in 1994 to 4.15% in 2000.[3]

To receive commissions from certain carriers and suppliers, agencies must be appointed by specific associations or other groups. For commissions on domestic air flights, appointment is needed from the Airlines Reporting Commission (ARC). International flight commissions require an IATAN (International Airlines Travel Agent Network) appointment. Appointment by the Cruise Lines International Association and AMTRAK is necessary for cruise and rail travel commissions. There is no requirement for appointments in making hotel, rental car, or other supplier reservations.

Although the average travel agency is quite small and has only six or seven employees, there are now a number of *mega-agencies* that employ thousands of agents. The leader of these agency superpowers in terms of total revenues is American Express, with 1999 gross sales of $13.7 billion. Carlson Wagonlit Travel, the sister company of Radisson, is the second largest U.S. mega agency, with 1999 sales of $11 billion. Other large agencies with 1999 sales of more than $1 billion were Rosenbluth International, World Travel Partners, Maritz Travel, Navigant International, Liberty Travel, and Sato Travel.[4]

There are several major trade associations representing travel agents in North America. They include the American Society of Travel Agents (ASTA), Association of Retail Travel Agents (ARTA), and the Association of Canadian Travel Agents (ACTA). The equivalent association in the U.K. is the Association of British Travel Agents (ABTA), while Australia has the Australian Federation of Travel Agents (AFTA). North America also has several smaller travel agency associations including the Society of Government Travel Professionals (SGTP) and the Independent Travel Agent Support Network (ITASN).

There are some important crossovers between the retail travel agency and corporate travel management. One of these is the inplant, a retail travel agency office that is located on the premises of a corporate client. According to the Airlines Reporting Corporation, the number of inplants in the United States trended downward during the 1980s.[5] The reason for this trend is that corporations are moving to other agency alternatives, including their own travel agency facilities and outside corporate travel agencies. Another option for corporations and government agencies is to pass along total responsibility for their travel arrangements to a corporate travel agency (a company specializing partly or wholly in corporate and government travel accounts). A few of these, for example Sato Travel, concentrate almost exclusively on government travel.

Did You Know?

✓ The number of traditional travel agencies in the United States has been declining.

✓ The following table shows this trend. The first column represents single-office, home, and branch locations. The figures in the second column include corporate on-site branches and restricted-access agencies.

Year	Traditional Agencies	All Full-Service Agencies
1994	32,913	33,106
1995	32,453	33,593
1996	31,617	33,715
1997	30,397	33,500
1998	28,801	32,688
1999	27,729	32,211
2000	25,585	30,026
Decrease 1994–2000	–7,328 (–22.3 percent)	–3,080 (–9.3 percent)

✓ The advent of commission caps is thought to be the main reason for this trend. The history of commission caps is as follows:

• February 1995: Delta capped domestic airline commissions.

• September 1997: United reduced its domestic commissions to 8 percent with caps.

• November 1998: United capped international airline commissions.

• October 1999: United reduced domestic commissions to 5 percent with caps.

Source: Fine, Phyllis. "As cap anniversary nears, agents look back—and ahead. "*Travel Weekly* 59 (11):2, (February 7, 2000).

Another example of greater specialization in the agency field are cruise-only agents (retail travel agents involved exclusively in selling and booking cruises).

Tour Wholesalers and Operators

As highlighted in Chapters 10 and 12, tour wholesalers and operators are one of the two main sources of vacation packages. A tour wholesaler is a company or individual who plans, prepares, markets, and administers travel packages, usually combining the services of several suppliers and carriers. Tour wholesalers normally do not sell packages directly to customers. This function is performed by retail travel agents. Like wholesalers of retail products, they buy in bulk from carriers and suppliers and re-sell through retail agency outlets. The wholesaler's administration function may or may not include operating the package or tour, meaning that it provides ground transportation, guides, and escort services. A tour operator is a tour wholesaler, other company, or individual who operates packages or tours (i.e., provides the necessary ground transportation and guide services). As you can see, the tour wholesaler performs a broader set of functions than the operator does, although it is common in the industry for the terms *tour operator* and *tour wholesaler* to be used interchangeably.

Although there are thousands of tour wholesalers and operators in the United States, the business is highly concentrated. Fewer than 100 firms control most of the revenue volume. Many of these high-volume firms are members of the United States Tour Operators Association (USTOA). To belong to USTOA, the active tour company members—who numbered about 60 in 2001—must have been in business for at least three years, must meet specific minimums in terms of passenger volumes or dollar tour volume, and must carry $1 million in consumer protection.[6] The other three major associations in this part of the industry are the National Tour Association (NTA), American Bus Association (ABA), and the United Motorcoach Association (UMA). Many of the regular members of these two groups are motor-coach tour wholesalers and operators. Both NTA and ABA hold large trade shows once each year, where suppliers, carriers, and destination marketing organizations can sell their wares to tour wholesalers and operators.

Tour wholesalers start developing tours and packages by doing careful marketing research, usually more than a year before the first tour departs.[7] About 12 to 18 months in advance, they negotiate bookings, fares, and rates with carriers and suppliers. They then establish tour or package prices and prepare brochures to distribute to travel agencies. Brochures may be developed by the wholesaler itself or in conjunction with a carrier, supplier, other intermediary, or destination marketing organization. Wholesalers' other promotional approaches include having sales representatives call on key agencies, advertising in consumer travel magazines, and trade advertising (print advertising in magazines and journals serving the travel trade).

Corporate Travel Managers and Agencies

A survey of corporate travel managers indicated three reasons for creating special in-house travel departments or consolidating travel arrangements in some other way. They are as follows:[8]

1. To cut business travel expenses
2. To provide better service to travelers
3. To increase corporate purchasing power

The traditional way of handling corporate travel was to have each department, division, or even individual manager make their own plans and reservations. Some of the problems of this approach are that the travelers may not necessarily come up with the most convenient travel schedules, the appropriate quality of services, or the most economical fares and rates. From the organization's standpoint, potential bargaining power with carriers and suppliers is lost. The recessionary period in North America forced many corporations, government agencies, and large, nonprofit organizations to cut costs wherever possible. Greater coordination and tightening of controls on travel has been one strategy used. According to American Express, nearly half of U.S. corporations have a travel manager/coordinator.[9]

Although many organizations agree that there are rich dividends in streamlining travel, the way they go about it varies. As mentioned earlier, some use inplants, while others farm out their business to corporate travel agencies (sometimes referred to as *outplants*). The remainder use full-service travel agencies or operate an in-house, fully accredited travel agency themselves.

The corporate (business) travel market is huge. In 2000, American Express estimated that travel and entertainment represented 7 percent of the total operating expenses of 600-plus of the world's largest companies.[10] *The 2000–2001 American Express Survey of Business Travel Management* found that 45 percent of U.S. companies' travel and entertainment expenses went toward air travel and 17 percent toward lodging.[11] Large U.S. corporations, such as General Electric, IBM, Digital Equipment, Hewlett-Packard, United Technologies, and Johnson & Johnson, have travel budgets in the hundreds of millions.[12] Competition for the corporate market is fierce among travel trade intermediaries, carriers, and suppliers. Corporate travel managers, who head up their organization's travel departments, collectively wield a tremendous amount of bargaining power. According to a survey of corporate travel managers, 96 percent of these managers are personally involved in negotiating rates and fares with carriers and suppliers (collectively known as *vendors* in the corporate travel business).[13] The concept of rebating also demonstrates companies' market power. Rebating occurs when an agency pays back a certain percentage of the commissions it earns to the corporation.

The trend toward centralizing corporate travel arrangements has been instrumental in creating other hospitality and travel industry changes. For example, it has spurred the development of mega travel agencies, corporate travel agencies, agency cooperatives and consortia, and franchised agency groups. It has also motivated large travel agencies, airlines, hotel chains, rental car firms, and others to mount national advertising campaigns aimed specifically at corporate travel managers.

The two major associations for corporate travel managers are the National Business Travel Association (NBTA) and the Association of Corporate Travel Managers (ACTE). With approximately 2000 members between them, NBTA and ACTE hold annual conferences and trade shows that provide an excellent opportunity for hotels, airlines, rental car firms, travel agency chains, and others to promote to the most influential travel managers.

Airline reservations systems have also had a great impact on corporate travel departments. A majority of the larger organizations have these on-line capabilities. Again, this highlights the importance of these systems to airlines and the desirability for suppliers, especially hotels and rental car companies, to have their information listed on one or more of these networks.

Incentive Travel Planners

Chapter 7 characterized incentive travel as a business travel segment that is experiencing significant growth. **Incentive travel** is used by an increasing number of companies as a motivational tool, by rewarding employees, dealers, and others who meet or exceed objectives.

What are the reasons for this trend? The bottom line is that the promise of travel as a reward is becoming increasingly lucrative to potential recipients. Traditionally, incentive travel has been used to recognize outstanding sales performances by company employees, dealers, or distributors, but the variety of applications is expanding. These other reasons include increasing production, encouraging better customer service, improving plant safety, introducing new products, selling new accounts, and enhancing morale and goodwill.

Many different organizations get involved in planning incentive trips. Some companies do all the work themselves, using their corporate travel departments, convention/meeting planners, or other management personnel. It is more common, however, for the incentive-trip packages to be developed by outside experts, either by full-service incentive houses, specialized incentive travel-planning firms, or travel agencies or tour wholesalers dabbling in this field. There are now about 400 to 500 specialized incentive travel-planning companies in the United States, most of which belong to the major trade association SITE (Society of Incentive & Travel Executives).

Incentive travel planners are really specialized tour wholesalers. The only difference is that they deal directly with their corporate clients. They assemble tailor-made packages that include transportation, accommodations, meals, special functions, theme parties, and tours. Like tour wholesalers, they negotiate with carriers and suppliers for the best prices and *blocks of space.* They also add a markup commission, which represents their fees for the planning service. Normally, the sponsoring corporate client pays all the costs of promoting the incentive trips to potential recipients.

Incentive travel is growing steadily in North America, Europe, and Asia. The original concept of incentive planning—sending only the top performers (usually salespersons) in large groups to exotic destinations—has been expanded to include non-sales personnel, *individual incentives,* cruise incentives, and multi-destination trips.[14] The growth in incentive travel has attracted the attention of many suppliers, carriers, and destination marketing organizations.

Convention/Meeting Planners

Conventions and meetings are a major part of North American business travel. According to a survey conducted by *Meetings & Conventions* magazine, total meeting expenditures reached a record high of $40.2 billion in 1999.[15] **Convention/meeting planners** plan and coordinate their organizations' external meeting events. They work for associations, corporations, large nonprofit organizations, government agencies, and educational institutions. Some combine the task of convention/meeting planning with that of corporate travel management, whereas other organizations split up the tasks. Typically, convention/meeting planners are involved in the following tasks:[16]

1. Preparing budgets
2. Selecting meeting sites and facilities
3. Negotiating group rates for accommodations and air and ground transportation
4. Developing meeting programs and agendas
5. Making reservations for participants
6. Developing meeting specifications and securing meeting space
7. Obtaining and coordinating entertainment
8. Planning food and beverage functions

9. Coordinating the production of printed and audiovisual support materials
10. Administering the meeting at the site

These planners attract the attention of many suppliers, carriers, other travel trade intermediaries, and destination marketing organizations. Promotion to them is usually split among advertising in special meeting planners' journals (e.g., *Meetings & Conventions, Successful Meetings, Meeting News*), exhibiting at major trade shows, and personal selling to individual planners. (Figure 13–3)

ON-LINE TRAVEL SERVICES

You have already heard in this chapter about on-line travel services, and perhaps you have even used them. They represent a brand new distribution channel for the hospitality and travel industry and function almost like an on-line intermediary. There are now so many of these services, it is hard to keep track of them. Figure 13–4 provides a partial list and identifies the major on-line travel services.

The on-line travel services provide several benefits for customers, the major of which are as follows:

1. Ability to self-book travel on-line
2. Assistance in planning travel trips
3. Availability of on-line pricing comparisons for hospitality and travel services
4. Convenience of accessing travel information at home or work
5. Immediate confirmation of travel bookings
6. Instant access to travel information
7. Potential of securing lower prices on hospitality and travel services

Several of these on-line travel services belong to a new association called the Interactive Travel Services Association (ITSA). The ITSA's mission is "to promote consumer choice, access, confidence, protection and information in the rapidly growing world of on-line travel."[17] The forecasts by expert industry consultants, such as PhoCusWright and Gartner Interactive, suggest that on-line travel bookings will increase by about 10 to 15 times between 1998 and 2001.[18] This growth is nothing short of extraordinary, especially considering that most of the major on-line services only date back to about 1994 to 1996.

Hospitality and travel marketers are already quite involved in working with this new distribution channel. In addition to having their own Web-based on-line booking systems, several organizations are buying *banner advertising* or offering special sales promotions on the on-line travel sites (Figure 13–5).

MARKETING TO THE TRAVEL TRADE

Travel trade intermediaries play a major role in generating business for suppliers, carriers, and destination marketing organizations. Their influence on customers is so great that they deserve separate attention in the marketing plan. Suppliers, carriers, and destination areas must treat them as a separate target market or markets.

◆ FIGURE 13–3   *Known locally as the "Armadillo," the Scottish Exhibition & Conference Centre advertises to meeting planners in one of their journals.* (Courtesy of the Scottish Exhibition & Conference Centre)

ON-LINE TRAVEL SERVICES	WEB ADDRESSES
Major On-line Travel Services	
• AOL Travel Channel (AOL)	• http://aolsvc.travel.aol.com/
• Expedia (Microsoft)	• http://www.expedia.com/
• Internet Travel Network (American Express)	• http://www.itn.com/
• Travelocity (Sabre)	• http://www.travelocity.com/
• Yahoo! Travel	• http://travel.yahoo.com/
• Priceline	• http://www.priceline.com/
Specialized On-line Travel Services	
• Biz Travel	• http://www.biztravel.com/
• Cheap Travel	• http://www.cheaptravel.com/
• Last Minute Travel	• http://www.lastminutetravel.com/
• Lowest Fare	• http://www.lowestfare.com/
• Web Flyer	• http://www.webflyer.com/
Other On-line Travel Services	
• Bye Bye Now	• http://www.byebyenow.com/
• Concierge	• http://www.concierge.com/
• Online Vacation Mall	• http://www.onlinevacationmall.com/
• Travelscape	• http://www.travelscape.com/
• Travel Now	• http://www.travelnow.com/
• Travel Store	• http://www.travelstore.com/
• Travel Web	• http://www.travelweb.com/
• Travel Zoo	• http://www.travelzoo.com/

◆ **FIGURE 13–4**   *On-line travel services—the new wave of hospitality and travel distribution.*

Should you promote to all trade intermediaries or only to selected ones? The answer is no different than for customers in general—it is usually more effective to use a segmented strategy. Not all travel agents, tour wholesalers, corporate travel managers, incentive travel planners, and convention/meeting planners are alike. They vary by their geographic locations, sales or booking volumes, types and volumes of clients served, areas of specialization, existing affiliations through perferred supplier or vendor relationships, and many other ways. A supplier, carrier, and destination must research each trade segment carefully to determine which companies are most likely to use its services.

A three-step process should be used in marketing to intermediaries: (1) research and select trade segments, (2) decide on the positioning approach and marketing objectives, and (3) establish a promotional mix for travel intermediaries.

ON THE WEB

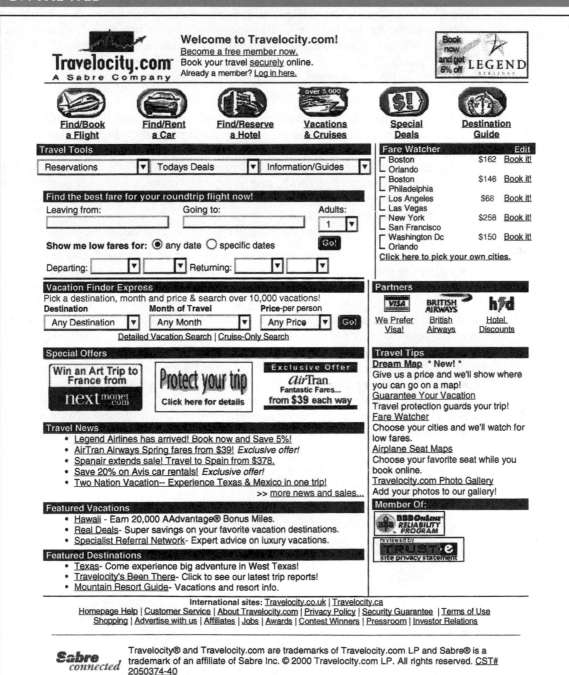

◆ FIGURE 13–5   *On-line travel services are becoming a popular place for promotions by hospitality and travel organizations.* (Courtesy of Travelocity.com.)

Research and Select Trade *Segments*

Internal reservation and registration records are often the best source of information for *trade marketing*. For lodging facilities, registration data indicate where customers live and work, as well as the names of travel trade companies that have made reservations for guests. Registration data should be analyzed frequently (or automatically through updating a computerized guest and travel agent database) to determine the following:

1. Key *feeder* market areas—cities or regions that provide the highest numbers of guests. There is a high probability that the most important trade intermediaries are located in these cities or regions.
2. Major corporate travel and convention/meeting accounts—the corporations, associations, government agencies, and nonprofit organizations that generate the largest numbers of guests. These organizations require constant follow-up to guarantee their future business.
3. Tour wholesalers and incentive travel planners that provide business.

Computerized reservations systems provide suppliers, carriers, and others with an excellent tool to target and evaluate the value of trade intermediaries. New hospitality and travel organizations, and ones targeting the travel trade for the very first time, have a tougher job. They have no in-house records upon which to base decisions and need to do primary (original) research to find the best travel trade prospects. The starting point for this research should be the organization's target markets, specifically their geographic locations and demographics. With key geographic markets pinpointed, the organization can survey travel agencies, corporate travel managers, and convention/meeting planners to determine which has the greatest future business potential. Other clues are found in what existing competitors are doing and which tour wholesalers, tour operators, convention/meeting groups, and incentive travel planners are currently using the destination.

Decide on Positioning Approach and Marketing Objectives

Every supplier, carrier, and destination area faces stiff competition for travel trade business. It is just as important for an organization to establish a distinctive image or position in the travel trade as it is to establish one with other customers. Again, one of the following six positioning approaches should be considered.

1. Specific product features
2. Benefits, problem solution, or needs
3. Specific usage occasions
4. User category
5. Against another product
6. Class dissociation

Holiday Inn advertises heavily in travel trade journals and has used the first positioning approach in several of these advertisements. The specific product feature it promoted to travel agents was the *Travel Agent Commission Program*. This program guarantees accurate, on-time payments of agents' commissions at all participating Holiday Inn properties. Commissions are conveniently mailed from a central location, rather than from each individual property. The first positioning approach (specific product features) tends to be the most popular in trade marketing, because it is commonly assumed that travel trade intermediaries make decisions based more on factual information than on the recommendations of other customers.

It is important to set marketing objectives for each travel trade segment targeted. Only by doing this can an organization plan trade promotions realistically and evaluate the success of these efforts. This can be done by apportioning some share of previously established objectives (discussed in Chapter 8) to specific travel trade segments. For example, a hotel may set an overall objective of a 5-percent increase in the number of pleasure travelers it attracts. It may project that 40 percent of this total will come through travel agents, thus apportioning 2 percent of the gain to agents.

Establish a Promotional Mix for Travel Intermediaries

The promotional mix is a combination of advertising, sales promotion, merchandising, personal selling, and public relations/publicity. Chapter 14 explores this concept in detail. It is essential that suppliers, carriers, and destination areas develop a separate promotional mix for the travel trade.

1. **Trade Advertising.** *Trade advertising* is paid advertising by suppliers, carriers, destination marketing organizations, and other intermediaries in specialized travel trade magazines, journals, and newspapers. Appendix 2–1 is a partial list of some of the principal publications oriented toward the trade. Direct mail is also used extensively with the travel trade. Advertising in these media should follow the guidelines and steps discussed in Chapter 15.

   One very important consideration in placing trade advertising is its timing. If travel agents are the audience, they need advance knowledge of the services so that they can provide their clients with accurate and complete information. In this case, trade advertising should precede consumer advertising.

2. **Directories and Computerized Databases.** Because of the sheer volume of travel alternatives, travel agents and other intermediaries are forced to rely on specialized directories and computerized databases. They cannot possibly be personally familiar with all the facilities and services available. Some of these directories allow advertising in addition to lists of facilities and services. Appendix 2–2 lists major directories that are used by the travel trade.

   There are a growing number of computerized and on-line databases that cover hospitality and travel facilities and services. The major ones are associated with the larger airline reservations systems. Because travel agents are increasingly relying on on-line information rather than on printed facts, it is becoming more important for suppliers, carriers, and destination marketing organizations to have their data on these reservation systems. The number of other on-line databases for personal computer use is also increasing.

3. **Trade Promotions.** Other items to be considered are special sales promotion activities aimed at travel trade intermediaries. These include the following:
   a. **FAMILIARIZATION TRIPS OR FAMS**—These are free or reduced-price trips given to travel agents and other intermediaries by suppliers, carriers, and destination marketing groups. They are an excellent promotion for

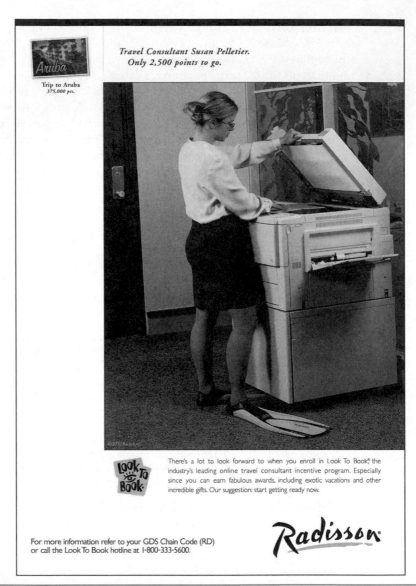

◆ **FIGURE 13–6**   *A travel agent incentive program offered by Radisson.* (Courtesy of Radisson Hotels & Resorts)

giving intermediaries a first-hand appreciation of the facilities and services being offered.

b. **CONTESTS, SWEEPSTAKES, AND INCENTIVE PROGRAMS**—Contests and sweepstakes are frequently used in the industry to obtain travel trade business, especially from travel agents. Figure 13–6 shows an example of an agent incentive program operated by Radisson. As you can see, Radisson's *Look to Book* program encourages agents to book Radisson properties, either through the agents' GDS system or Radisson's special agent hotline. Consumers who entered the sweepstakes won free trips to offshore destinations and their travel agents were awarded American Express travelers checks.

c. **SPECIALTY ADVERTISING GIVEAWAYS**—These are items bearing the sponsor's name that are given away to travel intermediaries.

d. **TRADE SHOWS**—Several travel trade associations hold annual trade shows where suppliers, carriers, destination marketing groups, and intermediaries can exhibit. Some are *marketplaces* where participants arrange interviews or discussions with each other. Some of the major trade shows in North America are those held by the National Tour Association, American Society of Travel Agents, American Bus Association, and National Business Travel Association. There are also many privately sponsored travel shows, where agents and others become more familiar with other organizations' services.

4. **Personal and Telephone Selling.** One of the most effective promotional techniques involves personal sales calls to selected travel intermediaries. Chapter 17 takes a detailed look at personal selling, and you will see that much of the personal selling in the industry is directed at the travel trade. There are two aspects of selling to the trade–field sales and telephone sales and service. Many suppliers, carriers, destination marketing groups, and other intermediaries employ full-time salespersons, who devote all or part of their time to calling on travel agents. Included are most airlines, cruise ship companies, hotel/resort chains, tour wholesalers, car rental firms, and passenger rail services. These salespersons often call on other intermediaries as well, including corporate travel managers, convention/meeting planners, and tour wholesalers.

An increasingly important part of travel trade sales and service is via telecommunications and electronics. Today it is almost essential for those dealing with the travel trade to provide a toll-free 800 number and dedicated website for travel agent information and reservations. In the lodging industry, Holiday Inn, Radisson, and Ramada are three of the leaders in providing excellent telephone reservation/information service to agents. Of course, the major airlines have the most elaborate linkages with travel agencies and corporate travel departments through their global distribution systems.

5. **Merchandising and Brochures.** Travel agencies are retail outlets, where the services and facilities of various suppliers, carriers, destination marketing groups, and tour wholesalers are merchandised. Each agency contains an extensive range of travel brochures, posters, and window and other merchandising displays. It is definitely in the best interests of other organizations to keep their key agencies well stocked with attractive brochures, posters and displays, and other sales tools that agents can use.

6. **Public Relations and Publicity.** Other companies in the hospitality and travel industry have a vested interest in maintaining open and cordial relationships with the travel trade. Activities designed to develop and maintain these positive relations should not be haphazard, but should be part of a carefully conceived public relations plan. Public relations and publicity are discussed in detail in Chapter 18. Typical trade public-relations activities include periodic news releases to travel trade magazines, participation in various travel-trade-association conferences and

EXCELLENCE CASE

Travel Trade Marketing:
The Cruise Line Industry in North America

One of the fastest-growing elements of travel in North America is cruising. This growth has been created by the increasing popularity of the type of all-inclusive vacations that cruise lines offer as well as the cruise lines' innovative marketing approaches. Another major reason has been the excellent *partnership* between the cruise lines and retail travel agents, particularly the way cruise lines have developed mutually beneficial relationships with agencies.

Formed in 1975, the Cruise Lines International Association (CLIA), with 23 member cruise lines and 95 percent of the current capacity, projects that the number of North American passengers on cruise ships will increase from 4.4 million in 1994 to 6.9 million in 2000. The Association estimates that 84 million passengers have taken deep-water cruises of two or more days since 1970. CLIA's research indicates that 50 percent of all adults over 25 with incomes above $20,000 have an interest in taking a cruise. It also estimates that 31 percent of adults, or about 43.6 million people, will definitely or probably cruise within the next five years. The assistance of retail travel agencies will be crucial in the cruise lines realizing this potential. With more than 20,000 travel agency affiliates, the CLIA cruise lines seem well positioned to do so.[1]

More than 95 to 97 percent of the cruises booked in North America are booked through retail travel agents. In fact, cruise lines are the only type of hospitality and travel organization that depends almost exclusively on travel agent bookings (indirect distribution). The cruise lines are highly supportive of the travel agent and clearly recommend in their promotions to consumers to "consult your professional travel agent for details and reservations." While airline commissions still represent the major share of travel agency revenues, the commissions earned from cruise lines are growing quite rapidly. In 1998, the cruise lines provided 18 percent of

U.S. travel agency sales ($22 billion)—the second largest individual source of agency revenues.[2] With the commission caps introduced by several U.S. airlines in early 1995, revenues from cruises are likely to become an even more important determinant of agency profitability.

The appeal of selling cruises to travel agents is based both on the dollar amount of commission earned and the rate of commission. The fully inclusive nature of cruise prices means that the agent can earn commissions on all elements of the package, including the airfare, lodging, meals and entertainment, and optional shore excursions. Agent commission rates begin at a standard 10 percent on the cruise package price but may go as high as 14 to 16 percent for *preferred* agencies. Thus, if a *preferred* agency sells a couple a seven-night cruise at $2,000 per person at a commission rate of 15 percent, this one sale alone is worth $600 to the agency.

The cruise lines offer a great diversity of ships and itineraries, and thus cruise package prices vary considerably. Per diems (daily cost per passenger) range from a low of $75 to $100 to more than $1,000 for some of the luxury lines' ships. These rates typically include round-trip airfare to the port of embarkation. Each ship contains a variety of inside and outside state-rooms and decks, and prices can vary quite significantly, even on the same ship, depending on the stateroom or suite selected. Cruise lines have positioned themselves differently based on their ship designs, types of passengers served, cruise themes, and types of itineraries. The *Travel Agent/Cruise Desk* issue in December 1994 divided the cruise line market into four segments—resort-style popular (54.7 percent of bed capacity), resort-style premium (32.7 percent), adventure/expedition (8.2 percent) and luxury (7.8 percent).[3] *Fodor's Cruises and Ports of Call* categorizes the types of cruises as traditional, party, cultural, senior, excursion, adventure, theme, and budget.[4]

continued

EXCELLENCE CASE *continued*

The utilization rate of cruise ship capacity is exceptionally high by our industry's standards. CLIA believes that it is around 90 percent, which is approximately 20 percentage points above the average occupancy rates for hotels and resorts in most regions of North America. This pinnacle of performance has been reached through a combination of excellent travel trade and consumer promotions and the provision of exciting and often highly programmed vacation experiences. In fact, the cruise lines have been among the most innovative users of packaging and programming within the hospitality and travel industry. For example, the Norwegian *Sports Afloat* program features themed sports cruises for motorsports, football, golf, tennis, ice hockey, basketball, skiing, baseball, and volleyball. Each of these cruises features well-known sports personalities, presentations, and participation or instruction in the given sport.

The cruise lines use the full range of promotion mix elements to appeal to and support travel agents. Major agent publications such as *Travel Agent* and *Travel Weekly* usually contain advertisements from industry leaders such as Carnival, Royal Caribbean, Princess, Holland America, and Norwegian. The amount of trade and consumer advertising by cruise lines is increasing. The advertising expenditures of one of the industry leaders, Royal Caribbean International, reached $172.6 million in 1999, making it the 145th largest advertiser in the United States.[5] The emerging presence of cruise lines was highlighted during the Super Bowl of 1994, when millions of people witnessed Norwegian's introduction of its dramatic *It's different out here* commercials.

The media advertising by the cruise lines is supported by a wide range of sales promotion, merchandising, and personal selling efforts aimed at the travel agent. Most of the major cruise lines use regional sales teams to liaise with individual agencies and to assist agencies in their advertising and sales promotion programs to their clients. Royal Caribbean advertisements use a *Scout* theme to encourage agents to use the services of RCL's

District Sales Managers. These sales representatives often help individual agencies with special promotions such as *cruise nights* where potential cruisers are invited to open houses to find out more about cruises. Cruise lines also frequently ask agencies to *sample* their ships through agent familiarization trips or in-port ship tours.

Brochures represent the main merchandising tool of the cruise lines and are prominently displayed in most agencies. These are usually of a very high quality, and most agents agree that they make cruises easier to sell. As well as presenting colorful images of their ships and cruise destinations, these brochures normally show deck-by-deck layouts indicating the location of every room and facility on each ship.

Agents make bookings directly with the cruise lines. Several cruise lines have also begun to make their inventories available through airline CRS systems, such as Princess' *Love Boat Link* and RCL's *Cruisematch 2000 On-line* programs' availability through the major CRS systems. For the travel agent, therefore, cruises are easy not only to sell but also to book because of the cruise lines' reservations/booking systems.

Other reasons for the popularity of cruises among travel agents are the very high rate of customer satisfaction with cruises and the relatively high rate of repeat cruising. According to a CLIA survey, 85 percent of first-time and 87 percent of frequent (taken three or more cruises in past six years) cruisers were *extremely* or *very* satisfied with their cruises. Eighty percent of frequent and 58 percent of first-time cruisers indicated that they would definitely take another cruise within the next two years.[7] The cruise lines themselves do a marvelous job of relationship and database marketing with their past passengers. Passengers are often asked to provide their mailing addresses and to complete questionnaires prior to disembarkation. With this, they join the *alumni* of the cruise line and receive its periodic newsletters and special offers.

continued

EXCELLENCE CASE *continued*

In summary, the relationship of cruise lines and North American travel agencies is one of mutual benefit and dependence. It is a shining example for the rest of the hospitality and travel industry of within-industry *relationship marketing*. As more mega cruise ships in the 2,000-plus passenger capacity range leave the shipyards, the linkage between agencies and cruise lines is likely to become even stronger. Certainly, retail travel agencies will be one of the keys to absorbing the major increase in cruise-ship capacity expected by 2005.

Discussion Questions

1. How have travel agencies in North America helped cruise lines achieve high rates of passenger growth and ship utilization?
2. What unique approaches have the cruise lines used in travel trade marketing?
3. What can other hospitality and travel organizations learn from the cruise lines in terms of marketing to the travel trade?

Web Site

http://www.cruising.org/

References

1. *Cruise Industry Overview: Marketing Edition-March 2001*. 2001. New York: Cruise Lines International Association.
2. *1998 U.S. Travel Agency Survey*. Travel Weekly. http://www.twcrossroads.com/
3. "The travel agent/cruise desk." *Travel Agent* December 5, 1994.
4. *Fodor's Cruises and Ports of Call 1993*.
5. *Advertisers Ranked 100 to 200*. Advertising Age, http://www.advge.com/database/

---

seminars, and development of press kits and *stock* photography for media and individual company use.

7. **Cooperative Marketing (Partnership).** Another element of the travel trade promotional mix should be marketing activities jointly funded with selected intermediaries. For example, airlines, hotels and resorts, and destination marketing groups often share the costs of developing brochures to distribute to travel agents and customers. Expenses of familiarization trips are frequently split by nonagent organizations, as are the costs of joint *sales blitzes* to travel-generating areas. Jointly sponsored consumer travel shows are another excellent example of cooperative marketing.

8. **Web site access.** Many organizations have created special sections of their Web sites for travel trade intermediaries. CVBs, for example, often have a meeting planner section, or information for tour operators. Hotel, cruise, and tour company sites have specially hyperlinked areas for travel agents. As the importance of on-line travel distribution increases, it is essential that Web sites be designed with these intermediaries in mind.

CHAPTER CONCLUSION

The distribution system in the hospitality and travel industry is very different from the one used by all other industries. The intermediaries are usually referred to as the *travel trade*. They include retail travel agents, tour wholesalers and tour operators, corporate travel managers and agencies, incentive travel planners, and convention/meeting planners. The travel trade performs several key roles, including widely disseminating information on available services and facilities. They also help other organizations by making hospitality and travel services more accessible and appealing to customers.

Marketing to the travel trade deserves separate attention in the marketing plan. In essence, intermediaries should be regarded as separate target markets, with their own strategies, positioning approaches, objectives, and promotional mix.

REVIEW QUESTIONS

1. What is the meaning of the terms distribution mix and travel trade?
2. What is the difference between direct and indirect distribution in the hospitality and travel industry?
3. How does the hospitality and travel industry's distribution system differ from that in other industries?
4. What are the eight roles that travel trade intermediaries play in the industry?
5. What are the roles of the five major travel intermediaries?
6. What are the three steps that other organizations should follow in marketing to the travel trade?
7. Which elements are normally included in the promotional mix used for the travel trade?

CHAPTER ASSIGNMENTS

1. Select a major carrier, supplier, or destination marketing organization and examine its distribution system. Does it use both direct and indirect distribution? Which trade intermediaries does it target? What positioning approach or approaches does it employ? What promotional activities are used for the travel trade? How could it expand or improve its travel trade marketing?

2. You are the marketing director for a new hotel chain, theme park, cruise line, rental car company, tour wholesaler, or airline. Which travel trade intermediaries would you target? How would you identify the specific travel trade companies to concentrate on? Would you use a segmented strategy? What positioning approach or approaches would you adopt? How would you promote to the travel trade?

3. A small, local-area hotel, resort, or attraction has asked you for some specialized advice on

marketing to the travel trade. Very little business has been received from intermediaries in the past, but the owners feel that there is good potential to develop additional revenues from this source. What steps would you recommend they follow? How would you describe the advantages and disadvantages of dealing with intermediaries? Which specific intermediaries would you suggest be targeted, and why? What promotional mix elements and activities would you recommend?

4. This chapter outlines eight roles played by travel intermediaries. Describe these roles, citing at least two actual examples of organizations that perform these roles. How important is cooperation with other organizations in providing services to customers? Are the organizations you selected performing their role effectively?

WORLD WIDE WEB RESOURCES

Airlines Reporting Corporation
http://www.arccorp.com/

Amadeus
http://www.amadeuslink.com/

American Express Travel Related Services
http://home3.americanexpress.com/
corporateservices/

American Society of Travel Agents (ASTA)
http://www.astanet.com/

AOL Travel Channel
http://aolsvc.travel.aol.com/

Apollo Galileo USA
http://www.galileo.com/

Association of British Travel Agents
http://www.abtanet.com/

Association of Canadian Travel Agents
http://www.acta.net/

Association of Corporate Travel Executives
http://www.acte.org/

Association Retail Travel Agents
http://www.artaonline.com/

Australian Federation of Travel Agents
http://www.afta.com.au/

Biz Travel
http://www.biztravel.com/

Bye Bye Now
http://www.byebyenow.com/

Carlson Wagonlit Travel
http://www.carlsonwagonlit.com/

Cheap Travel
http://www.cheaptravel.com/

Cruise Lines International Association
http://www.cruising.org/

Delta Airlines
http://www.delta.com/

Expedia
http://www.expedia.com/

Gartner Research
http://www.gartner.com/

Independent Travel Agent Support Network
http://www.itasn.com/

Interactive Travel Services Association
http://www.interactivetravel.org/

International Airlines Travel Agent Network
http://www.iatan.org/

Internet Travel Network
http://www.itn.com/

Last Minute Travel
http://www.lastminutetravel.com/

Liberty Travel
http://www.libertytravel.com/

Lowest Fare
http://www.lowestfare.com/

Mapquest
http://www.mapquest.com/

Maritz Travel Co.
http://www.maritztravel.com/

Media Metrix
http://www.mediametrix.com/

National Business Travel Association
http://www.nbta.org/

Navigant International
http://www.navigant.com/

Online Vacation Mall
http://www.onlinevacationmall.com/

PhocusWright Inc.
http://www.phocuswright.com/

Priceline
http://www.priceline.com/

Rosenbluth International
http://www.rosenbluth.com/content/home/home.htm

Sabre
http://www.sabre.com/

Sato Travel
http://www.satotravel.com/

Singapore Airlines
http://www.singaporeair.com/

Society of Travel Agents in Government
http://www.government-travel.org/index.html

Southwest Airlines
http://www.southwest.com/

Travel Now
http://www.travelnow.com/

Travelscape
http://www.travelscape.com/

Travel Web
http://www.travelweb.com/

Travel Zoo
http://www.travelzoo.com/

Travelocity
http://www.travelocity.com/

United Motorcoach Association
http://www.uma.org/

Web Flyer
http://www.webflyer.com/

Worldspan
https://www.worldspan.com/index.asp

World Travel BTI
http://www.worldtravel.com/

Yahoo! Travel
http://www.travel.yahoo.com/

REFERENCES

1. "The 1998 U.S. travel agency survey." *Travel Weekly* (1999). www.twcrossroads.com/

2. "The 1998 U.S. travel agency survey." *Travel Weekly* (1999). www.twcrossroads.com/

3. Fine, Phyllis. 2000. "As cap anniversary nears, agents look back—and ahead." *Travel Weekly*, 59 (11) 2000: 1–2, (February 7).

4. "Focus: 1999 top 50 travel agencies." *Travel Weekly* Section 2, 58 (51):F6 (June 28, 1998).

5. "ARC inplant listing shows 50% decline in 4 years." *Travel Weekly* 46 (83):B9–B13 (1987).

6. United States Tour Operators Association. http://www.ustoa.com/

7. Mill, Robert Christie, and Alastair M. Morrison. 1998. *The Tourism System: An Introductory Text.* 3rd ed. Dubuque, Iowa: Kendall/Hunt Publishing Company.

8. "The Fortune 1000 travel manager survey." *Travel Weekly* 46 (83):B6.

9. *The 2000-2001 American Express Survey of Business Travel Management.* American Express Corporate Services.

10. American Express. http://home3.americanexpress.com/corporateservices/

11. The 2000-2001 American Express Survey of Business Travel Management, www.acte.org/resources/annex/shtm/(Retrieved 5/30/01).

12. McNulty, Mary Ann, and Don Munro. "Corporate travel 100." *Corporate Travel* 9 (6):21–35 (1993).

13.

14. Juergens, Jennifer. "Incentive travel redefined: the industry's new twists." *Meetings & Conventions* 24 (4):71–82 (1989).

15. The Meetings Market Report 2000. *Meetings & Conventions,* http://www.meetings-conventions.com/

16. Meeting planning: a viable career option. 1987. Meeting Planners International.

17. Association of Destination Management Executives http://www.adme.org/

18. PhoCus Wright http://www.phocuswright.com/ and Gartner Interactive http://www.gartner.com/

For additional hospitality and travel marketing resources, visit our Web site at **www.Hospitality-Tourism.delmar.com**

Communications and the Promotional Mix

How Do We Get There?

Objectives

Having read this chapter, you should be able to:

◆ Define the term promotional mix.

◆ List the five elements of the promotional mix.

◆ List and explain the nine elements of the communications process.

◆ Explain the difference between explicit and implicit communications.

◆ List the three principal goals of promotion.

◆ Explain the relationship of the promotional mix and the marketing mix.

◆ Define the terms advertising, personal selling, sales promotion, merchandising, public relations, and publicity.

◆ List the advantages and disadvantages of each of the five promotional mix elements.

◆ Identify four factors that affect the promotional mix.

Overview

How does a hospitality and travel organization communicate its unique appeals and benefits to customers? The answer is through promotion and the combination of techniques known as the promotional mix. This chapter begins by explaining the relationship of promotion to

communications and looks at the objectives of promotion.

The five elements of the promotional mix are defined, and their individual advantages and disadvantages are discussed.

Key Terms

advertising	implicit communications	public relations
commercial sources	interactive media	receivers
communications process	medium	response
decode	merchandising	sales promotions
direct marketing	message	social sources
direct-response advertising	noise	source
encode	personal selling	surrogate cues
explicit communications	promotional mix	word-of-mouth advertising
feedback	publicity	

As a consumer of products and services, you are exposed to hundreds, perhaps even thousands, of promotions every week of your life. These include television and radio commercials, newspaper and magazine advertisements, billboards, coupon deals, ads received through the mail, store merchandising displays, various pieces of publicity covered by the media, and others. The human brain cannot possibly absorb all these messages, and it actually sifts out and retains few of them. This is a very perplexing problem for hospitality and travel organizations. They are faced with two known facts—there are a multitude of promotional alternatives available, but no matter which ones are chosen, the chances of being noticed are slim. The challenge, therefore, is to select the promotional technique that works best in the given situation and to use it in the way most likely to get the customer's attention and result in a purchase.

PROMOTION AND COMMUNICATIONS

Promotion is the communications part of marketing. In many ways, it is the culmination of all the research, analysis, and decisions we reviewed in Chapters 5 to 13. It is the way we tell the world our story, now that we know it ourselves! Promotion provides customers with information and knowledge in an informative and persuasive manner. This, we hope, will sooner or later result in sales of our services. The information and knowledge can be communicated using one or more of the five promotional techniques—advertising, personal selling, sales promotion, merchandising, and public relations and publicity. Taken together, these techniques are referred to as the promotional mix (the combination of advertising, personal selling, sales promotion, merchandising, and public relations and publicity approaches used for a specific time period).

The Communications Process

How many times have you noticed that what you intended to say was not what the other person or persons heard? Sure, they heard exactly what you said, but they interpreted it incorrectly. This occurs because communication is a two-way interaction between a sender and a receiver. To design effective promotional messages, hospitality and travel marketers (the sources) must first understand the target market (the receivers) and the communications process.

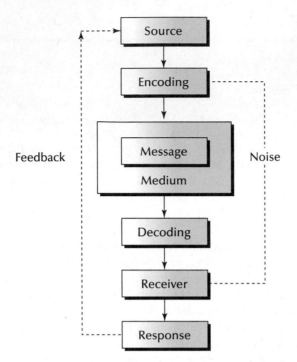

◆ FIGURE 14–1   *The communications process.* (Adapted from Kotler, Philip. 2000. Marketing Management: Millennium Edition. 10th ed. Prentice-Hall, Inc. Reprinted by permission of Pearson Education, Inc., Upper Saddle River, NJ 07458)

The communications process in the hospitality and travel industry has nine key elements (Figure 14–1). They are as follows:

1. Source
2. Encoding
3. Message
4. Medium
5. Decoding
6. Noise
7. Receiver
8. Response
9. Feedback

1. **Source.** The source is the person or organization (e.g., hotel chain, airline, travel agency, restaurant, state tourism department) that transmits the information to customers. There are two main sources—*commercial* and *social.* Commercial sources are advertising and other promotions that are designed by corporations and other organizations. Social sources (also known as word-of-mouth advertising) are interpersonal channels of information, including friends, relatives, business associates, and opinion leaders.

2. **Encoding.** Sources know exactly what they want to communicate, but they must translate or encode the information into an arrangement of words, pictures, colors, sounds, movements, or even body language. For example, the California Raisin Advisory Board wanted to remind people that raisins were healthful. Its advertising agency encoded this simple message into a television commercial featuring cartoonlike raisin characters marching to the Motown tune, "I Heard It through the Grapevine."

3. **Message.** The message is what the source wants to communicate and hopes that the receivers understand. For Wendy's in the classic "Where's the Beef?" commercials, the message was that Wendy's uses only fresh, unfrozen, 100 percent beef. In the memorable "Pizza Hut People" campaign, the message was that eating pizza is fun, and that Pizza Hut makes the best pizza in town.

4. **Medium.** The medium or media are the communications channels that sources select to pass their messages to receivers. The mass media—television, radio, newspapers, and magazines—are commonly used by commercial sources. However, the medium can simply be two-way communications between a salesperson and a potential customer. Therefore, the medium is either impersonal (mass media) or interpersonal (e.g., a presentation from a travel agent or hotel or airline salesperson, or a recommendation from a friend, relative, associate, or opinion leader).

5. **Decoding.** When you see or hear a promotional message, you decode it—you interpret it in such a way that it has real meaning for you. Of course, the source hopes that you hear or notice the encoded message and do not screen it out (remember perceptual screens and selective retention from Chapter 4?). It also hopes that you interpret the message in the way the source intended (remember perceptual biases from Chapter 4?).

6. **Noise.** Have you ever tried to tune into a radio station and given up because there was too much static or distortion? You could not hear the station's program because of the noise. In communications, noise can be a physical distraction such as the one you experience when you try to tune your radio. The background noise level may be so high that the source and receiver perceive different messages in a person-to-person or telephone conversation. In the mass media, the noise is different. The source's message is competing for the receiver's attention with messages from competitors and promotions of unrelated services and products.

7. **Receiver.** Receivers are the people who notice or hear the source's message. It is hoped that receivers will also decode the message's encoding.

8. **Response.** The ultimate objective of all promotion is to affect customer buying behaviors—to get a response. Many hospitality and travel advertisers do this by using a technique called *direct-response* advertising. Customers are asked to respond either by calling a toll-free number or sending back a completed coupon. The Australian Tourist Commission (ATC) includes on its Web site a link to a request for brochures, called "Order a Brochure" (Figure 14–2). By filling out the on-line form and e-mailing it to the ATC, potential travelers receive a variety of brochures on Australia, and on individual states and territories. This type of promotion tends to motivate customers to take action. In this case, it also helps the promoters (ATC) evaluate the effectiveness of their promotion and provides them with a valuable database of information on potential travelers.

9. **Feedback.** Feedback is the response message that the receiver transmits back to the source. In communications between two persons, feedback is relatively easy to judge. The receiver gives the source verbal and nonverbal (body language) feedback. When mass communications are used, feedback is much more difficult to evaluate. Obviously, feedback ultimately is expressed in the promotion's impact on sales. Special marketing research studies must usually be undertaken to determine the effect of mass-media promotions, especially advertising campaigns. There has been a definite trend in recent years for hospitality and travel promoters to place

ON THE WEB

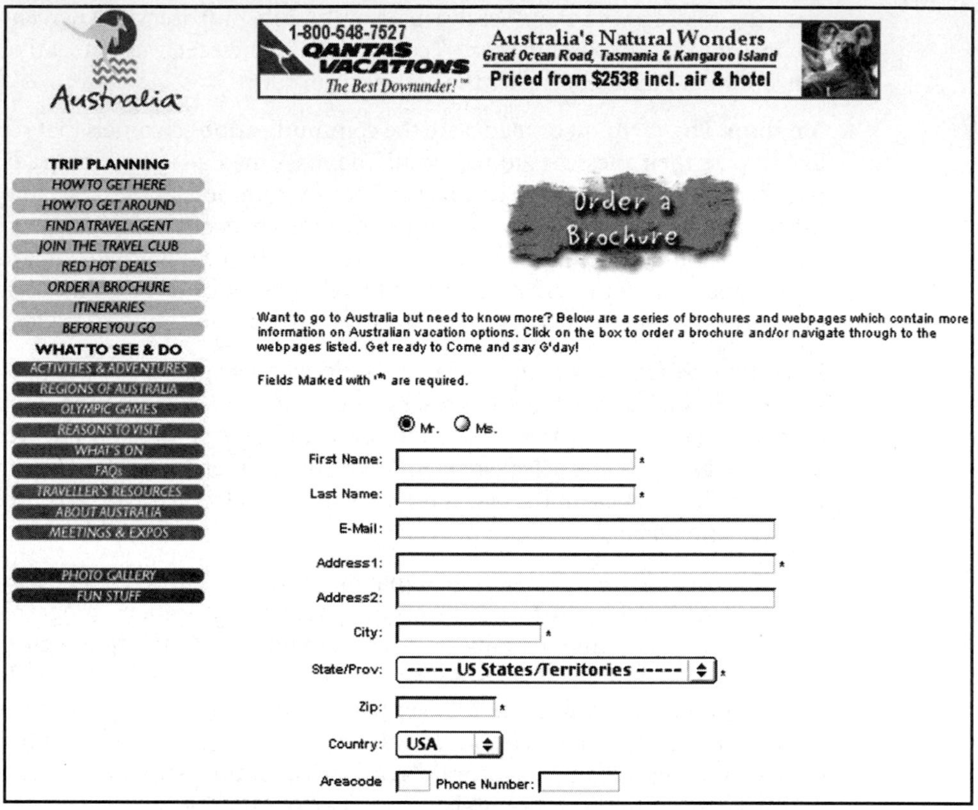

◆ **FIGURE 14–2**   *This Web-based survey form encourages travelers to respond and gives the Australian Tourist Commission an excellent database.* (Courtesy of the Australian Tourist Commission)

more emphasis on direct-response promotions, often referred to collectively as **direct marketing**. These are promotional techniques (including interactive Web and e-mail marketing, direct mail, telemarketing, direct-response advertising, and personal selling) that require customers to provide feedback by responding by phone, e-mail, mail, or in person. **Direct-response advertising** is a form of direct marketing that encourages the customer to take immediate action or make an immediate response directly to the advertiser.[1]

Figure 14–1 depicts the communications process.[2] It illustrates that promotion—a form of communications—is a system that begins with a source and ends with feedback from the receiver to the source. It also shows that the intended message (what we say) is often not the message that is actually received (what is heard and understood). The actual messages that receivers get result from their perceptual biases and decoding. The intended message, encoded for maximum impact, is what the promoter is trying to express through an advertisement, sales call, coupon promotion, press release, or other promotional tool.

In reviewing the model shown in Figure 14–1, it is also important to realize the social impact on the communications process. Research has shown that **word-of-**

mouth advertising (information relayed verbally between customers) further disseminates and reinforces messages. When customers buy hospitality and travel services, they are influenced more by interpersonal information from within their social network (friends, relatives, associates, opinion leaders) than by direct exposure to messages from the mass media. This is why so much attention is paid to developing promotions that generate widespread public interest and conversation, particularly among opinion leaders.

Another important point about the model is that, before customers can begin decoding, they must first pay attention to the messages. Hospitality and travel promoters go to great lengths to capture customers' attention by using the stimulus factors discussed in Chapter 4. These factors are used to encode messages and are expressed either through the service itself or in a symbolic way through words and pictures. Some effective techniques include novelty (*pop-out* sections in ads, upside-down ads), unusual uniforms worn by staff, intensity (full-page advertisements, speakers with deep, resonant voices), contrast (silence in TV commercials, white space in print advertisements, Figure 14–3), and motion (moving parts in billboards). Even in this case, marketers are walking a tightrope. They must use just the right amount of stimulation. If promotional messages have too strong an impact or too many stimuli, *internal noise* (a psychological state that inhibits customers from absorbing the message) can result. If customers are *overstimulated*, they may ignore or forget the main point of the message. The credibility of the promotion may also be lost.

The concept of *noise* needs further explanation. There are four principal sources of noise:

a. Directly competitive promotions
b. Noncompetitive promotions
c. The level of stimulation in the promotional message
d. The customer's state of readiness

When potential customers watch an evening's worth of television or read a travel magazine, they may be exposed to so many competitive advertisements that they do not notice the ad of one specific hotel company or airline. There is just too much competitive noise. The *clutter* of other noncompetitive promotions also severely taxes customers' patience and ability to notice and absorb messages. There are many examples that prove that customers have been oversaturated with commercial promotions. Many people make a point of visiting the refrigerator or bathroom during TV commercials; others automatically throw direct mail ads into the garbage. Another noise source is a customer's physical state at the time of exposure to the promotion. For instance, hungry customers are much more likely to notice fast-food billboards than are those who have just finished eating. As mentioned previously, some promotions are so complicated (overstimulating) that they create internal noise. Keeping promotions very simple, yet informative, is one of the key challenges (Figure 14–4).

Explicit and Implicit Communications

Explicit and implicit communications are the two basic ways that promotional messages are conveyed to customers. **Explicit communications** are definite messages that are given to customers through the use of language, either oral (e.g., television, radio,

Which is the only cruise line to listen to its guests and offer a truly smoke-free ship?

PARADISE

Today's ❯ Carnival sм

◆ **FIGURE 14–3**   *An excellent use of "white space" by Carnival makes this ad about its non-smoking ship, Paradise, stand out.* (Courtesy of Carnival Cruise Lines)

telephone, or personal sales) or written (e.g., the Web, e-mail, ad copy, sales proposals). Language is used to promote a common understanding between the seller and potential buyer (or source and receiver). Advertising, personal selling, sales promotion, merchandising, and public relations and publicity (the promotional mix elements) are used to transmit explicit communications to customers.

Somewhere, deep in your mind, is a child who grew up with dreams of adventure and romance.

A child who could turn a toy boat into a sailing ship. And a bathtub into the bounding main.

On a Royal Caribbean cruise, you could find yourself getting to know that child all over again.

You could spend seven, eight, ten, or even fourteen days discovering storybook islands ringed with palm trees and scented with hibiscus.

You could dance to the pulsating rhythm of steel drums. Dine on fresh pineapple and flaming babalu. Meet a neon-blue fish, face to face, in the lacy shadows of a coral reef.

Or stand high on a polished deck, with a warm breeze in your face, as your ship glides through an indigo sea that stretches all the way to the edges of your imagination.

Just see your travel agent about a Royal Caribbean cruise.

It can take you away to some of the most beautiful places on earth.

And take you back to some of the most beautiful times of your life.

ROYAL CARIBBEAN

Ever Since You Were A Kid, You've Wanted To Take A Cruise.

◆ **FIGURE 14–4** *A simple message communicates best.* (Courtesy of Royal Caribbean International)

Implicit communications are *cues* or messages conveyed through body language (e.g., facial expressions, gestures, other body movements). They can also be conveyed by other nonverbal means, including the following:

1. The inherent nature of the product/service mix (e.g., quality and variety of facilities and service, decor, staff uniforms, color schemes)
2. The prices, rates, or fares
3. The channels of distribution
4. The medium chosen for promotion
5. The media vehicle that carries the promotion (e.g., name of magazine or newspaper, television or radio station and type of program)
6. The partners chosen for cooperative promotions
7. The quality of packages and programs offered
8. The people managing and providing the service

With implicit communications or promotions, the salesperson, product/service, price, and distribution channels carry connotations for customers. This is the *evidence* mentioned in Chapter 2 as being so important to service businesses. Customers often make up their minds about services by looking at the clues they get from the facilities, services, prices, and distribution channels available. High prices usually connote high quality and are often used to communicate this level of service or facility. Spectacular atrium lobbies (such as those in many Hyatt Hotels), oriental carpets, marble, glass, copper, and brass are also clues to high-quality hotels, restaurants, and other hospitality/travel businesses. A hotel, restaurant, travel agency, or retail store in a trendy downtown location generates a different message than one in a low-income neighborhood. The packages, tours, cruises, and suppliers in which a travel agency specializes all carry a definite connotation. If the agency has many clients who buy Seabourn Cruises and Abercrombie & Kent tours, for example, this gives the impression that it serves primarily upper-income, more luxury-oriented customers.

Surrogate cues are product/service features that provide no direct use benefits, but convey a message about what is being offered. The name and size of an individual business or chain often convey a definite image. In the lodging industry, the names Econo Lodge and Thriftlodge transmit an impression of relatively low-cost accommodations. Thrifty and Payless Car Rental convey a similar image in their field.

Size is another important surrogate cue. Lodging customers expect more and different facilities in a 400-room hotel than they do in a 20-room motel. Generally, the larger the chain or company, the more services customers expect to be available. For example, most travelers would anticipate finding a frequent-guest awards program at a national hotel chain, but would not expect the same in a smaller regional company or independent hotel.

A Touch of Technology

The Internet, Intranets, and Extranets

- Business communications are being revolutionized by new technologies, including the Internet, Intranets, and Extranets.

- The Internet is the best known and understood of these three. The Internet functions include e-mail, the World Wide Web, gopher, and file transfer protocol.

- An Intranet is like a private Internet service and is most often used by individual companies to allow its employees to access certain information on-line. It provides faster access and transfers of data, and can result in significant cost savings.

- A person can access the Internet from an Intranet, but cannot access an Intranet from the Internet.

- Applications of Intranets in hospitality and travel include sites exclusively for members of the sales force, sites containing training materials, and sites containing databases of various types.

- Extranets are another offshoot of the Internet with the express purpose of exchanging information with business partners, customers, and suppliers. Again this interchange is private and limited to people within a certain group.

- An example of an Extranet in tourism is one operated by the Canadian Tourism Commission called the *Canadian Tourism Exchange* or CTX. CTX provides its members with research, statistics, and news about tourism.

What else did you notice about the list of *nonverbal,* implicit communications shown earlier? You are doing well if you realized that it includes all the other seven marketing-mix elements, excluding promotion. What do you think this means? Again, you are on the right track if you said that all eight marketing-mix elements must communicate the same message consistently. If the implicit communications do not support explicit promotions, these promotions will lack credibility. For example, the Hot'n Now hamburger chain's name and advertising campaign is supported by easy-to-access store locations and quick service through its double drive-through concept. If Hot'n Now offered a broad menu that took several minutes to prepare and serve, it would be guilty of creating a dramatic conflict between its explicit (promotional) and implicit communications. The reverse is also true—advertising and other promotions must support and be consistent with the other seven marketing-mix elements.

GOALS OF PROMOTION

The ultimate purpose of promotion is to modify behavior through communication. This requires helping customers through the various buying process stages so they eventually purchase or repurchase a particular service. As Figure 14–5 shows, promotion accomplishes this by informing, persuading, and reminding—the three principal goals of promotion.[3]

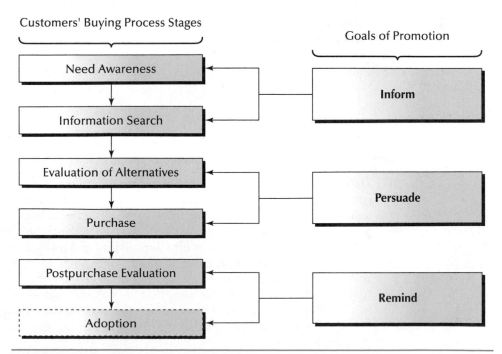

◆ FIGURE 14–5   *Goals of promotion and buying process stages.* (Adapted from *The Tourism System: An Introductory Text,* third edition by Robert Christie Mill and Alastair M. Morrison. Copyright © 1998 by Kendall/Hunt Publishing Company. Used with permission)

Informative promotions work best with new services or products (early product-life-cycle stages) and with customers in early buying process stages (need awareness and information search). These types of promotions tend to communicate data or ideas about the key features of services. Persuasive promotions are harder hitting. They are aimed at getting customers to select one particular company or brand over those of competitors, and to actually make the purchase. Advertisements that compare one company's services to another, and most sales promotions, fit into this category. Persuasive promotions work best in intermediate/late stages of the product life cycle (growth and maturity) and the buying process (evaluation of alternatives and purchase). Reminder promotions are used to jog customers' memories about advertising they may have seen, and to stimulate repurchases. They are most effective in the late product-life-cycle (maturity and decline) and buying process stages (postpurchase evaluation and adoption).

THE PROMOTIONAL MIX

The marketing mix (product, promotion, place, price, packaging, programming, partnership, and people) contains the eight elements that an organization must work with when it develops a marketing plan. Therefore, the promotional mix is only one element of the marketing mix. You already know that the promotional mix must complement the other seven parts of the marketing mix. We have also seen that these seven other elements themselves implicitly promote services, communicating definite messages to customers. The five promotional mix elements are as follows:

1. Advertising
2. Personal selling
3. Sales promotion
4. Merchandising
5. Public relations and publicity

Advertising

Advertising is the most widely visible and well-recognized element of the promotional mix. It is also the item on which most promotional dollars are spent.

1. **Definition.** *Advertising* is "paid, nonpersonal communication through various media by business firms, nonprofit organizations, and individuals who are in some way identified in the advertising message and who hope to inform and/or persuade members of a particular audience."[4] The key words in this definition are *paid, nonpersonal,* and *identified.* Hospitality and travel organizations always have to pay for advertising, either in money or in some form of barter (e.g., free meals from a restaurant in exchange for a radio ad). On the other hand, publicity is free. The communications approach is nonpersonal—neither the sponsors nor their representatives are physically present to give the message to customers. The word *identified* indicates that the paying organization is clearly identified in the advertisement.

Advertising messages do not always have to be aimed directly at creating a sale. Sometimes it is the sponsor's goal simply to convey a positive idea or a favorable image of the organization (often called *institutional* advertising). Coca Cola has sponsored ads during the children's Special Olympics, and McDonald's has advertisements centering on their Ronald McDonald House concept (accommodations for relatives of hospitalized children).

2. **Advantages.** There are several principal advantages of advertising, including the following:

   a. *Low Cost Per Contact.* Although the total costs of advertising campaigns often run into the millions of dollars, the cost per contact is relatively low when advertising is compared to alternative promotional approaches. One 30-second, prime-time television commercial often costs hundreds of thousands of dollars. However, with viewing audiences in the millions, the cost for each person who is exposed to this ad becomes a matter of cents.

   b. *Ability to Reach Customers Where and When Salespersons Cannot.* The salesperson usually cannot drive home with customers, spend an evening with them in their television room, or be on their doorstep every morning. They cannot successfully pass through the mail slot. However, advertisements can confront customers in almost every facet of their lives. They reach people in places and at times when salespeople cannot.

   c. *Great Scope for Creative Versatility and Dramatization of Messages.* Advertising provides limitless opportunities for creative approaches and for the dramatization of the promoter's message. This can be done through the brilliant colors of a magazine ad showing a destination's breathtaking scenery or through the reprise of an old ballad or rock-'n-roll song, such as Hyatt's "You've got the magic touch" and Jamaica's "Come to Jamaica and feel alright." Since there is so much advertising today, ads must stand out in the crowd. Figure 14–6 demonstrates this in an ad from the Bermuda Department of Tourism with the tag line, "They're up against breathtaking views." The deep blues of the Atlantic, pink beach, and deep green golf links help this ad stand out from other destinations' promotions.

   d. *Ability to Create Images that Salespersons Cannot.* Advertising is great at creating images in customers' minds. Television, with its use of sounds, colors, and movements, is especially effective at this. In 1994, Qantas used a favorite Australian song "I Still Call Australia Home" with famous landmarks like the Sydney Opera House and the Great Wall of China to create an image of nostalgia in its television advertising campaign.

   e. *Nonthreatening Nature of Nonpersonal Presentation.* Have you ever entered a store and been immediately confronted by an aggressive salesperson obviously eager to make a commission on your purchase? "Can I help you find what you want?" usually follows on the heels of a curt greeting. Many of us are threatened, or at least put on the defensive, by this type of approach. It is a face-to-face communication that forces us to come up with an answer or to make a decision quickly. Advertising, on the other hand, is a nonpersonal form of communications. Customers are not forced to respond, evaluate, or decide immediately. Because customers do not have their guards up, sponsors' messages often slip through consciously or unconsciously when other promotions would be resisted.

   f. *Potential to Repeat Message Several Times.* Some promotional messages work best if customers are exposed to them several times. For example, if you

GOLF COURSES IN BERMUDA ARE VERY COMPETITIVE.

THEY'RE UP AGAINST BREATHTAKING VIEWS.

Only two and a half hours from Toronto (and accessible from major Canadian hubs), it's easy for your clients to experience paradise—at exceptional value.

With more golf courses per square mile than in any other country, Bermuda is truly a golfer's paradise. Here, spectacular vistas— turquoise waters, our legendary pink beaches and quaint, white- roofed cottages—are par for the course. There's always something wonderful to experience in Bermuda, whether it's the thrill of tennis, scuba, deep-sea fishing and sailing regattas or the tranquility of our lush parks and nature reserves.

There's so much to discover.

Bermuda's new Heritage Passport provides unlimited admission to eight cultural attractions, all for one low price. Your clients can tour the Bermuda Aquarium & Zoo, unlock the secrets of the deep at the Underwater Exploration Institute and the Maritime Museum, stroll the historic streets of St. George and still find time to shop for local crafts at the Royal Naval Dockyard. Dining out in Bermuda is a true culinary adventure where your clients can savor a delectable array of international and Island cuisines.

Everything comes with a smile.

Our celebrated British heritage and charm and friendly local flair combine to take pampering to a whole new level. Not only will your clients feel welcomed and relaxed, they will also experience every amenity during their visit to Bermuda. Whether it's a full-service resort, comfortable guest house or cozy cottage colony, our choice of accommodations is as flexible as our rates. Discover why 46% of the people who visit, return to Bermuda.

TO ORDER YOUR BERMUDA RESOURCE GUIDE, *THE BLUE BOOK* **OR FOR MORE INFORMATION, CALL 1-800-223-6106 OR VISIT WWW.BERMUDATOURISM.COM**

◆ **FIGURE 14–6**   *An intriguing headline and beautiful photography make this Bermuda ad stand out from the crowd.* (Courtesy of the Bermuda Department of Tourism)

are driving to a vacation destination and have not made previous plans, you are definitely in the market for a hotel/motel room, meals, and perhaps a few quick side trips to attractions. The chances that you are aware of and choose a particular hotel, fast-food restaurant, or attraction increase with the number of their billboards you see en route.

g. ***Prestige and Impressiveness of Mass-Media Advertising.*** Advertising, and the specific advertising medium selected, can enhance the prestige and credibility of a hospitality and travel organization. An emerging hotel company that launches a national television advertising campaign signals that it has arrived in the big leagues. A tour wholesaler that places a full-page, four-color ad in *Smithsonian, National Geographic,* or *Fortune* gets almost instant credibility. Research shows that the more frequently a company or brand advertises nationally, the more customers perceive it as a high-quality product or service[5]

3. **Disadvantages.** The powerful, persuasive, and pervasive nature of advertising cannot be denied. It does, however, have its limitations and drawbacks.
   a. ***Inability to Close Sales.*** Advertising is strong in creating awareness, improving understanding (comprehension), changing attitudes, and creating purchase intentions, but it can seldom get the whole job done on its own. It rarely *closes the sale* (finally convincing customers to make reservations, buy tickets, make deposits, and take other actions that clinch the sale). Personal selling is far more effective than advertising in closing sales. This is especially true with high-involvement (extensive problem solving) decisions. In other words, advertising usually cannot, without the help of other promotional mix elements, guide customers through all their buying process stages.
   b. ***Advertising Clutter.*** The opportunities for advertising are limitless. This is both an advantage and disadvantage. Thousands of advertisements compete for your attention, but you remember few of them. Why? The human has a very limited memory and storage capacity. There are so many ads in so many places that they appear as a clutter of commercial messages. There are too many to notice and assimilate. Other promotional mix elements, particularly personal selling, allow a more individualized, personal presentation of the message.
   c. ***Customer's Ability to Ignore Advertising Messages.*** Although advertisers can be guaranteed of reaching their target audiences, there is no iron-clad assurance that everyone will notice them. Many of us automatically throw unopened, direct mail ads into the garbage. People find other things to do during the commercial breaks in TV and radio programs. Many avoid the advertising pages in the front of magazines with a quick flip to the lead article. Potential customers develop these advertising *avoidance* habits because they are oversaturated with commercial messages (advertising clutter). They know that advertising is *biased* toward the sponsor, and they do not even let messages pass through the attention filter.
   d. ***Difficulty Getting Immediate Response or Action.*** Advertising often does not cause the customer to respond quickly or to take immediate action. Other promotional mix elements, specifically sales promotions and personal selling, are usually more effective. As stated earlier, the increased emphasis on direct-response advertising by hospitality and travel promoters is helping the industry to overcome this problem.
   e. ***Inability to Get Quick Feedback and to Adjust Message.*** Without careful marketing research, it is very difficult to determine customer reactions to advertising. Ineffective ads may continue to run while research information is gathered. Personal selling, on the other hand, gives the organization immediate feedback and great flexibility in adjusting the message to suit the prospect. Advertising is powerful in its ability to influence the earlier stages of customers' buying processes, but not as effective as other promotional mix elements in later stages. The increasing use of direct-marketing techniques and interactive media is providing advertisers with more timely feedback from customers. **Interactive media**

involve some combination of electronic and communication devices (e.g., television, computers, phone lines) that permit the customers to interact with the sponsors' information or reservation services. For example, the Web and interactive television are becoming more popular, allowing customers to *home shop* by selecting and making travel reservations from their own living rooms.[6] These opportunities for direct booking will grow along with the increasing number of special travel shows on television and customer use of text-based on-line computer services such as America Online.

    f. ***Difficulty Measuring Advertising Effectiveness.*** So many variables influence customer purchases that it is usually difficult to separate the impact of advertising. The most troublesome issue is usually whether advertising led directly to a sale or whether it only assisted.

    g. ***Relatively High Waste Factor.*** Waste means having people who are not part of the target market see, hear, or read advertisements. Most forms of advertising involve significant *waste*. Newspapers, for example, have the advantage of broad coverage (they are read by many), but as a result they are not effective in appealing to specific target markets (except geographic ones). Direct mail advertising is the best advertising medium for targeting specific markets.

Personal Selling

1. **Definition.** Personal selling involves oral conversations. These are held, either by telephone or face-to-face, between salespersons and prospective customers.

2. **Advantages.**
    a. ***Ability to Close Sales.*** The most powerful feature of personal selling is its ability to close sales. As you will see in Chapter 17, one of the keys to a successful sales call is for the salesperson to *ask for the sale*. Experts refer to this as *using a close* or just *closing the sale*. The customer (or *prospect*) is persuaded to make a decision one way or the other. Other promotional mix elements allow customers to ignore the sales message completely or to postpone the purchase decision indefinitely.

    b. ***Ability to Hold the Customer's Attention.*** There is no better way to hold the customer's attention than in a face-to-face conversation. Customers, however, are completely free to ignore the messages carried by the four other promotional mix elements (advertising, sales promotion, merchandising, and public relations and publicity).

    c. ***Immediate Feedback and Two-Way Communications.*** The relative success in closing sales using personal selling results partly from the two-way communications involved and the ability to get quick customer feedback. All four other promotional mix elements use impersonal means of getting their messages across. A personal sales message can be adjusted based on the customer's reactions. The other four promotional mix elements are not as flexible.

    d. ***Presentations Tailored to Individual Needs.*** Personal sales presentations are tailor-made to fit the prospect's needs and requirements. Customers can ask questions and get answers. If they have objections (problems or concerns about the service or product), the salesperson can address these directly.

e. ***Ability to Target Customers Precisely.*** If an effective prospecting (choosing potential customers for sales presentations) job is done, there is very little *waste* in personal selling. In fact, good salespersons carefully screen and qualify customers (verify that the prospect is a potential buyer) before they arrange face-to-face meetings. The other promotional mix elements usually result in higher levels of waste.

f. ***Ability to Cultivate Relationships.*** With personal selling, the salesperson can develop an ongoing relationship with prospects. This does not mean that it is advisable for the salesperson to become best friends with all prospects—this is generally not recommended. What it does imply is that prospects can establish a more personal link with a company through a salesperson. Having this personal communications channel often is a more powerful inducement to customers to make repeat purchases than are the company's advertising and other promotions.

g. ***Ability to Get Immediate Action.*** As you saw earlier, advertising leads only indirectly to sales or it delays the purchase response. Personal selling always has the potential of producing immediate action from the prospect.

3. **Disadvantages.**

a. ***High Cost Per Contact.*** The major drawback to personal selling is its high cost per contact compared to the four other promotional mix elements. Whereas most other promotions usually cost no more than a few dollars per person reached, a field sales presentation often means salary and travel costs that exceed $100 per contact. Although personalizing the sales message is a powerful inducement for the customer to purchase, it involves a great deal of added expense. Some forms of personal selling are more efficient. For example, in-house and telephone selling do not require the travel costs necessary for field sales presentations.

b. ***Inability to Reach Some Customers as Effectively.*** Customers may refuse a salesperson's help or presentation. As noted earlier, some people are put on their guard by personal selling approaches. They are less defensive when it comes to impersonal communications such as advertising, sales promotion, merchandising, and public relations and publicity. Prospects may also be "inaccessible" for other reasons, such as their geographic locations and schedules.

Sales Promotion

1. **Definition.** Sales promotions are approaches other than advertising, personal selling, and public relations and publicity where customers are given a short-term inducement to make an immediate purchase. Like advertising, the sponsor is clearly identified and the communication is nonpersonal. Examples include discount coupons, contests and sweepstakes, samples, and premiums.

2. **Advantages.**

a. ***Combination of Some Advantages of Advertising and Personal Selling.*** In their ability to generate immediate purchases, sales promotions share this key advantage of personal selling. However, they have an added advantage over personal selling—they can be mass-communicated and distributed. For example, coupons can be sent through the mail, or customers can clip them out of magazines or newspapers.

b. ***Ability to Provide Quick Feedback.*** Many sales promotions offer incentives that must be claimed within a short time period. Most coupons must be redeemed before a specified date. Usually, there is also a deadline with contests, sweepstakes, and premiums. Customers must react quickly—thus, the sponsor gets rapid feedback on the offer.

c. ***Ability to Add Excitement to a Service or Product.*** An imaginative sales promotion can add excitement to a hospitality and travel service. The Singapore Tourism Board excited travel agents in 1999 with a colorful advertisement promoting *Millennia Mania* in Singapore. The ad announced 15 months of celebrations beginning in June 1999 including parades, festivals, and acts by various performers.

d. ***Additional Ways to Communicate with Customers.*** Sales promotions provide an added assortment of communications channels to customers. *Bounce-back* coupons can be attached to take-out and home-delivered food. Menus and coupon offers can be designed as doorknob hangers.

e. ***Flexible Timing.*** Another example of the flexibility of sales promotions is that they can be used on short notice and at almost any time. They are particularly helpful in building sales during off-peak times (e.g., two-for-one restaurant meals on Monday and Tuesday nights). If other promotional mix elements are unsuccessful in attracting forecasted sales volumes, a last-minute sales promotion may be used to fill the slack. Again, you can see that it is the ability of sales promotion to generate increased sales in the short term that is its key advantage.

f. ***Efficiency.*** Sales promotions can be very efficient. Both advertising and personal selling involve significant, up-front fixed costs. On the other hand, sales promotions can be launched with modest initial investments (e.g., printing coupons). Additional costs may vary directly with the number of customers taking advantage of the promotion (e.g., coupon redemptions, guests claiming frequent-flyer or frequent-guest awards).

3. **Disadvantages.**

a. ***Short-Term Benefits.*** The beauty of sales promotions is their quick payback in increased sales. It is paradoxical, but this is also their major shortcoming—sales promotions usually do not lead to long-term sales increases. A sales promotion tends to increase short-term revenues, but when the promotion is over, sales return to normal or below-normal levels. Furthermore, a company that offers too many *deals* runs the risk of having customers permanently undervalue its services.

b. ***Ineffective in Building Long-Term Loyalty for Company or Brand.*** Sales promotions are very appealing to *brand switchers,* who flip between competitive services based on which company offers the best deal at the time. They are not effective in developing true company or brand loyalty. Because most organizations are more concerned with building a long-term customer base, sales promotions are not as effective for them as other explicit and implicit promotions.

c. ***Inability to Be Used on Its Own in the Long Term Without Other Promotional Mix Elements.*** In the long-term, sales promotions are most effective if they dovetail with, and are supported by, the other promotional techniques. Frequent-guest programs must be advertised, *sold* to corporate accounts, and described in a brochure or brochures. For example, McDonald's Monopoly promotions over the years have been supported by significant media advertising.

d. ***Often Misused.*** Sales promotions are often used as *quick-fix* solutions for long-term marketing problems. Some national restaurant chains seem to offer a constant stream of sales promotion deals, seemingly buying customers away from competitors. They should, however, be concentrating on attracting loyal, long-term customers by improving menu selections, redesigning restaurants or reconcepting, repositioning, or upgrading service or food quality.

Merchandising (Point-of-Purchase Advertising)

It is a common practice to categorize merchandising as a sales promotion technique, because it does not involve media advertising, personal selling, or public relations and publicity. In this text, merchandising is separated from other sales promotion techniques because of its uniqueness and its importance to the industry.

1. **Definition.** Merchandising, or point-of-purchase advertising, includes materials used in-house to stimulate sales. These include menus, wine lists, tent cards, signs, posters, displays, and other point-of-sale promotional items.

2. **Advantages.** The advantages of merchandising are very similar to those for all sales promotions:
   a. Combining some of the advantages of advertising and personal selling
   b. Producing quick feedback
   c. Adding excitement to a service or product
   d. Providing additional ways to communicate to customers
   e. Allowing flexible timing
   Think of some of your recent trips to the supermarket or clothing store. You may have bought one or more grocery items on impulse because of a special aisle-end or other display. You may also have spent a few more dollars than you planned to on clothes, because of an attractive window display or arrangement inside the clothing store. Or perhaps you have visited a restaurant recently, and because of its unique menu or mouth-watering menu descriptions, significantly departed from your diet. Merchandising excites the visual senses at the point of purchase and often results in increased sales. There are two additional advantages of merchandising.
   a. ***Stimulation of Impulse Purchases and Higher Per Capita Spending.*** What we have just talked about is merchandising's ability to get you to make purchases you had not intended to make. You may be drawn into a travel agency by an attractive display for a cruise line or resort company. Once you are on the hospitality or travel business' premises, other visual merchandising may lead you to spend more than you planned.
   b. ***Support for Advertising Campaigns.*** Advertising campaign effectiveness can be greatly increased if customers receive a visual reminder at the point of purchase. Fast-food chains are masters of this technique. Through television advertising they promote children's meal *packages* that include certain toys or toy premiums with any purchases that customers make. Attractive, in-house displays are quick to remind children of this merchandise and to rivet their attention.

3. **Disadvantages.** The key difference between merchandising and other sales promotion techniques is that merchandising does not necessarily involve giving the customer a financial incentive. The impact of certain merchandising items can also be longer-term. A good menu can last for several years. In-store displays may be suitable for several months, as may posters, tents, and brochure displays.

   Although merchandising may have a longer-lasting positive impact, it is still not effective in building long-term loyalty for the company or brand. Although it can be used without support from other promotional mix elements, again it is much more effective if it is coordinated with personal selling and advertising.

   A third disadvantage of some merchandising may be its contribution to *visual clutter*. Some people are so annoyed by the number of tent cards on restaurant tables that they consciously or subconsciously ignore all of them.

Public Relations and Publicity

1. **Definition.** Public relations includes all the activities that a hospitality and travel organization engages in to maintain or improve its relationship with other organizations and individuals. Publicity is one public relations technique that involves nonpaid communication of information about an organization's services.

2. **Advantages.**
   a. *Low Cost.* Compared to other promotional mix elements, public relations and publicity costs relatively little. However, there is a common misconception that it is totally free. Effective public relations and publicity requires careful planning and considerable management and staff time.
   b. *Effective Because They Are Not Seen as Commercial Messages.* You saw earlier that media advertising is recognized as a biased form of communications. People do not treat public relations messages on radio and television, and in newspaper and magazine articles, with the same skepticism, because the services are being described by an independent party. Customers do not *turn off* as readily to this information as they do to media advertisements. Publicity has a way of slipping past perceptual defenses.
   c. *Credibility and Implied Endorsements.* If a travel critic writes favorably about a destination, hotel, or restaurant, this carries greater credibility than sponsors' paid advertisements. Customers also feel that they are receiving the reporter's endorsement.
   d. *Prestige and Impressiveness of Mass-Media Coverage.* Both publicity and advertising are carried by the mass media. Thus, publicity shares the advantage of prestige and impressiveness with advertising.
   e. *Added Excitement and Dramatization.* A writer's use of the English language, or the skills of a reporter or camera crew, can accentuate the benefits and unique features of a hospitality or travel business. Dramatic opening ceremonies for hotels or restaurants, inaugural departures of ships, or new airline routes are other examples of heightening the excitement of services.
   f. *Maintenance of a Public Presence.* Public relations activities ensure that an organization maintains a continued, positive presence in its various *publics*. These include local, media, financial, employees, and trade/industry segments.

3. **Disadvantages.**
   a. ***Difficult to Arrange Consistently.*** Receiving positive publicity is often a *hit-and-miss* proposition. Coverage is totally at the discretion of media people. Its timing cannot be controlled with the same degree of accuracy as other promotional techniques.
   b. ***Lack of Control.*** Another aspect of this lack of control is the inability to ensure that what is covered and said are exactly what you want. Reporters may fail to include key facts or selling ideas, or they may distort words and ideas.

Figure 14–7 provides a summary of the advantages and disadvantages of the five promotional mix elements.

FACTORS AFFECTING THE PROMOTIONAL MIX

You now understand the advantages and disadvantages of each promotional mix element. However, there are other factors that affect promotional mix decisions.

Target Markets

The effectiveness of the five promotional mix elements varies according to the target market. For example, in promoting its convention/meeting facilities, a lodging property might find that personal selling to key meeting planners is much more effective than advertising. On the other hand, using personal selling to attract individual pleasure travelers would not be feasible. Generally, the more complex the service, the greater the value of personal selling.

The geographic location of potential customers also has an impact. Where they are widely dispersed, advertising may be the most efficient and effective way to reach them.

Marketing Objectives

The promotional mix selected should flow directly from the objectives for each target market. For example, if the objective is to build awareness by a certain percentage, the emphasis may be placed on media advertising. If, on the other hand, it is to build sales significantly in a short time period, the focus may be put on sales promotion.

Competition and Promotional Practices

There is a distinct tendency in certain parts of the hospitality and travel industry for most competitive organizations to use the same *lead element* in promotional mixes. Fast-food chains focus on heavy television advertising, hotels and airlines are locked in a battle of frequent-traveler award programs, and cruise lines put a heavy emphasis on personal selling to travel agents. It is difficult and extremely risky for one competitor to *break from the pack* in this respect.

Promotional Budget Available

Obviously the funds available for promotion have a direct impact on choosing promotional mix elements. Smaller organizations with more limited budgets usually have to place greater emphasis on lower-cost promotions, including publicity and sales promotions. Larger organizations can better afford to use media advertising and personal selling.

	ADVERTISING	PERSONAL SELLING	SALES PROMOTION	MERCHANDISING	PUBLIC RELATIONS AND PUBLICITY
Advantages	• Low cost per contact • Ability to reach customers where salespersons cannot • Great scope for creative versatility and dramatization • Ability to create images that salespersons cannot • Nonthreatening nature of nonpersonal presentation • Potential to repeat message several times • Prestige and impressiveness of mass-media advertising	• Ability to close sales • Ability to hold the customer's attention • Immediate feedback and two-way communications • Presentations tailored to individual needs • Ability to target customers precisely • Ability to cultivate relationships • Ability to get immediate action	• Combination of some advantages of advertising and personal selling • Ability to provide quick feedback • Ability to add excitement to a service or product • Additional ways to communicate with customers • Flexible timing • Efficiency	• Ability to provide quick feedback • Ability to add excitement to a service or product • Additional ways to communicate with customers • Flexible timing • Stimulation of impulse purchases and higher per capita spending	• Low cost • Effective because they are not seen as commercial messages • Credibility and implied endorsements • Prestige and impressiveness of mass-media coverage • Added excitement and dramatization • Maintenance of a public presence
Disadvantages	• Inability to close sales • Advertising clutter • Customer's ability to ignore advertising messages • Difficulty getting immediate response or action • Inability to get quick feedback and to adjust message • Difficulty measuring advertising effectiveness • Relatively high waste factor	• High cost per contact • Inability to reach some customers as effectively	• Short-term benefits • Ineffective in building long-term loyalty for company or brand • Inability to be used on its own in the long term without other promotional mix elements • Often misused	• Does not necessarily give the customer a financial incentive • Ineffective in building long-term loyalty for company or brand • Contributes to visual clutter	• Difficult to arrange consistently • Lack of control

◆ **FIGURE 14–7** *Summary of the advantages and disadvantages of the five promotional mix elements.*

Promotional Mix:
Chi Chi's Restaurants

The increased popularity of ethnic and foreign cuisines has been a major trend in countries such as the United States, Canada, U.K., and Australia. Mexican food has become particularly popular both as a fast-food alternative (through chains like Taco Bell) and in dinner houses through companies such as Chi-Chi's, El Torito, Don Pablo's, and On the Border. The growth and development of Chi-Chi's provides an excellent example of how one company has capitalized on the rapidly increasing popularity of the Mexican cuisine during the past 25 years. The company has also made excellent use of various promotional mix elements to communicate its unique menu items to customers.

The first Chi-Chi's restaurant opened in 1976 in Minneapolis. At the time this case was written, there were approximately 150 units located in the U.S. Midwest and Eastern states.[1] Expansion of the chain was especially rapid in the early 1980s, and financial and managerial problems were experienced in the 1983–1986 period partly due to this rate of growth. In 1988, Foodmaker, Inc. of San Diego, California acquired Chi-Chi's. In 1994, Foodmaker divested Chi-Chi's and it became a subsidiary of Family Restaurants, Inc. or FRI (renamed as Prandium, Inc. since April 1999). At that time, FRI became the largest company of Mexican dinner houses with a combined total of nearly 300 restaurants under three brand names (Chi-Chi's, El Torito, and Casa Gallardo). Prandium has since then sold off some of its Mexican concepts and acquired different restaurant brands. It now operates three distinct brands (Chi-Chi's, Koo Koo Roo, and Hamburger Hamlet).

Part of Chi-Chi's initial development strategy was to concentrate its units in the Midwest and Eastern states of the U.S., where Mexican food was not yet as popular as in California and other Western states. El Torito, Chi-Chi's sister company between 1994 and 2000

(Photo courtesy of Chi Chi's Inc.)

until it was sold off, was already well established at that time on the West Coast. The number of Chi-Chi's restaurants continued to increase to over 200 in the mid-1900s. In the second half of the 1990s a major reorganization of the chain was initiated by the Irvine, California based Prandium. With the divesture of the poorer performing Chi-Chi's units in the mid to late 1990s, the chain has returned to its original location strategy. Another Prandium strategy was to renovate a large proportion of its Chi-Chi's units. During the period of 1998–2000, almost 100 Chi-Chi's restaurants were remodeled or "resalsafied" as the company calls this renovation process.

The heart of Chi-Chi's promotional mix is its menu and how the menu and supporting table tents, and staff merchandise the company's food and beverages. Chi-Chi's specializes in mildly spiced Mexican foods of the Sonoran variety, along with some Southwestern items. The chain's signature dishes are Sizzling Fajitas, the Outrageous Burrito, Presidente Enchiladas, Mexi-Grill Platter, Pepper-Rubbed T-Bone, and Mexican Fried Ice Cream. Chi-Chi's has been awarded the distinction of being selected as "America's Favorite Mexican Restaurant" for eight years in a row by a *Restaurant and Institution* consumer survey. With around 20 million guests per year, Chi-Chi's definitely is deserving of its claim to being "one

continued

EXCELLENCE CASE *continued*

(Photo courtesy of Chi Chi's Inc.)

of the most exceptional success stories in the foodservice industry."[2]

The mark of a business success story is that the company never stands still and Chi-Chi's changed approaches to promotions and merchandising in 1999–2000 certainly demonstrates this. In the last quarter of 1999, the company switched from broadcast media advertising to freestanding inserts (FSIs) in print media (e.g., newspapers). These FSIs featured several of Chi-Chi's signature dishes. In May 2000 and after several months of testing, Chi-Chi's introduced a new menu featuring 50 new recipes.[3] Noticing the public's growing preference for non-alcoholic specialty drinks, the company introduced a line of blended drink items known as *Cabo Coolers.* The menu changes were supported by a return to broadcast television advertising.

Apart from the modifications to the menu and advertising placements, Chi-Chi's placed a strong focus on staff training and guest service. With an overall theme of "Life always need a little salsa," the "Salsafied" concept introduced a more fun and high-energy atmosphere into Chi-Chi's restaurants.

Another part of Chi-Chi's success is also due to its moderate prices and large portions. In addition to the complimentary tortilla chips and

salsa (now a standard in Mexican restaurants), most entrees come with a choice of salsa rice, refried beans, black beans, or sweet corn cake.

Chi-Chi's has made excellent use of various promotional mix elements to carve a unique niche for itself in the restaurant market. In addition to the personal selling skills of the staff members and the Salsafied guest service program mentioned earlier, Chi-Chi's advertising, sales promotion, and merchandising have all been of a superior quality. This begins with the exterior, hacienda-style design of buildings. The theme is carried through in staff uniforms and interior design. The many dish combinations provide an appealing and convenient way for diners to sample various types of Mexican and Southwestern food. Table tents are frequently used to promote special menu items or drinks and are also of a high quality.

Aside from the growing pains that most companies encounter through different stages of their operating lives, Chi-Chi's is truly an excellent example of using the promotional mix and of capitalizing on new trends in the tastes of North Americans. The company was definitely the pioneer of the Mexican dinner house concept in North America, and has set the standard in so many ways for other companies to follow. With sales of $217.5 million in 2000,

(Photo courtesy of Chi Chi's Inc.)

continued

EXCELLENCE CASE *continued*

20 million customers per year, and a favored rating among Americans, Chi-Chi's seems poised to continue its success story in the new millennium.[4]

Discussion Questions

1. Which promotional mix elements does Chi-Chi's use, and what is unique about the way these are employed by the company?
2. How has Chi-Chi's capitalized on the trend toward the growing preferences for different national/ethnic food?
3. What can other hospitality and travel organizations learn and apply from Chi-Chi's promotional approaches?

Web Sites

http://www.chi-chis.com/
http://www.prandium.com/

References

1. Chi-Chi's Company Fact Sheet. *http://www.chi-chis.com/*
2. Chi-Chi's History. *http://www.chi-chi's.com/*
3. Prandium, Inc. 1999 Annual Report. *http://www.prandium.com/*
4. Prandium, Inc. Reports Fiscal 2000 Results. *http://www.prandium.com/*

CHAPTER CONCLUSION

Promotion involves all communications between an organization and its customers. Explicit promotion includes five techniques in the promotional mix: advertising, personal selling, sales promotion, merchandising, and public relations and publicity. The promotional mix is one of the eight elements of the marketing mix. The other seven elements implicitly communicate information about an organization to its customers.

Choosing a promotional program for an upcoming period requires very careful research and planning. Although target markets and marketing objectives provide the foundation for promotion selections, other factors must be considered. These include product-life-cycle stages, competitors and their promotional practices, and the promotional budget available.

REVIEW QUESTIONS

1. What are the five elements of the promotional mix?
2. Is the marketing mix an element of the promotional mix, or vice versa? Explain your answer.
3. Are the five promotional mix elements related, or is it better to develop them separately? Why do you think one approach is better than the other?
4. What are the nine elements of the communications process?
5. What is the difference between explicit and implicit communications? Is the promotional mix implicit or explicit? Are implicit and explicit promotions related?
6. What are the three principal goals of promotion? What is the ultimate purpose of promotion?
7. What are the advantages and disadvantages of each of the five promotional mix elements?
8. What factors influence the choice of promotional mix elements?

CHAPTER ASSIGNMENTS

1. Consider the following four purchases of hospitality and travel services:
   - Participating in clown face-painting at a theme park
   - Selecting a place to eat during a 30-minute lunch break
   - Selecting a restaurant for a twenty-fifth anniversary celebration
   - Deciding which country or fitness club to join

   Which of the four are usually high-involvement (extensive problem solving) and which are low-involvement (routine problem solving) decisions? Would the promotional techniques best suited for each decision type be the same? If not, how would they differ?

2. Select a part of the hospitality and travel industry in which you are most interested (e.g., hotel, airline, restaurant, travel agency, theme park, resort, tour operating). Assume you have just been hired as the marketing vice president. Your organization is not very satisfied with its past promotional activities, and you have been asked to recommend more effective promotional approaches. How would you present this information, making sure that you mention the advantages and disadvantages of each of the five promotional mix elements.

3. This chapter emphasizes the importance of keeping promotional messages simple. Review hospitality and travel promotions either at the local or national level. Find and describe at least five examples of promotions that use simple communications, and five examples of ones you feel are overly complicated. How could each of the latter messages be improved to communicate more effectively?

4. Both explicit and implicit communications influence how customers perceive an organization's services. Choose three organizations in your local community, or three national firms, and analyze their use of these two factors. How consistent are explicit and implicit communications in each case? Which of the three has the greatest consistency? What could each organization do to create greater consistency? Do you think consistency or the lack of it has influenced the success of these organizations? Why or why not?

WORLD WIDE WEB RESOURCES

Bermuda Department of Tourism
http://www.bermudatourism.org/

California Raisin Marketing Board
http://www.calraisins.org/

Carnival Cruise Line
http://www.carnival.com/

Chi Chi's
http://www.chi-chis.com/

Econo Lodge
http://www.econolodge.com/

Jamaica Tourist Board
http://www.jamaicatravel.com/

Payless Car Rental
http://www.paylesscar.com/

Royal Caribbean International
http://www.rccl.com/

Seabourn Cruise Line
http://www.seabourn.com/

Singapore Tourism Board
http://www.travel.com.sg/sog/

Thriftlodge
http://www.travelodge.com/

REFERENCES

1. Bennett, Peter D. 1988. *Dictionary of Marketing Terms*. Chicago: The American Marketing Association, 58.

2. Kotler, Philip. 2000. *Marketing Management: Millennium Edition*. 10th ed. Upper Saddle River, N.J.: Prentice-Hall, Inc.

3. Mill, Robert Christie, and Alastair M. Morrison. 1998. *The Tourism System: An Introductory Text*. 3rd ed. Dubuque, Iowa: Kendall/Hunt Publishing Company.

4. Bennett, Peter D. 1988. *Dictionary of Marketing Terms*. Chicago: The American Marketing Association, 4.

5. Dommermuth, William P. 1989. *Promotion: Analysis, Creativity, and Strategy*. 2nd ed. Boston: PWS-Kent Publishing Company, 44.

6. Fisher, Christy. "Travel takes an interactive route." *Advertising Age* 64 (33):3, 28 (1993).

For additional hospitality and travel marketing resources, visit our Web site at **www.Hospitality-Tourism.delmar.com**

Advertising
How Do We Get There?

Objectives

Having read this chapter, you should be able to:

◆ Describe the steps involved in planning the advertising effort.

◆ List the three categories into which advertising objectives can be divided.

◆ Explain the difference between consumer and trade advertising.

◆ Explain the three components of advertising message strategy and list the alternative creative formats.

◆ Explain the seven factors considered when selecting advertising media.

◆ List the advertising media alternatives.

◆ Describe the advantages and disadvantages of various advertising media alternatives.

◆ Explain how the hospitality and travel industry uses different advertising media.

◆ Describe the role of advertising agencies and the advantages of using them.

Overview

Advertising is perhaps the most pervasive and powerful promotional mix element. This chapter begins by emphasizing the need to integrate the planning of all promotional mix elements, and then provides a step-by-step approach for developing the advertising plan. The chapter also takes a detailed look at various media alternatives. The use of advertising in the hospitality and travel industry is explored. The role of advertising agencies is explained at the end of the chapter.

Key Terms

advertising	dominance	permanence
advertising agencies	fear appeal	persuasive impact
broadcast media	frequency	posttesting
celebrity testimonials	gross rating point (GRP)	pretesting
circulation	integrated marketing	print media
clutter	interactive marketing	reach
comparative advertising	interactive media	slice-of-life
consumer advertising	Internet	spots
cooperative advertising	lead time	testimonial advertisement
copy platform	media vehicles	tone
cost per thousand (CPM)	message format	trade advertising
database marketing	message idea	waste
designated market area (DMA)	message strategy	World Wide Web
direct mail	mood	
direct marketing	partnership	
direct-response advertising	pass-along rate	

In 1999, total advertising expenditures in the United States were $215.3 billion.[1] At $201.6 billion in 1998, advertising spending was up 6.8 percent in one year and more than 56 percent since 1993.[2] Most of you are probably not surprised by these figures. After all, you are exposed to some form of advertising all the time. Advertising is the most pervasive promotional mix element. You see it on the Internet, television, billboards, buses, and buildings. It comes in your mailbox at least once a day. You hear it on the radio and see it in newspapers, magazines, journals, flyers, posters, and other printed formats. People are so infatuated with advertising that they even pay money to carry advertising messages on their clothes! You only have to look at the popularity of Nike sportswear to see this.

The choices of advertising media and vehicles are almost limitless. Selecting the most effective ways to advertise is a complex and often perplexing process. As with all aspects of marketing, careful planning is the key to effective advertising. Many of the advertising dollars spent by our industry are wasted because of a lack of preplanning and clear advertising objectives.

ADVERTISING AND THE PROMOTIONAL MIX

Advertising is one of five promotional mix elements and can be defined as "paid, non-personal communication through various media by business firms, nonprofit organizations, and individuals who are in some way identified in the advertising message and who hope to inform/persuade members of a particular audience."[3] This highly varied promotional tool is probably the first one that comes to mind when most people think of promotion.

In many cases, other promotional mix elements have a greater impact on sales than advertising. Chapter 14 indicated that these choices must be based on careful consideration of target markets, marketing objectives, customer buying process stages, buying decision classifications, competitors and their promotional practices, and the total budget available for promotion.

Plan the Promotional Mix First

Once marketing objectives are set, there is a tendency to look at each promotional mix element separately. This is *not* the ideal or recommended approach. Promotion is much more effective if each of the five promotional mix elements is developed to support and complement the others (e.g., making sure that similar colors, graphics, and positioning statements are included in all written promotional materials). Another example is using advertising to create awareness and remind people about short-term sales promotions. Planning the promotional mix must come before the detailed planning for each of its elements. Broad promotional objectives should be established before advertising objectives are written, and a tentative promotional budget should be developed before a final advertising budget is set. In recent years, the term **integrated marketing** has started to be used for the planning and coordination of all the promotional mix elements.[4] It is also being used to refer to the closer coordination among a company's promotional consultants and advisors, including advertising agencies, sales promotion firms, and public relations consultants.

PLANNING THE ADVERTISING EFFORT

An organization should draw up a written plan for each promotional mix element, including advertising. The 10 steps involved in developing and implementing an advertising plan are as follows:

1. Set advertising objectives
2. Decide on in-house advertising or agency
3. Establish a tentative advertising budget
4. Consider cooperative advertising (partnerships)
5. Decide on advertising message strategy
6. Select advertising media
7. Decide on timing of advertisements
8. Pretest advertisements
9. Prepare final advertising plan and budget
10. Measure and evaluate advertising success

Set Advertising Objectives

As with all plans, the best way to start the advertising plan is by setting advertising objectives. These must meet the same types of criteria as overall marketing objectives, which were discussed in Chapter 8. Like marketing objectives, advertising objectives serve a dual purpose: they are guidelines for planning, but they are also a way to measure and evaluate success in implementation.

The three principal goals of promotion are to inform, persuade, and remind customers. Advertising objectives can usually be divided into these three categories also. Figure 15–1 illustrates some examples of how this can be accomplished. These examples are listed in general terms. They would have to be expressed more quantitatively for the most effective use.

1. INFORMATIVE ADVERTISING

- To create awareness of a newly introduced service (e.g., new airline route, cruise package, hotel, menu item)
- To explain the characteristics of a new service (e.g., cities served by a new airline route, ports visited on a new cruise package, facilities and services in a new hotel, ingredients of a new menu item)
- To inform customers and others of a price change
- To correct false impressions about the organization's services (e.g., to combat perceptions of poor service quality)
- To appeal to new target markets
- To reduce customers' apprehensions or fears about purchasing a service
- To build or enhance an organization's image

2. PERSUASIVE ADVERTISING

- To increase customer preference for the organization's services
- To increase customer loyalty to the organization or its brands
- To encourage customers to switch from using a competitor's services
- To convince customers to buy or book the service now or in the near future
- To change customers' perceptions about the quality or type of service provided

3. REMINDER ADVERTISING

- To remind customers about where they can buy or book the service
- To remind customers about facilities or services that are unique to the sponsoring organization
- To remind customers about when they should book or reserve services
- To remind customers of the existence of the service

◆ **FIGURE 15–1** *Sample advertising objectives by promotional goal.* (Adapted from Evans, Joel R., and Barry Berman. 2000. *Marketing.* 7th ed. Upper Saddle River, N.J.: Prentice-Hall, Inc.; Kotler, Philip. 2000. *Marketing Management: Millennium Edition.* 10th ed. Upper Saddle River, N.J.: Prentice-Hall, Inc. Reprinted by permission of Pearson Education, Inc., Upper Saddle River, N.J. 07458)

Most hospitality and travel organizations, with the exception of retail-only travel agencies, engage in the following two distinct branches of advertising:

◆ **Consumer Advertising**—Advertising to the customers who will actually use the services being promoted
◆ **Trade Advertising**—Advertising to travel trade intermediaries who will influence customers' buying decisions

Objectives should be defined for each of these two broad categories of advertising. An excellent 1999 advertising campaign by Royal Caribbean International will help you grasp these concepts. The campaign was done in advance of the introduction of a new ship, *Voyager of the Seas.* The ads were trade advertising placed in travel trade magazines. The theme was "Get Ready for Voyager of the Seas" and the ads were mainly of the informative variety, as they highlighted individual features of the new ship. An actual travel agent was featured in each of the ads, always in a somewhat humorous way. There was a persuasive element to these ads as well, since one of the cruise lines' marketing officials said that they were trying "to create a stronger partnership with agencies."[5]

Decide on In-House Advertising or Agency

Most medium-sized and large organizations within the hospitality and travel industry use outside agencies to develop and place their advertising. The services of these agencies are discussed later in this chapter. Obviously, this tends to be a one-time, rather

TARGET MARKET	TYPES OF PROMOTIONS	PROSPECTIVE PARTNERS
1. Individual Customers	• Brochures • Media Advertising • Direct Mail • Sales Promotions • Consumer Travel Shows • Internet (Web and e-mail)	• Airlines • Credit Card Companies • Tour Operators • Tour Wholesalers • Travel Agents • Travel Associations • Government Tourism Marketing Agencies • Other Complementary Tourism Businesses
2. Groups	• Brochures and Special Printed Materials • Specialized Magazine Advertisements • Personal Sales Calls • Advertising in Publications Aimed at Corporate and Group Markets • Internet (Web and e-mail)	• Airlines • Credit Card Companies • In-Bound Tour Operators • Travel Agents • Other Complementary Tourism Businesses
3. Travel Trade	• Brochures and Trade-Oriented Print Materials • Personal Sales Calls • Direct Mailings • Sales Promotions and Materials • Product Introductions, Agent Training, and Receptions • Trade Publication Advertising • Familiarization Trips for Agents, Tour Operators, and Travel Writers • Internet (Web and e-mail)	• Airlines • Tour Operators • Tour Wholesalers • Travel Associations • Government Tourism Marketing Agencies • Other Complementary Tourism Businesses

◆ FIGURE 15–2   *Cooperative promotional opportunities in hospitality and travel industry.* (Adapted from *Tourism Is Your Business: Marketing Management. 1986. Tourism Canada, 166.* Reproduced with the permission of the Minister of Public Works and Government Services Canada, 2001.)

than an annual, decision. However, an organization's choice of advertising agency is based more frequently on the success or failure of an agency's advertising campaigns.

Establish a Tentative Advertising Budget

Chapters 10 and 20 provide detailed descriptions of the available budgeting methods. As you will see, the objective-and-task approach is the one that this book recommends. This method involves building the budget on objectives and the specific activities needed to attain them. It would be nice, but unrealistic, if marketers felt that they would always get the promotion funds they need. Every organization has priorities other than marketing, and the funds available for marketing and promotion are greatly influenced by other activities and initiatives.

The realistic time to start budgeting for advertising is after setting a tentative total marketing and promotional budget. The portion of this total budget that is earmarked for the promotional mix should first be tentatively allocated to each of its elements.[6] When all the detailed plans for each promotional mix element have been developed, they should be costed out and compared to the tentative budget allocations. Individual plans may then have to be adjusted and recalculated to better align the tentative allocation with the plan's costs. In essence, this recommends a multi- rather than a single-stage budgeting process for the promotional mix and each of its elements.

Consider Cooperative Advertising (Partnerships)

This book clearly emphasizes the close relationship between many hospitality and travel organizations in delivering satisfying customer experiences. In a sense, they are *partners* in satisfying customer needs and wants. This partnership (cooperative marketing) opportunity is considered so vital that it has been singled out as one of the special Ps of the hospitality and travel marketing mix. Cooperation is possible for all elements of the promotional mix, including advertising. In cooperative advertising, two or more organizations share the costs of an advertisement or an advertising campaign.

There are many good examples of cooperative advertising in the hospitality and travel industry. The key is to find target markets and advertising objectives in which the *partners* share a mutual interest. The American Express Card shares a common goal with almost all carriers and suppliers—encouraging more people to travel and, incidentally, to use their green, gold, platinum, and now blue cards to reserve and pay for trips. For this reason, you will notice the American Express Card prominently displayed within the ads of many hotel chains, car rental firms, airlines, and some cruise lines. Another example is a 1999 cooperative advertisement between American Airlines and Blockbuster Video. This advertising promoted Blockbuster's Rewards program. For joining the Rewards program between August 11 and September 14, people received 250 frequent flyer miles in American Airlines program. In addition, those who joined were entered into a sweepstakes with a chance to win free flights on American Airlines.

There are several advantages of cooperative advertising. This form of advertising:

1. Increases the total budget available for advertising. This can result in more ad placements, using a more expensive medium, or increasing the ad size or its persuasive impact.

2. May enhance the image or positioning of the sponsor. For example, a hotel chain that associates with the American Express Card can augment its image by appealing to more affluent business and pleasure travelers.
3. Can communicate a better match between the customer's needs and the partners' services. Ads may be more convincing because of the convenient *packaging* of the partners' services or destinations.

Although these advantages are powerful, there are certain limitations with cooperative advertising.

1. More time is needed to plan advertisements so that all partners are satisfied with the arrangements.
2. Each partner sponsor has to give up absolute control over the advertising message strategy (how the ads will be developed and used).
3. Each partner loses the opportunity to *showcase* only its services or destinations.
4. Other compromises may also be required that need to be weighed carefully against the promotional goals and advertising objectives.

Figure 15–2 summarizes many of the cooperative promotional *partnership* opportunities available in the industry.

Decide on the Advertising Message Strategy

The fifth step in developing the advertising plan is to decide on the message strategy. Although writers use varying names for the components of the message strategy, the key ones are (1) message idea, (2) copy platform, and (3) message format.

1. **Message Idea.** The message idea is the main theme, appeal, or benefit to be communicated in the advertisement. The trade advertisement by Royal Caribbean International focused on the idea that *Voyager of the Seas* was *revolutionary* in terms of the facilities it provided.

2. **Copy Platform.** The copy platform is a statement that fully describes the message idea. It serves as the foundation for the copy (text) within an advertising campaign. It may fill as much as one page, and it is usually prepared by the advertising agency. The copy platform should cover the following seven items:[7,8]
   a. Target market or markets (Which customer or travel-trade market segments are being targeted?)
   b. The key appeal or benefit (What is the message idea?)
   c. Supporting information (Which statistics or other information will be used to support the sponsor's claims?)
   d. Positioning approach and statement (How does the sponsoring organization want to be perceived relative to competitors?)
   e. Tone (Will the key appeal or benefit be expressed emotionally or rationally? Will competitors be mentioned? How strongly should the message be delivered?)
   f. Rationale (How should these first five items work together to achieve advertising objectives?)
   g. Tie-in with other promotional mix elements (How should the ad mesh with other elements of the promotional mix?)
      Although you have already been exposed to most of these concepts, some elaboration is necessary. Chapter 8 outlined six alternative positioning approaches based on (1) specific product features, (2) benefits/problem solution/needs,

(3) specific usage occasions, (4) user category, (5) going against another competitive service, and (6) product class dissociation. The copy platform provides the first step in articulating the selected positioning approach so that it can be communicated to customers. The positioning statement is a short, memorable phrase or sentence that summarizes the chosen positioning.

The **tone** of an advertisement is the basic way that the message idea will be communicated. It is based on choosing between rational and emotional appeals, dealing with competitors' services versus not mentioning them, and the strength of the message.

Rational appeals or benefits are fact-based and are keyed to people's rational, physiological, and safety needs (remember Maslow's needs hierarchy from Chapter 4?). Emotional appeals play on psychological needs (e.g., belonging/social, esteem, self-actualization). There is much argument about which type of appeal is more effective, but the consensus seems to be that most hospitality and travel services are communicated more effectively with an emotional tone. There are exceptions, however. Trade advertising is thought to be communicated more effectively using rational appeals and information. The choice between a rational or an emotional tone ultimately depends on the organization's individual situation, including its audience (consumer vs. trade), product life-cycle stage, and the type of service provided. Rational appeals are thought to work best in early product-life-cycle stages, whereas emotional ones are more effective at later stages.

A heated debate also exists about the relative merits of a competitive tone, such as the one used in **comparative advertising** (ads that specifically mention competitors). In our industry, this approach is often common with fast-food, airline, and car rental companies. Positioning is by its very nature competitive, but its competitive tone varies with the approach that is selected. The fifth positioning approach—against a specific competitor or competitors—is the most direct and extreme. Usually this is used by the number two or a lower-level company against the market leader or leaders (e.g., Burger King vs. McDonald's, Avis vs. Hertz, or Northwest vs. American or United). This approach is not often encountered in the lodging industry.

Another component of tone is the strength of the message: How extreme or believable should the message be? You might think that the stronger the message, the more likely it will get people's attention and persuade them of the sponsor's arguments. This, however, is not always the case, depending on the positioning approach selected. The strength of an ad must be tempered with its believability. A great example of this occurred with Holiday Inn's early 1980s print and broadcast campaign, whose theme was "The Best Surprise Is No Surprise." The message was strong—you will find no unexpected surprises at any Holiday Inn. The ads implied that the traveler would find no service or maintenance problems. The campaign was not a success, however. Why? The basic claim was both unbelievable and undeliverable in every Holiday Inn operation. The tone was too strong and did not work. The company stuck its neck out too far. To be most effective, then, a strong message must be very believable to the target audience. You must also be able to deliver what is promised.

3. **Message Format.** The next stage in developing the message idea is to select a message format. This is a broad creative approach that is used to communicate the message idea to the target audiences. Some of these approaches have become associated with certain major advertising agencies and key agency executives. A description of several better-recognized formats follows.

a. ***Testimonial.*** In a testimonial advertisement, a celebrity, authority figure, satisfied customer (real or fictitious), or continuing character recommends or otherwise *endorses* the service or product.[9] This technique is used frequently in the hospitality and travel industry. Examples of celebrity testimonials include Jerry Seinfeld for American Express Travelers Cheques, Joan Rivers for Los Angeles, and Paul Hogan (Crocodile Dundee) for Australia. Celebrities attract attention to the ads and make them stand out from competitive promotions. They also support the advertiser's claim if they are in some way associated with the service, e.g., Gavin MacLeod, the "Love Boat" skipper, for Princess Cruises. If the same celebrity appears in several organizations' ads, however, each ad's effectiveness may be decreased.

   Authority figures, such as presidents of the companies that sponsor the ads, often deliver very effective testimonials. This approach has been used several times in the hospitality and travel industry, e.g., Dave Thomas for Wendy's, Bill Marriott for Marriott International, and Richard Branson for Virgin Atlantic (Figure 15–3).

   The third variety of testimonials uses actual customers (or travel trade staff members) or actors who play the part of customers.

   Continuing characters are the final type of testimonials. Applications in our industry include the koala bear for Qantas and Ronald McDonald for McDonald's.

b. ***Slice of Life.*** The slice-of-life format is a short *minidrama* or playlet from everyday life, where the sponsor's service or product is shown to solve customer problems. Some of the best examples in our industry are many McDonald's ads prepared by the Leo Burnett USA agency. Burnett's ads, thought to show great empathy for the *common folk* of Middle America, have upbeat, happy endings, e.g, a young boy leaving a small country town finds school friends in the big city, who invite him for some food and laughs at the local McDonald's.[10] The slice-of-life format is very popular because of its believability and close correlation to typical customer problems and concerns.

c. ***Analogy, Association, and Symbolism.*** This format uses analogies, association, or symbolism to communicate benefits to customers. A series of print ads from Preferred Hotels provides an excellent example (Figure 15–4). Under the heading "Which Do You Prefer?" one of the ads compared Preferred properties to fine gemstones, while others used fine paintings and vintage cars as the symbols. The message was clear—every Preferred Hotel is different, but they all share the same high-quality services and facilities.

d. ***Trick Photography or Exaggerated Situations.*** This approach is most often used in television commercials and print advertisements. It employs photographic *tricks,* special effects, or exaggerated situations to emphasize or clarify the advertiser's message. One excellent example is a magazine advertisement for Callaway Gardens, a resort in Pine Mountain, Georgia. With the headline "Deluxe Guest Blooms" (a made-up phrase), it shows a guest bed made from blooming flowers, with pillows of soft clouds against a blue sky and a headboard of sailboat sails (Figure 15–5). Obviously, the ad's intent was to emphasize the highly manicured and well-maintained gardens at the resort, in addition to its water-based attractions.

e. ***Word Plays and Made-Up Phrases.*** This format is used primarily with print (magazine and newspaper) media. The sponsor's approach is to get your attention and interest by using intriguing or humorous made-up phrases or word plays. Often these words or phrases appear in the ad headline, and they usually play against a photographic or other graphic element. In the mid-1980s, the

A Chairman who answers to passengers, not stockholders.

Good thing we're a privately owned airline. Because some of our amenities might be a little hard to explain to an auditorium of stockholders. Things like the free chauffeured limousines to and from each airport, and free massages and manicures on select flights for our business-class passengers. Or the 15″ of extra legroom where other airlines put a seat. Or even the personal video screen with a wide selection of entertainment channels for every passenger on the plane. All this might explain why our chairman, Richard Branson, doesn't check the financial pages to see how well we're doing. He just chats with the people on the planes.

For information or reservations, call your travel agent or Virgin Atlantic at (800) 862-8621.

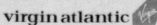

Virgin flies to London's Heathrow from JFK, Newark, Los Angeles and San Francisco, and to Gatwick from Boston, Miami, Orlando and Milwaukee (via Midwest Express).

◆ FIGURE 15–3   *Richard Branson conveys a message of personal service and attention to Virgin Atlantic passengers. (Courtesy of Virgin Atlantic)*

Which do you prefer?

Preferred Hotels offers the discriminating traveler a choice of 75 rare and beautiful hotels and resorts worldwide, each unique and extraordinary unto itself.

With so many of the world's most luxurious landmarks among our collection, choosing *one* Preferred Hotel can be a deliciously distracting experience.

Isn't it reassuring to know that any choice you make is the correct one?

For information on destinations, facilities and services, whatever your preference, write or call for our 1988 Member Directory.

PREFERRED HOTELS® WORLDWIDE

For reservations, contact your travel planner. For a free Preferred Directory call 1-800-323-7500 in North America. Or write: Executive Offices, Suite 220, 1901 S. Meyers Road, Oakbrook Terrace, IL 60148. Outside North America, have your travel planner contact Utell International.

◆ FIGURE 15–4 *Every Preferred Hotel is a gem—an example of symbolism in advertising.* (Courtesy of Preferred Hotels)

Australian Tourist Commission used this technique with great effect. Some of the interesting headlines they used in their campaign were "Dolls and Sense" (dollars and cents), "Yeggowan?" (You going?), "Icon Ardly Bleevit" (I can hardly believe it), "Emma Charthay" (How much are they?), "The Grade Owd Oars" (the great outdoors), and "Dopeys Prize" (Don't be surprised!) (Figure 15–6).

◆ FIGURE 15–5
Callaway Gardens gets its point across by using unusual photographic effects. (Courtesy of Resort Marketers, Berwyn, Penn.)

f. **HonestTwist.** The *honesttwist* format is an approach used by companies other than the market leader.[11] The sponsor first communicates its problem honestly (e.g., Avis' "When you're only No. 2"), and then *twists* (turns) the problem into an advantage (e.g., "You try harder. Or else.").

g. **Fear.** The fear appeal uses a negative emotional appeal to arouse or shock the customer into making a purchase or changing their attitude. This format is often used to sell insurance, traveler's cheques, and socially acceptable causes (e.g., AIDS prevention, nonsmoking, antidrug, and anti-drunk-driving messages). In a magazine advertisement, Frontier Airlines (now part of Continental) depicted a man with a clown face in a business suit. The message was aimed at convention/meeting planners and aroused their fears of badly planned events and the outcomes of such events. Using Frontier's special meeting planner's service was recommended. Experts have mixed feelings about the application of fear appeals. If the message is too strong, target customers may ignore it.

h. **Comparisons.** You have already read about this format. It involves direct comparisons between the sponsor and its competitors.

  You should realize that some of these formats can be combined. For example, the ads for American Express Traveler's Cheques used a *slice-of-life* minidrama (people losing cheques in foreign places) with a fear appeal. The effectiveness of ads can also be heightened by using humor and emotional appeals.

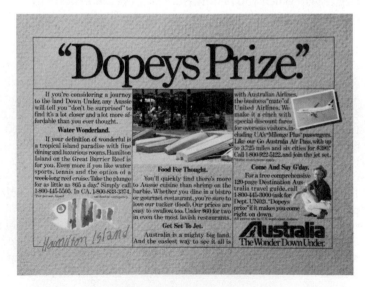

◆ FIGURE 15–6
Made-up phrases and Paul Hogan give Australia a unique appeal. (Courtesy of the Australian Tourist Commission, NY Ayer Advertising)

Select Advertising Media

Selecting the medium or media for the advertisement is usually the next step in drawing up the plan. This is often an extremely difficult choice to make, because of the variety of media and **media vehicles** (specific newspapers, magazines, journals, directories, television and radio stations) available. There are two main categories of media—print and broadcast. The **print media** contains all advertisements that appear in print, including those in newspapers, magazines, direct mail, and outdoor advertising. **Broadcast media** are advertisements displayed by means of electronics; they encompass television (including cable), radio, videotape, and computer-generated graphic presentations.

Media Selection Procedure.

Choosing the best media for advertisements is one of the most critical elements in the advertising plan. These selections must be based on the following seven considerations:

1. **Target Markets and Their Reading, Viewing, and Listening Habits.** Through marketing research, an organization should have established the media habits of chosen target markets. If potential customers live in defined metropolitan areas, then geographically specific media such as local newspapers, radio, television, direct mail, and outdoor advertising may be preferable. On the other hand, specialized travel trade journals may be the optimum mode of communications if the targets are travel trade intermediaries (trade advertising). Customers with special interests, such as golf, tennis, or scuba diving, might be reached most effectively through special-interest magazines.

2. **Positioning Approach, Promotional Goals, and Advertising Objectives.** The media, and media vehicles selected must support the image that the organization wants to convey, its promotional goals, and its advertising objectives. For example, if a company wants a luxury-oriented position, then *upscale* magazine advertising in publications such as *Smithsonian* may be the most appropriate. The promotional goal and associated advertising objective will determine the general suitability of each advertising media alternative. For example, television, considered the most persuasive of the media, may be selected if the goal is persuasion and the objective is to increase customer preference for the organization's services. Direct mail may work better with an informative promotional goal and the objective of explaining the characteristics of a newly introduced service.

3. **Media Evaluation Criteria.** An organization should use a battery of criteria to judge the appropriateness of each media alternative relative to the promotional goal and advertising objective. These criteria may include one or more of the following eight factors:
   a. *Costs.* This represents the total campaign costs *and* the average cost per reader, viewer, or listener. Often the latter is measured on a **cost-per-thousand** (or **CPM**) basis.
   b. *Reach.* The **reach** of a medium is the number of potential customers who are exposed to a given advertisement at least once. The **circulation** of a newspaper or magazine (number of households or others who subscribe) is one measure of reach. Some of the print media have *primary* and *secondary* audiences (**pass-along rate** of circulation). Most magazines, for example, are passed

EXCELLENCE CASE

Advertising:
Tourism British Columbia

How do you describe the spectacular beauty of a province like British Columbia? Super? Natural? How about, "Super, Natural British Columbia"? For several years this has been the theme (positioning statement) used by Tourism British Columbia, the provincial government travel promotion body, and its advertising agency Cosette Communication-Marketing. The campaigns have won many awards and are an excellent example of the basics of effective advertising discussed in this chapter.

Visitors to British Columbia tend to be older, better educated, and more affluent than the population in general. Given this general profile, Cosette and Tourism British Columbia have chosen to place the bulk of their media advertising budget in very specifically targeted consumer magazines. The six main advantages of magazine advertising are (1) tangibility, (2) high audience selectivity, (3) high reproduction quality, (4) long lifespan and good pass-along rate, (5) prestige and credibility, and (6) ability to communicate detailed information. According to Cosette, "magazines have a long shelf life, provide excellent four colour reproduction so we can show our products to their best advantage, and fit closely with the demographics we are after."

For advertising purposes, British Columbia's visitors are further segmented into touring/urban and outdoor/adventure visitors. Magazines chosen to reach the touring/urban travelers include such major consumer travel publications as *Travel & Leisure* and *National Geographic Traveler,* ones aimed at older travelers such as *Modern Maturity* (AARP) and *Mature Outlook,* city-oriented publications like *Los Angeles* and *Texas Monthly,* and others including *Reader's Digest, Sunset, Discovery,* and *Motorland.* For the outdoor and adventure oriented, the selected magazines include *Sports Illustrated, Field & Stream, Audubon, Outside, Sierra,* and *Esquire.* Reaching persons in Eastern Canada is done through in-flight magazines, and periodicals such as *Time, Maclean's, Equinox,* and *Canadian Geographic.* You can see from this that British Columbia practices multistage segmentation, using different combinations of geographic, demographic, purpose of trip, product-related, and lifestyle segmentation.

The ads used are of the informative variety, with the objective of creating and maintaining a high awareness of British Columbia as a travel destination.

The provincial government and its agency have found that the most effective magazine advertisements contain one *uncluttered* photograph, a very bold headline, and a minimum amount of copy (text). They keep advertisements as simple as possible. The *routes* ad is a brilliant example of this point. The heading or headline "An increasing number of Americans are discovering their routes in British Columbia" is bold and clearly stands out. Only one photograph is used. The photo is itself very simple and highly professional, showing off the great natural beauty of British Columbia's coastal tourism areas. The text is very limited and is placed at the top of the ad to attract a maximum amount of readership. The uniqueness and simplicity of this ad have the intended effect. It is attractive and different enough to be noticed by many magazine readers.

continued

EXCELLENCE CASE *continued*

Other advertisements in the same campaign as *routes* feature the same caliber of superior photography and creative, eye-catching headlines.

For the outdoor/adventure types there is the "Nearest car alarm: 140 km" ad showing a fisherman wading and casting in a beautiful river. For skiers, the "white open spaces" campaign clearly portrayed the great alpine skiing areas in the province. Another ad headed "Country vacation. City vacation. Just cross that bridge when you come to it" emphasizes the combination of city sophistication and rural charm in the Vancouver area. For the group tour market, the warmth of the message "We've been carving out our message of welcome for generations" is emphasized through a beautiful photograph of totem pole carving by first nations people. All ads, of course, boldly state

continued

EXCELLENCE CASE *continued*

the common theme "Super, Natural British Columbia."

The same creative approach is carried through in all Tourism British Columbia's other promotional materials, giving it the added advantage of consistency. For example, the back cover of the *British Columbia: First Nations Guide* uses the same *totem pole* ad with the heading "Why your next expedition should be to the poles."

Not only are these British Columbia ads an excellent example of brilliantly created, on-target implementation of advertising objectives, but they also reflect the importance of the preparatory work that must be done before advertisements are developed. Tourism British Columbia is a strong believer in marketing research and has spent thousands of dollars in research before making decisions on advertising

message strategies, media selection, and planning. This remarkable blend of careful research and top-quality advertising has paid rich dividends for the province. Tourism revenues have more than doubled in the past 15 years.

Discussion Questions

1. What factors make Tourism British Columbia's travel advertising so outstanding?
2. What could other tourism destinations learn and apply from Tourism British Columbia's advertising approaches?

Web Site

http://www.hellobc.com/

from the original subscriber or buyer to other persons, which results in additional *reach.*

c. *Frequency.* Frequency refers to the average number of times that potential customers are exposed to a given advertisement or advertising campaign. Some authors also use the word frequency to describe the number of times a specific medium can be used in a given time period.[12]

d. *Waste.* The waste factor represents the number of customers exposed to an advertisement who are not part of an organization's target markets. Newspapers, for example, are read by so many different types of people that significant waste circulation is often encountered.

A Touch of Technology

Wireless Internet Access

◆ Wireless Internet access is one exciting new innovation that will lead to increased use of the interactive media.

◆ Cellular phone users can now get onto the Internet through their phones.

◆ Wireless Internet access can also be provided to homes and offices in a manner similar to the satellite TV program distribution.

◆ Providers of this option claim download speeds much faster than on ISDN and ASDL lines.

e. ***Lead Time and Flexibility.*** **Lead time** refers to the space of time between the design of an ad and its actual appearance in the selected medium. Some media have long lead times (particularly magazines), whereas others have short ones (especially newspapers). The shorter the lead time, the greater the media's flexibility (i.e., the ability to adjust the campaign if necessary to better appeal to customers' needs).

f. ***Clutter and Dominance.*** **Clutter** represents the number of ads in one newspaper or magazine issue, or one radio or television program.[13] In a more generic sense, the word is used to describe the large number of ads that customers are exposed to each day. **Dominance** means a sponsor's ability to dominate a particular medium at a specific time period. In a highly cluttered medium, this is usually not possible.

g. ***Message Permanence.*** The **permanence** of a message refers to its life span and its potential for repeated exposures to the same customers.[14] A billboard on a busy commuter route has a relatively long life span, and it may be noticed many times by the same commuters. Radio and television ads, on the other hand, have very short life spans—15 to 60 seconds.

h. ***Persuasive Impact and Mood.*** Some media and media vehicles have a greater **persuasive impact** than others (ability of advertisement to convince customers in accordance with the advertiser's objectives). Television, for example, with its use of many stimuli (audio and visual), often has a high persuasive impact. **Mood** is the added enhancement or feeling of excitement that a particular medium or vehicle gives to an ad.[15] Again, television, with the availability of sound, movement, and other visual stimuli, tends to create the most added excitement or *mood.*

4. **Relative Strengths and Weaknesses of Each Media Alternative.** Once an organization has selected the criteria from this list of eight, it should evaluate the relative merits of each media alternative. For example, an ad placed in a special-interest magazine (e.g., *Golf Digest*) may have a smaller reach than if it appears in a major daily newspaper (e.g., the *New York Times*).

5. **Creative Requirements.** The creative format selected and the specific way it will be used also influence the choice of media and vehicles. For example, most travel destination ads require color and a visual presentation to have the greatest impact. Magazines, television, and direct mail brochures work best, whereas radio and newspaper ads do not generate the same excitement or mood.

6. **Competitive Media Placements.** Every organization must constantly keep one eye on its own marketing plan and the other on those of competitors. Often the market leader has the largest advertising budget available and may try to dominate certain media. Other companies are forced to respond with some level of presence in these media (e.g., Burger King, Wendy's, and Hardee's pursuing McDonald's in television advertising).

7. **Approximate Total Advertising Budget Available.** The tentative promotional budget allocated to advertising places a practical limit on the number of ads that can be run and the media that are selected. Many small hospitality and travel businesses have limited budgets and must use the least expensive media and vehicles (e.g., newspapers and radio). Making the jump into television advertising is often one of the most difficult decisions for small- to medium-sized businesses.

Decide on Timing of Advertisements

At this point in planning advertising, both the media and media vehicles have been chosen. Another difficult decision must be made about when and how often to place the ads. Different scheduling approaches are available, and the choice among them is based primarily on customers' decision processes and the sponsor's advertising objectives. Before looking at the alternative approaches, it is important to realize that there are really two decisions—macroscheduling and microscheduling.[16] Macroscheduling means in which seasons or months to advertise, whereas microscheduling refers to specific times of the week and day. The three major scheduling approaches available are:[17,18]

1. **Intermittent.** Here ads are placed intermittently over a certain time period. The number of ads placed in each flight or wave may be level or uneven. Cruise lines might use this approach because they emphasize different cruising areas at certain times during the year (e.g., the Caribbean and Alaska).

2. **Concentrated.** Using this approach, ads are concentrated in a specific part of the planning period and are not run at other times. Resorts open for only one season and downhill ski areas tend to use this approach by concentrating their ads in the months leading up to their peak operating periods.

3. **Continuous.** With the third scheduling method, ads are spread continuously throughout the planning period. Hospitality and travel businesses that need a steady, year-round and week-to-week flow of customers, including hotels and restaurants, tend to use this approach.

Pretest Advertisements

How does an organization know whether its advertising campaign will meet the advertising objectives? The answer is that it can never be 100-percent certain that ads will deliver the intended results, but there is a way of cutting the risk. **Pretesting** uses marketing research techniques to find out whether advertisements communicate information to customers in the manner the sponsor intended. Although pretesting can be put to many uses, it is most valuable in determining the effectiveness of the creative format and media selected.

Pretests serve three specific purposes: (1) testing *rough* ads before developing the finished versions, (2) testing *finished* ads before placing them in the media, and (3) deciding how often to use the individual ads initially in a campaign that has several different ones.[19] Many marketing research alternatives exist for pretesting, including direct ratings or rankings (customers are shown an ad or ads and are asked to rate or rank them), and portfolio tests (customers are shown an ad or ads and others not from the sponsor and are asked to indicate which ads they remember). Another alternative is theater/laboratory tests (e.g., customers in a theater are shown TV commercials and use electronic hand dials to express their emotions).[20] The choice of test should be based on the advertising objectives, which themselves are related to customers' buying decision process stages and the buying decision classification.

Prepare Final Advertising Plan and Budget

The pretests clear the way for preparing finished advertisements and finalizing the advertising plan and budget. Like the marketing plan itself, the written advertising plan must clearly state the objectives, research results, and assumptions that lead to choices, budget, and the implementation timetable. It must also outline the message strategy comprehensively. Detailed advertising costs will now be available and must be compared to the tentative advertising budget. This comparison may result in further modifications to the plan and to those for the other promotional mix elements.

Measure and Evaluate Advertising Success

Advertising planning does not end when the last page of the plan is written. It continues through the year. The success of individual ads and campaigns is carefully monitored and measured. Because campaigns often cost millions of dollars, they must be tracked carefully and continuously. Companies often *pull* campaigns, because of negative research findings and sales results, before their planned ending dates. Again, marketing research helps with these types of decisions.

Posttesting is a term commonly used for a variety of marketing research approaches to determine the effectiveness of ads after they have run. The choice of a posttest method is again based on the advertising objectives and the media used. The following criteria and measurements can be used, however:[21]

1. EXPOSURE MEASURES—How many potential customers were exposed to the advertising?
2. PROCESSING MEASURES—How did customers respond to the advertising?
3. COMMUNICATION EFFECTS MEASURES—Did customers react in the way intended by the advertising objectives?
4. TARGET-AUDIENCE-ACTION MEASURES—Did target customers take the actions that we wanted?
5. SALES OR MARKET-SHARE MEASURES—Did we achieve the sales or market share that we desired?
6. PROFIT MEASURES—Did we make the profit we wanted to?

There are also many specific marketing research and other measurement techniques that can be used for each of these six measurements. Gross rating points (GRP) is one useful exposure measure. It is calculated by multiplying the reach percentage (percentage of target-market customers who were exposed to the advertising) by the frequency (average number of exposures per target-market customer reached).[22] Recall tests are an example of a processing measure in which customers' ability to remember advertising is evaluated.

ADVERTISING MEDIA ALTERNATIVES

You already know about the criteria for selecting media, but we still must take a detailed look at each option. The major media alternatives are (1) newspapers, (2) magazines, (3) radio, (4) television, (5) outdoor advertising, (6) direct mail, and (7) interactive media. Several other media can also be used, including the Yellow Pages and specialized directories (e.g., AAA tour books and the *Hotel & Travel Index*).

1. **Newspapers.** Newspapers are the most popular medium for United States advertising, based on the total volume of spending. Some organizations in the hospitality and travel industry, particularly airlines, make heavy use of newspaper advertising.

This is not surprising because two-thirds of Americans read a newspaper every day and 74 percent of all households purchase them regularly.[23]

Advantages.
a. *High Reach.* Newspapers reach a very high percentage of the population, as we have just seen. They are read by people of both sexes, all ages, all income and occupational groups, and all ethnic segments. Some major dailies are read by more than a million persons each day.

b. *High Geographic Concentration.* Newspapers allow advertisers to be highly selective concerning the geographic markets they reach. Most major cities are served by at least one major daily. In 1999, the Newspaper Association of America (NAA) stated that it represented 1,800 newspapers in the United States and Canada, which was approximately 90 percent of U.S. daily newspaper circulation. Only 39 newspapers had circulation rates of 250,000 or more per day. There were 1,486 daily newspapers with circulations of 100,000 or less, most of which served specific local areas.[24] For organizations that use geography as part of their segmentation approach, newspapers should be considered for media placements. Most restaurants, for example, draw customers mainly from local markets, and they often find newspapers to be a very effective medium.

c. *Good Frequency.* Most newspapers are issued daily, and frequency (average number of times people are exposed to an ad) almost equals the number of issues.[25] Therefore, newspapers are a good medium for messages that must be repeated several times to achieve the highest impact (e.g., an airline announcing a new route from a particular city).

d. *Tangibility.* Newspapers are tangible. They allow readers to clip and save advertisements, coupons, or other offers and can also be easily shown or given to other people. They are useful when customers are being offered a sales promotion coupon, or in cases where they must provide further information by completing an address coupon.

e. *Short Lead Times.* Finished ads can be placed in newspapers on very short notice. Although a great deal depends on the ad itself and the amount of original artwork needed, a newspaper ad can be produced and published in as little as a few days. They are good, therefore, in announcing specials, price changes, or other updated information.

f. *Relatively Low Cost.* Compared with many of the other major media alternatives, newspapers are a relatively low-cost medium. For this reason, newspaper advertising is popular among small- and medium-sized organizations.

g. *Ability to Communicate Detailed Information.* Newspaper advertisements can convey more detailed information to potential customers than can many of the other media alternatives (i.e., television, radio, and billboards). Some larger advertisers convey even more information, either themselves or in cooperation with selected partners, by using freestanding inserts (FSI). These are separate, preprinted, and multipage sections that fit into a daily or Sunday edition.

h. *Ability to Place in Most Appropriate Location.* Most newspapers contain several specialized sections, which allows advertisers to choose the one that is most appropriate to their target markets. Many Sunday editions have travel sections—excellent locations for the ads of many organizations in our industry.

Some newspapers have daily or once-a-week dining and entertainment sections, which are ideal for restaurant and attraction advertisers. Companies targeting the business traveler usually find the business section the most appropriate.

    i. ***Ability to Schedule to Exploit Day-of-Week Factors.*** Advertising some hospitality and travel services is more effective on certain days of the week than on others. For example, advertising attractions, events, and dining-out facilities tends to produce more results on Thursdays and Fridays than it does on Mondays and Tuesdays. Advertisers have complete flexibility to choose the best days to run their ads.

Disadvantages.

    a. ***High Waste Factor and Inability to Target.*** Newspapers reach so many people that an organization using a segmented strategy will encounter a high waste factor. Organizations that use segmentation criteria other than geographic (e.g., demographic or psychographic) find that newspapers are a poor medium for pinpointing target markets.

    b. ***Limitations on Creative Format.*** Other media, especially television, allow the advertiser greater flexibility in choice of format. For example, newspapers do not allow for the most effective use of the slice-of-life format, nor can humor or other emotions be used as effectively. The lack of audio communications and the inability to show movement are shortcomings that newspapers share with magazines. There is no way to *talk person-to-person* in either of these two print media.

    c. ***Relatively Poor Reproduction Quality.*** Newspapers have relatively poor reproduction qualities when compared to other (visual) media alternatives. They lack the sharpness and range of color found in magazine, television, and even billboard advertising, although newspaper printing technology is advancing rapidly.

    d. ***Clutter.*** Newspaper advertising is so popular that a single advertiser faces stiff competition for the reader's attention each day. Many ads fill every newspaper issue, and only the largest ones stand out. Small advertisements tend to get lost.

    e. ***Short Life Span.*** Newspapers are usually read quickly, and they are tossed away just as quickly. Thus, the ads that they contain have a very short time to get the reader's attention. Given the creative limitations, this places an even greater premium on concepts that really stand out from those of competitors. Newspapers also do not have as high a (life-extending) pass-along rate as do magazines.

    f. ***High Cost of National Coverage.*** Running a national advertising campaign in newspapers can cost more than network television commercials. Although the per-newspaper expense is quite reasonable, there are so many newspapers that the total bill is in the hundreds of thousands of dollars.

2. **Magazines.** According to the National Directory of Magazines, 18,606 different magazines (mainly consumer) were published in 1998.[26] In that same year, the annual combined paid circulation of the 758 consumer magazines audited by the Audit Bureau of Circulations was 367 million.[27] Many hospitality and travel organizations, especially destination areas, hotels and resorts, and airlines, invest heavily in this medium. Some of its key attractions are its specialized readership groups, high reproduction qualities, and general prestige.

The number of magazines being published has increased rapidly in recent decades. Magazines run the gamut from major national consumer publications such as *TV Guide* and *Reader's Digest,* with circulations of over 10 million, to specialized business periodicals such as *Travel Weekly* and *Travel Agent,* with circulations of less than 100,000.

Because they are a print medium, magazines have some of the same advantages and disadvantages as newspapers. In some respects, such as in higher reproduction quality and greater targeting ability, they are superior to newspapers. However, they have lower reach and frequency, and longer lead times, than newspapers.

Advantages.

  a. ***Tangibility.*** Like newspapers, magazines are tangible and can be saved easily. Ads and coupons can be clipped and kept, or they can be passed along to others.

  b. ***High Audience Selectivity.*** Magazines lack the high reach and frequency of newspapers, but they offer the advertiser more selective audiences. They have less waste circulation and are very appropriate for organizations with segmented marketing strategies. Many magazines provide extensive demographic profiles of their subscribers, which gives advertisers the ability to select the magazines with reader characteristics most similar to their target markets.

     Magazines are also specialized by interest area. For example, there are several business-oriented magazines, such as *Business Week, Fortune,* and *Forbes,* for organizations that want to reach business travelers. There are consumer travel publications, including *Travel & Leisure, Travel-Holiday, National Geographic Traveler, and Condé Nast's Traveler,* that supply information to audiences primed for vacations. Many magazines appeal to enthusiasts of specific sports, hobbies, and other leisure-time pursuits, such as *Field & Stream* and *Golf Digest.* These are popular with organizations that cater specifically to these interest groups. Finally, there are many trade magazines that serve the travel trade.

  c. ***Good Reproduction Quality.*** The reproduction quality of magazines is much better than it is with newspapers. Many magazine ads are extremely attractive, with sharp and varied colors. Colors are a very important stimulus factor to most hospitality and travel advertisers. Whether it is the deep blues of the Caribbean water, the stark grays of an impressive mountain range, or the deep browns of a well-seared steak, color is an especially effective communicator in our industry. It has a great impact on creating the intended perception of the destination or service.

  d. ***Long Life Span and Good Pass-Along Rate.*** Magazines are read in a much more leisurely way than newspapers are. They are kept around the home or office longer, and they tend to be read intermittently over a period of days, rather than in a few minutes. You probably are like many others of us who are reluctant to throw them out because of their relatively high initial purchase price. Magazines are also passed along more frequently than newspapers to relatives, friends, and associates, giving them a *secondary* circulation. This added readership extends a magazine's life span and its reach.

     The result of these factors is that a magazine ad has more time to be noticed, read, and absorbed. If the magazine is reread, more than one exposure may result.

e. ***Prestige and Credibility.*** Unlike newspapers, magazines offer prestige because of their higher initial purchase price, reproduction quality, and, in some cases, the nature of their contents and editorial coverage. Customers also view their contents as being more believable than those communicated by other media, especially television. Advertisers that want to create a prestigious image, and to appeal to upscale or affluent customers, find that magazines are a particularly effective medium. For example, *National Geographic* has been published for many years and its contents are highly respected and credible. In fact, it is an authority in the field. In addition to a huge circulation of just under 10 million, the magazine has a high percentage of readers who are considered affluent.[28] Advertisers in *National Geographic* find that this prestige and credibility rubs off on their messages.

f. ***Ability to Communicate Detailed Information.*** Like newspapers, magazines are good at transmitting more detailed information about the service. They are, therefore, more effective than certain other media (e.g., television, radio, outdoor advertising) in situations where customers require more data (e.g., in extensive problem-solving, high-involvement purchases).

Although magazines have these six compelling strengths, they are not the best medium for every hospitality and travel organization. They are better suited for high-ticket items and extensive problem solvers—in situations where the purchase decision is protracted. Magazine advertising is not as persuasive nor does it have the same sense of urgency as certain other media, especially television. For these reasons, magazines are seldom used by fast-food companies, who prefer the greater persuasive impact and urgency of television.

Disadvantages.

a. ***Limitations on Creative Format.*** Although magazines can communicate emotionally oriented messages better than newspapers can, they do the same relatively poor job with the slice-of-life format and the use of humor. Again, the lack of an audio message and movement definitely limits the creative approaches that are feasible.

b. ***Clutter.*** Magazines suffer from the same clutter problem as do newspapers, although the problem is perhaps not quite as severe. Advertising in this medium is so popular that smaller ads may not be noticed.

c. ***Low Reach.*** Magazines have much more specialized audiences than do newspapers, and they lack their broad reach. Advertisers whose services and products have very widespread appeal, such as fast-food companies, find that the appeal of magazines is too fragmented for their purposes.

d. ***Low Frequency.*** Most magazines are published monthly, therefore, magazine advertisements have much lower frequencies than television, radio, and newspaper ads. These other media are more appropriate for messages that require greater repetition (e.g., special offers) and in cases where the customer's decision process is short (e.g., routine problem-solving choices such as which fast-food outlet to visit).

e. ***Long Lead Times.*** Newspapers ads can be developed and placed in a matter of days. For magazine ads, it is often several months. It takes much longer to prepare magazine ads, and the closing dates for placement are often two or more months before the magazine is published. Again, this means that magazine ads are better suited for higher-ticket purchases (e.g., vacation packages) and for services with distinct seasonal business patterns.

f. ***Relatively Expensive.*** Magazine advertising is significantly more expensive than newspaper ads. In a few instances, the cost can even exceed that of prime-time television commercials.

g. ***Difficulties in Geographic Targeting.*** Magazine readers are geographically dispersed, and this creates problems for organizations that want to target specific regions and cities. Other media alternatives offer the advertiser a greater ability to use geographic segmentation.

h. ***Inability to Schedule to Exploit Day-of-Week Factors.*** Although some magazines are published weekly, most are issued monthly. Because they are not available daily—like newspapers, radio, and television are—their advertisements cannot take advantage of day-of-week opportunities.

3. **Radio.** As is true with television, radio advertising can be placed nationally with a network or with local stations. However, unlike television, most radio advertising is carried on local rather than network stations. Radio advertisers also have the option of buying **spots**, or programs broadcast by the networks and local stations. Spot advertising is done between programs, whereas program sponsorship means that ads are aired on a specific program.

The Radio Advertising Bureau estimates that the average American listens to the radio for 3 hours and 18 minutes each weekday, and 5 hours and 45 minutes on weekends. There were 10,394 commercial radio stations in the United States in 1998, and the Radio Advertising Bureau estimates that radio reaches 75 percent of all American consumers on a daily basis.[29]

One of the major strengths of radio advertising, besides its reasonable cost, is its ability to target specific listening audiences based on the program format. Each format attracts certain specific groups of people. Following are the most popular radio formats based on station counts in the United States:[30]

1. Country
2. News, talk, business
3. Adult contemporary
4. Oldies
5. Adult standards
6. Spanish
7. Contemporary hit radio
8. Soft adult contemporary
9. Religion
10. Classic rock

Advantages.

a. ***Relatively Low Cost.*** Radio is one of the most affordable mediums for all sizes of organizations. It has one of the lowest cost-per-thousand (CPM) ratios among all the media alternatives.

b. ***Audience Selectivity.*** Radio offers a segmented audience for advertisers, according to program format. It is especially effective for organizations that target teenagers and young adults, because they make up most of the listeners of contemporary programs. Because radio stations serve distinct local areas, geographic segmentation is also possible. Most radio stations cover smaller geographic areas than their counterparts in television, which allows even greater precision in geographic targeting.

c. ***High Frequency.*** Advertisements on radio can be repeated more frequently than they can in almost any of the other media alternatives. Therefore, although radio ads do not have as high a reach as television ads, this is compensated for by the larger number of exposures per listener.

d. ***Short Lead Times.*** Radio advertisements can be produced on very short notice, often in a few days. The advertiser simply gives the radio station a script for the commercial or a prerecorded message.

e. ***Ability to Schedule to Exploit Day-of-Week and Time-of-Day Factors.*** Radio advertising has great timing flexibility, which allows sponsors to take full advantage of both day-of-week and time-of-day factors. For example, restaurants can air commercials just before major meal periods and whet listeners' appetites. Attractions can push special weekend admission discounts, and car rental firms can hype weekend rate deals.

Radio advertising seems best suited for advertisers of services and products that require low-involvement decisions (i.e., routine problem solving). These items seem to benefit most from the repetition that radio provides. Radio is not the ideal medium for communicating detailed information, or for services and destinations that benefit from a visual presentation.

Disadvantages.

a. ***No Visual Communications.*** All other media alternatives provide visual information to potential customers. Radio does not. This is a major shortcoming for marketing certain hospitality and travel services, including destination areas and many types of attractions. Some of the important stimuli, such as color and movement, are not present on radio, which makes it more difficult to create a desired image.

b. ***Inability to Transmit Complex Messages and Detailed Information.*** Radio is not a good medium for communicating complex messages and detailed information. Therefore, it is not very effective in advertising relatively expensive (high-involvement) services, such as cruise and vacation packages.

c. ***Short Life Span.*** The life span of a radio commercial is one minute or less. If only heard once, a radio ad can easily be forgotten. To be noticed, radio ads usually require considerable repetition.

d. ***Clutter.*** Although the number of commercials varies from station to station, and by program format, radio is generally a fairly cluttered medium. Therefore, it shares this disadvantage with both newspapers and magazines.

e. ***Shared Attention.*** Another hazard of radio advertising is that the radio often is not the main focus of the listener's attention. It may share the attention with some other activity (e.g., driving, doing homework, or cooking). Because of this, an advertiser's message can easily go unnoticed.

4. **Television.** There is no doubt today that television is the most persuasive media alternative. It appeals to all the senses, except smell. Television also allows advertisers to use all possible creative formats, including slice of life. For companies such as fast-food chains that are trying to reach national markets, television advertising seems the favored alternative.

As is true with radio, television advertisers can buy commercial time from local stations or, in the United States, from the four networks (ABC, CBS, NBC, and Fox). Each network has a stable of local station affiliates to which they supply programs. These affiliates give the network almost complete national coverage. Ads placed with the networks appear within their programs and are, therefore, broadcast throughout the country. Again, sponsors can purchase spots (between programs) or advertise within programs.

In the United States, television viewing audiences are divided geographically into **designated market areas (DMAs)**. These local viewing areas are larger than those served by radio stations, and they do not allow for the same precision in geographic targeting.

Advantages.
a. ***Potentially High Reach.*** According to the Television Bureau of Advertising, 98.2 percent of U.S. households—100.8 million households—owned at least one television set in 2000. Some 76.2 million households had two or more television sets. The four broadcast networks had between 76 and 85 percent penetration of TV households in 1999.[31] Network commercials have the potential of very high reach, to the millions of households and viewers. Although North Americans spend many hours watching TV every week, the likelihood of everyone seeing a one-time spot commercial is low. Therefore, reach is maximized by selecting many top-viewing market areas and repeating commercials several times in *prime time* over a number of weeks. Cable television advertising experienced rapid growth in the 1980s and 1990s, and a majority of United States households now have cable television services. In 1998, cable television represented 10 percent of the total measured media advertising in the United States.[32] The Television Bureau of Advertising estimated that 68 percent or about 68.6 million of the U.S. households with televisions had cable TV.

b. ***High Persuasive Impact.*** Television commercials can be highly persuasive because of their ability to employ all the creative formats and to make full use of emotions and humor to get viewers' attention and give added *mood*. Television is also an excellent medium to demonstrate services and products.

c. ***Availability of Uniform National Coverage.*** Television is very popular with major national companies, such as McDonald's, Burger King, and Wendy's, because they can conveniently purchase national coverage. They are almost guaranteed that commercials will be uniformly broadcast at the same time (according to time zone) throughout the country. This is definitely a lucrative feature for organizations with fairly standardized services and broad public appeal (the *combiners* you learned about in Chapter 8).

d. ***Ability to Schedule to Exploit Day-of-Week and Time-of-Day Factors.*** Television advertisements can be scheduled for different parts of the day and for certain days of the week. They share this advantage with radio ads.

e. ***Some Geographic and Demographic Selectivity.*** Television allows the segmenter some possibility of geographic and demographic targeting based on their choice of local stations and DMAs, and the program format. Other media, however, generally offer equivalent or even superior targeting possibilities.

Disadvantages.

a. *High Total Cost.* Although the cost-per-thousand ratio for television advertising can be quite reasonable, the absolute minimum that must be spent precludes many small and medium-sized businesses from using it. There are two significant cost items to be considered in television advertising—the cost of producing commercials and the cost of buying the time from the networks or local stations. Although production costs vary widely, they can be very significant. According to the *1998 Television Production Cost Survey* conducted by the Association of American Advertising Agencies (AAAA), the average cost of a 30-second national television spot was $295,000 in 1998. They sometimes cost in the millions of dollars during media events such as the Super Bowl.

b. *Short Life Span.* Television commercials, like those on radio, are very impermanent—they last only 60 seconds or less. They must be repeated several times to be effective, which increases the advertiser's costs significantly.

c. *Inability to Transmit Detailed Information.* Because of their short duration, television advertisements are not effective in communicating detailed information to potential customers. Other media alternatives, especially direct mail, magazines, and newspapers, do a much better job.

d. *Clutter.* Television is a highly cluttered medium, with dozens of ads each hour competing for the viewer's attention. So inundated are many people with TV commercials that they use commercial breaks to switch channels or leave the room to do something else. A television commercial must be very, very good to break through the high clutter level.

e. *Relatively High Waste Factor.* Television is not a highly precise medium for segmenters. Therefore, it leads to relatively high waste.

5. **Outdoor Advertising.** There are four general classes of outdoor advertisements: (1) posters, (2) painted bulletins, (3) *spectaculars,* and (4) signs at roadside and on buildings.[33] The first two categories include what the general public refers to as billboards. In outdoor advertising jargon, these are known as *poster panels* (large panels to which sheets are pasted) and *painted bulletins* (larger *boards* onto which a specific sponsor's sign is painted). *Spectaculars* are large and expensive displays, which are often illuminated and contain moving parts. They are found only in very high-traffic areas. Many hospitality and travel businesses use other roadside and on- or near-building signs to identify their locations. Another variant of outdoor advertising that has greatly increased in popularity is transit advertising (i.e., advertising on buses and taxis, and at bus stops).

Outdoor advertising plays an important role in the hospitality and travel industry partly because of the need to inform and direct travelers to unfamiliar places. In fact, some major outdoor advertisers in the United States are from our industry. Included among the top 25 outdoor advertisers in 1998 were McDonald's, Cendant Corp., Bass, Choice Hotels International, and CKE Restaurants.[34]

Advantages.

a. *High Reach and Good Frequency.* Although the average person's exposure to an outdoor ad is usually very short, there is the potential of high reach and frequency (Figure 15–7). Everyone who drives past a billboard is exposed to it (reach). If the billboard is located on a route that a person uses once a day, for example, several exposures occur in a month (frequency).

Fill 'em up.

Henry Ford Museum & Greenfield Village, Dearborn.

◆ **FIGURE 15–7**   *Two eyes and nine words get the driver's attention quickly and simply in this billboard.* (Courtesy of The Martin Agency)

b. ***Geographic Selectivity.*** The locations of outdoor advertising can be matched almost exactly to the sponsor's geographic target markets. For example, restaurants that serve a local market can place billboards and other signs within that area.

c. ***Relatively Uncluttered.*** Compared with other media alternatives, especially television and radio, an outdoor ad does not usually suffer from as high a clutter level. Although it seems that certain stretches of highway are littered with billboards and other signs, the number of advertising messages is generally fewer than the customer is exposed to in other media.

d. ***Long Life Span.*** Outdoor advertising is more permanent than most of the alternative media. Many signs are indeed permanent, or are at least intended to last for several years. Poster panels (billboards) are reserved by the month. Painted bulletins are either permanent, or are moved to other locations periodically.

e. ***Large Size.*** One visual stimuli that can have a positive impact on potential customers is the size of the advertisement. For example, full-page newspaper and magazine ads have a greater impact than smaller ones do. Outdoor signs can be very large, and their imposing size can be enough to catch the passerby's attention. Poster panels (billboards) are approximately 12 feet by 12 feet, and painted bulletins are even larger—14 feet by 48 feet.[35]

The real power of most outdoor advertising is its ability to communicate short, but memorable, messages. This advertising is especially effective with services that involve routine and limited problem solving, such as fast-food, other restaurant, and hotel-selection decisions (Figure 15–8).

(a)

(b)

◆ FIGURE 15–8   *(a) Distinctive buildings and signs make Pizza Hut stand out.* (Courtesy of Pizza Hut, Inc.) *(b) Red Lobster's outdoor signs are simple and attractive.* (Courtesy of Red Lobster)

Disadvantages.
a. ***High Waste Factor and Inability to Target.*** Although outdoor advertising can be geographically targeted, it does not permit any other form of segmentation. Like those in newspapers, outdoor messages are seen by all types of people, and a high waste factor results for segmenters that use criteria other than geography. Outdoor advertising is not as highly targeted a medium as others, particularly magazines, direct mail, and radio.

   b. ***Relatively Long Lead Times.*** Most billboards and signs take a relatively long
      time to design, print or paint, and place. This may be several weeks or months.
      In addition, there is an undersupply of locations for billboards and painted
      bulletins, which means that advertisers may have to wait to rent their chosen
      locations.

   c. ***Inability to Transmit Complex Messages or Detailed Information.*** Only a
      handful of words can be communicated effectively through an outdoor adver-
      tisement. Symbols often have to take the place of words, and messages must be
      short and to the point. Artwork must have strong visual appeal and be eye-
      catching. Therefore, it is not a suitable medium for high-involvement (extensive
      problem solving) purchases.

   d. ***Not Prestigious.*** Billboards and bulletins are not as prestigious a form of adver-
      tising as magazines and television. Many people consider highway advertising to
      be unaesthetic and feel that it spoils the natural character of the surroundings.
      In fact, certain forms of outdoor advertising are highly restricted or even illegal
      in some areas.

   e. ***Limitations on Creative Format.*** Outdoor advertising does not allow the ad-
      vertiser to use all the creative formats available. It is not particularly effective for
      humor or other emotional appeals or for the slice-of-life format. Many outdoor
      ads are, in fact, purely informative, rather than persuasive (i.e., they support
      other media advertising).

   f. ***Inability to Schedule to Exploit Day-of-Week and Time-of-Day Factors.*** With
      the exception of some signs that can be changed frequently, outdoor advertise-
      ments usually cannot take advantage of day-of-week and time-of-day opportu-
      nities. They share this limitation with magazine advertising.

6. **Direct Mail.** Direct mail advertising is one element of a broader category of techniques commonly referred to as direct marketing or direct-response marketing.
   The *direct* part of direct marketing means that no intermediaries are used. The
   producer of the services or products promotes directly to customers, takes their orders or reservations, and *distributes* the services or products directly. The major elements of direct marketing are direct mail and telemarketing (sales made over the
   telephone). Other forms of direct marketing include responses generated by television (via infomercials and cable programs), radio, and the Web. The effectiveness
   of direct marketing is increasing through a greater emphasis on database marketing. The National Center for Database Marketing defines this as "managing a computerized relational database system, in real time, of comprehensive, up-to-date,
   relevant data on customers, inquiries, and prospects, to identify our most responsive customers for the purpose of developing a high quality, long-standing relationship of repeat business by developing predictive models which enable us to
   send desired messages at the right time in the right form to the right people."[36] The
   growing sophistication of database marketing, principally through computer technology, is enhancing the advantages of direct mail advertising.

   The major direct marketing technique used in the hospitality and travel industry is direct mail advertising. Direct mail shares many of the same characteristics as newspaper and magazines, as it is usually in print format.

   Advantages.
   a. ***Audience Selectivity.*** Direct mail advertising is the most selective medium of all,
      because it allows segmenters to pinpoint their target markets with the smallest

amount of waste. This is one of the reasons for its great popularity in the hospitality and travel industry. It is especially effective with geographic segmentation and in cases where potential customers can be divided into distinctive groups such as travel agents, convention/meeting planners, or skiers, for example. The most powerful source of direct-mail mailing lists is an organization's own in-house records of past customers and inquirers. Many specialized lists can also be acquired from other organizations (e.g., membership directories) or from commercial mailing list brokers. These companies' lists can be rented for a fee and can be found in a directory published by Standard Rate & Data Service Inc.[37]

b. *Highly Flexible.* All the other media alternatives involve physical and time constraints that are not as severe in direct mail advertising. All ad placements must be made before media companies' deadlines, for example. Print and outdoor advertisements have to conform to size restrictions, and broadcast ads have very definite time limitations. Although physically controlled by postal regulations, direct mail ads give the advertiser greater freedom and flexibility in designing and *placing* them.

c. *Relatively Uncluttered.* Direct mail is a relatively uncluttered medium when compared to the other advertising alternatives. Each direct mail piece is physically separated and thus isolated from others, whereas there are many ads within most newspapers and magazines. Clutter does occur, however, when customers receive excessively large quantities of direct mail ads.

d. *High Level of Personalization.* All other media, with the exception of interactive media, are impersonal and do not communicate with customers effectively on a one-on-one basis. However, direct mail gives advertisers a great opportunity for more personalized communication. This is a trademark of the most effective direct mailing pieces (as it is of good mail questionnaire surveys). The more personalized the direct mail piece (e.g., postage stamp on envelope, hand-signed letter, and use of person's name in salutation—"Dear Ms. Brown," for example), the more likely it is to be opened and read.

e. *Ability to Measure Response.* It is easy to measure the impact of direct mail advertising. The sender knows exactly how many pieces were mailed (thus, the number of exposures) and can monitor the responses in a variety of ways (e.g., number of response/request cards mailed back, number of coupons redeemed). With other media, especially television and radio, it is more difficult to evaluate advertising response.

A growing portion of the advertising in the hospitality and travel industry is of the direct-response variety. The objective of these direct-response advertisements is usually to develop databases or mailing lists of inquiries. Once these inquiries have been generated—through devices such as toll-free numbers or mail-in coupon cards—the promoter *fulfills* the inquiry, often by mailing out *collateral* materials such as visitor guides, brochures, maps, or videotapes.

f. *Tangibility.* Direct mail gives customers something tangible to touch, feel, save, or pass on to others. In this sense, it is similar to newspaper and magazine ads.

g. *Low Minimum Cost.* Although direct mail is generally considered to be a relatively high-cost medium on a cost-per-thousand (CPM) basis, it has a relatively low minimum cost. There are certain minimum charges associated with newspaper, magazine, television, radio, and outdoor advertising. Sometimes these minimum rates are too high for smaller organizations. A limited direct mailing can be done for less than $500, making it affordable for organizations of all sizes.

h. *Short Lead Times.* Direct mail ads reach potential customers a few days after they are mailed. The lead time is short once the sender has assembled the mailing list and prepared the mailing.

Disadvantages.
a. *Junk Mail Syndrome and High Discard Rate.* *Junk mail* is a term we tend to use for mass-produced direct mail advertisements, the type that arrive addressed to "Dear Occupant" or "Resident." People are often irritated by the amount of this type of mail they receive and *junk* (discard) it without opening or reading it. Unfortunately, this negativism spills over to all direct mail advertisements, meaning that ads must be highly personalized or unique to avoid being thrown away immediately.
b. *Relatively High Total Cost.* Although the minimum cost can be low, direct mail is a relatively expensive medium on a cost-per-thousand (CPM) basis. To avoid the look of junk mail, it is often necessary to use first-class postage. At current postal rates, this means that, to mail 1,000 pieces, a company must incur a minimum CPM of $340 plus the cost of the mailing piece, list rental (if appropriate), and other expenses associated with the mailing. Even at bulk mail rates, the CPM is significantly higher than it is in the mass media, especially television.
c. *Limitations on Creative Format.* Although direct mail has fewer physical limitations than newspaper and magazine advertising, it is still only a visual medium. The slice-of-life format cannot be used, nor can emotional or humorous approaches be employed effectively.

7. **Interactive Media.** The interactive media are mainly those provided through the Internet and include the World Wide Web, e-mail, compact discs, and interactive television. Most of these media use some combination of computers, phone/cable lines, and televisions. They are a component of interactive marketing, which involves buyer-seller electronic communications in a computer-mediated environment in which the buyer controls the kind and amount of information received from the seller.[38]

Advantages.
a. *Cost Effectiveness.* These media are relatively inexpensive when compared with the other traditional advertising media.
b. *Easy to Modify.* Unlike most advertising that cannot be modified once it is placed, the interactive media can be modified almost instantly. Messages can be changed frequently and content can be kept current.
c. *Interactive Content.* The Internet allows a customer to communicate directly with a hospitality and travel organization. Customers can search databases online, and can request information and make travel reservations.
d. *International Reach.* By having a presence on the Internet, a hospitality and travel organization has the potential of reaching around the world.
e. *Expanding Market.* The number of people using the Internet and the World Wide Web is growing rapidly.
f. *Constant Availability.* The World Wide Web is available 24 hours per day and 7 days a week.
g. *Ease of Traffic Measurement.* In contrast to most other media, Internet technology allows marketers to know exactly how many customers see their mes-

sages. Through the use of access log file analyzer software programs, marketers can get very accurate traffic measurements for every page on their Web sites. *Cookie* technology also enables marketers to recognize return visitors to sites.

Disadvantages.

a. *Privacy Concerns.* Some customers are concerned that their privacy may be breached on the Internet, especially with respect to credit card transactions. There are also major problems with *spamming* in e-mail marketing, with customers receiving many unsolicited e-mail advertising messages.

b. *Partial Market Coverage.* While use of the Internet is growing rapidly, it does not yet provide the same level of market penetration as traditional media such as television, radio, and newspapers. There are uneven adoption rates of the Internet internationally. Internet use is highest in North America, but adoption rates in Europe and Asia are significantly lower.

c. *Navigation Problems.* There is so much information available on the Internet that it is often time-consuming and tedious for customers to find exactly what they want. Added to this is the fact that many consumers have slow modems and some Web sites are slow to download.

d. *Loss of Control.* The marketer gives up control to the customer in the interactive media. The customer chooses what to look at, as well as the time and place to view the information.

Did You Know?

✓ According to CommerceNet/Nielsen, the world is experiencing rapid growth in both its Internet and World Wide Web populations.

Year	Internet Population (millions)	World Wide Web Population (millions)
1995	22	14.3
1996	37.84	25.96
1997	58	48
1998	87.75	76.5
1999	110.25	101.25
2000	132.75	126
Growth	503%	781%

✓ The breakdown of the worldwide Internet population by region was estimated as follows:

- Africa (0.6%)
- Asia-Pacific (15.8%)
- Europe (23.4%)
- Middle East (0.5%)
- Canada and USA (53.7%)
- South America (3.1%)

ADVERTISING BY THE HOSPITALITY AND TRAVEL INDUSTRY

Now that you are familiar with the strengths and weaknesses of each of the media alternatives, you probably are interested in knowing more about how our industry uses these media. You will see that there are some distinct patterns to the industry's advertising, including the airlines' heavy emphasis on newspapers and the fast-food companies' focus on television commercials. You will also notice, however, that companies within the same part of the industry have quite different media-use patterns.

Several hospitality and travel companies are among the 100 leading national advertisers in the United States (Appendix 1–7). They include McDonald's, Tricon Global Restaurants, Cendant, Wendy's, and Starwood Hotels and Resorts. In 1998, McDonald's had the highest advertising expenditures in the industry at $1.025 billion.[39] Other companies that are divisions of larger parents would be among the leading advertisers if their advertising budgets were viewed separately. These companies include Walt Disney (cruise line, resorts, and theme parks) and Burger King (Diageo subsidiary).

Appendix 1–8 provides a more detailed breakdown of the 1999 advertising expenditures of our industry's leaders. The figures are for *measured media* only. That is, they are media statistics that are measured by various associations and service companies. Unmeasured spending occurs in media that are not measured by outside firms and associations. The data come from the sponsoring companies themselves. This latter category includes direct mail, other forms of advertising (e.g., Yellow Pages), and some sales promotion spending.

The total measured media spending in 1998 for travel, public transportation, hotels, and resorts was approximately $3 billion, while restaurants and fast food spent an additional $3.16 billion.[40] Note that these are measured-media-spending figures only, and they do not include regular (nonsupplement) newspaper and spot radio advertising.

ROLE OF ADVERTISING AGENCIES

Most medium-sized and large hospitality and travel organizations use the services of advertising agencies to develop and place their advertisements. **Advertising agencies** provide five distinct types of services:[41]

1. **Advertising Planning.** Most advertising agencies can put together the entire advertising plan for an organization, including all ten steps described earlier. Although this service exists, the sponsor should generally perform steps 1 to 4, and give the agency an indication of the message idea.

2. **Creative Services.** Creating effective advertisements is definitely an art, and ad agencies employ the most talented people to do this. Agencies develop the copy platform, decide on the message format, and select the advertising media and media vehicles. They are most often asked to do this for television, radio, newspaper,

and magazine advertising, but they can assist with all forms of advertising and sales promotion. Advertising agencies do not actually develop advertisements, but contract this function out to other specialized firms.

3. **Media Services.** Advertising agencies select the media and buy the time or space. In fact, agencies earn most of their money in commissions from the media companies with which they place advertisements. The commission rate is usually equal to 15 percent of the media *buy*. Agencies also monitor and control campaigns as they progress.

4. **Research Services.** All but the smallest agencies also offer marketing research services, particularly related to pretesting and posttesting advertisements. Again, the research is usually done under subcontract by specialized research firms, with the agency's supervision.

5. **Sales Promotion and Merchandising Services.** Many agencies provide creative services related to sales promotion and merchandising materials. Because these promotions are often supported by special advertising campaigns, this arrangement can be convenient.

A hospitality and travel organization has at least four options in creating and placing its advertising: (1) do it in-house, (2) use one advertising agency for all its advertising, (3) do some work in-house and some with an agency or agencies, and (4) use more than one agency or other specialists.

It is advisable for all hospitality and travel organizations, except those that are very small, to use advertising agencies. The principal advantages of using an agency are as follows:

a. Agencies employ the best creative minds in advertising and, because of their large client base, are able to compensate these individuals well.

b. Agencies have accumulated experience from working with diverse clients and, therefore, have a broader perspective than the client. They are an independent party and are more objective about the client's opportunities and problems.

c. Contracting an advertising agency may actually save the sponsor money. Hiring full-time advertising specialists for in-house positions normally is more expensive than using agency personnel.

d. Agencies are likely to be more familiar with the media and media vehicles than the sponsor.

CHAPTER CONCLUSION

Advertising is the most pervasive promotional mix element and is used by organizations of all types and sizes. It can be extremely powerful if it is well researched, carefully planned, and creatively implemented. Most advertising media are cluttered, and developing attention-getting, memorable advertisements is the key challenge.

Advertising is a minisystem in itself, beginning by establishing advertising objectives and ending by measuring results. Effective advertising is based on the research, analysis, and decisions from the situation analysis, marketing research results, marketing strategy, positioning approach, and marketing objectives. The advertising plan is one component of the overall marketing plan.

REVIEW QUESTIONS

1. What are the ten steps that should be followed when developing an advertising plan?
2. What are the three main categories of advertising objectives? When should each category be used?
3. What is the difference between consumer and trade advertising? Which media vehicles would be most appropriate for each of these?
4. What are the components of a message strategy?
5. What are the most popular creative formats used in advertising? Are all the media alternatives equally effective in using these formats? Why or why not?
6. Which seven factors should be considered when selecting an advertising medium?
7. What are the advantages and disadvantages of the major advertising media alternatives?
8. Does the hospitality and travel industry make uniform use of the media alternatives? Explain your answer.
9. Which five services do advertising agencies usually provide, and what are the advantages of using an agency?

CHAPTER ASSIGNMENTS

1. Select a part of the hospitality and travel industry in which you are most interested. Choose five or six of the leading companies or organizations in the field. Watch, listen to, or gather recent advertisements from each organization. Study the advertisements carefully and determine the message ideas and creative formats being used by the sponsors. Are the approaches similar and, if not, how do they differ? Which do you think are most effective, and why? Do all organizations tend to use the same types of media and media vehicles?

2. You are an executive with an advertising agency specializing in hospitality and travel company accounts. A new potential client (hotel or restaurant chain, airline, theme park, government tourism department, or other) has asked for your recommendations on which media it should use. What selection criteria would you suggest, and how would you assess each media alternative against these criteria? Which specific media and media vehicles would you recommend?

3. The owner of a small hospitality and travel business in the local community has asked you to develop an advertising plan. What steps would you follow in developing this plan? Who would you involve in the preparation of the plan? Prepare a detailed outline for the plan and, where possible, make specific recommendations on specific steps (e.g., media to use, message strategy, timing, amount of cooperative advertising).

4. This chapter emphasizes the importance of cooperative advertising. Either at the national, regional, or local level, find five good examples of cooperative advertising. Interview the participants in the cooperative programs to determine their feelings about joint promotional efforts. How beneficial have they found this type of advertising to be? What are its limitations or problems? Describe each of the ads or advertising campaigns. Based on your analysis, do you believe that more organizations in our industry should get involved in cooperative advertising? Why or why not?

WORLD WIDE WEB RESOURCES

American Association of Advertising Agencies
http://www.aaaa.org/

ABC
http://abc.go.com/

Advertising Age
http://www.adage.com/

Business Week
http://www.businessweek.com/

Callaway Gardens
http://www.callawaygardens.com/

CBS
http://www.cbs.com/

Condé Nast Traveler
http://www.cntraveler.com/

DDB Needham Worldwide
http://www.ddbn.com/

Direct Marketing Association
http://www.the-dma.org/

Field & Stream
http://www.fieldandstream.com/

Forbes
http://www.forbes.com/

Fortune Magazine
http://www.fortune.com/

Fox
http://www.fox.com/

Golf Digest
http://www.golfdigest.com/

Leo Burnett
http://www.leoburnett.com/

Magazine Publishers of America
http://www.magazine.org/

Martin Agency
http://www.martinagency.com/

NBC
http://www.nbc.com/

National Geographic Traveler
http://www.nationalgeographic.com/traveler/index
.html

Newspaper Association of America
http://www.naa.org/

Outdoor Advertising Association of America
http://www.oaaa.org/

Preferred Hotels
http://www.preferredhotels.com/

Radio Advertising Bureau
http://www.rab.com/

Readers Digest
http://www.readersdigest.com/

Smithsonian Magazine
http://www.smithsonianmag.si.edu/

Standard Rate & Data Service (SRDS)
http://www.srds.com/

Television Bureau of Advertising
http://www.tvb.org/

TV Guide
http://www.tvguide.com/

Time
http://www.time.com/

Tourism British Columbia
http://www.hellobc.com/

Travel Agent Magazine
http://www.advanstar.com/markets/travel.cfm

The Travel Channel
http://travel.discovery.com/

Travel/Holiday Magazine
http://www.travelholiday.com/

Travel & Leisure
http://www.travelandleisure.com/

REFERENCES

1. "National ad spending by media." *Advertising Age* (2000). http://www.adage.com/
2. "National ad spending by media." *Advertising Age* (2000). http://www.adage.com/
3. Bennett, Peter D. 1988. *Dictionary of Marketing Terms.* Chicago: The American Marketing Association, 4.
4. Levin, Gary. "Tearing down the fiefdoms." *Advertising Age* 64(46):S-14, (1993).
5. Fine, Phyllis. "Agents find 'soul mate.'" *Travel Weekly* 58 (69):37 (August 30, 1999).
6. Ray, Michael L. 1982. *Advertising & Communication Management.* Englewood Cliffs, N.J.: Prentice-Hall, Inc., 143–169.

7. Ray, Michael L. 1982. *Advertising & Communication Management*. Englewood Cliffs, N.J.: Prentice-Hall, Inc., 209–210.

8. Nylen, David W. 1993. *Advertising: Planning, Implementation, & Control*. 4th ed. Cincinnati, Ohio: South-Western Publishing Co., 459–461.

9. Moriarty, Sandra E. 1986. *Creative Advertising: Theory and Practice*. Englewood Cliffs, N.J.: Prentice-Hall, Inc. 75–77.

10. Ray, Michael L. 1982. *Advertising & Communication Management*. Englewood Cliffs, N.J.: Prentice-Hall, Inc., 285–286.

11. Ray, Michael L. 1982. *Advertising & Communication Management*. Englewood Cliffs, N.J.: Prentice-Hall, Inc., 296–297.

12. Evans, Joel R., and Barry Berman. 2000. *Marketing*. 7th ed. Upper Saddle River, N.J.: Prentice-Hall, Inc.

13. Evans, Joel R., and Barry Berman. 2000. *Marketing*. 7th ed. Upper Saddle River, N.J.: Prentice-Hall, Inc.

14. Evans, Joel R., and Barry Berman. 2000. *Marketing*. 7th ed. Upper Saddle River, N.J.: Prentice-Hall, Inc.

15. Ray, Michael L. 1982. *Advertising & Communication Management*. Englewood Cliffs, N.J.: Prentice-Hall, Inc., 365.

16. Kotler, Philip. 2000. *Marketing Management: Millennium Edition*. Upper Saddle River, N.J.: Prentice-Hall, Inc.

17. Kotler, Philip. 2000. *Marketing Management: Millennium Edition*. Upper Saddle River, N.J.: Prentice-Hall, Inc.

18. Belch, George E., and Michael A. Belch. 1993. *Introduction to Advertising & Promotion: An Integrated Communications Perspective*. 2nd ed. Homewood, Ill.: Irwin, 402–403.

19. Rossiter, John R., and Larry Percy. 2000. *Advertising Communications & Promotions Management*. 2nd ed. Boston: McGraw-Hill.

20. Derived from various sources including Dommermuth, William P. 1989. *Promotion: Analysis, Creativity, and Strategy*. 2nd ed. Boston: PWS-Kent Publishing Company, 537–538; Kotler, 594–597; Rossiter and Percy, 523–551; Ray, 327–331; Nylen, 629–659.

21. Rossiter, John R., and Larry Percy. 2000. *Advertising Communications & Promotions Management*. 2nd ed. Boston: McGraw-Hill.

22. Dommermuth, William P. 1989. *Promotion: Analysis, Creativity, and Strategy*. 2nd ed. Boston: PWS-Kent Publishing Company, 301.

23. Hulin-Salkin, Belinda. "Stretching to deliver reader's needs." *Advertising Age* 58 (45):S-1 (1987).

24. Facts About Newspapers: A Statistical Summary about the Newspaper Industry. 1999. Newspaper Association of America. http://www.noa.org/

25. Nylen, David W. 1993. *Advertising: Planning, Implementation, & Control*. 4th ed. Cincinnati, Ohio: South-Western Publishing Co., 333–335.

26. *The Magazine Handbook*. Magazine Publishers of America, 6 (1999). http://www.magazine.org/

27. *The Magazine Handbook*. Magazine Publishers of America, 6 (1999). http://www.magazine.org/

28. Leon, Hortense. "If you can't afford the cover price. . . ." *Advertising Age* 58 (45): S-26 (1987).

29. *Radio Marketing Guide and Fact Book*. 1999. Radio Advertising Bureau. http://www.rab.com/mgfb99/radfact.html

30. *Radio Marketing Guide and Fact Book*. 1999. Radio Advertising Bureau, http://www.rab.com/mgfb99/radfact.html

31. *TV Basics*. Television Advertising Bureau (1999). http://www.tvb.org/

32. "National ad spending by media." *Advertising Age* (2000). http://www.adage.com/

33. Nylen, David W. 1993. *Advertising: Planning, Implementation, & Control*. 4th ed. Cincinnati, Ohio: South-Western Publishing Co., 422–424.

34. "Top 25 outdoor advertisers." *Advertising Age* (1999). http://www.adage.com/

35. Nylen, David W. 1993. *Advertising: Planning, Implementation, & Control*. 4th ed. Cincinnati, Ohio: South-Western Publishing Co., 392.

36. Hughes, Arthur M. 1995. *The Complete Database Marketer: Second Generation Strategies and Techniques for Tapping the Power of Your Customer Database*. 2nd ed. Boston: McGraw-Hill Professional Publishing.

37. Standard Rate & Data Service, Inc. *Direct Marketing List Source*. Des Plaines, Ill. Published six times per year on a bimonthly basis.

38. Berkowitz, Eric N., Roger A. Kerin, Steven W. Hartley, and William Rudelius. 2000. *Marketing*. 6th ed. Boston: Irwin McGraw-Hill, 204.

39. "100 leading national advertisers." *Advertising Age* (1999). http://www.adage.com/

40. "100 leading national advertisers." *Advertising Age* (1999). http://www.adage.com/

41. Nylen, David W. 1993. *Advertising: Planning, Implementation, & Control*. 4th ed. Cincinnati, Ohio: South-Western Publishing Co., 71–74.

For additional hospitality and travel marketing resources, visit our Web site at **www.Hospitality-Tourism.delmar.com**

16

Sales Promotion and Merchandising

How Do We Get There?

Objectives

Having read this chapter, you should be able to:

◆ Define the terms sales promotion and merchandising.

◆ Explain the six roles of sales promotion and merchandising.

◆ Describe the steps involved in developing a sales promotion and merchandising plan.

◆ Explain the difference between special communication methods and special-offer promotions.

◆ List the various sales promotion techniques available.

◆ Explain the roles and advantages of each sales promotion technique.

Overview

Sales promotion and merchandising are two related promotional mix elements that can have a powerful influence on sales. This chapter begins by defining the two terms and explaining the roles they play. Again, it is emphasized that these two activities should be carefully planned in advance and should be coordinated with other promotional mix elements, especially advertising.

The chapter then describes the specific sales promotion and merchandising techniques available. Their roles and advantages are reviewed. The chapter outlines a step-by-step process that can be used to plan and implement sales promotions.

Key Terms

advertorial	frequent-flyer programs	sampling
affinity cards	frequent-guest award programs	self-liquidators
contests	games	special communication methods
continuity programs	merchandising	special offers
coupon redemption rates	premiums	specialty advertising
coupons	price-offs	sweepstakes
familiarization (fam) trips	recognition program	trade promotions
freestanding inserts (FSIs)	sales promotions	trade shows

As a consumer of many goods and services, you are probably more aware of sales promotion and merchandising than you think. As you stroll around the local mall, you are surrounded by merchandising. There are mannequins in store windows, end-of-aisle displays, eye-catching posters, and even moving objects designed to get your attention. When you pick up the newspaper or mail, you will find many coupons offering special prices on items ranging from pizza to pants. Many products you purchase come with a mail-in rebate offer. You can substantially add to your collection of glassware, dishware, or children's toys if you go to fast-food stores often enough. These are all examples of sales promotion and merchandising—visual and material inducements to get you to make purchases.

The total amount spent on sales promotion and merchandising in the United States has grown to be almost equal to media advertising expenditures. The amount spent on sales promotion per year in the United States is over $200 billion.[1] The total amount spent on advertising in 1998 was $201.6 billion.[2] Why has some of the emphasis shifted away from media advertising toward sales promotion and merchandising? The experts seem to agree on three reasons. First, the cost of media advertising has grown rapidly, forcing companies to look elsewhere to promote their products and services. Second, it is becoming increasingly difficult to appear unique in advertising, because of the great clutter as well as the present high quality of many advertisements. The third reason is that the results of sales promotions are measurable, whereas advertising effectiveness is more difficult to quantify.[3]

SALES PROMOTION, MERCHANDISING, AND THE PROMOTIONAL MIX

Definitions

Sales promotions are approaches other than advertising, personal selling, and public relations and publicity where the customer is given a short-term inducement to make an immediate purchase. Included are such items as coupons, free samples, and games. **Merchandising** or point-of-purchase advertising includes materials used in-house to stimulate sales (e.g., menus, wine lists, tent cards, signs, posters, displays, and other point-of-sale promotional items).

The two techniques are closely related, and some authors consider merchandising to be a sales promotion technique. Because of the great importance of merchandising in retailing hospitality and travel services, this book separates these two promotional mix elements.

Plan the Promotional Mix First

It is important to realize that organizations do not always look at sales promotion and merchandising as alternatives to advertising. Often all three promotional mix elements are part of a carefully coordinated communications campaign. They can work together in a powerful *three-punch combination.* Advertising creates the awareness, in-store merchandising jogs the customer's memory, and sales promotion induces the sale. The leading fast-food chains have perfected this three-tier approach. Television commercials make customers aware of the sales promotion (e.g., a child's toy at a reduced price, two-for-one or other price offer), exterior signs and interior displays and posters remind customers about the ads, and the availability of the offer in the restaurant creates the sale. In-house (personal) selling of the offer by servers further increases the promotion's effectiveness.

What this adds up to is that there can be great synergy among promotional mix elements if they are consistent and carefully coordinated. This takes careful preplanning and timing. Again, it also means that all promotional mix elements should not be planned independently, but should complement each other as much as possible.

Roles of Sales Promotion and Merchandising

Many people who have written about sales promotion say that it is frequently misused.[4] Managers tend to employ it as a quick fix for situations that need longer-term solutions. For example, an organization can have serious marketing problems, such as an inappropriate marketing strategy, wrong positioning approach or poor reputation, ineffective advertising, or inadequate service or variety. Sales promotions produce quick, positive results that mask these longer-term problems. Promotions can be introduced quickly and whenever management decides to do so. They make managers look good in the short term when sales expand. If each sales promotion is immediately followed by another, management may not even be aware that serious problems exist. When they find out that this is the case, it may be too late to correct the situation.

Many users of certain types of sales promotions, especially coupons, fail to recognize that these are forms of price competition. Competition based on price often degenerates into *price wars,* where there are no winners, and leads customers to always expect bargains. It erodes customer loyalty toward specific companies and brands, encouraging them to be bargain seekers, always switching to the lowest-price offer.

What then is the most appropriate role for sales promotion and merchandising? The simplest answer is that they should be used to take advantage of their principal strengths (listed in Chapter 14), particularly in meeting short-term objectives. On the other hand, sales promotions generally should not be used to satisfy objectives relative to which they are known to have weaknesses, such as building long-term company or brand loyalty.

There are exceptions to these rules, because not all sales promotions are alike. Coupons and other price offers usually do not change customers' basic attitudes toward a company or its brands. They do not encourage long-term use of the organization's services or products. However, giving customers free samples (e.g., a taste of a new menu item or wine, a free *upgrade* to a new level of service) may change their attitudes and they may eventually become loyal, long-term customers.

Sales promotions and merchandising should be used on an as-needed rather than a continuous basis. In this respect, they are unlike advertising, personal selling, and public relations, which require continuous, long-term use. They should be introduced periodically to meet short-term objectives such as the following:

1. **Getting Customers to Try a New Service or Menu Item.** This is frequently an objective of hospitality and travel companies when they introduce new services. British Airways handed out free unisex pajamas to its first-class passengers as one of the incentives to try a new type of first-class service on overnight, transatlantic flights.[5] KFC used a package price, advertising, and in-store merchandising to promote its Colonel's Rotisserie Gold chicken in a $14.99 family "Mega Meal."

2. **Increasing Off-Peak Sales.** This is a second key role of sales promotion, and it is applied frequently in the hospitality and travel industry. In January 2001, Amtrak introduced a special promotion program with the support of the American Society of Travel Agents (ASTA). The program offered travelers a ten percent discount on train fares booked and ticketed between January 12 and February 24, 2001. The offer was presented through coupons placed in *USA Today,* which travelers were required to redeem at a travel agency. The program represented a "win-win" partnership between Amtrak and travel agencies.[6] Amtrak received more business during an off-peak period, while travel agents collected more commissions.

3. **Increasing Sales in Periods that Coincide with Major Events, Vacations, or Special Occasions.** Each year there are several events and vacation periods when companies can use creative sales promotions and merchandising to boost sales well above their normal levels. Think about the Christmas season for a minute. You will quickly recognize that stores make a special effort to get your business during this festive time. Fast-food restaurants also intensify their sales promotions during certain seasons and holidays, especially Christmas. Increasingly, the fast-food business has begun to coordinate its sales promotions with the release of new children's or other family-oriented movies. For example, McDonald's and Disney entered into a partnership in 1999 to coincide with the release of the movie *Inspector Gadget.* During the four-week promotion, McDonald's included an *Inspector Gadget* toy (premium) in Happy Meals. As a result of the promotion, sales at McDonald's restaurants increased 9 percent over the same period in 1998. It was also the sixth best Happy Meal promotion of all time.[7]

   Sometimes an important sporting event, the release of a new movie, or a company's anniversary is the occasion. Megaevents such as the Summer and Winter Olympics, the World Cup, the Super Bowl, and the World Series are examples of sporting events that are often tied in with sales promotions. McDonald's sponsorship of the Olympic Games for the four years of 2001–2004 is a great example from our industry. Beginning with Sydney 2000 and ending with the Athens summer games in Greece, this promotion provides McDonald's with huge worldwide exposure.

4. **Encouraging Travel Intermediaries to Make a Special Effort to Sell Services.** Trade promotions frequently have this as their objective. Airlines, car rental firms, cruise lines, and others dangle extra commission points, free trips, and other prizes in front of travel agents if they supply business or client leads to the promotion's sponsors. Hyatt Resorts offered one night's accommodation for travel agents who

booked four nights for guests at one of the 18 participating resorts in the United States, Hawaii, and the Caribbean. You also know about preferred supplier relationships, in which travel agents are given extra commission rate points for their clients' business.

5. **Helping Sales Representatives Get Business from Prospects.** Certain types of sales promotions can be used to help sales representatives close sales (get a commitment for future business). Often companies provide *giveaway* items that are handed or mailed to prospects. These are often categorized as *specialty advertising* (various types of items carrying the sponsor's name).

6. **Facilitating Intermediary Sales.** Carriers, suppliers, and destination areas supply a variety of in-store merchandising materials to travel agents to help them sell their services. These include brochures, posters, displays of all types, and specialty advertising items (e.g., pens, balloons, tote bags).

PLANNING SALES PROMOTION AND MERCHANDISING EFFORTS

As is true with advertising, a written sales promotion and merchandising plan should be prepared and included in the marketing plan. The basic procedures for preparing this plan are quite similar to those used to draw up the advertising plan.

1. Set sales promotion and merchandising objectives
2. Choose between in-house or agency development
3. Establish tentative sales promotion and merchandising budget
4. Consider cooperative sales promotions
5. Select sales promotion and merchandising techniques
6. Select media for distributing sales promotions
7. Decide on timing of sales promotions and merchandising
8. Pretest sales promotions and merchandising
9. Prepare final sales promotion and merchandising plan and budget
10. Measure and evaluate sales promotion and merchandising success

Set Sales Promotion and Merchandising Objectives

Every sales promotion and merchandising activity should be based on a clear objective or objectives. As you should realize from previous discussions, these objectives are usually more short term than advertising objectives are. Sales promotion and merchandising must also meet the four basic criteria for all marketing objectives. These were discussed in Chapter 8. Sales promotion and merchandising objectives are generally persuasive. They induce sales in the short term by doing the following:[8]

1. Convincing new customers to try services and facilities, and convincing additional travel trade intermediaries to recommend them
2. Encouraging present customers and trade channels to use services and facilities more often

You should realize that advertising, sales promotion, merchandising, and personal selling objectives are often closely meshed within one *campaign*. In other words, sales promotion and merchandising objectives are seldom set in a vacuum. They are more likely closely related to longer-term advertising or personal selling objectives.

Choose between In-House or Agency Development

Every organization must decide whether it is better to produce sales promotion and merchandising materials internally or to use outside companies to develop and produce them. Most medium-sized and large companies choose the external route, contracting with advertising agencies or other promotions specialists. The advantages and disadvantages of the two alternatives are exactly the same as they are in advertising.

Establish Tentative Sales Promotion and Merchandising Budget

An approximate allocation from the total tentative promotional budget should be made for sales promotion and merchandising. This preliminary amount is used as a guide to select and design sales promotion and merchandising activities. The tentative budget can be reassessed once the actual costs of these activities are known.

Consider Cooperative Sales Promotions

The next step is to consider potential partnership approaches for sales promotion and merchandising. There are many opportunities for cooperative sales promotions in the hospitality and travel industry, just as there are for advertising promotions. For example, familiarization or fam trips are free or reduced-price trips for travel agents and tour wholesalers to encourage them to recommend or use the sponsoring organizations' or destinations' services. Frequently, the costs of these trips are shared among carriers, suppliers, and destination marketing groups.

Cross-promotional efforts are also possible with companies outside the hospitality and travel industry. You heard earlier in the chapter about McDonald's joint promotion with Disney. Another example was Pizza Hut's cooperative promotion in 1998 and 1999 with Sony Computer Entertainment America, manufacturer of the Sony PlayStation. Customers were given a PlayStation demo disk when they ordered a Pizza Hut Stuffed Crust Pizza. Sony produced 3.5 million demo disks in 1998 and 5 million in 1999 for the promotion. The program was a great success and both partners gained from it.[9]

Select Sales Promotion and Merchandising Techniques

The next question to consider is which sales promotion or merchandising techniques will be the most effective in achieving objectives. There are many alternatives available. Although not a direct parallel, choosing the right technique is similar to selecting the best message format in advertising.

Most hospitality and travel organizations are involved both in consumer and trade sales promotions. Some sales promotion programs and merchandising materials are geared directly toward customers, whereas others are aimed at travel trade intermediaries. Trade promotions are often referred to as a *push strategy,* which means *pushing* sales by promoting to intermediaries who, in turn, promote to customers. A *pull strategy* aims promotions at customers, whose demands *pull* services and products through distribution channels. Most parts of the hospitality and travel industry seem to favor the *push strategy,* primarily because there are far fewer travel trade intermediaries than potential customers. In certain cases, such as with restaurants, intermediaries are not used and a *push strategy* is, therefore, inappropriate. Before leaving this subject, you should realize that this is not simply an either/or situation. An organization may employ a combination of trade (push) and consumer (pull) promotions.

Some hospitality and travel organizations use promotions to intensify the personal selling efforts of their own salespeople. These are categorized as sales-force promotions.

Another way to divide available techniques is by *trial* and *usage* promotions. For example, coupons and sampling are considered quite effective in getting new customers to try a service or product. On the other hand, contests and sweepstakes are good at convincing present customers or trade channels to use services more often. Once again, an organization may decide to use a combination of *trial* and *usage* promotions.

In this book, sales promotion and merchandising techniques are categorized by their inherent characteristics. This route was selected because, as you will come to understand, the same techniques can be used for trade, consumer, and sales-force promotions.

Sales promotion and merchandising techniques can be divided into two groups: (1) **special communication methods** and (2) **special offers**.[10] The first group gives the promoter additional options for communicating with potential customers and travel trade intermediaries.

Special offers are short-term inducements given to customers, travel trade intermediaries, and sales representatives. Customers and intermediaries who use special offers are generally required to make a purchase or reservation. If not, they at least have to take some definite action (e.g., fill out and mail back a completed sweepstakes coupon). Offers come in many forms, including price reductions, gifts, free trips and meals, and extra commissions for intermediaries and sales representatives.

1. **Special Communication Methods.**
   a. *Specialty Advertising.* Specialty advertising (also sometimes referred to as *advertising specialties*) are free items given to potential customers or travel trade intermediaries. Often displaying the sponsor's name, logo, or advertising message, these items normally are either office products or unique or unusual gifts. They include pens, pencils, cups, glasses, paperweights, matchbooks, stationery, ashtrays, key rings, tote bags, balloons, T-shirts, and many other items. The in-room guest amenities found in many hotel rooms (soaps, shampoo, toothpaste, sewing kits, shower caps) also belong in this category, as do the *amenity packs* given out by some airlines. The most effective specialty advertising items satisfy four criteria:[11]
   - They are chosen for a specific target market or travel trade intermediary, and the items are either useful or attractive to these persons.
   - They are based on a specific promotional objective.
   - They tie in closely with other promotional mix elements.
   - They are creatively designed and have a long-term use or value to recipients.
   A program developed by Carlson Marketing Group for the Beefeater Restaurant & Pub Group (*http://www.beefeater.co.uk*) in the United Kingdom demonstrates how a specialty advertising item can meet these four criteria. Carlson was given a brief of adding value to the younger guest's (7--11 year olds) experience by developing appropriate at-table entertainment. The specific promotional objective was to make dining with young children a less stressful experience for parents. Carlson developed a themed activity booklet (the specialty advertising item) linking Beefeater with Warner Home Video. The booklet included a tear-off bookmark, seven games, a drawing for 100 Sony Playstation games, and a £1 voucher toward the purchase of the *Space Jam* video. The child's purchase of the videotape gave the promotion a longer value. Various in-restaurant merchan-

金陵飯店食譜 88

Jinling Hotel Recipe 88

◆ **FIGURE 16–1** *The Jinling Hotel's "Jinling Recipe Book 88," is an exquisite example of specialty advertising.* (Courtesy of Jinling Hotel Corporation)

dising materials supported the promotion. This program represented a "win-win" partnership for Beefeater and Warner.

Figure 16–1 shows an exquisite cookbook titled, *Jinling Hotel Recipe 88*, which is given away to special guests and prospects. The Jinling Hotel Corporation in Nanjing, China, designed the book for the five-star hotel in Jiangsu Province. Eighty-eight different dishes and their recipes are included in this excellent specialty advertising piece.

One of the advantages of specialty advertising items is their flexibility of use. They can be given to potential customers or to travel trade intermediaries or sales representatives. They can be handed out at trade or travel shows, mailed, or passed on by sales representatives in the field.

Did You Know?

✓ Now you can buy merchandise items from hospitality and travel organizations on-line.

✓ Some of the items available for on-line purchase carry the organization's name, so they are a variation on specialty advertising.

✓ Skyline's Cincinnati-style chili can be ordered from their Website. It is possible to order a whole case of 24 cans of the famous chili at http://www.skylinechili.com/

✓ Singapore Airline's Kris Shop features a diverse range of items from fashionware to Teddy Bears. Merchandise can be ordered on-line at http://www.krisshop.com/

✓ At the Albuquerque, New Mexico, web site, original art works, posters, note cards, and official Albuquerque phone cards are available. They can be ordered on-line at http://www.abqcvb.org/order/merchand.html

b. ***Sampling.*** Sampling means giving away free samples of items to encourage sales, or arranging in some way for people to try all or part of a service. This is much easier for manufacturers of products to do, because what they have to sell is tangible and can be mailed or handed out. As you will recall from Chapter 2, most hospitality and travel services are intangible. Therefore, they cannot be mailed or handed out. To sample them, the customer or travel trade intermediary must be invited to try services on a complimentary or no-additional-charge basis.

The one exception in our industry is establishments that serve food and beverages. Restaurants, bars, and lounges can, subject to certain legal restrictions, give customers free samples of menu items or beverages. Often this is done with new items or in an effort to boost sales in certain meal periods or food and beverage categories (e.g., breakfasts, desserts, appetizers, wines, mixed cocktails).

Familiarization trips by travel agents are a second good example of sampling. Another sampling technique is the free upgrade, where an airline, car rental firm, or hotel company allows travelers to enjoy a higher level of service than the one they paid for.

c. ***Trade and Travel Show Exhibits.*** Many hospitality and travel organizations exhibit at travel trade shows, exhibitions, or conventions, Figure 16–2. Generally, these occasions bring all parts of the industry (suppliers, carriers, intermediaries, and destination marketing organizations) together. Some of the major shows held in North America annually are the following:

- National Tour Association (NTA) Tour & Travel Exchange
- American Bus Association (ABA) Marketplace
- United States Tour Operators Association (USTOA) Annual Conference & Travel Mart
- American Society of Travel Agents (ASTA) World Travel Congress
- Affordable Meetings Exposition & Conference
- American Society of Association Executives Annual Meeting and Exposition (ASAE)
- Rendezvous Canada
- International Pow Wow (Visit USA travel show)

◆ FIGURE 16–2
*Fitur is Spain's
annual international
trade fair.* (Courtesy
of IFEMA)

- United Motorcoach Association (UMA) Motorcoach Expo
- National Business Travel Association (NBTA) Annual Convention
- Association of Retail Travel Agents (ARTA) Annual Cruise Conference

Internationally, the major travel shows include annual events such as the World Travel Market (London, England), ITB (Berlin, Germany), BIT (Milan, Italy), Travel Mart, and several others. FITUR (Madrid, Spain), IT&ME (Chicago), the PATA.

Exhibiting at a trade show is similar to putting together a *minipromotional mix*. Some exhibitors send out direct mail pieces (advertising) to intermediaries, inviting them to visit their booths. The booth displays (merchandising) attractively portray the available services and may be closely tied in with recent advertising campaigns. Representatives working the booth hand out brochures and other collateral, and try to develop sales leads (personal selling). They may also give away specialty advertising items (sales promotion). When the trade show is over, exhibitors often follow up with personalized mailings (direct mail advertising) and telephone or personal sales calls.

EXCELLENCE CASE

Sales Promotion:
Chick-fil-A

Which company was the first to introduce a boneless breast of chicken sandwich and chicken nuggets? Most of us would probably say McDonald's, but the correct answer is Chick-fil-A, the Atlanta-headquartered, quick-service restaurant chain. The company's CEO and Founder, S. Truett Cathy, began with the Dwarf House restaurant in an Atlanta suburb in 1946 and opened the first Chick-fil-A unit in an Atlanta shopping mall in 1967. As of May, 2001, the chain had grown to 950 restaurants in 35 states, and ranked in the top five chains specializing in chicken products.

Chick-fil-A attributes its success to three factors: (1) a unique entrepreneurial relationship with its restaurant operators, (2) a commitment to quality products, and (3) a commitment to creating a business atmosphere that attracts and keeps good people.

One important perk is a company-wide policy of being closed on Sundays. But perhaps the most unusual feature of this company's development is how it structures new unit openings. For a financial commitment of a mere $5,000, restaurant operators are set up in their stores, which in the case of a mall they sublease from the parent company. In return for this, they give 15 percent of gross sales and 50 percent of operating profits to Chick-fil-A. Part of Chick-fil-A's strategy has been to concentrate on development within regional shopping malls, whose customers represent a captive market for food facilities. More recently, the company has begun opening the types of freestanding units that are typical among quick-service chains.

An operator posting a significant increase in annual sales (based on the store concept and volume) over the previous year receives free use of one of eight different Ford automobiles. Even better, if this performance is repeated the next year, they receive the title to the car. Operators and their spouses are also treated to an all-expenses-paid, five-day trip to a luxury resort to attend the company's annual business seminar. In addition, Chick-fil-A has given away nearly $15 million since 1973 to college-bound students working with Chick-fil-A.

Another reason for the company's outstanding success is that most of its sales promotion efforts are among the most aggressive and unusual in the quick-service business. Unlike the leaders, who all have major national advertising campaigns, Chick-fil-A puts most of its promotional emphasis on local markets. Two of its most successful sales promotions are sampling and Be Our Guest Cards. Chick-fil-A excites shoppers' taste buds by giving away free samples of its chicken in malls. A high percentage of those tasting the samples either go directly to the restaurant or return to it to buy a chicken sandwich or other items. The company's Be Our Guest Cards are a variation of the gift certificates discussed in this chapter. In Chick-fil-A's case, these are given away by store operators and company executives to encourage recipients to try the chicken sandwich. Once tried, it is hoped that the person will return and comment favorably on the quality of the product to others.

Rapid growth in sales and units are not the only outcome of Chick-fil-A's unique management and promotional approaches. Independent surveys have also shown that the company's chicken products are favored over the competition. Respondents in the national "America's Choice in Chain Consumer Satisfaction Survey" carried out for *Restaurant & Institutions* magazine chose Chick-fil-A as the top chicken chain two years in a row. The unique taste of Chick-fil-A products is attributed to the company's secret seasoning batter and its use of peanut oil for frying. Through extensive use of sampling and free-trial certificates, Chick-fil-A ensures that many potential customers will have the opportunity to try the popular products for themselves.

continued

EXCELLENCE CASE *continued*

Discussion Questions

1. How does Chick-fil-A's location strategy and sales promotion programs differ from its closest competitors among chicken restaurants?

2. Sampling is a successful sales promotion technique for Chick-fil-A. How could other hospitality and travel organizations use sampling to increase their business volumes?

3. Are special communications more effective in generating increased business than special offers? What does this case suggest in this respect?

Web Site

http://www.chickfila.com

Trade shows are relatively expensive, because they involve travel costs, registration fees, display production, and other costs. However, they offer the exhibitor a highly specialized target audience and an efficient alternative to making sales calls to thousands of prospects.

There are also many privately operated trade shows that are held in major cities and that move across North America. Additionally, hospitality and travel organizations can exhibit at numerous consumer travel, recreation, and sports shows. Here, they promote directly to customers rather than to intermediaries. These range from small shows in local shopping malls to privately organized sports and recreation shows with hundreds of exhibitors.

d. ***Point-of-Purchase (P-O-P) Displays and Other Merchandising Materials.*** You already know about the importance of merchandising in our industry. This promotional technique is used most effectively at the point of purchase, hence its frequent abbreviation to point-of-purchase advertising. An enormous variety of display items and configurations is available. In the food and beverage industry, menus, wine and drink lists, and tent cards are the key tools (Figure 16–3). Some restaurants and bars also attach banners to building exteriors, or use signs that can be updated frequently, to announce special promotions. Others give away minimenus or post their full menus near front entrances. Brochures, posters, and window and standup displays are common in retail travel agencies. Hotels use a wide range of merchandising techniques, including in-room guest directories, room-service menus, elevator and lobby displays, and brochure racks.

e. ***Point-of-Purchase Demonstrations.*** Again because of the intangibility of services, it is much more difficult to demonstrate their use at the point of purchase. It is much easier to do this with products. You have probably seen many salespeople demonstrate the cleaning capabilities of vacuum cleaners or the chopping features of vegetable cutters. "The Pepsi Challenge" is another point-of-purchase demonstration with which we are all familiar. So how do you tangibly demonstrate the seemingly intangible? One method being used by an increasing number of travel agencies is to show travel promotion videotapes on in-store television monitors. Other possibilities include demonstrating cooking methods or mixing cocktails in restaurants and bars.

f. ***Educational Seminars and Training Programs.*** The hospitality and travel industry invests heavily in this type of sales promotion to inform and educate

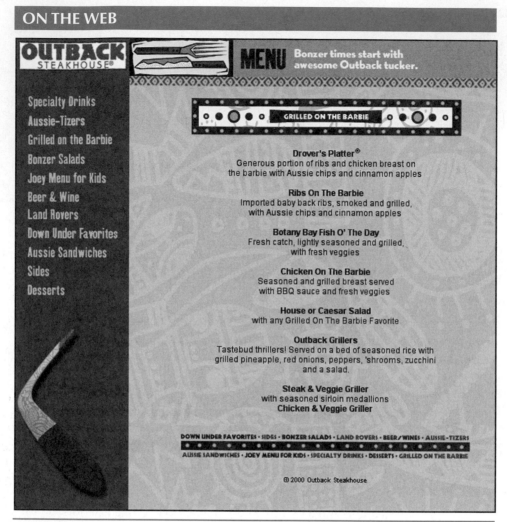

ON THE WEB

OUTBACK STEAKHOUSE®   **MENU**   Bonzer times start with awesome Outback tucker.

Specialty Drinks
Aussie-Tizers
Grilled on the Barbie
Bonzer Salads
Joey Menu for Kids
Beer & Wine
Land Rovers
Down Under Favorites
Aussie Sandwiches
Sides
Desserts

GRILLED ON THE BARBIE

Drover's Platter®
Generous portion of ribs and chicken breast on
the barbie with Aussie chips and cinnamon apples

Ribs On The Barbie
Imported baby back ribs, smoked and grilled,
with Aussie chips and cinnamon apples

Botany Bay Fish O' The Day
Fresh catch, lightly seasoned and grilled,
with fresh veggies

Chicken On The Barbie
Seasoned and grilled breast served
with BBQ sauce and fresh veggies

House or Caesar Salad
with any Grilled On The Barbie Favorite

Outback Grillers
Tastebud thrillers! Served on a bed of seasoned rice with
grilled pineapple, red onions, peppers, 'shrooms, zucchini
and a salad.

Steak & Veggie Griller
with seasoned sirloin medallions
Chicken & Veggie Griller

DOWN UNDER FAVORITES · SIDES · BONZER SALADS · LAND ROVERS · BEER/WINES · AUSSIE-TIZERS

AUSSIE SANDWICHES · JOEY MENU FOR KIDS · SPECIALTY DRINKS · DESSERTS · GRILLED ON THE BARBIE

® 2000 Outback Steakhouse

◆ FIGURE 16–3   *Menus are the key restaurant merchandising tool. Now, companies like Outback Steakhouse put their menus on the Web.* (Courtesy of Outback Steakhouse)

travel trade intermediaries. Airlines, cruise lines, tour wholesalers, and destination marketing organizations frequently sponsor these seminars, workshops, receptions, and training programs for travel agents. The primary objective is to pass on more detailed information and to help travel agents sell services to clients. Like trade shows, these events, often staged throughout the country, are relatively expensive, but they offer the sponsor a highly targeted and influential audience. A good example is the Shamrock Club course offered by the Irish Tourist Board in the United States (Figure 16–4). For a charge of $150, travel agents learn more about what Ireland offers visitors, and receive client referrals and other promotional support from the Irish Tourist Board.

g. ***Visual Aids for Sales Representatives.*** The intangibility of hospitality and travel services also poses a problem for field sales representatives. They cannot, like most salespeople representing products, demonstrate the service in the

Join the Shamrock Club, and more than just Irish eyes will be smiling!

The Shamrock Club is the Irish Tourist Board's official travel agent specialist program for Ireland, in association with the Northern Ireland Tourist Board. Take the course and not only will you satisfy your CTC Educational credits for the year, but you'll start growing your business, and your income, by

Irish Tourist Board

Ireland   Northern Ireland Tourist Board

becoming an expert on one of the most desirable destinations in the world. Ireland.

When you complete the Shamrock Club course, you'll enjoy privileges such as: client referrals, regular updates, dedicated toll-free lines direct to the Irish Tourist Board, VIP status at ITB events, promotional/point of sales materials, ongoing educational tools, and much more. Even the cost of the program will make you smile—only $150.00!

Build your business and increase your income by becoming a Shamrock Club member.

To have more Irish eyes smiling on you and your clients, return this coupon today to receive an official application form.

Please send me complete details and an application form for the Shamrock Club.

Name _____

Address _____

City _____ State ____ Zip ____

Phone Number _____

Best time to call _____

Mail to: Irish Tourist Board, Nichola Moss, 345 Park Avenue, New York, NY 10154

◆ **FIGURE 16–4** *The Shamrock Club is the Irish Tourist Board's educational program for travel agents.* (Courtesy of the Irish Tourist Board)

prospect's place of business. Visual aids play a key role in helping them give prospects an understanding of the quality and variety of their organizations' services. Materials used include three-ring binders containing photographs, Power Point and slide presentations, videotapes, standup displays, overhead transparencies, and many others.

2. **Special Offers.** The second main category of sales promotion techniques is special offers—short-term inducements to get people to act in certain ways, frequently to make purchases. These offers are usually run in conjunction with a media advertising campaign and are often supported by point-of-purchase merchandising.

a. *Coupons.* Coupons are one of the most popular sales promotion techniques. They are used extensively in the hospitality and travel industry, especially among restaurants. You will be interested to know that they are also the most misused. Coupons are vouchers or certificates that entitle customers or intermediaries to a reduced price on the couponed service or services. Coupons are considered the best tools along with sampling, for getting people to try services or products.[12]

North Americans are inundated by coupons. They are offered in the mail, newspapers, and magazines; on bulletin boards; and even with your pizza. According to the NCH NuWorld Marketing Limited, a staggering 248 billion coupons were distributed in the United States in 2000. Customers used 4.5 billion coupons worth approximately $3.6 billion. The average face value of a redeemed coupon was 79 cents.[13]

As you will see later, coupon redemption rates (percentage of total issued coupons used by customers) vary according to how the coupons are distributed. The coupons used by the hospitality and travel industry are mainly *manufacturer coupons.* They are developed and distributed directly to customers, not through travel trade intermediaries. There are five main methods of distributing these coupons:[14]

• Direct-to-customer distribution (mail or door-to-door delivery)
• Media distribution (newspapers, magazines, Sunday supplements)
• Merchandise distribution (in, on, or with packages)
• Specialized distribution (coupons on the backs of cash register tapes or automatic bank teller slips, and other novel approaches)
• On-line distribution via the Internet.

Why have coupons shown such spectacular growth and popularity? There are two sides to the story. Customers are more concerned with prices and *value for money* than ever before. Coupons deliver greater value in the form of a price reduction. The second reason is the increased competitiveness among manufacturers and service organizations. Advertising alone often cannot provide enough of a competitive edge. Coupons are most helpful in satisfying the following three promotional objectives:[15]

• Stimulating customers to try newly introduced services
• Generating temporary sales increases
• Adding excitement and appeal to media advertising

You should realize that most of the other special-offer promotions work well with these three objectives. Additionally, some experts recommend couponing as a way of combating competitive promotions.[16] This is definitely not a recommended approach for the long term, but it can blunt the success of competitors' advertising and sales promotions and stem the flow of customers away from a company. In the hospitality and travel industry, the use of this approach has led to many imitative promotions in different areas. Almost all national domestic airlines have frequent-flyer programs, most major hotel companies offer frequent-guest awards, nearly every pizza chain distributes coupons, and all large hamburger chains feature periodic premiums. Competitive pressures seem to force companies to use these approaches for long periods of time, but it is not yet known if these programs have long-term benefits to the companies or the industry as a whole. In other words, companies may be better off financially without them, but they are obligated to maintain them because competitors are keeping their programs.

Coupons come in many different varieties. For example, there are at least 14 variations used by restaurants:[17]

- Combination meal at a discount
- Multiple-item discount
- Buy one/get one free (also known as a *two-for,* short for two-for-one)
- Discounts on selected sizes
- Large item for the price of a smaller item
- Single-item discounts
- Discounts on specific purchase amounts
- Senior citizen and student discounts
- Free item with purchase of another item
- Children eat free
- Free item
- Early-bird discount
- Time-fused coupons
- Bounce-back coupons

Some of these require further explanation. A *time-fused* coupon offer includes several individual coupons that can be used during specified days, weeks, or months during the offer period. Taco Bell used this approach in its "See You in September" program. This combination stamp and coupon offer provided discounts on different menu items during the four weeks in September.

A *bounce-back* coupon is an offer that attempts to get the customer to use the restaurant or other service again. These are either handed to customers or glued, stapled, or inserted in packages. Domino's Pizza is just one national chain that uses this approach by gluing *bounce-backs* to the outside of pizza delivery boxes.

To be most effective, coupons should meet the following criteria.[18]

- Support a larger advertising and sales promotion campaign
- Use distribution methods that produce the highest redemption rates
- Have a definite target market or markets
- Influence both redeemers and non-redeemers
- Have a clearly defined expiration date
- Be pretested before use

b. ***Price-Offs.*** Price-offs are simply an advertised price reduction that does not involve using a coupon. These discounts are often limited to certain services (menu items, airline routes, cruise excursions), target markets (business travelers, senior citizens, children), geographic areas, or time periods. They are really a form of price discounting supported by promotion. Price-offs are popular because they can be introduced almost immediately.

Unfortunately, price-offs can quickly become *price wars,* as each competitor successively undercuts the last one to introduce the lowest price. This happens frequently among local gas stations, but has also occurred with airlines. Price-offs should not be used on their own, but as part of a carefully developed campaign promotional mix. They work best when introducing new services and when they are used for a short time at widely spaced intervals.[19]

c. ***Premiums.*** **Premiums** are merchandise items that are offered at a reduced price or free with the purchase of services or products. They differ from specialty advertising because there is a definite obligation to purchase. There are several varieties of premiums, including **self-liquidators** (sold at a price to recover the sponsor's costs) and free premiums (distributed by mail, in or on packages).[20] You have already heard about the extensive use of premiums by fast-food chains.

The most successful premiums require multiple-item purchases or multiple purchase occasions. In other words, they are *frequency* or *continuity* devices. Customers have to visit more than once to collect the *whole set* or must show several proofs of purchase. Another important guideline for premiums is that they must be consistent with the sponsor's image (position) and target market. This again is the *evidence* concept discussed in Chapter 2. An inexpensive, low-quality toy that falls apart after only a few minutes' use does not reflect the quality of food that most fast-food restaurants claim to serve. Conversely, it does not make much sense for a budget-oriented organization to promote top-of-the-line premiums.

Premiums should be thought of as another way to communicate the positioning approach and association with the selected target markets. The use of children's toys is very consistent with fast-food chains' appeal to and reliance on children. In summary, premiums must be of an appropriate quality and durability, be appealing, and have high perceived value to certain customer groups.[21]

d. ***Contests, Sweepstakes, and Games.*** You, like everybody else, love to win prizes or games. Entering contests, sweepstakes, or other forms of games is exciting. It elevates your interest in a subject, product, or service. **Contests** are sales promotions where entrants win prizes based on some required skill that they are asked to demonstrate. **Sweepstakes** are sales promotions that require entrants to submit their names and addresses. Winners are chosen on the basis of chance, not skill. **Games** are sales promotion events similar to sweepstakes, but they involve using game pieces, such as scratch-and-win cards.

The use of contests, sweepstakes, and games has been shown to increase advertising readership.[22] They can be very helpful in communicating key benefits, unique selling points (USPs), and other information. They are also good at elevating awareness and reminding people about the sponsor's services. Contests, sweepstakes, and games can be directed at customers, travel trade intermediaries, or sales representatives.

There are several different varieties of sweepstakes and games including the following:

- Sweepstakes
  i. Straight: entrants mail or hand in their names and addresses, and winners are selected randomly from all entries submitted.
  ii. Qualified: (1) programmed learning — entrants must read an advertising message and answer certain questions, and (2) automatic-entry coupons— entrants fill out a combination coupon and entry form.[23]

◆ FIGURE 16–5   *The Cayman Islands Department of Tourism* Seminars-in-Print *series offered a contest for travel agents.* (Courtesy of the Cayman Islands Department of Tourism)

- Games
  i. Match and win: entrants are required to match one game piece with another.
  ii. Scratch and win: entrants get scratch-card pieces and rub out certain areas to see whether they have won.

  How do you get more travel agents to read your advertisement, highlight key selling messages, and build up your mailing list of agencies? The Cayman Islands *Seminars-in-Print* series provides a good example (Figure 16–5.) This series of six, in-print seminars was run in *Travel Weekly* between April and September 1999. Travel agents had to read the materials provided in the **advertorial** that promoted the series, and then send in answers to the preprinted questions for all six seminars. The Grand Prize was round-trip airfare for two to Cayman Islands on Cayman Airways plus six nights accommodation at the Hyatt Regency Grand Cayman. This was an excellent example of a trade promotion contest using a *programmed learning* technique.

e. ***Travel Trade Inducements.*** As you have seen throughout this book, travel trade intermediaries can be a powerful ally to suppliers, carriers, and destination marketing organizations. Because of this, they are aggressively pursued by many organizations and are sometimes offered *inducements* of various kinds for reservations and confirmed bookings.

Travel agents, convention/meeting planners, and corporate travel managers are among the most hotly pursued travel trade intermediaries. Preferred supplier relationships and the offering of above-average commissions are becoming popular ways for carriers and suppliers to get more business from particular travel agencies. Convention/meeting planners and corporate travel managers often have enough bargaining power to convince suppliers, carriers, and destination marketing organizations to provide price discounts or other extras in order to secure their business.

You already know that other forms of inducements are used in trade promotions. They include specialty advertising items, familiarization trips, sweepstakes, and educational seminars.

f. ***Recognition Programs.*** A **recognition program** offers awards to travel trade intermediaries, sales representatives, or customers for achieving or providing certain levels of sales or business. The award may or may not involve cash. In fact, experts feel that noncash prizes are usually better motivators.[24] In other words, items such as free travel, trophies, wall plaques, or photographs in prominent journals are better at getting people to use the sponsor's services more often or to reach sales volume goals. **Frequent-flyer** and **frequent-guest award programs** are examples of recognition programs for customers. A good example of a customer recognition program is "Priority Club," Holiday Inn's frequent guest program and the first of its type in the lodging industry. This program has undergone several changes since its introduction in the early 1980s. A new twist on these types of programs is shown in Lufthansa's advertisement in Figure 16–6. Under the German airline's *Corporate Mileage Plan,* the company earns mileage points for its employees when they fly.

g. ***Continuity Programs.*** **Continuity programs** are sales promotions that require people to make several purchases, sometimes over a long period of time. Frequent-flyer and frequent-guest programs are continuity recognition programs. Travelers must stay at a hotel chain several times, or log a certain number of air miles, to earn rewards. Usually, the objective of a continuity program is either to stimulate more frequent purchases or to build long-term loyalty for a company or brand. They are considered one of the best sales promotions for building a long-term business.

Continuity programs are not really a different technique, but an approach that can be used with any of the sales promotions already described. For example, a *continuity premium* is a program where customers must make several purchases to collect a *set* of items (e.g., a set of four glasses, one available each week in a four-week period).

◆ **FIGURE 16–6**   *Lufthansa's Corporate Mileage Program awards points to a company.*
(Courtesy of Lufthansa German Airlines)

In recent years, credit-card and phone companies have become involved with the hospitality and travel industry's continuity recognition programs. For example, members of Northwest's WorldPerks frequent-flyer program receive miles for making phone calls with Sprint. Similarly, by charging any purchases to a special Citibank Visa card, members of American Airlines' AAdvantage program receive additional miles. As well as being a type of sales promotion, these are also a good example of partnerships in marketing hospitality and travel along with other industries' services.

While the airlines set the initial trend toward these affinity cards, others in hospitality and tourism were quick to emulate them. The Brown County Platinum Visa card gives people automatic membership in the Brown County Valued Visitors program. Every time the Brown County affinity card is used, the convention and visitors bureau receives part of the commission from First Bank USA. The American Museum of Natural History MBNA Platinum Plus Visa card works in a similar fashion, but there is the added benefit to the museum that MBNA makes a contribution each time a card is issued or renewed.

h. ***Gift Certificates.*** Gift certificates are vouchers or checks that are either selectively given away by the sponsor or sold to customers who, in turn, give them to others as gifts. The first type of certificate functions much like coupons encouraging recipients to try the services. Again, these are frequently used by restaurants. Gift certificates are also extensively promoted by restaurants, especially fast-food chains. A gift certificate pack may or may not feature a discount on its face value.

A Touch of Technology

Buying Restaurant Gift Certificates On-line

◆ If you want to buy a gift for a special person, what could be easier than getting on-line and ordering a gift certificate for them?

◆ Restaurant chains have definitely latched onto this idea and many sites allow you to order gift certificates on-line.

◆ T.G.I. Friday's offers gift certificates in $5, $10, $20, and $25 increments. In their *Gift Certificate Store,* the site visitor simply indicates how many certificates are wanted and then clicks to order at http://www.tgifridays.com/giftcertificates.htm/

◆ Joe's Crab Shack's gift certificates come in denominations of $25, $50, and $100. A 10 percent discount is given for gift certificate purchases between $500 and $1,999 and a 15 percent discount is given for purchases of $2,000 and more. Gift certificates can be purchased at http://www.joescrabshack.com/gifts.html/

◆ On Chick-fil-A's home page at http://www.chickfila.com/ is a link that says, "Click here to order a gift certificate." This takes you to http://www.gifttracker.com/ where you can order Chick-fil-A coupons in different denominations.

◆ You can also purchase certificates on-line from other restaurant chains, including Boston Market, Bennigan's, and Bonanza Steakhouse.

Select Media for Distributing Sales Promotions

Now that you know there are a great variety of sales promotion techniques to choose from, it is time to consider how your selected promotion will be distributed. The distribution method you selected is extremely important, because it influences the percentage of targeted persons who take advantage of a sales promotion.

The redemption rates on coupons illustrate this point. According to NCH NuWorld Marketing Limited, 82.4 percent of all coupons redeemed in the United States in 2000 were free-standing inserts (FSIs). These coupons were not included in the body of the newspaper itself or in any supplements. The second most popular were handout coupons, which accounted for 7.7 percent of all coupons redeemed.[25]

Decide on Timing of Sales Promotions and Merchandising

As you already know, sales promotions and merchandising schemes tend to be short term. They are often used to attack traditionally slow business periods, and this seems to be their most effective application. But there are really two parts to the timing question: (1) When is the best time to use sales promotions? and (2) How often should they be used? Overusing sales promotions can erode profitability and give an organization an unfavorable image. Some of the major dangers in using them too often include the following:

1. They may lead to temporary sales increases, masking longer-term problems in other marketing and promotional mix elements. Stated another way, they treat the symptoms, not the illness.
2. Sales promotions that promote special offers (e.g., coupons and premiums) are, in essence, a form of price competition (as you will see in Chapter 19). There are two basic problems with price competition: (1) it is an approach that competitors can easily imitate and (2) it loses its impact over the long term.
3. Sales promotions can be introduced quickly, and they produce almost immediate results. For this reason, they are often used hurriedly without sufficient consideration of their impact on other promotional and marketing-mix elements.

It is best to consider sales promotions as a supportive tool for advertising and personal selling. The timing of promotions, therefore, should be dictated by the schedules for advertising and personal selling activities. Sales promotions should be used when the marketer is confident that they can complement and increase the probability of achieving selling and advertising objectives.

Pretest Sales Promotions and Merchandising

Again, it is important to pretest sales promotions and merchandising materials before introducing them. This should be done by using marketing research techniques similar to those described for advertising in Chapter 15.

Prepare Final Sales Promotion and Merchandising Plan and Budget

With the pretesting completed, the final sales promotion plan and budget can be written. The sales promotion plan should describe the sales promotion objectives, research results, and assumptions leading to decisions, budget, and implementation timetable. Detailed sales promotion costs should then be compared with the tentative sales promotion budget and modifications made where necessary.

Measure and Evaluate Sales Promotion and Merchandising Success

Because sales promotion results are more immediate and short term, it is even more important to monitor their implementation closely. Marketing research techniques, including posttesting, should be used to determine if sales promotion objectives have been achieved.

CHAPTER CONCLUSION

Sales promotion is a powerful, but often misused, promotional mix element. Its power lies in creating almost immediate sales increases, which are especially helpful during off-peak periods. Overuse of sales promotions, however, carries serious dangers, including erosion of customer loyalty and reduced profitability.

Sales promotions should be carefully planned to coincide with and complement advertising and personal selling efforts. It is in a supportive role to these other promotional mix elements that the greatest benefits of sales promotion can be realized.

REVIEW QUESTIONS

1. How are the terms sales promotion and merchandising defined in this chapter?
2. What six roles do sales promotions and merchandising play in the marketing of hospitality and travel services?
3. Sales promotions are best used to support advertising and personal selling. Is this an accurate statement? Explain your answer.
4. How are special communication methods and special-offer promotions different?
5. Which sales promotion techniques are available to hospitality and travel marketers?
6. What are the advantages and disadvantages of each sales promotion technique?
7. What are the ten steps that should be followed when developing the sales promotion and merchandising plan?

CHAPTER ASSIGNMENTS

1. Select the part of the hospitality and travel industry in which you are most interested. Over a period of several weeks or months, track the sales promotion and merchandising activities of five or six leaders in the field. Collect items such as coupons, premiums, and contest/sweepstakes game materials. Are the techniques that are used similar and, if not, how do they differ? Do you feel that any of your selected companies are overusing sales promotions? Are sales promotions tied in with advertising and personal selling? Who has the most effective sales promotion program and why?

2. You are in charge of the marketing program for a travel agency, hotel, resort, airline, cruise line, restaurant, or other hospitality and travel organization. A period of traditionally low sales is approaching, and you have decided to use a sales promotion or promotions to boost sales. What technique(s) would you choose, and why? What steps would you follow in planning, implementing, and evaluating these activities? How would you tie the sales promotion(s) in with advertising and/or personal selling for maximum impact?

3. The owners of a small hospitality and travel business are considering using coupon promotions, and they have come to you for advice. What advantages and disadvantages of coupons would you discuss with them? What types of coupons would you recommend that they use? When and how should they be used? How should the success of these promotions be measured and evaluated?

4. Sales promotions can be divided into two distinct categories: (1) special communication methods and (2) special offers. Write a paper outlining the advantages and disadvantages of both approaches. Which of the approaches and specific techniques would you recommend to a hospitality and travel organization that has never used them before? How would you suggest these approaches and techniques be used for maximum effectiveness?

WORLD WIDE WEB RESOURCES

Albuquerque, New Mexico
   http://www.abqcvb.org/

American Museum of Natural History
   http://www.amnh.org/

Amtrak
   http://www.amtrak.com/

ASTA
   http://www.astanet.com/

Beefeater Restaurant & Pub
   http://www.beefeater.co.uk/

Brown County Convention & Visitors Bureau
   http://www.browncounty.com/

Carlson Marketing Group
http://www.carlsonmarketing.com

Cayman Islands Department of Tourism
http://www.caymanislands.ky/

Chick-fil-A
http://www.chickfila.com/

Cinnabon
http://www.cinnabon.com/

FITUR
http://www.fitur.ifema.es/

Hyatt Resorts
http://www.hyatt.com/hyatt_resorts/index.html

Irish Tourist Board
http://www.shamrock.org/

ITB Berlin
http://www.itb-berlin.com/

Joe's Crab Shack
http://www.joescrabshack.com/

Lufthansa's Corporate Mileage Program
http://www.lufthansa-usa.com/comp

National Business Travel Association
http://www.nbta.org/

National Tour Association (NTA)
http://www.ntaonline.com/

NCH NuWorld Marketing Limited
http://www.nuworld.com/

Promotional Marketing Association
http://www.pmalink.org/

Scandinavian Tourism Board
http://www.goscandinavia.com

Singapore Airlines
http://www.krisshop.com/

Skyline Chili
http://www.skylinechili.com/

T.G.I. Friday's Inc.
http://www.tgifridays.com/

World Travel Market
http://www.reedexpo.com/

REFERENCES

1. Berkowitz, Eric N., Roger A. Kerin, Steven W. Hartley, and William Rudelius. 2000. *Marketing.* 6th ed. Boston: Irwin McGraw-Hill, 534.

2. "National ad spending by media." *Advertising Age* (1999) http://www.adage.com/dataplace/

3. Frankel, Bud, and H. W. Philips. 1985. *Your Advertising's Great . . . How's Business?* Homewood, Ill.: Dow Jones-Irwin, 3–5.

4. Dommermuth, William P. 1989. *Promotion: Analysis, Creativity, and Strategy.* 2nd ed. Boston: PWS-Kent Publishing Company, 367.

5. McDonald, Michele. "BA hands out jammies, tucks in first class sleepyheads to London." *Travel Weekly* 52(7):1, 4 (1993).

6. Amtrak. (2001). "Amtrak announces special fares to drive business to travel agents." http://www.amtrak.com/

7. Reggie Silver Award Winners. "*Inspector Gadget.*" Promotional Marketing Association (1999). http://www.pmalink.org/html/99reggie.html

8. Rossiter, John R., and Larry Percy. 2000. *Advertising Communications & Promotions Management.* 2nd ed. Boston: McGraw-Hill.

9. "Pizza Hut and Sony Computer Entertainment America reunite for unprecedented holiday promotional program." Pizza Hut (1999). http://www.pizzahut.com/

10. Dommermuth, William P. 1989. *Promotion: Analysis, Creativity, and Strategy.* 2nd ed. Boston: PWS-Kent Publishing Company, 47–48.

11. Dommermuth, William P. 1989. *Promotion: Analysis, Creativity, and Strategy.* 2nd ed. Boston: PWS-Kent Publishing Company, 563.

12. Zikmund, William G., and Michael d'Amico. 2001. *Effective Marketing: Creating and Keeping Customers in an E-commerce World.* 3rd ed. Cincinnati, Ohio: South-Western College Publishing.

13. NCH NuWorld Marketing Limited. 2001. http://www.nuworld.com/

14. Lefever, Michael M., and Alastair M. Morrison. "Couponing for profit." *The Cornell Hotel and Restaurant Administration Quarterly* 28(4):59–60 (1988).

15. Dommermuth, William P. 1989. *Promotion: Analysis, Creativity, and Strategy.* 2nd ed.

Boston: PWS-Kent Publishing Company, 48, 368–372.

16. Schultz, Don E., William A. Robinson, and Lisa A. Petrison. 1998. *Sales Promotion Essentials: The 10 Basic Sales Promotion Techniques . . . and How to Use Them.* 3rd ed. Lincolnwood, Ill.: NTC Publishing Group.

17. Lefever, Michael M., and Alastair M. Morrison, "Couponing for profit." *The Cornell Hotel and Restaurant Administration Quarterly* 28 (4):62 (1988).

18. Lefever, Michael M., and Alastair M. Morrison. "Couponing for profit." *The Cornell Hotel and Restaurant Administration Quarterly* 28 (4):63 (1988).

19. Dommermuth, William P. 1989. *Promotion: Analysis, Creativity, and Strategy.* 2nd ed. Boston: PWS-Kent Publishing Company, 376–377.

20. Rossiter, John R., and Larry Percy. 2000. *Advertising Communications & Promotions Management.* 2nd ed. Boston: McGraw-Hill.

21. Frankel, Bud, and H. W. Philips. 1985. *Your Advertising's Great . . . How's Business?* Homewood, Ill.: Dow Jones-Irwin, 130.

22. Frankel, Bud, and H. W. Philips. 1985. *Your Advertising's Great . . . How's Business?* Homewood, Ill.: Dow Jones-Irwin, 132.

23. Frankel, Bud, and H. W. Philips. 1985. *Your Advertising's Great . . . How's Business?* Homewood, Ill.: Dow Jones-Irwin, 133–134.

24. Dommermuth, William P. 1989. *Promotion: Analysis, Creativity, and Strategy.* 2nd ed. Boston: PWS-Kent Publishing Company, 384–385.

25. "CPG Merger and Acquisition Activity Impacts Coupon Promotion Volume." NCH NuWorld Marketing Limited (2001). http://nuworld.com/

For additional hospitality and travel marketing resources, visit our Web site at **www.Hospitality-Tourism.delmar.com**

17

Personal Selling and Sales Management

How Do We Get There?

Objectives

Having read this chapter, you should be able to:

◆ Define personal selling.

◆ Explain the roles of personal selling.

◆ List the three categories of personal selling.

◆ Describe five major personal selling strategies.

◆ Explain the steps in the sales process.

◆ Describe the seven possible strategies for closing sales.

◆ Define sales management and explain its functions.

◆ Describe the characteristics of the successful salesperson.

◆ Describe the contents and role of the sales plan.

◆ Explain four characteristics of personal selling in the hospitality and travel industry.

Overview

Many consider personal selling to be the most powerful promotional mix element in its ability to generate sales. This chapter begins by defining personal selling and then discusses the role played by personal selling in the promotional mix.

*Personal selling varies in importance in different parts of the hospitality and travel indus-*try. The chapter explains the reasons for these differences and the role of selling in specific industry sectors.*

The steps involved in the personal sales process are also reviewed. The chapter ends by looking at the sales plan and sales management.

Key Terms

AIDA formula	outside sales	sales plan
approach	personal selling	sales presentation
blind prospecting	preapproach	sales process
canned sales presentations	prospecting	sales prospects
closing	qualifying	sales quotas
cold calling or canvassing	relationship selling	sales representative
customer relationship	sales blitz	sales territories
management (CRM)	sales calls	suggestive selling
field sales	sales demonstration	telemarketing
handling objections	sales lead	telephone sales
inside sales	sales management	up-selling
lead prospecting	sales management audit	

Have you ever gone into a store and bought much more than you thought you would? Have you recently consumed a calorie-laden dessert on the recommendation of a waitperson? How often have you heard the question, "Do you want fries with that?" and succumbed to the temptation? Was your new car, stereo, or outfit just a little more expensive than you thought it would be? If you answered yes to any of these questions, then you know how effective personal selling can be.

Advertising, sales promotion, and merchandising are impersonal and *mass* forms of communications. No matter how hard the companies that use them try, they are not dealing with you as an individual. You can turn the volume down on your radio or television when commercials are playing. Commercial time can easily become a convenient time for a trip to the refrigerator or bathroom. You can toss coupons in the garbage, along with direct mail ads. You can even completely ignore gimmicky, in-store merchandising. But if you are like most of us, you cannot turn off another human being quite as easily. People buy many of those extra desserts and french fries because they find it hard to say no to others presenting them with sales arguments. No matter how much you might come to resent the questions, "Can I help you with something?" or "Do you want _____ with that?" you cannot really ignore the messages because of the person who is delivering them. This is the real power of personal selling—the ability to deal one-on-one with customers and to develop rapport and personal relationships.

PERSONAL SELLING AND THE PROMOTIONAL MIX

Definition

Personal selling involves oral conversations, either by telephone or face-to-face, between salespersons and prospective customers. Unlike advertising, sales promotion, and merchandising, this promotional mix element is a form of personal communication, which introduces some unique advantages and potential problems.

The high degree of personalization that personal selling involves usually comes at a much greater cost per contact than does other mass communications techniques. Marketers must decide whether this added expense can be justified, or whether marketing objectives can be achieved by communicating with potential customers as groups. As you will see later, some hospitality and travel organizations favor personal selling far more than others. For them, the potential benefits greatly outweigh the extra costs. In other words, the strengths of personal selling are more important to some organizations than to others.

Plan the Promotional Mix First

Again, you should know up front that it is incorrect to think of personal selling as an alternative to advertising, sales promotion, merchandising, or public relations. Rather, they should all be viewed as the ingredients of a good recipe. Each ingredient in a recipe adds something special to the dish. Varying the quantities of ingredients can change the dish's flavor, taste, color, and texture. Forgetting to include an important ingredient can spoil the entire dish. Choosing a promotional mix in this way is similar to cooking. An organization can select its own combination of promotional mix elements. Like a garnish, personal selling tends to add the finishing touch to the promotional mix. An organization's sales representatives draw upon what has been communicated through mass communications channels.

Chapter 16 mentioned the three-punch combination of advertising, sales promotion, and merchandising. Each of these three elements builds on the other. This approach can be even more powerful in generating sales when it is finished off with personal selling. For example, many cruise lines use a combination of magazine and television advertising and the Web to make potential passengers aware of their departures. This media effort is supported by various forms of sales promotion and merchandising, including brochures, trade show exhibits, educational seminars and *fam* trips for travel agents, and retail travel agency displays. The final ingredient, and the one that really *closes* cruise sales, is personal selling by the retail travel agent. These knowledgeable people can fully explain the advantages of cruises over other forms of vacations, and they can excite clients about an individual cruise line's format. To make sure that agents stay well informed and enthusiastic, cruise lines have their own sales representatives, who call on travel agencies throughout the country. Whether it is a cruise line or a small, independent restaurant trying to increase its wine sales, the greatest success comes from the well-orchestrated and carefully preplanned use of personal selling in combination with advertising, sales promotion, merchandising, and public relations.

Roles of Personal Selling

What is the role of personal selling in marketing and the promotional mix? Let us start by saying that there is a role for personal selling in every hospitality and travel organization, although its relative importance varies. Why? The answer is that our business is service, and it is very difficult to separate good service from effective personal selling. When a desk clerk, waitperson, reservationist, or travel agent says the right things and pleases customers, this constitutes both good service and personal selling. Customers return primarily because of good service.

There are several important roles of personal selling in the hospitality and travel industry. The six that follow are the most important:

1. Identifying decision makers, decision processes, and qualified buyers
2. Promoting to corporate, travel trade, and other groups

3. Generating increased sales at the point of purchase
4. Providing detailed and up-to-date information to the travel trade
5. Maintaining a personal relationship with key clients
6. Gathering information on competitors' promotions

1. **Identifying Decision Makers, Decision Processes, and Qualified Buyers.** When targeting corporations, associations, and other groups, it is often very difficult to identify qualified buyers (the most likely purchasers of travel services), key decision makers (the person or persons who have the final say in travel decisions), and the decision processes used (the steps involved in making travel decisions). This important information can be gathered effectively through inquiries by sales representatives and sales calls on organizations. In this way, costly mistakes can be avoided, such as communicating with the wrong people (non-decision-makers) at an inappropriate time (e.g., too late in the decision process), or addressing irrelevant needs or requirements in sales presentations.

2. **Promoting to Corporate, Travel Trade, and Other Groups.** Many organizations find personal selling to be most effective in promoting to key travel decision makers and influencers, such as corporate travel managers, convention/meeting planners, tour wholesalers/operators, and retail travel agents. These people's decisions affect the travel plans of many individual travelers. Their purchasing power is impressive and there are relatively few of them, which justifies the added expense of personal selling.

3. **Generating Increased Sales at the Point of Purchase.** Used effectively at the point of purchase, personal selling can significantly increase the likelihood of a purchase and the amount spent by customers. Where are the points of purchase in the hospitality and travel industry? They include the hotel reservation (e.g., selling upgraded guest accommodations) and car rental desk (e.g., selling more expensive car models), the restaurant floor (e.g., selling more expensive or additional menu items and beverages), and the travel agency office (e.g., booking hotels and cars along with airline reservations). Another important place is where telephone inquiries are answered and reservations are accepted. Increased sales result from the proper training of service and reservations staff in personal selling techniques. To prove this point, think back to the unwanted desserts and french fries we talked about earlier.

4. **Providing Detailed and Up-to-Date Information to the Travel Trade.** Most forms of advertising and sales promotion can transmit only limited quantities of information. Direct mail advertising and the Web are the best in this respect. Personal selling not only allows an organization to pass on more detailed information, but it also provides the opportunity to deal immediately with a prospect's concerns and questions. This is especially important for an organization that relies on travel trade intermediaries for part or all of its business. It is very important for these professionals to fully comprehend an organization's services in order to communicate effectively with their clients and customers.

5. **Maintaining a Personal Relationship with Key Clients.** The key word in the term personal selling is undoubtedly *personal,* not *selling.* This promotional mix element, communicated through an organization's sales representatives and reservationists, gives it a personality that cannot be created as effectively through

the mass media. These people are a human reflection of an otherwise impersonal corporation or government agency. As such, they must mirror the quality levels and positioning of their organizations.

Most of us react more favorably if we are approached as individuals rather than as just one person in a group of people. Careful attention to individual needs and requirements is perhaps the most powerful form of marketing in the hospitality and travel industry. Personal selling, as one book reflects in its title, is "marketing personified."[1] Key customers really appreciate the personal attention they receive from professional sales representatives and reservationists. This normally pays off in increased sales and repeat use.

6. **Gathering Information on Competitors' Promotions.** Salespeople constantly rub shoulders with potential customers who are also the targets of competitors. Many sales prospects voluntarily pass on information about competitive promotional efforts. Thus, the sales force can be an important source of *competitive intelligence.*

CATEGORIES OF PERSONAL SELLING

There are three principal categories of personal selling in the hospitality and travel industry: field, telephone, and internal. Some organizations use all three, whereas almost everyone is involved in internal and telephone selling.

1. **Field Sales.** Field sales (external selling) are selling efforts that take place in person outside the hospitality and travel organization's place of business. Often referred to as sales calls, these involve face-to-face presentations to prospective customers (or sales prospects). Examples include outside sales agents of travel agencies and hotel sales representatives who call on corporations and convention/meeting planners and sales representatives from airlines, cruise lines, tour wholesalers, and car rental firms who visit travel agencies. This is the most expensive type of personal selling because it involves employing a sales force and adding travel costs when they are away from the home office. Additional funds also have to be invested in sales support materials, such as Power Point and slide presentations, videotapes, and presentation manuals with photographs.

   Another term that is found in the hospitality and travel industry is outside sales. For example, an outside sales person in a retail travel agency is someone who works outside the agency office to generate sales and leads for the agency.

2. **Telephone Sales.** Telephone sales are any communications via the phone that lead directly or indirectly to sales. Communications by telephone are playing an increasingly important role in many aspects of personal selling. Generally, this is now referred to as telemarketing. The phone is an efficient way of prospecting (identifying prospective customers) and qualifying (determining the potential value and ranking of) sales prospects. It is used to arrange appointments for sales calls, to gather important background information before making a field sales call, to follow up with promised information, and to confirm the details of a sales prospect's requirements. In some cases, especially where an organization cannot justify the travel and salary costs of a field visit, it substitutes for an in-person sales call.

   Another important role of the telephone in our industry is accepting phone reservations and handling inquiries. Although not as well recognized as a sales tool, the telephone, along with communications between computers, plays a huge role in distributing business among hospitality and travel organizations. Training employees who handle telephone calls to be an extension of the sales force rather than just order takers pays off handsomely, as does providing easy telephone access to information and reservations via toll-free numbers.

3. **Inside Sales.** Inside sales (internal selling) are efforts made within an organization's place of business to either increase the likelihood of a sale or to add to customers' average spending levels. You saw earlier that it is very difficult to draw a line between good service and effective inside sales. However, one readily discernible form of inside sales is suggestive selling or up-selling, where employees suggest or recommend additional or higher-priced items. Every retail situation at the point of purchase provides an opportunity for this form of selling.

Another type of selling that has emerged more recently is relationship selling, or the practice of building ties to customers based on a salesperson's attention and commitment to customer needs over time.[2] The focus here is not on just getting one sale or transaction, but on creating and keeping long-term customers. This is just one part of a process that has become known as customer relationship management (CRM).

Figure 17–1 shows a number of classified advertisements recruiting salespeople for travel organizations. You will notice that two of the positions are for District Sales Managers (Hawaiian Airlines and Classic Custom Vacations). Another is for an Inside Sales Representative, and the other for Outside Sales Agents (American Express Travel).

PERSONAL SELLING STRATEGIES

A sales representative or other staff member can select from several sales strategies when involved in field, telephone, or inside sales. The major ones are (1) stimulus response, (2) mental states, (3) formula, (4) need satisfaction, and (5) problem solving.[3]

1. **Stimulus Response or Canned Sales Presentations.** This approach is most often used with inside and telephone sales. Staff members are asked to memorize certain questions or phrases or consistently to behave in a specific fashion. By giving customers a stimulus (question, phrase, or behavior pattern), a predictable response is expected. For example, restaurants that train servers to ask patrons, "Can I interest you in one of our desserts?" or "Would you like _____ with that?" expect that the power of suggestion will stimulate customers to respond by ordering additional menu items. Likewise, travel agents who ask "Will you be needing a car or hotel room as well?" are likely to earn increased commissions.

This personal selling strategy ignores individual differences among customers, but it still works well in our industry. Canned sales presentations can also be used in field sales to guarantee that every sales representative communicates the same key messages to prospective customers. However, there is a greater need for a flexible approach in field sales that adapts to the needs and requirements of individual customers.

2. **Mental States Strategy.** The sales representative who uses this approach assumes that customers must go through sequential mental states before they make a purchase. Chapter 4 referred to these as *buying process stages*. Sales calls and follow-ups are planned and timed to correspond with the five buying process stages (need

NATIONAL·TRAVEL·MARKETPLACE

MARCH 13, 2000 **5**

THE BEST READ TRAVEL SECTION IN THE INDUSTRY

National Travel Marketplace is a twice-weekly feature on Mondays and Thursdays. Deadlines for the Monday issues are the Monday prior at 5:00pm EST. Deadlines for the Thursday issues are the Thursday prior at 5:00pm EST. Complete advertising information available by calling 201-902-1918 or fax 201-902-1928. 35 characters equal one line (count each letter, space and punctuation mark as a character). Add $10 for TWK Box Numbers. When replying to Travel Weekly Box Numbers, please use our complete address. TRAVEL WEEKLY (Box …), 500 Plaza Drive, Secaucus, NJ 07096.

POSITIONS OPEN

DISTRICT SALES MANAGER
SOUTHERN CALIFORNIA & SEATTLE

Hawaiian Airlines is seeking highly-motivated, dynamic, energetic, creative sales professionals to call on Travel Agents, Wholesalers and Corporate accounts in the Southern California and Seattle marketplace. The successful candidates must have a minimum of 3-5 years sales experience, preferably in airline and or travel related industry. Strong written and oral skills, PC literacy, self motivation, proven analytical ability, team player and knowledge of the Hawaii product are essential. Knowledge with the accounts within the territory is required. BS/BA preferred. Evening and weekend work sometimes required.

INSIDE SALES REPRESENTATIVE
LOS ANGELES

These full time (2) and part time (1) positions require a minimum of 1 year airline or travel related industry experience in sales, customer service or reservations. Sabre experience, strong PC literacy, Internet and Hawaii product knowledge required. Excellent oral and written skills necessary. Strong organizational experience required.

Hawaiian Airlines offers a competitive salary and comprehensive benefits package. Please send or fax your resume to: Hawaiian Airlines 6033 W. Century Blvd. Suite 810 Los Angeles, CA 90045. Fax: 310-641-4053. We will respond only to qualified candidates. No phone calls please.

We are an equal opportunity employer committed to diversity in the workplace.

DISTRICT SALES MANAGER
HOUSTON

Classic Custom Vacations, a wholly owned subsidiary of Global Vacation Group, is accepting applications for an experienced, motivated salesperson with strong communication skills & a resilient personality. Minimum of 3 years wholesale/retail travel management or airline sales experience. Must be Houston based and have loyal travel agency following and working knowledge of the territory that will encompass south Texas as far west as El Paso and central and south Louisiana. Fax or send resume to:

Classic Custom Vacations
One North First St., San Jose, CA 95113
Fax (770) 390-0891
e-mail: jobs@ccv.com
EOC

Home based, Franchisees & Smaller Retailers

CRUISE PROS ONLY!

100% COMMISSIONS

3 month trial offer with a $25 processing fee per cabin
— Minimum five unique bookings

Why pay franchise fees to earn TOP commissions? Get into the "net" with the fastest growing cruise retailer.

• No Start-up Costs or Fees   • Internet Leads
• No Monthly Franchise Fees   • Co-op Advertising
• Top-Notch Service and Support   • Ship Fams

Call Wayne @ 800-800-9552 x237
Your inquiry will be held in the strictest confidence

CRUISE.COM
AFFILIATES

Carlson Wagonlit Travel

AROUND THE WORLD TRAVEL

So. Florida's largest mgmt Co.
Continues to expand
Immediate Openings
• Corporate Agents
• Intl Tkt Agent
South Florida
Great Benefits/401K
Fax resume to: (305) 448-8290

CRUISE INTO THE FUTURE
WITH CRUISES INC.

We are the future! Join our sales crew and enjoy the benefits of a franchise without the large investment. This is an excellent opportunity for cruise selling agents. We take care of ticketing, processing, billing and more.

America's Cruise Specialists
CRUISES INC.

1-877-289-7746
www.cruisesinc.com

Cruise & Tour Specialist Wanted
Located in Woodland Hills, CA. Must have selling and closing exp. Contact Marsha 800-806-6444

API (Virtuoso) agency seeks experienced leisure agents. Independents welcome! BFH Ultimate Escape (Boca Raton, FL). Fax 561-241-5315; email ginny@bfhescapes.com

Experienced Agent / Assistant Manager for Leisure agency in Scarsdale, NY. Call Lee at 914-723-6611 or forward resume fax 914-723-6906 or email scarsdaltvl@AOL.com

---

With everything else we offer, our new benefit options are really the icing on the cake!

American Express is known for providing career advantages that make travel professionals' mouths water - and now we're topping things off with exciting benefit options for our Outside Sales Agents. Join us…we're #1 in *Travel Weekly's* list of agencies and in the top 100 of *Fortune's* "**best places to work!**" You'll also enjoy:

exciting BENEFITS options
• Medical/dental/vision eligibility
• Company-matched savings
• 401(k)
• And much MORE!
Plus, we continue to stand out with advantages such as:

AMERICAN EXPRESS®
Travel

• Generous commissions (accurately calculated and paid promptly)!
• Affiliations/partnerships with major travel providers (more lucrative selling opportunities for you)!
• The security of representing a world-class brand with over 150 years of leadership behind it!

We have openings nationwide for go-getters with 2 years of travel counselor experience, a solid base of existing clients, proven sales ability, and a make-it-happen attitude. Just call our National Sales Recruiter at **800-425-0497**, or forward your resume to his attention: **John Crater, Staffing Specialist, 7701 Airport Center Dr., Greensboro, NC 27409. Fax: 336-668-5610.**

what a **GREAT** place to **WORK!**

equal opportunity employer • www.americanexpress.com

Business Development Manager

Carlson Wagonlit Travel, a leader in the leisure travel industry, is seeking a travel professional with previous travel agency ownership/management experience to ensure retention, growth and satisfaction with our franchise offices in the midwest U.S. to help grow their business.

Requirements include:
• Marketing, Human Resources, Agency Operations and Financial Analysis experience
• BA/BS degree in related field or equivalent experience 5+ years
• Strong presentation skills
• Position is home-based out of the Kansas City, St. Louis, or Memphis markets
• Travel 80% of the time

Contact:
clghumanreosurces@carlson.com
or fax your resume along with salary requirements to:
612-212-2790. EOE.

Carlson Wagonlit Travel

TRAVEL CONSULTANT
Circle Travel, Chapel Hill, NC, is expanding. Need exp.agt. Comp. salary, benefits, profit sharing. Fax resume: (919) 967-1056

Travel Consultant/Sales
Est. Chapel Hill, NC Sabre agency. Top salary, incentives, bonuses, Full medical, dental, matching 401k. Fax resume 919-967-4770

Marketing Manager, travel industry sought by Travel Services Firm in Key Biscayne, FL. Must have Bach in Tourism & 2 yrs exp marketing in travel & tourism industry. Send resumes to Professional Travel Services, P.O. Box 1373, Key Biscayne, FL 33149

---

traveljobz.net

A new direction in recruitment

Our new internet based job board is dedicated to the travel, transport and leisure **industries** throughout North America.

It's fast and easy to use with regional and national focus, enabling you to search for positions and employees online.

TELEPHONE : 941 366 8040
EMAIL : info@traveljobz.net

www.traveljobz.net

TRAVEL CONSULTANTS/SALES
Fugazy Executive Travel is seeking CORPORATE agents in Boston and surrounding areas: branch offices and onsite locations. Top salary, Incentives, Bonuses, Full medical/dental/travel, Matching 401K. Fax resume: 617-692-5180/1-800-385-0999 http://www.fugazy.com

Business Travel, Inc. has CORPORATE agent openings in Boca Raton, FL; Chicago, IL; and Menlo Park, San Jose and San Francisco, CA. Full medical dental/travel, matching 401K, generous travel benefits, supportive management and upward mobility. Fax resume to 1-800-385-0999

AGENCIES WANTED

AGENCIES WANTED
Fugazy Executive Travel is growing again! We are seeking to acquire agencies of $20 million plus and a minimum of 60% corporate business. Open to all reservation systems. Call for confidential talk with Jeffrey Smith, President at 781-994-1203 http://www.fugazy.com

---

To Reply to a Classified Ad with a TWK Box Number, Please Send All Responses to:

Travel Weekly,
Box #
500 Plaza Drive,
Secaucus, NJ 07096

BUSINESS OPPORTUNITIES

YOU DESERVE MORE!!!

UNIGLOBE IN HOUSE TRAVEL
You can do it all from home/100% Commissions

UNIGLOBE cruise ship centers.
Proven Marketing System to grow your Cruise Business

UNIGLOBE Travel
20 years experience in supporting agencies worldwide

UNIGLOBE.com
Wired for Travel
Earn $$ with your own interactive.com

Recognized brand name, #1 Override Program, High Commissions, Merger/ Acquisition Assistance, Lead Generation, Customized, Interactive Web Site, Group Block Space, Negotiated Hotel Program, 7/24 Service, Marketing, Operations and Accounting Support…MUCH, MUCH MORE!!

CALL NOW!
1-800-863-1606
www.uniglobeinhouse.com

INCREASE YOUR INCOME!
★ 100% Commissions!
★ Low Fees!
★ SABRE and APOLLO

HOME OFFICE TRAVEL   Full Service
www.homeofficetravel.com   Support Center!
(800) 910-1240 x232

BUYING/SELLING
OPENING AN AGENCY?

BUYING OR SELLING?
Call us first!
We'll find the right Agent/Buyer for you and take care of the entire process!
Donna Conklin & Associates
703-644-9102
www.conklinandassociates.com

EARN HIGHER COMMISSIONS

ATTENTION OUTSIDE AGENTS
Keep up to 100% of your commissions! Nation's #1 support network, Toll-Free Helpline, Great Travel Benefits, FAMS, Worldspan Software, work at home or office, Full or Part Time, call us for free info.

Traveler's Choice
1 (800) 446-0096

Earn More! Run your travel business from your home or office, full or part time. CRS software, great commissions, marketing, training, travel benefits and much more.
HMI Travel
Call toll free 888-558-7600
www.hmitravel.com

OUTSIDE AGENTS WANTED 70% COMM
Best benefits & support. No fees, Sabre Incentive Connection www.ictravel.com 602-867-9606 or ictharvey@uswest.net

---

OBERAMMERGAU ARRANGEMENTS

OBERAMMERGAU TICKETS
Many dates • BUY • SELL • TRADE
Call Tom at 215-517-2100

◆ **FIGURE 17–1**   *Samples of advertisements looking for travel sales people.* (Courtesy of Travel Weekly)

awareness, information search, evaluation of alternatives, purchase, and post-purchase evaluation). This approach is used primarily for field sales and in cases where the purchase amount is large or very important to customers (i.e., high-involvement, extensive problem-solving decisions). Examples of these situations include travel agents who assist clients with plans for foreign vacations and hotel sales representatives who attempt to land an annual convention from a major association or a major corporate account.

3. **Formula Selling.** This is a variation of the *mental states* approach, and it assumes that customers' decisions and the sales process go through predictable and sequential steps. Based on these steps, sales representatives use a *formula* (preplanned sales process).

    The sales process model focuses on the steps that the sales representative must follow. Normally, there are four major steps: (1) the approach, (2) a sales presentation or demonstration, (3) handling customer questions and objections, and (4) closing the sale. This model is discussed in detail later. You should note at this point that this is an approach best suited for field sales and high-involvement purchase decisions.

    The AIDA formula is another example that assumes that the sales representative must do four things: (1) get the prospect's attention (the first *A*), (2) stimulate interest in the organization's services (*I*), (3) create a desire for these services (*D*), and (4) get the prospect to take action by reserving or buying the services (the last *A*).

    AIDA FORMULA
    Attention → Interest → Desire → Action

    The AIDA formula is another approach that is best suited to field sales and high-involvement decisions. Sales representatives can make the best use of AIDA by doing the following:
    a. Doing careful approach work before making sales calls (e.g., doing their homework on a prospect organization)
    b. Stimulating interest (e.g., through the presentations used in sales calls)
    c. Creating and holding desire by handling objections and demonstrating their services (e.g., complimentary trips for prospects)
    d. Using one of several methods to close the sale (e.g., asking the prospect to make some form of action-oriented decision).

4. **Need-Satisfaction Approach.** The three previous strategies are based on the assumption that all sales prospects are more or less alike. The need-satisfaction approach is more sophisticated and involves adapting the selling method to each prospect's individual needs and requirements.[4] It is a low-pressure, consultative form of personal selling.[5] It is particularly well suited for hospitality and travel organizations that act as advisors to their customers, such as travel agents and incentive travel planners. The need-satisfaction approach also works well in other situations where the customer is involved in significant amounts of pre-trip planning (e.g., an association planning a major national or international convention). There are four steps in this approach:
    a. Determining customer needs through discussion and questioning—summarizing the needs discovered

b. Presenting tailor-made services to satisfy the needs that have been mutually discovered

c. Obtaining customers' agreement that services meet their needs—addressing any remaining concerns or questions

d. Closing the sale—making sure customers' needs are satisfied

You should instantly recognize this as a *minimodel* of the marketing concept itself. It is a highly effective sales strategy, but one that requires considerable time and effort, as well as attention to individual details.

5. **Problem-Solving Approach.** The problem-solving approach, like need satisfaction, begins with the assumption that every customer's needs are unique. Even more time and effort are necessary to make this approach work, however. The sales representative begins by proving that the sales prospect has a problem. Let us assume that the prospect is a corporation. The problem could be that the company is spending an unnecessary amount of money on employee travel or on one specific travel element, such as lodging, airfares, car rentals, or other ground transportation. The sales representative could compare the prospect's expenses to typical situations to prove this point. Identifying such client problems often involves background research and several meetings with the client. Five steps are involved in this approach:[6]

a. Finding, defining, and demonstrating the problem to the sales prospect

b. Identifying alternative solutions to the problem

c. Suggesting criteria for choosing the optimum solution

d. Judging alternative solutions based on the criteria—recommending one solution

e. Closing the sale—making sure that the services purchased satisfy customer problems

You can see that this strategy differs from need satisfaction because prospects are usually unaware of the problems before they are contacted by sales representatives. In other cases, prospects are generally aware of the problem, but they have not defined or researched it. This approach requires considerable cooperation from prospects, as sales representatives research and define the problems.

You are probably now wondering which of the five personal selling strategies is the best. The answer is that it all depends on the individual situation. There is no universal approach to personal selling that fits every situation. An organization and its sales representatives must evaluate each selling opportunity and sales prospect carefully before deciding which strategy to use.

The factors that most influence the choice of selling strategy are the type of hospitality and travel service, the target market, and the size and complexity of the purchase. For example, fast-food and other restaurants are likely to use the least expensive and sophisticated stimulus-response approach. Their menu items have broad market appeal, are relatively inexpensive, and are purchased routinely. At the other end of the spectrum, corporate travel managers often coordinate travel budgets in the tens of millions of dollars. The decisions they make about which hospitality and travel services to use are complex and involve large sums of money. Here, the more expensive and time-consuming approaches of need satisfaction or problem solving are more justified. Similarly, carriers, suppliers, and other travel intermediaries may find these two more individualized strategies most appropriate for selling to travel agencies.

THE SALES PROCESS

Now that you know the specific approaches used in personal selling, it is time to look at the common steps followed in field sales, and some types of telephone selling. The step-by-step sales process described is usually more elaborate than the one required for inside sales. The sales process consists of the following steps:

1. Prospecting and qualifying prospective customers
2. Preplanning prior to sales calls
3. Presenting and demonstrating services
4. Handling objections and questions
5. Closing the sale
6. Following up after closing the sale

1. **Prospecting and Qualifying Prospective Customers.** What is another word for digging for gold and other precious metals or stones? Congratulations if you answered *prospecting.* The first step in the sales process is very similar to digging for gold—the sales representative has to explore and do research to find the most likely sources of business. *Prospecting,* or identifying sales prospects, includes a variety of techniques that sales representatives use to pinpoint potential customers. To be a sales prospect (often called a sales lead), a potential customer must meet three criteria.[7]
   a. Have an existing or potential need for the services
   b. Be able to afford the purchase or purchases involved
   c. Be authorized to purchase the services

   Whereas many pleasure-travel sales prospects walk into travel agency offices, it is much more common for hospitality and travel organizations to have to do prospecting outside their own places of business (field sales), by telephone, or through the Internet. There are several different types of prospecting. Blind prospecting involves using telephone directories and other published lists to find sales prospects.[8] The use of the adjective *blind* means that the sales representative has no prior knowledge of the groups or individuals on these lists and no idea if they are true sales prospects. This type of approach might be used by a new hotel that is trying to generate business from local industries, a travel agency that is attempting to attract group tour business from local clubs and organizations, or an incentive travel planner who is looking for companies interested in setting up incentive trips.

   A closely related technique is cold calling or canvassing. You already know what cold calling is if you frequently answer the door only to find someone trying to sell you something. Cold calling is really blind prospecting in the field. It is not a very systematic approach, but it often works. Sales representatives have no idea whether the individuals or organizations they visit will turn out to be sales prospects. The basic assumption here is that if the sales representative visits enough people with potentially similar requirements or needs, some of them will be prospects. A sales blitz, *blitzing,* or *concentrated canvassing* is an approach where several sales representatives cold call in the same, specific geographic area.[9] A blitz is usually only a one-time activity or is repeated infrequently.

   You are probably wondering why a systematic book such as this one is recommending such an unsystematic approach to prospecting. Is this not just a mini version of the undifferentiated marketing strategy discussed in Chapter 8? Are we not taking a *shotgun approach* to marketing? The answer to your dilemma is that there are better ways to prospect, but certain specific situations justify blind prospecting and cold calling. These include cases where the hospitality and travel business or service is new—the organization and potential customers are unfamiliar with each other. These prospecting approaches also are better justified if the potential purchase amounts are large relative to the organization's or business' current revenues (i.e., a very large potential sale). Another situation is where the organization is trying to get sales from a completely new geographic area or sales territory.

The most desirable way to do prospecting is to have *leads* to begin with. Some call this **lead prospecting**, or contacting individuals and organizations that have a high probability of being sales prospects.[10] There are many sources of leads including those shown in Figure 17–2.[11,12]

Not all sales prospects are worth pursuing, and the next step—*qualifying*—is used to narrow the list down to the most likely purchasers. Because the normal field sales call costs approximately $170, this procedure makes great financial as well as marketing sense. Qualifying means using preselected criteria to identify the best sales prospects. Following are typical criteria and questions used to qualify sales prospects:

a. If prospects are past customers, what volume of business did they provide?
b. Do prospects have needs or problems that the sales representative's services can satisfy?
c. Do prospects have the authority to make purchases?

1. Referrals (a prospect recommended by a current customer or by someone who is familiar with the service)
2. Endless chain referrals (sales representatives asking prospects or past customers for names of others who might be interested in services)
3. Referral letters and cards (sales representatives asking past customers to recommend the organization's services to potential customers either by writing letters of introduction or by filling out specially preprinted cards)
4. Friends and acquaintances
5. Directories (printed lists of potential customers in published directories)
6. Trade publications (hospitality and travel trade magazines and journals that provide information on organizations and people in the industry)
7. Trade and travel shows (persons visiting exhibits at shows who express an interest in receiving further information)
8. Telemarketing (prospects identified and qualified by telephone)
9. Direct-response advertising (inquiries received by telephone, mail, fax, computer, or in person in response to advertising)
10. Computerized database (prospects identified through maintaining and utilizing relational databases on computers)
11. Cold canvassing (cold calling on groups of potential customers)
12. Networking (building and maintaining groups of contacts who may, in the future, give advice on sales prospects)
13. Prospecting by nonsales employees (identification of prospects by nonsales employees)
14. Getting leads from the World Wide Web or by e-mail

◆ FIGURE 17–2 *Sources of sales leads.* (Adapted from Manning, Gerald L., and Barry L. Reece. 2001. *Selling Today: Building Quality Partnerships,* 8th ed. Prentice-Hall, Inc. Reprinted by permission of Pearson Education, Inc., Upper Saddle River, NJ 07458)

Did You Know?

✓ *Sales & Marketing Management* conducts an annual survey called the *S&MM Cost-Per-Call Survey*.

✓ In the 2000 survey, the average cost per sales call was estimated to be $169.64.

✓ The costs were also estimated for four different sales approaches: *transaction* (sell on price; product is a commodity); *feature/benefit* (price and features equally important); *solution* (tailor product to clients' needs; price is secondary); and *value-added* (use team-sell approach; solution more important than price).

✓ The average cost per call for each of these approaches in 2000 was as follows:
  • Transaction ($56.52)
  • Feature/benefit ($142.63)
  • Solution ($164.97)
  • Value-added ($211.56)

✓ The costs per call were also estimated by industry, and services had the highest cost per call:
  • Services ($199.59)
  • Industrial manufacturing ($262.35)
  • Wholesale/distribution ($132.67)
  • Manufacturing ($154.39)
  • Retail ($157.82)

✓ http://www.salesandmarketing.com/

d. Do prospects have the financial capabilities to pay for purchases?
e. Have the prospects entered into a long-term contract or arrangement with a competitor?
f. What volume of sales will prospects generate, and how profitable will their business be?

A fairly common approach is to divide prospects and past customers into *account* types. For example, an *A* account might be a person or organization that generates the highest levels of sales or profits. A *B* account would include those on the next level, and so on. The designation attached to each account usually determines the frequency of sales follow-ups and whether field or telephone sales are used.

You should think of qualifying as a smaller-scale version of market segmentation. Sales representatives use a continuous program of research to identify their target markets for future selling efforts. Obviously, internal records of sales volumes by customer are important here. For prospects other than past customers, a combination of secondary research and personal inquiries via the telephone or in person is often used. There are many excellent published sources of information on corporations, associations, and nonprofit organizations. Figure 17–3 shows a form used by Signature Inns (a midwestern, business-oriented, motor hotel chain) to gather qualifying data in the field. Notice the use of the endless chain referral approach to getting leads in questions 9 and 10. Notice also, in question 8, that the sales representative who completes the form asks for the opportunity to demon-

```
┌─────────────────────────────────────────────────────────────────────┐
│                        SIGNATURE INNS                                 │
│                        MARKET SURVEY                                  │
│                                                                       │
│ ┌───────────────────────────────────────────────────────────────┐   │
│ │ GENERAL INFORMATION: (attach business card)                   │   │
│ └───────────────────────────────────────────────────────────────┘   │
│                                                                       │
│  Name:_____       Title:_____   │
│  Company:_____       Decision Maker Name:_____   │
│  Address:_____       Phone #: (   )_____Ext:___   │
│  2nd Line:_____       Current Rate:_____   │
│  City:_____       Market Segment:_____   │
│  State, Zip:_____        Prospect or Client:_____   │
│  Phone #: (   )_____Ext:___      Known Name (Dear):_____   │
│  Fax #: (   )_____Ext:___      Prepared by:_____Date:____   │
│                                                                       │
│ ┌───────────────────────────────────────────────────────────────┐   │
│ │ MARKET SURVEY/SALES INFORMATION                               │   │
│ └───────────────────────────────────────────────────────────────┘   │
└─────────────────────────────────────────────────────────────────────┘
```

GENERAL INFORMATION: (attach business card)

Name:_____ Title:_____

Company:_____ Decision Maker Name:_____

Address:_____ Phone #: (___)_____Ext:_____

2nd Line:_____ Current Rate:_____

City:_____ Market Segment:_____

State, Zip:_____ Prospect or Client:_____

Phone #: (___)_____Ext:_____ Known Name (Dear):_____

Fax #: (___)_____Ext:_____ Prepared by:_____Date:_____

MARKET SURVEY/SALES INFORMATION

(1) What Does Company Do?:_____

(2) Other Contact People/Ph#:_____

(3) # Room Nights In Your SI Hotel (annual):_____

(4) # Room Nights in Your Market (annual):_____ (5) Chainwide (annual):_____

(6) Hotel Currently Using and Rate:_____

(7) Other SI Potential Cities (show Dir map):_____

(8) Factors Important in Selecting Hotel:_____

(9) Preferred Method of Making Reservation: ____Hotel Direct ____800# ____Travel Agency

(10) Travel Agency:_____

(11) T.A. Contact:_____ (12) Phone #:(___)_____Ext:_____

(13) 10% Comm. or Net-Non Rate: _____ (14) Publish Pref. Hotel Directory? _____

(15) GDS Systems Used: ___Amadeus ___Apollo ___Sabre ___System One ___Worldspan

(16) Travel Agency Consortium Affiliation: _____

(17) Other Clients of Travel Agency:_____

(18) Meeting Room Contact:_____ (19) Phone #:(___)_____Ext:_____

(20) Frequency:___Daily ___Bi-Wkly ___Mthly ___Qrtly ___Semi-Annual ___Annual ___Other:_____

(21) Average Group Size:_____ (22) Days/Times:_____

(23) # of Overnight Rooms Required with Meeting:_____

(24) Show Sales Kit Presentation - Tailor presentation to meet their lodging and meeting room needs.

NOTE PAD/COMMENTS:

_____
_____
_____
_____
_____
_____
_____
_____
_____
_____

Rev. 1/95

◆ FIGURE 17–3 *Signature Inns' lead-generating form.* (Courtesy of Signature Inns)

strate the company's lodging services. Data gathered on leads through secondary and primary research should be recorded and continually updated in individual sales prospect files.

2. **Preplanning Prior to Sales Calls.** A successful sales call, made either by telephone or in the field, requires careful preplanning and preparation. In this respect, it is

EXCELLENCE CASE

Personal Selling:
Signature Inns

How does an emerging, but as yet unrecognized, lodging chain successfully take on giants such as Holiday Inn, Ramada, and Marriott? The answer in Signature Inns' case was through an innovative approach to serving business travelers, an extensive internal sales/service program, and an aggressive personal selling effort in their local communities.

The first Signature Inn opened in Indianapolis in March, 1981. By 1995, the company had 26 properties in six Midwestern states (Illinois, Indiana, Iowa, Kentucky, Ohio, and Tennessee). A property in Michigan was sold by Signature Inns in the mid-1990s. In 1999, Signature Inns was merged with Jameson Inns of Atlanta, Georgia and became part of a hotel real estate investment trust (REIT). Signature Inns maintains one of the highest standards of operations in the industry because it has management control over all hotels and because there are no independent franchises. Virtually all the hotels are owned by affiliated limited partnerships, not company owned, to minimize the investment risk to the company. Signature Inns derives the vast majority of its business from five market segments: (1) business/corporate; (2) SMERF (social, military/government, educational, religious, and fraternal organizations and associations; (3) motorcoach; (4) special events; and (5) leisure.

The specific design features provided for business travelers include a well-lighted, 12-foot work center and a recliner in each guest room, a deluxe complimentary continental breakfast (Breakfast Express), free morning newspaper (Monday through Friday), free local phone calls, and free cable TV with movie channel (see advertisement headed "At Signature Inn, a lot of things just don't add up.") Also available are guest offices with typewriters and calculators, a phone equipped with a modem port for laptops, and private *telephone work centers* for one-on-one meetings. Each Signature Inn also offers five meeting rooms

(Photo courtesy of Signature Inns)

accommodating groups from five to eighty-five. A free meeting room is provided to groups that book fifteen or more guest rooms. The hotels have no restaurant or bar facilities, other than a small room where the Breakfast Express is provided. Each hotel arranges for participating local restaurants to give discounts to Signature Inn guests when they show their room keys.

Because Signature Inn rooms are moderately priced and appeal to the value-conscious traveler, only limited rate discounting is done, including discounts for senior citizens (AARP) and AAA cardholders, and for extended-stay guests. Guests aged seventeen or under stay free when sharing a room with their parents. In addition, the Corporate Sales and Marketing Department negotiates special rates on each hotel's behalf for listings in the preferred directories of Fortune 500 companies and travel agency consortia. Rates are always in the mid-price, moderate category.

It has been estimated that it costs at least five times more to attract a new guest than to retain an existing guest. Thus, Signature Inn, through its "Legendary Service" program (see attached advertisement headed "Stay with us and you never know what we'll surprise you with next") and the desire to go the extra mile with guest service, requires the General Manager and Guest Service staff to make many

continued

EXCELLENCE CASE *continued*

(Art courtesy of Signature Inns)

(Photo courtesy of Signature Inns)

contacts daily with their existing guests (e.g., thanking them for the business, getting to know them on a first-name basis, inquiring about potential business from associates, etc.). The company believes that an effective internal sales and service program carried out on a day-by-day basis is an essential prerequisite for an aggressive external sales effort.

Personal selling efforts are concentrated in each hotel's home and surrounding communities. Each Signature Inn has an Assistant General Manager, who is expected to complete at least 15 outside sales calls and mail out a substantial number of promotional packets each week. Local businesses of all sizes and other organizations are contacted. Various sources of information are used to generate leads, including Chambers of Commerce, local newspapers, industrial lists, and Yellow Pages. For example, newspaper announcements of engagements and upcoming weddings are used as a basis for mailing bride-to-be letters, encouraging them to

have their out-of-town guests stay at the Signature Inn.

A strict monthly duty of the Assistant General Manager is to make service calls (by telephone or in-person) to the 10 organizations generating the highest number of room nights the previous month. During 1993, the company installed a Marlboro property management system at each of its hotels. Guest profile and guest history data are accumulated in this system, which helps the hotel identify its top room-night generator. But that is not all. By carefully analyzing these data, Signature Inn also formulates more precise marketing and sales plans to attract non-Signature Inn guests who have similar profiles and who live in the company's primary geographical area. Recently, an automated sales and prospecting system, TeleMagic, has been implemented to more precisely manage the sales process at Signature Inns.

Each week, the Assistant General Manager does a Reader Board Survey, visiting all local competitors and finding out which organizations are having meetings and other functions. Often, the Inn's General Manager and Assistant General Manager will decide to target specific types of organizations (e.g., local churches, real estate companies, etc.), and the Assistant

continued

EXCELLENCE CASE *continued*

(Photo courtesy of Signature Inns)

(Art courtesy of Signature Inns)

General Manager will cold call them either in person or by phone. "Business colleague letters" are also sent to smaller businesses in surrounding communities, enclosing a brochure and other promotional materials. Referrals are used extensively to generate leads. Each prospect called on personally is asked if there are others they know of who might be interested in using the Signature Inn (see "Market Survey" form in Figure 17–3). The Market Survey information is then entered into the TeleMagic system for follow-up. Even the in-room, guest comment cards ask for similar referral information.

A variety of different approaches and tools are used to present and demonstrate Signature Inns' services. These include a manual with color photography of all Inn features as well as an attractive folder containing brochures, floor plans, rate card, and other printed information about Signature Inns. The company believes that one of its best selling points is the design of its guest rooms and other special services for the business traveler. What is the best way to

demonstrate these? Signature Inn has decided that the most effective approach is to invite prospective clients to take tours of their hotels personally guided by either the General Manager, Assistant General Manager, or Guest Service Manager.

Assistant General Managers use a five-step presentation for sales calls similar to the sales process described in this chapter: (1) warm-up, (2) front talk, (3) market survey, (4) presentation, and (5) close. Memorized phrases are used in presentations, when handling objections and questions, and in helping to close sales. Signature Inn believes in extensive after-sales follow-up. You have already heard about the monthly courtesy calls on top-10 accounts. The Guest Service Managers also follow up with meeting room users the day after their meetings to see if the events went well and if future meetings can be booked. VIP parties are periodically staged to acknowledge past customers and to attract new ones.

At the corporate level, additional sales work is done, concentrating on major travel

continued

EXCELLENCE CASE *continued*

"We are dedicated to providing opportunities for individuals to develop their God-given abilities to their fullest potential for the purpose of enhancing the success and quality of life for themselves, our company, our Guests and all mankind."

(Photo courtesy of Signature Inns)

trade shows (e.g., the National Tour Association's Tour & Travel Exchange and the National Business Travel Association annual trade show) and chain-wide corporate accounts. Individual properties also do some out-of-area promotions, primarily to travel agents and motor coach tour companies known to have tour or destinations through the local area.

A high level of professionalism is the hallmark of all Signature Inns and is the key reason for its growth history. Carefully designed

properties, rigorous maintenance and cleanliness programs, and extra-friendly staff members are examples of the chain's excellence. So too are its personal selling procedures, as well as the high value placed on local communities as generators of guest and meeting room rentals. Although, like other companies, Signature Inn has an extensive sales manual as a reference, there is a recognition that it is the sales team's (Assistant General Manager, Guest Service Manager, and General Manager) personal touch that makes the difference.

Discussion Questions

1. How has Signature Inns developed a unique approach to internal and external selling?
2. How does this approach help Signature Inns compete at the local level with the properties of larger hotel chains?
3. What can other hospitality and travel organizations learn and apply from Signature Inns' approaches to personal selling?

World Wide Web Resources

http://www.signatureinns.com/

very similar to a successful job interview in that the interviewee must think ahead about what he or she wants to say. There are two elements to preplanning a sales call: (1) the **preapproach**, and (2) the **approach**.[13] In the preapproach stage, sales representatives carefully review each sales prospect's files and other relevant information. If no file exists, the representative must use the information-gathering process discussed under qualifying. The objective is to develop enough familiarity with the prospect's situation to be able to establish a rapport during the sales call and to have the foundation on which to build the sales presentation itself.

The approach follows and involves all the activities that lead to the sales presentation. These include arranging the appointments with prospects or their secretaries, establishing rapport and confidence at the start of the sales call, and checking preliminary details prior to the sales presentation.[14] Sales representatives have three principal objectives in their approaches.[15] You will see that the last two objectives are the first two steps in the AIDA formula (attention-interest-desire-action) mentioned earlier.

a. To build rapport with the prospect
b. To capture a person's full attention
c. To generate interest in the product or service

It is important to recognize that some hospitality and travel organizations have no opportunity to do prospecting, qualifying, or preplanning. The first time they encounter customers is when they walk through the company's doors. Most travel agents face this problem with walk-in, phone-in, and Internet customers. Qualifying must be done when would-be clients first ask the agent for information.[16] Careful questioning and probing determine the inquirer's needs and their probability of making reservations. Other inside sales opportunities in the hospitality and travel industry require much less preplanning than field or telephone sales calls. Here, the stimulus-response, suggestive selling strategy is usually sufficient.

3. **Presenting and Demonstrating Services.** After the approach, the next step in the sales call is the sales presentation and demonstration. Sales representatives present facts and other information proving that their services can satisfy prospects' needs or solve their problems. In the sales demonstration, the ability of services to meet prospects' needs or problems is demonstrated. Because of the intangibility of hospitality and travel services, the opportunity to demonstrate them is much more limited. Visual aids, familiarization trips, and other on-site, inspection visits play a major role in overcoming the intangibility problem (question 8 in Figure 17–3).

During the sales presentation, sales representatives provide information about their organizations and services. Prospects' needs and problems are discussed and confirmed. Careful listening by the sales representative is as important as talking. Prospects are verbally shown how the services can satisfy their needs. The objective of the sales presentation is to be persuasive, creating a desire in the prospect to buy or reserve the services offered. Following are some of the keys to successful sales calls and presentations for sales representatives:[17]
   a. Preplan the sales call and presentation
   b. Have a specific reason and purpose for every sales call
   c. Have complete information on hand for the sales call
   d. Introduce themselves clearly
   e. Address sales prospects correctly
   f. Comprehensively, but briefly, describe the services for meeting prospects' needs
   g. Listen carefully and do not interrupt prospects when they are talking

The first step—preplanning the sales presentation—is the most important. Planned presentations save time for both sales representatives and prospects, ensure that presentations are complete, and help sales representatives anticipate probable questions and objections, and practice their responses.[18]

Sales presentations can be made in at least five different ways.[19]
   a. *Canned sales presentations*—sales representatives have memorized what they will say beforehand
   b. *Outlined*—sales representatives have a written outline of what they will say beforehand
   c. *Programmed*—cues such as photograph books or flip charts are used in a step-by-step presentation
   d. *Audiovisual*—PowerPoint, slide, slide-audio, or videotapes are shown
   e. *Multistage*—used often in the problem-solving approach; several sales calls are required

4. **Handling Objections and Questions.** When most sales presentations are completed, prospects ask questions and raise one or more objections. Objections come in

all forms, even through body language. Of course, the best thing is for sales representatives to anticipate typical objections in preplanning and address them in the sales presentation. Otherwise, sales representatives must spot and tackle objections, not ignore them. Prospects may voice a variety of concerns ranging from the price, characteristics, or timing of services to current economic constraints to purchasing them.

There are several effective ways for handling objections. One is to restate the objection and to prove diplomatically that it is not as important as it seems. Another is the *agree and neutralize* tactic or the *yes, but* approach. Here, sales representatives initially agree with the problem, but go on to show that the objection is not relevant or accurate. No matter which approach is used, objections must be met head-to-head. If they are not, an otherwise interested prospect may slip through the salesperson's hands. Listening is a key skill here, both in carefully hearing what is said and observing body movements.

5. **Closing the Sale.** If objections and questions have been handled effectively, sales representatives should then try to close sales. Closing means getting a sales prospect to agree with the objectives of the sales call, which normally implies making a definite purchase or reservation. In a multistaged presentation, it may involve getting a commitment for a follow-up visit or other additional discussions. A sales call without a close is definitely unsuccessful. Every sales representative must ask for the business or at least some commitment to continue the dialogue. Research shows, however, that salespeople often fear *no* answers and fail to close in the majority of sales calls.[20] Overcoming this psychological barrier is essential to effective personal selling.

Knowing when and how to close are the keys to success. As with objections, this again takes careful attention to the prospect's words and body language. Sales representatives must watch for verbal and nonverbal clues indicating that prospects have almost made up their minds. These include the following:[21]

a. *Verbal Closing Clues*
   - Questions ("When will the balance be due?" "How soon can we receive a written proposal from you?" "When can you give us confirmation of this reservation?").
   - Recognitions ("That really sounds good." "We've always dreamed of taking this type of trip." "Your organization's services definitely fit our needs." "Your price is certainly in our ball park.").
   - Requirements ("We'll need to get your lowest possible corporate rate." "This will have to be okayed by our finance department." "The departure will have to fit our vacation dates.").

b. *Nonverbal Closing Clues*
   - Signs of acceptance and agreement indicated by nodding of head.
   - Posture changes indicating greater interest in services being offered (e.g., leaning forward and listening more attentively, hands on chin, other signs of increased relaxation such as uncrossing legs and opening up hands and examining sales literature more thoroughly).

As soon as they notice any of these signals, sales representatives should use one of seven closing strategies:

a. *Trial Closes.* The sales representative who uses this strategy *tests the water* by asking questions that either determine a prospect's intentions to purchase or help them make a definite decision. The trial close also helps get a prospect to voice any remaining objections. For example, a travel agent could ask, "Shall I check on space availability for you?" A hotel representative might say, "Do you want one of our staff members to arrange the spouse's program?"

b. ***Assumptive Close.*** This is very similar to the trial close. The sales representative asks a question that assumes the prospect's willingness to buy. Examples include "Will you be paying for this in cash, by check, or with a credit card?" or "Would you like us to direct bill you?"

c. ***Summary or Summary-of-the-Benefits Close.*** The sales representative recapitulates the main points of the presentation or the major benefits to the prospect. The whole picture is put together, making an even more convincing argument for the purchase. This summarizing is immediately followed by a request for the reservation or purchase.

d. ***Special Concession Close.*** The sales representative offers a special inducement to the prospect if the reservation or sale is made.[22] The inducement is usually a further discount or a limited-time price or rate. For example, a travel agent in late 2001 might say, "If I book you on Princess before February 14, 2002, you can save up to $500 on the cruise."

e. ***Eliminating-the-Single-Objection or Final-Concern Close.*** Despite the sale representatives efforts, one important objection stands in the way of closing. One way to use this strategy is to say, "Assuming that we can solve this one problem, can we count on your reservation?" The Cruise Lines International Association in its "Cruise Counselor Training Program" suggests the following approach to a client's final concern on price:[23]

CLIENT: "I'm still not sure we should spend this much on this year's vacation."
COUNSELOR: "If we resolve this final issue, can we go ahead with your reservation?"

Another method is to point out that only one problem remains and to make another attempt to eliminate the objection.

f. ***Limited-Choice Close.*** The sales representative may have presented a prospect with a large number of alternatives (e.g., vacation packages, departure dates, banquet meals). When the prospect shows signs of nearing some type of commitment, the sales representative narrows the selection to a more limited number of alternatives, thereby making the prospect's decision easier.

g. ***Direct-Appeal Close.*** There is no mystery to this one: The sales representative flat-out asks for the sale or booking.

6. **Following Up After Closing the Sale.** The sales process does not end with a successful closing. On the contrary, this is the beginning of another cycle that leads up to additional sales to the prospect. Sales representatives' work is not done until they ensure that all the required steps and arrangements are made to deliver the promised services. In some cases, such as organizing major association conventions or planning incentive travel trips, this "delivery" work is extensive.

It is also advisable for sales representatives to give prospects some form of reassurance, to remove the cognitive dissonance discussed in Chapter 4. A simple letter complimenting the prospect on the decision is enough in most cases.

A third aspect of post-sale activities involves immediate follow-up after prospects or their clients have actually used the services. Many travel agents employ this effectively by telephoning clients soon after their trips to find out what they

A Touch of Technology

> ### Technology on the Road in Sales
>
> ◆ Sales executives and sales representatives are making great use of the latest information and communications technology to become more productive.
>
> ◆ The *State of Sales & Marketing Technology* study by *Sales & Marketing Management* magazine found that 92 percent of respondents felt that technology would make their jobs easier in the future.
>
> ◆ The most used technologies in 2000 were cellular phones (86%), laptop computers (73%), personal digital assistants (24%), pagers (13%), and audio-visual presentation equipment (10%).
>
> ◆ The most popular computer software applications were e-mail (85%), presentation (60%), contact management (55%), lead tracking (40%), proposal generation (34%), quote generation (32%), and mapping (15%).
>
> ◆ Fourteen percent of respondents indicated that they are using the Web for direct selling, and 22 percent of the companies had an Extranet.
>
> ◆ http://www.salesandmarketing.com/

liked and did not like. Some hotel companies touch base with key corporate clients monthly to ensure that these customers are pleased with the lodging services. In addition to being essential in maintaining a customer base, this is another form of prospecting. It might help if you think of the following analogy. Once prospectors find a trace of gold, they follow certain steps to mine it to its full potential. Maintaining close contact with past customers is very similar—the more effort that goes in, the more rewards that come out.

THE SALES PLAN AND SALES MANAGEMENT

You have already seen the importance of having individual plans for advertising and sales promotion. It is also advisable to have a personal selling or sales plan. The sales plan is a detailed description of personal selling objectives, sales forecasts, sales-force responsibilities, activities, and budgets. Besides being an important part of the overall marketing plan, the sales plan is a key tool in sales management (the management of the sales force and personal selling efforts to achieve desired sales objectives).

The task of preparing sales plans normally is assigned to sales managers, also sometimes known as directors of sales (DOS) or sales coordinators. The sales management functions for which these individuals are responsible include (1) sales-force staffing and operations, (2) sales planning, and (3) sales performance evaluation.[24] As you can see, there is much more to sales management than preparing sales plans.

Sales-Force Staffing and Operations

1. **Recruitment, Selection, and Training.** The sales director's first job is to hire competent people to fill available positions. In all industries, there are basically three categories of sales positions.[25]

a. ***Order Getters.*** These are the sales representatives that you have heard about in this chapter. They are the ones who are responsible for the sales process that was just discussed. They prospect and qualify customers, preplan sales calls, present and demonstrate services, handle objections and questions, close sales, and perform after-sales follow-up. One of their key jobs is to promote their organizations' services persuasively. In the hospitality and travel industry, these sales representatives spend most of their time on field sales, along with some telephone selling.

b. ***Order Takers.*** Order takers are inside salespeople, who in our industry may or may not work within the sales department itself. Examples include waitpersons in restaurants; servers in fast-food outlets; front desk clerks in hotels; airline ticket agents; and travel agency, hotel, car rental, cruise line, tour wholesaler, and airline reservationists. Their primary function is to accept reservations, orders, or inquiries and to process reservations or provide the services purchased.

   Although these people do not have the same level of persuasive responsibilities as sales representatives do, they should be well trained in inside sales techniques such as suggestive or up-selling. It is also important to repeat a key point mentioned earlier—the quality of service that is provided by these people, even if their only contact with customers is on the phone, *sells* future, repeat business.

c. ***Support Staff.*** The third category includes sales staff commonly referred to as *missionary salespersons* or *sales engineers.* They are employed directly by the sales department. The missionary salesperson's job is to distribute information about, and to describe the features of, new services. They do not, like sales representatives, make sales presentations. Sales engineers are resource people with specific technical knowledge who, when required, accompany sales representatives on sales calls.

   The hospitality and travel industry makes much less use of these support people than do other industries, including manufacturers of highly technical products (e.g., pharmaceuticals). The closest thing to missionary salespersons in our industry are the sales representatives who call on travel agencies, trying to *convert* agents to convince more clients to use their airline, car rental firm, hotel or resort, cruise line, packages or tours, attraction, or other travel services. These sales representatives do not normally close sales, although they often make sales presentations. It is the travel agent's function to close sales with their clients.

   Where does an organization find these staff members? Sources of new sales staff include in-house personnel, other related organizations (competitors; customers; other supplier, carrier, travel trade, or destination marketing organizations), hospitality and travel schools, executive placement consultants and employment agencies, and voluntary applications. In the hospitality and travel industry, it is uncommon for field sales representatives to be hired directly from college without prior sales experience. The more established practice is for entry-level people to be order takers, with eventual in-house promotion to sales representative. Hiring sales personnel from competitors and related outside organizations is also common. For example, many sales representatives who call on travel agents are former agents themselves. Given the more recent, increased emphasis on marketing and sales, many hospitality and travel organizations hire people with sales experience in other industries.

What are the characteristics of the successful salesperson? For many years, people thought that you had to be born with the gift of sales and could not learn the skills required. This has changed. Many people have written on how to determine success in personal selling, but the following three characteristics seem to be key:[26]

- **Sales aptitude**—the extent of an individual's ability to perform a given sales job, consisting of the following:
    i. Mental abilities (overall intelligence, oral communications skills, mental reasoning, mathematical abilities)
    ii. Personality traits (empathy, ego drive, sociability)
- **Skill levels**—skills obtained in personal communications and knowledge of services, obtained through the following:
    i. Sales training
    ii. Previous sales and operational experience
- **Personal characteristics:**
    i. Demographic profile, including educational background
    ii. Psychographic and lifestyle characteristics
    iii. Physical appearance and traits

Although these factors generally provide a good guide to an individual's potential success in personal selling, they are not foolproof. Research shows that there is no one set of physical characteristics, mental abilities, and personality traits that predict success in every situation. Salespersons' success depends more on the actual tasks assigned to them and the industrial environment in which they operate.[27] For example, a person given order-taking responsibilities may perform very well, but may not succeed as a field sales representative. The same can be true when a field sales representative is moved to inside sales. Research also shows that it is not particularly effective to recruit sales representatives who have characteristics that match those of customers.

Sales training programs are extremely important to continuing success in personal selling. Following are typical objectives of programs for new and existing sales staff:[28]

- Reduce turnover rates of sales personnel
- Improve relations with customers and prospects
- Enhance morale
- Generate more effective time management skills
- Improve control of sales personnel

Because of the high cost of field sales, the last two objectives play a key role in controlling sales costs.

The topics covered in sales training programs for new personnel usually include an orientation to the organization, its industry and target markets, a detailed description of the services offered, and territory management (if appropriate). Training may include lectures, discussions, demonstrations, role playing, videotapes, on-the-job instruction, use of an Intranet site, or some combination of these six approaches.[29]

There are several educational and training programs available to people in sales positions. In the hospitality and travel field, these include the certification programs provided by Hospitality Sales and Marketing Association International (the Certified Hospitality Marketing Executive or CHME) and the Educational Institute of the American Hotel & Lodging Association (the

Certified Hospitality Sales Professional or CHSP). The Sales & Marketing Executive International Association also offers certification for sales people in general.

2. **Leading, Motivating, and Compensating**. Just like any other manager, the sales manager must be an effective leader and have the respect and confidence of sales personnel. Sales managers must understand motivation theories (such as those discussed in Chapter 4), and provide financial and nonmonetary incentives to keep sales-force motivation at its peak. Enthusiasm among salespeople quickly rubs off on customers and prospects. Financial incentives include salary and commissions, and fringe benefits such as paid vacations, insurance programs, and medical/dental programs. In our industry, free travel is also a very important fringe, especially with travel agency and airline personnel. Nonmonetary compensation and motivators are award/recognition programs and job advancement opportunities (usually to a sales coordinator or director).

Several choices of financial compensation are available. *Straight salary* involves fixed salary payments with no commissions. Research shows that service organizations, including those in the hospitality and travel industry, like this approach the most.[30] Because a great deal of the field selling in our industry is to the travel trade and not to final customers, straight-salary compensation seems justified. It is also the approach best suited for inside sales. The second alternative is *straight commission,* payment based totally on the person's sales results. There are very few examples of this in the hospitality and travel industry. However, one is travel agencies that use outside salespeople and pay them a portion of the commissions earned on the reservations they generate. Straight-commission plans work best with smaller companies that cannot afford a sales department, and in cases where very little missionary selling is required.[31]

The third and most prevalent compensation method is a *combination approach*—a base salary plus commission and/or bonuses. Commissions are tied directly to the volumes of sales or profits generated by each salesperson. Bonuses are payments made when predetermined volumes of sales and profits, or *sales quotas,* are achieved. This third approach is most appropriate with field sales, when selling is being done to prospective final customers and in cases where sales result primarily from the sales representative's persuasive efforts.

Another motivator that can be used is the sales promotion that is aimed at the sales force. Chapter 16 pointed out that promotions tend to work best to achieve short-term objectives and are not advisable for the long term. Various forms of contests are popular in motivating sales representatives to intensify their efforts. They are most frequently used when an organization is attempting to (1) secure new customers or travel trade outlets, (2) promote the sale of specific services, (3) generate larger sales volumes per sales call, (4) counteract lower volumes in off-seasons, and (5) introduce new facilities or services.[32] Chapters 7 and 13 mentioned the growing role of incentive travel trips as rewards for outstanding sales performances. These can be used for sales contest winners.

Nonmonetary compensation also plays a large role in motivating salespeople, as it does with most employees. Normally, these are certificates, plaques, or cups that are awarded by sales managers at formal sales-force meetings or conventions.

Did You Know?

✓ Sales & Marketing Executives International conducts *The Sales & Marketing Compensation and Trends Survey.*

✓ The average Sales Manager made $173,305 in total compensation (salary plus bonus) in 1998.

✓ The average Sales/Account Representative made $115,679.

✓ The detailed statistics are shown in the table below:

Salary	Sales Manager	Both Marketing and Sales Manager	Sales/ Account Representative
Average Salary	$80,136	$77,427	$50,579
Average Bonus	$93,170	$84,792	$65,100
Average Total	$173,305	$162,219	$115,679

✓ http://www.sell.org/sme-statscomp.htm

3. **Supervising and Controlling.** Supervision and control of salespeople, especially those in the field, is more difficult for sales managers than it is for most other managers. Distance from home offices, extensive travel away from home, high levels of independence, and the continuous stress of peak performance complicate the supervisory function. Salespersons' abuse of expense accounts and above-average alcoholism rates are two fairly common supervisory problems.

The sales manager's supervisory methods and techniques include periodic, face-to-face meetings with individual staff members; telephone and e-mail conversations; sales-call reports and other written correspondence; compensation plan (especially with plans involving commissions and bonuses); sales territories; quotas; expense accounts; and sales management audit.[33] Sales meetings, conventions, or rallies provide another excellent opportunity for training and other communication with the sales force. A significant percentage of all meetings and conventions held in North America are of this type.

You should know something about sales territories and quotas before we leave this section on sales-force staffing and operations. Sales territories are specific areas of responsibility, usually geographic, that are assigned to individual sales representatives or branch offices. Territories can be based on geography, customers, services or products, or some combination of these three.[34] Small organizations that serve local markets, such as most restaurants and travel agencies, usually do not need to set up territories. Larger companies that serve regional or national markets, however, can often justify this move because of the following benefits of sales territories:[35]

a. Reduced selling costs

b. Improved supervision, control, and evaluation of sales representatives

c. Adequate coverage of potential markets
d. Improved relations with individual customers
e. Increased sales-force morale and effectiveness
f. Enhanced research and analysis of sales results

If you will recall the benefits of personal selling mentioned earlier, you will quickly realize the strength of territorial sales management. Two of the benefits were to target precisely and to cultivate relationships with potential customers. Effective sales representatives who remain in their territories for sufficient time develop strong relationships with customers and travel trade partners. Most national airlines organize sales personnel in this way. Regional sales managers supervise teams of sales representatives, with the regional headquarters based at or near a "hub" or other major airport.

Another major advantage you will see immediately is achieving greater efficiency in salespersons' travel expenses. It is obviously less expensive to send one person to a specific geographic area than it is to send two or more.

Sales quotas are performance targets periodically set for individual sales representatives, branch offices, or regions. They help sales managers motivate, supervise, control, and evaluate sales personnel. Quotas can be based on sales volumes, activities (e.g., total sales calls in a period, calls on new sales prospects), financial results (e.g., gross or net profit generated), travel-expenses-to-sales ratios, or some combination of these. Besides the obvious benefits from a human resources standpoint, quotas also reflect the fact that not all territories are alike, and that all offices or sales representatives cannot be expected to perform at exactly the same levels.

Sales Planning

The heart of sales planning is the sales plan, prepared periodically (usually annually) by the sales manager with information from the sales force. Its contents are quite similar to those of the advertising, sales promotion/merchandising, and public relations plans. The sales plan contains a detailed description of personal selling objectives, sales activities, and the sales budget. It normally differs from the other promotional plans in its sections on sales-force responsibilities, territories, and quotas. This is certainly the case with larger organizations that farm out all their advertising, sales promotion, and public relations work to outside agencies and consultants. The only in-house, promotional personnel they have to consider are in the sales department.

1. **Preparing Sales Forecasts.** Personal selling objectives are frequently set as forecasts of unit or sales volumes or some other financial target (e.g., gross or net profits) derived from expected sales levels. However, sales forecasts are not the only type of personal selling objectives. Nonfinancial ones may be equally important. These may include levels-of-activity objectives, such as numbers of sales calls, new sales prospects converted to customers, or volumes of inquiries answered successfully.

   You probably already realize that the sales forecast is very useful to others outside the sales department. In fact, it is a key planning tool for the entire organization. Expected sales levels influence the allocation of personnel and financial resources in many other departments.

2. **Developing Sales Department Budgets.** Given the relatively high costs of personal selling, this budget plays a key role in planning and controlling the sales effort. Typically, the sales budget has the following components:

a. *The sales forecast*—the dollar and/or unit sales volumes expected in an upcoming period.

b. *The selling-expenses budget*—the salaries, fringe benefits, commissions, bonuses, and travel expenses projected for the sales force.

c. *The sales administration budget*—the salaries, fringe benefits, and administrative costs of regional and head offices of the sales department.

d. *Advertising and sales promotion budget*—the amount to be spent on sales-force promotions (e.g., contests, recognition and award programs) and advertising that directly supports selling efforts. These amounts are also usually identified in the advertising and sales promotion budgets.

3. **Assigning Sales Territories and Quotas.** You have already been introduced to these concepts, but you should realize that they have an important function in sales planning. Sales managers normally derive financially based quotas from the overall sales forecast. They use a combination of past territory performance and market indices (a percentage or other numerical factor based on two or more factors related to a market) to allocate quotas for each territory.

Evaluating Sales Performance

The third and final function of sales management is measuring and evaluating sales performance. Instead of being viewed as the final step in a series of many, the sales management audit should be considered the first step in improving the effectiveness of an organization's personal selling efforts.

A **sales management audit** is a periodic analysis of the sales department's policies, objectives, activities, personnel, and performance. Sales analysis is a term most frequently used for the evaluation of performance. This can be done by considering total sales volumes or sales by territory, service or facility category, or customer groups.[36] One of the most important bases of evaluation is to judge actual results against sales forecasts and budgets.

PERSONAL SELLING IN THE HOSPITALITY AND TRAVEL INDUSTRY

You have seen frequent references in this chapter to personal selling within the hospitality and travel industry. In this final discussion, we will summarize a few key points.

1. **Importance of Personal Selling Varies.** Personal selling is not equally important to all hospitality and travel organizations. Smaller, more localized operations tend to limit their sales activities to inside sales. In this category are most restaurants and many travel agencies—the retail side of the industry.

The importance of personal selling within the promotional mix increases with the size of the organization, the geographical scope of its target markets, and its dependence on the travel trade and other decision makers who influence the travel behavior of groups of people. The types of organizations that are most likely to have teams of field sales representatives are the following:

a. Hotels, motor hotels, resorts, conference centers, and other lodging businesses

b. Convention and visitors bureaus, and convention/trade show centers

c. Airlines, cruise lines, passenger rail companies (e.g., Amtrak and Via Rail Canada)

d. Car rental firms

    e. Incentive travel-planning companies

    f. National and state government tourism-promotion agencies

      Other organizations also use sales forces. They include some travel agencies, tour wholesalers, and motorcoach tour operators.

2. **Inside Selling Closely Related to Service Levels.** In our industry, it is extremely difficult to draw the line between quality service to customers and internal selling. As Chapter 11 pointed out, the quality of service usually determines customer satisfaction. Although you can easily see that suggestive selling is part of personal selling, quality service is probably much more important in creating customer satisfaction and repeat patronage.

3. **No Generally Accepted Qualifications for Industry Sales Positions.** Sales does not tend to be an entry-level position in the hospitality industry. It is normally mandatory that you learn the ropes in operations or reservations before you become a sales representative. The rationale is that you know your product, customers, and sales prospects better after a stint in the actual workings of the organization.

      One serious problem that our industry has is the absence of generally accepted qualifications or criteria for hiring marketing and sales people. At the same time, there are few educational programs that specialize exclusively in hospitality and travel sales and marketing. The industry and its trade associations must establish standard criteria.

4. **Importance of Missionary Sales Work.** Chapter 13 highlighted the vital role played by travel trade intermediaries. You should realize that some intermediaries are themselves decision makers, whereas others are *decision influencers*. For example, decision makers include corporate travel managers and convention/meeting planners. Decision influencers include retail travel agents, tour wholesalers, and incentive travel planners. Selling approaches to these two categories of intermediaries are different. Keeping them informed and up to date—performing missionary sales work—is most important with decision influencers, whereas persuasive selling is more appropriate with decision makers. With the rapid pace of change in services, fares, prices, and facilities, missionary sales is very important in our industry.

      The magazine, *Selling Power,* conducts a survey called *The Selling Power 500,* which ranks U.S. companies by the size of their sales forces.[37] Several hospitality and travel organizations are in this group, and their presence emphasizes the importance of sales in our industry. The largest sales forces are shown in Figure 17–4.

Companies	Estimated Number of U.S. Salespeople	Rank Among Service Companies
Marriott International	10,000	15
Northwest Airlines	8,000	22
Delta Airlines	7,300	25
Southwest Airlines	7,039	27
Fairfield Communities	1,265	101

◆ **FIGURE 17–4**   *Largest sales forces among hospitality and travel organizations in the United States.* (Courtesy of SellingPower.com)

CHAPTER CONCLUSION

Nothing is as effective in getting sales as well-executed personal selling. It is much harder to say no to a personal presentation than to an impersonally communicated message in an advertisement or sales promotion. However, personal selling, especially the field sales element, is relatively expensive. Careful management of personal selling activities (sales management) is crucial. The heart of an effective sales program and sales management is the sales plan.

Following the step-by-step approach in the sales process usually produces the best results. This requires preplanning, effective presentation skills and methods, and follow-up. It is now believed that these skills can be learned. They are not necessarily inherent only in certain natural salespeople.

REVIEW QUESTIONS

1. How are the terms personal selling and sales management defined in this chapter?
2. What roles does personal selling play in the marketing of hospitality and travel services?
3. What are the three categories of personal selling?
4. Which five strategies can be used in personal selling, and how are they different?
5. What are the steps in the sales process, and what does each entail?
6. Which seven strategies can be used in closing sales, and what does each involve?
7. What are the functions of sales management?
8. To be effective in sales, one must be born with certain talents. Is this an accurate statement? Explain your answer, citing the characteristics of the successful salesperson.
9. What is the role of the sales plan, and what does it include?
10. Is personal selling in the hospitality and travel industry any different from that in other industries? Explain your answer, mentioning four distinct characteristics of selling in our industry.

CHAPTER ASSIGNMENTS

1. Arrange to spend a day accompanying a field salesperson in your favorite part of the hospitality and travel industry. At the end of the day, evaluate this person's performance. Did the sales representative follow the steps in the sales process? How successful was the person in achieving his or her objectives? Did you observe any closes, and what closing strategies were used? What did you like about the person's approaches? What did you dislike? Could you improve upon this salesperson's approaches and techniques? How?

2. Arrange to spend a day in a travel agency, hotel, or restaurant to observe its inside and telephone selling procedures. At the end of the day, evaluate the organization's sales techniques in these two areas. Were opportunities for inside and telephone sales used to their fullest potential, or do staff need further training in these areas? Did you see any evidence of suggestive or up-selling? What recommendations would you make to management to upgrade selling in these two categories?

3. You have been hired as the new sales manager of a hospitality and travel organization (real or hypothetical). Write your own job description for the position. What responsibilities would you have? What procedures would you use for (1) sales-force staffing and operations, (2) sales planning, and (3) evaluating sales performance? Be as specific as you can.

4. You are the sales manager of a hospitality and travel organization. Prepare a written set of

instructions for field sales representatives, being as specific as possible. What steps would you outline for prospecting and qualifying sales prospects? What advertising and sales promotions would you use to support sales representatives?

WORLD WIDE WEB RESOURCES

Educational Institute of the American Hotel & Lodging Association
http://www.ei-ahla.org/

Hospitality Sales & Marketing Association International (HSMAI)
http://www.hsmai.org/

Sales & Marketing Executives (SME) International
http://www.smei.org/

Sales & Marketing Executives Marketing Library
http://www.sell.org/

Sales & Marketing Management Magazine
http://www.salesandmarketing.com/

Selling Power
http://www.sellingpower.com/magazine/

Signature Inns
http://www.signatureinns.com/

REFERENCES

1. Balsley, Ronald D., and E. Patricia Birsner. 1987. *Selling: Marketing Personified.* Hinsdale, Ill.: The Dryden Press.
2. Berkowitz, Eric N., Roger A. Kerin, Steven W. Hartley, and William Rudelius. 2000. *Marketing.* 6th ed. Boston: Irwin McGraw-Hill, 552.
3. Balsley, Ronald D., and E. Patricia Birsner. 1987. *Selling: Marketing Personified.* Hinsdale, Ill.: The Dryden Press, 29–41.
4. Evans, Joel R., and Barry Berman. 2000. *Marketing.* 7th ed. Upper Saddle River, N.J.: Prentice-Hall, Inc.
5. Balsley, Ronald D., and E. Patricia Birsner. 1987. *Selling: Marketing Personified.* Hinsdale, Ill.: The Dryden Press, 33.
6. Balsley, Ronald D., and E. Patricia Birsner. 1987. *Selling: Marketing Personified.* Hinsdale, Ill.: The Dryden Press, 34.
7. Manning, Gerald L., and Barry L. Reece. 2000. *Selling Today: Building Quality Partnerships.* 8th ed. Upper Saddle River, N.J.: Prentice-Hall, Inc.
8. Evans, Joel R., and Barry Berman. 2000. *Marketing.* 7th ed. Upper Saddle River, N.J.: Prentice-Hall, Inc.
9. Balsley, Ronald D., and E. Patricia Birsner. 1987. *Selling: Marketing Personified.* Hinsdale, Ill.: The Dryden Press, 185.
10. Evans, Joel R., and Barry Berman. 2000. *Marketing.* 7th ed. Upper Saddle River, N.J.: Prentice-Hall, Inc.
11. Manning, Gerald L., and Barry L. Reece. 2000. *Selling Today: Building Quality Partnerships.* 8th ed. Upper Saddle River, N.J.: Prentice-Hall, Inc.
12. Balsley, Ronald D., and E. Patricia Birsner. 1987. *Selling: Marketing Personified.* Hinsdale, Ill.: The Dryden Press, 181–185.
13. Manning, Gerald L., and Barry L. Reece. 2000. *Selling Today: Building Quality Partnerships.* 8th ed. Upper Saddle River, N.J.: Prentice-Hall, Inc.
14. Balsley, Ronald D., and E. Patricia Birsner. 1987. *Selling: Marketing Personified.* Hinsdale, Ill.: The Dryden Press, 207.
15. Manning, Gerald L., and Barry L. Reece. 2000. *Selling Today: Building Quality Partnerships.* 8th ed. Upper Saddle River, N.J.: Prentice-Hall, Inc.
16. Davidoff, Philip G., and Doris S. Davidoff. 1994. *Sales and Marketing for Travel and Tourism.* 2nd ed. Englewood Cliffs. N.J.: Prentice-Hall Careers & Technology, 277–278.
17. Coffman, C. Dewitt. 1980. *Hospitality for Sale.* East Lansing, Mich.: Educational Institute of American Hotel & Motel Association, 55.
18. Balsley, Ronald D., and E. Patricia Birsner. 1987. *Selling: Marketing Personified.* Hinsdale, Ill.: The Dryden Press, 219.
19. Balsley, Ronald D., and E. Patricia Birsner. 1987. *Selling: Marketing Personified.* Hinsdale, Ill.: The Dryden Press, 234–236.

20. Davidoff, Philip G., and Doris S. Davidoff. 1994. *Sales and Marketing for Travel and Tourism.* 2nd ed. Englewood Cliffs, N.J.: Prentice-Hall Careers & Technology, 264.

21. Manning, Gerald L., and Barry L. Reece. 2000. *Selling Today: Building Quality Partnerships.* 8th ed. Upper Saddle River, N.J.: Prentice-Hall, Inc.

22. Manning, Gerald L., and Barry L. Reece. 2000. *Selling Today: Building Quality Partnerships.* 8th ed. Upper Saddle River, N.J.: Prentice-Hall, Inc.

23. Cruise Lines International Association. 1986. *Selling the Ultimate: The Cruise Vacation: Cruise Counselor's Handbook.* New York: Author, 28.

24. Stanton, William J., Rosann Spiro, and Richard H. Buskirk. 1998. *Management of a Sales Force.* 10th ed. Boston: McGraw-Hill.

25. Evans, Joel R., and Barry Berman. 2000. *Marketing.* 7th ed. Upper Saddle River, N.J.: Prentice-Hall, Inc.

26. Churchill, Gilbert A., Neil M. Ford, Orville C. Walker, et al. 1999. *Sales Force Management.* 6th ed. Boston: McGraw-Hill.

27. Churchill, Gilbert A., Neil M. Ford, Orville C. Walker, et al. 1999. *Sales Force Management.* 6th ed. Boston: McGraw-Hill.

28. Stanton, William J., Rosann Spiro, and Richard H. Buskirk. 1998. *Management of a Sales Force.* 10th ed. Boston: McGraw-Hill.

29. Stanton, William J., Rosann Spiro, and Richard H. Buskirk. 1998. *Management of a Sales Force.* 10th ed. Boston: McGraw-Hill.

30. Stanton, William J., Rosann Spiro, and Richard H. Buskirk. 1998. *Management of a Sales Force.* 10th ed. Boston: McGraw-Hill.

31. Stanton, William J., Rosann Spiro, and Richard H. Buskirk. 1998. *Management of a Sales Force.* 10th ed. Boston: McGraw-Hill.

32. Churchill, Gilbert A., Neil M. Ford, Orville C. Walker, et al. 1999. *Sales Force Management.* 6th ed. Boston: McGraw-Hill.

33. Stanton, William J., Rosann Spiro, and Richard H. Buskirk. 1998. *Management of a Sales Force.* 10th ed. Boston: McGraw-Hill.

34. Robertson, Dan H., and Danny N. Bellenger. 1980. *Sales Management.* New York: Macmillan Publishing Company, 296–299.

35. Stanton, William J., Rosann Spiro, and Richard H. Buskirk. 1998. *Management of a Sales Force.* 10th ed. Boston: McGraw-Hill.

36. Stanton, William J., Rosann Spiro, and Richard H. Buskirk. 1998. *Management of a Sales Force.* 10th ed. Boston: McGraw-Hill.

37. The Selling Power 500. *Selling Power,* http://www.sellingpower.com/magazine/

For additional hospitality and travel marketing resources, visit our Web site at **www.Hospitality-Tourism.delmar.com**

18

Public Relations and Publicity
How Do We Get There?

Objectives

Having read this chapter, you should be able to

◆ Define the terms public relations and publicity.

◆ Explain the roles of public relations and publicity in hospitality and travel marketing.

◆ List the *publics* served by a hospitality and travel organization.

◆ Describe the steps involved in developing a public relations plan.

◆ Identify and describe the techniques and vehicles used for public relations and publicity.

◆ Explain the steps involved in developing good relationships with the media.

◆ Describe the roles and benefits of using public relations consultants.

Overview

Hospitality and travel organizations deal with a wide variety of groups and individuals in a typical year. Because they provide intangible services and rely heavily on word-of-mouth advertising, maintaining positive relationships with all these external people is of paramount importance. This chapter begins by defining public relations and publicity. It then explains their importance in the hospitality and travel industry and identifies the targets of public relations and publicity efforts—known as publics.

A step-by-step procedure for preparing a public relations plan is outlined, and the techniques and media vehicles available for public relations and publicity are explained. The chapter also looks at the structure of media organizations and how good relationships are built with key individuals within these organizations. The role and advantages of specialized public relations consultants are reviewed.

Key Terms

community involvement	news (press) releases	public relations plan
feature stories	newsworthy	publicity
media (press) kits	preopening public relations	publics
media vehicles	public relations	
news (press) conferences	public relations consultants	

ave you ever been nice to someone you did not know, or to anyone you do not particularly like? Why on earth did you do this? Why bother to take the time? Could it be that you saw some long-term advantages to maintaining good relationships with these people? Maybe you realized that burning bridges behind you is not a good idea if you want to return to the same point some time in the future. Although you may not know it, you have used your own brand of public relations. When you think of it, you are your own *personal diplomat.*

Taking a broader perspective, have you ever heard the expressions "that's only PR" or "that's just a publicity stunt"? What you have listened to are uncomplimentary statements about the activities of *organizational diplomats,* those persons who coordinate public relations and publicity efforts. It seems that most nonmarketing people misunderstand or misinterpret the role of public relations. It is almost as if they see public relations and publicity as a smokescreen to hide company secrets or the inferior quality of products and services—promotion to manipulate the media and the general public.

Although this perception is quite widespread, it is a myopic and misguided view of this, the last promotional mix element. Public relations and publicity are valuable and important activities that help ensure the long-term survival of hospitality and travel organizations.

PUBLIC RELATIONS, PUBLICITY, AND THE PROMOTIONAL MIX

Definitions

Public relations includes all the activities that a hospitality and travel organization uses to maintain or improve its relationship with other organizations and individuals. Publicity is just one public relations technique, which involves nonpaid communication of information about an organization's services (e.g., news releases and press conferences).

Public relations and publicity are different from the other four promotional mix elements because with this element, the organization gives up total control of the promotion. Despite this drawback, public relations is a relatively low-cost and affordable promotional tool for organizations of all sizes. Another primary advantage of public relations and publicity is their persuasive impact, because they are not usually perceived as commercial messages.

Plan the Promotional Mix First

You should understand from the beginning that public relations and publicity are not substitutes for advertising, sales promotion, merchandising, or personal selling. The modern view of public relations is also that it is not an optional marketing activity, but one in which every organization, no matter how small, must engage. Public relations is affected by the four other promotional mix elements, and vice versa. Although this relationship initially is not as obvious as the one between advertising and sales promotion, for example, good public relations makes advertising, sales promotion, merchandising, and personal selling even more effective. Poor management of public relations usually has the opposite effect. Again, the objective of this short introduction is to show you that all five promotional mix elements must be planned together, not independently of one another.

Roles of Public Relations and Publicity

What roles do public relations and publicity play in marketing and the promotional mix? Let us start by returning to Chapter 2. You will remember that three of the differences between marketing services and products are the intangibility of services, more emotional buying appeals with services, and greater emphasis on stature and imagery with services. In Chapter 4, you learned about the great importance to hospitality and travel organizations of word-of-mouth information from social sources. What does this review add up to? It shows that personal opinions have an above-average impact on customers who are choosing hospitality and travel services. Customers cannot try them out before buying them. Friends, relatives, business associates, opinion leaders, and knowledgeable counselors such as travel agents are the *social* opinion sources that customers rely on heavily. Public relations activities try to ensure that these opinions are favorable. Therefore, the three most important roles of public relations and publicity in the hospitality and travel industry are as follows:

1. **Maintaining a Positive *Public* Presence.** The major function of public relations is to guarantee a continuing, positive relationship with individuals and groups with which an organization deals directly (e.g., customers, employees, other hospitality and travel organizations) and indirectly (e.g., the media, educational institutions, local citizens in general). Included are all individuals and groups who now, or in the future, can have an impact on the organization's marketing success.

2. **Handling Negative Publicity.** No matter how hard an organization tries to emphasize the positive aspects of its operations, it will encounter negative publicity once, if not many times, in its history. Examples are allegations of food poisoning in a restaurant, a fire in a hotel, travel agents whose passengers are left stranded by carriers, an airplane crash, or media stories that rate an organization's quality levels as substandard. Service organizations are especially vulnerable to the side effects of negative publicity because of the importance of word-of-mouth information sources. One author has gone as far as saying that there are two sides to public relations—proactive and reactive PR.[1] On the proactive side, steps are taken to generate positive public relations. Reactive PR or *vulnerability relations* is how negative public relations are handled. The key to *reactive PR* is to have a system for dealing with these undesirable situations and to have thought through some potential ways of handling them.

3. **Enhancing the Effectiveness of Other Promotional Mix Elements.** Chapter 17 compared the promotional mix to a good recipe, one with the right ingredients in the correct proportions. In many ways, good public relations management makes the other four promotional mix elements more palatable. Effective public relations

paves the way for advertising, sales promotion, merchandising, and personal selling by making customers more receptive to the persuasive messages of these elements. It increases the likelihood that these persuasive promotions will make it past customers' perceptual defenses.

HOSPITALITY AND TRAVEL INDUSTRY PUBLICS

What does the *public* in public relations mean? Does it imply the general public and, if so, what does this elusive term mean? The answer to these questions is that public relations involves communications and other relationships with various groups and individuals, both external and internal. Publics is a convenient name for all those with whom an organization interacts. Managing the relationships and communications with each and every public is essential to effective public relations. The hospitality and travel industry's publics include the following:

Internal Publics

1. Employees and employees' families
2. Unions
3. Shareholders and owners

External Publics

4. Customers and potential customers
5. Other complementary hospitality and travel organizations
6. Competitors
7. Industry community
8. Local community
9. Government
10. The media
11. Financial community
12. Hospitality and travel schools

1. **Employees and Employees' Families.** Imagine the great impact of having an organization paint or otherwise attach an advertisement to all its managers and other staff members. Maintaining good relationships with employees and their families is just like having walking-talking billboards. They pass on their enthusiasm about the organization to everyone else. Good human resources management results not only in more satisfied employees, but also in increased marketing effectiveness.

2. **Unions.** Several elements of the hospitality and travel industry are unionized, and management must always strive to maintain a harmonious relationship with these employee groups. To demonstrate this point, think about the union-management disagreements that have grounded air carriers, or the picketing of hotels by labor groups. Such cases can have a disastrous short-term impact on a company's performance and on customer confidence levels. During the summer of 2000 and through to early 2001, several of the major U.S. airlines suffered from labor disputes. American, Continental, Delta, and United experienced either strikes or work slowdowns from various groups of employees including pilots, flight attendants, and mechanics. In addition to shaking consumer confidence levels, these labor disputes led to many flight cancellations and lost revenues for the affected airlines.[2]

3. **Shareholders and Owners.** Corporations must be very concerned about their relationships with shareholders or other equity participants. These people primarily look to the company for a return on their investment, but they must also have pride in their association with the firm. The situation is slightly different for nonprofit organizations and government agencies. Nonprofits, such as associations and boards, need to maintain good relations with members, contributors, or benefactors. Government agencies must be concerned with their image among individual citizens and elected politicians.

4. **Customers and Potential Customers.** If you have not gotten the message already, customers and potential customers are the reason for marketing. Keeping on the right terms with them is not just advisable, it is essential.

5. **Other Complementary Hospitality and Travel Organizations.** In Chapter 13, you learned mainly about the importance of travel trade intermediaries to suppliers, carriers, and destination marketing organizations. Besides linking supplier, carriers, and destination marketing organizations to customers, travel trade groups are also an important promotional target of most other hospitality and travel organizations. Looking at it from the opposite perspective, you should realize that influencer intermediaries such as travel agents, incentive travel-planning companies, and tour wholesalers must maintain good relationships with suppliers, carriers, and destination marketing organizations. Therefore, public relations within the industry itself is a two-way process.

6. **Competitors.** Why worry about competitors? Are they not the opponents you are trying to beat in the first place? Yes, this is generally true, but there are times when cooperation is better in the long run than head-to-head, no-holds-barred competition. Sometimes competitive organizations must get together to satisfy the needs of certain clients (e.g., a large city-wide convention group that will need rooms in several hotels). Joint effort and planning may be needed to resolve issues that have a potentially negative impact on all competitors (e.g., an airport closing; the planned demolition of an important historic building; or the proposed imposition of a new, local tax). In other words, an antagonistic relationship with competitors should be avoided. Communication channels with competitors should be left open to allow for the exploration of areas of mutual interest in the future.

7. **Industry Community.** The hospitality and travel industry includes a large number of trade associations, most of which were mentioned in Chapter 10. These associations provide many important member services—lobbying against adverse legislation, upgrading professional skills, informing others about the importance of the industry, and holding periodic conventions and trade shows. At a minimum, an organization should belong to one key trade association. From a public relations standpoint, it is even better if an organization is more active. For example, managers may serve as association officers or as seminar and convention speakers.

8. **Local Community.** Many hospitality and travel organizations, including most travel agencies and restaurants, and many hotels, are highly dependent on their immediate local communities for customers. Others, such as convention and visitors bureaus, must have strong citizen and political support to be successful. Being an active and concerned local community member is a must for most organizations in our industry. Normally, this means that management should participate in local clubs and associations such as the chamber of commerce, convention and visitors bureau, and service clubs such as Rotary, Lions, and Kiwanis.

EXCELLENCE CASE

Public Relations:
McDonald's Corporation Ronald McDonald Houses

The Ronald McDonald House program is one of the best examples in our industry of a continuous public relations activity supported by a major corporation. It falls into the category of local community involvement, of which McDonald's Corporation and its individual franchisees are avid proponents. The now-famous program began in 1974, with the opening of the first Ronald McDonald House in Philadelphia with the help of the Philadelphia Eagles football team. The idea was that of former Philadelphia Eagles linebacker Fred Hill with creative assistance from Elkman Advertising, the ad agency for McDonald's franchisees in Philadelphia.[1] Fred Hill's daughter Kim had been hospitalized with leukemia and he wanted to help other families finding themselves in similar situations. The local franchisees, through a Shamrock Shake promotion, raised $40,000 for the first house. The next house was opened in 1977, in McDonald's home territory—the Chicago area. A major part of the funding for the second house again came through the local McDonald's franchisees, this time through an Orange Shake promotion, one of the colors of the Chicago Bears NFL team. The Chicago Bears football team also helped to promote its development.[2] By 2001, there were 206 houses in 19 countries.[3]

The worthy causes in this case are seriously-ill children requiring extended hospital care, and their families. A Ronald McDonald House is a home-away-from-home for the sick children and other family members when the children are receiving treatment. While many people are aware of the Ronald McDonald House concept and the services it provides, most are unfamiliar with the way the Houses are created.

Ronald McDonald Houses are planned, developed, and operated by local volunteer groups in not-for-profit (501 [c])[4] organizations. These organizations are eligible to receive start-up funding from the Ronald McDonald House

Charities (RMHC), which was established in 1984, in memory of Ray Kroc. RMHC awards grants to groups that benefit children in the areas of health care and medical research, including Ronald McDonald Houses, education and the arts, and civic and social services. Between 1984 and 2001, RMHC and its 110-plus local chapters in North America and overseas awarded more than $225 million to nonprofit organizations serving children. To qualify for funding under the Ronald McDonald House program, the applicant group must satisfy the following criteria:

1. The potential house must have *medical advisors* from area hospitals with a need for overnight housing for families of pediatric patients whose homes are great distances from the treatment centers.
2. There must be a *community volunteer organization,* often composed of parents who have children being treated for serious illnesses or who have been treated for such illnesses at the nearby hospital. The organization must also have other volunteers from community organizations, local businesses, or civic leaders who are willing to participate.
3. The project must have the *support of local McDonald's franchisees.*

The 206 Ronald McDonald Houses, located in 19 different countries, together contain more than 3000 bedrooms. The average house has fifteen bedrooms. The largest house is in New York City, with eighty-four rooms, and the smallest is in Youngstown, Ohio, with five rooms. Each house is located close to a major medical facility. McDonald's estimates that, at any given time, twenty new Ronald McDonald Houses are in various stages of development. Since 1974, the houses have served more than 10 million family members. McDonald's franchisees and their customers have contributed greatly to these most worthy projects.

continued

EXCELLENCE CASE *continued*

To oversee day-to-day operations, the local not-for-profit group hires a house manager. Families using the facility pay a small daily donation in the range of $5 to $20, if they can afford it. These donations and any other contributions are all channelled back into the Houses' maintenance and improvement, or into mortgage retirement. Family members also are expected to play the role of temporary volunteers sharing the tasks of cleaning, laundry, cooking, and grocery shopping.

McDonald's believes that the Ronald McDonald House program is a reflection of its business philosophy of giving something back to each of the communities in which it does business. There is no doubt that the Ronald McDonald House concept is one of the premier examples of community involvement in our industry. While the corporation and its franchisees fully realize the positive impact of positive public relations, it must be remembered that the Ronald McDonald House idea was someone else's in the first place.

Discussion Questions

1. What are the major public relations benefits that accrue to McDonald's from operating the Ronald McDonald House Program?
2. How does having a program like RMHC potentially impact the motivations of McDonald's employees and what are the possible roles that these employees could perform in furthering the program's goals?
3. What are the main lessons that other hospitality and travel organizations can learn from McDonald's leadership in this area?

Web Site

http://www.rmhc.com/

References

1. Love, John F. 1986. *McDonalds: Behind the Arches.* Toronto: Bartam Books, 213–214.
2. Kroc, Ray. 1977. *Grinding it Out: The Making of McDonald's.* New York: Berkley Medallion Books, 198–199.
3. http://www.rmhc.com
4. http://www.rmhc.com

9. **Government.** Various levels of government, including civic, county, state or provincial, and national agencies, affect a hospitality and travel organization. Compliance with the many pieces of legislation and regulatory measures is essential. It is also important to maintain good relations with key elected officials by keeping them informed of developments within the organization.

10. **The Media.** The media—newspapers, magazines, television, and radio stations— are the primary target of publicity efforts. Building open and cordial communications with them is one of the most important public relations functions. The topic of media relations is discussed in detail later in this chapter.

11. **Financial Community.** Banks, trust companies, and other lending agencies are important sources of short- and long-term capital for most corporations and many nonprofit organizations. It is very important to have a positive relationship with current lenders and others who might provide additional financing in the future.

12. **Hospitality and Travel Schools.** North America now has more than 500 colleges, universities, and private schools that offer specialized hospitality and travel education programs. The Council on Hotel, Restaurant and Institutional Education (CHRIE) is the major association of these educators. These range from proprietary schools that train travel agency reservationists to doctorate programs at major universities. Each year, hospitality and travel organizations are placing more emphasis on hiring people

with formal training and education in the field. It is beneficial for these organizations to be seen in the most positive light by the students and faculty in these programs.

PLANNING PUBLIC RELATIONS EFFORTS

Every hospitality and travel organization, no matter how small, should have a **public relations plan**. Like advertising, sales promotion, and sales plans, new public relations plans should be prepared periodically, at least once a year. There is a greater-than-average tendency to let this slip, however, because of the lack of deadlines for placing materials (as in advertising) and the fact that public relations often is not a responsibility of specific staff members. Many organizations mistakenly assign it a low priority and only engage in sporadic public relations efforts, often to counter negative publicity. One of the major points made in this chapter is that public relations must be a continuous activity, regardless of whether an organization has an in-house public relations specialist, uses an outside consultant, or does neither of the two.

There are nine steps involved in preparing the public relations plan.

1. Set public relations objectives
2. Decide on in-house public relations or agency
3. Establish tentative public relations and publicity budget
4. Consider cooperative public relations
5. Select public relations and publicity techniques
6. Select public relations and publicity media
7. Decide on timing of public relations
8. Prepare final public relations plan and budget
9. Measure and evaluate public relations success

Set Public Relations Objectives

The place to start any plan is with a clear set of objectives. You already know from Chapter 8 that overall marketing objectives are set by target market (if an organization is using a segmented strategy). Similarly, with public relations it is best to set objectives for each of the organization's publics. This ensures that all publics are continually kept in focus.

Public relations objectives are generally informative. They provide oral, written, or visual information about an organization to one or more of its publics. It is a *soft-sell* form of promotion that is aimed mainly at enhancing the organization's image. An example of setting a public relations objective is a restaurant that decides to improve its image in the local community. Again, although quite difficult to do with public relations, it is best to set measurable objectives. This requires taking measurements before and after implementing the public relations plan. In our restaurant example, this might involve conducting local surveys to measure the restaurant's image before and after the new public relations activities.

Decide on In-House Public Relations or Agency

The next decision concerns assigning responsibility for implementing the public relations plan. Many alternative approaches are used in the hospitality and travel industry:

1. Managers or owners assuming sole responsibility
2. Assigning public relations responsibilities to a multidepartment committee

3. Adding the public relations function to the responsibilities of one of the marketing department managers or directors (e.g., the director of marketing or the sales manager)
4. Appointing a full-time public relations director or manager to the marketing department
5. Hiring an outside public relations consultant or agency
6. Combining 2, 3, 4, and/or 5

The approach chosen depends primarily on the size of the organization. The larger the organization, the more likely it is to have a full-time public relations director and to use outside specialists. Smaller organizations generally use one of the first three approaches.

Establish Tentative Public Relations and Publicity Budget

There is a fairly common misconception that public relations and publicity are entirely free. However, staff costs are involved if there is a full-time public relations director and support staff. Outside public relations specialists charge consulting fees for their services. Even if public relations is handled by an in-house committee, the manager, or another manager, there are some charges for the time they devote to these activities. There are also definite costs incurred when an organization hosts the media, stages various public relations events, and prepares press releases. For example, preopening public relations for new hotels often involve spending hundreds of thousands of dollars.

Again, it is best to use a two-step process to set the public relations and publicity budget. First, a portion of the total promotional budget is tentatively allocated. This is followed by mapping out all the public relations activities for the upcoming period, based on objectives. Once the plan has been set, each activity is costed out and the final budget is determined.

Consider Cooperative Public Relations

Many opportunities for promotional partnerships exist with public relations and publicity that should be considered before going it alone. A good example is various suppliers and destination marketing groups from a specific area that jointly fund a media reception in a large city. Complementary hospitality and travel organizations may also get together to prepare press releases about new services they are offering jointly.

Select Public Relations and Publicity Techniques

A wide variety of public relations and publicity techniques are available to hospitality and travel organizations. They can be divided into three distinct categories (1) continuous activities; (2) preplanned, short-term activities; and (3) unpredictable, short-term activities (Figure 18–1).

1. **Continuous Public Relations Activities.** One important point about public relations is that it must be done continuously, not just when emergency situations or newsworthy stories arise. A hospitality and travel organization must maintain ongoing relationships with each of its publics. It must have a continuous *public presence*. For example, it is not enough to call the media only when a good story idea comes up. An organization must use an ongoing program of media contact.

CONTINUOUS PUBLIC RELATIONS ACTIVITIES

1. Local community involvement
2. Industry community involvement
3. Newsletters, newspapers, and company magazines
4. Employee relations
5. Media relations
6. Media kits and photography
7. Shareholder, owner, and financial community relations
8. Relations with hospitality and travel schools
9. Relationships with complementary and competitive organizations
10. Government relations
11. Customer relations
12. Advertising

PREPLANNED, SHORT-TERM ACTIVITIES

1. News (press) releases (traditional and on–line)
2. News (press) conferences
3. Ceremonies, openings, and events
4. Announcements
5. Feature stories
6. Press and travel trade seminars
7. Marketing research

UNPREDICTABLE, SHORT-TERM ACTIVITIES

1. Handling negative publicity
2. Media interviews

◆ FIGURE 18–1   *Public relations and publicity techniques.*

Dealing with publics is similar to operating a savings account. If you put no money into the account, you cannot make a withdrawal. Likewise, if an organization does not establish and continuously maintain a relationship with each of its publics, it cannot expect to draw on the goodwill that has been accumulated. When you deposit money into your savings account periodically, you know that you not only can make future withdrawals, but you will also earn interest. An organization must continuously and frequently communicate with each of its publics to build goodwill and to be able to ask for special favors when they are needed. For example, a hotel should get to know all the key people (editors, reporters, publishers) at local newspapers and television and radio stations, perhaps by hosting lunches or dinners for them periodically. Each of these people should always be sent announcements and stories (and perhaps even holiday and birthday cards) so that they are constantly up-to-date on what is happening at the hotel. By building these open and continuous channels of communication with media people, the hotel has a much greater likelihood that its news releases and announcements will be covered. Of course, paid advertising with each of the media also helps get additional *free* publicity.

What types of activities can a hospitality and travel organization conduct continuously? The major ones follow.

a. ***Local Community Involvement.*** Every hospitality and travel organization should constantly strive to be an exemplary *citizen* in the local community or communities that it serves. Local community involvement can mean making financial or in-kind (e.g., free services) donations to worthy local causes or charities, becoming a member and actively serving in local clubs and associations (e.g., chamber of commerce, Rotary, convention and visitors bureau, historical or museum board), and advocating support of community interests (e.g., economic development, social or environmental issues).

b. ***Industry Community Involvement.*** Membership and active participation in key trade associations is another must. The payoffs are perhaps less immediate, but they are nonetheless significant. They help improve the industry for all its component organizations. An organization can participate by attending annual conventions, serving on boards of directors or committees, attending and supporting professional development and educational programs, speaking at conventions and seminars, and being spokespersons on important industry issues. Appendix 2–3 identifies many of the industry's key trade associations.

c. ***Newsletters, Newspapers, and Company Magazines.*** Newsletters are an excellent way to maintain a steady flow of communications with employees and other publics. Many hospitality and travel organizations have house newsletters or newspapers that are distributed to employees. Some periodically publish newsletters or magazines that are given to customers and other external publics. Royal Caribbean International's *Crown & Anchor Society* provides a good example of the customer-directed newsletter, which the company calls its *special alumni magazine.* Details of this magazine and the entire repeat guest loyalty program are provided on Royal Caribbean's Web site at www.rccl.com (Figure 18–2). In-flight magazines are another good example. These provide their sponsoring airlines with both a public relations and an advertising vehicle.

   The distribution of newsletters through e-mail is gaining popularity in the hospitality and travel industry. A good example of this is also from the cruise line business. The World's Leading Cruise Lines (the cruise lines owned by Carnival Corporation) through its Web site invites people to subscribe to its electronic newsletter. This is a cost-effective alternative to distributing a newsletter when compared with the traditional methods of producing and distributing these publications.

d. ***Employee Relations.*** In-house newsletters and newspapers are just one technique among several that are used in human resources management. Others with definite public relations value are employee recognition programs (e.g., employee-of-the-month awards), cards or gifts that mark important dates such as birthdays and anniversaries, incentive programs (e.g., incentive travel trips, bonuses, other special awards), and promotions. Happy employees tend to provide better service, which leads to more satisfied customers and word-of-mouth advertising.

e. ***Media Relations.*** You have already read about the importance of continuous contacts with key media people. In many ways, this should be similar to an organization's system of staying in contact with important past customers and sales prospects. Follow-up should be made at predetermined intervals, which may involve face-to-face meetings either at media offices or at the organization's place of business.

ON THE WEB

◆ FIGURE 18–2   *Royal Caribbean's special alumni newsletter is announced on its Web site.* (Courtesy of Royal Caribbean Cruises Ltd.)

f. ***Media Kits and Photography.*** It is much better for an organization to anticipate media requests for information and photographs than it is to have to assemble these at the last minute. For example, the **media (press) kits** for hotels should include the items shown in Figure 18–3. Although some of these items must be written only once, others in the media kit must be updated constantly to reflect changes in facilities, services, and other factors.

The Internet has provided a completely new means for organizations to distribute news releases, photographs, and other materials to the media. These are usually found in the *company background* pages, but they often are accessed simply by clicking the *news releases* or *media/press* buttons on the home page. In

- A fact sheet (e.g., hotel's name, address, phone and fax numbers; e-mail and Web site address; general manager's name; number of rooms, restaurants, bars, and lounges; meeting room data; special facilities available)

- Biographies of the general manager and other key management staff (e.g., executive chef)

- A description, perhaps in news-release format, of the restaurants, bars, and lounges

- A description of the hotel's location

- A description of special features, facilities, and services (e.g., architectural or design features, unique facilities for specific target markets, special services)

- Previous press releases (if still current and accurate)

- Selected photographs of interior and exterior

◆ FIGURE 18–3   *Contents of a hotel's media kit.* (Reprinted by permission of Elsevier Science from *"Ink & air time: A public relations primer."* Cosse, Jacques C. *The Cornell Hotel and Restaurant Administration Quarterly, Vol. 21, No. 1, 1980, 37–40,* Copyright 1980 by Cornell University. *"Public relations for the hotel opening."* by Dee Zive, Jessica. *The Cornell Hotel and Restaurant Administration Quarterly, Vol. 22, No. 1, 1980, 19–28, Copyright 1981 by Cornell University*)

some cases, the news releases are supplemented with an on-line photo gallery, which allows media professionals to download individual photos with the click of a mouse. Company histories and *frequently asked questions* (FAQs) provide other useful information for the press. Another more recent digital technology innovation is for organizations to provide their photo galleries on CD-ROM.

Figure 18–4 shows a good example of the use of the Internet to distribute corporate information. Marriott International, in the *Corporate News & Information* section of its Web site, provides comprehensive company information for visitors. Included on the site are annual reports, news releases, *Marriott at a Glance,* and *Marriott Milestones.*

g. ***Shareholder, Owner, and Financial Community Relations.*** For legal, tax, and financial management reasons, hospitality and travel organizations must prepare annual reports and other financial statements. These reports and statements also have definite public relations value. In addition, periodic meetings with key shareholders, owners, and current and potential lenders are important in building positive relationships and open communications channels. Again, these are now often found on a company's Web site.

h. ***Relations with Hospitality and Travel Schools.*** Many hospitality and travel organizations recognize the value of staying in continuous contact with these educational institutions. Maintaining a positive image at these schools has both immediate payoffs (recruiting new staff members) and long-term benefits (faculty and former students spreading positive, word-of-mouth information on the organization). Because of their industry expertise, graduates and faculty members often are opinion leaders or are more influential in convincing others to use services than most people not associated with the schools.

One excellent example of an organization that has grasped this concept is Disney. Periodically, Disney World hosts an Educators' Forum on-site in Orlando, Florida, and invites faculty from North American schools and from overseas. After the forum the educators leave, Mickey Mouse ears in their suitcases, with a heightened regard for Disney.

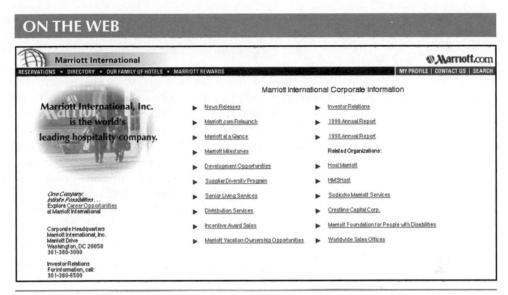

◆ **FIGURE 18–4** *Marriott International's Web site provides a wealth of information on the company.* (Courtesy of Marriott International, Inc.)

i. ***Relationships with Complementary and Competitive Organizations.*** It is essential for suppliers, carriers, and destination marketing organizations to stay on good terms with travel trade intermediaries. As you have seen in recent chapters, this involves placing advertisements in trade magazines, implementing trade-oriented sales promotions, and conducting personal selling. However, building a good and lasting relationship means doing more than this. It includes such techniques as joining travel trade associations as associate members, speaking publicly at travel trade conventions, mailing newsletters to individual travel trade organizations, and being advocates of travel trade groups.

j. ***Government Relations.*** Every hospitality and travel organization must comply with the laws and regulations that affect it. Failing to conform frequently results in negative publicity. Dealing with government should go further than mere compliance, however. There are many government agencies that are now involved in promoting and developing the hospitality and travel industry. Every state, province, and territory in the United States, Canada, United Kingdom, and Australia has a tourism or travel marketing department. Supporting the efforts of these agencies definitely benefits hospitality and travel organizations directly. An organization can serve on tourism advisory boards, help agencies publicize the economic importance of the hospitality and travel industry, and give moral support when agencies request increased budgets.

k. ***Customer Relations.*** Customers are the lifeblood of every organization, and techniques that improve relationships with them are very important to an organization's long-term survival. However, it is very difficult to draw a clear line between a public relations activity and advertising, sales promotion, and personal selling. For example, if a sales representative sends holiday cards to past customers and prospects, is this public relations or is it part of personal selling? Is a company-published magazine, such as the "Radisson News," a form of advertising or a form of public relations? Was the McDonald's advertising campaign highlighting the nutritional contents of its menu items pure advertising, or did it have a public relations purpose?

The answer is not simple, but it implies that persuasive promotions alone do not guarantee long-term success. It is equally important to do the little things for customers, such as remembering their birthdays—things that do not have immediate payoffs.

1. *Advertising.* How do you make sure that the media covers your public relations message exactly the way you want? The answer is to make it a paid advertisement. In 2001, with growing concerns over the outbreak of foot-and-mouth disease, the Irish Tourist Board mounted an advertising campaign reassuring tourists that there was no threat to humans. This book has talked several times about McDonald's nutrition-oriented advertisements. The same company in Canada used paid advertising to communicate the career success of its former employees. In early 2000, Fairmont Hotels launched a public relations effort, supported by paid advertising, to announce its acquisition of Canadian Pacific Hotels (Figure 18–5).

THE RICH TRADITIONS OF CANADIAN PACIFIC HOTELS HAVE JUST COME TOGETHER WITH FAIRMONT HOTELS.

LUCKILY, ONLY THE CODE HAS CHANGED.

As of December 3rd, all Canadian Pacific Hotels will move to the FA chain code in all Global Distribution Systems. This change will now give you access to 34 hotels within the Fairmont Hotels collection.

For complete details on this change, please refer to the following information pages:

Sabre: Y/HHL/WCP/NEWS or Y/HHL/QFA/NEWS   Apollo/Galileo: HODCP/NEWS or HODFA/NEWS

Worldspan: G/HTL/CPQ/NEWS or G/HTL/FAQ/NEWS   Amadeus: GGHTLCPNEW or GGHTLFANEW

HOTELS & RESORTS

Extraordinary Hotels. Extraordinary Places.

44-171-389-1126
www.fairmont.com

CITY HOTELS	SAN JOSE	ST. JOHN'S	RESORTS	MONTEBELLO	MEXICO:
UNITED STATES:	THE FAIRMONT SAN JOSE	*HOTEL NEWFOUNDLAND	UNITED STATES:	*LE CHÂTEAU MONTEBELLO	THE FAIRMONT ACAPULCO PRINCESS
BOSTON THE FAIRMONT COPLEY PLAZA BOSTON	CANADA:	TORONTO *ROYAL YORK	SCOTTSDALE THE FAIRMONT SCOTTSDALE PRINCESS	*KENAUK MONT-TREMBLANT *CHÂTEAU MONT	THE FAIRMONT PIERRE MARQUES
CHICAGO THE FAIRMONT CHICAGO	CALGARY *THE PALLISER EDMONTON	VANCOUVER *HOTEL VANCOUVER THE FAIRMONT	CANADA:	TREMBLANT ST. ANDREWS	BERMUDA: THE FAIRMONT SOUTHAMPTON
DALLAS THE FAIRMONT DALLAS	*HOTEL MACDONALD MONTREAL	VANCOUVER AIRPORT *THE WATERFRONT	BANFF *BANFF SPRINGS	*THE ALGONQUIN WHISTLER	PRINCESS
NEW ORLEANS THE FAIRMONT NEW ORLEANS	*THE QUEEN ELIZABETH OTTAWA	VICTORIA *THE EMPRESS	CHARLEVOIX *LE MANOIR RICHELIEU	*CHATEAU WHISTLER RESORT	
NEW YORK CITY **THE PLAZA	*CHÂTEAU LAURIER QUEBEC CITY	WINNIPEG *THE LOMBARD	JASPER *JASPER PARK LODGE		BARBADOS:
SAN FRANCISCO THE FAIRMONT SAN FRANCISCO	*LE CHÂTEAU FRONTENAC	BERMUDA: THE FAIRMONT HAMILTON PRINCESS	LAKE LOUISE *CHATEAU LAKE LOUISE		GLITTER BAY ROYAL PAVILION

*A CANADIAN PACIFIC HOTEL
** A FAIRMONT MANAGED HOTEL

◆ FIGURE 18–5   *Fairmont Hotels & Resorts announces its merger with Canadian Pacific Hotels.* (Courtesy of Fairmont Hotels & Resorts)

2. **Preplanned, Short-Term Activities.** These public relations and publicity activities are also planned in advance, but they are short term rather than continuous. A grand opening of a new restaurant, hotel, or travel agency is a good example, as are the activities publicizing an airline's inaugural flight on a new route. Another example is the news release. Although organizations should be producing these continuously, preparing each individual release is a short-term activity.

   a. *News* or *Press Releases.* A news or press release is a short article about an organization that is written in an attempt to attract media attention, which will then lead to media coverage of the materials contained within the news release. It is a publicity-generating tool that is used to communicate with publics without paid sponsorship. Preparing news releases is probably the most popular and widespread public relations activity.

   The contents of an effective news release are summarized in the following verse:[3]

   > I have six honest serving men;
   > They serve me well, I know,
   > Their names are Who and What and When,
   > And Where and Why and How.

   The news release should open with a paragraph that summarizes the main points of the news story by stating who did what, when, why, and where.
   Other important contents and details for news releases follow. They
   - Must be newsworthy, containing recent information with news value
   - Must have a date
   - Must list a contact person, phone number and e-mail
   - Are usually marked "for immediate release"
   - Are typed in double-space format
   - Should have a headline (e.g., Red Lobster Supports Local Communities through Programs for Environment, People with Disabilities)
   - Should be printed on a specially-designed, news-release paper, with a consistent heading on each release
   - Should be as brief as possible, generally not more than two pages
   - Should contain no grammatical or typographical errors
   - Should be very factual, avoiding unnecessary hype and flowery language
   - Must have the approval of all persons quoted in the release
   - Normally end with a *signature* (e.g., -30-, ###, -0-, or END)

   The contact person listed on the release must be ready to answer follow-up questions from the media, and perhaps to be interviewed for a news article or program. How important are news releases in communicating information about organizations? One source estimates that 50 percent to 75 percent of all newspaper stories are instigated by news releases.[4]

   b. *News or Press Conferences.* A news or press conference is a meeting where a prepared presentation is made to invited media people. These conferences are held infrequently, only when an organization has something really important to announce to all the media. Press conferences play a key role in preopening public relations and when an organization makes major changes to its facilities and services. Good examples are a hotel chain announcing plans to construct a new hotel in a particular city, an attraction owner publicizing a major park addition, a cruise line telling about its plans to build a new ship, or a new travel agency announcing a branch opening.

The persons making the presentations must be carefully chosen. Preferably, they should attract media attention themselves. This could include company presidents, mayors, other important political figures, tourism officials, or sports or entertainment stars. Besides having the opportunity to ask questions after the formal presentation, the media should be given a written summary of the news story. This can be in news-release format, or it can be set up as a fact sheet.

Think about the precision and planning that go into a president's or prime minister's periodic press conferences. You will soon realize how well these events are orchestrated to get consistent messages to the media.

c. ***Ceremonies, Openings, and Events.*** What is smashed when a newly built ship is launched? What gets cut when a new restaurant is opened? What is broken when construction of a new theme park is announced? You are doing well if you answered a champagne bottle, a ribbon, and the ground. These exercises are parts of traditional ceremonies to introduce new or expanded hospitality and travel facilities or services. All of the hoopla accompanying these events is important in creating a positive first impression. It is also important in building awareness. In among all the balloons, bands, and banners is a very clear public relations and publicity objective—to begin building positive relations with all publics.

Let us take the **preopening public relations** of a new hotel as an example. A carefully sequenced program of events should be used, including a groundbreaking or cornerstone ceremony (when construction starts), *topping-off* ceremony (when the building is completed), *soft* opening (only news reporters are invited), ribbon-cutting ceremony, press opening (all press are invited), grand opening (held a month after actual opening), and restaurant openings.[5] From this example it is important to realize that public relations begin months and sometimes years before operations begin. In many ways this is similar to the steps politicians take before they eventually get elected. With almost military precision, they make speeches and appearances, conduct debates and other activities, and then build these activities to near crescendo as election dates approach.

d. ***Announcements.*** Announcements are short news stories, often about one or more of an organization's employees. The events that are typically announced are internal promotions, hiring of new managers, or awards or other accomplishments of management or staff. The announcement usually features a photograph of the individuals involved, and the organization may be required to pay the print media that publishes the announcement. In addition to helping with public relations, announcements also play an important role in human resources management.

e. ***Feature Stories.*** Feature stories or *features* are articles of human interest that entertain, inform, or educate readers, viewers, or listeners. They are longer and have less immediate news value than news releases. In other words, they are unlikely to appear on the front page of a newspaper or at the beginning of a radio or television news broadcast. They are more likely to be published in a newspaper supplement (e.g., the travel, food, or entertainment section), in a magazine, or as a *backgrounder* or in a *feature* on a broadcast program.

Did You Know?

The National Credibility Index

✓ The Public Relations Society of America (PRSA) Foundation has developed the *National Credibility Index* to measure and track how the American public perceives the credibility of its leaders.

✓ The average score in the *National Credibility Index* was 61.5.

✓ The five groups of leaders with the highest credibility scores included the following:
  • Supreme Court justice (81.3)
  • Teacher (80.7)
  • National expert (78.6)
  • Member of the Armed Forces (73)
  • Local business owner (72.2)

✓ The lowest credibility scores were given to the following:
  • Head of a national interest group (51.3)
  • Political party leader (48.6)
  • Public relations specialist (47.6)
  • Famous entertainer (46.8)
  • TV or radio talk show host (46.6)

✓ http://www.prsa.org/nci/nci.html

There are two types of features—sponsor generated and media generated. A sponsor-generated feature is produced by the sponsoring organization; the other is a story idea developed by the media, in which an organization is asked to participate. Examples of media-generated features are the many articles on travel destination areas that appear in such magazines as *Travel & Leisure* and *Travel-Holiday.* Sponsor-generated stories come in many varieties, including life histories of company founders, company histories and descriptions, *backgrounders* on interesting or important customers, continuing contributions to important charities or worthy causes, and other unique organizational features and events.

   f. ***Press and Travel Trade Seminars.*** These are meetings that last longer than press conferences, where sponsoring organizations communicate detailed information. Although travel trade seminars are definitely a form of sales promotion, they also have public relations value. For example, a resort company or tour wholesaler may hold travel trade seminars when it introduces a new selection of vacation packages.

   g. ***Marketing Research.*** Marketing research can be used for public relations and publicity purposes when an organization wants to show that a public is sympathetic toward its point of view. For example, a transatlantic airline bothered by outbreaks of terrorism in Europe and the Middle East might survey its passengers to show others that their fears are misguided. A restaurant could publish survey results that show that it is considered the best in town for a particular food item.

3. **Unpredictable, Short-Term Activities.** Not all public relations activities can be carefully preplanned, but every organization must be prepared to deal with them. Management may be asked to do media interviews regarding news events or media-generated feature stories. Additionally, no matter how hard an organization tries, undesirable public relations and publicity are always a possibility. Although the exact nature of these events is certainly unpredictable, an organization should plan ahead and train its personnel to handle these situations.

   a. *Handling Negative Publicity.* What is the best approach with negative publicity? Should you avoid responding with the typical "no comment," or should you take the offensive and vehemently deny responsibility? Again, you can get a clue from observing politicians and how they react to bad publicity. Their typical response is to acknowledge the rumor or event and do one of the following:
   - Say that their staffs are looking into it
   - Say that they have set up a special committee or task force to investigate it
   - Offer their own or others' help in determining the accuracy of the rumor or event

      Of course, politicians can deny rumors outright or criticize the media and political opponents for spreading them. Taking the offensive immediately, however, is seldom the best tack. As Richard Nixon, Gary Hart, and Bill Clinton learned, it does not pay to cover up. Telling the truth pays off in the long run. If the facts are not readily at hand, one of the three previously listed approaches is best.

      Hospitality and travel organizations faced with negative publicity must also react with political aplomb. Some of the do's and don'ts include the following:[6,7]
   - Tell the truth and do not lie to the media.
   - Do not try to cover up. This will make the media want to dig even deeper.
   - Gather all the facts surrounding the incident and communicate them to the media.
   - Dismiss rumors by stating the facts correctly and completely.
   - Show a willingness to take action as a result of the incident.

      A good example of professionalism in handling an adverse situation is how Burger King handled the recall of Pokémon balls distributed in its restaurants in November and December 1999. The company mounted a major campaign to encourage people to discard these dangerous toys.

      How do you plan ahead for these kinds of situations if they are unpredictable? By far the best approach is for the persons responsible for public relations to anticipate the types of negative situations that may be encountered and to frame some possible responses to them.

   b. *Media Interviews.* Although some media interviews are a direct result of preplanned public relations activities, many are not. As you have just learned, some result from negative publicity, whereas others result from media-generated feature stories or from news stories where an organization's manager is asked to give an expert opinion.

      Media interviews can be nerve-racking for some people, especially under the bright glare of television-camera lights. Being comfortable and articulate during an interview takes both careful planning and practice:
   - When you are asked for the interview, get as many details as possible on the interview format, the interviewer, and the questions to be asked. Is it a live or taped interview? In which newspaper section or program will it appear? Why have you been chosen for the interview?

- Gather all the facts you need for the interview, and have these at your fingertips during the interview.
- Prepare responses to the questions you anticipate. Keep the answers short and factual. Avoid digressions.
- Practice your answers by asking someone else to role-play the reporter, and make any adjustments necessary after the role-playing session.
- Make sure that your appearance is neat.
- Establish a rapport with the reporter before the interview starts.

Select Public Relations and Publicity Media

As is true with advertising, many media vehicles are available for communicating information to publics. They include the Internet, broadcast media (radio, and network and cable television), newspapers (dailies, weeklies, and business), magazines (consumer and trade), and various in-house vehicles (company newsletters, newspapers, magazines, films, slide presentations, and videotapes). Chapter 15 showed you the relative strengths and weaknesses of most of these vehicles. Again, choosing from among them should be based on the publics targeted and the public relations objectives. For example, if you want to reach several publics in a local community, the broad coverage of a daily newspaper may be best. If, on the other hand, the target is travel trade intermediaries, then trade magazines such as *Travel Weekly* and *Travel Agent* are the right choice. Should you want to communicate with all employees, a company-generated newsletter may be the best route.

The same financial constraints found with advertising are not present when selecting media vehicles and specific newspapers, magazines, and radio and television stations. For example, adding a magazine to the mailing list for a news release costs much less than placing an ad in the same publication. This means that the sponsoring organization does not have to be as selective in placing publicity as it does in placing advertising.

Media Relations

You have already learned about the importance of building long-term relationships with the media and always providing them with honest, factual information. Another key to good media relations is not to show favoritism toward any individual stations, newspapers, or magazines. When an organization has a news release or other story, it should generally be given to all the media at the same time. It is then their prerogative to cover the story as quickly and as comprehensively as they choose. There are some situations that warrant releasing an *exclusive* story to one paper, station, or magazine. The rationale here is that the medium chosen for the exclusive story best fits the publics that an organization is targeting.

Which contacts should be developed within different media organizations? You need to understand more about the structure of media organizations to answer this question.

1. **Newspapers.** Major national newspapers such as the *New York Times* and *USA Today* have an extensive editorial staff. These include persons with titles such as editor, associate editor, managing editor, news editor, Sunday editor, city editor,

assistant city editor, and telegraph and cable editors.[8] Usually a newspaper also has several departments, each with its own editors. For example, there may be a food and entertainment editor, travel editor, sports editor, business editor, women's page editor, family/lifestyles editor, and others. Often these departmental editors are responsible for the special supplements you find inserted into the main newspaper. Additionally, newspapers have feature columnists, both national and local, who write periodic feature stories normally with the same theme. A good example is a local food or wine critic.

It is important to understand the roles of different editors before you approach them. City editors have overall responsibility for covering fast-breaking national, regional, and local news. If a hospitality and travel organization has a story with immediate news value, city editors should be contacted first, not the reporters who work for them. An example is when an important national figure or entertainer uses the organization's services and the individual's permission has been obtained to release this information.

Most stories generated by our industry do not, however, merit front-page news. They often fit better in specialized travel, food, entertainment, weekend, or lifestyle sections. In this case, the appropriate departmental editor should be the first person contacted.

The decision as to whom to contact first is also influenced by the size and the type of newspaper. If it is a small-town paper, the overall editor may be responsible for assigning all reporters. For a large-city daily, the correct procedure is to contact the city editor, as just discussed.

2. **Television.** As Chapter 15 mentioned, there are network, local, and cable television stations. Before you switch channels at the end of a news program, look at the titles and credits. You should see the names of producers, executive producers, news directors, editors, writers, and reporters. The key contacts in getting television coverage are assignment editors. They schedule stories, reporters, and film crews. Often this job is divided between two people—the morning and afternoon assignment editors.[9]

Getting television stations to cover an event such as a press conference means either directly contacting the stations or having the event listed in the *wire-service daybook.* This is an Internet news listing that all news directors and assignment editors check frequently.[10]

3. **Radio.** The key figures at radio stations are the station managers and news directors. Because of the immediacy of placing and airing radio news, radio tends to be a *feeder* for later coverage by television and newspapers. Again, the wire services, including UPI (United Press International) and AP (Associated Press), play a key role in distributing news stories of national interest. For local news, direct contact should be made with individual station managers or news directors.

4. **Magazines.** As you know, magazines do not carry the same amount of fast-breaking news as newspapers, television, and radio stations. Many of the pieces they print are feature stories. Some national weekly magazines, such as *Time* and *Newsweek,* have more current news than others published monthly, bimonthly, or quarterly. Several trade magazines, including *Travel Weekly, Travel Agent,* and *Nation's Restaurant News,* are published weekly and contain more news.

Appendix 2–4 lists the major consumer and trade magazines in the hospitality and travel field. Each magazine is structured differently, but contact names and titles can usually be found in the first few pages of an issue. Most have a publisher, an editor-in-chief or senior editor, a managing editor, and several departmental editors. For example, *Travel Agent* has editors for airlines, cruises, hotels, Florida, Caribbean/Bahamas/Bermuda/Latin America, car rentals, tour America, international tours, leisure travel, and business travel. Again, choosing the right person for the initial contact depends on the size of the magazine and its editorial departments.

Decide on Timing of Public Relations

You can see from the previous discussion that not all public relations activities can be scheduled precisely, ahead of time. Some situations are unexpected, but they must be dealt with promptly. You have also learned that there is a continuous part to this promotional mix element, including such activities as publishing a monthly employee newsletter, keeping up contacts with the media, and attending regular association and club meetings. Somewhere in between the unexpected and continuous are the preplanned, short-term activities such as news releases, press conferences, announcements, and feature stories. Therefore, a public relations plan must include a definite timetable for continuing and preplanned, short-term activities. It must also include a contingency plan to handle the unexpected.

Another important point is that an organization does not have the same control over the timing of publicity as it does with media advertising. For example, when a news release is mailed, follow-up inquiries may be immediate or they may take several weeks to surface. The media control the timing, the volume of coverage, and the position of the news or feature within their programs and publications. As you saw earlier, this is a drawback of publicity when compared with advertising, but nevertheless it has to be accepted because the organization is not paying for the coverage.

Prepare Final Public Relations Plan and Budget

Now that the activities and media vehicles have been chosen to satisfy public relations objectives, an organization can draft a final plan and budget. Again, it is wise in budgeting and overall planning to anticipate the unexpected by allocating specific persons and funds to handle such situations.

Measure and Evaluate Public Relations Success

Writing the last page of the plan is not the finale of the public relations planning process. It is important to understand how effective the public relations and publicity activities within the plan have been. Has each public's image or opinions of our organization improved, remained stable, or deteriorated? How many and which newspapers, magazines, and radio and television stations covered our news releases and feature stories? What other coverage did we get? What are the circulation rates of these magazines and newspapers, and how many people tuned into the radio and television programs? These are just a few typical questions that can be answered as part of the measurement and evaluation step. There are at least six different ways that public relations activities can be evaluated:[11]

1. **Evaluation by Those Responsible.** The evaluation can be based on the opinions and judgments of the public relations director, committee, or agent. This approach is not recommended on its own because the source has a definite interest in a positive evaluation. However, it can be used in conjunction with one or more of the other five methods.

2. **Visibility.** Here the organization measures the amount of publicity it received (e.g., press releases issued and covered, other positive mentions). This standard is also lacking because it focuses only on the publicity part of public relations, and usually ignores the counteractive effects of negative publicity. Again, it should not be used on its own, but in combination with other evaluation methods.

3. **Organizational Utility.** How available and prepared were public relations staff when negative publicity or other crisis situations emerged? It is crucial to an organization that its public relations team always be on the spot and ready to handle emergencies. Their ability to cope with the unexpected is definitely one evaluation standard that has great merit.

4. **Artistic Standards.** Did the public relations team follow principles, procedures, and practices generally considered acceptable by public relations professionals? What happens if a well-prepared news release does not get any media coverage? What if a press conference draws very few media because of an unexpected, competing news story of national significance? In other words, an organization may have followed all the right steps, but, because of circumstances beyond its control, the effectiveness of its efforts was not as great as intended. Therefore, evaluation must include consideration of not only what was and was not accomplished, but also how the public relations team tackled each activity.

5. **Change in Opinions, Attitudes, Images, and Issues.** This form of evaluation involves polling publics before and after implementing the plan or individual activities within it. Marketing research, frequently in the form of surveys, is used to determine changes in people's positions on certain issues or in their opinions, attitudes, or images of the organization and its services. This is a particularly valuable measurement and evaluation method, especially when it is used in conjunction with the next one.

6. **Evaluation by Objectives.** Did the plan meet its objectives? This is by far the best way to measure the success of a public relations plan. As this text has emphasized throughout, all objectives should be quantified, and measurements should be made to evaluate success. By how much did we want to improve people's attitudes toward our organization, and did we achieve this amount of change with our public relations plan? As you can see, the best approach to public relations evaluation is using a combination of methods 5 and 6. The other four methods should be used only to supplement these two approaches.

    The Institute for Public Relations gives some excellent suggestions for measuring public relations in a publication titled *Guidelines and Standards for Measuring and Evaluating PR Effectiveness.* This is available through the Institute's Web site at http://www.instituteforpr.com/. Four specific techniques are identified for measuring PR effectiveness:

a. Media content analysis—studying and tracking what is written and broadcast.
b. Cyberspace analysis—analyzing what is said about the organization in chat groups, forums, and news groups on the Web.
c. Trade shows and event measurement—assessing the benefits of attending trade shows and events.
d. Public opinion polls—determining if target audiences were exposed to particular messages, themes, or concepts, and then assessing their effectiveness through a survey.

PUBLIC RELATIONS CONSULTANTS

Public relations consultants perform a role quite similar to that of advertising agencies. They employ professionals who are skilled and experienced in public relations and publicity. Most of these public relations professionals belong to the Public Relations Society of America and abide by its "Code of Professional Standards for the Practice of Public Relations."

Like an advertising agency, the public relations firm assumes the responsibility for selecting, developing, and implementing all or some of an organization's public relations activities. Because of their size, salary scales, and degree of specialization, they attract and employ some of the best public relations professionals in the country. Some public relations firms are divisions of advertising agencies.

These outside experts help hospitality and travel organizations plan public relations and publicity activities. They do so by:

1. Helping to define public relations objectives
2. Selecting public relations activities and media vehicles
3. Using media contacts to get coverage for their clients
4. Providing creative services to develop various materials, programs, and events (e.g., preopening public relations programs, news releases, press conferences, feature stories) (Figure 18–6).
5. Conducting research to measure and evaluate the effectiveness of public relations activities and various aspects of an organization's image among its publics
6. Providing specialized assistance in dealing with specific publics (e.g., preparing an employee newsletter, liaising with the media, handling relations with government agencies, and preparing reports for shareholders)

Should a hospitality and travel organization hire a public relations consulting firm? The answer is exactly the same as it is for an advertising agency—if the organization can afford the firm's fees, it is advisable to retain their services. You should realize that many larger organizations have their own public relations departments with a full-time public relations director, but they still use outside professionals to carry out the work. Organizations choose to do this because the specialized agency has greater objectivity, media contacts, and breadth of experience than an in-house public relations department.

CHAPTER CONCLUSION

Public relations activities have a broader focus than other promotional mix elements. They involve an organization's relationships with all its publics, not just customers and travel trade intermediaries. The assumption is made that, in the long run, all the individuals and groups with whom an organization has contact have an impact on its success.

Contiki

EUROPE
AUSTRALIA
NEW ZEALAND
AFRICA
AMERICA
CANADA

Release At Will
July 1999

Contact: Christa Gesztasi/Anne Ryan
Herman Associates P.R.
(212) 338-0700
HermanPR@aol.com

YOUNGER TRAVELERS CAN NOW SEE THE
REAL TOUR EXPERIENCE VIA VIDEO ON CONTIKI'S WEBSITE

FOOTAGE FROM ACTUAL TOURS IS NOW VIEWABLE ON CONTIKI'S WEBSITE

Young travelers curious about the group tour experience can now see for themselves by watching video clips on the Contiki Holidays' Web site, located at www.contiki.com. The video clips feature actual footage shot on a Contiki European tour and Africa safari. Contiki is the world's largest tour company for 18- to 35-year-olds, offering a variety of escorted tours worldwide.

Twenty different video clips are available on the site, each running approximately one minute. The European clips feature one passenger's experience on tour, from arrival in London before meeting the tour group all the way through to the tour's conclusion. Viewers can watch her and the group enjoying sightseeing, evening entertainment at restaurants and clubs, actual hotel rooms on tour, traveling inside the motorcoach and more, providing a true sense of what can be expected when traveling with Contiki. Each clip is also accompanied by a short written travel journal entry, providing a well-rounded perspective on the entire experience.

The Africa video footage is of Contiki's Desert and Delta and Zambezi Discovery tours. Follow two passengers as they experience the sunrise over the dunes in Sossusvlei, cruise the wetlands of the Okavango Delta, enjoy the fun at Victoria Falls, relax on houseboats along Lake Kariba, and come in contact with monkeys, elephants, hippos and more.

"Younger travelers want to see for themselves what they might expect on a tour - not necessarily from pictures in a brochure," explains Lorraine Sharp, Contiki Holidays' vice president, sales and marketing. "Since these travelers may have some misconceptions about what a tour might be like, we thought showing real video footage would provide a more accurate picture of what they can expect."

The video is yet another way that Contiki is enabling younger travelers to research the tour experience in a more direct and personal way. The company's Web site already features message boards that enable

-more-

Contiki Holidays 2300 E. Katella Ave., #450 • Anaheim, CA 92806
Telephone: (714) 935-0808 • Reservations: (800) 266-8454 • Fax: (714) 935-2556
http://www.contiki.com

Contiki Holidays
Real Tour Experience/Page 2

potential travelers to pose questions to past passengers, as well as for future passengers to meet each other on-line before departing on tour. Another area enables travelers to correspond after their tours. The site also allows travelers to send customized E-mail postcards to friends and family back home while traveling abroad, plus a page featuring last-minute bargains (available exclusively online) and extensive information about the variety of tours available worldwide.

In business for 40 years, Contiki offers more than 100 different tours to Europe, the South Pacific, Africa and North America for 18- to 35-year-olds. Accommodations, most meals, transportation and sightseeing are all included in the tour price, which averages $75 per day. In addition, a young professional tour manager is always on hand to help along the way. Solo travelers can be matched with a same-sex roommate to avoid single supplement charges.

For more information and a free Contiki brochure, see your travel agent or call toll-free 1-800-CONTIKI; or log-on to www.contiki.com. Contiki is a member of USTOA.

###

◆ **FIGURE 18–6**   *An example of a news release prepared by a public relations agency.* (Courtesy of Contiki Holidays and Herman Associates Public Relations)

A plan is needed to guide the public relations effort. It should cover three types of activities—continuous; preplanned, short-term; and unpredictable, short-term. A contingency plan for negative publicity and other unexpected situations should be included.

Building positive relationships with the media is the key to getting the right type of publicity. The services of an outside public relations agency may help establish good media relations.

REVIEW QUESTIONS

1. How are the terms public relations and publicity defined in this chapter?
2. What are the roles of public relations and publicity in hospitality and travel marketing?
3. How important are public relations and publicity to hospitality and travel organizations? Explain your answer.
4. What are the twelve publics served by the hospitality and travel industry?
5. What are the nine steps that should be followed in developing a public relations plan?
6. What are the three basic categories of activities covered in a public relations plan?
7. Which techniques can be used to maintain positive relationships with publics?
8. What media vehicles are available for public relations, and which individuals should be contacted at each of them?
9. How can a hospitality and travel organization develop good media relations?
10. What are the roles and advantages of using public relations agencies and consultants?

CHAPTER ASSIGNMENTS

1. Interview the owner or manager of a hospitality and travel organization in your local area. Ask this person to define public relations or publicity. How does it compare with this book's definitions? What public relations activities does the organization undertake? What techniques and media vehicles are used? Does the organization have a public relations plan? Who is responsible for public relations? Based on your interview, can you recommend improvements in the organization's approaches to public relations and publicity? If so, what are they?

2. You have been asked to put together a public relations plan for an organization in our industry that is planning to introduce new services in an area (e.g., opening a new hotel, restaurant, travel agency, or car rental agency; or introducing a new air route or cruise excursion). What components would you include in the plan, and what steps would you follow? Which publics would be involved? How would you handle relations with the media? What, if any, special events would you use to publicize the new service or facilities? How would you evaluate the success of the plan?

3. Select a part of the hospitality and travel industry and examine the public relations activities of three of its leading organizations. Do they have a public relations department? How are they organized to handle the public relations function? Are outside agencies or consultants used? What public relations techniques and media vehicles are used? Have any of the organizations had to handle negative publicity recently, and how did they do this? Do you see similarities in their approaches, or are they all different? Which group does the best job of public relations, and why?

4. This chapter suggests that an organization must plan ahead to handle negative publicity. Assume that you are the public relations director for an organization in a specific part of our industry. What are five possible situations that might give your organization bad publicity? Be as specific as possible! Write a set of procedures for each situation that describes how you and others in your organization should handle these situations. In other words, how would you respond?

WORLD WIDE WEB RESOURCES

Associated Press
http://www.ap.org/

Burger King
http://www.burgerking.com/

Contiki Holidays
http://www.contiki.com/

Disney Company
http://www.disney.com/

Fairmont Hotels & Resorts
http://www.fairmont.com/

Institute for Public Relations
http://www.instituteforpr.com/

International Council on Hotel, Restaurant and Institutional Education (CHRIE)
http://www.chrie.org/

McDonald's Corporation
http://www.mcdonalds.com/

Marriott International
http://www.marriott.com/

Public Relations Society of America
http://www.prsa.org/

Radisson
http://www.radisson.com/

Red Lobster
http://www.redlobster.com/

Ronald McDonald House Charities
http://www.rmhc.com/

Royal Caribbean International
http://www.rccl.com/

United Press International
http://www.upi.com/

United Airlines
http://www.ual.com/

The Wire (News from the Associated Press)
http://wire.ap.org/

World's Leading Cruise Lines
http://www.leaderships.com/

REFERENCES

1. Goldman, Jordan. 1984. *Public Relations in the Marketing Mix.* Chicago: Crain Books, xi–xv.

2. Markey, Francis X. (2000). "Union clout is cleared for takeoff." http://www.dismal.com/.

3. Tourism Canada. 1982. *Planning and Operating a Festival.* Ottawa, Toronto: Author, 23–28.

4. Klein, Ted, and Fred Danzig. 1985. *Publicity: How to Make the Media Work for You.* New York: Charles Scribner's Sons, 126.

5. Zive, Jessica Dee. "Public relations for the hotel opening." *Cornell Hotel and Restaurant Administration Quarterly* 22 (1):2224 (1981).

6. Cosse, Jacques C. "Ink & air time: A public-relations primer." *Cornell Hotel and Restaurant Administration Quarterly* 21 (1):40 (1980).

7. Coffman, C. Dewitt. 1980. "Hospitality for sale." East Lansing, Mich.: Educational Institute of American Hotel & Motel Association, 103.

8. Klein, Ted, and Fred Danzig. 1985. *Publicity: How to Make the Media Work for You.* New York: Charles Scribner's Sons, 59.

9. Cosse, Jacques C. "Ink & air time: A public-relations primer." *Cornell Hotel and Restaurant Administration Quarterly* 21 (1):38 (1980).

10. Klein, Ted, and Fred Danzig. 1985. *Publicity: How to Make the Media Work for You.* New York: Charles Scribner's Sons, 4.

11. Crable, Richard E., and Steven L. Vibert. 1986. *Public Relations as Communication Management.* Edina, Minn.: Bellwether Press, 383–393.

For additional hospitality and travel marketing resources, visit our Web site at **www.Hospitality-Tourism.delmar.com**

19

Pricing
How Do We Get There?

Objectives

Having read this chapter, you should be able to:

◆ Describe the dual role of pricing.

◆ Explain pricing's role as an implicit promotional element.

◆ List and describe the unsophisticated and sophisticated pricing approaches.

◆ Explain the concept of target pricing.

◆ Describe break-even analysis and how it is used when making pricing decisions.

◆ Explain the multistage approach to pricing and, in the process, list the nine Cs of pricing.

◆ Explain the concept of value for money and how this relates to pricing.

Overview

Pricing is the final part of the marketing mix. This chapter begins by explaining that pricing is not only a direct determinant of profitability, but also a powerful promotional tool. Some inherent conflicts in the duality of pricing are identified.

There is a difference between the price of a service and the value for money that customers perceive they are receiving. The concept of

value for money is described. The chapter then points out that the hospitality and travel industry uses both unsophisticated and sophisticated pricing approaches. The recommended, cost-based method of pricing is discussed. The chapter ends by reviewing some specific pricing practices in different parts of the hospitality and travel industry.

Key Terms

break-even analysis	intuitive pricing	psychological pricing
competitive pricing	leader pricing	skimming
contribution margin	multistage approach to pricing	target pricing
cost-plus pricing	nine Cs of pricing	traditional (rule-of-thumb)
discounting	penetration	pricing
discriminatory pricing	price cutting	value for money
elasticity of demand	price discrimination	variable cost
fixed cost	price lining	yield management
follow-the-leader pricing	profit maximization	
Hubbart Formula	promotional pricing	

Have you ever watched the popular game show, "The Price Is Right?" If so, you know that contestants try to guess the prices of various products, ranging from groceries to expensive motor homes. Every show has several winners, an obvious necessity for staying on the air. Some people's guesses are surprisingly accurate, while others are way off the mark. What does this show have to do with marketing? The answer may surprise you—very little! When the pricing of hospitality services deteriorates into a guessing game, the price is definitely not right. Prices must be carefully researched. An organization must consider not only their impacts on revenues and profits, but also their effects on other marketing-mix elements.

There are good and bad approaches to pricing, all of which are evident in our industry. You have probably heard the term *price war* used in connection with airline, cruise, and hotel pricing. Like all other participants in wars, some companies are killed, others are wounded, and the fortunate ones return unscathed. Innocent bystanders sometimes are mortally injured in the crossfire. For example, travel agents see their commissions dwindling as airlines and suppliers offer deeper and deeper discounts. As you will see later, however, all price discounting is not necessarily bad if each party has a detailed knowledge of its costs and profit potential.

PRICING'S DUAL ROLE

One of the inherent problems with pricing is that it fulfills two sometimes contradictory roles. If you have taken a basic accounting or economics class, you already know that, along with costs and volumes of business, pricing is a direct determinant of profitability. The other role of pricing is as an implicit promotional-mix element. In a way, a price acts like a magnet—it attracts some customers and repels others. People tend to base their perceptions of services and products partly on the price. A price offer can also play a central role in an advertising campaign or sales promotion (e.g., a two-for-one sales promotion, looked at another way, is a 50-percent discount on two items).

Some authors say that pricing has both a *transactional* and *informational* dimension.[1] The dollar amount at which a service is offered for sale represents price's transactional dimension. Conventional wisdom suggests that the lower the price, the more of the service will be sold. Your economics class has probably described this relationship as a *downward-sloping demand curve.* As Figure 19–1 shows, the quantity

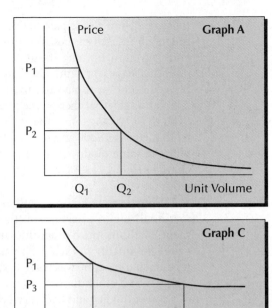

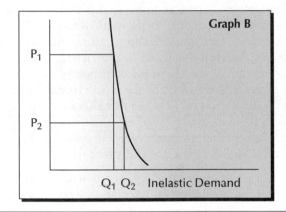

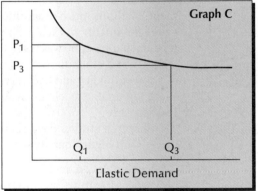

◆ **FIGURE 19–1**   *The transactional view of the price/quantity relationship.*

demanded falls as the price increases, but it increases when the price is lowered (graph A). The slope of the curve in Figure 19–1 varies with the **elasticity of demand** for the service. Demand elasticity measures the sensitivity of customer demand for services, to changes in their price. In an inelastic demand situation, customers are not very price sensitive. The slope of the demand curve is, therefore, very steep (graph B). On the other hand, customers are much more price sensitive when demand is elastic. Their demand curve is much flatter (graph C).

The graphs in Figure 19–1 are based on some very large assumptions. First, it is assumed that customers have full information on all hotels, airlines, restaurants, cruises, tour packages, travel destinations, or any other type of hospitality and travel service. Although this may be close to the truth for experts such as travel agents, most individual customers do not, in fact, have complete information on competitive offerings. A second major assumption is that customers gather information without considering the prices of each competitor's services. In other words, a price is a price, and it tells nothing else about the quality or features of services. This is often not the case, because customers tend to read a great deal into the prices of competitive items. A high price is frequently associated with high quality, whereas a low price has the opposite connotation.

Imagine that you are planning a trip to Europe and you are trying to choose a place to stay in London. Other than a long list of hotels with street addresses, numbers of rooms, and room rates, you have not been able to get complete information on the quality and range of services provided by each hotel. You narrow your list to five properties that are closest to the part of the city in which you want to stay. You cannot really tell much about each of these five possible hotels based on the number of rooms each has, and you know nothing about the streets and districts in which they are located. What does this leave you with? The answer, as you have probably already guessed, is the price of each hotel (or room rates in our example).

Let us say that there's one property with a room rate of £200 a night, three in the £100 to £120 range, and one at £40. What assumptions would you make about the hotel that charges £200 and the one that charges £40? Do you expect that each would provide the same quality and variety of services and facilities? What about the three that charge £100 to £120? Do you think that the services and facilities they offer would differ greatly?

Your answers to this hypothetical example should give you some idea of the informational role of pricing, and the function of pricing as an implicit promotional element. Without much other information on the London hotels, you had to use price to gauge the quality of each property. Let us see how you did. Did you think that the hotel that charges £200 was more luxurious, with top-quality service and a wide variety of facilities and amenities? Was your perception of the lowest priced property that it was of a lower quality and had very few of the frills provided by the most expensive hotel? Were you unable to tell much about the differences between the three hotels that charge £100 to £120?

Research studies have shown repeatedly that customers tend to associate higher prices with higher-quality services and facilities. This is especially true when:[2]

1. Customers do not have sufficient information or prior experiences to compare features of competitive offerings. As in our London example, they are forced to use price as their basis of comparison.
2. Services are perceived as complex, and there is a high risk of making a bad choice. Perhaps you will remember these as the extensive problem-solving or high-involvement decisions mentioned in previous chapters. Again, our London example is appropriate. For most of us, a trip to London and other parts of Europe involves complex decisions, with a relatively high risk of selecting unsatisfactory accommodations.
3. Services are perceived as having a certain snob appeal and carry social prestige. Can you think of any products that people buy for their snob appeal rather than their inherent qualities? How about Rolls Royce, Porsche, BMW, and Mercedes Benz automobiles? Maybe you thought of Rolex watches. In our London example, the prestige-conscious traveler would probably opt for the most expensive, £200 hotel.
4. The difference between the prices of competitive services is minimal. In this case, customers may choose the highest-priced service because they perceive an added guarantee of quality. In the London example, it is probable that you would select the highest-priced hotel in the £100 to £120 range, if the three hotels charge £107, £108, and £109, for example.

The graphs in Figure 19–1 all suggest that a higher price always results in less demand, and a lower price in greater sales. This is the transactional view of pricing. It is hoped that you now see that this is not always true because of pricing's impact as an implicit promotional element (its informational role). The demand curve for a prestige product or service looks more like the one shown in the graph in Figure 19–2. Demand actually increases, to a certain point, as the price goes up. The higher the price, the more exclusive and prestigious the services or products appear to certain customer groups.

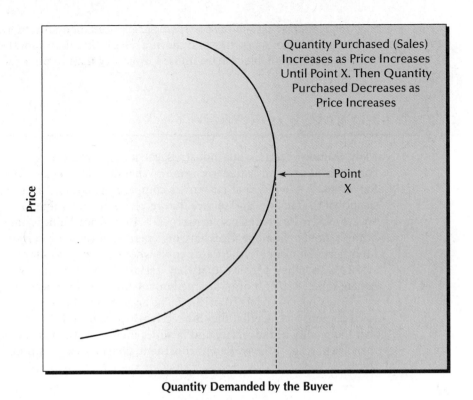

◆ FIGURE 19–2   *The demand curve for a prestigious hospitality and travel service.* (From Cohen, William A. 1988. *The Practice of Marketing Management,* Macmillan Publishing Company, 474)

The two-sided nature of pricing not only reflects its transactional and informational roles, but can also cause conflicts within hospitality and travel organizations. For example, sales representatives may feel internal pressure to build volumes (e.g., load factors on planes or occupied room nights in hotels) without sufficient regard for profitability. Price can be a powerful promotional tool in getting additional business, but merely having more volume does not necessarily increase an organization's profits. In other words, customers who are *bought* are not always profitable. American Airlines lost $50 million in 1979 when it imitated United Airlines, 50-percent-off coupons for future flights.[3] United was forced into this promotional approach because of a long labor dispute. American, however, had no such problem. American eventually dropped its discount coupon program, launching in its place the airline industry's first frequent-flyer program.

Hospitality and travel managers are often uneasy about having half-empty hotels, restaurants, cruise ships, or airplanes. In some ways, their concerns are very valid. As you will remember from Chapter 2, inventories of hospitality and travel services cannot be stored. They perish almost immediately. Therefore, is it better for managers and sales representatives to sell empty seats or rooms at any price than to lose their sale and use forever? Let us review the definition of marketing to help you answer this question. Marketing activities, including pricing, are designed to satisfy customers' needs *and* their organizations' objectives. For many organizations, the primary objective is to make a profit. Having a *fill-empty-spaces-at-any-cost* mentality, therefore, runs contrary to the definition of marketing and shows a sales rather than a marketing orientation. It is often more profitable to have unused inventory than to offer too large or too many price deals.

PRICING AND VALUE FOR MONEY

Many leading experts in our industry say that travelers are becoming increasingly value-conscious. They want **value for money**. What does this mean? One definition of value for money is the way that customers compare the amount of money they pay to the quality of the facilities and service they receive. For something to have value, it does not always have to be a bargain sold at a rock-bottom price. Value is only relevant in the eyes of the beholder. Some services have high perceived value for certain customers, but not for others. For example, there are people who pay high prices for luxury-oriented travel services, and they perceive that they get exceptional value for their money. Others equate value with economy-oriented or cut-rate travel services (e.g., economy hotels).

How does this relate to pricing? The answer is rather simple. A price must convey to customers a feeling that they are receiving value for money. They must be convinced that the quality of the service and facilities they are getting is consistent with the price they are paying. If the two are inconsistent, considerable customer dissatisfaction will result.

PLANNING PRICING APPROACHES

How do you know when the price is right? From Chapter 8 on, this book has stressed the importance of having objectives, and of basing the plans for each marketing-mix element on these objectives. The right pricing approach, therefore, begins with a set of clear pricing objectives. There are three steps involved in planning prices:

1. Set pricing objectives
2. Select pricing approaches
3. Measure and evaluate pricing success

Set Pricing Objectives

Most pricing objectives can be divided into three categories: (1) profit oriented, (2) sales oriented, and (3) status-quo oriented.[4]

1. **Profit-Oriented Pricing Objectives.** Prices can be established either to achieve certain targeted profit levels (**target pricing**) or to generate the maximum amount of profit (**profit maximization**). Target prices are usually expressed as certain percentage returns on investment or sales. Later in this chapter you will learn about a hotel pricing technique called the Hubbart Formula, which uses a target return on investment as its base. Target pricing is one of the best approaches to pricing available. With profit maximization, the company sets the price that will give it the greatest profits, based on forecasts of costs and customer demands. Profit maxi-

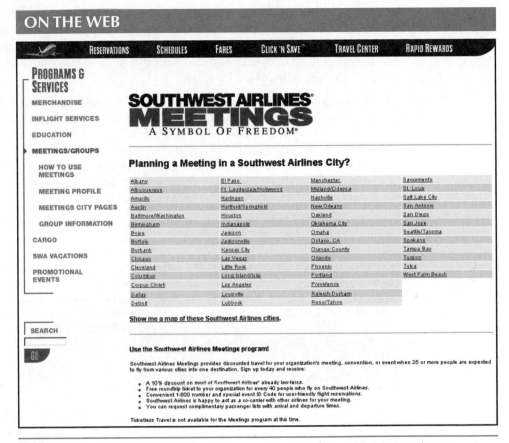

◆ **FIGURE 19–3**   *Southwest Airlines offers meeting attendees a 10 percent price cut.*
(Courtesy of Southwest Airlines)

mization objectives tend to be used more in the short term, whereas target pricing is more suitable for long-term application.

2. **Sales-Oriented Pricing Objectives.** Sales-oriented pricing emphasizes sales volumes rather than profits. The company uses price as a tool either to increase its sales to a maximum or targeted level or to get a larger share of the market. This chapter has already alerted you to the fact that sales-oriented pricing does not necessarily lead to increased profits. Despite the real need for caution, sales-oriented pricing approaches have proven extremely successful over several years for some companies. An example is grocery store chains that offer limited services, buy in bulk, and sell items at substantial discounts. Southwest Airlines is another good example of a *discounter* with sales-oriented objectives in our industry. With its low-fare and no-frills policy, Southwest was one of the few U.S. domestic airlines to operate profitably in the 1990s, Figure 19–3.

Sales-oriented pricing objectives can be either long or short term (Figure 19–4). In Motel 6's case, low rates are part of their long-term pricing approaches.

Short-term applications include many of those involved with sales promotions, which were discussed in Chapter 16. Couponing, for example, usually includes price discounting to increase sales in the short term. The seasonal demand patterns for many hospitality and travel services also force many companies to use price as an inducement in off-peak periods.

3. **Status-Quo-Oriented Pricing.** With status-quo objectives, the company tries to avoid large sales swings and maintain its position relative to competitors and travel trade intermediaries. The most common use of this approach is by companies that try to match competitors' prices closely (the **competitive pricing** approach). In certain parts of our industry, smaller-share companies adjust their prices to match more closely those of the market leaders (e.g., Burger King, Wendy's, and Hardee's following McDonald's price changes—the **follow-the-leader pricing** approach).

ON THE WEB

◆ FIGURE 19–4   *Low prices are the long-term pricing approach at Rent-A-Wreck.* (Courtesy of Rent-A-Wreck, Inc.)

EXCELLENCE CASE

Pricing:
Rent-A-Wreck, Inc.

This chapter mentions that some hospitality and travel companies start off with the intention of using low prices forever. Rent-A-Wreck, a division of Bundy American Corporation, is an excellent example of a successful application of this long-term, low-rate approach.

Rent-A-Wreck rents cars, vans, station wagons, and trucks for rates around 50 to 75 percent of those charged by the major car rental companies. How can it afford to do so? The answer is that it buys and rents used cars. Vehicles are generally between two and four years old and are in excellent operating condition. They're definitely not wrecks, as the company name seems to indicate. The positioning statement "Don't let the name fool you" makes sure that customers do not get the wrong impression.

The original idea of Rent-A-Wreck was conceived by David Schwartz in West Los Angeles in the early 1970s. Mr. Schwartz had an interesting background for the business, having worked his way through UCLA by buying and selling cars for his friends. He remains a driving force in the company and continues to operate a successful

(Photo courtesy of Rent-A-Wreck, Inc.)

franchise in the Los Angeles area. Through a franchising program introduced in 1978, the company now has more than 675 offices in United States, Australia, Canada, Holland, Norway, Sweden, New Zealand, and the United Arab Emirates. Shares in the company are publicly traded.

Rent-A-Wreck has two distinct target markets. First, there are people away from home, traveling for business, pleasure, or personal reasons. They are the travelers this book focuses on. Rent-A-Wreck also serves local markets, providing short- and long-term (3 to 12 month) rentals for those who are without their cars, are moving to another house, or have assorted other reasons. The company states that the average length of a car rental in the United States is about 3½ days. At Rent-A-Wreck it is about 9 days. Obviously, the company appeals to the more price-conscious renter and to persons who need vehicles for more than just a few days.

Traditionally, Rent-A-Wreck offices have not been at airports, but at the places of business of franchisees, many of whom are used- and new-car dealers. Again, this is an approach that helps the company keep its overhead costs and, therefore, its rental rates low.

Rent-A-Wreck is an excellent example of a hospitality and travel organization that is using sales-oriented pricing objectives and undercutting competition by maintaining low operating costs.

Discussion Questions

1. How is Rent-A-Wreck's approach to pricing unique and different from that of most of its competitors?
2. What types of customers would be most attracted to Rent-A-Wreck because of its pricing approach?
3. Which other hospitality and travel companies use a low-price approach, and how do they market themselves?

Web Site

http://www.rentawreck.com/

Did You Know?

Average daily rates on New Year's Eve 1999

✓ Smith Travel Research measured the average daily rates for hotels the evening before the new millennium.

✓ Here are the highest rates (with the occupancy percents shown in parentheses):
- Oahu, Hawaii, $342.62 (84.9%)
- New York, $301.20 (85.5%)
- New Orleans, $204.77 (80.1%)
- Miami, $196.27 (81.3%)
- Boston, $185.76 (65.1%)
- Chicago, $173.23 (77.1%)
- San Francisco, $157.38 (62.7%)
- Philadelphia, $139.94 (67.3%)

✓ Web site can be accessed at http://www.str-online.com/

SELECT PRICING APPROACHES

Once pricing objectives are understood, a company can make an informed choice among several available pricing approaches. These can be divided into three distinct categories—unsophisticated, sophisticated, and multistage.

Categories of Pricing Approaches

1. **Unsophisticated Approaches.** The approaches in this category are unsophisticated because they rely less on research and cost considerations than they do on the intuition of managers. They are generally not recommended, but are discussed here because they occur in our industry.

   a. *Competitive Approach.* As you have already seen, this is a status-quo approach to pricing—companies set prices based on their competitors' prices. It tends to be a reactive or *wait-and-see* method, because prices are moved up or down as competitors' price changes become known. In today's highly competitive hospitality and travel markets, it is essential to consider one's competitors when pricing, but this should not be the only consideration. Every individual organization has a different cost/profit structure and customer base. A certain price level may produce large profits for one company but result in no profits or a loss for another.

   b. *Follow-the-Leader Approach.* This is a modification of the general competitive pricing approach used mainly by smaller market-share companies. Again, it is a reactive rather than a preplanned method. Smaller companies wait for the new prices introduced by the market leader or leaders, and then they peg their own prices to these. In general, changes follow the direction (either up or down) of the larger firms. Because most smaller organizations operate with more slender profit margins than those of the market leaders (who enjoy considerable economies of scale), it can be dangerous for them to follow the leaders blindly. Market leaders, because of their volume advantage, can generally absorb larger cuts in prices. They also have more to gain from slight increases in prices.

c. *Intuitive Approach.* Intuitive pricing is the least scientific method, because it involves no research on costs, competitive prices, or customer expectations. Some have called it the *gut feel* approach because it relies most heavily on the manager's intuition.[5] You already know how important marketing research is to effective marketing decisions. Thus, you will quickly realize that this is not a good pricing approach.

d. *Traditional or Rule-of-Thumb Approach.* Over the years, certain traditional or rule-of-thumb pricing has developed in various parts of the hospitality and travel industry. In the lodging sector, it was believed in the 1970s that $1 should be charged for every $1,000 of capital invested per room in each property. For example, a hotel that cost $100,000 per room to build should have a room rate of $100. Another with a per-room investment of $150,000 should charge $150. Many now believe that this rule of thumb has become obsolete as hotel construction costs have escalated quickly and intense competition has held hotel rates down.[6] Because a 40-percent food cost was quite typical among restaurants in the 1970s, multiplying a dish's food costs by a factor of two and one-half was a common rule of thumb. The mechanics of this approach are very simple—just find out what the rule of thumb is and plug in your own numbers. However, you have probably already spotted serious flaws in this approach. Again, there is no research or consideration of customer expectations and competitive prices.

All four unsophisticated approaches have some common features. First, they are based on little, if any, research. Second, they take into account only one of the factors that influences prices—what competitors are charging. Third, they do not consider an organization's unique cost/profit structure or its customers' expectations and preferences.

Before we discuss the more sophisticated, research-based pricing approaches, you should know more about the variety of factors that influence prices. A discussion of these factors follows.

Customer Characteristics

The characteristics of customers should play a key role in determining prices. Some customers are extremely price-sensitive and will react quickly to even minor price changes (remember elastic demand?). Others do not change their buying habits, even after major price moves (inelastic demand). You will probably recall the discussion of high- and low-involvement purchase decisions. It is definitely easier to set high prices and to pass major price increases to high-involvement customers, because they are less price-sensitive.

Based on the target markets served, it may be possible to use price discrimination (also sometimes called discriminatory pricing). Here, two or more prices are set to appeal specifically to their respective target markets. Economy, business, and first-class airfares are an example, as are the array of rates that most large hotels offer (e.g., regular *rack,* commercial, tour group, government, and airline crew rates, Figure 19–5). The term yield management (or revenue management) refers to an application of price discrimination by target market. Yield management is a revenue management approach used by airlines, hotels, cruise lines, car rental firms, and others to maximize the sale of their perishable inventories by controlling prices and capacity.[7] In simpler language, yield management means selling the right inventory unit (seat, room, berth, or vehicle) to the right customer (target market) at the right time and for the right price.[8]

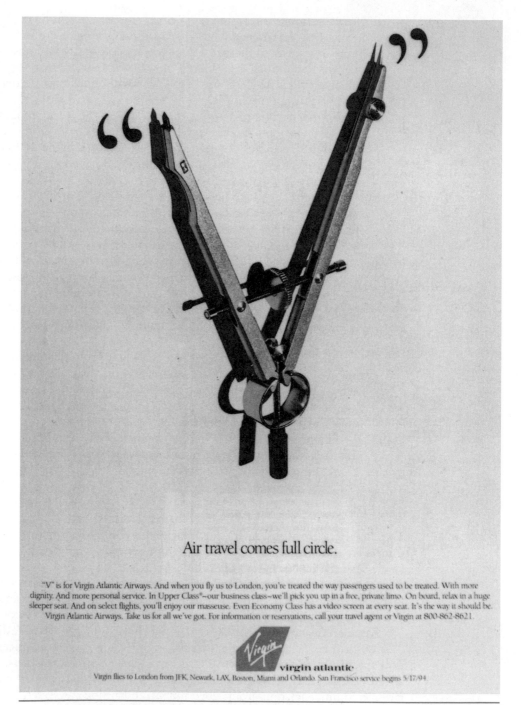

◆ **FIGURE 19–5**   *Virgin Atlantic demonstrates price discrimination by an airline. Business class becomes "upper class." (Courtesy of Virgin Atlantic)*

Corporate Objectives

Because prices are a direct determinant of profitability, the responsibility for pricing is not usually entrusted solely to the marketing manager. Prices must be set in the context of the overall corporate objectives that were discussed in Chapter 3. These objectives may, for example, be stated in terms of profit levels, market share, or sales-volume targets.

Corporate Image and Positioning

Prices should be consistent with the overall company image and positioning approaches. For example, a hotel company or cruise line that chooses to communicate a prestige or deluxe image should set prices well above the average. On the other hand, a hospitality and travel organization emphasizing economy would be advised to take the opposite tack.

Customer Demand Volumes

Another important part of the pricing equation includes the probable volumes of customer demand. The demand for most hospitality and travel services fluctuates widely by season, month, week, day of the week (weekend versus weekday), or even time of day. Added pressure is put on managers to fill off-peak periods because the services are so perishable (remember this from Chapter 2?). Price discrimination by time period is a tool heavily used by our industry to smooth out demand patterns. Examples include early-bird specials in restaurants, special weekend rates at city hotels, off-peak airfares on certain routes, preseason rates on cruise lines and at resorts, and reduced weekend car-rental rates.

Costs

Although discussed in more detail later, costs are another important consideration in arriving at prices. The weakness of most of the unsophisticated pricing approaches is their lack of regard for potential costs. Research into likely costs is a must in effective pricing.

Competition

Although the competitive pricing approach is not recommended on its own, no company should set prices without some reference to their competitors' price levels. Intensifying competition is expected in all parts of the hospitality and travel industry. Customers are also becoming increasingly value-conscious. Rather than using the *wait-and-see* or reactive method discussed earlier, it is much more effective for a company to use a proactive approach, anticipating how their organization's price changes will influence those of competitors.

Channels

When establishing prices for services to be sold through travel trade intermediaries, commissions must be taken into account. The actual revenues that airlines, hotels, car rental firms, tour wholesalers, and others realize through travel agent sales are some percentage below the price that the customer sees and pays. For example, domestic airlines receive 96 percent of fares after taxes, and after the typical 4 to 5 percent agent commission.

Complementary Services and Facilities

How will the price of one item affect the sales of others? This is another important consideration, because most companies in our industry sell a variety of services and facilities at different prices (e.g., different airline routes; cruising destinations; brands of lodging properties; menu items; and classes of automobiles, tours and vacation packages). One typical concern is that lowering the price of one item too much may draw sales away from higher-profit services. In other words, a company must adopt a portfolio approach to pricing, rather than pricing each item individually and ignoring the potential impacts on others.

Consistency with Marketing-Mix Elements and Strategy

Do you remember the traditional four Ps of marketing: product, price, place, and promotion? Throughout this book there is an emphasis on ensuring that these four marketing-mix elements are as consistent as possible. For example, higher prices seem appropriate if a company is providing a deluxe or premium service. Economical prices fit better with bare bones service concepts.

Have you noticed anything peculiar about the nine price-influencing factors just reviewed? Do you see something that they share in common? Give yourself some applause if you noticed that all nine factors begin with the letter *C*. You might recall these factors better if you think of them as the **nine Cs of pricing**.

2. **Sophisticated Approaches.** What you have just learned is that pricing involves balancing a variety of factors carefully. You now know that it is insufficient to look at one factor only, such as competitive prices. The more sophisticated pricing ap-

A Touch of Technology

Priceline.com

- ◆ Priceline.com is a Web-based service that allows travelers to bid the prices they want to pay for airline tickets and other travel services (cars and hotel rooms).

- ◆ Priceline.com started offering the service in April 1998.

- ◆ It uses a technique known as a *reverse auction*.

- ◆ Customers enter where and when they want to travel by air, name a price and commit to the price with a credit card, and then wait to see if any airlines accept the price offer.

- ◆ A number of U.S. domestic and international airlines provide their inventory through Priceline.com.

- ◆ The company hopes to expand its services by offering other nontravel products and services in the future.

- ◆ The Web site can be accessed at http://www.priceline.com/

proaches are normally used only after a company has carefully researched the consequences of pricing decisions.

a. ***Target Pricing.*** *Target pricing* is an example of a pricing approach based on a profit-oriented objective. The target is usually set in terms of a specific return on investment that the company wants to achieve. In some cases, the target may be expressed as a percentage of sales.

One target pricing method that is popular in the lodging industry is the Hubbart Formula. It is used to establish room rates and involves building an income statement up from the bottom to determine the rate that is necessary to provide a predetermined return on investment. Figure 19–6 shows how a *Hubbart Formula* room rate is calculated. The rate thus calculated does not include travel agent commissions and discounts offered to specific target markets. These two items must be projected before a final, advertised (or *rack*) rate can be estimated. Figure 19–7 provides a hypothetical example of such a calculation.

	Desired After-Tax Return on Investment
PLUS	
	Income Taxes
	Interest Charges
	Insurance
	Property Taxes
	Depreciation
	Administrative and General Expenses
	Marketing
	Energy Costs
	Property Operation and Maintenance
MINUS	
	Food and Beverage Department Revenues
	Telephone Department Revenues
	Other Department Revenues
PLUS	
	Food and Beverage Expenses
	Telephone Expenses
	Other Department Expenses
EQUALS	
	Required Room Profit
PLUS	
	Room Expenses
EQUALS	
	Required Room Revenues
ALL DIVIDED BY	
	Projected Number of Occupied Room Nights
EQUALS	
	Average Rate per Occupied Room Night After Discounts and Commissions

◆ FIGURE 19–6 *Example of target pricing: Hubbart formula method of determining room rates.* (Adapted from "Tourism is your business: Marketing management," 1986. Reproduced with the permission of Public Works and Government Services Canada, 2001.)

Required Room Revenues $555,476

Projected % of Occupied Room Nights = (total rooms ×
                                       365/year) × % occ
                                       Occupancy Rate = 0.65   11863

Target Average Net Rate Per Occupied Room Night = $46.83

Step Two: Calculate Specific Room Rates for Each Target Market

Target Markets	Occupied Room Nights	Percent	Discounts Offered	Avg. No. of Persons per room
Regular Business	593.13	5%	5.0%	1
Commercial Rate Business	593.13	5%	12.5%	1
Conference/Meeting Groups	4745.00	40%	20.0%	1.5
Motor Coach Tour Groups	1779.38	15%	25.0%	2
Pleasure Travellers	4151.88	35%	15.0%	2.5
TOTAL	11862.50	100%		1.5

Required Average Rate Before Discounting Equals $64.70

Required Average Rates by Target Market	Required Average Before Discount	Less Discount	Average Rate	Single Rate	Double Rate
Regular Business	$64.70	5%	$61.46	$61.46	—
Commercial Rate Business	$64.70	13%	$56.61	$56.61	—
Conference/Meeting Groups	$64.70	20%	$51.76	$49.26	$54.26
Motor Coach Tour Groups	$64.70	25%	$48.52	—	$48.52
Pleasure Travellers	$64.70	15%	$54.99	—	$54.99

Target Markets	Number of Room Nights	×	Average Rate		Revenues
Regular Business	593.125	×	$61.46	=	$36,456
Commercial Rate Business	593.125	×	$56.61	=	$33,578
Conference/Meeting (single)	2372.5	×	$49.26	=	$116,868
Conference/Meeting (double)	2372.5	×	$54.26	=	$128,731
Motor Coach Tour Groups	1779.375	×	$48.52	=	$86,343
Pleasure Travellers	4151.875	×	$54.99	=	$228,331
TOTAL ROOM REVENUES	11862.5	×	$53.13	=	$630,307

◆ FIGURE 19–7   *Hypothetical Hubbart Formula example for a hotel. How discounts and commissions are handled by the Hubbart Formula.*

Target pricing methods, such as the Hubbart Formula, are effective because they consider several of the nine Cs of pricing:

- A detailed forecast of costs and profit levels (Costs)
- Estimates of demand (Customer Demand Volumes)
- Consideration of price preferences of individual target markets (Customer Characteristics)
- Specifications of financial objectives (Corporate Objectives)
- Estimates of commissions paid to travel trade intermediaries (Channels)

Once the target rate is calculated, it may be adjusted slightly in relation to competitors' prices or for better alignment with the corporate image/positioning.

b. ***Price Discounting and Discrimination.*** **Discounting** is a common practice in certain parts of the hospitality and travel industry. Simply stated, it means offering fares, rates, or prices below those advertised. **Discriminatory pricing** (also sometimes referred to as price discrimination) is a form of discounting. In discriminatory pricing and discounting in general, services are sold to some customers at lower prices, Figures 19–8a & b. However, the price gap does not actually reflect any real difference in the costs of providing the service. Here are a few examples:

- Many fast-food chains offer discounts to senior citizens (often requiring customers to show proof of age or a *house* card certifying their status as senior citizens).
- Several major national airlines and lodging chains have clubs for older travelers. After paying a modest membership fee, these travelers receive discounts on airfares and related supplier services (e.g., hotels and car rentals). United Airlines' *Silver Wings Plus* offers people age 55 and over discounts on published fares, and many other travel price breaks, Figure 19–9.
- Most major car rental firms have corporate rate plans. Business travelers who join these plans automatically receive discounted rental rates.
- Almost all hotels and resorts have a multitiered list of rates. The corporate or commercial rate is by far the most common discounted rate, and it works much like the program used by car rental firms. Other *below-rack* rates often include those for government personnel, airline crews, tour groups, convention/meeting guests, seniors, and sports teams.

(a)

(b)

◆ **FIGURE 19–8**   *Why price discounting and discrimination? (a) Price discounting may have filled these seats. (b) Price discrimination may have put people in this room.* (Courtesy of Continental Companies)

◆ **FIGURE 19–9**   *United Silver Wings Plus program appeals to the 55 and overs.* (Courtesy of United Airlines)

Discounting and discriminatory pricing can be based on four different criteria. They include target market, form of service provided, image place, and time.[9]

- **Target market**—You have already read several examples of this type of discounting, for example, some target senior citizens and business travelers.
- **Form of service provided**—A few *add-on* services are not provided, but the discount that is offered is much greater than the cost of the deleted services. For example, an airline offering a discount fare may not issue boarding passes to passengers until check-in time.
- **Place**—Prices are varied according to the location of the facilities and services. For example, some resorts charge more for beachfront rooms, although other rooms are available at lower prices.
- **Time**—Discounting according to time period is a very common practice in our industry because of the perishability factor. The weekend packages now offered by most urban hotels are a good example. Room rates are discounted to attract pleasure travelers on weekends, when business volumes traditionally fall from their weekday highs. *Early-bird* discounts offered by restaurants are another example; diners are given a price break if they eat before rush periods.

Originated by the airlines, the practice of yield management is an example of discriminatory pricing based upon several of the previously mentioned criteria. You probably know about the advance-booking and nonrefundable fares that have become popular. In addition to the standard three-class system (economy/coach, business/club, and first class), typical restrictions include day of departure, minimum length of stay, Saturday stayovers, and the ability to modify or cancel the itinerary.

The types of price reductions involved in discounting are not the **price cutting** (or *price slashing*) variety used by companies that react quickly and often rashly to competitors' price moves. Discounts are carefully researched and preplanned pricing programs are designed to achieve specific objectives. They are based on a thorough review of the impact they will have on costs and profits. Discounting programs are often instituted for several months or years.

One technique that is most useful in establishing discount programs is **break-even analysis**. It involves developing charts that show the relationship of costs, customer demand volumes, and profits. These charts help managers determine the points at which certain prices or customer demand volumes will cover all the fixed and variable costs of providing the services. These are called the *break-even points*. A **fixed cost** does not vary with the volume of sales (e.g., property taxes on buildings, interest charges on equipment). A **variable cost** changes directly with sales volume (e.g., a 10-percent increase in sales produces a 10-percent increase in the variable cost item). Labor costs and materials used in the production process are normally variable costs. A good example is the cost of food in restaurant meals.

Figure 19–10 shows a break-even chart for a hypothetical situation. As you can see, the total units purchased are plotted on the horizontal axis. Costs and revenues are measured on the vertical axis. The break-even point is where the total revenue line intersects the total cost (fixed plus variable) line. Figure 19–10 assumes the following:

- The variable cost per unit sold is $30.
- The selling price per unit is $100.
- The **contribution margin** (difference between selling price and variable costs per unit) is $70 (i.e., $100 minus $30).
- Total fixed costs are $280,000.

The formula for calculating the break-even point is

$$\text{BREAK-EVEN POINT (UNITS)} = \frac{\text{TOTAL FIXED COSTS}}{\text{CONTRIBUTION MARGIN}}$$

$$= \frac{\text{TOTAL FIXED COSTS}}{\text{SELLING PRICE PER UNIT} - \text{VARIABLE COST PER UNIT}}$$

In the Figure 19–10 example, the break-even point is 4,000 units (which could, for example, be occupied room nights in a hotel, or airline or cruise passengers). The 4,000 figure was calculated as follows:

$$\text{BREAK-EVEN POINT (see Figure 19–10)} = \frac{\$280,000}{\$100 - \$30} = \frac{\$280,000}{\$70} = 4,000 \text{ units}$$

Total Costs & Revenues

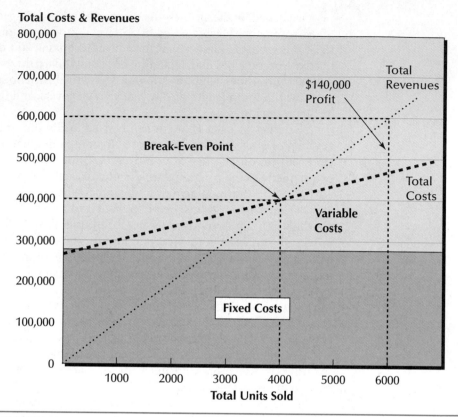

◆ FIGURE 19–10   *Break-even chart.*

What would happen if the selling price in Figure 19–10 was lower than $100—$65, for example? As you have probably guessed, the break-even volume of units would increase. In fact, it would double from 4,000 to 8,000 ($280,000/$65 − $30).

Besides helping to identify the break-even point, the charts can be used in target pricing. If the company knows how much profit it needs to generate a desired return on sales or investment, it can determine the required sales volumes in units and dollars. Take another look at Figure 19–10 and you will see how this works. Let us say that this company needs a profit of $140,000 to provide its targeted return on investment. To determine the break-even point, the following formula is used:

$$\text{BREAK-EVEN POINT} \atop \text{(for \$140,000 profit)} = \frac{\text{TOTAL FIXED COSTS + TARGET PROFIT}}{\text{SELLING} \atop \text{PRICE PER UNIT} - {\text{VARIABLE} \atop \text{COST PER UNIT}}}$$

$$= \frac{\$280,000 + \$140,000}{\$100 - \$30}$$

$$= \frac{\$420,000}{\$70} = 6,000 \text{ units}$$

The sales volume required to achieve the $140,000 profit objective is $600,000 (6,000 × $100 per unit).

There are some limitations to a break-even analysis, and you should be aware of them. First, such an analysis assumes that the variable cost per unit sold is exactly the same at every sales-volume level. But there are often some cost items that do not vary directly with sales volumes (e.g., a 100-percent increase in unit sales produces a 60-percent increase in costs, not a 100-percent increase). Second, break-even analysis assumes that fixed costs remain constant at all levels of production. This is not always the case, because fixed costs may increase at certain levels of sales (e.g., more equipment is required and the company borrows additional funds to finance the purchase, which results in increased interest charges). A third, questionable assumption is that price has no impact on market demand. Despite these limitations, break-even analysis is a useful tool for analyzing the relationships of costs, prices, customer demand volumes, and profits.

c. **Promotional Pricing.** Promotional pricing involves using short-term price reductions to stimulate temporary sales increases. Many types of sales promotions (which were outlined in Chapter 16) fit into this category, such as two-for-one and cents-off coupon offers.

d. **Cost-Plus Pricing.** Cost-plus pricing, also known as *markup* pricing, involves adding a certain dollar amount or percentage to the actual or estimated costs of a service to arrive at a final price. This dollar amount or percentage represents the desired contribution margin. For example, Figure 19–10 showed a mark-up of $3^{1}/_{3}$ on variable costs per unit of $30 (the selling price was $3^{1}/_{3}$ × $30, or $100). Using traditional, rule-of-thumb markups in a particular part of the industry is not recommended, as you saw earlier. In addition, using cost-plus pricing on its own is not the ideal approach. It is much better to combine cost-plus pricing with other techniques, such as break-even analysis, and also to consider other elements of the nine Cs of pricing besides costs.

e. **New-Product Pricing.** Many companies find that they can justify changing prices to correspond to the product life cycles of their services and facilities. Chapter 8 identified four potential strategies to introduce a new service: (1) rapid skimming, (2) slow skimming, (3) rapid penetration, and (4) slow penetration. In price skimming, the organization charges an artificially high price, because it knows that there are some customers who are willing to pay this price so they can be among the first users of the service.[10] A skimming price is artificial because the company knows that it will eventually have to reduce the price. For example, the first tourist into space in 2001 paid a premium to do so. Penetration pricing uses the opposite approach—introducing a new service at a low price to get a quick stronghold on a significant share of a market. The Southwest Airlines case discussed earlier is a good example. The company offers cut-rate fares to grab a sizeable share of the domestic airline travel market. A company using the penetration-pricing approach may or may not intend to continue it in the long run.

f. **Price Lining.** Price lining is a technique borrowed from the retailing industry, especially retailers of clothing. It involves preestablishing prices that the company feels confident will attract customers. For example, a restaurant may find from experience that the most popular prices for its entrees are $7.95, $9.95, and $11.95. When it changes its menus, therefore, it looks for dishes that can be sold for these prices and provide a satisfactory profit. Another example is a travel agency that establishes a range of prices for vacation packages that best suits its clientele.

g. ***Psychological and Odd Pricing.*** This is a *finishing-touch* pricing method, in which a price that has been set by using another pricing technique is modified slightly to provide added appeal. The basic strategy is to avoid prices set in round numbers, such as $10, $100, or $1,000. Psychological pricing means using slightly lower prices to give customers the perception of added value. The Club Med advertisement in Figure 19–11 is an example of psychological pricing. Instead of listing a price rounded off to the nearest $100, Club Med uses an $899 figure for its Family Escape package.

You will notice many prices that use some odd numbers, rather than only even numbers (e.g., prices ending with forty-five cents, forty-nine cents, ninety-five cents, ninety-nine cents, or ninety-nine dollars). These numbers are based on the belief that odd numbers induce greater sales than rounded, even ones such as fifty cents, one dollar, or one hundred dollars.[11]

h. ***Leader Pricing.*** Leader pricing is a form of promotional pricing in which a company offers one or more services or products for a short time at a price below its actual costs. These items are commonly referred to as *loss leaders*. Very common among retail stores, leader pricing is used by some hospitality and travel companies. For example, some pizza-delivery companies offer free Cokes with the purchase of a pizza (the Coke is the loss leader). The role of the reduced-price items is to induce sales of other items offered by the company (in this example, the pizza).

3. **Multistage Approach.** This chapter has outlined a wide variety of pricing techniques, some very unsophisticated and others more technically correct. You know that pricing should carefully consider nine factors (competitors, customer characteristics, customer demand volumes, costs, channels, corporate objectives, corporate image and positioning, complementary services and facilities, and consistency with marketing-mix elements and strategy). For effective pricing, therefore, a multistage approach is required, including the following steps:[12,13]

   a. Determine company objectives and specific pricing objectives (Corporate Objectives).
   b. Identify and analyze the target market or markets (Customer Characteristics).
   c. Consider the company's image and the positioning of services relative to target market or markets (Corporate Image and Positioning).
   d. Forecast the demand for services at various price levels (Customer Demand Volumes).
   e. Determine the costs of providing services (Costs).
   f. Evaluate potential competitive reactions to alternative prices (Competitors).
   g. Consider the impact of prices on travel trade intermediaries (Channels).
   h. Consider the impact of prices on sales of complementary services or facilities (Complementary Services and Facilities).
   i. Consider the impact of prices on other marketing-mix elements and other aspects of the marketing strategy (Consistency with Marketing-Mix Elements and Strategy).
   j. Select and use a pricing approach to arrive at a final price.

Club Med
Family Escape

Your clients pick the week. Club Med picks the beach.

Offer the Family Escape Package!
It's a great way for your clients to save money on their next family vacation. All they do is tell you which week they want to escape. Then for as low as $899 per person, we'll set up their dream vacation at one of our beautiful villages. One week prior to departure, we'll tell you which village they're going to enjoy.

And because it's Club Med, you can assure them that no matter where they go, they'll have everything they need for a wonderful time together. They can count on our experienced GO's, special facilities for kids, and lots of exciting activities for the entire family.

Caravelle, Guadeloupe
Huatulco, Mexico
Ixtapa, Mexico
Punta Cana, Dominican Republic
Sandpiper, Florida
St. Lucia, British West Indies

**7 NIGHTS
INCLUDING AIRFARE**
STARTING FROM
$**899***
PER ADULT
DEPARTURES MAY 6 TO AUGUST 26, 2000
CONVENIENT WEEKEND DEPARTURES

re-member, 120 villages worldwide!

At Club Med, it's all included: airfare, accommodations, all meals, unlimited beer and wine with lunch & dinner, most sports, entertainment, even trip insurance. As for tipping, it's simply not permitted.

Ask about our summer specials

Call 1-800 CLUB MED
Tour our website at clubmed.com

Departures are on Fridays, Saturdays or Sundays. Prices valid only for select dates/locations shown and are subject to change without notice. Prices are per person, double occupancy, standard room. Adult prices apply to all guests 12 years and older. Government, per person taxes/fees of between $23 and $189 are additional. A fuel surcharge of $50 is also additional. Annual Club Med Membership fees of $50 per Adult and $20 per child and one-time initiation fee of $30 per family are additional. Availability and seats are limited and may not be available on all flights or days. Some flights may be Club Med charters, see Operator-Participant Contract for details. Prices are for new individual booking. Not applicable for groups, or individuals traveling within groups. Other restrictions apply, including brochure terms and cancellation/change fees. Not responsible for errors or omissions. California Sellers of Travel CST 2020955-50.

Re-new ♆

◆ **FIGURE 19–11**   *Club Med uses psychological pricing in its trade advertisement.* (Courtesy of Club Med)

Using the multistage approach helps organizations decide which pricing approaches and specific price levels are most appropriate. As each stage is completed, the range of potential prices and pricing approaches narrows, making pricing decisions easier.

Measure and Evaluate Pricing Success

How did the selected pricing approach influence sales? This is the last of three steps in price planning, but no less important than the first two. While both price and sales changes are very measurable, it is often difficult to separate out the impact on sales by pricing alone. Other factors, such as the organization's nonprice promotions, changes in customer spending patterns, competition, local industrial activity patterns, and even the weather may also have had an impact on sales. Therefore, it is important when measuring the success of pricing to keep track of these other factors—especially competitors' prices—and to estimate their influence on sales. For example, in Chapter 15 through 18, you learned about some of the methods for measuring and evaluating the success of each promotional mix element.

The best way to evaluate pricing success is again through marketing research. Research studies can be designed to determine if new customers were attracted by price or whether other factors were more important. Noncustomers can be surveyed to find out why a new pricing approach did not appeal to them. Whatever research design is chosen, the most important factor is that thorough research and analysis be done to back up the measurement of price and sales changes.

CHAPTER CONCLUSION

Arriving at the right prices for hospitality and travel services is important for marketing as well as profitability reasons. Both unsophisticated and sophisticated pricing approaches are used in the hospitality and travel industry.

The most effective pricing results from a multistage approach that considers nine factors (corporate objectives, customer characteristics, corporate image and positioning, customer demand volumes, costs, competitors, channels, complementary services and facilities, and consistency with marketing-mix elements and strategy). Value for money is another important concept to be evaluated in arriving at the optimum prices.

REVIEW QUESTIONS

1. What are the two major roles of pricing and the inherent conflicts in these?
2. How does price play the role of an implicit promotional element?
3. What are the unsophisticated pricing approaches, and why are they not recommended?
4. What are some more sophisticated approaches, and why are they superior?
5. What does target pricing involve?
6. What is break-even analysis and how is it used in pricing?
7. Are there different pricing approaches that can be used when introducing new services? If so, what are they?
8. What does the multistage approach to pricing entail, and what factors are considered?
9. How does the concept of value for money affect pricing?

CHAPTER ASSIGNMENTS

1. Arrange to visit a local hospitality and travel business and interview its manager or owner. Ask this person to describe the pricing approaches that the business uses. Would you classify these as sophisticated or unsophisticated? Which of the nine Cs of pricing are considered? Is the multistage approach used? Are discounting, target pricing, or break-even analysis used? What recommendations would you make to management to improve their pricing approaches?

2. You are the marketing manager responsible for a newly launched hospitality or travel service (e.g., hotel, restaurant, airline route, travel agency, or other service). What steps would you follow in arriving at initial price structures for this operation? What specific factors would you consider? What would your prices be, and how would you justify them to senior management?

3. Select a part of the hospitality and travel industry in which you are most interested. Analyze the pricing approaches used. How would you categorize the approaches you have identified (i.e., unsophisticated or sophisticated)? Which specific approaches are used? Which of the nine Cs seem to have the greatest influence on price levels? Is there room for other organizations to enter the business using different approaches? Explain your answer.

4. Select a local business in our industry and show how it could use either target pricing or break-even analysis to make more effective pricing decisions. Illustrate your recommendations with numerical examples. How would you *sell* your recommendations to the owners?

WORLD WIDE WEB RESOURCES

Club Med
http://www.clubmed.com/

Priceline
http://www.priceline.com/

Rent-a-Wreck
http://www.rent-a-wreck.com/

Silver Wings Plus (United Airlines)
http://www.silverwingsplus.com/

Smith Travel Research
http://www.str-online.com/

Southwest Airlines
http://www.southwest.com/

United Airlines
http://www.ual.com/

Virgin Atlantic
http://www.virgin-atlantic.com/

REFERENCES

1. Dommermuth, William P. 1989. *Promotion: Analysis, Creativity, and Strategy.* 2nd ed. Boston: PWS-Kent Publishing Company, 32–34.

2. Dommermuth, William P. 1989. *Promotion: Analysis, Creativity, and Strategy.* 2nd ed. Boston: PWS-Kent Publishing Company, 34.

3. Cunningham, William H., Isabella C. M. Cunningham, and Christopher M. Swift. 1987. *Marketing: A Managerial Approach.* Cincinnati, Ohio: South-Western Publishing Co., 487.

4. Stanton, William J., Rosann Spiro, and Richard H. Buskirk. 1998. *Management of a Sales Force.* 10th ed. Boston: McGraw-Hill.

5. The Economic Planning Group of Canada. "Tourism is your business: Marketing management." Ottawa, Ontario: Tourism Canada, 92 (1986).

6. Rice, Faye. "Why hotel rates won't take off—yet." *Fortune* (October 4, 1993):124–128.

7. Lieberman, Warren H. "Debunking the myths of yield management." *The Cornell Hotel and Restaurant Administration Quarterly* 34 (1):34–41 (1993).

8. Kimes, Sheryl E. "Perceived fairness of yield management." *The Cornell Hotel and Restaurant Administration Quarterly* 35 (1):22–29 (1994).

9. Kotler, Philip. 2000. *Marketing Management: Millennium Edition.* 10th ed. Upper Saddle River, N.J.: Prentice-Hall, Inc.

10. Cunningham, William H., Isabella C. M. Cunningham, and Christopher M. Swift. 1987. *Marketing: A Managerial Approach.* Cincinnati, Ohio: South-Western Publishing Co., 496.

11. Carmin, JoAnn, and Gregory X. Norkus. "Pricing strategies for menus: Magic or myth?" *The Cornell Hotel and Restaurant Administration Quarterly* 31 (3):45–50.

12. Cunningham, William H., Isabella C. M. Cunningham, and Christopher M. Swift. 1987. *Marketing: A Managerial Approach.* Cincinnati, Ohio: South-Western Publishing Co., 546–550.

13. Evans, Joel R., and Barry Berman. 2000. *Marketing.* 7th ed. Upper Saddle River, N.J.: Prentice-Hall, Inc.

For additional hospitality and travel marketing resources, visit our Web site at **www.Hospitality-Tourism.delmar.com**

Controlling and Evaluating the Plan

20

Marketing Management, Evaluation, and Control

How Do We Make Sure We Get There? How Do We Know If We Got There?

Objectives

Having read this chapter, you should be able to

◆ Define marketing management and list its five components.

◆ Explain the benefits of marketing management.

◆ Describe the five different methods of organizing a marketing department.

◆ Explain the steps and procedures involved in staffing and managing marketing personnel.

◆ List the unsophisticated and sophisticated approaches to setting marketing budgets and identify the most effective method.

◆ Describe the building-block procedure for setting a marketing budget and explain its benefits.

◆ Define marketing control and marketing evaluation.

◆ Describe the process used to control the marketing plan.

◆ List and explain the techniques available for marketing evaluation.

Overview

This chapter discusses the management of marketing activities, often simply called marketing management, and identifies the benefits of effective marketing management. It emphasizes that it is not enough just to have a marketing plan. Even the best plan in the world may need
to be changed to adapt to unexpected circumstances. The five components of marketing management (research, planning, implementation, control, and evaluation) are highlighted.

The chapter looks at alternative ways of organizing a marketing department and discusses staffing and supervision. It also explains differ- ent ways of arriving at marketing budgets and suggests the best ways of doing this.

The last two questions of the hospitality and travel marketing system ("How do we make sure we get there?" and "How do we know if we got there?") are addressed in an explana- tion of marketing control and evaluation. The chapter ends by explaining several useful eval- uation techniques.

Key Terms

affordable budgeting	80–20 principle	marketing evaluation
arbitrary budgeting	iceberg effect	marketing management
budgeting	integrated marketing	objective-and-task budgeting
building-block procedure (for marketing budgets)	marginal economic budgeting	percentage-of-sales (rule-of- thumb) budgeting
competitive-parity budgeting	market share	performance measurement
conversion rate	marketing audit	sales analysis
e-commerce	marketing control	zero-based budgeting
efficiency ratios	marketing cost and profitability analysis	

Have you ever started the year with a set of New Year's resolutions, stuck with them for a few weeks or months, but eventually given them up? Do not feel em- barrassed. You are normal, just like the rest of us. Have you ever ended a year knowing that you have kept one or more of your resolutions? How did you accomplish this? It probably took great self-discipline, some encouragement from others, and a constant focus on your objectives. You might also have had to train yourself to modify your behavior—not eat as much, exercise more frequently, stop smoking, or study a cer- tain number of hours each day. Additionally, you probably had to plan and budget your time, money, and other resources. Above all, it took your single-minded determination and dedication to be better disciplined than you were at the beginning of the year. You had to *manage* yourself.

What does this have to do with marketing and marketing management? New Year's resolutions are very similar to an organization's marketing objectives and plan. They look good on paper and may have been very carefully thought out and re- searched. But as poet Robert Burns wrote, "the best-laid schemes o' mice an' men" often go wrong. Why? Usually, it is because we tend to relax after we have drawn up our objectives and plans. Developing them has sapped so much of our energy that there is not much left after the fact. In marketing, however, managing the marketing plan is every bit as important as thinking it up and writing it down on paper. Just as with New Year's resolutions, successful marketing management involves budgeting, motivation, training, changing people's behavior, and constant checking to ensure that the objectives are always in sight. Marketing management activities are designed to help the organization achieve objectives and to implement and, if necessary, adapt its marketing plan to changing circumstances. It is the way that the organization makes sure it gets where it wants to be. These activities answer the question, "How do we get there?"

MARKETING MANAGEMENT—DEFINITION AND COMPONENTS

Marketing management includes all the activities necessary to plan, research, implement, control, and evaluate the marketing efforts of a hospitality and travel organization. Chapters 4 through 19 discussed the first three functions—the *PRI* of the PRICE model discussed earlier—planning, research, and implementation. These functions together produce marketing strategies and plans. However, developing and implementing marketing strategies and plans involves organizing, staffing, and managing the marketing department, its staff, and any outside consultants that are used (e.g., advertising agencies, PR consultants). Marketing managers are also responsible for controlling and evaluating marketing efforts—the *CE* of the PRICE model—ensuring that strategies and plans are implemented as intended and that success is measured.

MARKETING MANAGEMENT BENEFITS

Effective marketing management not only provides rich benefits to an organization but is also an absolutely essential part of marketing. The major benefits of sound marketing management include the following:

1. Marketing efforts are accomplished in a well-planned, systematic way.
2. An adequate amount of marketing research and other marketing information is generated.
3. Marketing weaknesses are quickly spotted and corrected.
4. Funds and human resources available for marketing are used as efficiently and effectively as possible.
5. Marketing efforts are always under careful scrutiny. It is always believed that there is room for improvement.
6. The organization is in a better position to adapt to change among customers and competition, and in the industry.
7. Marketing is better integrated into all the organization's activities and within its various departments.
8. Marketing personnel and other staff members are more highly motivated toward achieving marketing objectives.
9. There is a much clearer understanding of marketing results, good and bad, and the reasons for successes and failures.
10. There is definite accountability for marketing.

MARKETING ORGANIZATION

One basic requirement for ensuring the successful achievement of goals, strategies, and objectives is to have the right marketing organization in place. There are several alternative ways to do this, depending mainly on the services provided by the organization, as well as its size and geographic coverage. The marketing organization or department is normally formed by using one of the following five criteria:[1]

1. Marketing and promotional mix elements
2. Facilities or services

3. Geography
4. Customer groupings
5. A combination of two of these criteria

1. **Marketing and Promotional Mix Elements.** Chapters 10 through 13 and 15 through 19 gave you information on each marketing and promotional mix element. Why not divide an organization's marketing specialists by each of these elements? For example, you might have individual managers responsible for product development and partnership (Chapter 10), services and service quality (Chapter 11), packaging and programming (Chapter 12), the distribution mix and the travel trade (Chapter 13), advertising (Chapter 15), sales promotion and merchandising (Chapter 16), personal selling (Chapter 17), public relations and publicity (Chapter 18), and pricing (Chapter 19). Many marketing departments in the hospitality and travel industry are set up in this way, especially smaller organizations and those with only one unit (e.g., a single hotel property). Some multiunit chains also organize the head-office marketing department in this way. The individual managers report to a director or vice president of marketing.

   Although this is a logical and convenient way to divide the marketing effort, it has its drawbacks. First, as earlier chapters mentioned, all marketing and promotional mix elements are interrelated. They work better if they are planned together. Some now call this practice integrated marketing (integrated planning of all or several marketing-promotional mix elements). When an organization allocates marketing responsibility to different managers and their support teams, there is a greater tendency for these groups to do their own thing, not working together as effectively as they could. Second, many larger companies have more than one *product*. These may be either various brands (such as with many of the major lodging chains) or completely different types of hospitality and travel businesses (e.g., an airline, a hotel company, and a car rental firm). Each of these products within the parent company may require a different marketing approach and, therefore, merit its own marketing organization.

2. **Facilities or Services.** The second alternative is to organize marketing by brand or division, each representing a specific type of facility or service. This approach is better suited to larger organizations, including those with several brands (e.g., large lodging and restaurant chains) and diversified hospitality and travel companies.

   The advantage of this approach over the first is that each brand or division is assured of an individualized and comprehensive marketing program. The potential drawback is that from a total-company standpoint, individual brands and divisions may not capitalize, to the fullest extent possible, on opportunities for joint marketing.

3. **Geography.** A third alternative is to divide the marketing team geographically. This is especially important for hospitality and travel organizations with multinational operations. Examples include many national government-tourism agencies, such as the Singapore Tourism Board, Canadian Tourism Commission, the British Tourist Authority, and the Australian Tourist Commission, each of which has marketing offices in several different countries. In these situations, separate marketing strategies and plans are required for each nation that has an office and for any neighboring countries for which individual offices also have the responsibility.

   As stated in Chapter 17, geography is also commonly used to organize a sales force. Each sales representative is allocated a territory.

4. **Customer Groupings.** A fourth way to divide marketing personnel is by assigning them to a specific target market or sets of target markets. This book has emphasized the need for separate approaches for each target market among organizations that choose segmented strategies. One of the best ways to assure the individual attention is by segmenting the marketing organization in this way. For example, several larger hotel properties divide up their sales staff by types of convention/meeting groups (e.g., national associations versus state associations).

5. **Combination Approaches.** There are many cases in which some combination of these four approaches is used. One of the most typical arrangements is to organize the marketing department by customer group, promotional mix element, or product, but to have the sales force divided by geographic territories.

   Another situation that requires a combination approach is in cases where the parent firm is involved in franchising. Franchising is common in many parts of the hospitality and travel industry, especially among restaurants, lodging facilities, travel agencies, and car rental firms. These companies usually have a national marketing plan that is prepared by a head-office marketing department, as well as individual unit marketing plans. In addition, groups of individual franchisees may get together at a city or regional level and develop marketing plans for their respective geographic areas.

   Whatever the organizational approach chosen, there is one principle that must be followed—the marketing organization should have full, or at least shared, responsibility (in the case of pricing) for all the marketing and promotional mix elements. This basic principle is violated in some parts of our industry. For example, some hotel properties have separate sales departments and public relations departments or directors. This book recommends placing all promotional mix elements within one division or department, under the direction of one director or manager.

STAFFING THE MARKETING ORGANIZATION

Another function of marketing management is hiring and retaining suitably qualified people. Where does the hospitality and travel industry find such individuals? Unfortunately, the answer is unclear, because little research has been done on the subject. However, some generalized comments can be made.

There is a strong tendency in the industry to require sales and marketing personnel to have some previous experience in operations, either with the subject organization or a similar one. Stated another way, this means that sales and marketing jobs tend not to be entry-level positions. Because of the rapid expansion of the industry, some organizations have hired experienced sales and marketing people from unrelated industries. There are few, if any, degrees and professional designations in hospitality and travel marketing, although some schools and professional associations are moving in this direction. Again, college/university and industry certification programs are strongly oriented toward producing people to fill operational roles, not marketing positions.

The hospitality and travel industry lags behind other industries in accepting marketing and the marketing concept. In other industries, graduates with marketing degrees usually enter directly into organizations' marketing departments without prior operational experience. This will take several years, and perhaps decades, to change in our industry. It demonstrates that operational skills and knowledge are valued more than marketing skills and knowledge.

MANAGING AND SUPERVISING MARKETING PERSONNEL

Because this is not a book on supervision and human resources management, it is inappropriate to discuss these subjects in great detail. However, it is important to mention that marketing managers at different levels, ranging from senior vice presidents to sales managers, must not only recruit and hire the right people, they must also motivate, coordinate, and communicate with them effectively. They must judiciously delegate authority and responsibility and build a feeling of teamwork directed toward achieving marketing objectives. This sense of common purpose is especially important in the hospitality and travel industry, because our people are so involved in providing customer service. The organizations that excel at motivating and communicating with their own employees are usually the ones that also provide excellent service.

SETTING MARKETING BUDGETS

Another important function of marketing management is budgeting—allocating human resources and money toward the implementation of the marketing plan. Chapter 19 mentioned that there are sophisticated and unsophisticated approaches to pricing. The same is true with budgeting.

1. **Unsophisticated Approaches.**
   a. *Arbitrary and Affordable Approaches.* These are budgeting methods involving the personal judgments of marketing managers or business owners. Many smaller businesses use the affordable budgeting method, spending only what they think they can afford for marketing. The arbitrary budgeting method usually means allocating a marketing budget approximately the same size as the one set in previous years.[2]
   b. *Percentage-of-Sales or Rule-of-Thumb Approaches.* With percentage-of-sales or rule-of-thumb budgeting marketing budgets are set as a percentage of last year's total sales or next year's expected total sales. The percentage figures are usually chosen because they are *rules of thumb* for that particular part of the hospitality and travel industry. These recommended percentages are commonly expressed in ranges. For example, several sources suggest that lodging properties should spend 2.5 percent to 5 percent of their total sales on marketing. Among food service operations, the given spread is often 1 percent to 8 percent.[3] Typically, these *rules of thumb* are based on published statistics that represent the averages for the industry segment. As you might already know from statistics, averages (arithmetic means) can be very misleading and often skewed by very high or very low individual figures.
   c. *Competitive-Parity Approach.* Competitive-parity budgeting is straightforward—find out what your closest competitors are spending on marketing and set your budget at the same or approximately the same level. How do you find this information? Annual reports are one good source of such statistics on

publicly-held corporations. Other sources include published articles on competitive organizations and various annual reports such as *Advertising Age's* series on the top 200 advertisers in the United States.

What are the advantages of using these three budgeting methods? The answer is their simplicity and the speed with which they can be determined. They do not require much research or significant other effort by the marketing manager. Can you spot any problems with using them? If you cannot right away, let us return to Chapter 8 when we began talking about marketing objectives. From that chapter on, this book has suggested that these objectives are the *building blocks* for the marketing plan. The marketing plan is written with the express purpose of achieving marketing objectives. Now, what is missing from all three unsophisticated budgeting approaches? None of them considers marketing objectives. Why on earth develop a detailed plan based on objectives, and then strike a budget based on sales volumes or competition? It should be obvious by now that what is needed is a budgeting procedure based on marketing objectives.

You might now be questioning the importance of competitors' spending levels and the affordability of marketing. Should organizations completely disregard what competitors are doing? Should they spend as much as it takes to get marketing done, without considering other priorities for funds within the organization? The answer to both questions is a resounding no. Competition and overall resources available within the subject organization are two factors that must be considered when establishing marketing budgets. They should not, however, be the primary and sole basis used to arrive at spending levels.

2. **Sophisticated Approaches.** You are right in thinking that a sophisticated approach would use marketing objectives as the primary basis for budgeting, but would also consider competition and affordability. In fact, the best budgeting approaches use a *building-block* procedure similar to the one depicted in Figure 20–1. The steps involved in this procedure are as follows:
   a. Allocate a tentative, overall budget to marketing or the marketing department.
   b. Determine the marketing objectives.
   c. Set objectives for each promotional mix element that are based on the overall marketing objectives.
   d. Tentatively split the overall budget allocation between communications (the promotional mix), and administrative and other marketing expenses.
   e. Divide the tentative communications budget on a provisional basis among advertising, sales promotion, personal selling, and public relations and publicity.
   f. Develop the marketing plan, specifying all the activities and tasks required for advertising, sales promotion, merchandising, personal selling, and public relations and publicity.
   g. Determine the final budget allocations for advertising, sales promotion, personal selling, public relations and publicity, and administrative and other elements, based on the activities included in the marketing plan. Further adjustments may be required to better fit the initial overall budget allocation to marketing or competitive expenditures.

You can see that setting the marketing budget requires a well-researched and carefully planned, step-by-step process. Look again at Figure 20–1. It seems to resemble a brick wall. As you know, a bricklayer starts a wall from the bottom and

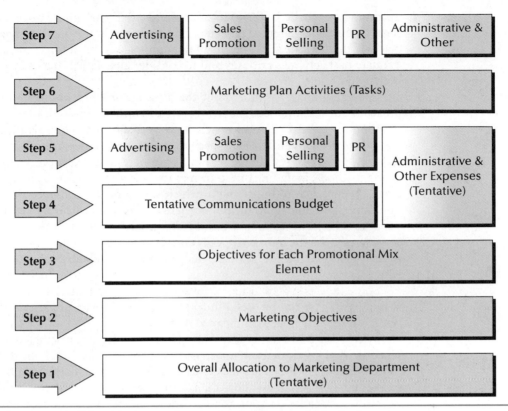

◆ FIGURE 20–1 *Building-block procedure for developing a marketing budget.*

works up, carefully cementing each new row of bricks to the one below. Establishing the marketing budget is much like wall building—each step builds on the preceding ones, using needed information and guidelines for allocating dollar amounts. Omitting certain steps is similar to the bricklayer leaving out some bricks and not cementing certain layers. The result is obvious—the wall will eventually fall down. Part of the building-block procedure just described reflects the use of a sophisticated budgeting approach known as the objective-and-task method.

a. ***Objective-and-Task Approach.*** The name given to this method aptly describes what is involved. The organization sets objectives, figures out what must be done to achieve them (the tasks), and then estimates the costs of completing the tasks (or activities). This three-step approach was used in Chapters 15 through 18 to set the final budget amounts for advertising, sales promotion, merchandising, personal selling, and public relations and publicity. It is the budgeting approach recommended in this book.

b. ***Zero-Based Budgeting Approach.*** There is a tendency in business to repeat activities from previous years without critically evaluating their worth. The reason for this is simple—there is some fear that discontinuing the activities that have contributed to success will lower performance. This often results in extending unproductive activities beyond their useful lives. Zero-based budgeting challenges this habit by requiring that each marketing-plan activity (or task) for an upcoming period be justified. In other words, the marketing budget starts at zero. There is no guarantee that any of the activities in the previous marketing plan will be continued. The beauty of this approach is that it forces managers to evaluate past activities critically and to consider alternatives that may produce even better results.

You are probably wondering if the *objective-and-task* and *zero-based* approaches can be combined. The answer is yes. In fact, objective-and-task is an application of the zero-based approach. Marketers start with clean slates each period and select activities that are specifically designed to meet chosen objectives.

c. **Other Approaches.** You should be aware that there are other sophisticated budgeting methods, including one known as the marginal economic method. (An idealistic approach to budgeting in which sponsors spend money on promotional-mix elements up to the point where the last dollar brings in exactly one dollar in sales.) This technique draws from general economic theory. Although considered to be the most technically correct approach, it is difficult to apply in actual practice. Objective-and-task budgeting is an acceptable substitute, and it is far easier to use.

Some experts suggest using various quantitative, statistical models to arrive at budgets. These can be useful in considering the impact of various assumptions, but they are not recommended on their own.

What you should realize is that effective budgeting, like pricing, uses a combination of sophisticated and unsophisticated approaches. Using one technique alone is insufficient. The key factors to be considered are marketing objectives, marketing-plan activities, affordability (amount of funds that an organization can realistically allocate to marketing), and competitive expenditure levels.

MARKETING CONTROL AND EVALUATION

Why have an elaborate marketing plan and budgeting process if you do not measure its progress and tally the results at the end? Marketing control includes all the steps that an organization takes to monitor and adjust the marketing plan as it progresses, as well as the procedures it selects to ensure implementation as planned. Marketing evaluation involves analyzing results to determine the success of a marketing plan. Marketing control helps answer the question. "How do we make sure we get there?" whereas marketing evaluation satisfies the "How do we know if we got there?" question. These are both part of the overall management concept of performance measurement.

The 80-20 Principle and the Iceberg Effect

Before discussing control and evaluation techniques, you should know about one common problem with marketing in our industry. This can best be described as the 80-20 principle, or putting 80 percent of the effort or resources into capturing only 20 percent of the total volume.[4] In other words, there is a tendency to put too much effort and budget into attracting certain types of customers and too little into others. Although the actual percentages may not be 80 percent and 20 percent, the important point is that many organizations in our industry are unaware of the problem in the first place. Efforts are often channeled away from higher- to lower-profit services and customers.

Marketing Effectiveness through Database Management:
Harrah's Entertainment, Inc.

The casino industry provides some of the best examples of good marketing management in the hospitality and travel industry. Harrah's Entertainment, Inc. is one of its brightest stars of late, achieving a 50 percent increase in revenues in 1999 over 1998. The core of Harrah's success is the company's unique marketing strategy based upon "the gaming industry's most detailed player *database* to develop leading-edge marketing programs that enhance customer loyalty."[1]

Harrah's has been in operation for more than 60 years and operates 21 casinos in 17 locations within the United States. The company also operates the Showboat and Rio casinos and has acquired the Players International casinos.[2] Harrah's has 38,000 employees and serves about 14 million guests per year.

As this chapter indicates, the key to measuring *marketing effectiveness* is for an organization to know how successful it has been in achieving its marketing objectives. Harrah's does this through masterful use of a proprietary database of 19 million players in the United States—more than the entire population of Australia. In 1997, Harrah's introduced a customer-loyalty (frequent player) program called Total Gold and each person that joined received a player card. When entered into slot machines, these cards allow Harrah's to record every aspect of each player's habits and preferences. With this intimate knowledge of each guest, the company offers an individually designed incentive to entice the guest to return to a Harrah's property. In the company's own words, it attracts customers repeatedly to Harrah's brands "by analyzing customer transaction data to gain insight into their preferences, then make marketing offerings specifically tailored to them. This highly customized approach is a key factor in gener-

ating increased customer loyalty, which drives increased profitability over time."[3]

It is interesting to note that Harrah's was struggling in the early 1990s in the increasingly competitive U.S. casino industry. Competitive companies were pouring millions of dollars into elaborate and sometimes highly themed properties in Harrah's existing locations. Harrah's response was to invest more in software technology and to focus more on its *bread-and-butter* market, the experienced and frequent slot player. Additionally, as outlined in a *Wall Street Journal* article, it conducted a series of carefully documented experiments with these players.[4] Harrah's research showed that these players were spending only 36 percent of their wagering dollars with the company, while the vast majority was going to its competitors. The strategy became how to get the players to spend more with Harrah's.

The resulting approach represented a superb application of the *PRICE model* (planning-research-implementation-control-evaluation). The company's plan was to select a strategy of increased customer loyalty with experienced slot players. This was based on the aforementioned research findings. Further research was done through *secondary data analysis,* by manipulating Harrah's existing player database using such factors as age, frequency of play, and average amount lost while playing. Following this, a series of carefully monitored implementation experiments were conducted. When each of these experiments had run its course, the results were evaluated. A *Wall Street Journal* article describes how two of the experiments were conducted and evaluated:

"One example: Harrah's chose two similar groups of frequent slot players from Jackson, Miss. Members of the control

continued

EXCELLENCE CASE *continued*

group were offered a typical casino-marketing package worth $125—a free room, two steak meals, and $30 of free chips at the Tunica casino. Members of the test group were offered $60 in chips. The more modest offer generated far more gambling, suggesting that Harrah's had been wasting its money giving its customers free rooms. Thereafter, profits from the revamped promotion nearly doubled to $60 per person per trip.

In another test, Harrah's focused on a group of monthly gamblers whom the company suspected could be induced to play more frequently because they lived nearby and displayed avid-gambler traits such as hitting slot buttons quickly. To entice them to make two back-to-back visits, Harrah's sent cash and food offers that expired in consecutive two-week periods. The group's average number of trips per month quickly rose to 1.4 from 1.1."[5]

Harrah's launched a new customer loyalty program in 2000, Total Rewards, which separates players into three levels—Gold, Platinum, and Diamond. Gold level players will reach the Total Platinum level when they earn 3,000 credits in a year. Eligibility for the Total Diamond level comes when 10,000 credits are earned in a year. Credits are earned by slot and table players based on amount spent, average bet, and length of time played. This program covers all of Harrah's properties and all of its other brands.[6]

It is hard to think of a better example than Harrah's to end the series of Excellence Cases in this book. The company's recent history clearly shows the importance of marketing planning, careful research, database development, and analysis. But what is perhaps the most outstanding aspect of this case is how Harrah's experimented and evaluated the results. While other casino operations continue to lavish many freebies on guests, Harrah's has taken the time to find out what its players want and then provide it.

Discussion Questions

1. Why does the Harrah's Entertainment case represent such a good application of the components of marketing management?
2. How does Harrah's multi-million person database allow it to effectively control and evaluate its marketing programs?
3. In what ways does Harrah's use relationship marketing to develop greater loyalty among its customers?
4. What can other hospitality and travel organizations learn from Harrah's example? Is the casino industry in a unique position to collect customer data, or can other hospitality and travel organizations do this as well?

Web Site

http://www.harrahs.com/

References

1. Harrah's Entertainment, Inc., *1999 Annual Report,* 13.
2. PR Newswire. 2000. *Harrah's Entertainment Unveils New Customer-Loyalty Program, Total Rewards; Gaming Industry's Only Nationwide Player Card Now Offers More Benefits,* April 4.
3. Harrah's Entertainment, Inc., *1999 Annual Report,* 14.
4. Binkley, Christina. "Lucky numbers. A casino chain finds a lucrative niche: The small spenders." *The Wall Street Journal* May 4, 2000: A1, A10.
5. Binkley, Christina. "Lucky numbers. A casino chain finds a lucrative niche: The small spenders." *The Wall Street Journal* May 4, 2000: A10.
6. Harrah's Entertainment Web site. http://www.harrahs.com/

Some also refer to this as the iceberg effect, meaning that managers often make decisions based on superficial information (they see only the tip of the iceberg). As every captain knows, it is the larger section of the iceberg under the water that can sink a ship. A wide course must be steered around this navigational obstacle. Likewise, a manager must take an in-depth look at a broad range of information to ensure that marketing activities are as effective as possible. How can the *80-20 principle* or the *iceberg effect* be avoided? The answer is by carefully controlling and comprehensively evaluating marketing-plan results.

Marketing Control

This book has emphasized two of the major functions of marketing management—research and planning. Controlling what goes on in an organization is another key management function. Basically, all systems of control include three steps: (1) setting standards based on plans, (2) measuring performance against standards, and (3) correcting deviations from standards and plans.[5] In most organizations, controls are devised for production, inventories, product/service quality, and financial resources. Chapter 2 stated that inventory and quality control are made more difficult in our industry because of the perishability and intangibility of services, and by the significant role of people who provide them.

How then do managers control their marketing plans? What are their standards? The two key measurement tools are marketing objectives and budgets. Marketing budgets assist with the financial control of the marketing plan. Periodic checks are made to see whether the budget is being spent according to the plan. Additionally, results are monitored periodically to determine progress toward achieving individual marketing objectives (expressed in numerical terms).

As you probably realize, the success of a marketing plan not only depends on the budget and how it is allocated, but also on the efforts of the many people who work in the organization. Some of these people are employed directly in marketing (e.g., sales representatives and public relations staff). Others are on the front line, providing service to customers. As you saw in Chapter 11, controlling the efforts of all staff members is more difficult than telling them what to do but is essential to effective marketing.

The main route to success is building a team spirit toward achieving marketing objectives. You read earlier in this chapter about the importance of recruiting and hiring the right people. This must be accompanied by effective leadership, motivation, orientation and training, and communications. Policies must be established to support individual aspects of the marketing plan, ranging from how employees should dress and wear uniforms to the proper ways of addressing customers. It is often the attention to these seemingly minute details that leads to outstanding success in this industry. Two dazzling examples of such success are the policies of the Disney theme parks and McDonald's. Marketing personnel may not be directly responsible for enforcing these standards and rules, but they must ensure that such systems exist and that compliance is checked periodically.

The marketing department, through the sales manager, is responsible for monitoring and controlling the productivity of sales representatives. Often this is accomplished through systems of sales quotas (the performance standards) and is measured through sales-call reports and other reports on sales by representatives. Again, controlling performance is easier if it is preceded by proper orientation and training of sales staff.

It is very unlikely that any marketing plan will proceed exactly as intended, because of the unpredictable nature of this industry and competitors. The controls that a manager uses provide an "early warning" system, highlighting problem areas and

Did You Know?

Using the Balanced Scorecard Approach in Marketing Evaluation

✓ In an interesting application of marketing evaluation, four researchers used the Balanced Scorecard Approach to assess the effectiveness of the Web sites of a group of small hotels in Scotland. Robert Kaplan and David Norton, who operate an organization called the Balanced Scorecard Collaborative, originally developed the Balanced Scorecard Approach.

✓ The researchers identified four distinct sets of measurement criteria, which they called critical success factors or CSFs:

- Customer CSFs
- Internal CSFs
- Marketing CSFs
- Technical CSFs

✓ Specific criteria and a scoring system were developed for each of the four groups of CSFs.

✓ The hotels' Web sites were then analyzed and scored.

✓ The researchers found that there were many ways in which these hotels' Web sites could be made more effective.

Source: Morrison, Alastair M., S. Taylor, Alison J. Morrison, and Allison D. Morrison. "Marketing small hotels on the World Wide Web." *Information Technology & Tourism* 2:97–113 (1999).

other deviations from the plan. If such situations are spotted early enough, corrective action can be taken.

Marketing Evaluation

Marketing evaluation techniques are used after the marketing-plan period has expired. Their two major purposes are to analyze the degrees of success in achieving individual marketing objectives and to more broadly evaluate an entire organization's marketing efforts.

1. **Sales Analysis.** Marketing objectives are frequently expressed in dollar or unit sales volumes (e.g., passenger counts, occupied room nights). Therefore, the most obvious evaluation techniques compare actual sales to desired objectives. The sales analysis shows the deviations between actual and desired sales results, and also attempts to explain the reasons for discrepancies. The more detailed the analysis, the better (remember the *iceberg principle?*). For example, larger companies will usually look at sales by target market, brand or division, type of service or facilities, and sales territory.

2. **Market-Share Analysis.** This is a variant of sales analysis, in which the organization compares its sales results to those for everyone in its specific part of the hospitality and travel industry. Market share is the percentage relationship of an organization's sales to total industry sales. It provides useful information on how the organization has performed relative to competition. For example, a drop in market share shows that the industry has outperformed the organization. An increase in-

dicates that the organization has outperformed the industry. In addition to its overall market share, an organization usually is also concerned about its performance relative to specific competitors (e.g., the industry leaders).

3. **Marketing Cost and Profitability Analysis.** Sales and market-share analyses provide only part of the required picture. An organization must evaluate the **marketing costs and profitability** associated with various parts of its marketing plan. Only by doing so will the *80-20 problem* be detected and corrected. A company analyzes income statements to determine sales, costs, and profits by one or more of the following:
   a. Target markets
   b. Sales territories
   c. Sales representatives
   d. Distribution channels
   e. Travel trade intermediaries
   f. Types of facilities or services
   g. Promotional mix elements and other marketing-expense areas

   Income statements are not normally designed so that these figures can be extracted easily. A careful and time-consuming allocation process is required, but the payoffs are worth it. This analysis can lead to dropping unproductive services or facilities, target markets, distribution channels, or specific travel intermediaries. It may also highlight the need for major reallocations of promotional expenditures, reorganization of sales territories, or retraining of sales representatives.

4. **Efficiency Ratios.** **Efficiency ratios** are statistical measurements that marketing managers use to evaluate the organization's efficiency in using promotional and distribution mix-elements. Figure 20–2 is a selected list of these ratios, which can be used as tools in the evaluation process.

   In hospitality and travel advertising, one of the popular measures of efficiency is to calculate the conversion rate of a specific advertisement or series of advertisements (advertising campaign). With direct-response advertising, in which the customer is given an address or phone number by the sponsoring organization, the organization can track the number of customer inquiries generated. The **conversion rate** of direct-response advertising is the percentage of customers who inquired that actually bought and used the sponsor's advertised hospitality or travel service. The costs of *converting* each inquiry can also be calculated (cost per converted inquiry), as can the customer spending per *converted* inquiry.[6] The sponsors usually have to conduct special research studies, known as conversion studies, to calculate conversion rates.

   Similarly, the efficiency of certain sales promotions, such as coupons, can be measured quite easily by tracking coupon redemption rates (the percentage of the coupons distributed that are used by customers). Other sales promotions are not as easily evaluated. For travel trade and consumer travel shows, some recommend a procedure like that used in calculating conversion rates of direct-response advertising. Here, an organization keeps track of the number of inquiries it receives at its booth or exhibit and then tracks the percentage of these inquiries that eventually result in bookings and sales.[7] The trade/consumer trade show cost per inquiry can be calculated by dividing the total costs of exhibiting at the show by the total number of inquiries received at the organization's booth. The show's converted cost per inquiry can be found by dividing total show costs by

1. SALES-FORCE EFFICIENCY
- Average number of sales calls per sales representative per day
- Average sales-call time per contact
- Average revenue per sales call
- Average cost per sales call
- Sales-force cost as a percentage of total sales

2. ADVERTISING EFFICIENCY
- Number of inquiries generated per ad
- Conversion rate
- Cost per inquiry
- Cost per thousand persons reached (CPM)
- Before-after measures of attitude toward services

3. SALES PROMOTION EFFICIENCY
- Percentage of coupons redeemed
- Number of inquiries generated per promotion
- Cost per inquiry

4. PUBLIC RELATIONS AND PUBLICITY EFFICIENCY
- Number of media organizations using press releases
- Number of mentions in print and broadcast media

5. DISTRIBUTION EFFICIENCY
- Percentage of sales through various distribution channels
- Percentage of sales by specific types of intermediaries

◆ FIGURE 20–2   *Selected list of efficiency ratios.*

either the number of converted booth inquiries or the total revenues resulting from these converted inquiries.

5. **Marketing-Effectiveness Rating Review.** This is an internal survey conducted among the managers of an organization, but it is not restricted to the marketing department. A three-point scale is used to get managers' opinions on five factors that reflect the organization's marketing orientation: (1) customer philosophy, (2) integrated marketing organization, (3) adequate marketing information, (4) strategic orientation, and (5) operational efficiency.[8] A total point score is calculated based on individual ratings of questions related to these five areas. This evaluation tool is very useful in getting other departments' opinions and perceptions on the strengths and weaknesses of marketing. Conducted annually, it can highlight marketing weaknesses that require further investigation.

6. **Marketing Audit.** The first four evaluation approaches strictly assess a single marketing plan. It is possible to go even further by conducting a full-blown marketing audit, which is a systematic, comprehensive, and periodic evaluation of an organization's entire marketing function, including its marketing goals, objectives, strategies, and performance.[9]

Figure 20–3 shows the topics to be considered in the marketing audit. You may notice some striking similarities between the marketing audit and the situation analysis described in Chapter 5. In fact, some people in our industry use these two terms interchangeably. Although it is true that all of the topics in a situation analy-

PART I: MARKETING-ENVIRONMENT AUDIT

Macroenvironment

1. Demographic
2. Economic
3. Ecological
4. Technological
5. Political
6. Cultural

Task Environment

1. Markets
2. Customers
3. Competitors
4. Distribution and Dealers
5. Suppliers
6. Facilitators and Marketing Firms
7. Publics

PART II: MARKETING-STRATEGY AUDIT

1. Business Mission
2. Marketing Objectives and Goals
3. Strategy

PART III: MARKETING-ORGANIZATION AUDIT

1. Formal Structure
2. Functional Efficiency
3. Interface Efficiency

PART IV: MARKETING-SYSTEMS AUDIT

1. Marketing Information System
2. Marketing Planning Systems
3. Marketing Control System
4. New Product Development System

PART V: MARKETING-PRODUCTIVITY AUDIT

1. Profitability Analysis
2. Cost-Effectiveness Analysis

PART VI: MARKETING-FUNCTION AUDITS

1. Products
2. Price
3. Distribution
4. Advertising, Sales Promotion, and Publicity
5. Salesforce

◆ FIGURE 20–3   *Components of a marketing audit.* (Adapted from Kotler, Philip. 2000. *Marketing Management: Millennium Edition,* 10th ed. Prentice-Hall, Inc. Reprinted by permission of Pearson Education, Inc., Upper Saddle River, NJ 07458)

sis are covered in the marketing audit, the audit is more extensive and because of the high level of effort required, may not be performed each year.

The major features of a good marketing audit process are that it is (1) comprehensive, (2) systematic, (3) independent, and (4) periodic.[10] An effective audit analyzes *all* aspects of an organization's marketing efforts, including planning and strategy setting, organization, marketing management, implementation, performance, and control and evaluation procedures. In other words, the process is similar to placing the entire hospitality and travel marketing system under a microscope. The marketing audit is systematic when it examines each aspect of marketing using the step-by-step procedure described in this book. It starts by investigating the information and decisions outlined in Chapter 5 and then moves chapter by chapter to the present one.

Most experts believe that it is better to get an outside, independent view of an organization's marketing strengths and weaknesses. There is a danger of bias if the marketing department performs the audit itself. Greater objectivity usually results by having the audit conducted by an independent management consulting firm, by another department, or by an internal task force.

In practice, many organizations carry out marketing audits only when they encounter serious problems. This is not the ideal approach because there is always room for improvement, even when things are going well. Because marketing audits are more expensive and time-consuming than situation analyses, they are not done as frequently. However, given the rapid pace of change in the hospitality and travel industry, this book recommends that audits be conducted every three-to-five years, and even more frequently if serious marketing problems arise.

A Touch of Technology

U.S. Foundation for Performance Measurement

◆ Marketing control and evaluation are a subset of the overall system of business performance measurement.

◆ The U.S. Foundation for Performance Measurement is a membership association of educators, business, government, and consultant specialists interested in improving organizational performance. It can be accessed at http://www.netmain.com/usfpm/

◆ Among other items, the site contains a number of presentations and briefings on performance measurement that can be downloaded or printed (located in the *Foundation Services* page). These include materials on the Balanced Scorecard Approach.

• Other sites on the Web that provide useful information on performance measurement are:

• The Work Measurement Institute at http://www.workmeasurement.com/

• Performance Pathways at http://www.itpolicy.gsa.gov/mkm/pathways/pathways.htm/

• Foundation for Performance Measurement at http://www.fpm.com/

• The Balanced Scorecard Institute, http://www.balancedscorecard.org/

THE FUTURE OF MARKETING

What lies ahead for marketing in the hospitality and travel industry? First, as this book has emphasized, marketing will be a much more important management function in the industry in the 2000s. Marketing budgets will continue to increase as competition grows. More people with marketing backgrounds will head major organizations in our industry. Associations of marketing professionals will grow in size and stature. We may even see specialized, four-year degree programs in hospitality and travel marketing being introduced by major educational institutions. Without question, the industry will become more sophisticated and creative in its marketing practices.

A second major trend that has been mentioned throughout this book is the use of new technologies to communicate information between organizations and their customers. There has been rapid growth in the use of the Internet and particularly in the use of e-mail and the World Wide Web. Customers are becoming increasingly comfortable buying products and services on the Internet, and e-commerce is booming. New technological innovations such as wireless Internet access will help accelerate this move to greater on-line purchasing. Travel is now one of the most popular items to purchase on-line, and there are many on-line travel services available. Travelers have an enormous amount of travel information to surf through on the Web that is both interactive and up to date. Hospitality and travel organizations have invested heavily in ensuring that they have a viable on-line presence.

The third trend that can be predicted with confidence is the continued splintering of the market for hospitality and travel services. Chapter 7 pointed out, both societal factors and the industry's reactions to them are combining to create an ever-expanding range of market segments.

A fourth trend is the increasing use of computer technology by the hospitality and travel industry, especially in database marketing and marketing research. As mentioned throughout this book, more and more marketers are recognizing the vital importance of maintaining detailed relational databases on past and potential customers. When used with direct-marketing programs, these databases offer hospitality and travel marketers a more effective and efficient means of achieving objectives. In research, the use of compact- and DVD technologies offers marketers great future potential in the use of research data. For example, many national hospitality/travel survey data sets are now available on CD-ROM and on the Internet.

Nothing is more inevitable than change. Through careful management, control and evaluation of marketing activities, an organization is much better equipped to adapt to change when it happens.

CHAPTER CONCLUSION

Having a marketing plan is not a prescription for success. Although marketing plans are vital, there are several other marketing management tasks that require attention, including organization, staffing, supervision, budgeting, control, and evaluation. A marketing management process that considers all these tasks is essential in today's competitive environment.

A marketing plan must be monitored carefully during its implementation, and corrective action must be taken when necessary. One of the key tools of control is the marketing budget, which should be developed on the basis of sound budgeting techniques such as the objective-and-task and zero-based approaches. Marketing objectives, stated in measurable terms, also play a key role.

An organization's marketing efforts should always be evaluated critically. There is no room for sacred cows and complacency in modern marketing. Several effective evaluation techniques are available, most notably the marketing audit, that can help an organization improve its marketing in the future.

REVIEW QUESTIONS

1. How is marketing management defined in this book?
2. What are the five components of marketing management?
3. Is marketing management an optional activity or is it essential? What are the benefits of effective marketing management?
4. What are the five different ways of organizing a marketing department, and in which situations does each work best?
5. How do organizations in the hospitality and travel industry recruit marketing personnel? Are they ahead or behind other industries in their recruitment approaches?
6. What are the steps and procedures involved in managing and supervising marketing personnel?
7. What are the best approaches to developing a marketing budget? Explain your answer by describing unsophisticated and sophisticated approaches.

8. How are marketing control and marketing evaluation defined in this book?

9. What steps are involved in controlling the marketing plan, and what roles do the marketing budget and plan play?

10. How important is marketing evaluation to the future success of an organization? Explain your answer by showing how the six evaluation techniques are used.

CHAPTER ASSIGNMENTS

1. Arrange to visit a hospitality or travel organization of your choice, and schedule an interview with the person responsible for marketing. Find out as much as you can about how the organization handles marketing management. How is marketing organized? How are marketing staff recruited? What is done to orient, train, and motivate them? What procedures are used to supervise and control the quality of service given by marketing and front-line staff? How are marketing budgets developed? Is their control of the marketing plan effective and, if so, how is this accomplished? How does the organization evaluate its marketing efforts? Summarize your conclusions in a report to senior management describing current procedures and including your recommendations on how marketing management could be made more effective.

2. Select three organizations in that part of the hospitality and travel industry in which you are most interested. Do they have marketing departments? How is marketing organized? Why do you think they are organized in this way? What are the advantages and disadvantages of their individual approaches? Which approach is best? Do they satisfy the basic principle that the person or persons responsible for marketing have at least joint responsibility for all marketing and promotional mix elements? How would you improve their organizational setups to increase marketing effectiveness?

3. A local hospitality and travel organization has asked you for help in developing a marketing budget. What approach would you recommend? Who would you involve in developing the budget? What sources of information would you use in developing the budget? Prepare a rough budget based on your analysis and findings.

4. Assume that you have been hired as a consultant by a hospitality and travel organization to improve the effectiveness of its marketing efforts. Explain the procedures you would recommend for using the five-step hospitality and travel marketing system. Make specific suggestions on how the organization should control and evaluate marketing. Describe the benefits the organization can expect from implementing your recommendations.

WORLD WIDE WEB RESOURCES

Balanced Scorecard Collaborative
http://www.bscol.com/

Balanced Scorecard Institute
http://www.balancedscorecard.org/

Foundation for Performance Measurement
http://www.netmain.com/usfpm/

Harrah's Entertainment, Inc.
http://www.harrahs.com/

Performance Pathways
http://www.itpolicy.gsa.gov/mkm/pathways/pathways.htm/

Work Measurement Institute
http://www.workmeasurement.com/

REFERENCES

1. Cunningham, William H., Isabella C. M. Cunningham, and Christopher M. Swift. 1987. *Marketing: A Managerial Approach.* Cincinnati, Ohio: South-Western Publishing Co., 776–780.
2. Ray, Michael L. 1982. *Advertising & Communication Management.* Englewood Cliffs, N.J.: Prentice-Hall, Inc., 148.
3. Reid, Robert D., and David Bojanic. 2000. *Hospitality Marketing Management.* 3rd ed. New York: John Wiley & Sons, Inc.
4. Stanton, William J., Rosann Spiro, and Richard H. Buskirk. 1998. *Management of a Sales Force.* 10th ed. Boston: McGraw-Hill.
5. Fulmer, Robert M. 1987. *The New Management.* 4th ed. New York: Macmillan Publishing Company.
6. Burke, James F., and Lisa A. Lindblom. "Strategies for evaluating direct response tourism marketing." *Journal of Travel Research* 28 (2):33–37.
7. Pizam, Abraham. "Evaluating the effectiveness of travel trade shows and other tourism sales-promotion techniques." *Journal of Travel Research* 29 (1):3–8 (1990).
8. Kotler, Philip. 2000. *Marketing Management: Millennium Edition.* 10th ed. Upper Saddle River, N.J.: Prentice-Hall, Inc.
9. Stanton, William J., Rosann Spiro, and Richard H. Buskirk. 1998. *Management of a Sales Force.* 10th ed. Boston: McGraw-Hill.
10. Kotler, Philip. 2000. *Marketing Management: The Millennium Edition.* 10th ed. Upper Saddle River, N.J.: Prentice-Hall, Inc.

For additional hospitality and travel marketing resources, visit our Web site at **www.Hospitality-Tourism.delmar.com**

Appendix 1
Industry Profile

The author and Delmar affirm that the Web site URLs referenced herein were accurate at the time of printing. However, due to the fluid nature of the Internet, we cannot guarantee their accuracy for the life of the edition.

◆ APPENDIX 1–1A   *The 25 Leading U.S. Lodging Brands*[1]

HOTEL BRAND	PARENT COMPANY	U.S. PROPERTIES	FOREIGN PROPERTIES
1. Holiday Inn Hotels, Select, and Sunspree	Bass Hotels & Resorts	1,179	506
2. Best Western Hotels	Best Western International	2,120	1,942
3. Days Inn of America	Cendant Corp.	1,806	111
4. Ramada	Cendant Corp.	997	0
5. Super 8	Cendant Corp.	1,868	75
6. Marriott Hotels, Resorts, & Suites	Marriott International	262	110
7. Hampton Inns/Inn & Suites	Hilton Hotels Corp.	983	16
8. Comfort Inns	Choice Hotels International	1,253	345
9. Hilton Inns/Hotels	Hilton Hotels Corp.	279	13
10. Motel 6	Accor Economy Lodging	815	2
11. Holiday Inn Express/Express & Suites	Bass Hotels & Resorts	965	138
12. Sheraton Hotels, Inns, & Resorts	Starwood Hotels & Resorts Worldwide	193	196
13. Courtyard by Marriott	Marriott International	452	41
14. Hyatt Hotels & Resorts	Hyatt Hotels Corp.	118	77
15. Radisson Hotels	Carlson Companies	232	178
16. Quality Inns	Choice Hotels International	430	310
17. Doubletree Hotels	Hilton Hotels Corp.	158	1
18. Econo Lodge	Choice Hotels International	682	30
19. Howard Johnson	Cendant Corp.	429	85
20. Fairfield Inn	Marriott International	426	0
21. La Quinta Inns/Inns & Suites	The Meditrust Companies	301	0
22. Red Roof Inns	Accor Economy Lodging	350	0
23. Residence Inn by Marriott	Marriott International	327	0
24. Travelodge	Cendant Corp.	483	89
25. Embassy Suites	Hilton Hotels Corp.	146	6

SOURCE: "The Brand Report." *LH/Lodging Hospitality* 56(11):45 (August 2000).

[1]Ranked by the number of U.S. rooms available in 1999.

◆ **APPENDIX 1–1B**   *The Largest Lodging Chains in the World*[1]

HOTEL CHAIN	HEADQUARTERS	ROOMS	PROPERTIES
1. Cendant Corp.	Parsippany, NJ, USA	542,630	6,315
2. Bass Hotels & Resorts	London, England	471,680	2,886
3. Marriott International	Washington, DC, USA	355,900	1,880
4. Accor	Evry, France	354,652	3,234
5. Choice Hotels International	Silver Springs, MD, USA	338,254	4,248
6. Best Western International	Phoenix, AZ, USA	313,247	4,037
7. Hilton Hotels Corp.	Beverly Hills, CA, USA	290,000	1,700
8. Starwood Hotels & Resorts Worldwide	White Plains, NY, USA	217,651	716
9. Carlson Hospitality Worldwide	Minneapolis, MN, USA	114,161	616
10. Hyatt Hotels/Hyatt International	Chicago, IL, USA	85,743	195
11. Wyndham International	Dallas, TX, USA	73,215	303
12. Sol Meliá	Palma de Mallorca, Spain	69,178	260
13. Société du Louvre	Paris, France	65,970	990
14. Hilton International	Watford, England	61,889	217
15. Forte Hotel Group	London, England	58,636	449
16. FelCor Lodging Trust	Irving, TX, USA	50,000	188
17. TUI Group	Hanover, Germany	42,379	172
18. La Quinta Inns	San Antonio, TX, USA	39,250	302
19. Extended Stay America	Fort Lauderdale, FL, USA	38,300	362
20. Club Méditerranée	Paris, France	36,510	127
21. Westmont Hospitality Group	Houston, TX, USA	34,769	296
22. U.S. Franchise Systems	Atlanta, GA, USA	32,722	400
23. Millennium & Copthorne Hotels PLC	Horley, England	30,247	117
24. Interstate Hotels Corp.	Pittsburgh, PA, USA	29,379	158
25. MeriStar Hotels & Resorts	Washington, DC, USA	29,348	116

SOURCE: *Hotels' Corporate 300 Ranking*:50 (July 2000). http://www.hotelsmag.com

[1]Ranked by the total number of rooms available worldwide in 1998.

◆ **APPENDIX 1–1C** *The Largest Hotel Markets in the United States*

CITY	NUMBER OF GUEST ROOMS
1. Las Vegas, Nevada	105,800
2. Orlando, Florida	87,200
3. Los Angeles—Long Beach, California	79,100
4. Atlanta, Georgia	70,300
5. Chicago, Illinois	69,400
6. Washington, DC	68,500
7. New York, New York	65,800
8. Dallas, Texas	47,600
9. San Diego, California	47,600
10. Anaheim, California	44,300
11. San Francisco, California	42,900

SOURCE: Hotel & Motel Management. http://www.hmmonline.com/

◆ **APPENDIX 1–2A**　*The 25 Leading U.S. Food Service Chains*[1]

CHAIN NAME	CONCEPT	NUMBER OF UNITS	TOTAL SALES 1999 (MILLIONS)
1. McDonald's	Sandwich	12,629	$19,006.0
2. Burger King	Sandwich	8,139	8,659.0
3. Wendy's	Sandwich	4,868	5,250.3
4. Taco Bell	Sandwich	6,875	5,111.0
5. Pizza Hut	Pizza	8,084	5,000.0
6. KFC	Chicken	5,182	4,300.0
7. Aramark Global Food/Leisure Services	Contract	2,818	3,757.3
8. Subway	Sandwich	12,008	3,200.0
9. Domino's Pizza	Pizza	4,629	2,560.0
10. Applebee's Neighborhood Bar & Grill	Dinner House	1,142	2,305.0
11. Arby's	Sandwich	3,069	2,260.0
12. Dairy Queen	Sandwich	5,113	2,145.0
13. Hardee's	Sandwich	2,673	2,138.8
14. Denny's	Family	1,715	2,079.0
15. Dunkin' Donuts	Snack	3,650	2,007.0
16. Red Lobster	Dinner House	625	2,005.0
17. Jack in the Box	Sandwich	1,517	1,757.2
18. Outback Steakhouse	Dinner House	574	1,729.0
19. Olive Garden	Dinner House	464	1,610.0
20. Sonic Drive-In	Sandwich	2,113	1,588.5
21. Chili's Grill & Bar	Dinner House	626	1,555.0
22. Papa John's Pizza	Pizza	2,254	1,426.0
23. Marriott Hotels, Resorts, & Suites	Hotel	501	1,400.0
24. T.G.I. Friday's	Dinner House	452	1,364.0
25. LSG/Sky Chefs	Contract	89	1,321.0

SOURCE: "NRN' Top 100, 2000." *Nation's Restaurant News* 29 (31):84.

[1]Ranked by the total U.S. sales volume in 1999.

◆ **APPENDIX 1–2B** *The Top Five Restaurant and Food Service Chains by Total U.S. Sales in Each Category*[1]

CATEGORY/CHAIN	CATEGORY/CHAIN

1. SANDWICH CHAINS
- McDonald's
- Burger King
- Wendy's
- Taco Bell
- Subway

2. CHICKEN CHAINS
- KFC
- Popeye's
- Chick-fil-A
- Boston Market
- Church's Chicken

3. PIZZA CHAINS
- Pizza Hut
- Domino's Pizza
- Papa John's Pizza
- Little Caesars Pizza
- Sbarro, The Italian Eatery

4. DINNER-HOUSE CHAINS
- Applebee's Neighborhood Grill & Bar
- Red Lobster
- Outback Steakhouse
- Olive Garden
- Chili's Grill & Bar

5. FAMILY CHAINS
- Denny's
- Cracker Barrel Old Country Store
- International House of Pancakes
- Shoney's
- Perkins Restaurant and Bakery

6. CONTRACT CHAINS
- Aramark Global Food/Leisure Services
- LSG/Sky Chefs
- Sodexho Marriott Corporate Services
- Sodexho Marriott Healthcare Services
- Sodexho Marriott Education Services

7. HOTEL CHAINS
- Marriott Hotels, Resorts, & Suites
- Hilton Hotels
- Sheraton Hotels
- Holiday Inns
- Radisson

8. GRILL-BUFFET CHAINS
- Golden Corral
- Ryan's Family Steak House
- Ponderosa Steakhouse
- Sizzler
- Western Sizzlin'

SOURCE: "NRN' Top 100, 2000." *Nation's Restaurant News* 29 (31):84.

[1]Ranked in descending order by the total U.S. sales volume in 1999.

◆ **APPENDIX 1–2C**   *The Estimated Market Shares of Restaurant Chain Brands in the United States*[1]

CHAIN BRAND	ESTIMATED MARKET SHARE
SANDWICH/HAMBURGER	
McDonald's	34.7%
Burger King	15.8%
Taco Bell	9.6%
Wendy's	9.5%
Subway	5.9%
Hardee's	4.6%
Arby's	3.9%
Dairy Queen	3.8%
Others	11.7%
PIZZA	
Pizza Hut	21.4%
Domino's	11.3%
Little Caesars	7.4%
Papa John's	5.2%
Others	54.7%
CHICKEN	
KFC	57.0%
Boston Market	12.6%
Popeye's	11.4%
Chick-fil-A	8.4%
Others	10.6%
DINNER HOUSE/CASUAL DINING	
Applebee's Neighborhood Grill & Bar	16.7%
Red Lobster	15.9%
Olive Garden	12.2%
Outback Steakhouse	11.9%
Chili's Grill & Bar	11.3%
T.G.I. Friday's	9.1%
Others	22.6%

SOURCE: *US Business Reporter.* http://www.activemedia-guide.com

[1]Ranked by the share of category sales in the United States in 1999.

◆ APPENDIX 1–3   *The Major Cruise Lines Serving North America*[1]

CRUISE LINE	NUMBER OF SHIPS	NUMBER OF LOWER BERTHS
1. Carnival	14	26,885
2. Royal Caribbean	12	24,714
3. Princess Cruises	9	14,670
4. Norwegian Cruise Line	8	12,306
5. Holland America Line	9	11,742
6. Celebrity Cruises	5	8,218
7. Costa Cruise Line	6	7,047
8. Premier Cruise Line	5	5,022
9. Norwegian Coastal Voyage, Inc./Bergen Line Services	11	4,263
10. Renaissance Cruises	9	3,692
11. First European	5	3,622
12. Disney Cruise Line	2	3,508
13. Mediterranean Shipping Cruises	4	3,449
14. Royal Olympic Cruises	6	3,277
15. Cunard Line, Ltd.	5	3,131
16. Crystal Cruises	2	1,884
17. Radisson Seven Seas Cruises	5	1,524
18. Commodore Cruise Line	2	1,177
19. Delta Queen Steamboat Co.	3	1,024
20. Regal Cruises	1	873
21. American Hawaii Cruises	1	867
22. Orient Lines, Inc.	1	845
23. Europamerica Rivers	5	792
24. Windstar Cruises	4	756
25. Seabourn Cruise Line	3	612
26. Silversea Cruises	2	592
27. Star Clipper	3	572
28. Club Med	1	386
29. American Canadian Cruise Line	3	244
30. Clipper Cruise Line	2	240
31. America West Steamboat Co.	1	163
32. Classical Cruises	1	140

SOURCE: "Cruise Industry Overview: Marketing Edition." *Cruise Lines International Association*, August 2000. http://www.cruising.org/

[1]Ranked by the number of lower berths available at the beginning of 2000.

◆ APPENDIX 1–4   *The Major U.S. Car Rental Companies*[1]

COMPANY	FLEET SIZE (CARS)	U.S. LOCATIONS	AIRPORT TRANSACTIONS (PERCENT)	LOCAL MARKET TRANSACTIONS (PERCENT)
MAINLY AIRPORT SALES				
1. Hertz	280,500	1,220	80%	20%
2. Avis	210,000	1,000	85%	15%
3. Alamo	150,000	101	90%	10%
4. Budget	146,000	1,056	65%	35%
5. National	140,000	500	86%	14%
6. Dollar	70,000	250	72%	28%
7. Thrifty	46,000	548	66%	34%
8. Payless	7,500	66	80%	20%
9. Ace	7,500	40	65%	35%
10. Inter American Car Rental	4,600	12	70%	30%
MAINLY LOCAL SALES				
1. Enterprise	399,941	3,600	5%	95%
2. FRCS (Ford)	48,000	3,353	1%	99%
3. Car Temps U.S.A.	38,000	440	0%	100%
4. DRAC (Chrysler)	22,000	1,200	1%	99%
5. Rent-A-Wreck	15,000	523	5%	95%
6. U-Save	13,000	460	10%	90%
7. Advantage	11,000	125	40%	60%
8. Auto Rental Resource Center	8,500	850	15%	85%
9. Affordable/Sensible	4,300	175	0%	100%
10. Americar	3,800	17	0%	100%
OTHER BRANDS	17,750	612	n/a	n/a
INDEPENDENTS	90,000	7,200	30%	70%
TOTALS	1,733,391	23,338		

SOURCE: "U.S. Car Rental Market." *Auto Rental News.* http://www.fleet-central.com/ARN/

[1]Ranked by the fleet size (total number of vehicles) in 1999.

◆ APPENDIX 1–5A   *The Top 25 Theme Parks in North America*[1]

THEME PARK	ATTENDANCE (MILLIONS)
1. The Magic Kingdom at Walt Disney World, Florida	15.4
2. Disneyland, Anaheim, California	13.9
3. EPCOT at Walt Disney World, Florida	10.6
4. Disney-MGM Studios at Walt Disney World, Florida	8.9
5. Disney's Animal Kingdom at Walt Disney World, Florida	8.3
6. Universal Studios at Universal, Orlando, Florida	8.1
7. Islands of Adventure at Universal, Orlando, Florida	6.0
8. Universal Studios Hollywood, California	5.2
9. Seaworld Florida	5.2
10. Busch Gardens Tampa Bay, Florida	5.0
11. Sea World California, San Diego, California	3.6
12. Six Flags Great Adventure, Jackson, New Jersey	3.5
13. Knott's Berry Farm, Buena Park, California	3.46
14. Cedar Point, Sandusky, Ohio	3.43
15. Morey's Piers, Wildwood, New Jersey	3.3
16. Six Flags Magic Mountain, Valencia, California	3.3
17. Paramount's King's Island, King's Island, Ohio	3.2
18. Santa Cruz Beach Boardwalk, California	3.0
19. Adventuredome at Circus Circus, Las Vegas, Nevada	2.977
20. Paramount Canada's Wonderland, Maple, Ontario	2.975
21. Six Flags Great America, Gurnee, Illinois	2.88
22. Six Flags Over Texas, Arlington, Texas	2.78
23. Knott's Camp Snoopy, Bloomington, Minnesota	2.6
24. Hersheypark, Hershey, Pennsylvania	2.45
25. Six Flags Over Georgia, Atlanta, Georgia	2.4

SOURCE: "Top 50 North American Amusement/Theme Parks." *Amusement Business* (December 25, 2000):84–85.

[1]Ranked by the estimated total attendance in 2000.

◆ APPENDIX 1–5B   *The Top 25 Fairs in North America*[1]

FAIRS	ATTENDANCE
1. State Fair of Texas, Dallas	3,300,000
2. Houston Livestock Show & Rodeo	1,889,861
3. State Fair of Oklahoma, Oklahoma City	1,702,888
4. Minnesota State Fair, St. Paul	1,682,685
5. Canadian National Exhibition, Toronto	1,350,000
6. Western Washington Fair, Puyallup	1,312,332
7. Del Mar Fair, California	1,169,150
8. Los Angeles County Fair, Pomona	1,280,000
9. Calgary Stampede, Alberta	1,218,851
10. Eastern States Exhibition, West Springfield, Massachusetts	1,210,961
11. Illinois State Fair, Springfield	1,162,000
12. Tulsa State Fair, Oklahoma	1,091,508
13. Pacific National Exhibition, Vancouver	1,055,292
14. San Antonio Stock & Rodeo Show	1,027,064
15. Erie County Fair, Hamburg, New York	1,006,000
16. Ohio State Fair, Columbus	980,819
17. New York State Fair, Syracuse	979,326
18. Iowa State Fair, Des Moines	978,841
19. California State Fair, Sacramento	965,840
20. Wisconsin State Fair, West Allis	904,059
21. Evergreen State Fair, Monroe, Washington	892,083
22. Arizona State Fair, Phoenix	855,553
23. North Carolina State Fair, Raleigh	846,724
24. Orange County State Fair, Costa Mesa, California	808,552
25. Southwestern Expo & Livestock Show, Fort Worth, Texas	792,800

SOURCE: "Top 50 North American Fairs." *Amusement Business* (December 25, 2000):96–97.

[1]Ranked by the estimated total attendance in 2000.

◆ APPENDIX 1–6 *The Market Shares of Major U.S. Airlines*[1]

AIRLINES	1999
1. United	20.7%
2. American Airlines	18.2%
3. Delta Air Lines	17.3%
4. Northwest Airlines	12.2%
5. Continental Airlines	9.6%
6. US Airways	6.9%
7. Southwest	6.1%
8. TWA	4.3%
9. America West	2.9%
10. Alaska Airlines	1.9%
Total Revenue Passenger Miles (RPMs) (in $ billions)	606.6

SOURCE: "Top 10 U.S. Airlines." *Advertising Age* (September 25, 2000). http://www.adage.com/dataplace/index.html

[1]Ranked by the share of total revenue passenger miles (RPMs) in 1999. RPM estimates provided by the U.S. Department of Transportation.

◆ APPENDIX 1–7   *The Leading Hospitality and Travel Advertisers*[1]

COMPANY	RANK	TOTAL U.S. ADVERTISING
Hospitality and Travel Industry Companies		
McDonald's	14	$1,134,802.3
Tricon Global Restaurants (KFC, Pizza Hut, Taco Bell)	31	858,780.2
Cendant Corp.	48	564,298.4
Wendy's International	95	282,060.1
Starwood Hotels & Resorts	99	264,066.1
Marriott International	116	232,900.0
Delta Air Lines	127	200,600.0
Bass PLC	131	197,200.0
Promus Hotel Corp. (now Hilton)	135	185,500.0
Darden Restaurants	139	178,200.0
Royal Caribbean International	145	172,600.0
AMR Corp. (American Airlines)	146	169,200.0
UAL Corp. (United Airlines)	157	149,800.0
Domino's Pizza	159	148,400.0
Southwest Airlines	175	124,800.0
Triarc Cos. (Arby's)	176	123,500.0
Advantica Restaurant Group (Denny's)	177	122,300.0
CKE Restaurants (Hardee's, Carl's Jr.)	184	114,400.0
Jack in the Box	188	109,500.0
Parents of Hospitality and Travel Industry Companies		
Ford Motor Co. (Hertz)	7	1,639,761.5
Walt Disney Co.	11	1,304,002.2
Diageo (Burger King)	13	1,198,445.2
Anheuser-Busch Cos.	40	654,391.1
American Express	54	518,798.8

SOURCE: "100 Leading National Advertisers/Advertisers Ranked 101 to 200." *Advertising Age* (September 25, 2000). Available online: http://www.adage.com/dataplace/index.html

[1]Ranked among leading U.S. advertisers in 1999. Figures are in thousands of dollars.

◆ **APPENDIX 1–8** *The Advertising Expenditures by Major Hospitality Companies by Media Type*[1]

TYPE OF ADVERTISING	MCDONALD'S	TRICON	CENDANT	WENDY'S	STARWOOD
Type of Measured Media					
Magazine	$5,382.8	$1,075.9	$15,551.7	$6,638.6	$24,876.9
Sunday Magazine	3,116.1	110.0	37.5	–	538.0
Newspaper	1,776.5	1,277.7	23,219.4	30.5	17,626.6
National Newspaper	768.8	293.6	7,085.3	135.0	16,564.7
Outdoor	28,916.4	4,809.4	15,646.8	5,057.9	3,444.1
Network TV	296,766.1	287,897.1	46,338.2	103,714.9	257.8
Spot TV	179,444.6	191,620.5	3,444.5	50,038.1	2,111.5
Syndicated TV	42,470.0	7,753.8	4,635.6	24,147.7	59.7
Cable TV	70,206.9	37,148.1	20,783.3	27,691.6	1,597.3
Network Radio	36.9	45.0	1,449.6	–	–
National Spot Radio	3,238.9	19,550.3	5,275.4	2,552.6	2,614.5
Internet	599.6	273.5	7,536.3	–	286.4
Yellow Pages	–	6,352.2	7,000.0	–	–
Total Measured Media Spending	632,723.6	558,207.1	158,003.6	220,006.9	69,977.5
Total Unmeasured Media Spending	502,078.6	300,573.1	406,294.8	62,053.2	194,088.6
Total Spending	$1,134,802.3	$858,780.2	$564,298.4	$282,060.1	$264,066.1

SOURCE: "100 Leading National Advertisers." *Advertising Age* (September 25, 2000). http://www.adage.com/dataplace/index.html

[1]Figures are in thousands of dollars and are for 1999.

◆ APPENDIX 1–9   *The Top 25 U.S. Travel Agencies*[1]

COMPANY	TOTAL SALES (MILLIONS)
1. American Express, New York, New York	$13,700.0
2. Carlson Wagonlit Travel, New York, New York	11,000.0
3. WorldTravel Partners, Atlanta, Georgia	4,300.0
4. Rosenbluth International, Philadelphia, Pennsylvania	4,200.0
5. Navigant International, Englewood, Colorado	3,300.0
6. Maritz Travel, St. Louis, Missouri	1,740.0
7. Liberty Travel, Ramsey, New Jersey	1,390.0
8. Sato Travel, Arlington, Virginia	1,200.0
9. Travelocity.com, Fort Worth, Texas	1,200.0
10. Expedia, Inc., Bellevue, Washington	832.0
11. McCord Travel, Chicago, Illinois	813.4
12. Total Travel Management, Troy, Michigan	749.0
13. Travel & Transport, Omaha, Nebraska	650.0
14. Omega World Travel, Fairfax, Virginia	645.0
15. VTS Travel, New York, New York	588.5
16. Cheap Tickets, Inc., Honolulu, Hawaii	495.3
17. Travel Incorporated, Duluth, Georgia	475.0
18. Northwestern Travel, Minneapolis, Minnesota	472.2
19. Fugazy Executive Travel, Boston, Massachusetts	325.0
20. Travel Management Partners, Raleigh, North Carolina	316.0
21. AAA Auto Club South, Tampa, Florida	310.0
22. Boeing Travel, Hazelwood, Missouri	305.0
23. Garber's Travel Service, Boston, Massachusetts	289.0
24. World Wide Travel Service, Little Rock, Arkansas	276.0
25. Sea Gate Travel, New York, New York	275.0

SOURCE: "The Top 50." *Travel Weekly* (June 23, 2000). http://www.twcrossroads.com

[1]Ranked by the total company sales in 1999.

◆ APPENDIX 1–10A   *The Budges of U.S. State Tourism Offices*[1]

STATE	BUDGET	STATE	BUDGET
1. Hawaii	$60,000,000	26. Arizona	$8,849,300
2. Illinois	55,507,500	27. Alabama	8,790,604
3. Florida	54,287,750	28. Colorado	7,300,000
4. Pennsylvania	34,370,996	29. Georgia	7,246,382
5. Texas	30,875,113	30. Kentucky	7,177,800
6. New York	20,808,010	31. Vermont	6,985,079
7. Virginia	19,200,000	32. Montana	6,841,624
8. Iowa	17,589,711	33. Alaska	6,668,500
9. Louisiana	16,758,578	34. New Jersey	6,600,000
10. Wisconsin	15,525,000	35. Ohio	6,380,000
11. Michigan	15,450,883	36. Connecticut	6,094,297
12. Missouri	15,148,409	37. South Dakota	5,547,000
13. Massachusetts	14,162,000	38. Idaho	5,314,027
14. South Carolina	13,543,771	39. Utah	4,829,500
15. California	13,200,000	40. Indiana	4,536,000
16. West Virginia	13,028,002	41. Maine	4,512,158
17. New Mexico	12,868,500	42. Kansas	4,500,000
18. Minnesota	12,770,311	43. Wyoming	4,406,460
19. Mississippi	12,681,198	44. Washington	3,875,020
20. Tennessee	12,052,200	45. New Hampshire	3,502,202
21. Arkansas	11,397,938	46. Nebraska	3,290,000
22. Maryland	10,736,310	47. Oregon	3,122,082
23. North Carolina	10,658,626	48. Rhode Island	2,632,718
24. Oklahoma	9,665,611	49. North Dakota	2,187,513
25. Nevada	9,381,380	50. Delaware	1,176,600
		TOTAL	$644,032,663

SOURCE: *Survey of State and Territory Tourism Offices 1999–2000*, Travel Industry Association of America (February 2000): 4.

[1]Ranked by the projected budget for 1999–2000.

◆ **APPENDIX 1–10B**   *The Promotional Budgets of the 10 Leading National Tourism Administrations*[1]

COUNTRY	PROMOTIONAL BUDGET
1. Australia	$88
2. United Kingdom	79
3. Spain	79
4. France	73
5. Singapore	54
6. Thailand	51
7. Netherlands	50
8. Austria	47
9. Ireland	38
10. Portugal	37

SOURCE: "Top Ten NTA/NTO Promotional Budgets, 1995." *World Tourism Organization.*

[1]Ranked by promotional budget in millions of U.S. dollars in 1995.

◆ **APPENDIX 1–11**   *The Leading Tourism Destinations in the World by Country*

COUNTRY	1998	1999
International Tourist Arrivals	(millions)	(millions)
1. France	70,040	73,042
2. Spain	47,403	51,772
3. United States	46,395	48,491
4. China and Hong Kong	36,648	38,375
5. Italy	34,933	36,097
6. United Kingdom	25,745	25,740
7. Canada	18,867	19,557
8. Mexico	19,810	19,236
9. Russia	15,805	18,496
10. Poland	18,780	17,950
International Tourist Receipts		
1. United States	$71,250	$74,448
2. Spain	29,737	32,913
3. France	29,931	31,699
4. Italy	29,866	28,357
5. China and Hong Kong	19,685	21,308
6. United Kingdom	20,978	20,972
7. Germany	16,429	16,828
8. Austria	11,184	11,088
9. Canada	9,396	10,025
10. Greece	6,188	8,765

SOURCE: "International Tourist Arrivals by Region." *World Tourism Organization* (August 2000). http://www.world-tourism.org/

◆ **APPENDIX 1–12**   *The Most Visited Travel Sites on the World Wide Web*[1]

TRAVEL WEB SITE	UNIQUE AUDIENCE	AVERAGE TIME SPENT AT SITE[2]
1. Mapquest.com	4,335,152	0:09:30
2. Travelocity.com	4,235,552	0:19:26
3. Expedia.com	3,996,625	0:14:00
4. Maps.yahoo.com	3,950,103	0:09:46
5. Travel.yahoo.com	1,513,479	0:02:11
6. Itn.net	1,420,423	0:13:01
7. Southwest.com	1,171,427	0:09:47
8. AA.com	1,131,745	0:11:03
9. Delta-air.com	1,053,340	0:15:12
10. Mapblast.com	1,046,939	0:09:29
11. Nwa.com	932,181	0:07:46
12. Usairways.com	857,113	0:09:36
13. Mapsonus.com	831,109	0:01:15
14. Ual.com	773,673	0:04:34
15. Trip.com	716,600	0:08:31

SOURCE: "Top 15 Travel Sites, at Work." *Advertising Age.* http://www.adage.com/dataplace/index.html

[1]Ranked by the number of unique visitors to the sites for the week ending July 23, 2000.

[2]Time is shown in minutes and seconds.

Appendix 2
Industry Resources

The author and Delmar affirm that the Web site URLs referenced herein were accurate at the time of printing. However, due to the fluid nature of the Internet, we cannot guarantee their accuracy for the life of the edition.

◆ **APPENDIX 2–1**   *Travel Trade Intermediaries and Trade Publications*

INTERMEDIARY/PUBLICATION	WEB ADDRESS
1. RETAIL TRAVEL AGENTS, CORPORATE TRAVEL MANAGERS, AND AGENCIES	
• ACTE Quarterly	http://www.acte.org/
• Business Travel News	http://www.btnonline.com/
• Cruise Trade	http://www.traveltrade.com/cruisetrade/
• Frequent Flyer	http://www.frequentflyer.oag.com/
• JAX FAX Travel Marketing Magazine	http://www.jaxfax.com/
• Travel Agent Magazine	http://www.advanstar.com/
• Travel Daily News	http://www.traveldailynews.com/
• Travel Management Daily	http://www.tmdaily.com/
• Travel Trade	http://www.traveltrade.com/
• Travel Weekly	http://www.twcrossroads.com/
• Web Travel News	http://www.webtravelnews.com/
2. TOUR WHOLESALERS AND OPERATORS	
• Courier (NTA)	http://www.ntaonline.com/
• The Group Travel Leader	http://www.grouptravelleader.com/
• Specialty Travel Index	http://www.spectrav.com/
3. INCENTIVE TRAVEL PLANNERS	
• CIM	http://www.cim-publications.de/
• Corporate Meetings & Incentives	http://www.meetingsnet.com/
• Incentive	http://www.incentivemag.com/
• Motivation Strategies	http://www.info-now.com/
• Potentials	http://www.potentialsmag.com/
• Promo Magazine	http://www.promomagazine.com/
4. CONVENTION AND MEETING PLANNERS	
• Association Management	http://www.asaenet.org/magazine/
• Association Meetings	http://www.meetingsnet.com/
• Association Meetings International	http://www.cat-publications.com/
• Insurance Conference Planner	http://www.meetingsnet.com/
• Medical Meetings	http://www.meetingsnet.com/
• Meetings & Conventions	http://www.meetings-conventions.com/
• Meetings & Incentive Travel	http://www.cat-publications.com/
• Meeting News	http://www.meetingnews.com/
• Religious Conference Manager	http://www.meetingsnet.com/
• Sales & Marketing Management	http://www.salesandmarketing.com/
• Successful Meetings	http:www.successmtgs.com/
• Training	http://www.trainingmag.com/
• Training & Development	http://www.astd.org/
• Technology Meetings	http://www.meetingsnet.com/

◆ APPENDIX 2–2   *Major Directories of Hospitality and Travel Facilities and Services*

DIRECTORY NAMES	WEB ADDRESS
• Berlitz Complete Guide to Cruising & Cruise Ships	http://www.berlitz.com/
• Cruise Line & Ship Profiles	http://www.cruising.org/
• Hotel & Travel Index	http://www.cahners.com/
• OAG Pocket Flight Guide	http://www.oag.com/
• OAG Flight Guide North America	http://www.oag.com/
• Official Corporate & Incentive Travel Directory	http://www.d-net.com/
• Official Cruise Guide	http://www.cahners.com/
• Official Meeting Facilities Guide	http://www.omfg.com/
• World Travel Guide	http://www.wtgonline.com/

◆ **APPENDIX 2–3**   *Key Trade Associations in the North American Hospitality and Travel Industry*

INDUSTRY GROUP	WEB ADDRESS
1. CARRIERS	
• Airlines Reporting Corporation	http://www.arccorp.com/
• Air Transport Association	http://www.air-transport.org/
• American Automobile Association	http://www.aaa.com/
• American Bus Association	http://www.buses.org/
• Amtrak (National Passenger Transport Corporation; government agency)	http://www.amtrak.com/
• International Air Transport Association	http://www.iata.org/
• International Airlines Travel Agency Network	http://www.iatan.org/
• Recreation Vehicle Industry Association	http://www.rvamerica.com/
• Regional Airline Association	http://www.raa.org/
• United Motorcoach Association	http://www.uma.org/
• Via Rail Canada	http://www.viarail.ca/
2. SUPPLIERS	
• American Bed & Breakfast Association	http://www.abba.com/
• American Gaming Association	http://www.americangaming.org/
• American Hotel & Lodging Association	http://www.ahma.com/
• American Resort Development Association	http://www.arda.org/
• American Sightseeing International	http://www.americansightseeing.org/
• Canadian Restaurant and Foodservices Association	http://www.crfa.ca/
• Convention Industry Council	http://www-c-l-c.org/
• Cruise Lines International Association	http://www.cruising.org/
• Hotel Association of Canada	http://www.hotels.ca/
• Hotels Sales and Marketing Association International	http://www.hsmai.org/
• International Association of Amusement Parks and Attractions	http://www.iaapa.org/
• International Association of Assembly Managers	http://www.iaam.org/
• International Association of Conference Centers	http://www.iacconline.com/
• International Association for Exhibition Management	http://www.iaem.org/
• International Association of Fairs and Expositions	http://www.iafenet.org/
• International Council of Cruise Lines	http://www.iccl.org/
• International Festivals & Events Association	http://www.ifea.com/
• National Association of RV Parks and Campgrounds	http://www.gocampingamerica.com/
• National Park and Recreation Association	http://www.activeparks.org/
• National Restaurant Association	http://www.restaurant.org/
• Professional Association of Innkeepers International	http://www.paii.org/
• Society of Independent Show Organizers	http://www.siso.org/
• World Waterpark Association	http://www.waterparks.org/
3. THE TRAVEL TRADE	
• Adventure Travel Society	http://www.adventuretravel.com/
• Association of Canadian Travel Agents	http://www.acta.ca/
• American Society of Association Executives	http://www.asaenet.org/
• American Society of Travel Agents	http://www.astanet.org/
• Association of Corporate Travel Executives	http://www.acte.org/
• Association of Destination Management Executives	http://www.adme.org/
• Association of Retail Travel Agents	http://www.artaonline.com/
• Canadian Institute of Travel Counsellors	http://www.citc.ca/
• Institute of Certified Travel Agents	http://www.icta.com/

(continued)

◆ **APPENDIX 2–3** *Continued*

INDUSTRY GROUP	WEB ADDRESS
• Meeting Professionals International	http://www.mpiweb.org/
• National Association of Commissioned Travel Agents	http://www.nacta.org/
• National Business Travel Association	http://www.nbta.org/
• National Tour Association	http://www.ntaonline.com/
• Professional Convention Management Association	http://www.pcma.org/
• Receptive Services Association	http://www.rsana.com/
• Religious Conference Management Association	http://www.rcmaweb.org/
• Reunion Network	http://www.reunionfriendly.com/
• Society of Corporate Meeting Professionals	http://www.scmp.org/
• Society of Government Travel Professionals	http://government-travel.org/
• Society of Incentive & Travel Executives	http://www.site-intl.org/
• U.S. Air Consolidators Association	http://www.usaca.com/
• U.S. Tour Operators Association	http://www.ustoa.com/

4. DESTINATION MANAGEMENT AND SUPPORT SERVICES

• Association of Travel Marketing Executives	http://www.atme.org/
• Council on Hotel, Restaurant, and Institutional Education: CHRIE	http://www.chrie.org/
• International Association of Convention & Visitor Bureaus	http://www.iacvb.org/
• International Society of Travel & Tourism Educators	http://www.istte.org/
• Society of American Travel Writers	http://www.satw.org/
• The International Ecotourism Society	http://www.ecotourism.org/
• Tourism Industry Association of Canada	http://www.tiac-aitc.ca/
• Travel Industry Association of America	http://www.tia.org/
• Travel and Tourism Research Association	http://www.ttra.com/
• Western Association of Convention & Visitors Bureaus	http://www.wacvb.com/

◆ **APPENDIX 2–4**   *Major Consumer, Academic, and Trade Journals in the Hospitality and Travel Field*

1. CONSUMER MAGAZINE

- Arthur Frommer's Budget Travel
- Backpacker Magazine
- Budget Travel
- Caribbean Travel and Life
- Condé Nast Traveler
- Consumer Reports Travel Letter
- Cruise Travel
- Endless Vacation
- Expedia Travels
- Gourmet
- Islands
- Midwest Living
- National Geographic Traveler
- Outdoor Life
- Outside Magazine
- Resorts and Great Hotels
- Southern Living
- Travel 50 and Beyond
- Travel & Leisure
- Travel & Leisure Golf
- Travel/Holiday
- Travel America
- Vacations Magazine

2. ACADEMIC AND TRADE JOURNALS (TJ)

- ACTA Turistica
- ANATOLIA
- Annals of Tourism Research
- Asia Pacific Journal of Tourism Research
- Australian Journal of Hospitality Management
- Club Management (TJ)
- Cornell Hotel and Restaurant Administration Quarterly
- Current Issues in Tourism
- Event Tourism
- FIU Hospitality Review
- Gaming Research & Review Journal
- Hotel & Motel Management (TJ)
- Hotels (TJ)
- Information Technology & Tourism
- International Journal of Contemporary Hospitality Management
- International Journal of Hospitality Management
- International Journal of Hospitality and Tourism Administration
- Journal of Convention & Exhibition Management
- Journal of Ecotourism
- Journal of Foodservice Systems
- Journal of Gambling Studies
- Journal of Hospitality & Leisure Marketing
- Journal of Hospitality Financial Management
- Journal of Hospitality & Tourism Education
- Journal of Hospitality & Tourism Research
- Journal of Nutrition for the Elderly
- Journal of Nutrition in Recipe & Menu Development
- Journal of Quality Assurance in Tourism
- Journal of Restaurant & Foodservice Marketing
- Journal of Sports Tourism
- Journal of Sustainable Tourism
- Journal of Teaching in Travel & Tourism
- Journal of The American Dietetic Association
- Journal of Tourism Studies
- Journal of Travel Research
- Journal of Travel & Tourism Research
- Journal of Travel & Tourism Marketing
- Journal of Vacation Marketing
- Lodging (TJ)
- LH/Lodging Hospitality (TJ)
- NACUFS Journal
- Nation's Restaurant News (TJ)
- Pacific Tourism Review
- PRAXIS: The Journal of Applied Hospitality Management
- Restaurant Business (TJ)
- Restaurants and Institutions (TJ)
- Restaurants USA (TJ)
- Scandinavian Journal of Hospitality and Tourism
- School Foodservice Journal
- Teoros International
- The Tourist Review
- Tourism Analysis
- Tourism: An International Interdisciplinary Journal
- Tourism, Culture & Communication
- Tourism Economics
- Tourism Geographies
- Tourism and Hospitality Research
- Tourism Management
- Tourism Recreation Research
- Tourismus Journal
- Tourist Studies
- Travel & Tourism Analyst

Glossary

accountability research—Research done to measure the results of a marketing plan, particularly, to determine if marketing objectives were achieved.

advertising—Any paid form of nonpersonal presentation or promotion of ideas, goods, or services by an identified sponsor (American Marketing Association definition).

advertising agency—A specialized company that provides advertising services to hospitality and travel organizations.

advertorial—An advertising message that is presented in an editorial format and is usually lengthier than a standard advertisement.

affinity cards—Credit cards issued by a bank or other financial institution that are linked with a specific hospitality and travel company, attraction, tourism destination, or nonprofit organization.

affinity group packages—Vacation packages or tours arranged for groups that share some form of affinity, usually a close social, religious, or ethnic bond.

affordable budgeting—A method of budgeting for marketing, often used by small businesses, in which only what can be afforded is spent.

AIDA formula—An acronym for attention, interest, desire, action. This is a formula approach to personal selling. It is also used to describe the functions that advertisements need to play (get attention, create interest and a desire, and cause action).

all-inclusive packages—A generic term for packages that include all or nearly all the elements that travelers require for their trips including airfare, lodging, ground transportation, taxes, and gratuities.

American Plan (AP)—A rate that includes accommodation and three meals per day—typically breakfast, lunch, and dinner.

appointed—A retail travel agency receives a designation from an association, airline, cruise line, or other supplier or carrier to act as a sales agent for them.

approach—This is part of the second step in the sales process. It includes various activities leading up to the sales presentation including making appointments with prospects, establishing rapport, and checking out preliminary details.

arbitrary budgeting—Allocating a marketing budget of approximately the same size as previous years.

attitude(s)—Predisposition to evaluate some symbol, object, or aspect of the world in a favorable or unfavorable manner.

baby boomers—A demographic segment of the population consisting of people born between 1946 and 1964.

balanced scorecard approach (BSC)—A performance measurement approach for a company that was originally developed by R. Kaplan and D. Norton.

banner advertisements—Advertisements placed on a World Wide Web site, usually by an organization other than the one that owns the site.

Bed and Breakfast (B & B)—A rate that combines a night's accommodation with a breakfast the following day that can be either a full or continental breakfast.

behavioral segmentation—Divides customers by their usage rates, usage status and potential, brand loyalty, use occasions, and benefits sought.

benefit segmentation—A type of behavioral segmentation. It groups customers according to similarities in the benefits they look for in specific products or services.

blind prospecting—Involves the use of telephone directories and other published lists to find sales prospects. The sales representative has no prior knowledge of the people on the lists and has no idea if they are true sales prospects.

blocking space—Reserving groups (blocks) of rooms or seats for tour wholesalers or other group customers.

brand loyalty—The extent to which a customer repeatedly buys a specific brand of product or service.

brand segmentation—Developing brands that are designed to appeal to a specific target market or sets of target markets.

branding—Developing a mark (logo), symbol, set of words, or combination of these to differentiate an organization from others.

break-even analysis—A technique used in pricing based on the consideration of fixed and variable costs, customer volumes, and profit margins.

broadcast media—Advertisements displayed by means of electronics, encompassing television (including cable), radio, videotape, and computer-generated graphic presentations.

budgeting—Allocating human resources and money toward the implementation of marketing plans.

building-block procedure (for marketing budgets)—A carefully sequenced, step-by-step process for developing a marketing budget. Also known as the objective-and-task approach.

business travel market—One of the two main divisions of the hospitality and travel market. This includes people traveling and dining out for business purposes, and those attending conventions and meetings.

buying process—Stages that customers go through before and after making a purchase. The five stages are need awareness, information search, evaluation of alternatives, purchase, and postpurchase evaluation.

canned sales presentations—Methods for making sales presentations in which sales representatives know exactly what they will say beforehand. All or part of the presentations are memorized.

cannibalize—A situation where one of an organization's brands takes customers away from one or more of the organization's other brands.

capital budget—A projection of the capital investment expected in a new hospitality and travel business.

carriers—Airlines, railways, bus, ship, and ferry companies.

case studies—A primary research technique that produces in-depth, qualitative information on comparable hospitality and travel organizations or other specific situations relating to marketing hospitality and travel customers.

celebrity testimonials—A type of advertising message format in which a well-known celebrity recommends or otherwise *endorses* the service or product.

change—As one of the five Cs of marketing research, this refers to trends that have occurred among customers and competitors.

channel-of-distribution segmentation—Dividing up travel intermediaries (the travel trade) by function and by common characteristics shared by functional groups.

channels of distribution—Direct or indirect (through the travel trade) distribution arrangements used by suppliers, carriers, and destination marketing organizations.

charter tour—A trip or package where the aircraft or other equipment is chartered (rented) by a tour wholesaler, tour operator, or another individual or group.

circulation—The number of households who subscribe to a given magazine or newspaper. It is one of the measures of reach in advertising.

closing—Getting a sales prospect's agreement on the objectives of the sales call, normally implying a definite sale or reservation.

clutter—This is a factor considered when evaluating advertising media alternatives. It represents the number of ads in one newspaper or magazine issue, or one radio or television program.

co-branding—Also sometimes referred to as dual branding, this is the offering of two or more brands at one location, e.g., combining a KFC restaurant with a Taco Bell.

cognitive dissonance—Also sometimes called post-purchase doubt, this is a feeling of anxiety that a person experiences after making a purchase.

cold calling or canvassing—A type of blind prospecting in the field. Sales representatives call on individuals or organizations with no idea if these people will turn out to be true sales prospects.

combiners—Organizations that recognize that they serve different market segments but choose to ignore these differences when marketing. This is one of four alternative marketing strategies available to organizations.

comment cards—In-house, self-administered surveys that typically generate a low response rate.

commercial information sources—The advertising and other promotional materials designed by corporations and other organizations.

commercial sources—(See commerical information sources.)

commission caps—First initiated by Delta Air Lines in 1995, these caps place a maximum amount in dollar terms on the amount of commission paid by the airlines.

commissionable (packages)—Packages where suppliers, carriers, and destination marketing organizations agree to pay the travel agent a commission.

communications process—The process through which hospitality and travel marketers communicate with customers consisting of nine elements—source, encoding, message, medium, decoding, noise, receiver, response, and feedback.

community involvement—Various activities undertaken by a hospitality and travel organization and its employees to help or serve the local community. This is considered part of the public relations effort.

comparative advertising—An advertising message format in which direct comparisons are made between the sponsor and specific competitors.

competition—For hospitality and travel organizations, this includes: (1) direct competition, (2) substitute services, and (3) indirect competition.

competitive budgeting—(see competitive-parity budgeting)

competitive-parity budgeting—An unsophisticated approach to setting a marketing budget. Marketing expenditures are set at approximately the same amount as competitors.

competitive pricing—A marketing approach in which companies try to match competitors' prices closely.

competitors—Organizations with similar services or products competing to satisfy the needs of the same customer groups.

concentrated marketing strategy—An approach to marketing where a few market segments are chosen from among several and attention is concentrated on these selected market segments.

conclusive research—Information gained through research that helps solve a business problem or assess a marketing opportunity.

confidence—One of the five Cs of marketing research in which the marketer believes that a prediction or decision is more likely to be accurate or successful.

consumer advertising—Advertising aimed at the customers who will actually use the services being promoted.

contests—A sales promotion technique where entrants win prizes on the basis of some skill requirement that they are asked to demonstrate.

contextual differences—Unique characteristics of organizations in the service industries, including hospitality and travel, that exist because of the ways they have been managed and regulated.

Continental Plan (CP)—A meal and accommodation package that includes a room and a cold breakfast.

contingency planning—This is where some flexibility is built into marketing plans and budgets to allow for unexpected events.

continuity programs—Sales promotions that require people to make several purchases, sometimes over a long period of time.

contribution margin—The difference between the selling price and the variable costs per unit.

convention and visitors bureau (CVB)—A term coined in North America for an organization, typically nonprofit, that is responsible for marketing a specific destination. A CVB is a type of destination marketing organization. In the United States, the majority of funding comes through room taxes.

convention/meeting packages—Special packages offered by resorts, hotels, and conference centers to attract conventions and meetings. Normally, they include accommodation and meals, but they may also incorporate local tours, attraction admissions, special events, or programs.

convention/meeting planners—Persons who plan and coordinate meetings and conventions. Some belong to major national associations, large nonprofit organizations, government agencies, educational institutions, and large corporations. Others work for specialized convention management consulting firms.

conversion rate—Used with direct-response advertising, this is the percentage of customers who inquire that actually buy or use the sponsor's advertised hospitality and travel service.

cooperative advertising—A situation where two or more organizations share the costs of an advertisement or advertising campaign.

cooperative promotion (partnership)—A situation where two or more organizations share the costs of a promotional effort (advertising, sales promotion, personal selling, public relations, or publicity).

copy platform—A statement that fully describes the (advertising) message idea and serves as the foundation for the copy (text) within an advertising campaign.

core principles of marketing—The seven basic principles of marketing: the marketing concept, marketing or customer orientation, satisfying customers' needs and wants, market segmentation, value and the exchange process, product life cycle, and marketing mix.

corporate travel agencies—Also known as *outplants*, these are retail travel agencies specializing, either partly or wholly, in handling corporate or government accounts.

corporate travel managers—Individuals employed by corporations, associations, government agencies, and other types of organizations to coordinate the organization's travel arrangements.

cost per thousand (CPM)—This is a criterion used to evaluate alternative advertising media and vehicles based on the cost per thousand readers, viewers, or listeners reached.

cost-plus pricing—Also known as mark-up pricing, this pricing approach involves the addition of a certain dollar amount or percentage to the actual or estimated costs of a service to arrive at a final price.

coupon redemption rates—The percentages of total coupons issued that are used (redeemed) by customers.

coupons—Vouchers or certificates that entitle customers or intermediaries to a price cut on the couponed product or services.

credibility—One of the five Cs of marketing research referring to the level of believability attached to the marketer's information or facts.

critical success factor (CSF)—A characteristic, strategy, or approach that industry experts believe is required for success in a particular area of business.

cruise-only agents—Retail travel agencies involved exclusively in selling and booking cruises.

culture—A combination of the beliefs, values, attitudes, habits, traditions, customs, and forms of behavior that are shared by a group of people.

customer behavior—The ways in which customers select, use, and behave after they have purchased hospitality and travel services.

customer mix—The combination of customers that use or are attracted to a specific hospitality and travel organization.

customer needs—Gaps between what customers have and what they would like to have.

customer relationship management (CRM)—A business strategy to select and manage customers to optimize long-term value (http://www.CRMguru.com/).

customer wants—Needs of which customers are aware.

customers—One of the five Cs of marketing research referring to the importance of gathering and analyzing data on past and potential guests.

database marketing—Managing a computerized relational database system, in real time, of comprehensive, up-to-date, relevant data on customers, inquiries, and prospects, to identify our most responsive customers for the purpose of developing a high quality, long-standing relationship of repeat business by developing predictive models which enable us to send desired messages at the right time in the right form to the right people (National Center for Database Marketing definition).

databases—Detailed information on individual customers maintained in computerized systems by individual hospitality and travel organizations.

decline stage—This is the final stage in the product life cycle when the sales of a service begin to fall.

decoding—Part of the communications process. This is when customers interpret promotional messages in such a way that the messages have real meaning for them.

demand-led trends—The six industry trends that resulted from newly emerging customer needs include changing age structure; changing household structure; changing household roles and responsibilities; an increasing importance of minorities; changing social/cultural patterns and lifestyles; and an increased demand for specific travel alternatives.

demographic segmentation—Dividing up markets based on population statistics.

destination management companies (DMCs)—A professional services company possessing extensive local knowledge, expertise, and resources, specializing in the design and implementation of events, activities, tours, transportation and program logistics.

destination marketing organizations (DMOs)—Government agencies, convention and visitors bureaus, travel associations, and other bodies that market travel to their respective destination areas.

designated market area (DMA)—the geographic area composed of all the counties that a specific television station influences.

destination mix—A unique relationship found in the hospitality and travel industry involving attractions and events, facilities, infrastructure and transportation amenities, and hospitality resources.

destination package—A travel package characterized by the destination it features.

differential pricing—(see **price discrimination**)

differentiated marketing strategies—Marketing approaches that recognize differences between target markets by using individualized marketing mixes.

digital marketing—All the types of marketing communication that involve digital technologies, including the World Wide Web, e-mail, CD-ROM, and other forms of transmission of text and images in a digital format.

direct distribution—Where the organization itself assumes the total responsibility for promoting, reserving, and providing services to customers.

direct mail—An advertising medium involving the mailing of promotional materials to customers and intermediaries.

direct marketing—A form of hospitality and travel promotion in which no intermediaries are used. Booking is made or information requested directly from the sponsoring organization. The major elements of direct marketing are direct mail, telemarketing, and home shopping through television and by personal computer.

direct-response advertising—A form of direct marketing which encourages the hospitality and travel customer to take immediate action or make an immediate response directly to the advertiser (American Marketing Association definition).

discounting—A common pricing practice in the hospitality and travel industry in which fares, rates, or prices are below the advertised figures. This is usually done by target market.

discriminatory pricing—(see **price discrimination**)

disintermediation—Giving the customer direct access to information or reservations, often electronically. This enables the customer to bypass intermediaries.

distribution channel—A particular direct or indirect distribution arrangement used by a supplier, carrier, or destination marketing organization.

distribution mix—The combination of direct and indirect distribution channels used by a hospitality and travel organization to make customers aware of its services and to reserve and deliver them.

dominance—the ability of an advertising sponsor to dominate a particular medium at a specific time.

double occupancy basis—A rate for a lodging property that is based on the assumption that two persons will be sharing the room or unit.

e-commerce—The online purchasing of hospitality and travel services, mainly through the World Wide Web and by e-mail.

economic environment—The overall condition of the economy at the local, regional, national, and international levels.

economic feasibility—The analysis of a development project to determine if it will produce a sufficient return on investment.

efficiency ratios—Statistical measurements that marketing managers use to evaluate their organizations' efficiency in using promotional and distribution mix elements.

eight Ps—Product, place, promotion, price, people, packaging, programming, and partnership—the eight elements of a hospitality and travel organization's marketing mix.

80-20 principle—A common problem found in marketing in which 80% of the effort or resources is put into capturing 20% of the total sales volume.

elasticity of demand—The sensitivity of customer demand to changes in the prices of services.

empowerment—Giving hospitality and travel employees the authority to identify and solve guest problems or complaints on the spot and to make improvements in work processes when necessary.

encoding—Part of the communications process in which the sponsor translates the information to be communicated into an arrangement of words, pictures, colors, sounds, movements, and even body language.

escorted tours—Packages that follow a predetermined itinerary and provide tour escorts and guides to accompany the travelers.

European plan (EP)—An accommodation-only rate that includes no meals.

evaluation research—Research that is completed to determine the effectiveness of a hospitality and travel organization's marketing efforts, also referred to as *accountability research.*

event packages—Packages developed around special, one-time events, festivals, entertainment and cultural performances, or other occurrences.

evidence—Tangible clues on which customers rely when they purchase services.

evoked set—The set of hospitality or travel brands, or destinations, from which the customer selects for a specific purchase occasion.

exchange process—A process through which suppliers of hospitality and travel services and their customers trade items of value.

executive summary—A few pages usually positioned at the beginning of a marketing plan that sum up the plan's main sections.

experimental research—A category of primary research in the hospitality and travel industry. It involves tests of various kinds to determine the likely reactions of customers to new services or products.

explicit communication—Promotional messages explicitly (clearly and intentionally) given to customers through the use of language, either orally (e.g., via television, radio, telephone, or personal selling) or in a written format (e.g., via direct mail, magazine or newspaper ads, or sales proposals).

exploratory research—Information-collection techniques that shed more light on a research problem or opportunity but that do not help solve or assess the problem or opportunity.

exposure—A term used in advertising to describe the numbers of customers who read, see, or hear advertisements.

external customers—The guests or customers of a hospitality and travel organization.

external environment—Events (marketing environment factors) that are completely beyond the control of the marketing manager and that shape the way business is done.

external secondary research data—Previously published information obtained from sources outside the hospitality and travel organization, including government agencies, destination marketing organizations, magazines, journals and newspapers, research companies and private consulting organizations, and universities.

familiarization (fam) trips—Free or reduced-priced trips given to travel agencies, tour wholesalers and operators, travel writers, and other intermediaries by suppliers, carriers, and destination marketing organizations.

family life-cycle—Predictable stages that families pass through over a period of time.

family vacation packages—Vacation packages that provide something for everyone in parent-children households.

FAQs (frequently asked questions)—A set of predetermined questions and answers that are supplied on a Web site.

fear appeal—An advertising message format that uses a negative emotional appeal to arouse or shock the customer into a purchase or change of attitude.

feasibility analysis—A study of the potential demand and economic feasibility of a business or other type of organization.

feature stories—Also known as *features,* these are articles or stories of human interest that entertain, inform, or educate readers, viewers, or listeners.

feedback—An element of all systems, feedback is used in two slightly different ways in this book. First, it is said that there must be feedback mechanisms in the hospitality and travel marketing system. This is necessary to gather information from customers and others to make future marketing decisions. Second, feedback is said to be an element in the communications process (a system itself). Here it is the response message that the receiver (customer) transmits back to the source (sponsor).

field sales—Also known as external selling, these are selling efforts taking place in person outside the hospitality and travel organization's place of business.

five Cs of research—The five major reasons for doing marketing research including customers, competition, confidence, credibility, and change.

five Ds of positioning—These are five sequential steps that an organization should follow for effective positioning—documenting, deciding, differentiating, designing, and delivering.

fixed costs—Costs that remain the same no matter how many customers buy the package or other services.

fly-cruise packages—Mostly offered by cruise line companies, these are packages that include round-trip airfare to a port of departure plus a cruise.

fly-drive packages—Single-price packages with round-trip airfare and car rental at destinations.

fly-rail packages—A type of hospitality and travel package that includes air and railway travel.

focus group—A form of personal interviewing in which the researcher directs questions to a small group of people.

follow-the-leader pricing—A pricing approach where, if one company (e.g., Burger King) raises its prices, others (McDonalds and Wendy's) do so also.

foreign independent tour (FIT)—Custom-designed packages arranged by travel agents or other foreign independent travel specialists that fit individual client's needs while traveling in foreign countries.

four Ps—The four factors traditionally considered to comprise an organization's marketing mix—product, price, place, and promotion.

freestanding inserts (FSIs)—Advertising materials of various sizes that are inserted into newspapers but which are not attached to the newspaper. These may or may not incorporate coupons.

frequency—A criterion for evaluating alternative advertising media based on the average number of times potential customers are exposed to a given advertisement or advertising campaign.

frequent-flyer programs—Continuity recognition programs first introduced by domestic airlines in the early 1980s. This sales promotion technique awards free trips, upgrades, and other prizes to fliers after they have logged certain numbers of air miles with the airline.

frequent-guest award programs—Continuity recognition programs, similar to frequent-flyer programs, first introduced by lodging chains in the early 1980s. This sales promotion technique awards free accommodation, upgrades, and other prizes to guests after they have spent certain numbers of room nights with the chain.

frequent travelers—People, especially business travelers, who take a more than average number of trips.

frequently asked questions (FAQs)—A set of predetermined questions and answers that are supplied on a Web site.

full-coverage marketing strategy—A marketing strategy, often followed by industry leaders, where the company appeals to all market segments in the total market with a tailor-made approach for each market segment.

games—Sales promotion events, very much like sweepstakes, that involve the use of game pieces, such as scratch-and-win cards.

general positioning approach—An approach to creating an image for an organization or destination that promises more than one benefit. These benefits may not be very obvious to the customer.

generation X—A demographic segment of the population consisting of those people born between the early 1960s and early 1980s.

generic differences—Unchangeable differences shared by all services that affect the marketing of services.

geodemographic segmentation—A two-stage market segmentation approach using the geographic and demographic characteristics of customers.

geographic segmentation—Dividing the market into groups of customers who share the same geographic location.

gross rating point (GRP)—An exposure measure used in evaluating advertising success. It is calculated by multiplying the reach percentage (percent of target market customers exposed to advertising) by the frequency (average number of exposures per target market customer reached).

group inclusive tour (GIT)—An all-inclusive package with a specified minimum size (number of travelers) involving one or more groups traveling on scheduled or chartered air service.

growth stage—The second stage of the product life cycle when sales climb rapidly and profit levels improve.

guests—The customers of a hospitality and travel organization.

handling objections—Techniques that sales representatives use to address objections that prospects raise or indicate about sales presentations. This is a step in the sales process.

heavy-half or use-frequency segmentation—Dividing the overall market based on the number of times a service is purchased or upon each segment's share of total demand.

historical budgeting—A form of arbitrary budgeting that involves taking last year's marketing budget and adding a certain dollar amount or percentage to it.

horizontal integration—Developing or acquiring similar businesses.

hospitality and travel industry—A group of interrelated organizations providing personal services to customers who are away from home.

hospitality and travel marketing environment—All the factors to be considered when making marketing decisions.

hospitality and travel marketing system—A five-step, systematic process for marketing a hospitality and travel organization based on answering the questions: (1) Where are we now? (2) Where would we like to be? (3) How do we get there? (4) How do we make sure we get there? (5) How do we know if we got there?

hosts—The people who work within hospitality and travel organizations and that serve guests.

Hubbart Formula—A target-pricing method used by lodging facilities. This involves building an income statement up from the bottom to determine the room rates necessary to provide a predetermined return on investment.

iceberg effect—When marketing managers make decisions based on superficial information.

implementation plan—One of the main parts of the marketing plan, this details the marketing budget, staff responsibilities, activities, timetable, and methods of controlling, measuring, and evaluating activities.

implicit communication—Promotional cues or messages conveyed through body language or other nonverbal means.

incentive packages—All-inclusive packages given by corporations and other organizations as a reward for outstanding performance from employees, dealers, and others.

incentive travel—Travel by persons who have received incentive packages as a reward for outstanding performance.

incentive travel planners—Specialized tour wholesalers who assemble incentive packages for sponsoring organizations.

indirect distribution—A situation in which part of the responsibility for promoting, reserving, and providing services is given to one or more other hospitality and travel organizations, especially travel trade intermediaries.

individual customers—Individual people or families who make their own hospitality and travel decisions.

individual depth interviews—A qualitative research technique involving a meeting of one interviewer and one interviewee for about 45 minutes to one hour.

inplants—An office of a retail travel agency located on the premises of a corporate client.

inseparability—Some hospitality and travel services (e.g., restaurants and tennis camps) are closely associated with the individuals who provide them. Without these individuals, the services would not have the same appeal.

inside sales—Also known as internal selling, these are personal selling efforts within an organization's place of business to either increase the likelihood of a sale or to add to customers' average spending levels.

institutional advertisements—An advertising message format in which the philosophy or goodwill of an organization or industry sector is promoted.

intangibility—A generic difference shared by all services. It means that most services have to be purchased in order to experience them.

integrated marketing—The planning and coordination of all the promotional mix elements so that they are as consistent and mutually supportive as possible.

This is also used to refer to the closer coordination of a hospitality and travel organization's promotional consultants and advisors (advertising agencies, sales promotion firms, public relations consultants).

interactive marketing—Using interactive media to enable buyer-seller electronic communications in a computer-mediated environment. The customer controls the type and amount of information that is received from the organization.

interactive media—A combination of electronic and communication devices (e.g., television, personal computers, phone lines) that permit customers to interact with a hospitality and travel organization's information or reservation services.

interdependency (interdependent)—This unique characteristic of the hospitality and travel industry occurs because several organizations usually contribute to satisfying customers' needs and wants.

interests—Things that people spend time on and that get their attentions including families, homes, jobs, hobbies, recreational pursuits, communities, clothes, food and drink preferences, and other items.

intermediaries—Also known as the travel trade and channels of distribution, these include retail travel agents, tour wholesalers and operators, corporate travel managers and agencies, incentive travel planners, and convention/meeting planners.

internal customers—All of the employees of a hospitality and travel organization.

internal marketing—Includes all the efforts in which an organization engages to communicate with its employees in support of its customer marketing efforts.

internal secondary research data—Customer databases and other information contained within a hospitality and travel organization's own records.

internal sources—Information stored in a person's mind, including past experiences with a service and recollections of related promotions.

Internet—A system connecting millions of computers around the world. The Internet's main elements include the World Wide Web, e-mail, file transfer protocol (FTP), and gopher.

interpersonal factors—The outside influence of other people on customer behavior including factors such as cultures and subcultures, reference groups, social classes, opinion leaders, and the family.

introduction stage—The first stage in the product life cycle when a new service is first offered to the public.

intuitive pricing—An unscientific pricing approach based solely on management's intuition.

lead prospecting—Techniques used by sales representatives to pinpoint *leads* or potential sales prospects.

lead time—The space of time between the design of an advertisement and its actual appearance in the selected medium.

leader pricing—A form of promotional pricing where one or more services or products is offered for a short time at a price below its actual costs.

learning—A personal factor that influences customer behavior and that develops through a combination of factors including needs, motives, objectives, cues, responses, and reinforcement.

legislation and regulation—An uncontrollable factor in the hospitality and travel marketing environment consisting of various laws and regulations set by government agencies.

lifestyle—The way people live based on their attitudes, interests, and opinions.

lifestyle segmentation—Also known as psychographic segmentation, this is a market segmentation approach that divides the market by lifestyle categories.

lifetime value (LTV)—A concept associated with relationship marketing and customer relationship management (CRM) in which the lifetime value of individual customers is considered. The customer is viewed as a long-term asset of the organization rather than as a one-time transaction.

location and community analysis—A step followed in market, feasibility, and situation analyses to determine how a given site and community will contribute to a business' success.

long-term planning—Also known as strategic planning, this involves planning for a period of three or more years into the future.

macrosystem—Every organization in the hospitality and travel industry.

management contract—A contract between the owners of a hotel and a hotel management company that specifies the duties of each party and the formula for sharing revenues and profits.

marginal economic budgeting—An idealistic approach to budgeting in which sponsors spend money on promotional mix elements up to the point where the last dollar spent brings in exactly one dollar in sales.

market analysis—A study of the potential demand for a new hospitality and travel business.

market potential analysis—A research component of a market or feasibility analysis that determines if there are enough potential customers for a new hospitality or travel business.

market segment—An identifiable component group of an overall market, whose members have something in common, and to which a specific service appeals.

market segmentation—The division of the overall market for a service into groups of customers with common characteristics.

market segmentation analysis—A two-step process in which a hospitality and travel organization first segments the market and then selects its target markets from among the resulting market segments.

market share—The percentage relationship of an organization's sales to total industry sales.

marketing—A continuous, sequential process through which management in the hospitality and travel industry plans, researches, implements, controls, and evaluates activities designed to satisfy customers' needs and wants, and their own organization's objectives. To be most effective, marketing requires the efforts of everyone in an organization and can be made more or less effective by the actions of complementary organizations.

marketing audit—A systematic, comprehensive, and periodic evaluation of the entire marketing function in an organization including its marketing goals, objectives, strategies, and performance.

marketing-company era—The second stage of the marketing-organization era when companies realized that marketing was a long-term organizational concern and not just the responsibility of the marketing department.

marketing-company orientation—The view that marketing is a long-term, organized concern where the success of the company hinges not only on satisfying the customers' short-term needs, but the long-term needs as well.

(the) marketing concept—Acting on the belief that satisfying customers' needs and wants is the first priority in business.

marketing control—Steps that an organization takes to ensure that its marketing plans are successful. This includes setting standards, measuring performance against standards, and correcting deviations from standards and plans.

marketing cost and profitability analysis—A marketing evaluation technique in which income statements are analyzed to determine sales, costs, and profits.

marketing-department era—The first stage in the marketing-orientation era, this was a period when manufacturing and packaged-goods companies began to accept the need to set up new departments to coordinate all marketing activities.

marketing environment analysis—A step completed in a situation market or feasibility analysis examing the organization's marketing environment (i.e., the economy, society, culture, government, technology, and population/demographics) that will affect its direction and success. This analysis provides a foundation for the organization's marketing plans and strategic market plans.

marketing environment factors—Events and other factors completely beyond the direct control of the marketing manager, but which must be analyzed in marketing planning. There are six factors in this part of the hospitality and travel marketing environment: competition, legislation and regulation, economic environment, societal and cultural environment, technological environment, and organizational objectives and resources. They are also often referred to as the uncontrollable factors.

marketing evaluation—Techniques used after the marketing plan period to analyze success in achieving individual marketing objectives and to more broadly assess the entire organization's marketing efforts.

marketing management—All the activities necessary to plan, research, implement, control, and evaluate the marketing efforts of a hospitality and travel organization.

marketing manager—The person with overall responsibility for marketing in an organization or individual unit.

marketing mix—Includes the controllable factors, including product, price, place, promotion, packaging, programming, people, and partnership (8 Ps), that an organization selects to satisfy customer needs.

marketing myopia—A term coined in 1960 by Theodore Levitt to describe many of the thirteen symptoms of production and sales orientations.

marketing objective—A measurable goal for a target market that a hospitality and travel organization attempts to achieve within a specific time period—typically one to two years.

marketing orientation—This means acceptance of the marketing concept—that customer needs are the first priority in a hospitality and travel organization.

marketing-organization era—The second stage in the marketing-orientation era, this was the period after the marketing-department era when manufacturing and packaged-goods companies began to see marketing as not only one department's responsibility, but as a long-term organizational concern.

marketing plan—A written, short-term plan—for a period of two years or less—that details how a hospitality or travel organization will use its marketing mix(es) to achieve its marketing objectives.

marketing position and plan analysis—A step followed in market, feasibility, and situation analyses to determine how best a new or existing organization should be positioned and marketed.

marketing research—The function of marketing that links the consumer, customer, and public to the marketer through information (American Marketing Association definition).

marketing research program—A plan developed by an organization to investigate several opportunities or problems.

marketing research project—An individual element of a marketing research program where a specific problem or opportunity is investigated.

marketing strategy—The selection of a course of action from among several alternatives that involves specific customer groups (target markets), communication methods, distribution channels, and pricing structures.

marketing strategy factors—The elements of the hospitality and travel marketing environment that a marketing manager can control. These factors are the elements of a hospitality and travel organization's marketing mix. They are also often referred to as the controllable factors.

market-share analysis—A marketing evaluation technique that analyzes an organization's market share and the market-share performance of its competitors.

maturity stage—The third stage in the product life cycle when there is a slowdown in the rate of sales growth.

media (press) kits—A selection of press releases, articles, and photographs assembled for use by the press.

media vehicles—Specific newspapers, magazines, journals, directories, Web sites and television and radio stations where advertising can be placed.

medium—A means of communicating, including print and broadcast, with customers through advertising. In the broader context of the communications process, media are the communication channels that sources (sponsors) select to pass their messages to receivers (customers).

megacarriers—A term commonly used in North America to refer to the major domestic airlines such as United and American Airlines.

menus—A merchandising tool used in restaurants and other food and beverage operations that lists all food and beverage items available.

merchandising—Also sometimes referred to as point-of-purchase advertising, this includes all in-house materials used to stimulate sales (menus, wine lists, tent cards, posters, displays).

message—This is part of the communications process. It is what the source (sponsor) wants to communicate in the hope that the receivers (customers) understand.

message format—Broad creative approaches in advertising to communicate the message idea to customers.

message idea—The main theme, appeal, or benefit communicated in an advertisement.

message strategy—The way an advertising message is communicated including the message idea, copy platform, and message format.

microsystems—Individual organizations in the hospitality and travel industry. The hospitality and travel marketing system is a microsystem.

milestones—Subobjectives with specific time deadlines that are established within a marketing plan.

mission—A broad statement about an organization's business and scope, services or products, markets served, and overall philosophy.

mission statement—A broad statement about a hospitality and travel organization's business and scope, services or products, markets served, and overall philosophy. It summarizes the organization's role in society.

Modified American Plan (MAP)—Packages that include accommodation and two meals per day, normally breakfast and dinner.

moments of truth—A term used to describe service encounters or when a customer directly interacts with an employee of a hospitality and travel organization.

mood—The added enhancement or feeling of excitement that a particular medium or vehicle gives to an advertisement.

motivation—Inner drives that customers have that cause them to take action to satisfy their needs.

motives—Individual drives or desires that customers have to satisfy their wants.

multistage approach to pricing—The pricing approach this book recommends based on step-by-step consideration of nine factors—corporate objectives, customer characteristics, corporate image and positioning, customer demand volumes, costs, competition, channels, complementary services and facilities, and consistency with marketing mix elements and strategy.

multistage segmentation—An approach to market segmentation in which more than two segmentation bases are used.

needs—(see **customer needs**)

news (press) conferences—A meeting where a prepared presentation is made to invited media people.

news (press) releases—Short articles about organizations that try to attract media attention, leading to media coverage of the materials contained within the releases.

newsworthy—This means that a story is of enough interest and with sufficient recency that the media are likely to cover it.

nichers—Organizations that choose the marketing strategy of appealing only to one target market (single-target-market approach).

niching—Using a strategy to appeal only to small or narrow target markets.

nine Cs of pricing—Nine factors that influence prices including customer characteristics, corporate objectives, corporate image and positioning, customer demand volumes, costs, competition, channels, complementary services and facilities, and consistency with marketing mix elements and strategy.

noise—This is a factor that affects the communications process and includes the distractions (other promotional messages) that draw the customer's attention away from the sponsor's message.

noncommercial sources—Independent, objective assessments of hospitality and travel services such as ratings by the American Automobile Association, Mobil, Michelin, and restaurant critics.

nonprobability sampling—A subjective sample-selection approach used in marketing research where every person in the group does *not* have a known probability of being in the sample.

objective-and-task budgeting—A sophisticated approach to setting the marketing budget where the actions (tasks) required to achieve marketing objectives are determined and then costed.

objective criteria—Factors that the customer uses to choose between alternative hospitality and travel services or destinations that include prices, locations, physical characteristics of facilities, and services offered.

observational method—A category of primary research in the hospitality and travel industry that involves watching and noting how customers behave.

observational research—Includes both human and mechanical observational research methods. Human observation is watching and noting how customers behave. The other method uses mechanical or electronic devices to collect data.

occasion-based segmentation—A form of behavioral segmentation in which customers are categorized according to when they buy and the purpose of their purchases (e.g., honeymoon vacationers).

on-line advertising—Generally considered to involve advertising on the Internet, particularly the World Wide Web.

on-line marketing—Marketing of a hospitality and travel organization or destination using the Internet, mainly the World Wide Web and e-mail.

on-line research—Marketing research conducted using the Internet.

on-line surveys—Surveys conducted on the Internet.

on-line travel services—Sites on the World Wide Web that provide travel information and that enable the customers to book travel, including Travelocity, Expedia, Priceline, and others.

open systems—The microsystems or individual organizations in the hospitality and travel industry that are dynamic, constantly undergoing change.

opinion leaders—People in various social groups who exert an above-average influence, through word-of-mouth communication, on the behavior of their peers.

opinions—Beliefs that people have, accurate or inaccurate, about a variety of subjects, including the political scene, the economy, the educational system, products, future events, sports, countries, and so on.

organizational buying behavior—The ways in which people in organizations select, use, and behave after they have purchased hospitality and travel services.

organizational objectives and resources—Overall, long-term goals of an organization—usually in for-profit companies—set as profitability, market share, and sales volume targets.

outside sales—A term used mainly in the travel agency business for people who sell the agency's services outside of its retail location.

packaging (and programming)—The combination of related and complementary hospitality and travel services into a single-price offering.

partnership—Cooperative promotions and other cooperative marketing efforts by hospitality and travel organizations.

pass-along rate—An element in the reach of a medium, it is the rate at which magazines and newspapers are passed along from primary to secondary audiences.

penetration—In common usage this means the share of the total market available that a service captures. It also is used to describe a low price set to capture a large share of the market.

penetration strategies—Strategies used when a new service is first introduced involving setting low prices to capture as much of the market as possible.

people—All of an organization's employees who provide services to customers.

percentage-of-sales (rule-of-thumb) budgeting—An arbitrary, unsophisticated approach to setting a marketing budget based on industry-average percentages of sales.

perception—The mental process customers employ using their five senses—sight, hearing, taste, touch, and smell—to size up hospitality and travel services and the industry's promotional messages.

performance measurement—The tools used to evaluate the success of an organization's marketing efforts.

perishability—A generic difference shared by all services. It means that services cannot be stored. If they are not sold when they are available, that sale is lost forever.

permanence—The lifespan of a promotional message and its potential for repeated exposures to the same customers.

personal factors—Psychological characteristics of individual customers that influence their behavior—needs, wants, and motivation; perception; learning; personality; lifestyle; and self-concept.

personal selling—Involves oral conversations, either by telephone or face-to-face, between salespersons and prospective customers.

personality—All the things that make a person unique—motivation, perception, learning, and emotions—and the different ways that every person thinks and acts.

persuasive impact—The ability of an advertisement to convince customers in accordance with the advertiser's objectives.

place—The plan that the organization makes to allow it to work with other complementary groups in the distribution channel.

plan—The outcome of the process of planning. In this text, a plan is defined as a written document that details how a hospitality or travel organization has decided to try to achieve its marketing objectives.

planning—The process that produces plans. Planning is a management activity in which choices are made between alternative marketing approaches.

pleasure and personal travel market—One of the two main divisions of the hospitality and travel market, this includes people traveling and dining out for pleasure and other personal, nonbusiness reasons.

positioning—The development of a service and marketing mix to occupy a specific place in the minds of customers within target markets.

positioning statement—Phrases reflecting the image the organization wants to create.

posttesting—The use of marketing research techniques to determine the effectiveness of an advertisement after it has been run.

preapproach—A step in the sales process, this is the review of each sales prospect's files and other relevant information in preparation for the sales call.

preferred suppliers or vendors—An example of relationship marketing in which airlines, hotel companies, rental car firms, cruise lines, and tour operators try to increase their shares of selected travel agencies' business by offering extra commission percentage points or other incentives.

premiums—Items of merchandise offered at a reduced price or free with the purchase of services or products.

pre-opening public relations—A program of public relations activities used before the opening of a new hospitality and travel business.

press (or news) conferences—Prearranged meetings where prepared presentations are made to invited media people.

pretesting—The use of marketing research techniques to find out whether an advertisement communicates information to customers in the manner the sponsor intended.

price—The dollar value at which services are offered.

price cutting—This is not the same as discounting but happens when companies react quickly and rashly (without careful analysis) to competitors' price moves.

price discrimination—Also known as discriminatory or differential pricing, this is where services are set to appeal to specific target markets with some markets receiving rates lower than others.

price lining—Preestalbishing price lines (levels) that the company feels confident will attract customers.

pricing—One of the marketing mix elements (8 Ps) that is a marketing technique and a major profit determinant. Pricing should include all special rates and discounts in addition to regular pricing.

price-offs—A type of special-offer sales promotion where there is an advertised price reduction that does not involve using a coupon.

pricing objectives—The first step in price planning, these fall into three categories: (1) profit-oriented, (2) sales-oriented, and (3) status-quo-oriented.

primary competitor analysis—A step followed in market, feasibility, and situation analyses to determine the strengths and weaknesses of primary competitors (competitive organizations who market similar services to some or all of the subject organization's target markets).

primary groups—Customers' family and friends who influence what they purchase.

primary research—Data collected for the first time by a method other than secondary research, to answer specific questions.

primary segmentation base—The characteristic that is most important in determining the customer's choice of a service.

print media—Newspapers, magazines, direct mail, outdoor advertising, and other printed materials in which advertising can be placed.

probability sampling—A sampling procedure used in marketing research where every person in the group to be researched has a known probability of being in the sample.

product—The range of services and facilities (product/service mix) a hospitality and travel organization provides to customers.

product adoption curve—A concept suggested by Everett M. Rogers that divides the population into five groups known as the innovators, early adopters, early majority, late majority, and laggards.

product life cycle (PLC)—A concept that suggests that all hospitality and travel services pass through four predictable stages: (1) introduction, (2) growth, (3) maturity, and (4) decline.

product-related segmentation—A market segmentation approach that uses some aspect of the service to classify customers.

product/service mix—The assortment of services, facilities, and products that an organization provides to customers.

product/service mix length—The number of related services provided by an organization.

product/service mix width—The number of different services provided by an organization.

production orientation—A production-oriented organization puts most of its emphasis on producing and selling services that are the easiest and most efficient to produce, and not on satisfying the needs and wants of its customers.

production-orientation era—The first evolutionary stage in the development of marketing among manufacturing and packaged-goods companies. This was a period when the concept of mass production began.

profit maximization—Setting a price to achieve the maximum amount of profit.

pro forma **(projected) income statement**—A forecast of the income and expenses for a hospitality and travel organization or development project for 5 to 20 years in the future.

programming—The development of special activities, events, or programs to increase customer spending or give added appeal to a package or other hospitality/travel service.

promotion—All the techniques that hospitality and travel organizations use to promote their services.

promotional mix—The combination of advertising, sales promotion, merchandising, personal selling, public relations-publicity approaches used by a hospitality and travel organization for a specific time period.

promotional pricing—The use of short-term price reductions to stimulate temporary sales increases, particularly as part of sales promotion efforts.

prospecting—A step in the sales process, these are the various techniques that sales representatives use to identify sales prospects.

psychographic segmentation—A market segmentation approach based on psychographics.

psychographics—The development of psychological profiles of customers and psychologically based measures of distinctive modes of living or lifestyles.

psychological pricing—Using slightly lower prices to give customers the perception of added value.

public relations—All the activities that a hospitality and travel organization uses to maintain or improve its relationships with other organizations and individuals.

public relations consultants—Specialized companies that provide public relations and publicity services to hospitality and travel organizations.

public relations plan—A written plan that outlines all the public relations and publicity activities to be carried out over a specific period of time.

publicity—Nonpaid communication of information about an organization's services.

publics—All those individuals and groups with whom an organization interacts.

purpose-of-trip segmentation—A market segmentation approach based on dividing hospitality and travel markets according to the customer's primary trip purpose.

qualifying—This is a sales process step and involves using preselected criteria to identify the best sales prospects.

qualitative data—Data that is non-numerical.

qualitative information—Nonnumerical market research information.

quantitative data—Data that is numerical.

quantitative information—Numerical market research information.

questionnaire—A printed form used in surveys that lists questions and provides spaces for answers.

rail-drive packages—A type of hospitality and travel package that includes travel by railway and car or other vehicle.

rationale—The part of the marketing plan that explains the facts, analyses, and assumptions on which the plan is based.

reach—The number of potential customers exposed to a given advertisement at least once.

receiver—An element in the communications process, this is the person who notices or hears and decodes the source's (sponsor's) encoded message.

recognition programs—A sales promotion technique that makes awards to travel trade intermediaries, sales representatives, or customers for providing certain levels of sales or business.

reference groups—Groups with which customers identify.

relationship marketing—A marketing principle that emphasizes the importance of building long-term relationships with individual customers and with other organizations in the distribution chain.

relationship selling—The practice of building ties to customers based on a salesperson's attention and commitment to customer needs over time. This is an element of the relationship marketing and customer relationship management concepts.

repositioning—Using various promotional programs and physical changes in the product/service mix to change the image of an organization in customers' minds.

response—An element in the communications process. This is the manner in which receivers (customers) react to sponsors' messages.

response rate—The percentage of all people surveyed who supply answers to the researcher's questions.

retail travel agents—A specialized travel trade intermediary that sells the services of carriers, suppliers, other travel trade intermediaries, and destination marketing organizations, earning commissions for providing the service.

rule-of-thumb budgeting—(see **percentage-of-sales budgeting**)

sales analysis—A marketing evaluation technique that compares actual sales with sales objectives.

sales blitz (blitzing or concentrated canvassing)—An approach in which several sales representatives cold call in the same, specified geographic area.

sales call—An in-person visit by a sales representative to a sales prospect.

sales demonstration—The sales representative demonstrates the ability of the organization's services to meet the prospect's needs.

sales leads—Another name for sales prospects or customers who may be interested in purchasing the organization's services.

sales management—The management of the sales force and personal selling efforts to achieve desired sales objectives.

sales management audit—A periodic analysis of the sales department's policies, objectives, activities, personnel, and performance.

sales orientation—A sales-oriented organization places most of its emphasis on outselling the competition, and not on satisfying the needs and wants of its customers.

sales-orientation era—The second evolutionary stage in the development of marketing among manufacturing and package-goods companies. This was a period—beginning in the 1930s and lasting through the 1940s—when the emphasis switched from production to outselling the competition.

sales plan—A detailed description of personal selling objectives, sales forecasts, sales-force responsibilities, activities, and budgets.

sales presentation—A presentation, either verbal, written or both, through which a sales representative tries to convince a prospect to make a purchase.

sales process—The step-by-step process used in conducting personal selling efforts.

sales promotions—Approaches other than advertising, personal selling, and public relations and publicity where customers are given a short-term inducement to make an immediate purchase.

sales prospects—The prospective customers of an organization.

sales quotas—Performance targets periodically set for individual sales representatives, branch offices, or regions.

sales representative—A person who works in the sales department of a hospitality and travel organization and who is directly involved in personal selling.

sales territories—Specific areas of responsibility, usually geographic, that are assigned to individual sales representatives or branch offices.

sampling—A sales promotion technique in which free samples are given away or another type of arrangement is made so that people can try out all or part of a service.

satellite ticket printers—A travel agency branch that has an attended or unattended airline ticketing machine.

secondary groups—Groups to which customers belong including churches, workplaces, clubs, and societies.

secondary research—Published marketing research information available from other sources, either internal or external.

segmentation bases—The characteristics used to divide a market into segments.

segmentation criteria—The specific criteria or techniques that a hospitality and travel organization uses to divide up markets into subgroups.

segmented marketing strategy—Also known as differentiated marketing strategies, these are approaches that recognize differences between target markets by using individualized marketing mixes.

segmenters—Organizations that use segmented marketing strategies.

self-concept—Mental pictures that customers have of themselves, consisting of four different elements: the real self, ideal self, reference-group self, and self-image. These are personal factors that influence how customers behave.

self-liquidating premiums—Merchandise items sold at a reduced price that recover the sponsor's costs.

self-liquidators—Premiums which are sold at a price to recover the sponsor's costs.

service encounter—A period of time when a customer directly interacts with a service.

service industries—Organizations, including those within the hospitality and travel industry, primarily involved in the provision of personal services.

services analysis—A step followed in market, feasibility, and situation analyses to determine what new or improved services can be provided to better match the needs of customers.

services marketing—A concept based on a recognition of the uniqueness of all services. It is a branch of marketing that specifically applies in the service industries.

SERVQUAL—A technique developed by Parasuraman, Zeithaml, and Berry to measure service quality (*see* Chapter 11).

seven core principles (of marketing)—The basic principles of marketing comprising the marketing concept, marketing orientation, satisfying customers' needs and wants market segmentation, value and the exchange process, product life cycle, and marketing mix.

shared room basis—*See* double-occupancy basis.

short-term planning—The process of preparing plans for a period of two years or less.

simulation—A category of primary research that involves using computers to simulate marketing situations.

single-stage segmentation—A market segmentation approach where only one of the seven categories of segmentation bases is used.

single supplement—An added charge to packages and tours for people who book on a single-occupancy basis.

single-target-market strategy—A marketing strategy approach where the organizations select only one target market from several market segments and market exclusively to the chosen target market.

situation analysis—Similar to a market analysis, this is a study of the marketing strengths, weaknesses, and opportunities of a business or other type of organization.

skimming strategies—Strategies used when a new service is first introduced involving high prices to achieve the highest possible gross profit.

slice-of-life—An advertising message format that shows a short mini-drama or playlet from everyday life where the sponsor's service or product solves customers' problems.

social classes—A system of classifying the population based on such factors as occupation, sources of income and accumulated wealth, highest level of education achieved, place of residence, and family history.

social information sources—Interpersonal channels of information—also known as word-of-mouth advertising—that influence customer behavior.

social sources—Interpersonal channels of information.

societal and cultural environment—An uncontrollable factor in the hospitality and travel environment, these are the changes in society and culture that affect organizations and individual customers.

societal-marketing-orientation era—Beginning about the 1970s, this is the fourth and final evolutionary era of marketing. It is when organizations started to recognize their social responsibility in addition to their profit and customer-satisfaction objectives.

source—An element of the communications process. This is the person or organization (sponsor) transmitting the information to customers.

special communication methods—This is one of the two main groups of sales promotion techniques—the other being special offers. It includes specialty advertising, sampling, trade/travel show exhibits, point-of-purchase displays and demonstrations, educational seminars and training programs, and sales representatives' visual aids.

special-interest packages—The primary attraction in these packages is the special activities, programs, and events—sports instruction, hobbies, continuing education topics—arranged by one or more of the providers.

special offers—This is one of the two main groups of sales promotion techniques—the other being special communication methods. It includes coupons, price-offs, premiums, contests, sweepstakes and games, travel trade inducements, recognition programs, and continuity programs. They offer short-term inducements to customers, travel trade intermediaries, and sales representatives.

specialty advertising—A sales promotion technique in which free items are given to customers or travel trade intermediaries displaying the sponsor's name, logo, or advertising message.

specific positioning approach—An approach to creating an image for an organization or destination. Only one customer benefit is selected and the concentration is on that one benefit.

spot advertising—Advertising that is done between programs.

spots—Local and network radio and television advertisements that are aired between programs.

strategic alliances—A form of relationship marketing, these are special long-term relationships formed between two or more hospitality and travel organizations or between a hospitality and travel organization and one or more other types of organizations.

strategic market plan—Also known as long-term planning, this is a written plan for marketing a hospitality or travel organization covering a period of three or more years in the future.

strategic marketing planning—The process that produces strategic (long-term) market plans. It is a management activity in which long-term choices are made between alternative marketing approaches.

subcultures—Cultures within a broader overall culture. In the United States, subcultures include ethnic minorities (Black-, Hispanic-, and Asian-Americans) and religious-based groups.

subjective criteria—Intangible factors used by the customer to choose between alternative hospitality and travel services, or destinations, such as the image of the organization or destination.

suggestive selling—Also known as *up-selling,* this is where employees suggest or recommend additional or higher-priced items or services.

suppliers—Organizations that operate facilities (lodging, restaurant and food service), attractions and events, cruise lines, car rental agencies, casinos, ground transportation, and other support services in or between travel destinations.

surrogate cues—Product/service features that provide no direct benefits in use but convey a message about what is being offered, e.g., a company name like Econo Lodge.

survey research—The most popular of the four primary research categories. This includes personal interview, mail, and telephone surveys.

sweepstakes—Sales promotions in which entrants submit their names and addresses, and where winners are chosen on the basis of chance and not skill.

SWOT analysis—Short for strengths, weaknesses, opportunities, and threats, this is an analysis technique used as the foundation of an organization's strategic market plan and marketing plan. Often it is used interchangeably with the term situation analysis.

synergism—An outcome of partnership (cooperative marketing). It is the combined action of two or more organizations producing a result that individually would not have been possible.

system—A collection of interrelated parts that work together to achieve common objectives.

tactical planning—The process by which short-term (2 years or less) marketing plans are developed, implemented, controlled, and evaluated.

target market—A market segment selected by a hospitality and travel organization for marketing attention.

target pricing—A sophisticated pricing approach where the target is usually set in terms of a specific return on investment that the company wishes to achieve.

technology—Methods or processes for handling specific technical problems.

telemarketing—Personal selling efforts conducted via the telephone.

telephone selling—Any communications via the phone that lead directly or indirectly to sales. This is one of the three main categories of personal selling.

test marketing—An experimental research technique in which new services or products are tested in locations thought to be representative of the population as a whole.

testimonial advertisement—An advertisement in which a celebrity, authority figure, satisfied customer (real or fictitious), or continuing character recommends or otherwise endorses the service or product.

tone—The basic way an advertising message is communicated based on choices between rational and emotional appeals, dealing with competitors' services versus not mentioning them, and the strength of the message.

total quality management (TQM)—A process designed to cut down on an organization's defects, to determine its customer requirements, and to satisfy those requirements.

tour operator—A tour wholesaler, other company, or individual who operates packages or tours, i.e., provides the necessary ground transportation and guide services.

tour wholesaler—A company or individual who plans, prepares, markets, and administers travel packages, usually combining the services of several suppliers and carriers.

trade advertising—Advertising to travel trade intermediaries who will influence customers' buying decisions.

trade-area analysis—A research study that analyzes the market within an organization's surrounding trading area.

trade promotions—Sales promotions directed at travel trade intermediaries including trade show exhibits, recognition programs, sweepstakes and contests, price offs, and other trade inducements.

trade shows—Events where all parts of the industry (suppliers, carriers, intermediaries, and destination marketing organizations) are brought together to share information.

trading area—The geographic area from which an organization (or similar organizations) tends to attract the majority of its customers.

traditional (rule-of-thumb) pricing—An unsophisticated pricing approach based on traditional ways of arriving at prices—usually using some sort of formula—in various parts of the hospitality and travel industry.

travel agency appointments—Processes by which travel agencies are approved to sell and receive commissions by specific supplier and carrier associations.

(retail) travel agent—A person or organization who sells and reserves the services of suppliers, carriers, other travel trade intermediaries, and destination marketing organizations to individual and group customers, and receives commissions for these efforts.

travel demand generators—The primary reasons for travel including attractions, events, and business-related facilities.

travel trade—A term commonly used in the hospitality and travel industry to describe all intermediaries.

travel trade intermediary—One of several specialized indirect distribution channels, including retail travel agents, tour wholesalers and operators, corporate travel managers and agencies, incentive travel planners, and convention/meeting planners, in the hospitality and travel industry.

two-stage segmentation—A market segmentation approach in which a primary segmentation base is chosen and then customers are further subdivided using a second segmentation base.

undifferentiated marketing (strategy)—A marketing strategy approach that overlooks segment differences, using the same marketing mix for all target markets.

up-selling—(see **suggestive selling**)

use-frequency segmentation—(see **heavy-half segmentation**)

VALS™2—A psychographic segmentation scheme for the U.S. population developed by SRI Consulting Business Intelligence.

value or value for money—Mental estimates that customers make of a hospitality or travel service's ability to satisfy their needs and wants.

variability—A generic difference shared by all services. This results from the difficulty of standardizing services because of the heavy involvement of different people in their provision.

variable (direct) costs—Costs that vary in direct proportion to the number of customers buying the package or other hospitality/travel service.

vertical integration—Expansion up and down the distribution channel by a hospitality and travel organization (e.g., a travel agency chain acquiring a lodging company).

vision—A marketing objective describing the organization's view of where they would like to be in the future.

vision statement—A formal step in the marketing plan comprised of a written statement outlining the organization's view of where they would like to be in the future.

wants—(see **customer wants**)

waste—The number of customers exposed to an advertisement who are not part of an organization's target markets.

word-of-mouth advertising—Information about a service experience passed orally from past (and other social information sources) to potential customers.

World Wide Web—The collection of text, graphics, video, and sound that can be accessed on the Internet through the use of URLs or Web site addresses.

yield management—A revenue-management approach used by airlines, hotels, cruise lines, car rental firms, and others to maximize the sales of their perishable inventories by controlling prices and capacity.

zero-based budgeting—A sophisticated approach to setting a marketing budget that requires that each marketing plan activity (task) for an upcoming period is justified, i.e., the budget begins at zero.

zip-code demographics analysis—An analysis of the demographic characteristics of the people living within a specific zip code area.

Index